Y0-BBX-254

Business relationships can go sour—very sour. Colleagues turn on each other; friends turn into enemies; and satisfied customers turn irate. And boom—someone's crossed the line, and they land in court. Watch and listen as these associates argue, defend, present the facts, and provide evidence. Then prepare your ruling...**You Be The Judge.**

TURN THE PAGE...

...to access your copy of the You Be the Judge DVD

CASE TOPICS INCLUDED ARE:

Religious Discrimination—Dress Code Flips Burger Joint

Fraud—Blind Dates Go Bust

Sexual Harassment—Did Sexy Prank Kill Promotion?

Defamation—Trashing the French Maid

Partnership—You Sunk My Partnership

Warranty—Who's Distorting What?

Verbal Agreement—Recording Studio Blues

Liability—Office Party Blame Game

Property—Subtracting The Addition

Privacy/Employment-at-will—Fired For Whistling?

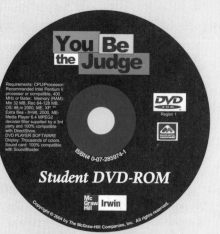

This new DVD-Rom is available FREE with each new copy of the book.

THE LEGAL & REGULATORY ENVIRONMENT OF BUSINESS

THIRTEENTH EDITION

LICENSE AGREEMENT FOR MCGRAW-HILL SOFTWARE

This agreement gives you, the customer, certain benefits, rights, and obligations. By using the software, you indicate that you have read, understood, and will comply with the terms.

Terms of Agreement:

1. McGraw-Hill licenses and authorizes you to use the software specified below only on a microcomputer located within your own facilities.

2. You will abide by the Copyright Law of the United States. The law provides you with the right to make only one back-up copy. It prohibits you from making any additional copies, except as expressly provided by McGraw-Hill. In the event that the software is protected against copying in such a way that it cannot be duplicated, McGraw-Hill will provide you with one back-up copy at minimal cost or no charge.

3. You will not prepare derivative works based on the software because that also is not permitted under the Copyright Law. For example, you cannot prepare an alternative hardware version or format based on the existing software.

4. If you have a problem with the operation of our software or believe it is defective, contact your nearest McGraw-Hill Book Company office about securing a replacement. We cannot, however, offer free replacement of software damaged through normal wear and tear, or lost while in your possession. Nor does McGraw-Hill warrant that the software will satisfy your requirements, that the operation of the software will be uninterrupted or error-free, or that the program defects in the software can be corrected. Except as described in this agreement, software is distributed "as is" without any warranties of any kind, either express or implied, including, but not limited to, implied warranties of merchantability and fitness for a particular purpose or use.

5. Additional rights and benefits may come with the specific software package you have purchased. Consult the support materials that come with this program, or contact the nearest McGraw-Hill Book Company office in your area.

NOTICE: THIS PACKAGE IS NOT RETURNABLE IF SEAL IS BROKEN.

THE LEGAL & REGULATORY ENVIRONMENT OF BUSINESS

THIRTEENTH EDITION

O. LEE REED
Professor of Legal Studies, University of Georgia

PETER J. SHEDD
Professor of Legal Studies, University of Georgia

JERE W. MOREHEAD
Professor of Legal Studies, University of Georgia

ROBERT N. CORLEY
Distinguished Professor of Legal Studies Emeritus, University of Georgia

McGraw-Hill Irwin

Boston   Burr Ridge, IL   Dubuque, IA   Madison, WI   New York   San Francisco   St. Louis
Bangkok   Bogotá   Caracas   Kuala Lumpur   Lisbon   London   Madrid   Mexico City
Milan   Montreal   New Delhi   Santiago   Seoul   Singapore   Sydney   Taipei   Toronto

The McGraw-Hill Companies

McGraw-Hill
Irwin

THE LEGAL AND REGULATORY ENVIRONMENT OF BUSINESS
Published by McGraw-Hill/Irwin, a business unit of The McGraw-Hill Companies, Inc., 1221 Avenue of the Americas, New York, NY, 10020. Copyright © 2005, 2002, 1999, 1996, 1993, 1990, 1987, 1984, 1981, 1977, 1973, 1968, 1963 by The McGraw-Hill Companies, Inc. All rights reserved. No part of this publication may be reproduced or distributed in any form or by any means, or stored in a database or retrieval system, without the prior written consent of The McGraw-Hill Companies, Inc., including, but not limited to, in any network or other electronic storage or transmission, or broadcast for distance learning.
Some ancillaries, including electronic and print components, may not be available to customers outside the United States.

This book is printed on acid-free paper.

4 5 6 7 8 9 0 VNH/VNH 0 9 8 7 6

ISBN 13: 978-0-07-288111-0

ISBN 10: 0-07-288111-9

Vice president and editor-in-chief: *Robin J. Zwettler*
Editorial director: *John E. Biernat*
Senior sponsoring editor: *Andy Winston*
Senior developmental editor: *Sarah Reed*
Marketing manager: *Lisa Nicks*
Producer, Media technology: *Mark Molsky*
Project manager: *Laura Griffin*
Production supervisor: *Gina Hangos*
Designer: *Kami Carter*
Photo research coordinator: *Judy Kausal*
Supplement producer: *Lynn M. Bluhm*
Senior digital content specialist: *Brian Nacik*
Typeface: *10.5/12 Times New Roman*
Compositor: *Carlisle Communications, Ltd.*
Printer: *Von Hoffmann Corporation*

Library of Congress Cataloging-in-Publication Data
The legal and regulatory environment of business / O. Lee Reed . . . [et al.].—13th ed.
    p. cm.
    Includes index.
    ISBN 0-07-288111-9 (alk. paper)
    1. Trade regulation—United States. 2. Business law—United States. 3. Industrial laws and legislation—United States. I. Reed, O. Lee (Omer Lee)
KF1600.C6 2005
346.7307—dc22
                                     2003067410

www.mhhe.com

ABOUT THE *authors*

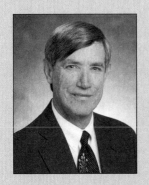

O. LEE REED

Professor Reed holds a J.D. degree from the University of Chicago and a B.A. degree from Birmingham-Southern College. Presently, he is Professor of Legal Studies at the University of Georgia. The author of many scholarly articles, he is former editor-in-chief of the *American Business Law Journal.* He also has served as president of the Academy of Legal Studies in Business and of SEALSB. Professor Reed has received teacher-of-the-year awards from both undergraduate and graduate student organizations. He has been co-author of *The Legal and Regulatory Environment of Business* since 1977.

PETER J. SHEDD

Professor of Legal Studies in the Terry College of Business at the University of Georgia where he received his B.B.A. and J.D. degrees, Professor Shedd has extensive experience as a teacher, researcher, and author of business-related texts. His teaching at the undergraduate and MBA levels has been recognized numerous times. Professor Shedd is an active member of the Academy of Legal Studies in Business and its Southeastern Regional. He served as president of the National Academy during 1999–2000. In addition to being a member of the State Bar of Georgia, Professor Shedd is a member of the American Arbitration Association. He is an experienced mediator and arbitrator.

(continued)

JERE W. MOREHEAD

Professor Morehead is a Professor of Legal Studies at the University of Georgia where he received his J.D. degree. Prior to joining the Georgia faculty, Professor Morehead served as an Assistant United States Attorney in the Department of Justice, where he specialized in the prosecution of white-collar crime. He has served as editor-in-chief of the *American Business Law Journal* and is past president of the International Law Section of the Academy of Legal Studies in Business. Professor Morehead is the recipient of several distinguished teaching awards and has served as a visiting faculty member at the University of Michigan. He has authored many scholarly articles on the subjects of jury selection, export controls, and peer review. He currently serves as associate provost and director of the Honors Program at the University of Georgia.

ROBERT N. CORLEY

Professor Corley is a Distinguished Professor of Legal Studies Emeritus of the University of Georgia. He received his J.D. and B.S. degrees from the University of Illinois, where he taught for 18 years. He was admitted to the Illinois Bar in 1956. Professor Corley is past president of the American Business Law Association and a past member of the editorial board of the *American Business Law Journal.* In 1985 he was awarded the Senior Faculty Award of Excellence by the American Business Law Association. Winner of numerous teaching awards at both the undergraduate and graduate levels, he has also taught in several national executive development programs. Since 1964 he has been senior author of *The Legal Environment of Business.* His contributions have shaped the content of the entire legal environment of the business field.

preface

We welcome you to this thirteenth edition. For the adopters of past editions, we hope you will find this edition continues our long tradition of setting the standard as an introduction to the legal and regulatory environment of business. This edition continues to provide an overview of the structure of the legal and regulatory environment, examples of how businesses and their people are regulated, and discussions of legal issues impacting the conduct of business.

For our past as well as new adopters, we trust you will find this edition full of historical analyses as well as current explanations from recent examples of corporate fraud. Even as new issues are presented, this edition continues to emphasize and illustrate that the rule of law is a necessary foundation for construction of a successful system of private markets in the modern nation. Kofi Annan, the secretary-general of the United Nations stated, "Without good governance, without the rule of law, predictable administration, legitimate power, and responsive regulation—no amount of funding, no short-term economic miracle will set the developing world on the path to prosperity." Every student who uses this text should understand that the prosperous nations of the world owe the conditions for their wealth to their historically vibrant private economies, which in turn rest on a rule of law that fundamentally enables their existence. Because an understanding and appreciation of the concept of the rule of law is so critical, the recent events involving corporate fraud must be examined to ensure that today's business students learn what must not be repeated to protect our system of private enterprise.

RECENT EVENTS AND CORPORATE GOVERNANCE

News stories, since the twelfth edition appeared, have brought into everyday conversations corporate names, such as Enron, Arthur Andersen, WorldCom, Salomon Smith Barney, Tyco, Adelphia, Imclone, and HealthSouth. A common thread running through these news stories is the lack of corporate governance within each organization. This failure of proper internal corporate governance causes significant harm to employees and the investing public. When an organization's internal corporate governance fails, the need arises for an examination of how businesses operate and how governmental legislation and regulation focus on the conduct of business organizations and their leaders.

The themes of internal organizational and governmental corporate governance appear throughout this edition. Even though these themes were important in prior editions, the focus is enhanced in this edition. Each chapter in this edition incorporates an examination of the role of corporate governance. In our collective roles as teachers of the next generation of business leaders, each of us worries whether we are doing all we should. It is our hope this edition will assist in ensuring your students are well educated in ways that prevent a repetition of corporate fraud.

CHANGES IN THE THIRTEENTH EDITION

This thirteenth edition places new emphases in several key areas. These emphases result in new chapters and new cases while maintaining the broad coverage of past editions. For example, the need for enhanced ethical leadership within business organizations is the subject matter of Chapter 2. This chapter focuses on the interrelationship between ethical management and legal mandates.

The emphasis on the important role of property as the foundation of our legal system continues in this edition. Because of the growing significance of intellectual property to businesses and businesspeople, Chapter 7 focuses on this topic.

As highlighted above, corporate governance and its various meanings are themes that run through each chapter. This special focus particularly is highlighted in Chapters 11 and 12 with respect to the creation and operation of various business organizations and the administrative agencies regulating business activities.

To emphasize the renewed energies in the field of regulating securities, this edition dedicates Chapter 16 to this topic. The recent passage of the Sarbanes-Oxley Act receives special attention.

PEDAGOGY

Each chapter contains the following pedagogical elements:

Business Decisions—This element, introduced first in the ninth edition, is continued here. At the beginning of each chapter is a statement of facts that highlights one or more of the substantive aspects of the chapter. Each chapter in this edition contains a new Business Decision, many of which are based on recent news stories.

Cases—We have included portions of actual court decisions that illustrate the parties' arguments and the courts' resolutions of the issues raised. From these cases, we have deleted most of the procedural aspects, citations, and footnotes. Although the resulting edited cases are much shorter than in their original form, the heart of the opinions remain.

Case Questions—Following each case is a series of questions that are designed to help the student understand the key points raised in the case.

Concept Summaries—When it is most helpful, a summary of the preceding textual discussion is provided. In this way, complex or lengthy presentations are easily reviewable by the reader.

Key Terms—At the conclusion of the text of each chapter is a list of words or phrases that are introduced in the chapter. The glossary, at the end of the book, contains definitions for these key terms.

Business Discussions—The last item in each chapter is a factual situation designed to stimulate conversation as a means to provide student review of the chapter's contents.

SUPPLEMENTS

INSTRUCTOR'S RESOURCE MANUAL

This manual consists of the teaching outline section, transparency masters, a case brief supplement, and video guide.

The teaching outline section makes up the bulk of this Instructor's Manual, which is organized by text chapter. This section corresponds with the headings in the text, and typically includes suggestions on points of emphasis, answers to the case questions that appear within each chapter of the text, cases for discussion, and additional matters for discussion. Each chapter of this manual also includes a list of references that might be useful secondary sources of information; a suggested answer to the Business Decision that begins each chapter of the text; and suggested answers to all case questions and responses to the end-of-chapter review questions. The Case Brief section of the Instructor's Manual contains a brief of each edited case found in the text. For ease of use, the briefs are numbered by chapter in the order they appear in the text. There is a reference to the page in the text where the edited case appears. The tear-out format of this supplement allows instructors to remove any material and incorporate it into their lecture notes.

POWERPOINT PRESENTATION SLIDES

A useful supplement to this edition is the PowerPoint Presentation slides. These slides and an outline for classroom lectures are replications of those used by the authors.

TEST BANK

The Test Bank was written by Michael Katz of the University of Delaware. Instructors can test students' mastery of concepts as the instructors create exams with the use of this Test Bank. Organized by chapter, the Test Bank contains at least 40 multiple-choice questions, 20 true/false questions, and 10 essay questions per chapter. Many of the questions have been modified to correspond with the text's revision. Answers immediately follow each question.

COMPUTERIZED TEST BANK (WINDOWS VERSION)

The computerized Test Bank contains all the multiple-choice, true/false, and essay questions included in the above-described print Test Bank. This powerful system allows tests to be prepared quickly and easily. Instructors can view questions as they are selected for a test; scramble questions; add, delete, and edit questions; select questions by type, objective, and difficulty level; and view and save tests. For Mac copies, please contact your Irwin/McGraw-Hill sales rep.

IRWIN/MCGRAW-HILL BUSINESS LAW CASE DVD/VIDEOS

The exclusive You Be the Judge DVD features 10 interactive case videos that showcase courtroom arguments of business law cases. This interactive DVD gives you the opportunity to watch profile interviews of the plaintiff and defendant, read background information, hear each case, review the evidence, make your decision, and then access an actual, unscripted judge's decision and reasoning. Cases include topics such as sexual harassment, fraud, liability, and oral contracts.

WOULD YOU LIKE A STUDY TOOL TO HELP YOU REVIEW?

Our Student Study Guide, written by author O. Lee Reed, is available for purchase. This workbook contains bonus test questions and study material like chapter outline and learning hints that will help you review and study the main concepts for each chapter. To get your copy of the Study Guide, talk to someone at your bookstore or call us at 1-800-338-3987.

ACKNOWLEDGMENTS

Finally, we would like to thank a number of people. First, without the typing skills of Mary Evans and Donna Ward, the manuscript would not have been so professionally presented. The authors are once again grateful for their work with manuscript drafts.

Second, we are indebted to Andy Winston, our editor; Lisa Nicks, our marketing manager; Sarah Reed, our development editor; and Laura Griffin, our project manager. Together, they provided the support needed to make this edition the best yet.

Third, the following colleagues provided valuable insight during the review process for which each author is grateful. We thank them all for sharing their expertise with us.

Jay Ballantine	University of Colorado
Kerri Bauchner	Montclair State University
Robert B. Bennett	Butler University
Judith Robb Bullock	North Carolina Wesleyan College
Marisa S. Campbell	Meredith College
Laura Marini Davis	Bloomburg University
Richard F. Golen	University of Massachusetts–Dartmouth
Dwayne R. Lambert	California State University, Hayward
James MacDonald	Weber State University
Ann Morales Olazábal	University of Miami
Roger W. Reinsch	University of Wisconsin–La Crosse
Bruce L. Rockwood	Bloomsburg University
Ron Washburn	Bryant College

Finally, but certainly not last, we want to thank all of the professors and students who have used or are using this text. Your feedback has been and continues to be important. Please feel free to share your thoughts with us. You may contact any of the coauthors directly at the Terry College of Business, University of Georgia, Athens, Georgia, 30602, or through the Irwin/McGraw-Hill Publishing Company.

O. LEE REED
PETER J. SHEDD
JERE M. MOREHEAD
ROBERT N. CORLEY

TO THE *student*

HOW TO STUDY THE LEGAL AND REGULATORY ENVIRONMENT OF BUSINESS

To gain the most from this textbook, you should learn how to study written material effectively. You can achieve effective study through use of the SQ3R method, a method widely taught by study-skills psychologists for learning textual material.

SQ3R stands for **survey, question, read, recite,** and **review.** As a study method, it has dramatically improved the grade-point averages of most students who have practiced it. It is based upon the concept that active study of written material improves memory and comprehension of information far better than passive reading. Unfortunately, many students have not recognized the difference between active study and mere passive reading.

Students often read a textbook chapter exactly as they would read a novel or a magazine article. They begin with the first sentence of the chapter and read straight through the material, pausing only to underline occasionally. This way of reading may be suitable for a novel, but it is quite inappropriate for a textbook. Psychologists insist that an active study method must begin with a **survey** of the material to be read. If you plan to spend two hours studying a 30-page chapter, take three to five minutes in the beginning and survey the chapter. First, read the bold-type section headings (each chapter of this book is divided into numbered sections). Second, read a sentence or two from the text of each section. The purpose of this survey is to familiarize you with the topics covered in the chapter. Fight the tendency to stop your surveying process in order to comprehend all of the concepts you are surveying. Comprehension is not the goal of surveying.

Following the survey of all the sections, go back to the beginning of the chapter: Ask yourself a **question** before reading each section. Ask it aloud, if possible, but silently if circumstances demand. The important thing is actually to "talk to yourself." Normally, each section heading can easily be turned into a question. If the section heading reads *Stare Decisis,* ask yourself the question, "What does *stare decisis* mean?"

Only after asking a question are you finally ready to **read** a chapter section. In reading keep your question in mind. By so doing you will be reading for a purpose: To discover the answer to your question.

Upon finishing each section, stop and **recite** the answer to your question. As an example, at the end of the section on *stare decisis* say to yourself, "*Stare decisis* refers to the legal tradition that a judge in a given case will follow the precedent established in similar cases decided by courts in the jurisdiction." According to psychologists, to recite this way greatly aids memory. Recitation also lets you know whether or not you have understood the material just read.

The last step of the SQ3R method is **review.** When devoting two hours to the study of a chapter, take the final 15 minutes of the time to review the material.

Review the questions taken from the headings of each chapter section and recite the answers to them, rereading material if necessary to answer accurately.

While the SQ3R method may be used effectively to study any subject, the **case briefing system** is uniquely designed to aid in the study of court decisions. In studying law, students frequently write up case briefs of each decision they read. Whether you are required to write up every decision is up to your individual instructor. However, the case briefing system provides an excellent framework for comprehending complicated judicial reasoning processes, and you should brief cases whether required to do so or not.

To avoid getting lost in a maze of judicial terminology, you should ask yourself a standard set of questions about each case decision and read to discover the answers to these questions. These standard questions lie at the heart of the case briefing system. They are:

1. Who is the plaintiff and who is the defendant?
2. What are the facts of the case? (Who did what to whom? What is the behavior complained of?)
3. Did the plaintiff or the defendant win in the lower court(s), and which party is appealing? (All decisions in this textbook come from appellate courts.)
4. What was the legal issue or issues appealed?
5. Does the plaintiff or the defendant win on the appeal?
6. What rules of law and reasoning does the appellate court use in deciding the issue?

Here is an illustration of a written case brief. It is a brief of the first case in the book, which is found on page 73. Before looking at the brief you should now read that case. To understand the case you need to know several terms: (1) "bench trial"—a trial before a judge without having a jury; (2) "District Judge"—the judge in a federal district court where trials are held; (3) "Sixth Circuit Court of Appeals"—the federal court that decides appeals of law from the district courts in Michigan and several other Midwestern states; (4) "petition for a writ of certiorari"—the document filed in a supreme court when asking that court to determine whether the court of appeals has properly decided an appeal of law; (5) "affirmed"—what a higher court says when it agrees with the decision of a lower court; it is the opposite of "reversed" or "vacated"; and (6) "dissent"—the opinion that one or more judges of an appellate or supreme court write when they disagree with what the majority of the judges have written.

CASE BRIEF

GRUTTER v. BOLLINGER, 2003 U.S. LEXIS 4800 [The notation following the name of the case indicates that this 2003 case can be found in the computerized LEXIS reporting system.]

Plaintiff and Defendants The plaintiff (who brings the lawsuit against the defendant by filing a complaint) is Barbara Grutter, an applicant to the University of Michigan Law School. The defendants include the law school and Lee Bollinger, president of the university.

Facts The plaintiff Grutter is a white female whose admission to the University of Michigan Law School was denied. She sued the defendants claiming that she was being discriminated against on the basis of her race because the school's admission process allowed a flexible consideration of race and ethnicity that tended to favor groups historically discriminated against.

Lower Courts The district court ruled that the use of race as a factor in admissions was unlawful. The full federal court of appeals reversed the district court, concluding that the law school's use of race was "narrowly tailored," i.e., appropriately narrow, since it was only a potential "plus" factor in admission.

Issue Appealed Does the Equal Protection clause of the Fourteenth Amendment prohibit as unconstitutional the race factor weighing system used in the law school admission process?

Who Wins? The defendants win.

Reasoning
1. Racial classifications are permissible under constitutional equal protection only if they are "narrowly tailored" to "further a compelling state interest."
2. The law school's admission process is narrowly tailored in that it adequately weighs many factors applying to all applicants and assigns weight based on race only within a sensitive, flexible system.
3. The law school has a compelling interest in "attaining a diverse student body."
4. Thus, the Equal Protection Clause is not violated.

Dissent (Four of the nine justices [judges] dissented.)
1. The school's admission process is not narrowly tailored.
2. The school seeks a "critical mass" of students from various backgrounds but does not explain what this means or why it varies from one racial group to another.
3. The "goal of critical mass is simply a sham." Thus the means to attaining its desired end amounts merely to prohibited "racial balancing," similar to a quota.
4. The admissions process is also unconstitutional and not narrowly tailored because it lacks a "reasonably precise time limit" for the racial favoritism given.

GUIDED TOUR

chapter

1

LAW AS THE FOUNDATION OF BUSINESS

BUSINESS DECISION *Darden's Land*

Three years ago the Darden Corporation bought a thousand acres of land that borders the Potowac River in Washam County. While waiting on development opportunities, Darden cut timber to help repay the mortgage loan it took out to buy the land. On March 2, the Washam County Commission proposed an ordinance to establish a 250-foot-wide greenway along the south side of the Potowac that will effectively ban both development and timbering on nearly 80 acres of Darden's land. The same day in an unrelated accident a Darden truck ran over a hunter who was hunting without permission on the company's land. Darden immediately contacted an attorney in Washam City.

What is law?

What does it mean to say that Darden has "property" in the land? That the hunter has "property" in himself?

What sources of law will the attorney have to understand in order to advise Darden about the proposed greenway? The company's potential responsibility to the hunter?

INTRODUCTION

To understand the legal and regulatory environment of busine ate the role of law as the foundation for business practice in t tem. The purpose of this book is to explain the legal system a lations that provide the foundation for the private market. No maintains, however, that not just any kind of law creates a ba ness practice. Only a property-based legal system does this. the foundation of business and the private market, we first ex causes of national wealth.

The thirteenth edition has a timely focus on corporate governance woven into key areas.

BUSINESS DECISION

Each chapter opens with a Business Decision vignette to stimulate student thinking and provoke classroom discussion. These situations are designed to enhance the student's interest by portraying the real-world relevance of the chapter material.

CHAPTER 1   LAW AS THE FOUNDATION OF BUSINESS   19

concept SUMMARY   *Legal Sanctions*

1. Persons and businesses convicted of criminal conduct may be fined, imprisoned, or both.
2. A party that breaches a contract may be required to pay as compensatory damages to the other party the sum of money required to make the victim whole. In addition, special circumstances may justify consequential damages.
3. A tort victim is entitled to collect as damages the amount of money necessary to compensate the injured

party for the total harm caused by the intentional or negligent conduct of the wrongdoer.
4. Punitive damages may be awarded in the case of intentional torts.
5. Statutes and regulations issued by government agencies often authorize sanctions similar to those used in the criminal law, contracts, and torts. They usually go further by using a multiplier for damages and award attorney's fees as well.

2. Courts may use a court order called an **injunction** either to prevent future violations or to correct the impact of past violations. The injunction may prevent anticompetitive behavior or it may even force the breakup of a corporation, as it did for the former American Telephone and Telegraph Company.

3. Persons who suffer injury as a result of noncompliance may sue wrongdoers for *triple* damages.

4. Any property owned in violation of the act that is being transported from one state to another is subject to seizure by and forfeiture to the United States.

Other areas of the law discussed later in this text have similar sanctions. Violations of the securities regulations can result in both criminal sanctions and civil damages. They are covered in Chapter 16. Labor law authorizes the awarding of back pay with job reinstatement to workers who are victims of unfair labor practices. It is covered in Chapter 14. The laws on discrimination in employment have similar sanctions. They are covered in Chapter 15. As you study the various aspects of regulation, keep in mind that the administrative sanctions are modeled after the traditional sanctions for violating statutes. However, they often go further and impose attorney's fees as well.

A PROPERTY-BASED LEGAL SYSTEM AND CORPORATE GOVERNANCE

Under the rule of law in a property-based legal system, all persons have an equal right to their resources. Property problems arise when one person harms another's resources or takes them without permission or authorization. When a stranger takes your car without permission, we call this "theft," and it is easy to appreciate how it violates your right of property under the rule of law. However, more complex property problems can arise.

Much, if not most, business in the United States is transacted through large corporate business organizations. A **corporation** is a business that is chartered by the state to do business as a legal person in a certain form of organization

---

CONCEPT SUMMARY

Critical concepts are recapped in Concept Summaries at various places in each chapter.

CASES

Cases are in the language of the court and carefully edited to give students insight into the law's interface with business actions.

FRIENDS OF THE EARTH V. LAIDLAW ENVIRONMENTAL SERVICES

528 U.S. 167 (2000)

Laidlaw Environmental Services bought a facility in Roebuck, South Carolina, that included a waste-water treatment plant. Shortly thereafter, the South Carolina Department of Health and Environmental Control (DHEC) granted Laidlaw a National Pollutant Discharge Elimination System (NPDES) permit. The permit authorized Laidlaw to discharge treated water into the North Tyger River, but limited, among other things, the discharge of pollutants into the waterway. Laidlaw began to discharge various pollutants into the waterway; these discharges, particularly of mercury, an extremely toxic pollutant, repeatedly exceeded the limits set by the permit. DHEC and Laidlaw reached a settlement requiring Laidlaw to pay $100,000 in civil penalties and to make every effort to comply with its permit obligations. Friends of the Earth (FOE) and Citizens Local Environmental Action Network, Inc., notified Laidlaw of their intention to file a citizen suit against it under the Act.

FOE filed this citizen suit against Laidlaw, alleging noncompliance with the NPDES permit and seeking declaratory and injunctive relief and an award of civil penalties. Laidlaw moved for summary judgment on the ground that FOE lacked Article III standing to bring the lawsuit.

achieved substantial compliance with the terms of its discharge permit. The court did, however, assess a civil penalty of $405,800. The total deterrent effect of the penalty would be adequate to forestall future violations, the court reasoned, taking into account that the defendant will be required to reimburse plaintiffs for a significant amount of legal fees and has, itself, incurred significant legal expenses.

To satisfy Article III's standing requirements, a plaintiff must show (1) it has suffered an "injury in fact" that is (a) concrete and particularized and (b) actual or imminent, not conjectural or hypothetical; (2) the injury is fairly traceable to the challenged action of the defendant; and (3) it is likely, as opposed to merely speculative, that the injury will be redressed by a favorable decision. An association has standing to bring suit on behalf of its members when its members would otherwise have standing to sue in their own right, the interests at stake are germane to the organization's purpose, and neither the claim asserted nor the relief requested requires the participation of individual members in the lawsuit.

Laidlaw contends first that FOE lacked standing from the outset even to seek injunctive relief, because the plaintiff organizations failed to show that any of their members had sustained or faced the threat of any injury in fact from Laidlaw's activities.

---

17.   *For Violating Statutes and Regulations*
    (a)   What types of sanctions are used for the violation of statutes and regulations?
    (b)   What is an injunction?

A Property-Based Legal System and Corporate Governance
    (c)   Why do corporate owners sometimes have difficulty protecting their property interest?
    (d)   Define corporate governance in a specific sense. In a general sense.

TERMINOLOGY REVIEW

For each term in the left-hand column, match the most appropriate description in the right-hand column.

1. Precedent	a. A classification of law that focuses on how many people are impacted by the law
2. *Stare decisis*	b. A court order to stop some action or event
3. Private v. public law	c. A legislative enactment at the local level
4. Procedural law	d. A judge's decision or opinion that is to be followed in the future
5. Ordinance	
6. Dicta	e. A remedy that orders a contracting party to complete what was promised
7. Specific performance	
8. Injunction	f. Rules that guide how the law is to be created or enforced
9. Rule of law	g. The doctrine that means "let the decision stand"
10. Property	h. An opinion of a judge that goes beyond what is needed to decide the merits of a case
	i. A set of exclusive private rights
	j. A system of generally and equally applied laws

BUSINESS DISCUSSION

As the vice president of finance for a company producing and selling electronic switchboards, you are considering foreign investment to build a plant to assemble electronic components. A source in Russia advises you that a town near Moscow may be an excellent location for a new plant. Russians are well educated and willing to work for reasonable wages. Projected construction costs are acceptable. Both rail lines and airports are nearby, and the current Russian government seems politically stable. The town even has a technical college that will be an excellent source for skilled employees. The plant will ship most of the finished electronic components back to the United States.

Do you know everything you need to make an investment decision?

If not, what else do you need to know about investment in foreign countries?

What does it mean to say that law is the foundation of the private enterprise system?

BUSINESS DISCUSSION

Each chapter closes with a Business Discussion to bring critical thinking full circle. Open-ended questions encourage students to use their newly developed understanding of legal and managerial interaction.

TOBACCO INDUSTRY *insight*

Consider the ethical significance of the following facts:

Tobacco products have been consumed in the United States since at least the early 1600s.

Hundreds of thousands of people are involved in the growing, manufacturing, distributing, and selling of tobacco products.

In the first 20 years of tobacco litigation, juries did not award plaintiffs a single penny against tobacco companies.

Scientists and doctors accept that tobacco consumption is an important contributing factor in cancer and heart disease. Excess consumption of fatty foods and lack of exercise are also contributing factors to these diseases.

Between 300,000 and 400,000 people in the United States die annually due to tobacco consumption.

The average age of beginning tobacco consumption is around 16.

Almost no one begins tobacco consumption past age 21. Three thousand new teenagers begin tobacco consumption every day.

Tobacco companies spend approximately $5 billion annually in advertising and promoting tobacco sales. The main strategy of tobacco promotion is to associate glamour, excitement, sex, and desirable life images with tobacco consumption.

The law requires that health warnings accompany the advertising and sale of tobacco products.

The nicotine in tobacco is considered addictive. However, millions have stopped tobacco consumption.

TOBACCO INDUSTRY INSIGHT

These boxes portray the role of the judicial courts in dealing with big industry cases like those of the tobacco industry that question the protection of the Constitution's free-speech clause.

CYBER LAW *connection*

New developments in society raise fresh issues of law because law is the principle social force ordering society. Consider the following questions of public and private law raised by computers, the Internet, and the Information Age.

- Do the creators of software have a property interest in the "look and feel" of the software? A property interest in what it does (i.e., in its functionality)?
- How do we create legally binding agreements over the Internet?
- Is it unconstitutional for the FBI to monitor e-mail transmissions without a search warrant through software that can detect possible evidence of criminal communication?
- Do the purchasers of copyrighted music and video have a legal right to give copies of that expression to others?
- Do employers violate federal labor law by monitoring employee e-mail and disciplining employees for criticizing the employers?
- Can Congress constitutionally regulate sexually explicit materials transmitted over the Internet?
- Can states prohibit in-state delivery of untaxed alcoholic beverages ordered from out-of-state sellers over the Internet?
- Are Internet providers like America Online ever liable for what users say over their services?

The chapters of this textbook discuss these and other questions of cyber law. Answers to these questions will come through a series of court cases that interpret and apply existing public and private law, prior case precedents, and new legislation and regulations. This emphasis on the courts is a hallmark of the common law legal system.

CYBER LAW CONNECTION

The addition of Cyber Law Connection boxes throughout demonstrates the author's passion for keeping the text in line with the high level of interest in this area.

SUPPORT MATERIALS

INSTRUCTOR'S MANUAL

The Instructor's Manual consists of objectives, suggestions for lecture preparation, recommended references, answers to problems, and problem cases. It also includes answers to the Student Study Guide questions.

TEST BANK

The Test Bank consists of true/false, multiple-choice, and short essay questions in each chapter. Approximately 35 questions are included per chapter. The Test Bank is also available in computerized format so you can create your own tests.

POWERPOINT PRESENTATION

The PowerPoint presentation includes hundreds of slides that provide lecture outline material, as well as slides that expand on important concepts and figures in the text.

INSTRUCTOR'S RESOURCE CD

The Instructor's Resource CD includes the Instructor's Manual, the computerized Test Bank, and the PowerPoint presentation all on one CD so you can format your lectures.

STUDENT STUDY GUIDE

The Student Study Guide contains additional test questions for students so they can review and study the main concepts for each chapter.

POWERWEB

PowerWeb is an online tool that provides high-quality, peer-reviewed content including up-to-date articles from leading periodicals and journals, current news, weekend updates with assessments, interactive exercises, Web research guide, study tips, and much more! Access PowerWeb through the Online Learning Center or at www.dushkin.com/powerweb. Access to PowerWeb is provided with each new copy of the book.

ONLINE LEARNING CENTER

www.mhhe.com/reed13e

The Online Learning Center (OLC) is a website that follows the text chapter by chapter. The thirteenth edition OLC contains case updates, Business Law in the News updates, quizzes and review terms for students to study from, downloadable supplements for the instructors, and links to professional resources for students and professors.

YOU BE THE JUDGE DVD-ROM

This new DVD features interactive case videos that showcase courtroom arguments of business law cases. This interactive DVD gives students the opportunity to watch profile interviews of the plaintiff and defendant, read background information, hear each case, review the evidence, make their decisions, and then access an actual, unscripted judge's decision and reasoning. There are also instructor's notes available with each video to help prepare you for classroom discussion.

VIDEOS

Two video packages are available. One includes 120 minutes of business law cases taken from the business law telecourse videos. The other includes the video material from the DVD (profile interviews, courtroom arguments, and the judge's verdict) reformatted for VHS for those who may not have access to a DVD player in the classroom.

BRIEF TABLE OF *contents*

TABLE OF *contents*

3   THE COURT SYSTEM   57

13 ANTITRUST LAWS — REGULATING COMPETITION 379

16 SECURITIES REGULATIONS   477

17 ENVIRONMENTAL LAWS AND POLLUTION CONTROL   507

TABLE OF *cases*

LAW AS THE FOUNDATION OF BUSINESS

BUSINESS DECISION   *Darden's Land*

Three years ago the Darden Corporation bought a thousand acres of land that borders the Potowac River in Washam County. While waiting on development opportunities, Darden cut timber to help repay the mortgage loan it took out to buy the land. On March 2, the Washam County Commission proposed an ordinance to establish a 250-foot-wide greenway along the south side of the Potowac that will effectively ban both development and timbering on nearly 80 acres of Darden's land. The same day in an unrelated accident a Darden truck ran over a hunter who was hunting without permission on the company's land. Darden immediately contacted an attorney in Washam City.

What is law?

What does it mean to say that Darden has "property" in the land? That the hunter has "property" in himself?

What sources of law will the attorney have to understand in order to advise Darden about the proposed greenway? The company's potential responsibility to the hunter?

INTRODUCTION

To understand the legal and regulatory environment of business, you must appreciate the role of law as the foundation for business practice in the private market system. The purpose of this book is to explain the legal system and its rules and regulations that provide the foundation for the private market. Note that Chapter 1 maintains, however, that not just any kind of law creates a basis for modern business practice. Only a property-based legal system does this. To appreciate law as the foundation of business and the private market, we first examine some possible causes of national wealth.

1. WHY NATIONS ARE PROSPEROUS OR POOR

Why some nations are prosperous and others poor is of great importance in the world today. Poverty causes immense human suffering. Worldwide, 30,000 children die every day from malnourishment and largely preventable diseases. In poverty lie the roots of much discontent, despair, revolution, and terrorism.

According to the World Bank, 19 nations in 2000 had national income per capita (head) above $20,000 a year, with the figure in the United States being $34,100 annually. In contrast 30 countries had per capita incomes of a dollar a day or less, under $365 a year. The wealthier nations tend to be in Europe, North America, and along the Pacific Rim, whereas the poorer nations are found in the rest of the world, but sometimes they are side by side. For instance, although the United States and Mexico share a common border, the former has seven times the national income per capita that the latter has.

People have put forth several reasons attempting to explain why nations are prosperous or poor. One is *dependency theory,* which asserts that prosperous nations exploit the resources and labor of poor nations through trade, so the wealthy countries are prosperous *because* the poor nations are poor. Yet the fact is that prosperous countries invest and trade much more with each other than they do with poorer nations, and even in the poorest nations, international trade makes up only a small fraction of their economies. Whatever trade-related abuses have occurred in poor countries over the years do not account in any important way for why these nations remain poor.

Some nations have superior natural resources and more fertile land than others, but this does not explain why nations are prosperous or poor. Wealthy Japan has relatively few natural resources and little fertile land but poor Russia has an abundance of both. Many poor regions of South America and Africa actually possess considerable fertile lands, minerals, and other natural resources. Likewise, education and technology certainly play an important role in the prosperity of nations, but these things alone do not account for the differences between prosperous and poor countries. In some parts of the world, well-educated people have no job opportunities, and powerful technologies can be fairly easily transferred between countries. The advantages produced by education and technology development are actually more a result of wealthy economies than their cause.

Business students learn about the significant contribution the private market makes to the greatest wealth of nations. No state planning system seems to have the flexibility and coordinating power for producing new resources that the private market does. When private sellers and buyers are free to make and exchange goods and services, the most likely possibility exists for the economic growth that creates wealth. However, the problem with this view is that it tells only a partial truth. Although all prosperous countries have private markets, so do some poor ones. After the Soviet Union ended and Russia terminated much state planning and freed individuals to carry on business in the private market, many experts expected the Russian economy to take off. Instead, it declined 42 percent over the next seven years. In spite of the end of state control over production, something vital was missing in order to have a successful private market and the prosperity it produces.

That something was an adequate legal system. Increasingly, it is recognized that law itself is the foundation for the private market in the prosperous modern nation. Not just any kind of law will do, however. Only a legal system that gives incentives to the production and exchange of the resources that people need or want creates the potential for prosperous nations. Chapter 7 discusses this assertion in greater detail.

This chapter examines three concepts that establish the foundation for such a legal system: law, the rule of law, and property. It then examines basic classifications of law, outlines the sources of law in our legal system, explains the judicial process and judicial review, and, finally, explores the enforcement of law and legal sanctions such as money damages. Chapter 1 also introduces the important topic of corporate governance, a topic which most of the chapters will emphasize.

LAW, THE RULE OF LAW, AND PROPERTY

Three concepts establish the most effectively functioning marketplace for business in the modern nation: law, the rule of law, and property. Note how they connect to each other.

2. LAW

In the last 10,000 years, human society has moved from roving bands of hunter gatherers to large modern nations with populations in the hundreds of millions. The social forces that hold together societies range from custom and religion to law and economic ties. In the modern nation, however, the most significant of the social forces is **law** because law can glue together diverse peoples of different backgrounds into very large, organized groups. Law is known by everyone as being intended to tell members of society what they can or cannot do. Strangers to a society may not understand or appreciate complex and subtle customs of behavior, but they can observe the formal laws governing what kinds of activities are permitted and prohibited in society. Lawyers, judges, and other trained interpreters of the rules can help them in this process.

A simple definition of law follows:

- Law is made up of rules.
- These rules are laid down by the state and backed up by enforcement.

Law is a formal social force, meaning that laws come from the state and are usually written down and accessible so those who need to understand and obey them can. To maintain order in society, adequate enforcement institutions such as courts and the police are a necessary part of the legal system. As the countries of the former Soviet Union are finding out, written laws mean little unless they can be promptly and fairly enforced. Without adequate enforcement, resources can be taken from those who have them, and agreements can be disregarded. Unless there is confidence in fair and neutral enforcement institutions, the certainty and trust necessary to make complex, long-term business arrangements are absent. People must spend much of their time guarding their resources rather than developing them.

3. THE RULE OF LAW

In a modern nation, law is important to implement either the commands of a dictator or the will of the people in a democracy. However, only in democracies is there true concern for the rule of law, which goes beyond merely thinking of law as governmental commands backed up by force. Under the **rule of law,** laws that are made are *generally* and *equally* applicable. They apply to all or most members of society and they apply to various groups in the same way.

Under the rule of law, law applies to lawmakers as well as to the rest of society. Thus, lawmakers have an incentive to make laws that benefit everyone. Rule-of-law nations adopt laws supporting the private marketplace because it is in everyone's interest, including the lawmakers'.

In today's international business environment, more and more voices are calling for the rule of law. The secretary-general of the United Nations says that "without confidence based on the rule of law; without trust and transparency—there could be no well-functioning markets." The managing director of the International Monetary Fund asserts that "high quality" economic growth depends "in particular on the rule of law" which is a "lodestar for all countries." Observes the managing director of J. P. Morgan and Co.: "An environment in which courts cannot be relied upon to adhere to the rule of law is an environment in which businesses will be reluctant to invest and in which development will be stunted." He calls the rule of law "a cornerstone of free trade."

Unfortunately, the rule of law is an ideal rather than a complete fact in even the most democratic nation. Special interest groups attempt to persuade lawmakers to benefit these groups at the expense of others. And it is not always clear what it means to apply laws generally and equally. Still, in a democracy well-educated voters who understand the importance of the rule of law can hold to account lawmakers who excessively favor special interests.

4. PROPERTY

The third concept that founds the marketplace in the modern nation is **property,** which establishes private exclusive rights in resources. It is through the law of property that individuals and business organizations can possess, use, and transfer their private resources. Without law that guarantees property in resources, there is little incentive for anyone to develop resources since they may be seized by the state or by others who want them. Where there is inadequate property law, individuals either have few resources or must guard their resources by force, and the conduct of modern business is almost impossible due to lack of trust.

Even attorneys sometimes confuse the right of property with the resources, especially the physical resources, that property guarantees. We think of "my land" as being the same thing as "my property," but in a legal sense it is not. Consider the following example: *Tree* is a general word that can describe all sorts of specific things like *oak, pine, elm,* or *maple.* You may even see a new leafy thing and ask, "What kind of tree is that?" However, *property* is not a general word meaning *land, car, widget,* or *banana,* and you do not see a new thing for the first time, for example, a new automobile, and ask, "What kind of property is that?"

To understand property, think of the word as meaning *ownership.* If you own a piece of land you enjoy the right of property to it. The legal significance of property is that an owner of land (one who has property in it) can exclude or keep others from interfering with the land. Owners can exercise their right of property by having the police or courts keep others from interfering with what they own.

The enforcement of the property right under the rule of law gives people incentive to develop the resources they own. Something deeply natural to human beings encourages them to exert the greatest productive effort only when they can prevent others from taking the resources they produce. Only when people control what they

HOW PROPERTY PROTECTS THE POOR

Many people have difficulty grasping how property protects the poor. After all, do the poor even have "property"? Legally, the answer is "yes," because property is an exclusive right to keep others from interfering with one's resources, not the resources themselves, and under the rule of law, this right protects the resources of the poor as well as those of the wealthy.

In many parts of the world that have no adequate property systems, poor "squatters" lack formally recognized ownership of the land they live on. They spend much of their time defending their possession and cannot use their houses and land to secure loans that would allow them to start small businesses. Peru, however, has begun recognizing and registering the legal ownership of these squatters in their homes.

Princeton graduate student Erica Field compared areas of Peru where legal property has been formally secured with areas where it is yet to be recognized. She found the granting of the right of property to the "average squatter family" was associated with a 17 percent total household work increase, a 47 percent increase in the probability of working outside the home, and a 28 percent decline in the likelihood of child labor in the family. Her 2002 study concluded that formal ownership means the families no longer have to spend as much time protecting their homes and can engage in more productive work, which makes them less poor.

The ownership program in Peru was initiated following the ideas of economist Hernando de Soto. De Soto's ideas and work have spread to other countries, and he has gained support from many world leaders, including Presidents George W. Bush and Bill Clinton. De Soto believes that western and Pacific Rim nations are the world's most wealthy because they have had the rule of law and the law of property the longest. He maintains that law is the "hidden architecture" of the modern private market.

produce will they give production their maximum effort. It is a property-based legal system that enables such control by allowing people to exclude others from interfering with what their efforts produce. Importantly, such a system protects and assists the poor as well as the wealthy. (See the box "How Property Protects the Poor.")

State-controlled production does not come close to matching the national levels of goods and services produced under private property systems (capitalism). This illustrates that the incentive to maximum effort comes from the property right. The countries that have enjoyed strong property systems for the past several centuries uniformly have the highest national incomes, and those countries that do not protect private productive efforts under a strong property system are the world's poorest. The exclusionary right of property provides a basis for the private market and modern business. Scholars have traced the economic flourishing of Western civilization during the last several hundred years to the increasing recognition of the right of property in the nations of the West.

5. PROPERTY IN ITS BROADEST SENSE

Property can be thought of as the central concept underlying Western legal systems. (See the figure "The wheel of property.") Most of the topics discussed in this book relate to the exclusionary right of property. Contract law enables an owner to exchange resources (Chapter 8), especially at a future date. Tort law compensates owners whose resources are wrongfully harmed by the actions of others (Chapter 9). Criminal law punishes those who harm an owner's resources in particular ways, for example, by theft (Chapter 10). The law of business organizations identifies how individuals can own and use private resources in groups (Chapter 11).

Regulatory law both protects ownership and sets limits on private resource use (Chapter 12). Antitrust law forbids owners from monopolizing classes of resources and sets rules for how businesses can compete to acquire ownership in new resources (Chapter 13). Securities laws regulate the transfer of ownership in certain

The Wheel of Property

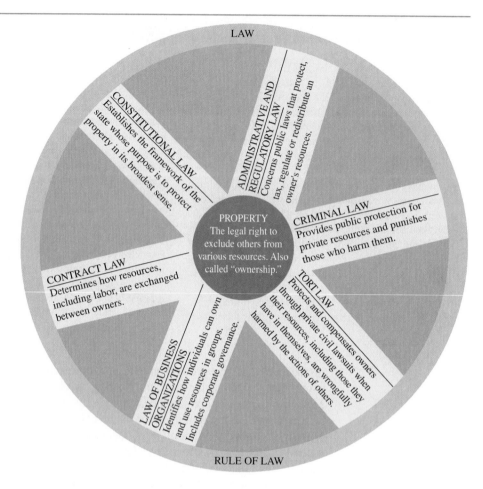

profit-making opportunities (Chapter 16). Environmental law controls how owners can use their resources when creating pollution (Chapter 17). Even labor laws and antidiscrimination laws involve property in the sense they protect the employees' right to exclude employers from interfering with certain self-ownership interests of the employees (Chapters 14 and 15). Finally, a theme of the entire book, corporate governance, specifically concerns the law protecting the owners of a business organization from the managers who run it for them. Generally speaking, corporate governance also refers to any law regulating and limiting private owners' productive resources and their use.

In its broadest sense, property includes an ownership of individual constitutional and human rights in ourselves that excludes the state from interfering with these rights. Today, we usually call our relationship to these rights "liberty," but liberty and property in this sense have almost identical meanings. John Locke, the seventeenth-century English philosopher who greatly influenced the framers of the Constitution, asserted that private property begins with the right we have in ourselves and in our efforts and actions. He said that an individual is the "proprietor [owner] of his own person, and the actions or labour of it" and that this is "the great foundation of property." Later, James Madison wrote that property "in its larger and juster meaning . . . embraces everything to which a man may attach

RUSSIA'S PROPERTY PROBLEMS

When the former Soviet Union collapsed, many observers thought that the new private market would promptly improve Russia's economy. However, that economy went into a serious decline from which it has been slow to recover. Why? Most now consider that Russia's lack of the rule of law and the law of property account for its poor economy.

The government still controls over half of the resources in Russia. Much of what private control of resources exists in Russia has been gotten through force, fraud, and corruption. One study in Moscow found that small business owners must pay over $30,000 a year in bribes to corrupt officials and extortionists. Developing property law in Russia often does not allow a single individual to control all the ways that land can be used. When disputes over agreements arise, businesses cannot depend on the courts to resolve issues justly and impartially.

Generally and equally applied property rights, their transfer by contract, and the support of adequate enforcement institutions like courts will provide a necessary basis to move the Russian economy toward prosperity. But the Russian people will have to be educated about the legal foundation of the wealth of nations.

value and have a right. . . . [A] man has property in his opinions and free communication of them. . . . In a word, as a man is said to have a right to his property, he may be equally said to have a property in his rights." For Madison and other constitutional framers, property protected not only physical resources like land but also human rights like freedom of speech, freedom of religion, and freedom from unreasonable intrusion by the government. The individual's very relationship to society was defined by the word *property*. Scholars have pointed out that the modern understanding of human rights began with the concept of property.

Nearly two million students study business in the United States; one hundred thousand of them are from other countries. As necessary as it is for them to grasp technical business subjects involving computers, debits and credits, balance sheets, quality control circles, and consumer behavior, it is equally vital for them to appreciate how law and the legal concept of property found conditions for the private marketplace in society. The secret to social prosperity and the wealth of nations lies in the adequate foundation of property law and the legal system to implement it. For an example of the difficulties that occur when a nation tries to implement a private marketplace without the enforcement of proper laws see the box titled "Russia's Property Problems."

CLASSIFICATIONS OF LAW

Even when you understand the significance of law, the rule of law, and property to the private marketplace, you still have much left to know about the legal and regulatory environment of business. In large part, learning about law demands an extensive vocabulary of legal terms and concepts. It will be useful in organizing this vocabulary to examine several major classifications of law.

6. COMMON LAW AND CIVIL LAW

The world has two major legal systems: common law and civil law. The United Kingdom, the United States, Canada, Australia, Jamaica, New Zealand, and a few other countries—all colonized by England—follow the common law. The **common law** legal system emphasizes the role of judges in determining the meaning of laws and how they apply. It arose beginning in the eleventh and twelfth centuries as the English monarch appointed royal judges to ride circuits around the English countryside and to resolve disputes in the name of the king (or queen). As there was little formal law to apply to many disputes, the decisions handed down by the judges literally made the law.

By the time the English legislature (Parliament) emerged, a huge body of written judicial decisions was "common" to all of England. The role of judges in making and interpreting law was in place. English colonists then brought the common law to what became the United States and various other countries. The common law continues its development even today, and so significant is the role of judges in the United States that they determine the meaning of the Constitution and can declare void the legislation of Congress and the acts of the president.

The world's nations not colonized by England generally observe civil law legal systems. The **civil law** relies more on legislation than judicial decisions for law. Like common law courts, civil law courts decide the facts in a disputed case (e.g., who did what, who committed a crime or breached a contract), but civil law courts defer to the legislature for answers to legal issues. Civil law systems do not recognize judge-made law. Nor does civil law recognize the importance of prior judicial decisions, called precedents. Only Louisiana, among the U.S. states, follows a partial civil law system. This is due to Louisiana's historical ties with France rather than England.

7. PUBLIC AND PRIVATE LAW

Another way of classifying the law is to divide it into matters of public law and matters of private law. **Public law** involves those matters that involve the regulation of society as opposed to individuals interacting. Examples of public law include constitutional law, administrative law, and criminal law.

Constitutional law involves the interpretation and application of either the federal or a state constitution. **Administrative law** describes the legal principles that apply to government agencies, bureaus, boards, and commissions. **Criminal law** encompasses all legal aspects of crime. In each of these areas, society, or "the people," are directly involved in the issues. Their interests are represented by a governmental agency, officer, or official whose obligation it is to see that justice is accomplished and the ends of society achieved. Public law provides a major portion of the legal environment of business. For this reason much of the material in subsequent chapters deals with constitutional and administrative areas of public law and their application to business.

Private law encompasses those legal problems and relationships that exist between individuals. Private law is traditionally separated into the law of property, the law of contracts, and the law of torts.

As the beginning of this chapter explains, **property law** involves the state's recognition of an individual's exclusive rights in both tangible (physically touchable) and intangible resources. Special areas of property law concern land, goods, copyrights, patents, and trademarks. **Contract law** covers when agreements to exchange resources can be enforced. These agreements transfer from one person to another property in various resources ranging from land to information to services in one's work. **Tort law** addresses when law allows one to recover damages from another for injuries that do not arise from breaches of agreement. The table "Classifications of Legal Subjects" provides a further breakdown of these private law topics.

Classifications of Legal Subjects

The Law of Property	The Law of Contracts	The Law of Torts
Real property	Sales of goods	Assault and battery
Personal property	Commercial paper	Slander and libel
Leases	Secured transactions	Invasion of privacy
Bailments	Bank deposits and collections	Interference with contracts
Wills	Creditor's rights	Conversion
Trusts and estates	Consumer protection	Negligence
Mortgages	Debtor protection	Product liability
Intellectual property		

We live in a time of the rapid generation and distribution of new information through computers and technology. This development raises many issues of property, contract, and tort law. The text contains chapters on each of these areas of the private law. See the box "Cyber Law Connection" for examples of new questions of public and private law.

CYBER LAW *connection*

New developments in society raise fresh issues of law because law is the principle social force ordering society. Consider the following questions of public and private law raised by computers, the Internet, and the Information Age.

- Do the creators of software have a property interest in the "look and feel" of the software? A property interest in what it does (i.e., in its functionality)?
- How do we create legally binding agreements over the Internet?
- Is it unconstitutional for the FBI to monitor e-mail transmissions without a search warrant through software that can detect possible evidence of criminal communication?
- Do the purchasers of copyrighted music and video have a legal right to give copies of that expression to others?
- Do employers violate federal labor law by monitoring employee e-mail and disciplining employees for criticizing the employers?
- Can Congress constitutionally regulate sexually explicit materials transmitted over the Internet?
- Can states prohibit in-state delivery of untaxed alcoholic beverages ordered from out-of-state sellers over the Internet?
- Are Internet providers like America Online ever liable for what users say over their services?

The chapters of this textbook discuss these and other questions of cyber law. Answers to these questions will come through a series of court cases that interpret and apply existing public and private law, prior case precedents, and new legislation and regulations. This emphasis on the courts is a hallmark of the common law legal system.

8. CIVIL LAW AND CRIMINAL LAW

Another means of classifying the law is to divide it into civil law and criminal law. For administrative purposes, courts usually separate criminal actions from all other lawsuits. *Civil* cases may include suits for breach of contract or tort cases, such as suits for personal injuries. Typically, they involve a request for damages or other appropriate relief that does not involve punishment of the wrongdoer. *Criminal* cases involve a representative of government attempting to prove the wrong committed against society and seeking to have the wrongdoer punished by the court system.

9. SUBSTANTIVE LAW AND PROCEDURAL LAW

Another important classification or distinction in law is between substance and procedure. **Substantive law** defines the legal relationship of people with other people or between them and the state. Thus, the rules of law governing the creation or enforcement of a contractual promise are substantive in nature. **Procedural law** deals with the method and means by which substantive law is made and administered. The time allowed for one party to sue another and the rules of law governing the process of the lawsuit are examples of procedural laws. Thus, substantive rules of law define rights and duties, while procedural rules of law provide the machinery for enforcing those rights and duties.

Judicial procedures involve the conduct of lawsuits and appeals and the enforcement of judgments. The rules for conducting civil trials are different from those for criminal trials. For example, each party may call the other party to the witness stand for cross-examination in a civil trial, but the defendant may not be required to testify in a criminal case. Procedural problems sometimes arise concerning papers filed in lawsuits, the admission of evidence, and various other techniques involved in trying the case. They are the rules of the game. In Chapter 4, you will study these procedural aspects of law in greater depth.

SOURCES OF LAW

The Business Decision that introduces this chapter asks you about the sources of law that the Darden Corporation's attorney must consider in order to evaluate its problems. The next sections answer that question.

10. CONSTITUTIONS

The constitutions of the states and federal government are the highest laws of the nation. An attorney advising you about a legal problem knows that as a source of law, constitutions override all other sources. The U.S. Constitution establishes the federal government, and its amendments guarantee basic rights and liberties to the people of the nation. State constitutions also provide a general structure for state government, dividing it into legislative, executive, and judicial branches, giving each branch checks and balances on the others, and defining the powers and functions of the various branches. Like the U.S. Constitution, the state constitutions guarantee various rights and liberties.

In consulting constitutional sources of law, your attorney will look closely to determine if regulations or legislation that affect you violate your constitutional rights. If your rights are violated, the laws violating them are void, (i.e., these laws have no legal effect on you). Chapter 6 examines more closely how the U.S. Constitution in particular applies to business practice.

An important distinction exists between the federal and state constitutions. The U.S. Constitution contains grants of authority from the states to the federal government. All powers not specified in the federal constitution are retained by the states. This means that the U.S. Constitution identifies what the federal government can do, but the state constitutions tell the state governments what they cannot do.

11. LEGISLATION

After the constitutions, your attorney will consult formal written laws known as **legislation** as the most significant source of law. Our elected representatives serving in the legislative branch of government create and adopt legislation. Legislative bodies exist at all levels of government, including not only the federal Congress but also state general assemblies, city councils, and many other local government bodies that adopt or enact laws. Legislation in its broad sense also includes treaties entered into by the executive branch of government and ratified by the Senate.

Legislation adopted by Congress or a state legislature is usually referred to as a **statute** or **act.** Laws passed by local governments are frequently called **ordinances.** Compilations of legislation at all levels of government are called **codes.** For example, we have local traffic codes covering such matters as speed limits, and state laws, such as the Uniform Commercial Code, that cover all aspects of commercial transactions. The statutes of our federal government are compiled in the United States Code.

Uniformity of Legislation Because Congress, 50 state legislatures, and countless local governments enact statutes and ordinances, there is concern about lack of uniformity in the law. If the law lacks uniformity, it decreases the certainty necessary for the conduct of business and the general ordering of society.

Legislators can achieve uniformity in the law through two methods. First, Congress can enact a single law that preempts (overrides) varying state laws. Second, the state legislatures can all adopt a single uniform law in a particular area. The latter method has been attempted by a legislative drafting group known as the National Conference of Commissioners on Uniform State Laws. These commissioners endeavor to promote uniformity by drafting model acts. When approved by the National Conference, proposed uniform acts are recommended to the state legislatures for adoption.

More than 100 uniform laws, mostly related to business activities, have been drafted and presented to the various state legislatures. The response of the states in adopting these proposed laws has varied. A few of the uniform laws have been adopted by all the states. Sometimes a state adopts the uniform law in principle but changes some of the provisions to meet local needs. As a result, there are "nonuniform state laws."

The most significant uniform law for business is the **Uniform Commercial Code (UCC).** It was prepared for the stated purpose of collecting in one body the law that "deals with all the phases which may ordinarily arise in the handling of a commercial transaction from start to finish." Thus it covers the law as it relates to the sale of goods, the use of commercial paper to pay for them, the banking system, and the giving of security to ensure that the purchase price will be paid. The Uniform Commercial Code is limited to commercial transactions involving personal property and is not applicable to contracts for the sale of real estate or to contracts for personal services. Although the UCC, due to its private law orientation, is not a matter of significant focus in this text, its provisions are discussed in Chapter 8 on contracts.

Interpretation of Legislation   Legislation often is written in general terms. The precise meaning of the law often is unclear. In our legal system, it is up to the judiciary to determine the meaning of general language in a legislative enactment and apply it to the limited facts of a case. The court's purpose in interpreting a statute or an ordinance is to determine the intent of the legislature when the statute was enacted. Such a process is called **statutory construction.** Considering the legislative history of statutes, applying rules for interpreting specific types of legislation, and using rules for interpreting various kinds of statutory words are all a part of statutory construction.

12. ADMINISTRATIVE REGULATION

Whatever legal problem your business has, your attorney must consider administrative regulation as a major source of law. As previously stated, legislatures often enact statutes in broad, general terms. Legislative bodies, recognizing the need for greater specificity, often authorize the creation of administrative agencies to provide clarity and enforcement of a legal area. Examples of such actions include the establishment of the Environmental Protection Agency (EPA), the Securities and Exchange Commission (SEC), and the Occupational Safety and Health Administration (OSHA).

Each of these agencies and hundreds more regulate business activities through the adoption of rules and regulations. Administrative agencies also can be empowered to investigate businesses to determine if laws have been violated. Many agencies can hold their own hearings resulting in findings of a business's guilt or innocence. Other agencies can prosecute alleged violations of the rules and regulations.

Section 17 of this chapter discusses possible penalties for violations of administrative rules, regulations, and decisions. Chapter 12 provides further details on the creation, operation, and impact of agencies. Suffice it, for now, to say that almost every business activity is regulated to some degree by the administrative process at the federal, state, or local level.

13. JUDICIAL DECISIONS

Finally, your attorney must consult the decisions of judges as a source of law. Even after considering constitutional language, reading legislation, and referring to administrative regulation, your attorney must still know the judicial decisions, called "case law," that apply to your legal problem. These decisions interpret the relevant constitutional, legislative, and regulatory laws. As previously discussed, judges also make and interpret the common law.

When judges, especially judges who decide appeals from trial courts, make decisions on legal issues, they write their decisions, or **opinions,** setting out reasons. These case opinions are collected and published in book volumes known as "reporters," and these opinions now become **precedents** for future cases involving similar facts and legal issues. To locate prior precedents, it is helpful to know the **citation** for the case where a precedent is found. For example, a case opinion cited as 313 N.W.2d 601 (1982) can be located on page 601 of volume 313 of the *Northwestern Reporter,* second edition, a case decided in 1982. Knowing a case citation, you can easily locate the case in a library or through computer databases. Keyword searches through law digests can also find case precedents on given legal topics.

The extensive reliance of our legal system on judicial decisions has both advantages and disadvantages. It is useful to summarize these.

Advantages The precedent-oriented nature of the common law system is founded on the doctrine of **stare decisis.** This common law doctrine means that, when possible, judges in current cases follow the meaning of law determined by judges in prior cases. *Stare decisis* arose from the desire of courts as well as society for certainty and predictability in the law. In addition, following precedent was expedient. The common law, through precedent, settled many legal issues and brought stability into many areas of the law, such as contracts. Relying on prior decisions, individuals could then act with reasonable certainty as to the legality of their conduct.

Disadvantages The benefits of the doctrine of *stare decisis* and the common law system are counterbalanced by some significant disadvantages. While these burdens are discussed in the remainder of this section, you should keep in mind that we do not consider these disadvantages as destroying the benefits of certainty, predictability, and stability.

Volume, Time, and Expense. First, notwithstanding the fact that common law arose out of a desire for certainty and is designed to create it, common law creates a great deal of uncertainty in the law. The sheer volume of judicial decisions, each possibly creating precedent, makes the "law" beyond the comprehension of lawyers and judges, let alone the rest of us. Large law firms employ lawyers whose sole task is to search the case reports for the law to be used in lawsuits and in advising clients. Access to hundreds of volumes of cases is required. Due to this volume of cases, the common law system does not provide the level of certainty and predictability envisioned by its English creators so many centuries ago.

Instead, it may require hundreds of hours of research time. Since lawyers often charge by the hour, the cost of doing research to "find the applicable law" is becoming increasingly expensive. Although computer search tools are helpful in reducing the time required to locate appropriate cases, the increasing volume of such cases that must be read carefully causes expenses to climb.

Furthermore, conflicting precedents frequently are discovered. Additional time and expense is required to prepare persuasive arguments as to which of the precedents found is the most applicable to resolving the current case.

No Precedent Exists. Second, in many cases the law cannot be found by searching cases. The law that is used to decide many cases must be made as part of the decision process. Many years ago legal philosopher Jeremy Bentham, in discussing this aspect of case law, observed:

> It is the judges that make the common law. Do you know how they make it? Just as a man makes laws for his dog. When your dog does anything you want to break him of, you wait till he does it, and then beat him for it. This is the way you make laws for your dog: and this is the way the judges make laws for you and me. They won't tell a man beforehand what it is he should not do—they won't so much as allow of his being told: they lie by till he has done something which they say he should not have done, and then they hang him for it. What way,

then, has any man of coming at this dog-law? Only by watching their proceedings: by observing in what cases they have hanged a man, in what cases they have sent him to jail, in what cases they have seized his goods, and so forth.

Dicta. Third, there is an important distinction between precedent and unnecessary opinions of judges. A judicial decision, as precedent for future cases, is limited by the facts upon which it is founded and the rules of law upon which the decision actually is based. Frequently courts make comments on matters not necessary to the decision reached. Such expressions, called **dicta,** lack the force of a judicial settlement. Strictly speaking, they are not precedent that courts will be required to follow within the rule of *stare decisis.* However, dicta may be followed if they are sound and just, and dicta that have been repeated frequently are often given the force of precedent. Moreover, even though a statement by a court is not pure precedent, it does express the court's opinion, and to the extent that the court is knowledgeable about the subject matter, the court's opinion carries some weight.

Rejecting Precedent. Fourth, one of the major reasons that the case law system leads to uncertainty is that a precedent may be changed or reversed. Since case law is susceptible to change, absolute reliance on it is not possible.

Case law created by the judiciary can be changed by the judiciary. The common law is not set in stone to be left unchanged for decades and centuries. As Justice William O. Douglas observed:[1]

> Inherent in the common law is a dynamic principle which allows it to grow and to tailor itself to meet changing needs within the doctrine of *stare decisis,* which, if correctly understood, was not static and did not forever prevent the courts from reversing themselves or from applying principles of common law to new situations as the need arose. If this were not so, we must succumb to a rule that a judge should let others "long dead and unaware of the problems of the age in which he lives, do his thinking for him."

Courts usually hesitate to reject a precedent or to change case law. The assumption is made that a principle or rule of law announced in a former judicial decision, if unfair or contrary to public policy, will be changed by legislation.

Precedent has more force in trial courts than in courts of review, which have the power to make precedent in the first instance. However, *stare decisis* does not mean that former decisions *always* will be followed, even by trial courts. A former ruling may have been erroneous or the conditions upon which it was based may have changed or may no longer exist. The doctrine does not require courts to multiply their errors by using former mistakes as authority and support for new errors. Thus, just as legislatures change the law by new legislation, courts change the law, from time to time, by reversing or modifying former precedents.

Judges are subject to social forces and changing circumstances just as are legislatures. The personnel of courts changes, and each new generation of judges has a responsibility to reexamine precedents and to adapt them to changing conditions. This responsibility is especially present in cases involving constitutional issues. A doctrine known as *constitutional relativity* stands for the proposition that the meaning of the language found in the Constitution is relative to the time in which

---

[1] *The Eighth Annual Benjamin N. Cardozo Lecture delivered before the Association of the Bar of the City of New York on April 12, 1949. By permission from Justice William O. Douglas.*

it is being interpreted. The doctrine has been used frequently by the Supreme Court to give effect to society's attitudes. Under this concept, great weight is attached to social forces and needs, as the court sees them, in formulating judicial decisions. As the attitudes and problems of society change, precedent changes.

Some comments from justices indicate their attitude toward precedent. For example, Justice Wanamaker in the case of *Adams Express Co. v. Beckwith,* 100 Ohio St. 348 (1919), said:

> A decided case is worth as much as it weighs in reason and righteousness, and no more. It is not enough to say "thus saith the court." It must prove its right to control in any given situation by the degree in which it supports the rights of a party violated and serves the cause of justice as to all parties concerned.

Or as Justice Musmanno stated in the case of *Bosely v. Andrews,* 393 Pa. 161 (1958):

> *Stare decisis* is the viaduct over which the law travels in transporting the precious cargo of justice. Prudence and a sense of safety dictate that the piers of that viaduct should be examined and tested from time to time to make certain that they are sound, strong and capable of supporting the weight above. . . . A precedent, in law, in order to be binding, should appeal to logic and a genuine sense of justice. What lends dignity to the law founded on precedent is that, if analyzed, the particularly cited case wields authority by the sheer force of its self-integrated honesty, integrity, and rationale. A precedent cannot, and should not, control, if its strength depends alone on the fact that it is old, but may crumble at the slightest probing touch of instinctive reason and natural justice.

The extent to which precedent is followed varies a great deal depending on the subject matter of the litigation. If the dispute involves subject areas of private law, such as torts, contracts, or property, there is much greater deference to precedent than if the subject area is constitutional law. The fact that precedent is to be given great weight in the areas of private law does not mean that courts will continue to follow a rule of private law where the reasoning behind the rule no longer exists. Even here, precedents are reversed as the needs of society change. The belief that the meaning of the Constitution is relative to the times in which it is being interpreted results in less deference to precedent in constitutional law cases. To the extent that courts provide leadership in bringing about social, political, and economic change, they are likely to give less weight to precedent and more weight to other factors.

Conflict of Laws. A fifth disadvantage of *stare decisis* arises because our country consists of 50 sovereign states. Each creates its own body of common law. The law as it develops on a case-by-case basis in different states varies from state to state. Moreover, the federal legal system is superimposed on the state systems, thus creating additional bodies of judge-made laws.

When a controversy involves more than one state, the difficulty arising from conflicting precedents is compounded. In case law, differences among the states are common and exist in every area of the law.

In cases involving transactions with contact with more than one state, the question must always be asked: Which state law applies? To answer this question a body of law has developed primarily through judicial decisions, which is referred to as **conflict of laws.** The decisions that constitute this body of law simply determine which state's substantive law is applicable to any given question when more than one state is involved. This usually arises where all or some of the facts occur in one state and the trial is held in another. For example, the conflict-of-laws rules

Now you should be able to answer the questions posed by the Business Decision that begins this chapter. Law is a series of rules laid down by and enforced by the state. The Darden Corporation has "property" in the land because it has acquired the land through voluntary exchange without force, fraud, or theft and as a result can exclude others, usually including the state as well, from interfering with (often called "trespassing" on) the land. Likewise, under many circumstances the hunter has a right to exclude others from interfering with his person. It is a bit old-fashioned to say that the hunter "owns himself," but the exclusionary right that protects land, widgets, and new engine designs and the exclusionary right that protects one's person have many similarities.

To advise Darden about the applicable sources of law, the attorney will have to understand both the U.S. Constitution and the relevant state constitution, especially the "takings," or eminent domain, clauses (see Chapter 7). The attorney will also need to read carefully the ordinance itself, which is a type of legislation, and may have to know about the legal rules of various regulatory agencies like the Environmental Protection Agency. The attorney will have to identify the case law that has interpreted the eminent domain clause of the Constitution, legislation like the greenway ordinance, and applicable regulatory rules. Additionally, the attorney will have to know how common law tort decisions apply to the accident involving the hunter, how to appreciate *stare decisis,* and how to distinguish the holding of a case from its dicta.

---

for tort cases are, in most instances, that the law of the place of injury applies. If a car accident occurred in Missouri, but the plaintiff sued the defendant in Illinois, the judge would apply the law of Missouri. In contract disputes some courts apply the law of the state where the contract was made. Other courts favor the law of the state where the parties perform the contract. A few courts use the law of the state with "the most substantial contact" with the contract.

LEGAL SANCTIONS

The enforcement of the law is vital to the rule of law and a "proper" legal system. Law enforcement officials and the courts use several methods to encourage or to force compliance with the obedience to the law. These methods, often called **sanctions,** may be used against a person who has failed to comply with the law. The sanctions are in effect a form of punishment for violating the law. Sanctions also have a preventive function. The threat of sanctions usually results in compliance with the requirements of law.

Because punishment is used to secure obedience to the law, the Fourteenth Amendment to the Constitution of the United States provides in part: "No State shall . . . deprive any person of life, liberty or property without due process of law." This provision recognizes that the law is enforced by taking a person's life, freedom, or the resources that he or she owns. The taking of an owner's resources may be (1) for the benefit of society generally, as when land is taken through eminent domain; (2) to punish someone, as with a traffic fine; or (3) for the benefit of another person, as an award of damages. The right of an individual to take another person's resources (especially money) because that person has failed to meet the requirements of the law (e.g., the breach of a contract) is known as a **remedy.** As you study the following sections, identify the remedies available to those seeking through the courts what belongs to another.

14. FOR CRIMINAL CONDUCT

A *crime* is a public wrong against society. Criminal cases are brought by the government on behalf of the people. The people are represented by a state's attorney or U.S. attorney or other public official. When a person is convicted of a crime, one of the following punishments may be imposed:

1. Death
2. Imprisonment
3. Fine
4. Removal from office
5. Disqualification from holding any office and from voting

Among the purposes of such punishment are to protect the public and to deter persons from wrongful conduct.

15. FOR BREACH OF CONTRACT

The conduct of business is primarily a series of contracts, or legal relationships created between individuals by their own agreement. Business organizations are based on the law of contracts, which in the law of promises by which the parties create the legal rights and duties enforceable by courts.

When one party to a contract fails to do what he or she agreed to do, a **breach of contract** has occurred. The usual remedy for a breach is a suit for dollar damages. These damages, called **compensatory damages,** are awarded to make the victim of the breach "whole" in the economic sense. Such damages compensate the party for all losses that are the direct and foreseeable result of the breach of contract. The objective is that the party be in as good a position as he or she would have been in had the contract been performed. Damages do not make most parties totally "whole," however, because they do not as a general rule include attorney's fees. Unless the contract or some special law provides to the contrary, parties to the contract litigation pay their own attorneys.

In addition to compensatory damages, breach-of-contract cases may award consequential damages when the breaching party knew or had reason to know that special circumstances existed that would cause the other party to suffer additional losses if the contract were breached.

There are other remedies available for a breach of contract. If a breach by one party is serious enough, the other party may be permitted to rescind or cancel the contract. In some circumstances, the remedy of an injured party may be a decree of **specific performance**—an order by the court commanding the other party actually to perform the bargain as agreed. Much of the litigation today, especially in the federal courts, involves one corporation suing another for breach of contract.

16. FOR TORTIOUS CONDUCT

A **tort** is a civil wrong other than a breach of contract committed against persons and their property for which the law gives a right to recover damages. It differs from a crime, which is a wrong against society, although the same act—assault, for example—may be a wrong both against a person and against society.

Tort liability is based on two premises:

1. In a civilized society, persons will not intentionally injure others or their property.
2. All persons will exercise reasonable care and caution in their activities.

The first premise has resulted in a group of torts called **intentional torts.** These include such traditional wrongs as assault and battery, false imprisonment, libel, slander, trespass, and conversion of personal property. This group of torts also includes relatively new torts such as interference with contractual relationships and invasion of privacy. The second premise has led to the general field of tort liability known as **negligence.** Negligence is the failure to exercise the degree of care the law requires under the circumstances. Conduct that is negligent under some circumstances may not be negligent in others.

Each of these premises creates liability for wrongful conduct because a party is at fault. Our legal system in effect says, "If you are at *fault* and cause injury to another or his or her resources, you shall compensate the injured party for the loss with money." Such compensation often involves hundreds of thousands or even millions of dollars. Before concluding that some verdicts are too large, ask yourself, "How much money would it take to make the plaintiff whole?" Keep in mind that the objective of a damage award in a tort case is to compensate the plaintiff for a proven loss or injury caused by the intentional or negligent conduct of another. The award is designed to compensate the injured party in full measure for the total harm caused.

In addition to compensatory damages, some tort cases allow plaintiffs to recover **punitive** or **exemplary damages.** These are money damages awarded one party to punish the other's conduct and to deter others from such conduct in the future. These awards often bear little or no relationship to the actual damages sustained. Punitive damages are frequently awarded in intentional tort cases. They can also be awarded when business conduct is oppressive, malicious, or otherwise indicative of the breaching party's intent to harm the other party.

17. FOR VIOLATING STATUTES AND REGULATIONS

Statutes at both the federal and state levels of government impose a variety of sanctions for violating the statutes or regulations of administrative agencies adopted to accomplish statutory purposes. These sanctions are often similar to those imposed for criminal conduct, breach of contract, or tortious conduct. Many statutes, for example, impose a fine for a violation and authorize damages to injured parties as well.

The laws designed to protect our competitive economic system from anticompetitive behavior provide a good example of the use of sanctions to control business conduct. The Sherman Antitrust Act of 1890 as amended authorizes four sanctions to enforce its provisions:

1. It is a crime punishable by fine, imprisonment, or both to violate many of the provisions.

---

concept SUMMARY   *Legal Sanctions*

1. Persons and businesses convicted of criminal conduct may be fined, imprisoned, or both.

2. A party that breaches a contract may be required to pay as compensatory damages to the other party the sum of money required to make the victim whole. In addition, special circumstances may justify consequential damages.

3. A tort victim is entitled to collect as damages the amount of money necessary to compensate the injured

party for the total harm caused by the intentional or negligent conduct of the wrongdoer.

4. Punitive damages may be awarded in the case of intentional torts.

5. Statutes and regulations issued by government agencies often authorize sanctions similar to those used in the criminal law, contracts, and torts. They usually go further by using a multiplier for damages and award attorney's fees as well.

---

2. Courts may use a court order called an **injunction** either to prevent future violations or to correct the impact of past violations. The injunction may prevent anticompetitive behavior or it may even force the breakup of a corporation, as it did for the former American Telephone and Telegraph Company.

3. Persons who suffer injury as a result of noncompliance may sue wrongdoers for *triple* damages.

4. Any property owned in violation of the act that is being transported from one state to another is subject to seizure by and forfeiture to the United States.

Other areas of the law discussed later in this text have similar sanctions. Violations of the securities regulations can result in both criminal sanctions and civil damages. They are covered in Chapter 16. Labor law authorizes the awarding of back pay with job reinstatement to workers who are victims of unfair labor practices. It is covered in Chapter 14. The laws on discrimination in employment have similar sanctions. They are covered in Chapter 15. As you study the various aspects of regulation, keep in mind that the administrative sanctions are modeled after the traditional sanctions for violating statutes. However, they often go further and impose attorney's fees as well.

A PROPERTY-BASED LEGAL SYSTEM AND CORPORATE GOVERNANCE

Under the rule of law in a property-based legal system, all persons have an equal right to their resources. Property problems arise when one person harms another's resources or takes them without permission or authorization. When a stranger takes your car without permission, we call this "theft," and it is easy to appreciate how it violates your right of property under the rule of law. However, more complex property problems can arise.

Much, if not most, business in the United States is transacted through large corporate business organizations. A **corporation** is a business that is chartered by the state to do business as a legal person in a certain form of organization. Chapter 11 will explain to you the details of corporate legal ownership but, briefly, a corporation is owned by *shareholders* who have *stock* in the business. They vote to elect the *board of directors* who legally run the business but who often hire *managers* to be in charge of day-to-day business operations. In large corporations, few shareholders sit on the board of directors or are managers of these businesses, and thus ownership is usually separate from resource control.

Because of the separation of ownership and control, corporate governance is very important. **Corporate governance** refers to the legal rules that structure, empower, and regulate the *agents* (primarily the board of directors and managers) of corporations and define their relationship to the owners (shareholders). Specifically, corporate governance rules protect the property interest that the owners have in corporations.

Because of the complexity of modern corporations, there are sometimes breakdowns in corporate governance. Managers like the president, vice presidents, or chief financial officer of a corporation can abuse their control of its resources to benefit themselves in ways that impair or even destroy the corporation's value to the shareholders. For example, often these top managers have salaries, bonuses, or stock options that are tied to the corporation's profitability or stock price. If they manipulate the corporation's profit by puffing up assets or concealing debts, they may be able to raise their incomes by millions of dollars even as they mislead their owners about the true value of the corporation and risk corporate collapse when the true situation is disclosed. Other examples of corporate misgovernance include managers' engaging in insider trading of stock, running up stock prices in order to exercise stock options, and taking advantage of business opportunities that rightfully belong to the corporation and its shareholders.

All of these corporate governance failures adversely affect the owners of the corporation, especially when the misgovernance becomes publicly known. Only a relatively few business leaders may engage in such illegal conduct, but in recent years some spectacular failures of corporate governance have occurred. Managers at companies like Enron, Qwest, Global Crossing, Tyco, Health South, Kmart, WorldCom, Adelphia, and ImClone have been criminally prosecuted and/or civilly sued. Tens of billions of dollars in shareholder value have been destroyed. At Enron alone, thousands of workers whose retirements were based on stock ownership of that mismanaged corporation have lost their entire pensions.

In a general sense, corporate governance applies not just to the property relations between the owners and agents of a corporation. Broadly speaking, it refers to the legal property relations that large businesses have with each other, with their customers, and with society. The issue becomes how large businesses, which are mostly corporations, are limited by the rule of law to ensure that they recognize the equal right of other owners in our property-based legal system. How the law protects us from injury-causing products, harmful pollution, destructive (rather than constructive) competition, and certain employment discriminations can also be called corporate governance.

The chapters of this book deal with the specific and general issues of corporate governance in the property-based market. (See the table "Corporate Governance Summary.") In most chapters we will show how the issues of corporate governance relate to your understanding of a "proper" legal system. By the time you complete your reading, you should appreciate how law, the rule of law, and property provide the foundation for our business economy and how effective corporate governance contributes to the wealth of nations.

Corporate Governance Chapter Summary

Examples of the specific and general senses of corporate governance.

Chapter	Topic	Example
Chapter 1	Law and private market	Importance of effective corporate governance in a "proper" legal system.
Chapter 2	Law and business ethics	The moral significance of managerial respect for corporate owners.
Chapter 3	The court system	The role of impartial judges in enforcing corporate governance.
Chapter 4	The litigation process	How the threat of lawsuits helps preserve the integrity of corporate ownership.
Chapter 5	Mediation and arbitration	The advantages of keeping private the resolution of disputes between corporate owners and their agents.
Chapter 6	The Commerce Clause	The constitutional basis for corporate governance in the general sense.
Chapter 7	Intellectual property	Importance of keeping businesses from misappropriating each others' patents, copyrights, trademarks, and trade secrets.
Chapter 8	Agreements with managers	How contracts made by the board of directors with managers help or hurt effective corporate governance.
Chapter 9	Wrongful conduct by corporations and their managers	Tort law as the substantive civil enforcement mechanism of corporate governance.
Chapter 10	Illegal conduct by corporations and their managers	Prosecutions for fraud and lying as the substantive criminal enforcement mechanism of corporate governance.
Chapter 11	Business organizations	The structure of corporate governance in the specific sense.
Chapter 12	Public regulation of business	The agencies that administer corporate governance in the general and specific senses.
Chapter 13	Monopoly and restraints on trade	Antitrust and corporate governance in the general sense: the regulation of competition.
Chapter 14	Labor/management relations	The government's general regulation of the corporation's relationship with employees.
Chapter 15	Employment discrimination	The government's regulation preventing employers from harming employees through certain discriminations.
Chapter 16	Securities regulation	Corporate governance and the public regulation of fraud against shareholders.
Chapter 17	Clean Air Act and Clean Water Act	Corporate governance in the general sense prohibiting environmental pollution.
Chapter 18	International business regulation	Problems of inadequate corporate governance in Russia and many other countries.

KEY TERMS

REVIEW QUESTIONS AND PROBLEMS

Introduction

1. *Why Nations Are Prosperous or Poor*

   (a)   Identify several reasons put forth to explain why nations are prosperous or poor.

   (b)   What does this section say is the foundation of the private market and prosperity?

Law, the Rule of Law, and Property

2. *Law*

   (a)   Define law. Compare and contrast law and custom.

   (b)   What role do the courts and police play in the legal system?

3. *The Rule of Law*

   (a)   Define the rule of law. How does the rule of law differ from law as the commands of the state?

   (b)   Explain why the rule of law is "an ideal rather than a complete fact."

4. *Property*

   (a)   What is property? How does property differ from "resources"?

   (b)   Why is property important to society? To private enterprise?

5. *Property in Its Broadest Sense*

   (a)   Explain why property can be thought of as the central concept underlying Western legal systems.

   (b)   What does James Madison mean when he says we have property in our opinions "and free communication of them."

Classifications of Law

6. *Common Law and Civil Law*

   (a)   What is "common law"? Why is the United States a "common law country"?

   (b)   What is the primary distinction between common law and civil law legal systems?

7. *Public and Private Law*
   (a)   What is public law? Give three examples of public law.
   (b)   Explain private law. Give three examples.

8. *Civil Law and Criminal Law*
   (a)   What is the difference between civil law and criminal law?
   (b)   Explain the two ways that the words *civil law* are used in this chapter.

9. *Substantive Law and Procedural Law*
   (a)   Define substantive law and procedural law.
   (b)   Is contract law substantive law or procedural law? How about a rule specifying that a defendant has 30 days to respond to a complaint?

Sources of Law

10.   *Constitutions*
   (a)   Explain what it means to say that constitutions are the "highest laws of the nation"?
   (b)   Explain the important distinctions between state and federal constitutions.

11.   *Legislation*
   (a)   Give two additional terms for *legislation.*
   (b)   Why is uniformity of law important to business? How can legislators achieve uniformity of the laws affecting business? What is the most significant uniform law affecting business?
   (c)   What is statutory construction?

12.   *Administrative Regulation*
   (a)   Where do administrative agencies come from?
   (b)   For what purposes do administrative agencies exist?

13.   *Judicial Decisions*
   (a)   Define *stare decisis.* What are its advantages? Disadvantages?
   (b)   What is the distinction between a precedent and dicta in judicial decisions, and how does this distinction relate to *stare decisis*?
   (c)   Alex was on a coast-to-coast trip by automobile. While passing through Ohio, Alex had a flat tire. It was fixed by Sam's Turnpike Service Station, and later, while Alex was driving in Indiana, the tire came off and Alex was injured. Alex was hospitalized in Indiana, so he sued Sam in Indiana for the injuries. What rules of substantive law will the Indiana court use to determine if Sam is at fault? Explain.

Legal Sanctions

14.   *For Criminal Conduct*
   (a)   What is a sanction? A remedy?
   (b)   What are the criminal sanctions?

15.   *For Breach of Contract*
   (a)   What is the purpose of compensatory damages?
   (b)   What is specific performance of a contract?

16.   *For Tortious Conduct*
   (a)   What are the two premises of tort liability?
   (b)   When are punitive damages appropriate in a tort case?

17.   *For Violating Statutes and Regulations*

(a)   What types of sanctions are used for the violation of statutes and regulations?

(b)   What is an injunction?

A Property-Based Legal System and Corporate Governance

(c)   Why do corporate owners sometimes have difficulty protecting their property interest?

(d)   Define corporate governance in a specific sense. In a general sense.

TERMINOLOGY REVIEW

For each term in the left-hand column, match the most appropriate description in the right-hand column.

1. Precedent
2. *Stare decisis*
3. Private v. public law
4. Procedural law
5. Ordinance
6. Dicta
7. Specific performance
8. Injunction
9. Rule of law
10. Property

a. A classification of law that focuses on how many people are impacted by the law
b. A court order to stop some action or event
c. A legislative enactment at the local level
d. A judge's decision or opinion that is to be followed in the future
e. A remedy that orders a contracting party to complete what was promised
f. Rules that guide how the law is to be created or enforced
g. The doctrine that means "let the decision stand"
h. An opinion of a judge that goes beyond what is needed to decide the merits of a case
i. A set of exclusive private rights
j. A system of generally and equally applied laws

BUSINESS DISCUSSION

As the vice president of finance for a company producing and selling electronic switchboards, you are considering foreign investment to build a plant to assemble electronic components. A source in Russia advises you that a town near Moscow may be an excellent location for a new plant. Russians are well educated and willing to work for reasonable wages. Projected construction costs are acceptable. Both rail lines and airports are nearby, and the current Russian government seems politically stable. The town even has a technical college that will be an excellent source for skilled employees. The plant will ship most of the finished electronic components back to the United States.

Do you know everything you need to make an investment decision?

If not, what else do you need to know about investment in foreign countries?

What does it mean to say that law is the foundation of the private enterprise system?

2

THE ETHICAL BASIS OF LAW AND BUSINESS MANAGEMENT

The research director of PharmCo, a midsize pharmaceutical company, tells top management of an important new discovery. After years of effort, one of the company's research teams has discovered a drug that will reverse pattern baldness, the leading cause of male hair loss. The potential for profit from such a drug is enormous, but the director cautions that two of the eight principal researchers on the team believe that the drug may also increase the possibility of potentially fatal cerebral aneurysms in a very tiny percentage of users.

> If follow-up animal studies of the new drug do not show significant side effects, would it be ethical for the company to tell the two researchers to keep quiet about their concerns?
>
> Is it ethical to put animals at risk in order to test the drug's safety?

Many poor men in the world will be unable to afford the new drug if PharmCo sets the price too high.

> Is it morally right for PharmCo to maximize its profit even if it means that many men will have to remain bald?
>
> Does your answer change if the drug cures rheumatoid arthritis? AIDS?

Historian Barbara Tuchman was asked, "What's happened to the world of Washington, Adams, and Jefferson?" She replied that we suffer today from "a loss of moral sense, of knowing the difference between right and wrong, and being governed by it." In recent years the emphasis on business ethics shows concern about regaining this moral sense. The close connection between ethics and law makes a discussion of moral sense especially significant to a book on the legal environment.

Justice Oliver Wendell Holmes wrote, "The law is the witness and external deposit of our moral life. Its history is the history of the moral development of the race." Ethical (or moral) values underlie much law, including the law of how business operates and is regulated, making it important for business students to know about the nature of ethics, sources of ethics, and problems of achieving an ethical business organization. This chapter introduces the study of business ethics by examining the current concern over business ethics. It explores the relationship of morality and ethics and then of ethics and law. Two principal approaches to ethics are presented: formalism and consequentialism.

Next, the chapter looks at ethical values for business decision making. It examines trends and looks at four sources of ethical values:

- Legal regulation
- Professional codes of ethics
- Codes of ethics from business organizations
- Individual values

The chapter also considers the problems faced in achieving an ethical business organization. When in groups, people often decide and act differently from the way they act as individuals. This fact has special significance for ethics in business corporations. The chapter examines how the profit motive and business bureaucracy put pressure on ethical decision making and how ethical reform must begin with the top leadership of business organizations. The importance of open communication to the ethical life of a business organization is emphasized, and several strategies for implementing corporate ethics are presented.

Finally, the chapter examines the morality of property, the legal right to exclude others from the resources one has or acquires. The concept of property has moral implications because it recognizes an exclusive private sphere of effort and resources on which the community and the state have no legal claim. It also permits individuals to acquire unequal amounts of the resources that others may need or want. In the broad sense, property reflects moral values concerning the resource relationships among people.

CONTEMPORARY BUSINESS ETHICS

U.S. customs agents caught the president of Ann Taylor, a large chain store, trying to avoid paying duty on $125,000 worth of wristwatches for his personal collection. A substantial civil penalty was proposed. At an Ann Taylor board of directors meeting, one director told the president: "This calls into question your integrity." The president resigned from the company.

More than ever before, business ethics are of concern to the business community and to society. In the 1980s few corporations hired people as ethics officers. Today over 20 percent of big companies have ethics officers whose job is to develop ethics policies, listen to complaints of ethics violations, and investigate ethics abuses. Why have business ethics become so important? Several developments help explain the phenomenon.

1. ETHICS AND SOCIETY

Ours is a diverse society, formed from many ethnic backgrounds, races, and religions. As a result, we have few shared ethical values to guide behavior. When a business decision maker does not share common values with society in general, any decision made has a greater likelihood of arousing ethical concern than if there is a common code of behavior and universally accepted values. Diversity fosters concern over values, and in recent years American society has become more openly pluralistic.

The rising concern over business ethics also responds to a decline in public education and the family structure as sources for ethical teaching. Increasingly sensitive to challenges of bias, school systems have reduced their involvement in promoting shared ethical values and increased their emphasis on the teaching of "value-free" facts. At the same time, the rising divorce rate and numbers of single parents, as well as the tendency of both spouses to work outside the home, has decreased the time families spend together and their power in sharing and shaping ethical values.

Increasing economic interdependence also promotes concerns about business ethics. Not even farm families are self-sustaining. Each of us depends on business and industry for our every necessity—food, clothing, shelter, and energy. The marketplace dominates all aspects of life, and how the marketplace is conducted concerns us. The decisions people in business make have a significant impact on us. When there is a labor-management dispute in the coal industry, one source of electricity is threatened. When manufacturers conspire to raise prices, the cost of our goods goes up. The sale of dangerous pesticides or impure drugs threatens our health. A management decision to close a plant may threaten our jobs.

At the same time, the increasing role of the news media makes us more aware of business decisions than ever before. It has become increasingly difficult for large organizations, including businesses and governments, to hide behavior that is questionable. From the coverage concerning stock market manipulations to accounts of Enron's collapse, the news media heighten public attention and concern. What used to be considered purely private is now considered public. The ethical issues that surround nearly every significant business decision are easier to see than they once were.

In part, business ethics have become of increasing concern because there is evidence in society generally that certain values are declining. For evidence of the decline among high school students, see the box "From Bad to Worse."

FROM BAD TO WORSE

In 2002 the nonpartisan Josephson Institute of Ethics surveyed 12,000 high school students. The following percentages of students admitted to various behaviors in the past year when compared to a similar 1992 study.

	1992	2002
Cheated on an exam	61%	74%
Stole something from a store	33	38
Lied to parents	83	93
Lied to teachers	69	83

In the year 2000 questions were added to the biannual survey. The following percentages admitted to holding these beliefs.

	2000	2002
Willing to "lie to get a good job"	28%	37%
Agreed that "a person has to lie or cheat sometimes in order to succeed"	34	43

2. ETHICS AND GOVERNMENT

These changes in society have been accompanied by changes in the role of government. When business fails to make ethical decisions, when it fails to live up to society's expectations for ethical behavior, government may step in. As the chapters in this book demonstrate, in the last century, government has been increasingly active in regulating business.

In response, business leaders have become increasingly concerned with business ethics precisely because they want to limit further governmental regulation. They recognize that by encouraging ethical conduct and self-regulation within business organizations, they will prevent outside standards from being imposed on them through public law. As a consequence, both business and industry have, in recent decades, developed codes of ethics. Such efforts by professions and businesses to set standards of behavior are evidence of the increasing tendency toward self-regulation.

Federal law also encourages self-regulation. Federal sentencing guidelines reduce criminal fines for legal violations in companies that have taken specific steps to self-police ethical/legal conduct.

THE NATURE OF ETHICS

In 1759 Adam Smith wrote, "However selfish man believes himself to be, there is no doubt that there are some elements in his nature which lead him to concern himself about the fortune of others, in such a way that their happiness is necessary for him, although he obtains nothing from it except the pleasure of seeing it." With this statement the author of *The Wealth of Nations,* perhaps the most famous book on economic theory ever written, recognized a moral element in human nature that goes beyond self-interest.

What is it that makes us care about the fortunes of others? The next sections examine the nature of ethics. What is morality? What are ethics? How are morality and ethics similar? How do ethics relate to law? What are the major ethical systems? How do these systems apply to business decision making? When you have finished reading these sections, come back to these questions and see if you can answer them.

3. ETHICS AND MORALITY

Since earliest childhood we have been told about "right and wrong," "good and bad." It is right (good) to tell the truth. It is right to help others. It is right to obey your parents. It is wrong (bad) to lie. It is wrong to cheat and steal. It is wrong to hurt others. Through such teaching we develop values about right and wrong. These values that guide our behavior constitute our **morality.** In a larger sense, morality is also society's value system.

In society at large the sharing of moral values promotes social cooperation and is a significant means of social control. Shared moral values lead us to accept and trust others. Shared values allow us to recognize when there is proper behavior in others and where limits to behavior rightfully belong. Shared moral values create social harmony.

The sharing of values in business life is as important as it is in other aspects of our lives. Today many businesses try to foster shared moral values in employees. It is right to strive for quality in products and service. It is wrong to discriminate against or harass a person because of race, gender, or religion. One of the successes of many Japanese companies has been to instill shared moral values in their employees.

Internationally, businesses often face problems when they do business with nations with different moral values. What is wrong in the United States may be right somewhere else and vice versa. Is it right to bribe customs officials so that your company's goods can enter a country? Is it wrong for a woman to appear in public without her face covered? Is it right to eat meat and consume alcohol? Is it wrong to talk business on Sunday? On Saturday? On Friday evening? To succeed in international operations, businesses must be sensitive to differences in moral values.

If morals involve what is right and wrong, **ethics** is a systematic statement of right and wrong together with a philosophical system that both justifies and necessitates rules of conduct. In the Judeo-Christian tradition, for example, private ownership of land and goods is highly valued. It is wrong to take something that does not belong to you—hence the rule "Thou shalt not steal."

Ethics involves a rational method for examining our moral lives, not only for recognizing what is right and wrong but also for understanding why we think something is right or wrong. "The unexamined life is not worth living," said the Greek philosopher Socrates. In other words, ethical self-examination is necessary for a meaningful human life.

The end result of ethical examination is what philosophers call **the good.** The concept of the good is central to the study of morality. *The good* may be defined as those moral goals and objectives we choose to pursue. It serves to define who we are. Thus, *leading a good life* means more than *having the good life.* It means more than material possessions and luxury. It means pursuing intangibles, being concerned, as Adam Smith put it, about the fortunes of others. That many in contemporary society do not achieve the good is evident. Mortimer Adler has observed: "Go on a hiking trip with a typical American and listen to what he talks about. . . . He'll talk about food, the weather, football, money, sex. He may seem to be having a good time, but he lacks much that is needed for the good life." Too often, we confuse a good time with a good life.

In summary, morality involves what we mean by our values of right and wrong. Ethics is a formal system for deciding what is right and wrong and for justifying moral decisions. In everyday language, the terms *morality* and *ethics* are often used interchangeably. This chapter will also sometimes use the two words to mean the same thing.

4. ETHICS AND LAW

Ethics and law have similar or complementary purposes. Both consist of rules to guide conduct and foster social cooperation. Both deal with what is right and wrong. Society's ethical values may become law through legislation or court decisions, and obedience to law is often viewed as being ethically correct.

However, there are also differences between ethics and law. Unlike ethical systems, the legal system is an institution of the state. The state enforces legal rules through civil and criminal sanctions, like monetary damage awards, fines, and imprisonment. Many ethical values (regarding the treatment of animals, for example) are not enforced by the state, and many laws (regarding traffic violations, for example) do not address ethical concerns.

Another difference between ethics and law concerns motivation. Although values found in ethics may be imposed on an individual (by the family, the company, or the law), the motivation to observe moral rules comes from within. On the other hand, even though the values found in law may also be personal ethical values of an individual, the motivation to observe the law comes from outside the individual in the form of state sanctions. As Justice Oliver Wendell Holmes explained:

> You can see very plainly that a bad man has as much reason as a good one for wishing to avoid an encounter with the public force, and therefore you can see the practical importance of the distinction between morality and law. A man who cares nothing for an ethical rule which is believed and practiced by his neighbors is likely nevertheless to care a good deal to avoid being made to pay money, and will want to keep out of jail if he can.

Ethical systems also involve a broader-based commitment to proper behavior than does the law. Law sets only the minimum standards acceptable to a society. As a former chief executive officer of Procter & Gamble points out: "Ethical behavior is based on more than meeting minimum legal requirements. It invariably involves a higher, moral standard."

Ultimately, the commitment to ethical values is superior to mere observance of the law in ensuring responsible business behavior. Legal rules can never be specific enough to regulate all business actions that may have socially undesirable or even dangerous consequences. And lawmakers often do not have the information to know whether specific conduct threatens employees, consumers, or the public generally. They may also lack the consensus to act quickly, or to act at all, in the face of potentially harmful business actions. However, a commitment to acceptable business ethics will usually ensure responsible business behavior.

TWO SYSTEMS OF ETHICS

Two principal systems of ethics dominate thinking about morality in Western civilization. They are formalism and consequentialism. Although these two systems are not mutually exclusive in the outcomes of their moral analyses, they begin from different assumptions. Most people adopt elements of both systems in making ethical choices. *It is very important to appreciate how these systems have influenced your own values and moral beliefs even though until now you may have been unaware of it.*

5. FORMALISM

Formalism (also called **deontology**) is an approach to ethics that affirms an absolute morality. A particular act is in itself right or wrong, always and in every situation. For example, lying is wrong. There are no justifications for it, and its wrongness does not depend on the situation in which the lie is told. Formalism is primarily a duty-based view of ethics. To be ethical, you have a **duty,** or moral obligation, not to lie. You have a duty to keep promises. You have a duty not to divulge confidences.

For the formalist (one who expresses the ethics of formalism), the ethical focus is on the worth of the individual. Individuals have rights, and these rights should not be infringed, even at the expense of society as a whole, because they have an intrinsic moral value to them. The Bill of Rights illustrates this view of the rights of individuals. When the First Amendment states "Congress shall make no law . . . abridging the freedom of speech," it takes the formalist approach.

For the formalist thinker Immanuel Kant (1724–1804), to be ethical requires that you act with a good intent. To have a good intent, you have to act in ways that are ethically consistent. This emphasis on consistency Kant called the **categorical imperative.** You are compelled to act in the way you believe everyone should act. You should never act in a certain way unless you are willing to have everyone else act in the same way. You cannot make an exception for your own action. You cannot say, "I can lie (cheat) (steal) (cause injury), but others should not do this to me (to my family) (to my friends)." Kant said that to make an exception for your own behavior is immoral and unethical. Note the similarities between Kant's categorical imperative and the Golden Rule: "Do to others as you would have others do to you."

Formalist thinking raises many questions for business ethics. Are you treating your employees with respect for their rights as individuals, or are you treating them only as units of production to make a profit? If you are willing to lie about your ability to meet a production schedule in order to get a new customer, are you willing to have the customer lie to you about his or her ability to pay? If you pass on information that was told to you in confidence, are you willing to have your confidences passed on? Can business function with widespread lying, cheating, and stealing and without respect for the rights of individuals?

In his novel *The Turquoise Lament,* John D. MacDonald puts words into the mouth of his Travis McGee character that illustrate well a formalist approach:

> Integrity is not a conditional word. It doesn't blow in the wind or change in the weather. It is your inner image of yourself, and if you look in there and see a man who won't cheat, then you know he never will. Integrity is not a search for the rewards for integrity.

The table "Examples of Ethical Formalism" presents other statements that reflect a formalist approach to ethics in business and nonbusiness situations.

The Social Contract   The social contract theory of Harvard philosopher John Rawls furnishes an important recent example of how formalism has influenced thinking about business and personal ethics. This theory is based not on duty but on contract (agreement).

Social contract theory concerns itself with how to construct a just society given the many inequalities of wealth, knowledge, and social status. Rawls suggests a simple first step in determining the ethical values on which a just society

Examples of Ethical Formalism	
Statement	*Source*
"We hold these truths to be self-evident."	Declaration of Independence
"Thou shalt not steal."	The Ten Commandments
"A sale made because of deception is wrong. . . . The end doesn't justify the means."	Caterpillar Code of Ethics
"There are fundamental values that cross cultures, and companies must uphold them."	Thomas Donaldson, business ethics scholar
"Openness in communications is deemed fundamental."	Business Roundtable
The moral sense is "the sense of what is inherently right and wrong. . . ."	Barbara Tuchman, historian

can be built. We should assume that we do not know our age, gender, race, intelligence, strength, wealth, or social status. This step is vital because it keeps us from being self-interested in the ethical values we consider. For example, not knowing our sex or race, will we agree that it is ethical to discriminate in employment compensation based on sex or race? Not knowing our wealth, will we agree that owning property is a fair prerequisite to being able to vote? Not knowing our age or work status, will we agree that it is just for a company to have mandatory retirement of its officers at age 65? Freeing ourselves of self-knowledge, Rawls argues, improves our ability to evaluate the terms of a fair agreement (contract) under which we enter society or join an organization like a corporation.

Placing himself behind a veil of self-ignorance, Rawls proposes two ethical principles. First, everyone is entitled to certain equal basic rights, including liberty, freedom of association, and personal security. Second, although there may be social and economic inequalities, these inequalities must be based on what a person does, not on who a person is, and everyone must have an equal opportunity for achievement. Since there are natural differences of intelligence and strength and persistent social differences of wealth, class, and status, defining "equal opportunity" is crucial to this second ethical principle. Rawls insists that individuals in a just society have the right to an equal place at the starting line. This is as true within a corporation as it is within a country.

Because of its emphasis on individual rights and self-worth, social contract theory has its origin in formalism. It provides a powerful process for ethical business decision making. Social contract theory is especially valuable in international business. In this arena, in the absence of much law, businesses from various cultures must agree as to the terms under which international business is to take place.

6. CONSEQUENTIALISM

The second principal system of ethics is consequentialism. **Consequentialism** (also called **teleology**) concerns itself with the moral consequences of actions rather than with the morality of the actions themselves. For the consequentialist, lying itself is not unethical. It is the consequences, or end results of lying, that must be evaluated for their ethical implications. It is the loss of trust or harm done by lying that is unethical.

If formalism focuses on individual rights, consequentialism focuses on the common good. The ethics of actions are measured by how they promote the common good. If actions increase the common good, they are ethical. If actions cause overall harm to society, they are unethical.

The dominant form of consequentialism is **utilitarianism.** Utilitarianism judges actions by *usefulness,* by whether they serve to increase the common good. For utilitarians, the end justifies the means. But to judge the utility of a particular action, it is necessary to consider alternative courses of action. Only after you consider all reasonable courses of action can you know whether a particular one has the greatest utility.

In 1992 the International Franchising Association (IFA) adopted a new code of ethics. Officers of the association indicated that an important reason for adopting the new code was to head off government regulation of franchising through self-policing. The code states that when a franchiser is going to make a decision about adding a new franchise outlet into an area where a franchisee already owns an existing outlet, it should weigh "the positive or negative effect of the new outlet on the existing outlet." Another factor to be considered is "the benefit or detriment to

Examples of Ethical Consequentialism	
Statement	*Source*
"There is no doubt that ethics pays off at the bottom line."	CEO, Procter & Gamble
"Loss of confidence in an organization is the single greatest cost of unethical behavior."	CEO, KPMG
"The strongest argument for raising the ethics bar boils down to self-interest."	CEO, KPMG
"Cost-benefit analysis (used by various governmental agencies and in business and finance)."	Economic theory, finance theory, and policy studies
"The greatest happiness of the greatest number is the foundation of morals and legislation."	Jeremy Bentham (1748–1832), English social philosopher

the franchise system as a whole in operating the new outlet." The motivation of the IFA in adopting the new ethics code and the quoted language of the code suggest a consequentialist ethical view. The table "Examples of Ethical Consequentialism" illustrates consequentialism in business and nonbusiness situations.

Although business ethics reflect elements of both formalism and consequentialism, they focus more heavily on the latter. Business leaders feel a need to justify what they do in terms of whether or not it produces dividends for their shareholders. Their primary goal or end is to produce a profit. This orientation reflects consequentialism.

The many statements of business leaders that ethics are "good for business" illustrate this point. These statements imply that certain values are important because their end result is useful in increasing productivity and profit rather than because the values are intrinsically good. The way business managers evaluate alternative courses of action through cost-benefit analysis is a form of consequentialism.

One approach to business ethics, called "values-based management," also illustrates consequentialism. The emphasis of this approach teaches ethical values to employees that enhance the profitability of the company. Examples include why it is wrong to use company computers for personal entertainment during work hours and why it is unethical to use company long-distance phone service to contact friends and relatives. (See the box "Virtual Morality.") Note that these examples involve misappropriation of an employer's resources and thus violates the employer's property right.

The Protestant Ethic   In part, the current focus on consequentialism in business ethics is due to the decline in business life of what has been described as the **Protestant ethic.** With the Protestant Reformation of the sixteenth century came a new emphasis on the importance of the individual. Instead of relying on the intercession of a church hierarchy to achieve grace, each person, Protestants asserted, had the means to address God personally. Thus religion provided the impetus to hard work and achievement. Human desire and indulgence, said Protestants, should be bent to God's will through self-denial, rational planning, and productivity. The Protestant ethic was rooted in a formalist approach: honesty and keeping promises were intrinsically good.

CYBER LAW *connection*

Computers and the ease with which employees can use them for personal as well as employment reasons raise many ethical issues, which some have begun terming *virtual morality.* Is it wrong to use the Internet from work for holiday shopping? To help one's children with schoolwork? To send personal e-mail to a friend on the other side of the country? To hunt for a new job? Some businesses prohibit all personal use of company computers. Others, such as Boeing Company, permit personal use of computers during working hours, but limit such use to "reasonable duration and frequency." Even then such use should not cause "embarrassment to the company."

From the perspective of values-based management, it is easy to see that keeping employees from wrongful computer use may improve the profitability of the employer. On the other hand, improper use of what another owns raises individual moral issues as well. Similarly, if an employer has purchased the time and effort of an employee, is it morally right for the employee to use those resources for personal reasons?

Increasingly, employers are monitoring how employees use their computers. Currently, over a third of large U.S. companies use software to monitor employee e-mails and website visits.

The Protestant ethic was a boon to capitalism. The quest for economic independence fueled commercial growth, which fueled industrial growth, which created our modern consumer society. English social philosophers promoted self-interest as the means to securing the greatest good for society, and American entrepreneurs asserted that "What's good for business is good for America." Along the way, however, the religious basis of the Protestant ethic was eroded by rising wealth and the encouragement of mass consumption. The part of the ethic that supported hard work, success, and rational planning continued, but without the original absolute moral values. The Protestant ethic became transformed into an organizational ethic that supports the modern bureaucratic managerial system. The sociologist Robert Jackall identifies this system as having "administrative hierarchies, standardized work procedures, regularized timetables, uniform policies, and centralized control." The goal of this system is to produce profit. Business actions are justified by their usefulness in accomplishing the goal. The religious formalism of the Protestant ethic has become a type of utilitarian consequentialism.

7. COMPARING THE TWO ETHICAL SYSTEMS

Formalists and consequentialists can arrive at the same conclusion for an ethical course of action, but they use a different evaluation process (see the Figure "Formalism versus consequentialism"). Take as an example a company's decision whether or not to secretly monitor its employees' use of the e-mail system. The company suspects that some employees are using the system for personal business and to spread damaging rumors about the company and its executives. How would formalists and consequentialists approach this decision?

Formalists might say that secret monitoring treats employees only as a means to the end of increasing organizational efficiency and does not respect their self-worth as individuals. The monitoring also does not respect their dignity and their privacy. Formalists might conclude that secret monitoring is unethical. Explaining

Formalism Versus
Consequentialism

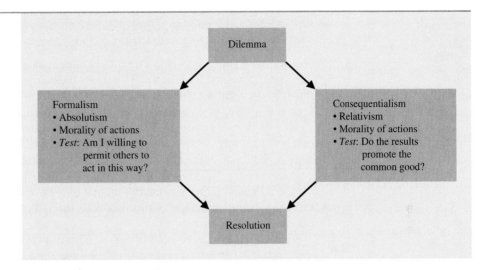

the problem to the employees and asking for their consent to monitor would be a more ethical action to take.

For a consequentialist, the act of secret monitoring itself is ethically neither right nor wrong. It is the end result that is ethically important. Secret monitoring and the punishment of wrongdoers are useful in improving productivity, which is an appropriate company goal and beneficial to society at large. To that extent, secret monitoring is ethically acceptable. But the punishment of wrongdoers will likely reveal to all employees that their e-mail has been secretly monitored. This breach of trust can lower employee morale and lessen employee loyalty to the company. Overall productivity may fall. In examining alternative solutions to the problem, a more beneficial overall solution, and thus a more ethical one, might be to explain the problem to the employees and ask for their consent to monitor all e-mail messages.

This example of the thinking processes of formalists and consequentialists does not exhaust all of the possible approaches that these groups might take to the e-mail problem. It does emphasize the fact that both formalist and consequentialist thinking can lead to the same business decision.

One of the most complex problems of contemporary business ethics concerns the promotion and sale of tobacco products. As you think about the information in the "Tobacco Industry Insight" box, bring to bear your new knowledge of formalism and consequentialism.

SOURCES OF VALUES FOR BUSINESS ETHICS

There are at least four sources of values for business ethics. The sections that follow identify them as:

- Legal regulation
- Professional codes of ethics
- Organizational codes of ethics
- Individual values

BUSINESS DECISION   REVISITED

Consider now your answers to PharmCo's ethical dilemma in the Business Decision that begins this chapter. How does the company treat the concerns of two of the eight researchers when animal studies do not show side effects? If the two researchers are wrong, publicity about their concerns could frighten away many people from using the new baldness product. If the researchers are correct, however, people could die from its use. Almost certainly, it would be unethical for PharmCo's management to tell the researchers to keep quiet within the company or before a regulatory agency like the Food and Drug Administration that may have to approve the product for use. A careful weighing of this product's safety is essential to its ethical introduction in the marketplace.

Whether it is ethical to experiment on animals provokes much controversy today. A formalist may contend that it is always immoral to harm other living creatures for the benefit of humans but may also claim that human welfare is a supreme moral value. A consequentialist may balance the benefits to many humans against the harm to a few animals. Note that arriving at ethical conclusions seldom has the certainty of looking up a recipe in a cookbook. A business must consider many factors in deciding whether or how to experiment on animals. To make the effort is itself ethically very important.

Many students may think that it is ethically insignificant how PharmCo decides to price its baldness product, but the ethical issues involved become clearer when serious disease cures are involved. Currently, tens of millions of people around the world are dying of AIDS and very few of them can afford $1,000 a month or more to buy the drugs that will stop or drastically slow the advance of this hideous disease. Pharmaceutical companies are criticized for pricing AIDS drugs beyond the reach of the world's poor. Should companies be stripped of their intellectual property right (patent) in AIDS-related drugs? What would this do to the incentive for them to create new drugs for AIDS or other diseases? Should governments buy the drugs from the companies for redistribution to the needy?

Evaluation of complex ethical issues often seems to raise more questions than it answers. But many pharmaceutical companies are now making AIDS drugs available at greatly reduced prices for some of the world's poorest.

---

8. LEGAL REGULATION

Insider trading, bribery, fraudulent practices, and conflicts of interest are often cited as examples of ethical failures. But these practices are illegal as well. That the unethical may be illegal and vice versa is often confusing to students.

The way to understand the ethical-legal relationship is to realize that in our society ethical values frequently become law and that legal regulation can reflect society's ethical values. For example, society's ethical commitment to equal opportunity became law in the Civil Rights Act of 1964, which prohibits employment discrimination based on "race, sex, color, religion, and national origin."

TOBACCO INDUSTRY *insight*

Consider the ethical significance of the following facts:

Tobacco products have been consumed in the United States since at least the early 1600s.

Hundreds of thousands of people are involved in the growing, manufacturing, distributing, and selling of tobacco products.

In the first 20 years of tobacco litigation, juries did not award plaintiffs a single penny against tobacco companies.

Scientists and doctors accept that tobacco consumption is an important contributing factor in cancer and heart disease. Excess consumption of fatty foods and lack of exercise are also contributing factors to these diseases.

Between 300,000 and 400,000 people in the United States die annually due to tobacco consumption.

The average age of beginning tobacco consumption is around 16.

Almost no one begins tobacco consumption past age 21. Three thousand new teenagers begin tobacco consumption every day.

Tobacco companies spend approximately $5 billion annually in advertising and promoting tobacco sales. The main strategy of tobacco promotion is to associate glamour, excitement, sex, and desirable life images with tobacco consumption.

The law requires that health warnings accompany the advertising and sale of tobacco products.

The nicotine in tobacco is considered addictive. However, millions have stopped tobacco consumption.

At the same time, the very existence of legal regulation can influence society's view of what is ethical. In 1964, when the Civil Rights Act was passed, few people were concerned about sex discrimination in employment. Opponents of the bill inserted the prohibition against sex discrimination in hopes of preventing its passage. Obviously, these legislators believed that sex discrimination in employment was acceptable and that many others agreed with them. Despite their efforts, however, the Civil Rights Act passed, and over the years, as legal battles involving sex discrimination in employment were fought, Americans' moral sense of the importance of equal employment opportunity regardless of sex caught up with the law. Today a great majority of Americans believe women should not be discriminated against in employment simply because they are women and that such discrimination is wrong. To a significant extent, the law itself contributed to the change in values.

Legal regulation is, then, a significant source of values for business ethics. In fact, many business and professional organizations look to the law when drawing up their codes of ethical conduct. At least five major ethical rules can be drawn from the law. These include:

- Respect for the liberty and rights of others
- The importance of acting in good faith
- The importance of exercising due care
- The importance of honoring confidentiality
- Avoidance of conflicts of interest

The following sections elaborate these concepts. These values derived from legal regulation are appropriate for use in ethical business decision making even when decisions do not involve legal issues.

Liberty and Rights   First, the law requires respect for the liberty and rights of others. We see this requirement in legislation protecting the right of privacy, promoting equal employment opportunity, and guaranteeing freedom of expression and due process of law. In one form or another, these legal rights often appear in ethical codes. Do you think that the concern for individual rights represents formalism or consequentialism?

Remember from Chapter 1 that respect for individual rights is historically connected to the legal concept of private property. To have exclusive legal rights over what you say (freedom of speech), for example, is quite similar to having exclusive rights to an area of land or a piece of machinery. The philosopher John Locke, who influenced the framers of the U.S. Constitution, even referred to "lives, liberties, and estates which I call by the general name *property.*"

Good Faith   The law requires that good faith be demonstrated in various economic and other transactions. An example comes from the Uniform Commercial Code, adopted in 49 of the 50 states. Article 2 of the UCC on sales law requires that all sales of goods transactions be carried out in *good faith,* which has been interpreted as meaning "honesty in fact" and honesty in intent.

The reverse of good faith is *bad faith,* which can be understood as dishonesty in intent. In cases involving a bad faith withholding of amounts due under insurance policies, some courts and juries have severely punished defendant insurance companies with large punitive damage awards. Acting with an honest intent is the key to understanding good faith. Is looking at the intent of parties to a business contract evidence of formalism or consequentialism?

Due Care   Another ethical value reflecting legal rules requires the exercise of *due care* in our behavior. This value comes from the law of torts, which Justice Oliver Wendell Holmes said "abounds in moral phraseology." Due care derives from society's expectations about how fair and reasonable actions are. Due care promotes the common good. In negligence law, failure to exercise due (or reasonable) care is the principal element that triggers liability against the defendant. Courts have examined due care in negligence cases in terms of a balancing test. The likelihood that the defendant's conduct will cause harmful consequences, taken with the seriousness of the harmful consequences, is balanced against the effort required to avoid the harmful consequences. The balancing test is central to the concept of due care.

Consider the following problem of due care. Bridgestone/Firestone became aware that certain of its tires were showing defects at much higher rates than what might be thought of as normal. Still, the tires operated perfectly on hundreds of thousands of vehicles. Was the company ethically required to warn the public about the tires? To recall the tires? A very small fraction of all tires showed defects. What level of defect is acceptable without warning those who use a product? Ford Explorer sport utility vehicles used the Firestone tire, and Ford decided to recall and replace the tires in Saudi Arabia. But Ford did not notify U.S. safety authorities or the public about what it was doing overseas, even though the same tires were on Ford Explorers in the United States. Was Ford acting ethically? What would you need to know in order to decide?

Another form of the requirement to exercise due care comes from the Federal Guidelines for Sentencing for Criminal Convictions, which focus specifically on corporate white-collar crime. In determining what punishment a company should receive for the illegal business acts of its employees, the guidelines look at whether the company has "an effective program to prevent and detect violations of the law." An effective program is measured by whether "the organization exercised due diligence in seeking to prevent and detect criminal conduct by its employees and other agents." *Due diligence* is another way of saying "due care."

As with the determination of due care in negligence law, the determination of due diligence in sentencing guidelines requires use of a balancing test. Considering the significance of the balancing test to the exercise of due care (or due diligence), do you think that formalist or consequentialist values are reflected?

Confidentiality Honoring confidentiality is the fourth major ethical value emerging from the law and legal regulation. The legal requirement of honoring confidentiality appears in agency law generally and in the professional-client relationship in particular. For a CPA to share with unauthorized third parties what has been learned during a client's audit is professional malpractice. Likewise, it is malpractice for an attorney, physician, real estate broker, or any professional agent to tell others what a client (principal) has related in confidence.

In addition to not telling others of a confidence, an agent must in many instances not act on the confidence related by a principal. The insider trading scandals of the 1980s and early 1990s occurred largely because agents improperly traded in the stock market on confidential information provided to them by their principals. The securities laws make it a crime for agents to trade improperly on confidential information.

The legal requirement of honoring confidences contains both formalist and consequentialist ethical values. Can you identify these values?

Conflicts of Interest Often embodied in business codes of ethics, avoiding conflicts of interest is a final ethical value flowing from the law, especially from agency law. A conflict of interest occurs when one attempts to "serve two masters," and no agent or employee of one principal can secretly work for another whose interest competes with that of the first principal. That is why a real estate agent may not represent both the seller and the buyer in a real estate transaction without permission from both parties.

Sometimes when corporations "go public" or otherwise sell new stock issues, they will give employees of their customers or suppliers the option of buying a number of the new stock shares at a special fixed price. If the market value of the stock rises, exercise of the stock options can be quite valuable to these employees as they resell the stock at market price. Is it a conflict of interest for employees of other companies to accept these stock options? Does it impair their objective judgment about continuing to do business with the corporation that has given them such a gift? Compaq Computer Corporation, Cisco Systems, and SBC Communications specifically forbid employees from accepting stock options from their suppliers or customers.

Conflicts of interest also arise in public service. For instance, it is a conflict of interest for a judge or administrative regulator to make a decision involving a company in which he or she owns stock. Note that in this instance the conflict of interest does not involve "serving two masters." The conflict arises because of the

concept SUMMARY   *Ethical Values from Legal Regulation*

- Respect the liberty and rights of others.
- Act in good faith.
- Exercise due care.
- Honor confidentiality.
- Avoid conflicts of interest.

ownership of property that will make it difficult for the judge or regulator to make an unbiased decision. In terms of formalism and consequentialism, how do you evaluate the prohibition against conflicts of interest?

9. PROFESSIONAL CODES OF ETHICS

Another important source of business ethics comes from the historic tradition of the professional codes of ethics. Professions such as law and medicine have long traditions of codes of ethical conduct. Other professions, and more recently business and industry in general, have developed and adopted codes of ethical conduct. Here we use portions of professional codes to demonstrate sources of ethical values that come from the development of group standards for ethical conduct.

We begin with selected excerpts from codes of conduct for two professions: law and accounting. These codes are the American Bar Association Model Rules of Professional Conduct, shown below, and the American Institute of Certified Public Accountants Code of Professional Conduct, which appears on page *41.*

AMERICAN BAR ASSOCIATION MODEL RULES OF PROFESSIONAL CONDUCT

As a public citizen, a lawyer should seek improvement of the law, the administration of justice and the quality of service rendered by the legal profession. As a member of a learned profession, a lawyer should cultivate knowledge of the law beyond its use for clients, employ that knowledge in reform of the law and work to strengthen legal education. A lawyer should be mindful of deficiencies in the administration of justice and of the fact that the poor, and sometimes persons who are not poor, cannot afford adequate legal assistance, and should therefore devote professional time and civic influence in their behalf. A lawyer should aid the legal profession in pursuing these objectives and should help the bar regulate itself in the public interest.

Many of a lawyer's professional responsibilities are prescribed in the Rules of Professional Conduct, as well as substantive and procedural law. However, a lawyer is also guided by personal conscience and the approbation of professional peers. A lawyer should strive to attain the highest level of skill, to improve the law and the legal profession and to exemplify the legal profession's ideals of public service. . . .

In the nature of law practice . . . conflicting responsibilities are encountered. Virtually all difficult ethical problems arise from conflict between a lawyer's responsibilities to clients, to the legal system and to the lawyer's own interest in remaining an upright person while earning a satisfactory living. The Rules of Professional Conduct prescribe terms for resolving such conflicts. Within the framework of these Rules many difficult issues of professional discretion can arise. Such issues must be resolved through the exercise of sensitive professional and moral judgment guided by the basic principles underlying the Rules. . . .

The Rules do not, however, exhaust the moral and ethical considerations that should inform a lawyer, for no worthwhile human activity can be completely defined by legal rules. The Rules simply provide a framework for the ethical practice of law.

Take into account that what follows are only short excerpts. These codes in full run many pages.

In spite of their Rules of Professional Conduct, lawyers are sometimes viewed as acting unethically. Is this because unethical people are attracted to the practice of law? Is it because the power conferred by knowing the law corrupts lawyers? Or is it because most nonlawyers do not understand the legal process, so that when they lose legal disputes, they feel it must be because of the other side's "dishonest" lawyers? Is it the emotion invested in legal cases that makes it easy for us to blame others when things do not turn out to our satisfaction? In answering these questions, think about the relationship between law and justice. Does law ensure justice? Are we wrong to hope that it should?

Another important set of group standards is the ethical code of certified public accountants.

From these excerpts, the ethical values expressed in the codes of ethics for lawyers and accountants may seem overly general in nature. But each code has pages of rules that apply to specific situations arising in the lawyer-client and accountant-client relationship. As the state does not enforce these codes, it is not proper to call them law. Yet the professional organizations that have adopted these codes employ specific sanctions to back them up. Lawyers may be disbarred for ethical breaches. Because the state will likely regulate these professions if they do not do so themselves, it is appropriate to term their ethical codes **self-regulation.**

AMERICAN INSTITUTE OF CERTIFIED PUBLIC ACCOUNTANTS CODE OF PROFESSIONAL CONDUCT

These Principles of the Code of Professional Conduct of the American Institute of Certified Public Accountants express the profession's recognition of its responsibilities to the public, to clients, and to colleagues. They guide members in the performance of their professional responsibilities and express the basic tenets of ethical and professional conduct. The Principles call for an unswerving commitment to honorable behavior, even at the sacrifice of personal advantage.

In carrying out their responsibilities as professionals, members should exercise sensitive professional and moral judgments in all their activities.

As professionals, certified public accountants perform an essential role in society. Consistent with that role, members of the American Institute of Certified Public Accountants have responsibilities to all those who use their professional services. Members also have a continuing responsibility to cooperate with each other to improve the art of accounting, maintain the public's confidence, and carry out the profession's special responsibilities for self-governance. The collective efforts of all members are required to maintain and enhance the traditions of the profession.

Members should accept the obligation to act in a way that will serve the public interest, honor the public interest, and demonstrate commitment to professionalism.

A distinguishing mark of a profession is acceptance of its responsibility to the public. The accounting profession's public consists of clients, credit grantors, governments, employers, investors, the business and financial community, and others who rely on the objectivity and integrity of certified public accountants to maintain the orderly functioning of commerce. This reliance imposes a public interest responsibility on certified public accountants. The public interest is defined as the collective well-being of the community of people and institutions the profession serves.

In discharging their professional responsibilities, members may encounter conflicting pressures from among each of those groups. In resolving those conflicts, members should act with integrity, guided by the precept that when members fulfill their responsibility to the public, clients' and employers' interests are best served.

10. ORGANIZATIONAL CODES OF ETHICS

There are few industrywide codes of ethics, so many businesses have adopted ethical codes at the individual organization level. Nearly all large corporations now have their own codes of business ethics, often called codes of conduct. These codes are obviously an important source of business ethics.

The Business Roundtable, a national group of senior business leaders, has identified a general list of topics that organizational codes of business ethics should cover. These include:

- Fundamental honesty and adherence to the law
- Product safety and quality
- Health and safety in the workplace
- Conflicts of interest
- Fairness in selling/marketing practices
- Financial reporting
- Supplier relationships
- Pricing, billing, and contracting
- Trading in securities/using inside information
- Payments to obtain business/Foreign Corrupt Practices Act
- Acquiring and using information about others
- Security
- Political activities
- Protection of the environment
- Intellectual property/proprietary information

Individual companies take different approaches to ethical codes. The Hertz Corporation has a one-page statement of general ethical principles. In part that statement reads: "We will conduct business ethically and honestly in dealing with our customers, suppliers and employees. We will treat our employees in the same fashion as we expect them to treat our customers—with dignity and respect."

Hertz's statement provides only general guidelines to ethical conduct rather than detailed definitions of what kind of ethical behavior the company expects in specific instances. Other companies spell out their expectations for employees' behavior in considerable detail. For instance, the Martin Marietta Corporation Code of Ethics and Standard of Conduct is 17 pages long and covers a wide variety of company activities and practices.

Many codes of business ethics contain both general statements of shared ethical values and more specific applied examples of these values. General statements of shared values remind employees what their companies stand for and at the same time serve to encourage ethical behavior in situations not covered by specific ethical guides. The applied examples address specific types of business conduct like those listed above by the Business Roundtable.

A majority of organizational codes of business ethics provide sanctions for their violation, up to and including employee termination. As with professional codes of conduct, it is appropriate to call these organizational codes self-regulation. Whether companies pursue ethical self-regulation with enthusiasm and commitment or the codes are mere window dressing to satisfy the government and the general public is an important issue in determining the value of these codes.

11. INDIVIDUAL VALUES

The ultimate source of ethical values for business decision making comes from the individual. Others can tell you what is right or wrong. They can sanction you for failing to live up to their expectations. But only you can make your behavior ethical. Only you can intend your actions to be honest and fair or to serve the common good.

How to act ethically in every business situation is beyond the scope of this chapter, or that of any book, for that matter. Business life is just too complex. There is no way to create enough rules to cover all possible ethically significant situations, even if they could be identified in advance. However, there are five questions that you can ask yourself that will help you explore your ethical values before making personal or business decisions about what to do.

1. **Have I thought about whether the action I may take is right or wrong**? John Smale, former CEO of Procter & Gamble, has said that "there is an ethical dimension to most complex business problems." If this is so, then you should consider whether any decision you propose to make to solve such a problem is ethical or not. The philosopher Hannah Arendt explained that evil often comes from a kind of thoughtlessness. Plato wrote that immoral behavior often flows from ignorance. A major goal of this chapter is to encourage you to think about the ethical implications of what you decide and what you do. It is the first step in leading a good life.

2. **Will I be proud to tell of my action to my family? To my employer? To the news media**? An excellent way to uncover whether there are ethical difficulties with a possible decision is to consider how proud you would be to share it with others. Before reaching an important business decision, consider how you would feel about telling your decision to your family, your employer, and the public through the news media. The less proud you are to share your decision with others, the more likely your decision is to be unethical. As Stephen Butler, CEO of KPMG said, "An essential part of an ethics process is identifying issues that would mortify a chief executive if he were to read about them on the front page of the newspaper."

3. **Am I willing for everyone to act as I am thinking of acting**? With this question you encompass a major principle of ethical formalism. If you consider suggesting to a coworker that it would be advantageous for him or her to develop a sexual relationship with you, are you willing to have your superior suggest this relationship to you? Or to your friends or a member of your family? Trying to convince yourself that it is acceptable for you to do something but not acceptable for others in your situation to do it is virtually always immoral.

4. **Will my decision cause harm to others or to the environment**? Asking this question exposes a significant principle of ethical consequentialism: promotion of the common good. Promoting the common good within your business organization is important, but it is even more important to consider whether your decision is good for society.

    You can approach this issue of the common good by asking whether your decision will cause harm. If the decision will cause no harm and will advance your business interests, it will also usually advance the good of society by increasing productivity, efficiency, or innovation.

Many business decisions, however, do cause harm to others or to the environment. It is difficult to construct an interstate highway without workers being injured and trees being cut. The point of asking yourself the question about potential harm is so you can weigh the harm against the increase in the common good and so you can evaluate whether an alternative course of action might bring about the same increase in the common good with less harm.

Note also that if the harm caused would be avoidable, legal problems can arise from a decision to accept the costs of the harm. An internal memorandum at General Motors that estimated the cost at $2.40 per car of settling fire-related claims due to the gas tank design in GM cars has plagued that company in lawsuits for years. Plaintiffs' lawyers have claimed that GM was willing to spend this average amount per car in order to avoid having to change a defective gas tank design. Juries have assessed huge punitive damage awards against GM.

Recall that ethical formalists maintain that harm to some individual rights is never justified by an increase in organizational or common good. But as ethical decision making in business often involves a mixed approach, including both formalism and consequentialism, it is appropriate for you to evaluate potential business decisions by weighing harms against benefits to the common good.

5. **Will my actions violate the law**? Both formalists and consequentialists believe that you have an ethical duty to obey the law except in very limited instances. The law provides only minimum standards for behavior, but they are standards that should be observed. Thus, to be ethical, you should always consider whether any business decision you make will require illegal actions.

   Sometimes it is not clear whether proposed actions will violate the law. Then you should consult with legal counsel. Many regulatory agencies will also give legal advice about whether actions you are considering are legal or not.

   When you are convinced that a law itself is morally wrong, you may be justified in disobeying it. Even then, to be ethical, you must be willing to make public your disobedience and to accept the consequences for it. Both Mohandas Gandhi and Martin Luther King, Jr., deliberately disobeyed laws they thought were morally wrong, and they changed society by doing so. Ultimately they changed both laws and ethics. But they made their disobedience to these laws public, and they willingly accepted punishment for violating them. Dr. King wrote: "I submit that an individual who breaks a law that conscience tells him is unjust, and who willingly accepts the penalty of imprisonment in order to arouse the conscience of the community over its injustice, is in reality expressing the highest respect for the law."

Now, you should be able to answer the questions presented in the Business Decision that begins the chapter. See Business Decision Revisited on page 36 for our suggested answers, but try on your own first.

Leading an ethical business life may be difficult at times. You will make mistakes. You will be tempted. It is unlikely that you will be perfect. But if you want to be ethical and will work hard toward achieving your goal, you will be rewarded. As with achieving other challenging business objectives, there will be satisfaction in ethical business decision making.

In business as well as in personal life, the key to ethical decision making is wanting to be ethical and having the will to be ethical. If you do not want to be ethical, no code of conduct can make you ethical. Potential harm you may cause to individuals and to society will best be deterred by the threat of legal punishment and the sanctions of professional and corporate codes. You may never get caught, lose your job, or go to jail. But, as Mortimer Adler observed, you will lack "much that is needed for the good life."

ACHIEVING AN ETHICAL BUSINESS CORPORATION

The dominant form of organization in modern business is the corporation. Currently, the top 100 manufacturing corporations produce more than two-thirds of the nation's entire manufacturing output. In 1840 the largest manufacturing firm in the United States, the Springfield Armory, employed only 250 workers. Today, many corporations have tens of thousands of employees. Some have hundreds of thousands. In substantial part, the development of the corporate form of business organization made possible this growth in business size.

Ethical problems, however, arise in corporate life that are not present in one's individual experience. In a study published of Harvard MBAs during their first five years following graduation, 29 of 30 reported that business pressures had forced them to violate their own ethical standards. The next sections focus on the ethical problems of an individual in the corporation and suggest several ways of dealing with them.

12. THE OBSTACLES

Some may contend that the corporation by its very nature, with its dependence on a competitive edge and on profit and its limited liability, is so constituted as to make ethical behavior unlikely. That is not true, but there are certain obstacles to ethical corporate behavior that deserve serious consideration.

concept SUMMARY	*Self-Examination for Self-Regulation*

- Have I thought about whether the action I may take is right or wrong?
- Will I be proud to tell of my action to my family? To my employer? To the news media?
- Am I willing for everyone to act as I am thinking of acting?

- Will my decision cause harm to others or to the environment?
- Will my actions violate the law?

The Emphasis on Profit The primary goal of the modern business corporation is to produce profit. Management demands it, the board of directors demands it, and shareholders demand it. Making profit motivates our entire economic system, and it promotes the common good by providing incentive for job creation and the efficient fulfillment of social needs for goods and services.

Unfortunately, with the decline of the Protestant ethic, emphasis on corporate profit alone sometimes conflicts with ethical responsibility. How a profit is made becomes less important than that it is made. Various business scandals illustrate this point.

In many corporations the responsibility for profit making is decentralized. The home office expects a plant in another state to meet certain profit goals, but the home office does not know much about the particular operations of that plant. Meeting profit goals places enormous pressure on the local plant manager. The manager's career advancement depends on the plant's profitability, yet the home office does not appreciate the difficulties under which the plant is operating. In such a situation the overemphasis on profit can easily lead to the manager's taking ethical and legal shortcuts to ensure profit.

An example of such shortcuts involved Columbia/HCA Healthcare Corporation, one of the major national hospital chains. Following a government investigation, many units of the company were accused of enhancing profits by improperly billing Medicare for laboratory tests and home health care services. It was also alleged that managers were "upcoding," or exaggerating patient illness, in order to get greater reimbursements from the Medicare system. Several managers were criminally indicted and convicted. The company's CEO resigned. To settle charges, the company agreed to pay the federal government $745 million to resolve fraud allegations. As part of its response, the company also stationed ethics and compliance officers in nearly every hospital, in part to prevent managers from "looking good" by producing profits through improper billings.

The Effect of the Group The social critic Ambrose Bierce once remarked that the corporation is "an ingenious device for obtaining individual profit without individual responsibility." He was referring to the fact that individuals in large groups such as the corporation feel less responsibility for what happens in the group than they do for what happens in their individual lives. They may also act differently, and to some extent less ethically, in a group.

That individuals will do unethical things as part of a mob which they would never do alone is widely recognized, and the same pattern can be observed in corporate behavior. Within corporations it becomes easy for a researcher not to pass on lately discovered concerns about the possible (yet not certain) side effects of a new skin lotion that upper management is so enthusiastic about. In corporate life it is not difficult to overlook the unethical behavior of a superior when many fellow employees are also overlooking it. And of course, "I did it because everyone else did it" is a common rationalization in groups of all kinds. "Just following orders" is a similar rationalization.

That individuals in groups may feel a diminished sense of responsibility for decisions made and actions taken invites ethical compromise. Coupled with an overemphasis on profit, the group effect increases the difficulty of achieving an ethical business corporation.

THE CONTROL OF RESOURCES BY NONOWNERS

In the modern corporation, the owners or shareholders are often not in possession and control of corporate resources. Top management of many corporations effectively possess and control vast resources that they do not own. This produces the problems of corporate governance mentioned in Chapter 1. Managerial agents like the president and vice presidents of a large corporation have ethical and legal duties to manage the corporate resources for the benefit of their owners. But because they control corporate resources, it may be easy to manipulate the resources in their own interest and difficult for others to find out that they have done so. In other words, managers may be in an ideal position to infringe on the property interest of the corporate owners.

Sometimes, managers embezzle corporate money or abuse expense accounts. At other times they misrepresent the financial condition of the corporation in order to exercise stock options, obtain huge bonuses, or prop up loans they have secured with company stock. Because the very nature of corporate structure gives managers the opportunity to abuse and misappropriate corporate resources owned ultimately by the shareholders, ethical business practice is made more important yet more difficult. Consider the box, "Corporate Governance Failure at WorldCom?"

13. THE STEPS

Despite the obstacles that sometimes stand in the way of ethical corporate behavior, certain steps can be taken to promote business ethics in corporate life.

Involvement of Top Management   To encourage corporate ethics, it is not enough merely to adopt a code of conduct. For the code to change behavior, corporate employees must believe that the values expressed by the code represent the values of the corporation's top management. Top management must act as a role model for values it wishes corporate employees to share.

CORPORATE GOVERNANCE FAILURE AT WORLDCOM?

Bernard J. Ebbers, chief executive officer and founder of the telecommunications giant WorldCom, had a problem. He owed the corporation $375 million from a loan secured by company stock he owned. WorldCom's stock was rapidly declining in market value, and the stock value securing his loan was now far below what he owed. Investors (owners) and potential investors were concerned about WorldCom's liquidity (ability to pay debts with cash) and its accounting practices, including manipulations that kept corporate liabilities from public view.

On February 2, 2002, Mr. Ebbers engaged in a conference call with several important Wall Street stock analysts whose opinions help drive stock prices in the market. Characterizing investors' concerns as mostly "unfounded nonsense," he said "we stand by our accounting," "are free cash flow positive ahead of time," and have only "a very minimal amount" of scheduled debt payable. "Bankruptcy or a credit default is not a concern. To question WorldCom's viability is utter nonsense." "It has been 10 years since WorldCom has been so well positioned from an operating perspective." The day of Mr. Ebbers's statements, the corporation's stock rose 12.4 percent in market value.

Five months later WorldCom filed for bankruptcy, its finances in shambles. Do you understand that in propping up the value of the corporation's stock, Mr. Ebbers was misrepresenting the corporation to the new investors who were buying stock and becoming owners of the corporation? His statements represent a type of corporate misgovernance. Were the statements unethical? Illegal? Mr. Ebbers was arrested in fall 2003.

The sociologist Robert Jackall attributes the importance of a corporation's top management in encouraging business ethics to the bureaucratic system for career advancement. Each employee owes loyalty to his or her immediate corporate superior. As a practical matter, career advancement for the employee is generally tied to career advancement for the superior. In turn, that supervisor has a corporate superior to whom loyalty is owed, and so on up the corporate bureaucratic hierarchy.

Beyond a certain level in corporate bureaucracy, argues Jackall, social indicators about how well an employee "fits in" to the company management are as important as merit performance in securing further career advancement. For this reason, corporate employees tend to be very sensitive to the values of top corporate management and take these values as their own. Due to the interlocking system of loyalties that run between employment levels of the corporate hierarchy, top management's values filter down quite effectively to lower-level employees.

The values adopted by lower-level employees, however, will be top management's *real* values. So if the corporation has a code of conduct that expresses excellent ethical values, but top management shows that it expects profit at any cost, then the values adopted by lower-level employees will likely relate to profit at any cost rather than to values appearing in the code of conduct.

Top management must really believe in the ethical values expressed in codes of conduct for these values to take hold throughout the corporation. But if they do believe them and will communicate this belief through the corporation, there is an excellent chance that these values will be adopted within the corporate group. As Stephen Butler, CEO of KPMG says, "I really believe that corporate ethics are essential for a successful business today, and the CEOs of corporate America are the only ones who can institutionalize them."

Openness in Communication For ethical corporate values to make their most significant impact on decision making, corporate employees must be willing to talk with each other about ethical issues. "Openness in communication is deemed fundamental," states the Business Roundtable. Openness promotes trust, and without trust even the best-drafted code of ethics will likely fall short of achieving an ethical business corporation.

Beyond helping establish trust, openness in communication is necessary for ethical corporate decision making because of the complexity of information required to evaluate the implications of many business decisions. Without open discussion of these implications among employees and between employees and their superiors, ethical decision making is severely hindered. Information crucial to making an ethical decision may be lacking.

For example, consider the complexity of a firm's decision to sell in other countries a pesticide that is banned for sale in the United States. Evaluating the ethical implications of the sale (assuming there are no legal ones) will demand considerable information. To make a fully informed decision the firm must know:

- What the effects of the pesticide on humans and the environment are
- Why the pesticide was banned in the United States
- Why the pesticide is useful in other countries
- Whether in spite of its ban for use in the United States there may be good reasons to use the pesticide in other countries
- Whether there are alternatives to its use in other countries

The sharing of information about the implications of this pesticide sale will greatly assist the making of an ethical decision about its use. Openness in communication among employees on these implications will be vital in reaching an ethically informed corporate decision about this complex matter.

How is openness in communication on ethical issues promoted within the corporation? There is no single answer. For top management to provide a good role model of concern for speaking out on ethical issues is certainly a right beginning. Another possibility is for employees to meet periodically in small groups to consider either real or hypothetical ethical problems. In general, a shared corporate commitment to the ideal of ethical decision making is important to openness in communication.

CONSIDERATION OF ALL STAKEHOLDERS

Large corporations affect the interests of many different groups in society, which are called "stakeholders" because they have something at risk when the company acts and thus have a "stake" in it. Investor-owners, employees, the board of directors, and managers typically have a stake in the actions of large corporations, but so do customers, suppliers, financial creditors like banks, and the community in which a company is located. If a company pollutes as a by-product of production, society itself may have a stake in what actions a corporation takes.

The consequentialist ethics known as **stakeholder theory** maintains that ethical corporate behavior depends on managers who recognize and take into account the various stakeholders whose interests the corporation impacts. Stakeholder theory includes but goes beyond the responsibilities of corporate governance, which focuses on the *legal* responsibilities of managers to society and to the investor-owners of the corporation. Stakeholder theory suggests that through its managers, an ethical corporation

- Considers the concerns of all proper stakeholders and weighs their interests when making decisions.
- Allows stakeholders to communicate with decision makers and informs them about risks to their interests that may arise from corporate action.
- Adopts communication methods that are appropriate to the sophistication levels of various stakeholders.
- Realizes the interdependence of all stakeholders and demonstrates fairness toward both voluntary stakeholders (e.g., employees) and involuntary stakeholders (e.g., the community).
- Works actively and cooperatively to reduce the risk of corporate harm to all stakeholders and to compensate them when harm occurs.
- Avoids risks to stakeholders which, if explained, would be clearly unacceptable.
- Acknowledges the potential conflict between managerial self-interest and the ethical responsibility of managers to other stakeholders, and promotes open procedures that allow managers to monitor their own ethical performance.

For an example of ethical collapse within the top management of a major U.S. firm, see the box "The Demise of Arthur Andersen."

THE DEMISE OF ARTHUR ANDERSEN

For much of the last century, the firm of Arthur Andersen was one of the largest and most influential accounting firms in the world. Yet in 2002 it collapsed following the firm's criminal prosecution for obstruction of justice in shredding the documents of Enron, one of its clients known for massive corporate governance problems. In the end, three of the five largest bankruptcies ever recorded involved Arthur Andersen clients with financial accounting problems.

In her book *Final Accounting: Ambition, Greed and the Fall of Arthur Andersen,* business ethicist and former Harvard professor Barbara Ley Toffler recounts what led to the demise of the accounting firm. Although the firm employed thousands of honest accountants, its top management cut ethical and legal corners in the auditing of some of its biggest clients, clients from whom the firm also collected millions of dollars in financial consulting fees. Within a business culture that encouraged loyalty, conformity, and obedience to the leadership of its senior partners, the conflicts of interest between impartial accounting and partisan consulting set the stage for the final corruption leading to the fall of the firm.

Companies attract investors (and lenders) who depend on the reputation of the accountants who audit the companies' books for accurate financial information about the companies. When almost all their clients abandoned them after their prosecution, Arthur Andersen fell. The firm's demise illustrates Robert Jackall's emphasis on the importance of top management on the ethical values within business organizations.

14. THE REWARDS

Of the world's 100 largest economies, 49 of them are countries and 51 are companies. General Motors has greater annual sales than the gross national products of Denmark, Thailand, Turkey, South Africa, or Saudi Arabia. Wal-Mart's economy is larger than that of Poland, Ukraine, Portugal, Israel, or Greece. Because of the size and influence of modern corporations, business ethics take on special significance. Although there are unique problems with promoting ethical corporate decision making, the rewards for making the attempt are important both to business and society.

The Spanish journal *Boletín Círculo* makes four observations about business ethics. A paraphrase of these observations provides a good way to highlight a chapter on ethics and self-regulation:

1. Profits and business ethics are not contradictory. Some of the most profitable businesses have also historically been the most ethical.
2. An ethical organizational life is a basic business asset that should be accepted and encouraged. The reverse is also true. Unethical behavior is a business liability.
3. Ethics are of continuing concern to the business community. They require ongoing reevaluation. Businesses must always be ethically sensitive to changes in society.
4. Business ethics reflect business leadership. Top firms can and should exercise leadership in business ethics.

Business plays a vital role in serving society, and we cannot isolate the impact of important business decisions from their social consequences. For businesses merely to observe the law is not sufficiently responsible. Legal regulation lacks flexibility and is inadequately informed to be the only social guide for business decision making. Ethics belong in business decision making. A business that does not act ethically severs itself from society, from the good, and ultimately from its own source of support.

In reading the next chapters on the regulatory environment, consider how passage of much of the regulation was preceded by breaches of business ethics. If ethical self-regulation does not guide business behavior, legal regulation often follows quickly.

15. THE MORALITY OF PROPERTY

This chapter has approached business ethics in a way to illustrate the moral problems and ethical approaches of individuals in the corporate world. It might have taken a different approach and discussed the morality of business from the perspective of "stakeholders" such as stock owners, but also including employees and others in the community whom business decisions affect. It could have considered techniques of values-based management, a how-to implementation of business ethics for managers. But with its emphasis on the basics, this chapter has examined the moral dilemmas of individual ethical choice in business organizations.

One important issue of business ethics remains. It goes to the heart of whether it is ethical to engage in modern private enterprise. It concerns the fundamental morality of the law of property that is the foundation of private enterprise, which we call "business."

Throughout history some people have criticized property and what it stands for (see "Moral Criticism of Property"). They have challenged the morality of property, which is the legally enforced exclusive right to possess, use, and transfer resources. The primary criticism is the moral question of how some can possess more resources than they need while others go hungry and homeless. How can the wealthy ignore the plight of the poor and how can society endure a system that permits it? Property critics seem to long for a time when the abundant resources of nature were a common property, sufficient to satisfy the needs of all and free for the taking.

Of concern also to the critics is the power over others conveyed by the possession of great capital resources. Karl Marx saw capitalists as oppressing workers

---

Moral Criticism of Property

"I do nothing but go about persuading you all . . . not to take thought for your persons or your properties, but first and chiefly to care about the greatest improvement of the soul."—Socrates (circa 400 B.C.)

"Private property is the fruit of inequity."—Clement of Alexandria (circa second century)

"Property hath no rights. The earth is the Lord's, and we are his offspring. The pagans hold the earth as property. They do blaspheme God."—St. Ambrose (fourth century)

"Property is theft."—Judah ibn Tibbon (twelfth century)

"This 'I and mine' causes the whole misery. With the sense of possession comes selfishness and selfishness brings on misery."—Vivekanda (nineteenth century)

"In actual history it is notorious that conquest, enslavement, robbery, murder—briefly, force—play the great part [in the original accumulation of property]."—Karl Marx (1867)

"It is the preoccupation with possession, more than anything else, that prevents men from living freely and nobly."—Bertrand A. Russell (twentieth century)

"Property is not theft, but a good deal of theft becomes property."—Richard H. Tawney (1926)

"Private property does not constitute for anyone an absolute and unconditional right. No one is justified in keeping for his exclusive use what he does not need when others lack necessities."—Pope Paul VI (1967)

and exploiting their labor resources. "[T]he theory of the Communists," wrote Marx, "may be summed up in a single sentence: Abolition of private property." Religious critics often associate greed with property and argue that property discourages sharing and deprives us of a spiritual focus to life. They argue the Bible says that "the love of money is the root of all evil" and that it is easier to thread "a camel through the eye of a needle than for a rich man to enter the kingdom of heaven." Finally, critics observe that humans are social creatures who live in community. The culture of values, education, and information that surrounds us and influences us in every way is not the creation of any individual but of all of us. What then is the moral basis for an individual's exclusive property in resources that the community may need?

Supporters of property (see the table "Moral Support for Property") counter with a strong moral defense that begins with the acknowledgment that we cannot go back to some time in nature, possibly imaginary, when there were no resource allocation problems. Given limited resources, considerable evidence exists that the more resources that can be put under the legal system of property the less wastefully those resources will be treated. People are more careful with their own resources than with resources that are common to all. For example, the destruction of the world's rainforests is not caused by a system of property, but because property in these important resources largely does not exist, prompting a free-for-all clear-cutting of the forests.

Further, adequate property in resources maximizes total wealth in society. It provides incentives for individuals and groups to develop both physical and human resources to produce the goods that society values. Since property is not limited to legal rights in physical resources, but also includes one's creative, scientific, and

Moral Support for Property

"The end of government being the good of mankind points out its great duties: it is above all things to provide for the security, the quiet, the happy enjoyment of life, liberty, and property."
—James Otis (1764)

It is an "essential, unalterable right in nature . . . that what a man has honestly acquired is absolutely his own, which he may freely give, but cannot be taken from him without his consent."
—Samuel Adams (1768)

"The rights of man in society are liberty, equality, security, and property."—Declaration of the Rights and Duties of Man and the Citizen (1795)

"The natural tendency of every society in which property enjoys tolerable security is to increase in wealth."—Thomas B. Macaulay (1835)

"Property is desirable, is a positive good in the world. Let not him who is houseless pull down the house of another, but let him work diligently and build one for himself, thus by example assuring that his own shall be safe from violence when built."—Abraham Lincoln (1864)

"Private property was the original source of freedom. It still is its main bulwark."—Walter Lippmann (1937)

"The system of private property is the most important guarantee of freedom, not only for those who own property, but scarcely less for those who do not."—Fredrich A. Hayek (1944)

"Private property is a natural fruit of labor, a product of intense activity of man, acquired through his energetic determination to ensure and develop with his own strength his own existence and that of his family, and to create for himself and his own an existence of just freedom, not only economic, but also political, cultural, and religious."—Pope Pius XII (1944)

"A fundamental interdependence exists between the personal right to liberty and the right to property. Neither could have meaning without the other."—Justice Potter Stewart (1972)

technological innovations, societies that recognize property flourish more than societies that do not in almost all areas. Over the years the economic and social disparity between property-strong and property-weak societies grows ever wider.

Property supporters maintain that enforcing legally exclusive rights to resources is also a just system. It protects the resources of the poor as much as those of the rich. And the poor may actually benefit from an adequately enforced property system more than the rich since the rich are often able to guard their resources better than the poor and are less likely to have their resources coerced from them. Property also supports personal freedoms and individual autonomy, a fact recognized by the framers of the U.S. Constitution who believed that personal rights to speech, religion, and privacy were possessed by individuals as a type of property. Wrote John Adams, the second president of the United States: "The moment the idea is admitted into society that property is not as sacred as the laws of God, and there is not a force of law and public justice to protect it, anarchy and tyranny commence."

Acquisitiveness and territoriality appear to be very important parts of human nature. They are also seen in many other species and are a tendency connected to personal survival and mating. Capable of cooperative effort and the reciprocal sharing of resources within fairly small groups, we tend to resist strangers who take what is "ours," although we will trade with strangers for mutual benefit when we feel secure that our resources will not be tricked or coerced from us. In modern society the legal recognition of our natural acquisitiveness and territoriality is called "property."

With the worldwide decline of socialism and communism, those who support the morality of property are strengthened in the argument that the law of property provides the most moral social foundation known for encouraging prosperity and personal freedom. However, both critics and supporters of property recognize that moral controversy concerning the distribution of resources continues. Moral questions about property concern the legitimacy of the original acquisition of resources, how voluntary an exchange of resources is, whether one's use of resources interferes with another's resources, the limits to taxation, and society's responsibility to its weak, old, young, and sick members. Ultimately, business ethics and the morality of property embrace many of the most important issues of society.

Property as a System of Personal Ethics

Once you understand property as a "right" rather than a "thing," you appreciate how property can be the basis for a system of personal ethics. Property is a system of law enforced by the state but the values underlying this system are moral ones.

Property provides an ordering of relations between people. It acknowledges that each person has an exclusive sphere for private resources that all other persons must observe. If in the broad sense we apply property not only to the external resources that a person has lawfully acquired, but also—as James Madison did—to a person's internal resources, we must acknowledge that to harm others' safety and health, freedom of choice, or liberty of movement is to infringe their right of property. It is to deprive others of what is "proper" to them.

Property applies both to what is mine and to what is yours. As a part of the system of property, you must recognize what is mine but I also must recognize what is yours. Morally, as well as legally, each must respect the equal right of others to what is proper to them. It is as unethical for an employer to fail to warn employees of safety risks in the workplace as it is for the employee to embezzle money from the employer.

The property system does not explain which resources belong in the first instance within the exclusive sphere of property's protection. Some property critics are uncomfortable with this result, yet long tradition, custom, and law place almost all resources that are originally possessed (e.g., your liberty) or are acquired without force, fraud, or theft within this personal exclusive sphere. Once within this sphere, these resources become proper to private persons. By law and morality, each must not interfere with or harm (common law said "trespass" on) the resources of others, and this value applies as much in as out of the workplace.

The rule of law and property are fundamental not only to the structure but also to the values of the private market and of ethical behavior in the business community. The next three chapters concern when the values that underlie law are not enough to resolve disputes and legal enforcement becomes necessary.

KEY TERMS

Categorical imperative 31	Protestant ethic 33
Consequentialism 32	Self-regulation 40
Deontology 30	Social contract theory 31
Duty 30	Stakeholder theory 49
Ethics 29	Teleology 32
Formalism 30	The good 29
Morality 28	Utilitarianism 32

REVIEW QUESTIONS AND PROBLEMS

Contemporary Business Ethics

1. *Ethics and Society*

   Describe the reasons for the rising concern over business ethics.

2. *Ethics and Government*

   How has government action in recent years encouraged increased business attention to ethical matters?

The Nature of Ethics

3. *Ethics and Morality*

   Compare and contrast ethics and morality. What do philosophers call the end result of ethical examination?

4. *Ethics and Law*

   A marketing consultant to your firm comments that being ethical in business means nothing more than obeying the law. Discuss.

Two Systems of Ethics

5. *Formalism*

   As amended in 1988, the Foreign Corrupt Practices Act prohibits bribery as a practice for U.S. companies to use in obtaining business in other countries. In passing the act, Congress expressed the concern that bribery was inherently wrong. Which major system of ethical thought does this concern suggest? Explain.

6. *Consequentialism*

   A recent headline from *The Wall Street Journal* read "U.S. Companies Pay Increasing Attention to Destroying Files." The article discussed how many companies are routinely shredding files in the ordinary course of business to prevent future plaintiffs from obtaining the files and finding incriminating evidence. Is this practice unethical? Evaluate.

7. *Comparing the Two Ethical Systems*

   (a)   Is it ethical to advertise tobacco products in association with a desirable, exciting, or sophisticated lifestyle?

   (b)   Is it ethical to advertise these products in association with a cartoon character that is appealing to young people?

Sources of Values for Business Ethics

8. *Legal Regulation*

   Explain how in our society, ethical values frequently become law, and how legal regulation can promote change in ethical values. Describe several common ethical values that are found in law.

9. *Professional Codes of Ethics*

   Discuss why lawyers are sometimes viewed as being unethical. Is the average lawyer more or less ethical than the average business manager?

10. *Organizational Codes of Ethics*

    A study of one major company's code of ethics by the Business Roundtable found that the lower the level of employees on the corporate ladder, the greater their hostility and cynicism toward codes of business ethics.

    (a)   Why might this be true?

    (b)   What can top business management do to change this view?

11. *Individual Values*

    In addition to the five questions listed in the text, can you think of questions to ask yourself to help explore your ethical values before making a business (or personal) decision?

Achieving an Ethical Business Corporation

12. *The Obstacles*

    A *Newsweek* article on business ethics concludes, "Even in today's complex world, knowing what's right is comparatively easy. It's doing what's right that's hard." Explain why this statement may be true in modern corporate decision making.

The Control of Resources by Nonowners

13. *The Steps*

    Another article from *The Wall Street Journal* carries the headline "Tipsters Telephoning Ethics Hot Lines Can End Up Sabotaging Their Own Jobs." Discuss why whistle-blowing is unpopular within the corporation. Apply to your discussion what sociologist Robert Jackall said about a subordinate's loyalty to supervisors within the corporation. Is whistle-blowing an appropriate subject for corporate ethics codes?

Consideration of All Stakeholders

14. *The Rewards*

Why are formal legal rules alone not an adequate ethical system for business?

15. *The Morality of Property*

Define *property* and discuss its morality.

TERMINOLOGY REVIEW

For each term in the left-hand column, match the most appropriate description in the right-hand column.

1. Morality
2. Ethics
3. The good
4. Formalism
5. Consequentialism
6. Duty
7. Categorical imperative
8. Protestant ethic
9. Social contract theory

a. The total values that we choose to pursue
b. Deontology
c. Teleology
d. A formal statement of values together with a rational method to justify the values
e. Concept that to be ethical, actions should be appropriate for universal adoption
f. Helped the early success of Western capitalism
g. Advocated by John Rawls to construct a just society
h. Concepts of right and wrong
i. Moral obligation

BUSINESS DISCUSSION

As the chief executive officer of a Silicon Valley software company, you become aware that your chief competitor is working on a new computer program that will revolutionize interactive voice-based applications. You know that if you can find out about several key functions relating to your competitor's program, your own programmers can duplicate the function of the program without actually copying its code.

Is it ethical for you to hire away from your competitor a secretary who may have overheard something that will be useful to you?

Is it ethical for you to send an attractive employee to a bar where your competitor's programmers hang out in the hope of getting the information you want?

Is it ethical for you to have someone hunt up and read everything published by your competitor's programmers in case they may have let slip something that will help you?

THE COURT SYSTEM

BUSINESS DECISION

You are the president of a large corporation which is in the business of manufacturing, among other things, chemical products used to eradicate termites.
You have just reviewed a confidential report, prepared by one of your top
scientists, questioning the effectiveness of the product and the claims your
business has been making to homeowners, pesticide treatment firms, and the
general public. You have heard rumors that a lawsuit will be filed shortly
against your corporation claiming that this product is ineffective.

> Who should you turn to for advice?
> Should you destroy the report?
> In which court can a lawsuit be filed?
> If you lose the lawsuit at trial, can you appeal?

Corporate governance, in a property-based legal environment, is dependent
on a viable court system. This chapter deals with the court system and
how courts have the authority to decide disputes between parties. First it examines the personnel who operate our courts, including the role of judges, jurors,
and lawyers in a case. It next explores the organizational structure of both the
state and federal courts and the differences between trial courts and appellate
courts. Finally, the chapter examines the U.S. Supreme Court and the concept
of judicial review and the role of courts in interpreting the Constitution, state
and federal legislation, and the making of common law in the process of deciding cases (*stare decisis*).

To appreciate how law affects business, a manager needs a thorough understanding of the court system. Managers frequently are involved in the litigation
process as either parties or witnesses in a case.

By the time you have completed this chapter, you should have an understanding
of the court system and a greater sensitivity for how the courts apply the law.

CORPORATE GOVERNANCE AND THE
SOARING COST OF LEGAL REPRESENTATION

How much does it cost to defend a company and its executives when a lawsuit is filed? In some cases, the mere investigation may run into the tens of millions. Massive legal expenses are a major concern for corporate executives and shareholders alike. Legal fees can bankrupt a small business. In a recent accounting fraud investigation, Qwest Communications International spent $75 million on legal fees in one year. Tyco International spent about $50 million to defend and investigate its practices. Problems with corporate governance and rising legal fees go hand in hand.

PERSONNEL

Before we look at the court system, some background and understanding of the individuals who operate our court system is helpful. Judges apply the law to the facts. Jurors find or determine the facts from conflicting evidence, and the facts as found by the jury are given great deference. In the process of representing clients, lawyers present evidence to the jury and argue the law to the court. Collectively, these persons conduct the search for truth.

1. JUDGES AND JUSTICES

The individuals who operate our courts are called judges or magistrates. In some appellate courts, such as the U.S. Supreme Court, members of the court are called justices. In this discussion, we will refer to trial court persons as judges and reviewing court persons as justices.

In all cases, the function of the trial judge is to determine the applicable rules of law to be used to decide the case. Such rules may be procedural or substantive. In cases tried without a jury, the judge is also responsible for finding the facts. In cases tried before a jury, the function of the jury is to decide questions of fact. In all cases, the judge is responsible for deciding questions of law.

Trial judges are the main link between the law and the citizens it serves. The trial judge renders decisions that deal directly with people in conflict. These judges have the primary duty to observe and to apply constitutional limitations and guarantees. They bear the burden of upholding the dignity of the courts and maintaining respect for the law.

Justices do more than simply decide an appeal—they often give reasons for their decisions. These reasoned decisions become precedent and a part of our body of law that may affect society as a whole as well as the litigants. So in deciding cases, justices must consider not only the result between the parties but also the total effect of the decision of the law. In this sense, their role is similar to that of legislators. When reviewing appeals, justices are essentially concerned with issues of *law;* issues of *fact* normally are resolved at the trial court level.

For these reasons, the personal characteristics required for a justice or appellate judge are somewhat different from those for a trial judge. The manner of performing duties and the methods used also vary between trial and reviewing courts. A trial judge who has observed the witnesses is able to use knowledge gained from participation as an essential ingredient in his or her decisions. A justice must spend most of the time in the library studying the briefs, the record of proceedings, and the law in reaching decisions.

The judiciary, because of the power of judicial review, has perhaps the most extensive power of any branch of government. This issue will be extensively examined later in the chapter. Lower court judges' decisions may be reviewed by a reviewing court, but they have almost absolute personal immunity from legal actions against them based on their judicial acts.

2. JURORS

It is important to understand the role of the jury as a fact-finding body. Since litigation may involve both questions of law and questions of fact, the deference given to the decisions of a jury is very important. Trial by jury is a cherished right guaranteed by the Bill of Rights. The Sixth and Seventh Amendments to the Constitution guarantee the right of trial by jury in both criminal and civil cases. The **petit jury** is the trial jury that returns a verdict in both situations.

Although juries are used in only a very small percentage of all cases, they remain critical to the administration of justice. In civil cases the right to trial by a jury is preserved in suits at common law when the amount in controversy exceeds $20. State constitutions have like provisions guaranteeing the right of trial by jury in state courts.

Historically, a jury consisted of 12 persons. Today many states and some federal courts have rules of procedure that provide for smaller juries in both criminal and civil cases. Such provisions are constitutional since the Constitution does not specify the *number* of jurors—only the *types* of cases that may be brought to trial before a jury at common law. Several studies have found no discernible difference between results reached by a 6-person jury and those reached by a 12-person jury. As a result, many cases are tried before six-person juries today.

In most states, a jury's decision must be unanimous because many believe that the truth is more nearly to be found and justice rendered if the jury acts only on one common conscience. However, there is growing evidence that the requirement of unanimity is taking its toll on the administration of justice in the United States. Holdout jurors contribute to mistrials and many cases are routinely deadlocked by margins of 11–1 or 10–2. Many states have eliminated the requirement of unanimity in their courts in civil cases and two states have done so in criminal cases. Several legal commentators have argued that unanimous jury verdicts are not constitutionally mandated and should be eliminated to help restore public confidence in our jury system.

Thanks to a series of sensationalized trials, the jury system has been subject to much criticism. Many argue that jurors are not qualified to distinguish fact from fiction, that they vote their prejudices, and that their emotions are too easily swayed by skilled trial lawyers. However, most members of the bench and bar feel the right to be tried by a jury of one's peers in criminal cases is as fair and effective a method of ascertaining the truth and giving an accused his or her "day in court" as has been devised.

As Jeremiah Black, the attorney for the defendant in the famous case of *Ex Parte Milligan,* 71 U.S. 2 (1886), observed:

> I do not assert that the jury trial is an infallible mode of ascertaining truth. Like everything human, it has its imperfection. I only say, that it is the best protection for innocence and the surest mode of punishing guilt that has yet been discovered. It has borne the test of longer experience, and borne it better than any other legal institution that ever existed among men.

Several reforms in the jury system have been launched in recent years. Several states now permit jurors to have a more active role. In several jurisdictions, jurors now are permitted to take notes during trials. Some states allow jurors to submit questions directly to the judges who, using their discretion, may require witnesses to answer during their testimony. A few jurisdictions even permit jurors during the trial to discuss the evidence as the case progresses rather than waiting until the end of the proceeding to begin deliberations. Most of these recent reforms are based upon the belief that active and engaged jurors, who do more than merely listen, pay closer attention to the evidence during the course of the trial and make better decisions.

Jurors normally do not give reasons for their decisions, although some special verdicts may require juries to answer a series of questions. Actually, it would be almost impossible for the jury to agree on the reasons for its verdict. A jury may agree as to the result but disagree on some of the facts, and different jurors may have different ideas on the significance of various items of testimony.

Many individuals attempt to avoid jury duty. Some lose money because of time away from a job or profession. Others may feel great stress in having to help make important decisions affecting the lives of many people. Because so many potential jurors seek relief from jury duty, many trials often end up with more jurors who are unemployed or retired than would otherwise be the case. Today, there is a strong trend toward requiring jury duty of all citizens, irrespective of any hardship that such service may entail. Courts often refuse to accept excuses because jury duty is seen as a responsibility of all citizens in a free society.

One of the most difficult issues facing the judicial system is the right to a trial by jury in very complex and complicated cases that frequently take a long time to try. For example, many antitrust cases involve economic issues that baffle economists, and such cases may last for several months or even years. The average juror may not comprehend the meaning of much of the evidence, let alone remember it when the time to reach a verdict arrives. As a practical matter, many persons cannot serve on a jury for several weeks or months. How does a free and democratic society deliver trial juries of one's peers, if busy people are excused from jury service? For these and other reasons, some experts recommend that the right to a trial by jury be abolished in very complex and time-consuming cases.

Complex cases can result in huge verdicts as juries send important messages to the business community. In 2002 the nation's 10 largest jury verdicts included 2 over a billion dollars (table on next page). Only 10 years earlier the largest award by a jury was $75 million, which would not even make a top 10 list today.

Many of the largest jury verdicts involve product liability, fraud, or breach of contract. Juries have been increasingly generous to plaintiffs who suffer death or serious physical injury. Many plaintiffs' lawyers now contend that million dollar awards—once the standard for measuring a successful case—are no longer indicative of a major victory.

3. LAWYERS

Our court system is an adversarial one. Although private parties to proceedings in a court may represent themselves without a lawyer, as a practical matter, lawyers are required in most cases. Since knowledge of court procedures and substantive law is required as a bare minimum in most cases, lawyers serve as

10 Largest Jury Verdicts of 2002		
1. Bullock v. Phillip Morris	Fraud, products liability	$28.00 billion
2. Hayes v. Courtney Jackson	Personal injury	$2.225 billion
3. Kinetic Concepts v. Hillenbrand Industries	Antitrust	$520.7 million
4. IGEN International v. Roche Diagnostics	Breach of licensing agreement	$505 million
5. City of Hope Medical Center v. Genentech	Breach of contract	$500.2 million
6. Steele Software v. First Union	Breach of contract	$276 million
7. Johnson v. Equitable Resources	Personal injury	$270 million
8. Burns v. Prudential Marion	Breach of fiduciary duty	$261.7 million
9. Benavides v. Ford Motor	Product liability	$225 million
10. In Re Real Estate Associates	Malicious prosecution	$185 million

Source: www.law.com.

the representative advocates in our court system. They present the evidence, the points of law, and the arguments that are weighed by juries and judges in making their decisions.

A lawyer's first duty is to the administration of justice. As an officer of the court, he or she should see that proceedings are conducted in a dignified and orderly manner and that issues are tried on their merits only. The practice of law should not be a game or a battle of wits, but a means to promote justice. The lawyer's duties to each client require the highest degree of fidelity, loyalty, and integrity.

A lawyer serves in three capacities: counselor, advocate, and public servant. As a counselor, a lawyer by the very nature of the profession knows his or her client's most important secrets and affairs. A lawyer is often actively involved in the personal decisions of clients, ranging from their business affairs and family matters such as divorce to their alleged violations of the criminal law. These relationships dictate that a lawyer meet the highest standards of professional and ethical conduct.

The tension between the business community and the legal profession has been growing in recent years. This conflict has been fueled by the increasing number of lawsuits filed by lawyers on behalf of their clients, by resistance from organized lawyer advocacy groups like the American Bar Association to products liability reform, and by the high costs of attorney fees that businesses must absorb into their costs of doing business. As the size and revenue generated by law firms grows every year, many of the nation's largest law firms take on the look of a large business enterprise. The table on the next page lists the 10 largest firms.

It is obvious that if a lawyer is to give competent advice and adequate representation, he or she must know to the fullest extent possible all the facts involved in any legal problem presented by the client. In attempting to ensure that a lawyer may be fully advised of a client's problems and all matters affecting them, the rules of evidence provide that confidential communications to a lawyer are privileged. The law does not permit a lawyer to reveal such facts and testify against a client, even if called to do so at a trial. This is the attorney-client privilege, and it may extend to communications made to the lawyer's employees in certain cases. This is especially important today because law firms frequently use paralegals to gather facts and assist attorneys.

Top 10 Law Firms of 2001

Firm	Headquarters	Gross Revenue	Number of Lawyers
1. Skadden, Arps, Slate, Meagher & Flom	New York, NY	$1.225 billion	1,602
2. Baker & McKenzie	Chicago, IL	$1.000 billion	3,031
3. Jones, Day, Reavis & Pogue	Cleveland, OH	$790 million	1,481
4. Lathan & Watkins	Los Angeles, CA	$769.5 million	1,165
5. Sidley Austin Brown & Wood	Chicago, IL	$715 million	1,276
6. Shearman & Sterling	New York, NY	$619.5 million	1,039
7. White & Case	New York, NY	$603 million	1,315
8. Weil, Gotshal & Manges	New York, NY	$581 million	845
9. Morgan, Lewis & Bockius	Philadelphia, PA	$574.5 million	1,083
10. Mayer, Brown & Platt	Chicago, IL	$573 million	893

Source: www.law.com.

concept SUMMARY   *Personnel*

1. Trial judges determine the applicable law, and in cases without a jury, they also are responsible for finding the facts.
2. Appellate courts act as reviewing courts and generally are concerned with issues of law.
3. The petit jury is the trial jury that returns a verdict.
4. The nation's top 10 jury verdicts include 2 in the billions of dollars.
5. Lawyers serve three roles: counselor, advocate, and public servant.

ORGANIZATION OF THE COURT SYSTEM

There are two major court systems in the United States: the federal courts and the 50 state courts. The federal court system and those in most states contain three levels—trial courts, courts of appeals, and supreme courts. Lawsuits are begun at the **trial court** level, and the results are reviewed at one or more of the other two **appellate court** levels.

4. STATE COURTS

State court systems are created, and their operations are governed from three sources. First, state constitutions provide the general framework for the court system. Second, the state legislature, pursuant to constitutional authority, enacts statutes that add body to the framework. This legislation provides for various courts, establishes their jurisdiction, and regulates the tenure, selection, and duties of judges. Other legislation may establish the general rules of procedure to be used by these courts. Each court sets forth its own rules of procedure within the statutory bounds. These rules are detailed and may specify, for example, the times when various documents must be filed with the court clerk.

Trial Courts Depending upon the particular state, a general trial court can take on any number of names: the *superior court,* the *circuit court,* or the *district court.* In the trial courts, parties file their lawsuits or complaints seeking to protect their

Typical state court system

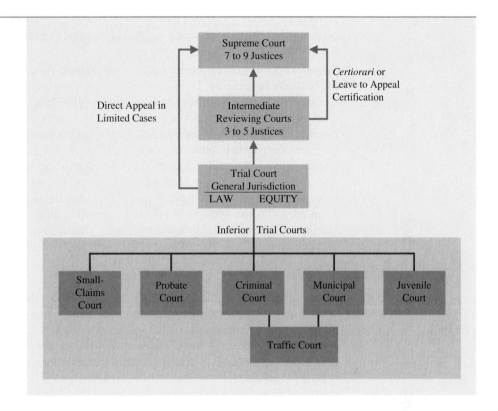

property rights or redress a wrongdoing. The complaint describes the parties (John Doe versus Sally Smith), the facts and law giving rise to a cause of action, the authority of the court to decide the case, and the relief requested from the court. (See Chapter 4 for a more complete explanation of the litigation process.) The trial court is responsible for determining both the facts and law in the case. Of course, 95 to 98 percent of all complaints are settled or fully resolved at the trial level.

Appellate Courts The parties to litigation are entitled as a matter of right to a review of their case by a higher court, or an **appeal,** if the requirements of procedural law are followed in seeking the review. In some states there is only one appellate court, which is usually called the supreme court of the state. In more populous states, there often are two levels of reviewing courts—an intermediate level and a court of final resort. In states with two levels of review, the intermediate courts are usually called the **courts of appeal,** and the highest court is again called the **supreme court.** In states with two levels of reviewing courts, most appeals are taken to the lower of the two courts, and the highest court of the state will review only very important cases. Intermediate courts of review typically consist of three to five judges, while seven to nine judges typically make up a state supreme court.

Reviewing courts review are essentially concerned with questions of law. Although a party is entitled to one trial and one appeal, he or she may obtain a second review if the higher reviewing court, in the exercise of its discretion, agrees to such a review. The procedure for requesting a second review is to file what is called in some states a *petition for leave to appeal* and in others a petition for a ***writ of certiorari.*** These procedures are explained more fully in section 5 in this chapter. Deciding such requests is a major function of the highest court in each state. As a practical matter, less than 5 percent of all such requests are granted.

Small-Claims Courts One court of limited jurisdiction is especially important to the business community. This court, usually known as **small-claims court,** handles much of the litigation between business and its customers. Small-claims courts are used by businesses to collect accounts and by customers to settle disputes with the business community that are relatively minor from a financial perspective. Such suits are often quite important from the standpoint of principle. Landlord-tenant disputes are an example of controversies decided in these courts. Small-claims courts have low court costs and simplified procedures. The informality of the proceedings speeds up the flow of cases. The services of a lawyer are not usually required, and some states do not allow lawyers to participate in these proceedings. Lawsuits filed in small-claims courts usually are subject to a dollar limitation, such as a maximum of $25,000, often ranging from $500 to $5,000.

5. FEDERAL COURTS

Article III of the Constitution (see Appendix) provides that judicial power be vested in the Supreme Court and such lower courts as Congress may create. The judicial power of the federal courts has been limited by Congress. Essentially, it extends to matters involving (1) questions of federal law (federal question cases), (2) the United States as a party, (3) controversies among the states, and (4) certain suits between citizens of different states (diversity of citizenship). Federal question cases and diversity of citizenship cases require further discussion as presented in the following paragraphs.

Federal question cases may be based on issues arising out of the U.S. Constitution or out of federal statutes. Any amount of money may be involved in such a case, and it need not be a suit for damages. For example, a suit to enjoin a violation of a constitutional right can be filed in a federal court as a federal question case. These civil actions may involve matters based on federal laws such as those dealing with patents, copyrights, trademarks, taxes, or employment discrimination. The rights guaranteed by the Bill of Rights of the Constitution also may be the basis for a federal question case.

Diversity of citizenship requires that all plaintiffs be citizens of different states from all defendants. If a case involves a party on one side that is a citizen of the same state as a party on the other, there will then be no diversity of citizenship and thus no federal jurisdiction. Courts have held that it is the citizenship of the real party in interest in the case that determines whether diversity of citizenship exists. For example, diversity jurisdiction is based on the citizenship of all members of a partnership.

The fact that business corporations, which are considered persons before the law, are frequently incorporated in one state and have their principal place of business in another state also causes problems in determining when diversity of citizenship exists. For purposes of diversity jurisdiction, a corporation is a citizen of the state of incorporation and also a citizen of the state in which it has its principal place of business. Thus, a Delaware corporation with its principal place of business in Illinois is a citizen of both Delaware and Illinois for purposes of diversity. If any party on the other side of a lawsuit with such a corporation is a citizen of either Illinois or Delaware, there is then no diversity and no federal jurisdiction.

Moreover, questions arise regarding the state in which a corporation has its principal place of business. The total activity of the corporation is examined to determine its principal place of business. This test incorporates both the *place of activities* and the *nerve center* tests. The nerve center test places general emphasis on the locus of the managerial and policy-making functions of the corporations. The place of activities test focuses on production or sales activities. The *total activity* test is not an equation that can provide a simple answer to the question of a corporation's principal place of business. Each case necessarily involves somewhat subjective analysis.

In diversity of citizenship cases, the federal courts have a jurisdictional amount of more than $75,000. If a case involves multiple plaintiffs with separate and distinct claims, *each* claim must satisfy the jurisdictional amount. Thus, in a class-action suit, the claim of each plaintiff must be greater than the $75,000 jurisdictional amount.

One of the reasons Congress provides for diversity of citizenship jurisdiction is to guard against state court bias against the nonresident party in a lawsuit. Since the biggest increase in federal lawsuits in recent years has been over businesses suing one another in contract disputes (transfer of property rights), diversity jurisdiction preserves the sense of fairness in such situations when one of the parties is out of state.

District Courts The federal district courts are the trial courts of the federal judicial system. There is at least one such court in every state and the District of Columbia. These courts have subject matter jurisdiction over all the cases mentioned above. These courts have the authority to review lawsuits, receive evidence, evaluate testimony, impanel juries, and resolve disputes. Most significant federal litigation begins in this court. The **Federal Rules of Civil Procedure** provide the details concerning procedures to be followed in federal court litigation. These rules are strictly enforced by the courts and must be followed by the parties in every lawsuit.

Appellate Courts Under its constitutional authorization, Congress has created 12 U.S. Courts of Appeal plus a special Court of Appeals for the Federal Circuit as intermediate appellate courts in the federal system. This special reviewing court, located in Washington, D.C., hears appeals from special courts such as the U.S. Claims Court and Contract Appeals as well as from administrative decisions such as those made by the Patent and Trademark Office. Other courts, such as the Court of Appeals for Armed Forces, have been created to handle special subject matter. The following chart illustrates the federal court system and shows the relationship of state courts and administrative agencies for appellate review.

In addition to these courts of appeal, the federal court system provides for a Supreme Court. Because the litigants are entitled to only one review, or appeal, as a matter of rights, a subsequent review by the U.S. Supreme Court must be obtained through a petition for a *writ of certiorari* to the Supreme Court which is explained in the next section of this chapter.

6. DECISIONS BY THE U.S. SUPREME COURT

A petition for a *writ of certiorari* is a request by the losing party in the Courts of Appeal for permission to file an appeal with the U.S. Supreme Court. In such situations, the Supreme Court has discretion as to whether or not it will grant the

The federal court system

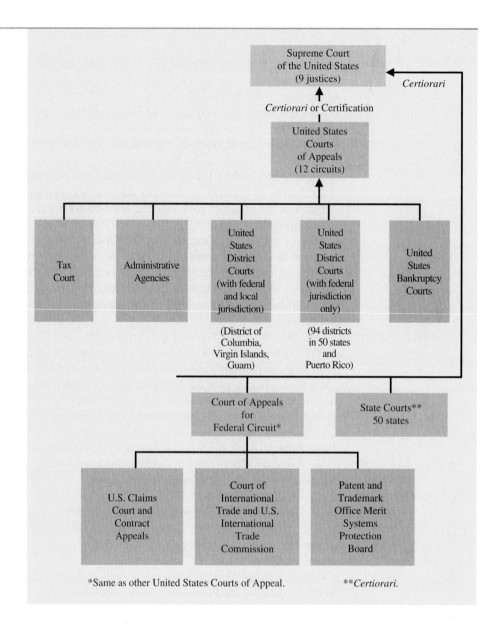

petition and allow another review. This review is not a matter of right. *Writs of certiorari* are granted only in cases of substantial federal importance or where there is an obvious conflict between decisions of two or more U.S. Circuit Courts of Appeal in an important area of the law that needs clarification. The Supreme Court's decision becomes the law of the land and reconciles the division of opinion between the lower courts.

When the U.S. Supreme Court reviews petitions for a *writ of certiorari,* the writ is granted if four of the nine justices vote to take the case. The Supreme Court spends a great deal of time and effort in deciding which cases it will hear. It is able to pick and choose those issues with which it will be involved and to control its caseload. The Supreme Court normally resolves cases involving major constitu-

THE VERY SLIM ODDS

Every year between seven and eight thousand petitions are filed in the U.S. Supreme Court from parties seeking review of adverse decisions issued by federal circuit courts of appeal or state supreme courts. Parties pay a $300 filing fee and thousands of dollars to appellate lawyers to prepare their petitions. However, the odds heavily favor the decisions issued by the lower courts. In the 2001–2002 term of court, the Supreme Court agreed to hear only 88 cases. In the 2002–2003 term of court, that number fell to just 84 cases or about 1 percent of the petitions filed.

tional issues or interpretation of federal law. In recent years, the Court has been very reluctant to review many lower court decisions. In the 2002–2003 term of the U.S. Supreme Court, only 84 cases were heard.

The Supreme Court is far more likely to review and reverse a decision rendered by the Ninth Circuit Court of Appeals—treating it, as one commentator noted, like a wayward child. Many commentators attribute the difference to the judicial activism of the Ninth Circuit, which often is at odds with the philosophy of judicial restraint found in the Supreme Court in recent years. In contrast, decisions rendered by the Fourth Circuit Court of Appeals tend to be far more conservative or consistent with the philosophy of judicial restraint. A more thorough discussion of these two philosophies will follow in sections 7 and 8 of this chapter.

The federal district courts and the courts of appeal cannot review, retry, or correct judicial errors charged against a state court. Final judgments or decrees rendered by the highest court of a state are reviewed only by the Supreme Court of the United States. State cases reviewed by the U.S. Supreme Court must concern a federal question involving the validity of state action on the grounds that the statute is repugnant to the Constitution, treaties, or laws of the United States. If the case does not involve a federal question, the decision of the highest state court is not subject to review by the Supreme Court of the United States.

THE ROLE OF THE REVIEWING COURT

Since reviewing courts create case law or precedent in the process of deciding cases, most final decisions of reviewing courts are published in order to make the precedent of each case available for inclusion into the total body of law. The opinions usually include the procedures which have been followed, the facts of the case, the law applicable to the facts, the decision of the court, and the reasons for the decision. Opinions may be written in the name of the author of the opinion or they may be written *per curiam*—by the court without identifying the author.

It is not surprising that the decisions of a reviewing court often are not unanimous. In fact the decisions of the U.S. Supreme Court are unanimous less often than not. Many Supreme Court of the United States decisions are closely divided and 5–4 or 6–3 decisions in cases involving highly controversial issues are quite common. A recent circuit court of appeals decision was 9–7. The *Roe v. Wade* decision legalizing abortions and the cases involving abortions which followed have been decided 5–4 or 6–3. Presidential appointments to the Supreme Court are evaluated, in part, on their potential effect on the court alignment as perceived in the close decisions of the past.

The written opinions in the cases in this textbook reflect the majority opinion of the reviewing court and as such they reflect the current status of the law. Dissenting opinions of the court also make a contribution to our jurisprudence and to the public debate on important social and public policy issues. Dissents often provide the foundation for changes in public policy and they often provide guidance to legislative bodies on issues under consideration.

concept SUMMARY   *Organization of the Court System*

1. The court system—both at the federal and state level—operates on three levels: the trial court, the court of appeals, and the supreme court.

2. Trial courts focus on the law and facts while reviewing courts focus only on the law.

3. The parties to litigation are entitled as a matter of right to one review of their case by a higher court.

4. Federal courts typically obtain jurisdiction upon diversity of citizenship or federal questions.

5. The highest legal authority in the United States is the U.S. Supreme Court.

6. Parties seek permission to bring their case to the Supreme Court through a petition for a *writ of certiorari.*

THE POWER OF JUDICIAL REVIEW

In the United States the most significant power of the courts, or "judiciary," is **judicial review,** which is the power to review laws passed by the legislative body and to declare them to be unconstitutional and thus void. It also allows the courts to review actions taken by the executive branch and to declare them unconstitutional. Although the Constitution does not expressly provide that the judiciary shall be the overseer of the government, the net effect of this power is to make it so. Chief Justice John Marshall in *Marbury v. Madison,* 5 U.S. 137 (1803), announced the power of judicial review using in part the following language and reasoning:

> It is a proposition too plain to be contested, that the constitution controls any legislative act repugnant to it; or that the legislature may not alter the constitution by an ordinary act. . . .
>
> It is, emphatically, the province and duty of the judicial department, to say what the law is. Those who apply the rule to particular cases, must of necessity expound and interpret that rule. If two laws conflict with each other, the courts must decide on the operation of each. So, if a law be in opposition to the constitution; if both the law and the constitution apply to a particular case, so that the court must either decide that case, conformable to the law, disregarding the constitution; or conformable to the constitution, disregarding the law; the court must determine which of these conflicting rules governs the case: this is of the very essence of judicial duty. If then, the courts are to regard the constitution, and the constitution is superior to any ordinary act of the legislature, the constitution, and not such ordinary act, must govern the case to which they both apply.

As the next section reveals, however, the U.S. Supreme Court rarely exercises its extraordinary powers and has developed carefully crafted rules as self-imposed limits on its authority as individual jurists.

As individual jurists exercise the power of judicial review, they do so with varying attitudes and philosophies. Some judges believe that the power should be used very sparingly, although others are willing to use it more often. Those who believe that the power should not be used except in unusual cases are said to believe in **judicial restraint.** Those who think that the power should be used whenever the needs of society justify its use believe in **judicial activism.** All members of the judiciary believe in judicial restraint and all are activists to some extent. Often a jurist may be an activist in one area of the law and a firm believer in judicial restraint in another. Both judicial restraint and judicial activism describe attitudes or tendencies by matters of degree. Both terms are also used to describe general attitudes toward the exercise of the power of judicial review as the next two sections explain.

In recent years, judicial restraint has been associated with conservative judges often appointed by Republican presidents. Judicial activism primarily is linked to

THE PROCESS OF CHOOSING A JUDGE

The process of choosing state judges varies from state to state. In some states, the judges are appointed and in others the judges are elected. In the federal system, the U.S. Constitution gives the president the power to appoint federal judges, including Supreme Court justices, with the advice and consent of a majority in the U.S. Senate. However, in recent years, confirmation has required a supermajority of 60 votes when the opposition has mounted a filibuster to forestall a vote on the judge's confirmation.

The breakdown in the confirmation process for federal judges is demonstrated most vividly by the following statistics: During the first two years of George W. Bush's presidency, only 53 percent of his circuit court nominees were confirmed by the Senate. Those statistics compare with 100 percent for Jimmy Carter, 95 percent for Ronald Reagan, 96 percent for George Bush, and 86 percent for Bill Clinton.

liberal judges generally appointed by Democratic presidents. The tension between these philosophies has become more pronounced in the past several years often leading to bitterly divided confirmation hearings before the U.S. Senate where less attention often is paid to a nominee's qualifications than to his or her political views. The box above, describes the process of becoming a judge.

7. JUDICIAL RESTRAINT

The philosophy of judicial restraint developed naturally from the recognition that, in exercising the power of judicial review, the courts are overseeing coequal branches of government. When the power of judicial review is used to set aside decisions by the other branches of government, the courts are wielding great power. It follows that logic and a commitment to the constitutional system dictate that this almost unlimited power be exercised with great restraint.

Those who believe in judicial restraint think that many constitutional issues are too important to be decided by courts unless absolutely necessary and are to be avoided if there is another legal basis for a decision. They believe the proper use of judicial power demands that courts refrain from determining the constitutionality of an act of Congress unless it is absolutely necessary to a decision of a case. This modest view of the role of the judiciary is based on the belief that litigation is not the appropriate technique for bringing about social, political, and economic change.

The philosophy of judicial restraint is sometimes referred to as *strict constructionism,* or *judicial abstention.* Strict constructionists believe that the Constitution should be interpreted in light of what the Founding Fathers intended. They place great weight on the debates of the Constitutional Convention and the language of the Constitution. Those who promote judicial abstention hold that courts should decide only those matters they must to resolve actual cases and controversies before them. Courts should abstain from deciding issues whenever possible, and doubts about the constitutionality of legislation should be resolved in favor of the statute. Cases should be decided on the facts if possible and on the narrowest possible grounds.

Those who believe in judicial restraint believe that social, political, and economic change in society should result from the political process rather than from court action. Justice John Harlan, in *Republic v. Sims,* 84 S.Ct. 1362 (1964), epitomized the philosophy of judicial restraint in a famous dissenting opinion contained in the box labeled "Understanding Judicial Restraint."

WHO ARE THE JUSTICES ON THE SUPREME COURT?

William Rehnquist, Chief Justice of the United States (born 1924). He received a B.A., an M.A., and an LL.B. from Stanford University and an M.A. from Harvard University. President Nixon nominated him to the Supreme Court, and he took his seat as an associate justice in 1972. Nominated as chief justice by President Reagan, he assumed that office in 1986.

John Paul Stevens, Associate Justice (born 1920). He received an A.B. from the University of Chicago, and a J.D. from Northwestern University School of Law. President Ford nominated him as an associate justice of the Supreme Court, and he took office in 1975.

Sandra Day O'Connor, Associate Justice (born 1930). She received her B.A. and LL.B. from Stanford University. President Reagan nominated her as an associate justice of the Supreme Court, and she took office in 1981.

Antonin Scalia, Associate Justice (born 1936). He received his A.B. from Georgetown University and the University of Fribourg, Switzerland, and his LL.B. from Harvard Law School. President Reagan nominated him as an associate justice of the Supreme Court, and he took office in 1986.

Anthony Kennedy, Associate Justice (born 1936). He received his B.A. from Stanford University and the London School of Economics, and his LL.B. from Harvard Law School. President Reagan nominated him as an associ-

ate justice of the Supreme Court, and he took office in 1988.

David Souter, Associate Justice (born 1939). He received his A.B. from Harvard College, was a Rhodes Scholar at Oxford University where he received another A.B. and an M.A. He received his LL.B. from Harvard Law School. President Bush nominated him as an associate justice of the Supreme Court, and he took office in 1990.

Clarence Thomas, Associate Justice (born 1948). He attended Conception Seminary and received an A.B., cum laude, from Holy Cross College, and a J.D. from Yale Law School. President Bush nominated him as an associate justice of the Supreme Court, and he took office in 1991.

Ruth Bader Ginsburg, Associate Justice (born 1933). She received her B.A. from Cornell University, attended Harvard Law School, and received her LL.B. from Columbia Law School. President Clinton nominated her as an associate justice of the Supreme Court, and she took office in 1993.

Stephen Breyer, Associate Justice (born 1938). He received an A.B. from Stanford University, a B.A. from Magdalen College, Oxford, and an LL.B. from Harvard Law School. President Clinton nominated him as an associate justice of the Supreme Court, and he took office in 1994.

UNDERSTANDING JUDICIAL RESTRAINT

The vitality of our political system, on which in the last analysis all else depends, is weakened by reliance on the judiciary for political reform. . . . These decisions give support to a current mistaken view of the Constitution and the constitutional function of this Court. This view, in a nutshell, is that every major social ill in the country can find its cure in some constitutional "principle," and that this Court should "take the lead" in promoting reform when other branches of government fail to act. The Constitution

is not a panacea for every blot upon the public welfare, nor should this Court, ordained as a judicial body, be thought of as a general haven for reform movements. The Constitution is an instrument of government, fundamental to which is the premise that in a diffusion of governmental authority lies the greatest promise that this nation will realize liberty for all its citizens. This Court, limited in function in accordance with that premise, does not serve its high purpose when it exceeds its authority, even to satisfy justified impatience with the slow working of the political process.

Judges who identify with judicial restraint give great deference to the political process. They believe that the courts, especially the federal courts, ought to defer to the actions of the states and of the coordinate branches of government unless these actions are clearly unconstitutional. They allow the states and the federal legislative and executive branches wide latitude in finding solutions to the nation's problems.

Judicial restraint jurists have a deep commitment to precedent. They overrule cases only when the prior decision is clearly wrong. They try to refrain from writing their personal convictions into the law. They do not view the role of the lawyer and the practice of law as that of social reform. To them, reform is the function of the political process.

Followers of judicial restraint often take a pragmatic approach to litigation. Whenever possible, decisions are based on the facts rather than a principle of law. Reviewing courts exercising judicial restraint tend to accept the trial court decisions unless they are clearly wrong on the facts or the law. If there is any reasonable basis for the lower court decision, it will not be reversed. Such courts often engage in a balancing approach to their decisions. They weigh competing interests. For example, justices who adhere to judicial restraint often weigh the rights of the person accused of crime with the interests of the victim and of society in determining the extent of the rights of the accused in criminal cases.

Throughout most of our history, judicial restraint has been the dominant philosophy. Today, most of the justices of the U.S. Supreme Court usually follow this philosophy, but all courts to some degree are activist. The box below illustrates typical judicial restraint decisions. The court allowed these decisions by other branches of government and the political process to stand.

8. JUDICIAL ACTIVISM

Those who believe in the philosophy of judicial activism believe that courts have a major role to play in correcting wrongs in our society. To them, courts must provide leadership in bringing about social, political, and economic change because the political system is often too slow or unable to bring about those changes necessary to improve society. Activists tend to be innovative and less dependent on precedent for their decisions. They are value oriented and policy directed. Activist jurists believe that constitutional issues must be decided within

TYPICAL JUDICIAL RESTRAINT DECISIONS

1. Male-only draft is not a denial of equal protection of the law.
2. States can regulate nuclear power.
3. States can tax the foreign income of multinational corporations.
4. Prayer in the legislature does not violate the First Amendment.
5. Unanimous verdicts are not required, and juries may consist of fewer than 12 persons.
6. A federal law cannot require state law enforcement officers to conduct background checks on gun purchasers.
7. Class-action suits require actual notice to members of the class.
8. Congress cannot create religious freedoms pursuant to Section 5 of the Fourteenth Amendment.
9. Seniority has preference over affirmative action layoffs.
10. State and local employees are subject to the Federal Fair Labor Standards Act.

TYPICAL JUDICIAL ACTIVIST DECISIONS

1. Welfare recipients have a right to travel among states and be treated like others in their new states.

2. The Pledge of Allegiance is an unconstitutional endorsement of religion when recited in public schools because of the reference to "under God."

3. No prayer is to be permitted in school.

4. The *Miranda* warning shall be given to all criminal suspects prior to interrogation.

5. Statutes outlawing abortion are unconstitutional.

6. Female pensions must be the same as male pensions, even though, on average, females live longer.

7. There shall be equal pay for comparable worth.

8. Residency requirements for public assistance violates equal protection.

9. State laws that require teaching "creation science" as well as evolution are unconstitutional.

10. Certain public employees, such as public defenders, cannot be fired because of political affiliation.

the context of contemporary society and that the meaning of the Constitution is relative to the times in which it is being interpreted. Activists believe that the courts, and especially the Supreme Court, sit as a continuing constitutional convention to meet the needs of today.

During the 1950s and 1960s, there was an activist majority on the Supreme Court. This activist majority brought about substantial changes in the law, especially in such areas as civil rights, reapportionment, and the criminal law. For example, the activist court of this period ordered desegregation of public schools and gave us the one-man, one-vote concept in the distributing of legislative bodies. Earl Warren, Chief Justice during that period, used to request that lawyers appearing before the Court address themselves to the effect of their clients' positions on society. "Tell me why your position is 'right' and that of your opponent is 'wrong' from the standpoint of society" was a common request to lawyers arguing cases before him.

Activist courts tend to be more result conscious and to place less reliance on precedent. Activists are often referred to as liberals, but that description is too narrow to explain their belief in the role of the judiciary as an instrument of change. Activists also believe that justices must examine for themselves the great issues facing society and then decide these issues in light of contemporary standards. Otherwise, they believe we are governed by the dead or by people who are not aware of all of the complexities of today's problems.

The box above illustrates typical judicial activist decisions. These examples are of decisions in which that judiciary has imposed its will on society.

Chief Justice William Rehnquist has presided over the Supreme Court since 1986. The Court's decisions are often split along 5–4 lines with Justices Sandra Day O'Connor and Anthony Kennedy usually deciding whether the consistently conservative triage of Rehnquist, Antonin Scalia, and Clarence Thomas or the more activist foursome of John Paul Stevens, David Souter, Ruth Bader Ginsburg, and Stephen Breyer prevail. In many cases, Justices O'Connor and Kennedy join to create a conservative majority favoring judicial restraint as illustrated in the table on the next page.

Typical Alignment of Justices		
Judicial Activism	*Moderate*	*Judicial Restraint*
Stevens		Rehnquist
Souter		Scalia
Ginsburg		Thomas
Breyer	O'Connor →	
	Kennedy →	

Mirroring societal trends, the Supreme Court's divided decisions are often peppered with angry words about each other. In a recent decision about states' rights, Justice Kennedy used phrases like "scanty and equivocal evidence" and "analytical confusion" and Justice Souter used words such as "unrealistic" and "indefensible" in response. The importance of the issues and the close division of the Court contributes to the tension found in many divided opinions. Although dissenting opinions usually are not included in this textbook, they remain an important part of the process of judicial review. Many dissenting views may become the law of the land in the future as the composition and views of the Supreme Court change over time.

A Sample Case To illustrate the role of the United States Supreme Court in creating laws through the exercise of judicial review, the following case is presented. When this case opinion was announced, the media called it the most important decision of the 2002–03 Supreme Court term. The constitutionally permissible limits of affirmative action programs are critical to businesses as well as institutions of higher education.

We present the following case at the outset of this edition as an example of how the Supreme Court influences critically important areas of the law. This case also shows how controversial issues often are decided by a single vote. Note that the following decision involves a split of 5 to 4 among the nine Supreme Court justices. Although case examples throughout this text usually are limited to only the majority opinion, the following includes language from a dissenting opinion.

Finally, this case is so important to business that your professor likely will make reference to it when you study the Equal Protection Clause of the United States Constitution in Chapter 6 and employment discrimination laws in Chapter 15.

GRUTTER V. BOLLINGER

2003 U.S. LEXIS 4800; 71 U.S.L.W. 4498 (2003)

In 1996, Barbara Gutter, a white female and resident of Michigan, applied to the University of Michigan Law School. Ms. Gutter was denied admission despite a 3.8 grade point average and an LSAT score of 161. She filed a lawsuit in federal district court claiming she was discriminated against on the basis of her race in violation of the Equal Protection

Clause of the Fourteenth Amendment. The Law School, and the other defendants, including Lee Bollinger, the President of the University of Michigan, defended its admission policy as focusing on the applicants' academic ability coupled with a flexible assessment of the applicant's talents, experiences, and potential to contribute to the learning

[CONTINUED]

environment as well as the life and diversity of the Law School. Of particular importance to the Law School was diversity based on race and ethnicity. The Law School especially desired to include students from groups that have been historically discriminated against, like African-Americans, Hispanics, and Native Americans.

Following a 15-day bench trial, the District Judge ruled that the Law School's use of race as a factor in admissions decisions was unlawful. The Law School appealed to the Sixth Circuit Court of Appeals. The full court reversed the District Judge and concluded that the Law School's use of race was narrowly tailored since race was used only as a potential plus factor in making an admission decision. The Supreme Court granted Ms. Gutter's petition for a writ of certiorari.

O'CONNOR J.: . . . We last addressed the use of race in public higher education over 25 years ago. In the landmark *Bakke* case, we reviewed a racial set-aside program that reserved 16 out of 100 seats in a medical school class for members of certain minority groups. 98 S. Ct. 2733 (1978). The decision produced six separate opinions, none of which commanded a majority of the Court. . . . The only holding for the Court in *Bakke* was that a State has a substantial interest that legitimately may be served by a properly devised admissions program involving the competitive consideration of race and ethnic origin. . . .

Since this Court's splintered decision in *Bakke,* Justice Powell's opinion announcing the judgment of the Court has served as the touchstone for constitutional analysis of race-conscious admissions policies. Public and private universities across the Nation have modeled their own admissions programs on Justice Powell's views on permissible race-conscious policies. We therefore discuss Justice Powell's opinion in some detail.

Justice Powell began by stating that the guarantee of equal protection cannot mean one thing when applied to one individual and something else when applied to a person of another color. If both are not accorded the same protection, then it is not equal. In Justice Powell's view, when governmental decisions touch upon an individual's race or ethnic background, he is entitled to a judicial determination that

the burden he is asked to bear on that basis is precisely tailored to serve a compelling governmental interest. . . . .

Justice Powell approved the university's use of race to further only one interest: the attainment of a diverse student body. . . . Justice Powell emphasized that nothing less than the nation's future depends upon leaders trained through wide exposure to the ideas and mores of students as diverse as this Nation of many peoples. In seeking the right to select those students who will contribute the most to the robust exchange of ideas, a university seeks to achieve a goal that is of paramount importance in the fulfillment of its mission. Both tradition and experience lend support to the view that the contribution of diversity is substantial.

Justice Powell was, however, careful to emphasize that in his view race is only one element in a range of factors a university properly may consider in attaining the goal of a heterogeneous student body. For Justice Powell, it is not an interest in simple ethnic diversity, in which a specified percentage of the student body is in effect guaranteed to be members of selected ethnic groups, that can justify the use of race. Rather, the diversity that furthers a compelling state interest encompasses a far broader array of qualifications and characteristics of which racial or ethnic origin is but a single though important element. . . .

[F]or the reasons set out below, today we endorse Justice Powell's view that student body diversity is a compelling state interest that can justify the use of race in university admissions. . . .

We have held that all racial classifications imposed by government must be analyzed by a reviewing court under strict scrutiny. This means that such classifications are constitutional only if they are narrowly tailored to further compelling governmental interests. Absent searching judicial inquiry into the justification for such race-based measures, we have no way to determine what classifications are benign or remedial and what classifications are in fact motivated by illegitimate notions of racial inferiority or simple racial politics. We apply strict scrutiny to all racial classifications to smoke out illegitimate uses of race by assuring that government is pursuing a goal important enough to warrant use of a highly suspect tool.

. . . Although all governmental uses of race are subject to strict scrutiny, not all are invalidated by

[CONTINUED]

it. . . . When race-based action is necessary to further a compelling governmental interest, such action does not violate the constitutional guarantee of equal protection so long as the narrow-tailoring requirement is also satisfied.

Context matters when reviewing race-based governmental action under the Equal Protection Clause. . . . Not every decision influenced by race is equally objectionable and strict scrutiny is designed to provide a framework for carefully examining the importance and the sincerity of the reasons advanced by the governmental decisionmaker for the use of race in that particular context.

With these principles in mind, we turn to the question whether the Law School's use of race is justified by a compelling state interest. Before this Court, as they have throughout this litigation, respondents assert only one justification for their use of race in the admissions process: obtaining the educational benefits that flow from a diverse student body. In other words, the Law School asks us to recognize, in the context of higher education, a compelling state interest in student body diversity.

. . . Today, we hold that the Law School has a compelling interest in attaining a diverse student body.

The Law School's educational judgment that such diversity is essential to its educational mission is one to which we defer. The Law School's assessment that diversity will, in fact, yield educational benefits is substantiated. . . . Our scrutiny of the interest asserted by the Law School is no less strict for taking into account complex educational judgments in an area that lies primarily within the expertise of the university. Our holding today is in keeping with our tradition of giving a degree of deference to a university's academic decisions, within constitutionally prescribed limits.

We have long recognized that, given the important purpose of public education and the expansive freedoms of speech and thought associated with the university environment, universities occupy a special niche in our constitutional tradition. In announcing the principle of student body diversity as a compelling state interest, Justice Powell invoked our cases recognizing a constitutional dimension, grounded in the First Amendment, of educational autonomy: The freedom of a university to make its own judgments as to education includes the selection of its student body. From this premise, Justice Powell reasoned that by claiming the right to select those students who will contribute the most to the robust exchange of ideas, a university seeks to achieve a goal that is of paramount importance in the fulfillment of its mission. Our conclusion that the Law School has a compelling interest in a diverse student body is informed by our view that attaining a diverse student body is at the heart of the Law School's proper institutional mission, and that good faith on the part of a university is presumed absent a showing to the contrary.

. . . The Law School's claim of a compelling interest is further bolstered by its amici, who point to the educational benefits that flow from student body diversity. In addition to the expert studies and reports entered into evidence at trial, numerous studies show that student body diversity promotes learning outcomes, and better prepares students for an increasingly diverse workforce and society, and better prepares them as professionals.

These benefits are not theoretical but real, as major American businesses have made clear that the skills needed in today's increasingly global marketplace can only be developed through exposure to widely diverse people, cultures, ideas, and viewpoints. . . .

We have repeatedly acknowledged the overriding importance of preparing students for work and citizenship, describing education as pivotal to sustaining our political and cultural heritage with a fundamental role in maintaining the fabric of society. This Court has long recognized that "education . . . is the very foundation of good citizenship." Brown v. Board of Education, 74 S. Ct. 686 (1954). For this reason, the diffusion of knowledge and opportunity through public institutions of higher education must be accessible to all individuals regardless of race or ethnicity. . . . Effective participation by members of all racial and ethnic groups in the civic life of our Nation is essential if the dream of one Nation, indivisible, is to be realized.

Moreover, universities, and in particular, law schools, represent the training ground for a large number of our Nation's leaders. Individuals with law degrees occupy roughly half the state governorships, more than half the seats in the United States Senate, and more than a third of the seats in the United

[CONTINUED]

States House of Representatives. The pattern is even more striking when it comes to highly selective law schools. A handful of these schools accounts for 25 of the 100 United States Senators, 74 United States Courts of Appeals judges, and nearly 200 of the more than 600 United States District Court judges.

In order to cultivate a set of leaders with legitimacy in the eyes of the citizenry, it is necessary that the path to leadership be visibly open to talented and qualified individuals of every race and ethnicity. All members of our heterogeneous society must have confidence in the openness and integrity of the educational institutions that provide this training. . . . Access to legal education (and thus the legal profession) must be inclusive of talented and qualified individuals of every race and ethnicity, so that all members of our heterogeneous society may participate in the educational institutions that provide the training and education necessary to succeed in America. . . .

Even in the limited circumstance when drawing racial distinctions is permissible to further a compelling state interest, government is still constrained in how it may pursue that end: The means chosen to accomplish the government's asserted purpose must be specifically and narrowly framed to accomplish that purpose. . . .

Since *Bakke,* we have had no occasion to define the contours of the narrow-tailoring inquiry with respect to race-conscious university admissions programs. That inquiry must be calibrated to fit the distinct issues raised by the use of race to achieve student body diversity in public higher education. . . .

To be narrowly tailored, a race-conscious admissions program cannot use a quota system—it cannot insulate each category of applicants with certain desired qualifications from competition with all other applicants. Instead, a university may consider race or ethnicity only as a plus in a particular applicant's file, without insulating the individual from comparison with all other candidates for the available seats. In other words, an admissions program must be flexible enough to consider all pertinent elements of diversity in light of the particular qualifications of each applicant, and to place them on the same foot-

ing for consideration, although not necessarily according them the same weight.

We find that the Law School's admissions program bears the hallmarks of a narrowly tailored plan. As Justice Powell made clear in *Bakke,* truly individualized consideration demands that race be used in a flexible, nonmechanical way. It follows from this mandate that universities cannot establish quotas for members of certain racial groups or put members of those groups on separate admissions tracks. Nor can universities insulate applicants who belong to certain racial or ethnic groups from the competition for admission. Universities can, however, consider race or ethnicity more flexibly as a plus factor in the context of individualized consideration of each and every applicant.

We are satisfied that the Law School's admissions program . . . does not operate as a quota. . . .

The Law School's goal of attaining a critical mass of underrepresented minority students does not transform its program into a quota. . . . Some attention to numbers, without more, does not transform a flexible admissions system into a rigid quota. . . .

That a race-conscious admissions program does not operate as a quota does not, by itself, satisfy the requirement of individualized consideration. When using race as a plus factor in university admissions, a university's admissions program must remain flexible enough to ensure that each applicant is evaluated as an individual and not in a way that makes an applicant's race or ethnicity the defining feature of his or her application. The importance of this individualized consideration in the context of a race-conscious admissions program is paramount.

Here, the Law School engages in a highly individualized, holistic review of each applicant's file, giving serious consideration to all the ways an applicant might contribute to a diverse educational environment. The Law School affords this individualized consideration to applicants of all races. . . . [T]he Law School awards no mechanical, predetermined diversity bonuses based on race or ethnicity. . . .

We also find that . . . the Law School's race-conscious admissions program adequately ensures that all factors that may contribute to student body diversity are meaningfully considered alongside race in admissions decisions. With respect to the use of

[CONTINUED]

race itself, all underrepresented minority students admitted by the Law School have been deemed qualified. By virtue of our Nation's struggle with racial inequality, such students are both likely to have experiences of particular importance to the Law School's mission, and less likely to be admitted in meaningful numbers on criteria that ignore those experiences.

The Law School does not, however, limit in any way the broad range of qualities and experiences that may be considered valuable contributions to student body diversity. . . . The Law School seriously considers each applicant's promise of making a notable contribution to the class by way of a particular strength, attainment, or characteristic—e.g., an unusual intellectual achievement, employment experience, nonacademic performance, or personal background. All applicants have the opportunity to highlight their own potential diversity contributions through the submission of a personal statement, letters of recommendation, and an essay describing the ways in which the applicant will contribute to the life and diversity of the Law School.

What is more, the Law School actually gives substantial weight to diversity factors besides race. The Law School frequently accepts nonminority applicants with grades and test scores lower than underrepresented minority applicants (and other nonminority applicants) who are rejected. This shows that the Law School seriously weighs many other diversity factors besides race that can make a real and dispositive difference for nonminority applicants as well. By this flexible approach, the Law School sufficiently takes into account, in practice as well as in theory, a wide variety of characteristics besides race and ethnicity that contribute to a diverse student body. . . .

We acknowledge that there are serious problems of justice connected with the idea of preference itself. Narrow tailoring, therefore, requires that a race-conscious admissions program not unduly harm members of any racial group. . . .

We are satisfied that the Law School's admissions program does not. Because the Law School considers all pertinent elements of diversity, it can (and does) select nonminority applicants who have greater potential to enhance student body diversity over underrepresented minority applicants. . . .

We agree that, in the context of its individualized inquiry into the possible diversity contributions of all applicants, the Law School's race-conscious admissions program does not unduly harm nonminority applicants.

We are mindful, however, that a core purpose of the Fourteenth Amendment was to do away with all governmentally imposed discrimination based on race. Accordingly, race-conscious admissions policies must be limited in time. This requirement reflects that racial classifications, however compelling their goals, are potentially so dangerous that they may be employed no more broadly than the interest demands. Enshrining a permanent justification for racial preferences would offend this fundamental equal protection principle. We see no reason to exempt race-conscious admissions programs from the requirement that all governmental use of race must have a logical end point. The Law School, too, concedes that all race-conscious programs must have reasonable durational limits. . . .

We take the Law School at its word that it would like nothing better than to find a race-neutral admissions formula and will terminate its race-conscious admissions program as soon as practicable. It has been 25 years since Justice Powell first approved the use of race to further an interest in student body diversity in the context of public higher education. Since that time, the number of minority applicants with high grades and test scores has indeed increased. We expect that 25 years from now, the use of racial preferences will no longer be necessary to further the interest approved today.

In summary, the Equal Protection Clause does not prohibit the Law School's narrowly tailored use of race in admissions decisions to further a compelling interest in obtaining the educational benefits that flow from a diverse student body. . . . The judgment of the Court of Appeals for the Sixth Circuit, accordingly, is affirmed.

It is so ordered.

DISSENT: REHNQUIST, C. J. with whom SCALIA, J., KENNEDY, J., THOMAS, J. join, dissenting. I agree with the Court that, in the limited circumstance when drawing racial distinctions is

[CONTINUED]

permissible, the government must ensure that its means are narrowly tailored to achieve a compelling state interest. I do not believe, however, that the University of Michigan Law School's (Law School) means are narrowly tailored to the interest it asserts. The Law School claims it must take the steps it does to achieve a critical mass of underrepresented minority students. But its actual program bears no relation to this asserted goal. Stripped of its critical mass veil, the Law School's program is revealed as a naked effort to achieve racial balancing.

As we have explained many times, any preference based on racial or ethnic criteria must necessarily receive a most searching examination. Our cases establish that, in order to withstand this demanding inquiry, respondents must demonstrate that their methods of using race fit a compelling state interest with greater precision than any alternative means.

Before the Court's decision today, we consistently applied the same strict scrutiny analysis regardless of the government's purported reason for using race and regardless of the setting in which race was being used. We rejected calls to use more lenient review in the face of claims that race was being used in good faith because more than good motives should be required when government seeks to allocate its resources by way of an explicit racial classification system. . . .

Although the Court recites the language of our strict scrutiny analysis, its application of that review is unprecedented in its deference.

Respondents' asserted justification for the Law School's use of race in the admissions process is obtaining the educational benefits that flow from a diverse student body. They contend that a critical mass of underrepresented minorities is necessary to further that interest. Respondents and school administrators explain generally that *critical mass* means a sufficient number of underrepresented minority students to achieve several objectives: To ensure that these minority students do not feel isolated or like spokespersons for their race; to provide adequate opportunities for the type of interaction upon which the educational benefits of diversity depend; and to challenge all students to

think critically and reexamine stereotypes. These objectives indicate that critical mass relates to the size of the student body. . . .

In practice, the Law School's program bears little or no relation to its asserted goal of achieving critical mass. Respondents explain that the Law School seeks to accumulate a critical mass of each underrepresented minority group. But the record demonstrates that the Law School's admissions practices with respect to these groups differ dramatically and cannot be defended under any consistent use of the term *critical mass.*

From 1995 through 2000, the Law School admitted between 1,130 and 1,310 students. Of those, between 13 and 19 were Native American, between 91 and 108 were African-Americans, and between 47 and 56 were Hispanic. If the Law School is admitting between 91 and 108 African-Americans in order to achieve critical mass, thereby preventing African-American students from feeling isolated or like spokespersons for their race, one would think that a number of the same order of magnitude would be necessary to accomplish the same purpose for Hispanics and Native Americans. Similarly, even if all of the Native American applicants admitted in a given year matriculate, which the record demonstrates is not at all the case, how can this possibly constitute a critical mass of Native Americans in a class of over 350 students? In order for this pattern of admission to be consistent with the Law School's explanation of critical mass, one would have to believe that the objectives of critical mass offered by respondents are achieved with only half the number of Hispanics and one-sixth the number of Native Americans as compared to African-Americans. But respondents offer no race-specific reasons for such disparities. Instead, they simply emphasize the importance of achieving critical mass, without any explanation of why that concept is applied differently among the three underrepresented minority groups. . . .

Respondents have never offered any race-specific arguments explaining why significantly more individuals from one underrepresented minority group are needed in order to achieve critical

[CONTINUED]

mass or further student body diversity. They certainly have not explained why Hispanics, who they have said are among the groups most isolated by racial barriers in our country, should have their admission capped out in this manner. True, petitioner is neither Hispanic nor Native American. But the Law School's disparate admissions practices with respect to these minority groups demonstrate that its alleged goal of critical mass is simply a sham. . . . Surely strict scrutiny cannot permit these sort of disparities without at least some explanation. . . .

I do not believe that the Constitution gives the Law School such free rein in the use of race. The Law School has offered no explanation for its actual admissions practices and, unexplained, we are bound to conclude that the Law School has managed its admissions program, not to achieve a critical mass, but to extend offers of admission to members of selected minority groups in proportion to their statistical representation in the applicant pool. But this is precisely the type of racial balancing that the Court itself calls patently unconstitutional.

Finally, I believe that the Law School's program fails strict scrutiny because it is devoid of any reasonably precise time limit on the Law School's use of race in admissions. We have emphasized that we will consider the planned duration of the remedy in determining whether a race-conscious program

is constitutional. Our previous cases have required some limit on the duration of programs such as this because discrimination on the basis of race is invidious.

The Court suggests a possible 25-year limitation on the Law School's current program. Respondents, on the other hand, remain more ambiguous, explaining that the Law School of course recognizes that race-conscious programs must have reasonable durational limits, and the Sixth Circuit properly found such a limit in the Law School's resolve to cease considering race when genuine race-neutral alternatives become available. These discussions of a time limit are the vaguest of assurances. In truth, they permit the Law School's use of racial preferences on a seemingly permanent basis. Thus, an important component of strict scrutiny—that a program be limited in time—is casually subverted. The Court, in an unprecedented display of deference under our strict scrutiny analysis, upholds the Law School's program despite its obvious flaws. We have said that when it comes to the use of race, the connection between the ends and the means used to attain them must be precise. But here the flaw is deeper than that; it is not merely a question of fit between ends and means. Here the means actually used are forbidden by the Equal Protection Clause of the Constitution.

CASE QUESTIONS

1. What is the procedural background of this lawsuit resulting in this Supreme Court decision?

2. How does Justice O'Connor explain the University of Michigan Law School's use of race and ethnicity in its admission policy?

3. What type of scrutiny does the Court use in analyzing the Law School's use of race and ethnicity?

4. Why is the concept of "narrow-tailoring" important in the use of race and ethnicity?

5. How does the Court resolve the issue of a limited time duration for the use of race and ethnicity in admissions policies?

6. What is the central theme of Chief Justice Rehnquist's dissent?

9. THE NATURE OF THE JUDICIAL PROCESS

In deciding cases and in examining the powers discussed in the prior sections, courts are often faced with several alternatives. They may decide the case by use of existing statutes and precedents as they of necessity have a deep commitment to the common law system. Yet they may also refuse to apply existing case law or may declare a statute to be void as unconstitutional. Also, if there is no statute or case law, the court may decide the case and create law in the process. However, case law as a basis for deciding controversies often provides only the point of departure from which the difficult labor of the court begins. The court must examine and compare cases cited as authority to it so it can determine not only which is correct but also whether the principles or rules of law contained therein should be followed or rejected as no longer valid. In reaching and preparing its decision, the court must consider whether the law as announced will provide justice in the particular case and whether it will establish sound precedent for future cases involving similar issues.

The foregoing alternatives raise several questions: Why do courts reach one conclusion rather than another in any given case? What formula, if any, is used in deciding cases and in determining the direction of the law? What forces tend to influence judicial decisions when the public interest is involved?

There is, obviously, no simple answer to these questions. Many people assume that logic is the basic tool of the judicial decision. But Justice Oliver Wendell Holmes stated, "the life of the law has not been logic; it has been experience."[1] Others argue that courts merely reflect the attitudes of the times and simply follow the more popular course in decisions where the public is involved.

Justice Benjamin Cardozo, in a series of lectures on the judicial process,[2] discussed the sources of information judges utilize in deciding cases. He stated that if the answer were not clearly established by statute or by unquestioned precedent, the problem was twofold: "He [the judge] must first extract from the precedents the underlying principle, the *ratio decidendi;* he must then determine the path or direction along which the principle is to work and develop, if it is not to wither or die." The first part of the problem is separating legal principles from dicta so that the actual precedent is clear. Commenting on the second aspect of the problem, Cardozo said:

> The directive force of a principle may be exerted along the line of logical progression; this I will call the rule of analogy or the method of philosophy; along the line of historical development; this I will call the method of evolution; along the lines of the customs of the community; this I will call the method of tradition; along the lines of justice, morals and social welfare, the *mores* of the day; and this I will call the method of sociology.

In Cardozo's judgment, the rule of analogy was entitled to certain presumptions and should be followed if possible. He believed that the judge who molds the law by the method of philosophy is satisfying humanity's deep-seated desire for certainty. History, in indicating the direction of precedent, often illuminates the path of logic and plays an important part in decisions in areas such as real property. Custom or trade practice has supplied much of the direction of the law in the area of business. All judicial decisions are at least in part directed by the judge's view-

---

[1] *Holmes,* The Common Law 1 *(1938).*

[2] *Cardozo,* The Nature of the Judicial Process *(1921). Excerpts are used by permission from the Yale University Press.*

point on the welfare of society. The end served by law must dictate the administration of justice, and ethical considerations, if ignored, will ultimately overturn a principle of law.

Noting the psychological aspects of judges' decisions, Cardozo observed that it is the subconscious forces that keep judges consistent with one another. In so recognizing that all persons, including judges, have a philosophy that gives coherence and direction to their thought and actions whether they admit it or not, he stated:

> All their lives, forces which they do not recognize and cannot name, have been tugging at them—inherited instincts, traditional beliefs, acquired conviction; and the resultant is an outlook on life, a conception of social needs, . . . which when reasons are nicely balanced, must determine where choice shall fall. In this mental background every problem finds its setting. We may try to see things as objectively as we please. None the less, we can never see them with any eyes except our own. To that test they are all brought—a form of pleading or an act of parliament, the wrongs of paupers or the rights of princes, a village ordinance or a nation's charter.

In the following comments, Cardozo summarized his view of the judicial process.

THE NATURE OF THE JUDICIAL PROCESS

BENJAMIN N. CARDOZO

. . . My analysis of the judicial process comes then to this, and little more: logic, and history, and custom, and utility, and the accepted standards of right conduct are the forces which singly or in combination shape the progress of the law. Which of these forces shall dominate in any case must depend largely upon the comparative importance or value of the social interests that will be thereby promoted or impaired. One of the most fundamental social interests is that law shall be uniform and impartial. There must be nothing in its action that savors of prejudice or favor or even arbitrary whim for fitfulness. Therefore in the main there shall be adherence to precedent. There shall be symmetrical development, consistently with history or custom when history or custom has been the motive force, or the chief one, in giving shape to existing rules, and with logic or philosophy when the motive power has been theirs. But symmetrical development may be bought at too high a price. Uniformity ceases to be a good when it becomes uniformity of oppression. The social interest served by symmetry or certainty must then be balanced against the social interest served by equity

and fairness or other elements of social welfare. These may enjoin upon the judge the duty of drawing the line at another angle, of staking the path along new courses, of marking a new point of departure from which others who come after him will set out upon their journey.

If you ask how he is to know when one interest outweighs another, I can only answer that he must get his knowledge just as the legislator gets it, from experience and study and reflection; in brief, from life itself. Here, indeed, is the point of contact between the legislator's work and his. The choice of methods, the appraisement of values, must in the end be guided by like considerations for the one as for the other. Each indeed is legislating within the limits of his competence. No doubt the limits for the judge are narrower. He legislates only between gaps. He fills the open spaces in the law. How far he can go without traveling beyond the walls of the interstices cannot be staked out for him upon a chart. He must learn it for himself as he gains the sense of fitness and proportion that comes with years of habitude in the practice of an art. Even within the gaps,

[CONTINUED]

restrictions not easy to define, but felt, however impalpable they may be, by every judge and lawyer, hedge and circumscribe his action. They are established by the traditions of the centuries, by the example of other judges, his predecessors and his colleagues, by the collective judgment of the profession, and by the duty of adherence to the pervading spirit of the law. . . . Nonetheless, within the confines of these open spaces and those of precedent and tradition, choice moves with a freedom which stamps its action as creative. The law which is the resulting product is not found, but made. The process, being legislative, demands the legislator's wisdom. . . .

---

concept SUMMARY   *Judicial Review*

1. Judicial review allows the courts to review actions taken by legislative and executive branches of government.
2. The philosophy of judicial restraint is sometimes referred to as strict constructionism or a conservative approach.
3. Supporters of judicial activism believe the courts are the appropriate body to bring about social, political, and economic change.
4. The Supreme Court is deeply divided between these two competing views of judicial decision making.

KEY TERMS

Appeal   63
Appellate court   62
Courts of appeal   63
Diversity of citizenship   64
Federal question cases   64
Federal Rules of Civil Procedure   65
Judicial activism   68

Judicial restraint   68
Judicial review   68
Petit jury   59
Small-claims court   64
Supreme Court   63
Trial court   62
Writ of certiorari   63

REVIEW QUESTIONS AND PROBLEMS

Personnel

1. *Judges and Justices*

   What are the essential responsibilities of a trial judge?

2. *Jurors*

   Why have several states eliminated the requirement of unanimity in jury trials?

3. *Lawyers*

   Name the three critical roles a lawyer serves in society. Why have many lawyers and their business clients had such conflict in recent years?

Organization of the Court System

4. *State Courts*

   What role do reviewing or appellate courts play in the judicial process? How do they differ from trial courts?

5. *Federal Courts*

   XYZ makes and markets a product that it believes will help control weight by blocking the human body's digestion of starch. The Food and Drug Administration (FDA) has classified the product as a drug and orders it removed from the market until it can evaluate its use through testing. XYZ disputes the FDA's action and seeks to bring suit in the federal courts. Will the federal courts have jurisdiction to hear the case? Why or why not?

6. *Decisions by the U.S. Supreme Court*

   Susan files a petition for certiorari in the U.S. Supreme Court following an adverse decision in the Illinois Supreme Court on a claim arising under a breach of contract. What chance does Susan have of the Supreme Court granting the petition? What special circumstances would she need to show?

The Power of Judicial Review

7. *Judicial Restraint*

   Define the power of judicial review. How do advocates of judicial restraint exercise that power?

8. *Judicial Activism*

   Define judicial activism. Compare and contrast judicial restraint and judicial activism.

9. *Nature of the Judicial Process*

   What are the forces that Justice Cardozo says shape the judicial process? How is the law made? In light of the liberal versus conservative divisions in the courts, are Cardozo's observations still relevant?

TERMINOLOGY REVIEW

For each term in the left-hand column, match the most appropriate description in the right-hand column.

1. Petit jury
2. Judicial activism
3. *Writ of certiorari*
4. Dissenting opinion
5. Trial court
6. Equity
7. Appeal
8. Diversity of citizenship
9. Judicial review
10. Judicial restraint

a. When the highest court grants review of a lower court's ruling
b. A belief that courts have a major role in correcting wrongs in our society.
c. Initial stage of litigation between the parties
d. The fact-finding body during trial
e. The position advanced by the minority on a judicial panel
f. Use of moral rights and conscience
g. A situation in which plaintiffs and defendants are from different states
h. Review of case by higher court
i. When constitutional issues are too important to be decided by courts unless absolutely necessary
j. Power to review laws by the legislative body or actions taken by the executive branch

BUSINESS DISCUSSION

You have just graduated from college and have started working as a financial analyst for an investment banking firm. You are working 60 to 70 hours per week as part of a highly competitive team of recent college graduates. Suddenly and without any warning you receive a notice from the clerk of court summoning you for jury duty before the United States District Court. You are advised to expect jury service to require between two to four weeks of your uninterrupted time. By the way, your team manager has just assigned you to a new project which he estimates will require 200 hours over the next three weeks.

What options do you have?

How will jury duty impact your career?

Where does your duty lie?

What does the law require of your firm?

THE LITIGATION PROCESS

BUSINESS DECISION

You are a local manager for a major international corporation. The corporation has been embroiled in a lengthy class-action employment discrimination suit. Today, you received a notice of deposition from opposing counsel. You know your testimony could hurt your firm by documenting widespread discrimination. You worry that your testimony will damage your chances for future promotion. You've been told by your supervisor that losing a class-action lawsuit could devastate the firm's financial picture.

> What is a class-action lawsuit?
>
> How do depositions operate?
>
> Can you decline to testify at the deposition?
>
> How do you reconcile your career aspirations with your obligation to the court?

The court system and the litigation process help the business community resolve actual disputes over corporate governance under the rule of law. An impartial enforcement and dispute resolution process is essential to any system that preserves private property interests. Effective business leaders need to develop an appreciation and understanding of the litigation process. Lawsuits and the threat of lawsuits impact every business regardless of size. By the time you have completed this chapter, you should have acquired a knowledge base regarding litigation and greater sensitivity to how a lawsuit is an immense drain of time, money, and energy on everyone involved in the case.

In this chapter, you will study the parties to litigation and the barriers presented to the resolution of a case in court. You will study the lawsuit itself—from pretrial procedures to the trial. Finally, you will learn about the process for resolving appeals and ultimately the enforcement of a final judgment.

LITIGATION—AN OVERVIEW

To fully understand the litigation process, you need to be familiar with the terminology used to describe the parties who are adversaries in lawsuits. The next section reviews a variety of relevant terms. Following that, the legal concepts of when a party has the right to file a lawsuit, when a court has power over the parties, and when one person might sue on behalf of a much larger number of other persons, are discussed.

The first of these issues is generally described as *standing to sue.* It is discussed in section 2. If a plaintiff has standing to sue, the court next must determine if it has *personal jurisdiction* over the defendant. This area is discussed in section 4. The third problem area relates to *class-action suits,* which involve one or more individuals suing on behalf of all who may have the same grounds for suit. These suits are discussed more fully in section 5.

1. PARTIES

The party who files a civil action is called the **plaintiff.** The party sued is known as the **defendant.** The term *defendant* also is used to describe the person against whom a criminal charge is filed by the prosecuting state or federal government. When a defendant wants to sue the plaintiff, the defendant files a **counterclaim.** Most jurisdictions use the terms **counterplaintiff** and **counterdefendant** to describe the parties to the counterclaim. Thus, the defendant becomes a counterplaintiff and the plaintiff becomes a counterdefendant when a counterclaim is filed.

When the result at the trial court level is appealed, the party appealing is usually referred to as the **appellant,** and the successful party in the trial court is called the **appellee.** Most jurisdictions, in publishing decisions of reviewing courts, list the appellant first and the appellee second, even though the appellant may have been the defendant in the trial court. As a result, the names used in a case are somewhat misleading. When a petition for certiorari is filed to the Supreme Court, the party initiating the petition is the **petitioner** and the other party is known as the **respondent.**

Litigating Parties		
Action Filed	*Party Filing the Action*	*Party against Whom the Action Is Filed*
Civil case	Plaintiff	Defendant
Criminal case	State or federal government as represented by a prosecutor	Defendant
Appeal	Appellant	Appellee
Petition for a *writ of certiorari*	Petitioner	Respondent

In most state jurisdictions and in federal courts, the law allows all persons to join in one lawsuit as plaintiffs if the causes of action arise out of the same transaction or series of transactions and involve common questions of law or fact. In addition, plaintiffs may join as defendants all persons who are necessary to a complete determination or resolution of the questions involved.

In addition, if a defendant alleges that there cannot be a complete determination of a controversy without the presence of other parties, he or she may bring in new third parties as **third-party defendants.** This procedure usually is followed when there is someone who may have liability to a defendant if the defendant has liability to the plaintiff. For example, assume Never-Fail, Inc., supplies brake shoes to the Ready-to-Go Mechanics Corporation. Ready-to-Go worked on your brakes, and thereafter you were injured when your car failed to stop at an intersection. After you filed a lawsuit against Ready-to-Go, it could bring Never-Fail, Inc., into the case as a third-party defendant. In essence, Ready-to-Go is arguing that if it is liable to you, then Never-Fail is liable to Ready-to-Go since the cause of the accident easily could be faulty brake shoes.

2. STANDING TO SUE

A court's power to resolve a controversy may be limited by the subject matter involved in the case. This power we called subject matter jurisdiction. In addition to showing the court that it has subject matter jurisdiction, a plaintiff must establish that he or she is entitled to have the court decide the dispute, that is, he or she has **standing to sue.**

To establish the required standing, a plaintiff must allege two things. First, the plaintiff must allege that the litigation involves a case or controversy. Courts are not free to litigate matters that have no connection to the law. For example, one business cannot maintain a suit against another business just because the two are competitors. There must be some allegation of a wrong that would create a dispute between plaintiff and defendant.

Second, the plaintiff must allege a personal stake in the resolution of the controversy. This element of standing prevents any individual from asserting the rights of the general public or of a group of which we are not a member. For instance, only a shareholder of one of the two companies involved in a merger could sue to stop the combination of these companies, despite the fact that such a merger may have a substantial adverse impact on competition in general.

In essence, through the standing-to-sue requirements, courts are able to insist that there be an adversarial relationship between plaintiff and defendant. This adversarial relationship helps present the issues to be litigated in sharper focus. To establish standing, plaintiffs must assert their personal legal positions and not those of third parties. Without the requirements of standing, courts would be faced with abstract legal questions of potentially wide public significance, questions generally best left to legislative bodies or administrative agencies.

It is very important to note that standing to sue does not depend upon the merits of the plaintiff's contention that particular conduct is illegal. The presence of standing is determined by the nature and source of the plaintiff's allegations. Standing is determined at the outset of the litigation, not by the outcome. The following case illustrates the critical nature of standing in winning a lawsuit.

FRIENDS OF THE EARTH v. LAIDLAW ENVIRONMENTAL SERVICES

528 U.S. 167 (2000)

Laidlaw Environmental Services bought a facility in Roebuck, South Carolina, that included a wastewater treatment plant. Shortly thereafter, the South Carolina Department of Health and Environmental Control (DHEC) granted Laidlaw a National Pollutant Discharge Elimination System (NPDES) permit. The permit authorized Laidlaw to discharge treated water into the North Tyger River, but limited, among other things, the discharge of pollutants into the waterway. Laidlaw began to discharge various pollutants into the waterway; these discharges, particularly of mercury, an extremely toxic pollutant, repeatedly exceeded the limits set by the permit. DHEC and Laidlaw reached a settlement requiring Laidlaw to pay $100,000 in civil penalties and to make every effort to comply with its permit obligations. Friends of the Earth (FOE) and Citizens Local Environmental Action Network, Inc., notified Laidlaw of their intention to file a citizen suit against it under the Act.

FOE filed this citizen suit against Laidlaw, alleging noncompliance with the NPDES permit and seeking declaratory and injunctive relief and an award of civil penalties. Laidlaw moved for summary judgment on the ground that FOE lacked Article III standing to bring the lawsuit.

GINSBURG, JUSTICE: This case presents an important question concerning the operation of the citizen-suit provisions of the Clean Water Act. Congress authorized the federal district courts to entertain Clean Water Act suits initiated by "a person or persons having an interest which is or may be adversely affected." To impel future compliance with the Act, a district court may prescribe injunctive relief in such a suit; additionally or alternatively, the court may impose civil penalties payable to the United States Treasury. In the Clean Water Act citizen suit now before us, the District Court determined that injunctive relief was inappropriate because the defendant, after the institution of the litigation,

achieved substantial compliance with the terms of its discharge permit. The court did, however, assess a civil penalty of $405,800. The total deterrent effect of the penalty would be adequate to forestall future violations, the court reasoned, taking into account that the defendant will be required to reimburse plaintiffs for a significant amount of legal fees and has, itself, incurred significant legal expenses.

To satisfy Article III's standing requirements, a plaintiff must show (1) it has suffered an "injury in fact" that is (a) concrete and particularized and (b) actual or imminent, not conjectural or hypothetical; (2) the injury is fairly traceable to the challenged action of the defendant; and (3) it is likely, as opposed to merely speculative, that the injury will be redressed by a favorable decision. An association has standing to bring suit on behalf of its members when its members would otherwise have standing to sue in their own right, the interests at stake are germane to the organization's purpose, and neither the claim asserted nor the relief requested requires the participation of individual members in the lawsuit.

Laidlaw contends first that FOE lacked standing from the outset even to seek injunctive relief, because the plaintiff organizations failed to show that any of their members had sustained or faced the threat of any injury in fact from Laidlaw's activities. In support of this contention Laidlaw points to the District Court's finding, made in the course of setting the penalty amount, that there had been "no demonstrated proof of harm to the environment" from Laidlaw's mercury discharge violations.

The relevant showing for purposes of Article III standing, however, is not injury to the environment but injury to the plaintiff. Focusing properly on injury to the plaintiff, the District Court found that FOE had demonstrated sufficient injury to establish standing.

We have held that environmental plaintiffs adequately allege injury in fact when they aver that they use the affected area and are persons "for whom the

[CONTINUED]

aesthetic and recreational values of the area will be lessened" by the challenged activity.

The affidavits and testimony presented by FOE in this case assert that Laidlaw's discharges, and the affiant members' reasonable concerns about the effects of those discharges, directly affected those affiants' recreational, aesthetic, and economic interests.

In this case we need not explore the outer limits of the principle that civil penalties provide sufficient deterrence to support redressability. Here, the civil penalties sought by FOE carried with them a deterrent effect that made it likely, as opposed to merely speculative, that the penalties would redress FOE's injuries by abating current violations and preventing future ones—as the District Court reasonably found when it assessed a penalty of $405,800.

We are satisfied that FOE had standing under Article III to bring this action.

CASE QUESTIONS

1. What parties are authorized to file lawsuits under the Clean Air Act?

2. How does a party satisfy Article III's standing requirements?

3. How do environmental plaintiffs adequately allege an injury in fact?

3. SUBJECT MATTER JURISDICTION

Jurisdiction refers to the power of a court, at the state or federal level, to hear a case. For any court to hear and decide a case at any level, it must have **subject matter jurisdiction,** which is the power over the issues involved in the case. Some state trial courts have what is called general jurisdiction, or the power to hear any type of case. Other state courts have only limited jurisdiction, or the power to hear only certain types of cases. Jurisdiction may be limited as to subject matter, amount in controversy, or area in which the parties live. For example, small-claims courts have jurisdiction only if the amount in the controversy does not exceed a certain sum.

Courts, especially those of limited jurisdiction, may be named according to the subject matter with which they deal. Probate courts deal with wills and the estates of deceased persons, juvenile courts with juvenile crime and dependent children, criminal and police courts with violators of state laws and municipal ordinances, and traffic courts with traffic violations. In Chapter 3, you learned how subject matter jurisdiction in the federal courts revolves around diversity of citizenship and federal question issues.

Even courts of general jurisdiction cannot attempt to resolve every dispute or controversy that may arise. Some issues are simply nonjusticiable. For example, courts would not attempt to referee a football or basketball game. They would not hear a case to decide how English or math should be taught in the public schools. Moreover, courts do not accept cases involving trivial matters.

4. PERSONAL JURISDICTION

Power to hear a case means a court must have authority not only over the subject matter of the case but also over the parties to the case. This latter authority is called **personal jurisdiction.** Personal jurisdiction over the plaintiff is obtained when the plaintiff files the suit. Such action indicates voluntary submission to the court's power.

Personal jurisdiction over the defendant usually is obtained by the service of a **summons,** or notice to appear in court, although in some cases it is obtained by the publication of notice and mailing a summons to the last known address. This delivery of notice is referred to as *service of process.* Service of a summons on the defendant usually is valid if it is served upon any member of the household above a specified age and if another copy addressed to the defendant is mailed to the home.

For many years, a summons could not be properly served beyond the borders of the state in which it was issued. However, states now have what are called **long-arm statutes,** which provide for the service of process beyond their boundaries. Such statutes are valid and constitutional if they provide a defendant with due process of law. Under the Fifth Amendment to the Constitution, no person shall "be deprived of life, liberty, or property without due process of law." The Fourteenth Amendment provides that states must also guarantee due process protection. Due process requires that if a defendant is not present within the state where the lawsuit is filed, he or she must have certain minimum contacts with the state so that maintenance of the suit does not offend "traditional notions of fair play and substantial justice."

The typical long-arm statute allows a court to obtain jurisdiction over a defendant even though the process is served beyond its borders if the defendant:

1. Has committed a tort within the state.
2. Owns property within the state that is the subject matter of the lawsuit.
3. Has entered into a contract within the state or transacted the business that is the subject matter of the lawsuit within the state.

WORLD-WIDE VOLKSWAGEN CORP. v. WOODSON

100 S.CT. 559 (1980)

The *World-Wide Volkswagen* case is the leading case on the constitutional limits associated with personal jurisdiction on out-of-state defendants. In this case, the plaintiff filed a products liability lawsuit in Oklahoma to recover for personal injuries sustained in an automobile accident in that state. The defendants were the German manufacturer of the automobile, the importer of the car, the wholesale distributor, and the retail dealership. The wholesaler and retailer were located in New York State, and they challenged personal jurisdiction because they did not do business in Oklahoma and had no ties or contacts to the state. The court held in favor of the defendants, under the due process clause of the Fourteenth Amendment to the U.S. Constitution, because these defendants had not "purposefully availed" themselves of the privilege of conducting business in Oklahoma. The plaintiff should have sued these defendants in New York State. The manufacturer and importer were proper defendants in Oklahoma since they envisioned that the cars they made and imported had contacts with all states, including Oklahoma.

Long-arm statutes do not authorize out-of-state service of process in all cases. Personal jurisdiction is obtained under long-arm statutes only when requiring an out-of-state defendant to appear and defend does not violate due process. In the case which follows, the court examines the issue of personal jurisdiction in the modern context of the Internet.

TOYS "R" US, INC.; GEOFFREY, INC. V. STEP TWO, S.A.; IMAGINARIUM NET, S.L.

2003 U.S. APP. LEXIS 1355 (3RD CIR. 2003)

Toys "R" Us, a Delaware corporation with its head-quarters in New Jersey, owns retail stores worldwide where it sells toys, games, and numerous other products. The retailer was Step Two, a Spanish corporation that owns or franchises toy stores in Spain and nine other countries. The retailer did not operate any stores, maintain any offices or bank accounts, or have any employees anywhere in the United States. It did not pay taxes to the U.S. or to any U.S. state. It maintained that it had not directed any advertising or marketing efforts toward the United States. However, a portion of the merchandise sold at its stores was purchased from vendors in the United States. Additionally, its president attended the New York Toy Fair once each year.

OBERDORFER, J.: Toys "R" Us, Inc. and Geoffrey, Inc. ("Toys") brought this action against Step Two, S.A. and Imaginarium Net alleging that Step Two used its Internet web sites to engage in trademark infringement, unfair competition, misuse of the trademark notice symbol, and unlawful "cybersquatting," in violation of the Lanham Act and New Jersey state law. The District Court denied Toys' request for jurisdictional discovery and, simultaneously, granted Step Two's motion to dismiss for lack of personal jurisdiction. We hold that the District Court should not have denied Toys' request for jurisdictional discovery. We therefore reverse and remand for limited jurisdictional discovery, relating to Step Two's business activities in the United States, and for reconsideration of personal jurisdiction with the benefit of the product of that discovery.

Toys owns retail stores worldwide where it sells toys, games, and numerous other products. In August 1999, Toys acquired Imaginarium Toy Centers, Inc., which owned and operated a network of "Imaginarium" stores for the sale of educational toys and games. As part of this acquisition, Toys acquired several Imaginarium trademarks, and subsequently filed applications for the registration of additional Imaginarium marks. Prior to Toys' acquisition, the owners of the Imaginarium mark had been marketing a line of educational toys and games since 1985 and had first registered the Imaginarium mark with the United States Patent and Trademark Office in 1989. Toys currently owns thirty-seven freestanding Imaginarium stores in the U.S., of which seven are located in New Jersey. In addition, there are Imaginarium shops within 175 of the Toys "R" Us stores in the U.S., including five New Jersey stores.

Step Two is a Spanish corporation that owns or has franchised toy stores operating under the name "Imaginarium" in Spain and nine other countries. It first registered the Imaginarium mark in Spain in 1991, and opened its first Imaginarium store in the Spanish city of Zaragoza in November 1992. Step Two began expanding its chain of Imaginarium stores by means of a franchise system in 1994. It has registered the Imaginarium mark in several other countries where its stores are located. There are now 165 Step Two Imaginarium stores. The stores have the same unique façade and logo as those owned by Toys, and sell the same types of merchandise as Toys sells in its Imaginarium stores. However, Step Two does not operate any stores, maintain any

[CONTINUED]

offices or bank accounts, or have any employees anywhere in the United States.

At the time this lawsuit was filed, four web sites operated by Step Two were interactive, allowing users to purchase merchandise online. When buying merchandise via Step Two's web sites, purchasers are asked to input their name and email address, as well as a credit card number, delivery address, and phone number. At no point during the online purchase process are users asked to input their billing or mailing address. The web sites provide a contact phone number within Spain that lacks the country code that a user overseas would need to dial. Moreover, the prices are in Spanish pesetas and Euros, and goods ordered from those sites can be shipped only within Spain. Step Two's Imaginarium web sites are entirely in Spanish.

The advent of the Internet has required courts to fashion guidelines for when personal jurisdiction can be based on a defendant's operation of a web site. Courts have sought to articulate a standard that both embodies traditional rules and accounts for new factual scenarios created by the Internet. Under traditional jurisdictional analysis, the exercise of specific personal jurisdiction requires that the plaintiff's cause of action is related to or arises out of the defendant's contacts with the forum. Beyond this basic nexus, for a finding of specific personal jurisdiction, the Due Process Clause of the Fifth Amendment requires (1) that the defendant have constitutionally sufficient minimum contacts with the forum, and (2) that subjecting the defendant to the court's jurisdiction comports with traditional notions of fair play and substantial justice.

The precise question raised by this case is whether the operation of a commercially interactive web site accessible in the forum state is sufficient to support specific personal jurisdiction, or whether there must be additional evidence that the defendant has "purposefully availed" itself of the privilege of engaging in activity in that state. Prior decisions indicate that such evidence is necessary, and that it should reflect intentional interaction with the forum state. If a defendant web site operator intentionally targets the site to the forum state, and/or knowingly conducts business with forum state residents via the site, then the purposeful availment requirement is satisfied.

Based on the facts established in this case thus far, Toys has failed to satisfy the purposeful availment requirement. Step Two's web sites, while commercial and interactive, do not appear to have been designed or intended to reach customers in New Jersey. Step Two's web sites are entirely in Spanish; prices for its merchandise are in pesetas or Euros, and merchandise can be shipped only to addresses within Spain. Most important, none of the portions of Step Two's web sites are designed to accommodate addresses within the United States.

At best, Toys has presented only inconclusive circumstantial evidence to suggest that Step Two targeted its web site to New Jersey residents, or that it purposefully availed itself of any effort to conduct activity in New Jersey.

Absent further evidence showing purposeful availment, Toys cannot establish specific jurisdiction over Step Two. However, any information regarding Step Two's intent vis-à-vis its Internet business and regarding other related contacts is known by Step Two, and can be learned by Toys only through discovery. The District Court's denial of jurisdictional discovery is thus a critical issue, insofar as it may have prevented Toys from obtaining the information needed to establish personal jurisdiction.

We are persuaded that the District Court erred when it denied Toys' request for jurisdictional discovery. The court's unwavering focus on the web site precluded consideration of other Internet and non-Internet contacts—indicated in various parts of the record—which, if explored, might provide the "something more" needed to bring Step Two within our jurisdiction.

For all of the reasons set forth above, we reverse the District Court's denial of Toys' request for jurisdictional discovery, vacate the District Court's dismissal of Toys' complaint, and remand the case for limited jurisdictional discovery guided by the foregoing analysis, and for reconsideration of jurisdiction with the benefit of the product of that discovery.

Reversed.

[CONTINUED]

CASE QUESTIONS

1. When may a court exercise personal jurisdiction over a defendant?

2. What standards should be applied in determining whether a court has personal jurisdiction over a website?

3. Why does the court permit jurisdictional discovery in this case?

In criminal suits, the crime must have been committed within the state for the court to have jurisdiction of the case. Jurisdiction over the person of the defendant is obtained by arrest. In the event of arrest in a state other than that in which the crime was committed, the prisoner must be transported back to the state where the crime occurred. This is done by the governor of the state of arrest voluntarily turning the prisoner over to the governor of the requesting state. The process of requesting and transporting the prisoner from one state to another is called **extradition.**

Regardless of the type of case, a defendant may decide not to object to a court's exercise of personal jurisdiction. In other words, a defendant may agree to submit to a court's authority even though personal jurisdiction may not be obtained under the rules discussed in this section. In essence, a defendant may waive or forgo any objection to a court's exercise of personal jurisdiction.

5. CLASS-ACTION SUITS

A **class-action suit** is one in which one or more plaintiffs file suit on their own behalf and on behalf of all other persons who may have a similar claim. For example, all sellers of real estate through brokers were certified as a class in an antitrust suit against the brokers. All persons suing a drug company, alleging injuries from a product, constituted a class for a tort action. Class-action suits may also be filed on behalf of all shareholders of a named corporation. The number of people constituting a class is frequently quite large. Class-action suits are popular because they often involve matters in which no one member of the class would have a sufficient financial interest to warrant litigation. However, the combined interest of all members of the class not only makes litigation feasible, it quite often makes it very profitable for the lawyer who brings the suit. In addition, such litigation avoids a multiplicity of suits involving the same issue, especially when the issues are complex and the cost of preparation and defense is very substantial.

At the federal level, the Supreme Court has tended to discourage class-action suits. Federal cases require that members of the class be given notice of the lawsuit; actual notice and not merely notice by newspaper publication is usually required. This notice must be given to all members of the class whose names and addresses can be found through reasonable efforts. In addition, those plaintiffs seeking to bring the class-action suit must pay all court costs of the action, including the cost of compiling the names and addresses of those in the class. If the trial

PERSONAL JURISDICTION AND THE INTERNET

The issue of personal jurisdiction and the Internet is one of growing interest to many litigants. International computer-based communication firms transcend state and national borders and create new issues for regulating the Internet and holding offending parties liable in the courts. In one recent case, a court refused to find personal jurisdiction over an allegedly infringing Florida website adver-

tiser who had no minimum contact with Arizona other than maintaining a home page which is accessible to citizens of Arizona over the Internet. Typically, courts have refused to find personal jurisdiction based solely on a passive or purely informative website. However, jurisdiction may be appropriate in situations where the defendant has purposefully directed an activity, in a substantial way, into the state seeking to assert jurisdiction.

court denies the plaintiff a right to represent the class, that decision cannot be appealed until there is a final decision in the lawsuit itself. Denial of class-action status making it impractical to continue the litigation does not give grounds for an immediate appeal.

One legal commentator has described the class-action suit as the law's version of a nuclear weapon—it is so destructive no side wants to set it off. A plaintiff's threat to aggregate thousands of individual claims is so powerful that it can destroy a defendant business. However, if the class action fails, the plaintiff wins nothing and loses the investment in the litigation. Simple cost-benefit analysis leads the litigants to settle a class-action suit.

In the past, the federal courts routinely approved class-action settlements provided there was some benefit to the class and a release of all class members' claims. Typically large attorneys' fees were included in the settlements. However, in recent years, the federal courts have begun carefully examining class-action settlements and have developed a much higher standard for approving settlements. A tougher standard is especially important where settlements have been proposed because of the risk that the class representatives and their lawyers could sacrifice the interests of the class in order to financially benefit themselves. Class-action suits in federal courts may be settled on a classwide basis only if the settlement's terms are fair and equitable and only if all the class certification requirements for trial have also been met.

If a class-action suit is in federal court because of diversity of citizenship, the claim of each member of the class must meet the jurisdictional amount of $75,000. This requirement and the aforementioned requirement of notice and settlement have greatly reduced the number of such suits in federal courts. However, the

EXAMPLES OF RECENT CLASS-ACTION LAWSUITS

- A $490 million settlement filed over the merger of NationsBank and BankAmerica Corporation.
- An estimated $13.2 billion paid by Wyeth to settle all claims from the approximately 370,000 who used the diet drugs Redux and Pondimin (Fen-Phen).
- $180,000,000 settlement for 63,000 people exposed to a toxic chemical cloud.

- A $125,760,000 settlement from three manufacturers of infant formula for an alleged nationwide price-fixing conspiracy.
- $456,000,000 from State Farm for alleged violations of the terms of its policies and breaches of contract with its policyholders.

Source: www.bigclassaction.com.

CERTIFYING A CLASS

In the spring of 2003, MasterCard and Visa entered into a $3 billion settlement of an antitrust lawsuit before a single witness testified at trial. After the court certified a class of four million merchants, including Wal-Mart and Sears, the defendants chose not to gamble on losing a case where damage claims could have reached $100 billion. One commentator noted that with potential damages of $100 billion, tripled under the Sherman Act, the class needed only a 1 percent chance of victory to justify the $3 billion settlement. Merchants had claimed in the lawsuit that Visa's and Mastercard's intercharge fee was too high for purchases made with debit cards.

practice of consumers' and plaintiffs' lawyers of combining a single grievance into a lawsuit on behalf of every possible litigant is quite common in state courts. Numerous state class-action statutes allow consumers and others to file suit in state courts on behalf of all citizens of that state. So although the Supreme Court has attempted to reduce class-action cases, it is apparent that public companies are still subject to this type of claim.

concept SUMMARY — *Litigation—An Overview*

1. The party who files a civil action is called the plaintiff and the party sued is known as the defendant.
2. To establish standing to sue, a plaintiff must establish that a case or controversy exists and that he or she has a personal stake in the resolution of the case.
3. Long-arm statutes are constrained or limited by the requirement the defendant has sufficient minimal contacts with the state.
4. Many requirements must be met to bring a class-action suit, particularly in a federal court.

PRETRIAL PROCEDURES

How does a lawsuit begin, and how are issues presented to a court? How does a court decide whether it is the proper place for the lawsuit to be tried? To what extent do the parties in a civil lawsuit learn of the opposing party's legal arguments and factual presentations? How can one party test the validity of the other party's claims prior to trial? And what are the protections against one party harassing another by filing improper or unwarranted lawsuits? The following sections provide the answers to these questions.

6. PLEADINGS

The legal documents that are filed with a court to begin the litigation process are called **pleadings.** Through the contents of the pleadings, the issues to be resolved are brought into sharper focus. Lawsuits begin by a plaintiff filing a pleading, called a **complaint,** with the court clerk. The complaint contains allegations by the plaintiff and a statement or request of the relief sought. The clerk issues the summons, and a court official (usually a sheriff or marshal) delivers the summons and a copy of the complaint to the defendant.

The summons provides the date by which the defendant must respond to the complaint. This response usually takes the form of a written pleading, called an **answer.** The defendant's answer will either admit or deny each allegation of the

---

Pretrial Proceedings

Plaintiff files complaint.

Complaint and summons served on defendant.

Defendant files motion or answer with possible counterclaim and defenses.

Court rules on motions.

Plaintiff files reply to answer.

Attorneys conduct discovery procedures.

Parties may file motions for summary judgment or judgment on pleadings.

Court conducts pretrial conference.

---

plaintiff's complaint and may contain affirmative defenses that will defeat the plaintiff's claim. The answer may also contain causes of action the defendant has against the plaintiff. These statements are called *counterclaims*. If the defendant does not respond in any way, the court may enter an order of **default** and grant the plaintiff the relief sought by the complaint.

After receiving an answer that contains one or more counterclaims, the plaintiff files a reply that specifically admits or denies each allegation of the defendant's counterclaims. The factual issues of a lawsuit are thus formed by one party making an allegation and the other party either admitting it or denying it. In this way, pleadings give notice of each party's contentions and serve to set the boundary lines of the litigation.

7. STEPS IN DISCOVERY

Lawsuits are often high drama in the movies and on television. Inevitably in these dramatized courtroom scenes, some element of surprise is the turning point, thereby ensuring a favorable outcome for the popular client or lawyer. In reality, civil litigation seldom concludes with a surprise witness or new piece of evidence. The reason the surprises do not occur is the process of **discovery.**

Purpose Discovery procedures are designed to take the "sporting aspect" out of litigation and ensure that the results of lawsuits are based on the merits of the controversy and not on the ability, skill, or cunning of counsel. Historically, an attorney who had a weak case on the facts or law could win a lawsuit through a surprise witness at the trial. Today, the law is such that verdicts should not be based on the skill of counsel but on the relative merits of the controversy. Discovery practice is designed to ensure that, prior to trial, each side is fully aware of all the facts involved in the case and of the intentions of the parties. One of its purposes is to aid trial preparation by permitting the parties to learn how a witness will answer questions prior to the actual questioning at the trial. Discovery, in this way, provides a "dress rehearsal" for the trial. Another, perhaps even more important, purpose of discovery is to narrow the issues disputed by the parties. In this way, discovery encourages the settlement of the lawsuit, thereby avoiding the actual trial.

Methods During the discovery phase of litigation, clients and lawyers need to work very closely together. Several methods of discovery can be utilized, or it might be decided that some methods will not produce new information and thus will be skipped. It is only through the aid of a client that a lawyer can gain the confidence that the discovery is complete and that the case is ready to go to trial.

Typically the least expensive method of discovery is to present a series of written questions to the opposing parties. These questions, called **interrogatories,** must be answered by the party to whom they have been delivered. It is fairly common for plaintiff and defendant to attach a series of interrogatories to their respective pleadings. A common interrogatory is "Please furnish the names and addresses of all persons known to you that witnessed the occurrence which is the subject matter of this lawsuit."

After answers to the interrogatories are received, either party might ask the other to produce specific documents, called **request for production of documents,** that are important to the lawsuit's outcome. For example, a buyer of merchandise who is suing the seller can request that this defendant produce the original sales contract that contains certain warranties covering the merchandise.

In a personal injury action, the defendant can require the plaintiff to submit to a physical examination by the defendant's expert physician. Although the plaintiff may object to the specific doctor, a general objection to the physical examination is not permissible.

The most expensive method of discovery is also the most revealing with regard to preparing for the trial. To conduct discovery to the greatest extent possible, the lawyers will want to take **depositions** of all potential witnesses. In a deposition, the lawyer orally asks questions of the possible witness and an oral response is given. All the spoken words are recorded by a court reporter, and a written transcript is prepared. In this way, a permanent record of the anticipated testimony is created. With depositions, lawyers seldom need to ask a question during a trial to which they do not already know the answer.

Finally, after some or all of these methods of discovery are used, either party may request the other to admit that certain issues presented in the pleadings are no longer in dispute. By the **request for an admission,** issues are narrowed, and settlement may become more likely.

8. SCOPE OF DISCOVERY

The discovery procedures are intended to be used freely by the parties to litigation without the court's direct supervision. At times a question about the scope of what is discoverable arises, and the party objecting to discovery seeks the judge's opinion. In this setting, a ruling must be given. Generally, judges provide a very broad or liberal interpretation of the degree of discoverable information. The usual rule is that as long as the information sought in discovery will lead to evidence admissible during the trial, the information is discoverable and an objection is overruled.

Although the use of discovery is essential to our system of litigation, it also carries significant costs. In a recent survey of 1,000 judges, abusive discovery was rated highest among the reasons for the high cost of litigation. Discovery imposes several costs on the litigant from whom discovery is sought. These burdens include the time spent searching for and compiling relevant documents; the time, expense, and aggravation of preparing for and attending depositions; the costs of copying and shipping documents; and the attorneys' fees generated in interpreting discovery requests, drafting responses to interrogatories and coordinating responses to production requests, advising the client as to which documents should be disclosed and which ones withheld, and determining whether certain information is privileged. The party seeking discovery also bears costs, including attorneys' fees generated in drafting discovery requests and reviewing the opponent's objections and responses. Both parties incur costs related to the delay discovery imposes on reaching the merits of the case. Finally, discovery imposes burdens on the judicial system; scarce judicial resources must be diverted from other cases to resolve discovery disputes.

The following case illustrates the perils for a business when a judge fails to properly monitor the abuses in the discovery process.

CHUDASAMA V. MAZDA MOTOR CORP.

123 F. 3D 1353 (11TH CIR. 1997)

Bhupendra Chudasama and his wife, Gunvanti B., purchased a used 1989 Mazda MPV minivan (the "MPV minivan") from Jays Dodge City, a Columbus, Georgia, Dodge dealer. Gunvanti Chudasama was injured when Bhupendra Chudasama lost control of the minivan and it collided with a utility pole. Mrs. Chudasama sustained a broken pelvis and broken facial bones; Mr. Chudasama was uninjured. Mrs. Chudasama's medical bills totaled approximately $13,000, and she lost approximately $5,000 in wages. The accident left the MPV minivan, worth approximately $11,000, beyond repair.

The Chudasamas filed a products liability action against the defendants—Mazda Motor Corp. ("Mazda Japan"), a Japanese company, and Mazda Motor of America, Inc. ("Mazda America"), an American subsidiary of Mazda Japan (collectively "Mazda"). The complaint pointed to two alleged defects in the MPV minivan as the cause of the Chudasamas' accident and resulting injuries. Their complaint contained four counts: three standard products liability counts—strict liability, breach of implied warranty, and negligent design and manufacture—and one count of fraud. Each count sought compensatory damages to cover Mrs. Chudasama's medical bills and lost wages, and to compensate her for her pain and suffering, Mr. Chudasama for his loss of his wife's "society, companionship and services," and the loss of the vehicle. All but the breach of implied warranty count also sought punitive damages. Following a protracted discovery dispute, the district court entered a default judgment against

Mazda for failing to comply with a court order compelling discovery, and the defendant appealed.

TJOFLAT, J.: As has become typical in recent years, both sides initially adopted extreme and unreasonable positions; the plaintiffs asked for almost every tangible piece of information or property possessed by the defendants, and the defendants offered next to nothing and took several steps to delay discovery. In this case, however, the district court never attempted to resolve the parties' disputes and force the parties to meet somewhere in the middle of their respective extreme positions. As a result, what began as a relatively common discovery dispute quickly deteriorated into unbridled legal warfare.

We see no useful purpose in describing the drawn-out discovery battle in detail; a relatively brief summary will suffice. The Chudasamas served Mazda with their first interrogatories and requests for production. Both documents were models of vague and overly broad discovery requests.

The production requests all but asked for every document Mazda ever had in its possession and then some. For example, the Chudasamas sought detailed information about practically all of Mazda's employees worldwide. They requested production of all documents relating to organizational charts, books or manuals of Mazda . . . which will or may assist in identifying and locating those operating divisions, committees, groups, departments, employees, and personnel . . . involved in the conception, market analysis, development, testing, design safety engi-

[CONTINUED]

neering and marketing of the product for all years during which the product has been developed, designed, manufactured and marketed. . . .

In response to the Chudasamas' excessively broad discovery requests, Mazda adopted four different strategies. First, it objected to almost every production request and interrogatory on almost every imaginable ground. While some of its objections were clearly boilerplate and bordered on being frivolous, many were directly on point and raised bona fide questions of law.

Mazda pursued a second strategy for countering the Chudasamas' vague and overbroad discovery requests. It filed a motion to dismiss their fraud count for failure to plead fraud with particularity. Mazda contended that the Chudasamas had failed to point to any specific misrepresentation made by Mazda. . . .

In its motion to dismiss the fraud count, Mazda contended that the Chudasamas failed to allege the "time, place and content of the alleged misrepresentations." The Chudasamas' memorandum in opposition to Mazda's motion argued that the misrepresentations were made in advertisements they had viewed in the past. They needed discovery from Mazda, they said, to find out which particular advertisements they had viewed and relied upon.

Despite the fact that both parties fully briefed Mazda's motion to dismiss, the district court never ruled on it. Although Mazda frequently reminded the district court—over a period of time exceeding a year and a half—that the motion was pending, the only indication in the record that the district court even acknowledged the motion was a statement made at a hearing (over nine months after the motion was filed) suggesting that the motion would be considered after discovery. . . .

Mazda's third strategy was to seek a protective order. Much of the information requested by the Chudasamas involved confidential documents that went to the heart of Mazda's business. They sought marketing studies, internal memoranda, and documentation on the history of the development and design of the MPV minivan and other vehicles. Fearing disclosure of this information to its competitors or to other potential plaintiffs, Mazda sought a "nonsharing" protective order that would keep the information un-

der seal and prohibit the Chudasamas from sharing Mazda's proprietary information with anyone. . . .

Perhaps because it realized that the district court had no intention of ruling on its motion to dismiss the fraud count or its various objections, Mazda adopted a fourth strategy; it withheld a substantial amount of information that it later conceded was properly discoverable.

The district court based its decision to impose sanctions on the Federal Rules of Civil Procedure.

[The Federal Rules] authorize a district court to impose such sanctions "as are just" against a party that violates an order compelling discovery. Included in the list of possible sanctions is an order striking a defendant's answer and entering a default. District courts enjoy substantial discretion in deciding whether and how to impose sanctions. When reviewing an order striking a defendant's pleadings, our review should be particularly scrupulous lest the district court too lightly resort to this extreme sanction, amounting to judgment against the defendant without an opportunity to be heard on the merits.

We recognize that district courts enjoy broad discretion in deciding how best to manage the cases before them. This discretion is not unfettered, however. When a litigant's rights are materially prejudiced by the district court's mismanagement of a case, we must redress the abuse of discretion. The mismanagement of two key parts of this case—Mazda's motion to dismiss the Chudasamas' fraud claim and Mazda's resistance to the Chudasamas' discovery requests—indicates that the district court abused its discretion. . . .

Turning to the facts of the instant case, we note that even the most cursory review of the Chudasamas' shotgun complaint reveals that it contains a fraud count that is novel and of questionable validity. Upon reading the complaint, the district court should have noted that the fraud count dramatically enlarged the scope of the Chudasamas' case. Without the fraud theory, the scope of discovery likely would have been limited to information tending to show that the MPV minivan was a defective product and that Mazda was negligent in designing it. With the fraud theory in the case, on the other hand, the scope of discovery broadened to include Mazda's marketing strategies and safety testing. As a result,

[CONTINUED]

the Chudasamas could seek much broader discovery with the fraud count in the complaint than without it.

We conclude that this claim was dubious enough to require the district court to rule on Mazda's motion to dismiss. When the court refused to do so and, instead, allowed the case to proceed through discovery without an analysis of the fraud claim, it abused its discretion. By and large, the Federal Rules of Civil Procedure are designed to minimize the need for judicial intervention into discovery matters. They do not eliminate that need, however.

Having determined that the district court abused its discretion in ordering Mazda to respond to the Chudasamas' requests, we turn to the subsequent sanctions order to determine whether it fell within the district court's broad discretion. The answer is fairly clear: the district court would have been hard pressed to fashion sanctions more severe than those included in its order. Mazda lost nearly everything that was at stake in the litigation and more. In addition to granting costs and attorneys' fees to the Chudasamas, the court struck Mazda's answer and ordered that a default be entered on all claims, reserving damages as the only issue to be tried on the merits. These sanctions were so unduly severe under the circumstances as to constitute a clear abuse of discretion.

For the foregoing reasons, we VACATE both the district court's order compelling discovery and its order granting the appellee's amended motion for sanctions and REMAND this case with the instruction that the Chief Judge of the Middle District of Georgia reassign the case to a different district judge for further proceedings consistent with this opinion.

CASE QUESTIONS

1. How can a party protect itself from an abusive discovery process?

2. What is the practical consequence of a default judgment being entered against the defendants?

3. Is a ruling of this nature likely to have any impact on the litigation process in this country?

9. MOTIONS

During the pretrial phase of litigation, either plaintiff or defendant or both may attempt to convince the court that there are no questions about the factual setting of the dispute. An argument is presented that there are only questions of law for the judge to resolve. For example, the parties may be in complete agreement that the plaintiff has not been paid by the defendant for the merchandise that was delivered by the plaintiff and received by the defendant. The dispute between these parties is simply whether, under the stated facts, the defendant must pay the plaintiff. This dispute presents only an issue of law, not of fact.

When a question of law is at issue, the parties can seek a pretrial determination of their rights by filing a **motion** with the court. These motions can be made at any point in the litigation process. First, the defendant may, instead of filing an answer, file a pleading that at common law was called a *general demurrer*. Today we call this a *motion to dismiss for failure to state a cause of action*. By this pleading the defendant, in effect, says to the court, "Even if everything the plaintiff says in his complaint is true, he is not entitled to the relief he seeks." For example, the defendant in the case involving the nonpayment for merchandise can argue the plaintiff failed to allege that the defendant ordered the goods. By federal law, merchandise sent unsolicited does not have to be paid for even when it is kept. In essence, the defendant, in the motion to dismiss, argues that the plaintiff failed to plead an essential element of a valid claim.

TYPICAL MOTIONS

Motion to dismiss.	*Motion in limine* or to exclude evidence.
Motion for summary judgment.	Motion for discovery sanctions.
Motion to compel discovery.	Motion for judgment not withstanding verdict.

In addition, a defendant may move to dismiss a suit for reasons that as a matter of law prevent the plaintiff from winning his or her suit. Such matters as a lack of jurisdiction of the court to hear the suit, or expiration of the time limit during which the defendant is subject to suit, may be raised by such a motion. This latter ground is usually referred to as the **statute of limitations.** Each state has prescribed a time limit after which a suit cannot be filed. For example, if the plaintiff fails to sue within the stated period, the defendant is not liable for the nonpayment of the merchandise. (Typically in a situation like the merchandise example, the statute of limitations will be four years from the time the merchandise is received.)

The rules of procedure in the federal court system and in most of the state systems provide for motions for a **judgment on the pleadings** or for **summary judgment.** In the former motion, a party is asking the judge to decide the case based solely on the complaint and the answer. If in the example involving the nonpayment for the merchandise the complaint does contain all the elements needed to state a claim and if the defendant offers no explanation or excuse for nonpayment in the answer, the judge can enter a judgment that the defendant must pay the plaintiff a specified amount. Through this motion, a time-consuming but unnecessary trial can be avoided.

A motion for summary judgment seeks a similar pretrial conclusion to the litigation. However, the party filing this motion is asking the judge to base a decision not only on the pleadings but also on other evidence. Such evidence usually is presented in the form of sworn statements called **affidavits.** The judge also may conduct a hearing and allow the lawyers to argue the merits of the motion for summary judgment. If there is no question of material fact, the judge will decide the legal issues raised by the facts and enter a judgment in favor of one party over the other.

10. FRIVOLOUS CASES

Either on a motion by a party or on their own initiative, judges may terminate the litigation process if there is a finding that the lawsuit is frivolous, that is, totally lacking in merit. The difficulty is in the determination of what is frivolous. What initially may appear to be a frivolous complaint may upon the presentation of evidence become a legitimate case.

During the past decade, courts within the federal judiciary and most state court systems have increased the frequency of assessing fines against lawyers who file frivolous cases. For example, Rule 11 of the Federal Rules of Civil Procedure authorizes the imposition of fines for filing frivolous papers. These fines are justified because Rule 11 states:

> The signature of an attorney or party constitutes a certificate by the signer that the signer has read the pleading, motion, or other paper; that to the best of the signer's knowledge, information, and belief formed after reasonable inquiry it is well grounded in fact and is warranted by existing law, and that it is not interposed for any improper purpose, such as to harass or to cause unnecessary delay or needless increase in the cost of litigation.

Most states have a rule similar to Federal Rule 11. The courts have upheld fines against lawyers and clients who sign frivolous documents. These holdings make it essential that businesspeople have thorough discussions with their lawyers about litigation strategies.

---

concept SUMMARY   *Pretrial Procedures*

1. Lawsuits typically are won and lost at the discovery stage of litigation.
2. Interrogatories are a series of written questions that must be answered by the opposing party.
3. Substantial penalties can be imposed by courts for thwarting the discovery process.
4. Abusive discovery is one of the primary reasons for the high cost of litigation.
5. A motion for summary judgment seeks to resolve the case without a trial.

THE TRIAL

If efforts to resolve a case through pretrial motions or negotiations have been unsuccessful, the case will proceed to trial. A trial normally involves the presentation of evidence to a jury to determine the actual facts in dispute. After the evidence is presented, the judge explains the applicable law to the jury. The jury is asked to deliberate and render a verdict and the trial court must then decide whether to enter a judgment based on the jury's verdict.

11. JURY SELECTION

As the case is called, the first order of business is to select a jury. Prior to the calling of the case, the court clerk will have summoned prospective jurors. Their names are drawn at random from lists of eligible citizens, and the number of jurors required, between 6 and 12, is selected or called into the jury box for the conduct of *voir dire* examination. **Voir dire** literally means to speak the truth. This examination is a method by which the court and often the attorneys for each party examine each potential juror as to his or her qualifications and ability to be fair and impartial. A party to a lawsuit is entitled to fair and impartial jurors in both civil and criminal cases. Prospective jurors are sworn to give truthful answers to the questions on *voir dire*.

TRIAL STEPS

Voir dire—Parties and their attorneys select jury.

Attorneys present opening statements.

Plaintiff presents evidence through witnesses.

Defendant moves for directed verdict.

Defendant presents evidence through witnesses.

Attorneys present closing arguments.

Court instructs jury on the law.

Jury deliberates and makes decision (verdict).

Judge enters judgment on verdict.

Losing party files posttrial motion.

CORPORATE GOVERNANCE AND THE JURY SELECTION PROCESS

In 2003, a judge in Corpus Christi, Texas, asked a district attorney to investigate Bayer, a giant drug company based in Germany, after the firm sent thousands of letters to residents in the community before jury selection in a lawsuit involving its anticholesterol drug, Baycol. Bayer sent the letters describing its position in the case and noting that it employs nearly 2,000 individuals at several Texas operations. The letter asked recipients to "keep an open mind" about the drug company. Bayer claimed the letter was "a miscommunication" intended only for members of the local chamber of commerce. Was Bayer's explanation reasonable? Did the court properly respond or over react?

Either party in the lawsuit may challenge or excuse a prospective juror for a specific reason, or cause. For example, if a prospective juror is related to one of the parties or to a witness or the juror admits bias favoring one side, that person may be excused as a juror because of the specific reason. In addition to the excuses for cause, the plaintiff and defendant are given a certain number of challenges, known as **peremptory challenges,** for which no cause or reason need be given to excuse a prospective juror. The number of peremptory challenges varies from court system to court system and on the type of case being tried. The number also may vary between the parties. For instance, in a criminal case, the defendant may have twelve peremptory challenges, and the government may have only six. The process of voir dire examination continues until all the peremptory challenges are exhausted and a full jury panel is selected.

Based upon a series of U.S. Supreme Court decisions, beginning with *Batson v. Kentucky,* 476 U.S. 79 (1986), outlawing racial discrimination in jury selection, the jury has become increasingly more representative of the racial diversity in the United States. *Batson* represented a major development in Supreme Court jurisprudence allowing lawyer misconduct in a single case to establish discriminatory motive in making peremptory strikes. The Court banned gender discrimination in jury selection in the following case.

J. E. B. v. ALABAMA EX REL. T.B.

114 S. CT. 1419 (1994)

At petitioner's paternity and child support trials, the court assembled a panel of 36 potential jurors, 12 males and 24 females. After the court excused three jurors for cause, only 10 of the remaining 33 jurors were male. The State of Alabama then used 9 of its 10 peremptory challenges to remove male jurors. The petitioner used all but one of his strikes to remove female jurors. As a result, the trial court empaneled an all-female jury. The court rejected peti- *tioner's claim that the Equal Protection Clause of the Fourteenth Amendment prohibits peremptory strikes based solely on gender. The jury subsequently found petitioner to be the father of the child in question and the trial court ordered him to pay child support. After the Alabama Court of Civil Appeals affirmed the decision, the Supreme Court granted certiorari.*

[CONTINUED]

BLACKMUN, J.: . . . We have reaffirmed repeatedly our commitment to jury selection procedures that are fair and nondiscriminatory. We have recognized that whether the trial is criminal or civil, potential jurors, as well as litigants, have an equal protection right to jury selection procedures that are free from state-sponsored group stereotypes rooted in, and reflective of, historical prejudice.

Although premised on equal protection principles that apply equally to gender discrimination, all our recent cases . . . involved alleged racial discrimination in the exercise of peremptory challenges. Today we are faced with the question whether the Equal Protection Clause forbids intentional discrimination on the basis of gender, just as it prohibits discrimination on the basis of race. We hold that gender, like race, is an unconstitutional proxy for juror competence and impartiality. . . .

Discrimination on the basis of gender in the exercise of peremptory challenges is a relatively recent phenomenon. Gender-based peremptory strikes were hardly practicable for most of our country's existence, since, until the 19th century women were completely excluded from jury service. So well-entrenched was this exclusion of women that in 1880 this Court, while finding that the exclusion of African-American men from juries violated the Fourteenth Amendment, expressed no doubt that a State may confine the selection of jurors to males.

Many states continued to exclude women from jury service well into the present century, despite the fact that women attained suffrage upon ratification of the Nineteenth Amendment in 1920. States that did permit women to serve on juries often erected other barriers, such as registration requirements and automatic exemptions, designed to deter women from exercising their right to jury service. . . .

This Court consistently has subjected gender-based classifications to heightened scrutiny in recognition of the real danger that government policies that professedly are based on reasonable considerations in fact may be reflective of "archaic and overbroad" generalizations about gender, or based on "outdated misconceptions concerning the role of females in the home rather than in the marketplace and world of ideas. . . .

Far from proffering an exceptionally persuasive justification for its gender-based peremptory challenges, respondent maintains that its decision to strike virtually all the males from the jury in this case "may reasonably have been based upon the perception, supported by history, that men otherwise totally qualified to serve upon a jury might be more sympathetic and receptive to the arguments of a man alleged in a paternity action to be the father of an out-of-wedlock child, while women equally qualified to serve upon a jury might be more sympathetic and receptive to the arguments of the complaining witness who bore the child."

Even if a measure of truth can be found in some of the gender stereotypes used to justify gender-based peremptory challenges, that fact alone cannot support discrimination on the basis of gender in jury selection. We have made abundantly clear in past cases that gender classifications that rest on impermissible stereotypes violate the Equal Protection Clause, even when some statistical support can be conjured up for the generalization. . . .

Discrimination in jury selection, whether based on race or on gender, causes harm to the litigants, the community, and the individual jurors who are wrongfully excluded from participation in the judicial process. . . . When state actors exercise peremptory challenges in reliance on gender stereotypes, they ratify and reinforce prejudicial views of the relative abilities of men and women. Because these stereotypes have wreaked injustice in so many other spheres of our country's public life, active discrimination by litigants on the basis of gender during jury selection invites cynicism respecting the jury's neutrality and its obligation to adhere to the law. . . .

Our conclusion that litigants may not strike potential jurors solely on the basis of gender does not imply the elimination of all peremptory challenges. . . . Parties still may remove jurors whom they feel might be less acceptable than others on the panel; genders imply may not serve as a proxy for bias. **The judgment of the Court of Civil Appeals of Alabama is reversed and the case is remanded.**

[CONTINUED]

CASE QUESTIONS

1. Is a peremptory challenge peremptory if you have to give a nondiscriminatory reason to justify striking a particular juror?

2. What facts made this case an easy one for detecting the existence of discrimination? Will it always be so easy?

3. Is a trial judge normally able to tell whether a lawyer is using peremptory challenges improperly?

12. OTHER STEPS DURING A TRIAL

After selecting jurors to hear the case, the attorneys make their opening statements. An opening statement is not evidence; it familiarizes the jury with the essential facts that each side expects to prove. So that the jury may understand the overall picture of the case and the relevancy of each bit of evidence as presented, the lawyers inform the jury of the facts they expect to prove and of the witnesses they expect to call to make such proof.

After the opening statements, the trial continues with the plaintiff introducing evidence to establish the truth of the allegations made in the complaint. Evidence is normally presented in open court by the examination of witnesses and production of documents and other exhibits. After the plaintiff has presented his or her evidence, the defendant may make a motion for a **directed verdict.** The court can only direct a verdict for one party if the evidence, taken in the light most favorable to the other party, establishes as a matter of law that the party making the motion is entitled to a verdict. Just as a plaintiff must *allege* certain facts or have the complaint dismissed by motion to dismiss, he or she must have some *proof* of each essential allegation or lose the case on a motion for a directed verdict.

CHALLENGING THE USE OF A PEREMPTORY STRIKE

As a result of cases like *Batson v. Kentucky* and *J. E. B. v. Alabama Ex Rel. T. B.,* a complex evidentiary framework has developed for evaluating claims of discrimination in jury selection. First, the moving party must offer evidence of racial or gender discrimination in his opponent's use of a peremptory strike. At that point, the burden shifts to the party making the peremptory strike to offer a race or gender neutral reason for the strike. If he does so, the moving party must carry the burden of convincing the judge that the peremptory strike was motivated by a discriminatory purpose.

Given all of the criticism raised about juries today, particularly their ability to decide cases involving celebrity criminal defendants or complex civil issues, we are likely to see further decisions by the Supreme Court clarifying the permissible uses of peremptory challenges in jury selection. Several legal commentators have suggested following the example of England and eliminating the use of peremptory challenges altogether.

TECHNOLOGY IN THE COURTROOM

As a result of several initiatives by federal and state judges, courtrooms across the nation are being updated with computer technology—laptops, flat-screen monitors, Power-Point presentations, and video clips—which have invaded the courtroom. One commentator noted that "we are a TV generation now," and jurors expect to see information pre-sented to them in a way that seems up-to-date and accessible. Improved technology also makes it easier for jurors to sift through what has become increasingly greater amounts of evidence presented in recent years. The lawyer's previous tools, ballpoint pens and Magic Markers, appear to be in the past. Of course, one commentator observed that "[t]he goal is justice at all times, not technology."

After the parties have completed the presentation of all the evidence, the lawyers have an opportunity to summarize the evidence. Unlike the opening statements, which involved simply a preview of what was to come, the lawyers in closing argument attempt to convince the jury (or judge if no jury is used) of what the case's outcome should be.

Following the closing arguments, the judge acquaints the jury with the law applicable to the case. These are the **jury instructions.** As the function of the jury is to find the facts and the function of the court is to determine the applicable law, the purpose of jury instructions is to bring the facts and the law together in an orderly manner that will result in a decision. A typical jury instruction might be:

> The plaintiff in his complaint has alleged that he was injured as the proximate cause of the negligence of the defendant. If you find from the evidence that the defendant was guilty of negligence, which proximately caused plaintiff's injuries, then your verdict should be for the plaintiff.

In this instruction, the court is in effect saying that the plaintiff must prove that the defendant was at fault. Thus, the jury is instructed as to the result to be returned if the jurors have found certain facts to be true. At the conclusion of the jury instructions, the judge informs the jurors to begin their deliberations and to return to the courtroom when they have reached a decision.

13. BURDEN OF PROOF

The term **burden of proof** has two meanings depending on the context in which it is used. It may describe the burden or responsibility that a person has to come forward with evidence on a particular issue. The party alleging the existence of certain facts usually has the burden of coming forward with evidence to establish those facts.

Burden of proof may also describe the responsibility a person has to be persuasive as to a specific fact. This is known as the *burden of persuasion.* The party with this burden must convince the trier of fact on the issue involved. If a party with the burden of persuasion fails to meet this burden, that party loses the lawsuit. Thus, the burden of persuasion is a legal device used to help determine the rights of the litigating parties.

Criminal Cases   The extent of proof required to satisfy the burden of persuasion varies, depending upon the issue and the type of case. There are three distinct levels of proof recognized by the law. For criminal cases, the burden of proof is described as **beyond a reasonable doubt.** This means that the prosecution in a

TELEVISING JURY DELIBERATIONS

A raging debate has developed in recent years over televising jury deliberations. Some legal scholars believe that jurors are oblivious to the cameras and that the televised proceedings better inform the public in the modern age of mass communication. They argue that the American jury system is excellent and that we should not be ashamed to see how it works. Other scholars think that televising the jury deliberation process is a terrible idea because it will turn a civic duty into a public performance. They fear it could adversely impact the jury deliberations by turning them into a form of reality television. What do you think?

criminal case has the burden of convincing the trier of fact, usually a jury, that the defendant is guilty of the crime charged and that the jury has no reasonable doubt about the defendant's guilt. This burden of proof does not require evidence beyond any doubt, only beyond a reasonable doubt. A reasonable doubt is one that a reasonable person viewing the evidence might reasonably entertain. This standard is not used in civil cases.

Civil Cases In civil cases the party with the burden of proof is subject to one of two standards: the **preponderance of evidence** standard or the **clear and convincing proof** standard. The preponderance of evidence standard is used most frequently. It requires that a party convince the jury by a preponderance of evidence that the facts are as he or she contends. Preponderance of evidence is achieved when there is greater weight of evidence in support of the proposition than there is against it. The scales of justice, in other words, tilt more one way than the other. The clear and convincing proof standard is used in situations where the law requires more than a simple preponderance of the evidence but less than proof beyond a reasonable doubt. The scales of justice must tilt heavily one way. Unless the evidence clearly establishes the proposition, the party with the burden of proof fails to sustain it and loses the lawsuit.

14. DECIDING THE CASE

The principal job of the jury is to determine what the facts are and to apply the law, as instructed by the judge, to these facts. The jury's decision is called a **verdict,** and it is announced in the courtroom when the jury's deliberations are completed. An example of a verdict might be "We, the jury, find in favor of the plaintiff and award $1,000,000 to be paid by the defendant" or "We, the jury, find the defendant is not liable to the plaintiff and should pay nothing." The judge must decide whether to accept the verdict. If the judge agrees with the verdict, a **judgment** is entered in favor of the party that won the jury's verdict.

The party who is dissatisfied with the jury's verdict may file a posttrial motion with the judge seeking a **judgment notwithstanding the verdict,** often called JNOV. The judge may enter a judgment opposite to that of the jury's verdict if the judge finds that the verdict is erroneous as a matter of law. The test used by the judge is the same one used to decide a motion for a directed verdict. To grant a motion for a judgment notwithstanding the verdict, the judge must find that reasonable persons viewing the evidence would not reach the verdict the jury returned. Because jurors are presumed to be reasonable, this motion is not frequently granted.

The party who receives the adverse judgment may file a motion for a new trial. This motion may be granted if the judge is convinced that a legal mistake was made during the trial. Because a judge is not usually inclined to acknowledge that mistakes have been made, a motion for a new trial is usually denied. It is from the ruling on this motion that the losing party appeals.

---

concept SUMMARY   *The Trial*

1. Peremptory challenges may not be based upon race or gender discrimination.
2. A direct verdict may be granted when the evidence establishes, as a matter of law, that the moving party is entitled to a verdict.
3. Jury instructions are used to acquaint the jury with the law applicable to the case.
4. In most civil cases, the preponderance standard is used to evaluate the case.
5. A judgment notwithstanding the verdict may be entered if the verdict is erroneous as a matter of law.

POSTTRIAL ISSUES

Even after the trial, a number of issues may still exist. First among these is this one: How can a disappointed litigant obtain a review of the trial judge's legal rulings? If the trial court's judgment is final, what can the victorious party do to collect the dollar damages awarded? Finally, can the same subject matter be relitigated? These questions are the subject of the final three sections of this chapter.

15. APPEALS

Each state prescribes its own appellate procedure and determines the jurisdiction of its various reviewing courts. Although having knowledge of the procedure used in an appeal is essentially a responsibility for the lawyer, understanding certain aspects of this procedure may assist you in understanding our judicial system.

Appellate Procedures   Courts of appeal deal with the record of the proceedings in lower court. All the pleadings, testimony, and motions are reduced to a written record, which is filed with the court of review. The court of appeal studies the issues, testimony, and proceedings to determine whether prejudicial errors occurred or whether the lower court reached an erroneous result. In addition to the

---

APPELLATE REVIEW

Party receiving adverse judgment files notice of appeal.

Parties file briefs in reviewing court.

Oral argument made in reviewing court.

Reviewing court announces decision.

Further review may be requested by petition to higher court.

Higher court allows or denies further review.

Final decision (successful party may require judicial assistance in enforcing the final decision).

record, each party files a **brief,** which contains a short description of the nature of the case, the factual situation, the points and authorities on which the party relies, and the argument for reversing or affirming the decision of the lower court, depending on whether the party is an appellant or appellee.

In addition to the brief, the reviewing court is often given the benefit of **oral argument** in deciding the case. The attorneys are given a specified amount of time to explain orally to the court their position in the case. This also gives the court of review an opportunity to question the attorneys about various aspects of the case.

After oral argument, an initial vote of the judges' or justices' impressions is usually taken. The case is assigned to one judge or justice to prepare an opinion. Each judge or justice has a staff of clerks assisting in the preparation of opinions. After the opinion is prepared, it is circulated among the other members of the court. If a majority approve the opinion, it is adopted. Those who disagree may prepare a dissenting opinion. If the review is conducted by an intermediate appellate court, the losing party may petition the highest court in the system for a *writ of certiorari.*

Deference to Trial Courts   Courts of appeal are essentially concerned with questions of law. However, a reviewing court may be asked to grant a new trial on the ground that the decision in the lower court is contrary to the manifest weight of the evidence found in the record. In the federal courts and in many states, appellate courts are not allowed to disturb factual findings unless they are clearly erroneous. This limitation recognizes the unique opportunity afforded the trial judge in evaluating the credibility of witnesses and weighing the evidence. Determining the weight and credibility of the evidence is the special function of the trial court. An appellate court cannot substitute its interpretation of the evidence for that of the trial court simply because it construes the facts or resolves the ambiguities differently.

16. ENFORCEMENT OF JUDGMENTS AND DECREES

After a judgment in a court of law or a decree in a court of equity has become final, either because of the decision on appeal or because the losing party has failed to appeal within the proper time, it may become necessary for the successful party to obtain judicial assistance in enforcing the court decision. The judgment debtor, for example, may not have voluntarily paid the amount of the judgment to the judgment creditor.

APPEALING AN EVIDENTIARY RULING

Judges are required to make split second rulings on the admissibility of evidence during trial. Lawyers, in order to preserve an argument for appeal, must show the following:

1. An objection is made
2. In a timely manner
3. Challenging the evidence on specific grounds
4. The lower court's ruling was wrong and
5. The error harmed your client.

PREVENTING LAWSUITS

1. Make sure key officials have access to legal advice and use it before a situation becomes a major dispute.

2. Encourage employees to use preventive planning and develop cooperative working relationships to avoid mistakes.

3. Develop internal grievance, mediation, and other alternative dispute-resolution mechanisms to avoid court action.

4. Perform regular audits and other reviews to locate and deal with sources of risk and possible litigation.

5. Require a legal impact statement as a part of the review before taking significant action.

The primary enforcement mechanism is for the judgment creditor to request the court's assistance to have the **execution** of the judgment or decree. An execution of a judgment occurs when a court official, such as a sheriff or marshal, seizes some property of the debtor, sells it at public auction, and applies the proceeds to the creditor's claim.

Another form of execution is **garnishment.** This method of enforcement involves having a portion of the debtor's wages paid to the court, which in turn pays the creditor.

17. RES JUDICATA

Once a decision of the court has become final, it is said to be *res judicata* (the thing has been decided), meaning that a final decision is conclusive on all issues between the parties, whether raised in the litigation or not. *Res judicata* means either that the case has been finally decided on appeal or that the time for appeal has expired and a cause of action finally determined by a competent court cannot be litigated by the parties in a new proceeding by the same court or in any other court. *Res judicata* prevents successive suits involving the same factual setting between the same parties and brings disputes to a conclusion. A matter once litigated and legally determined is conclusive between the parties in all subsequent proceedings.

KEY TERMS

REVIEW QUESTIONS AND PROBLEMS

Litigation—An Overview

1. *Parties*

   A building contractor is sued by homeowners alleging that their homes were poorly constructed resulting in several defects. The contractor adds to the lawsuit a building supplier that it claims provided faulty support beams. How can the contractor add the building supplier as a party to the lawsuit? What is this procedure called and how does it work?

2. *Standing to Sue*

   A group of environmentalists filed a lawsuit challenging commercial fishing in Glacier Bay National Park and sued the secretary of the interior and the National Park Service in order to prevent more commercial fishing.

   (a)   What must the environmentalists show in order to satisfy the requirement of standing to sue in this case?

   (b)   At what point should the issue of standing be decided by the court during the course of litigation?

3. *Subject Matter Jurisdiction*

   Mark, a citizen of Georgia, was crossing a street in Atlanta when he was struck by a car driven by David, a citizen of New York visiting Atlanta. The car was owned by David's employer, a Delaware corporation that has its principal place of business in Atlanta, Georgia. Mark sues both David and the corporation in federal district court in Atlanta alleging damages in the amount of $500,000. Does the court have subject matter jurisdiction? Why or why not?

4. *Personal Jurisdiction*

   The New York Gazette is a New York corporation with its principal place of business in New York City. Although the *Gazette* sells the majority of its newspapers in the greater New York City area, the *Gazette* also distributes its newspapers throughout the United States and places its printed articles on a website that is read around the world. Shirley, a California resident, brought suit in San Francisco against the *Gazette* over a published article about her and seeks damages for defamation, invasion of privacy, and intentional infliction of emotional distress.

(a)   Is the defendant subject to the jurisdiction of the California courts?

(b)   How should a court analyze a jurisdiction issue of this kind?

5. *Class-Action Suits*

What are the key requirements for federal courts to permit class-action suits?

Pretrial Proceedings

6. *Pleadings*

Describe the purpose of a complaint and an answer in civil litigation. What is the function of the pleading stage in a lawsuit?

7. *Steps in Discovery*

(a)   Why do surprises rarely occur at trial?

(b)   What are some of the key devices a litigant can use in discovery?

8. *Scope of Discovery*

How do abusive discovery practices raise the cost of litigation?

9. *Motions*

Under what circumstances may a court grant a motion for summary judgment?

10. *Frivolous Cases*

Federal Rule 11 sanctions are available against both lawyers and their clients to curb frivolous litigation. Under what circumstances may sanctions be imposed?

The Trial

11. *Jury Selection*

In light of recent court decisions restricting the use of peremptory challenges, should they be eliminated from litigation altogether? Would the elimination of peremptory challenges improve the efficiency of the trial process?

12. *Other Steps during a Trial*

When is a directed verdict appropriate?

13. *Burden of Proof*

There are three distinct levels of proof required by law depending upon the kind of case involved. Describe them and when they are used.

14. *Deciding the Case*

Under what circumstances would a judge enter a judgment notwithstanding the verdict?

Posttrial Issues

15. *Appeals*

What normally is contained in an appellate brief? An oral argument?

16. *Enforcement of Judgments and Decrees*

How does the court enforce judgments?

17. *Res Judicata*

Why is the notion of *res judicata* important in civil litigation?

TERMINOLOGY REVIEW

For each term in the left-hand column, match the most appropriate description in the right-hand column.

1. Interrogatories
2. Plaintiff
3. Beyond a reasonable doubt
4. Personal jurisdiction
5. Standing to sue
6. Class-action suit
7. Depositions
8. Peremptory challenges
9. Directed verdict
10. Preponderance of evidence

a. The burden of proof used in criminal cases
b. The power of a court over the parties involved in litigation
c. Typically granted to a defendant when the plaintiff fails to present sufficient evidence at trial to justify a jury verdict
d. Written questions to the opposing party
e. The party who files a civil action
f. The burden of proof normally applied in civil cases
g. A type of case in which one or more plaintiffs file a lawsuit on behalf of a much larger group
h. A discovery process that involves the sworn questioning of potential witnesses outside of court
i. Demonstrating a personal interest in the lawsuit as a plaintiff
j. The power granted each litigant to reject a certain number of prospective jurors

BUSINESS DISCUSSION

You are the owner of a small firm that manufactures lawn mowers. While using one of your products, a person suffers severe injury and now is suing, claiming that your product was negligently designed because it did not adequately protect the user. You have no experience with the legal system. You learn that lawyers charge as much as $250 per hour and must be paid whether they win or lose their cases. You are surprised at what must happen before a trial can occur to determine who is at fault. First, your lawyer may move to dismiss the case on jurisdictional grounds. If that fails, both sides will take costly depositions of likely witnesses. You will have to turn over reams of internal documents related to the design of your mower. Each side also will have to pay several hundred dollars per hour for experts as the lawyers prepare the case. These experts will have to be paid again when they testify at trial. As the time for the trial approaches, each side will spend money trying to discern the most sympathetic type of jury. Years after the lawsuit was first filed, the parties will be sitting in the courtroom waiting for jury selection to begin. More money will have been spent defending this case than the plaintiff was seeking when the lawsuit was first filed. Many questions come to mind:

Should you have settled the case at the beginning?

Has your attorney been getting rich at your expense?

Is discovery more of a burden than a help?

ALTERNATIVE DISPUTE RESOLUTION SYSTEMS

As the vice president for sales of a company that manufactures and sells commercial carpet, you notice an alarming increase in the number of customers filing complaints with your company service representatives. Of particular importance is the number of complaints that involve claims in excess of $10,000. Because these large dollar amounts can lead to lawsuits being filed, you want to investigate what is causing the increase in complaints and how your company can be processing these complaints to avoid burdensome litigation.

> What steps should you take to discover, in the most accurate and efficient manner, the reasons customers are filing complaints?
>
> What is the distinction between mediation and arbitration?
>
> Should your company's sales contracts include a clause that requires the parties to attempt resolution of dispute by mediation? By arbitration? By some other mechanisms?
>
> If your company's sales contracts did include a dispute resolution (other than litigation) clause, when can the courts still be used?

As the previous chapter points out, the process of litigation may not always be the best way to settle disputes due to its expense and time-consuming nature. In business relationships, it is neither feasible nor desirable to litigate each dispute that arises. Time is money, and one small delay in the court proceedings can cause larger and longer delays down the line. In addition, the emotional and financial costs of litigation often are overwhelming and destructive of the relationship.

Business relationships can be irreparably damaged through litigation. To help avoid this harm and to help ensure productive, ongoing relationships, a number of alternatives to litigation have developed. These are known as alternative dispute resolution (ADR) systems.

The figure on the next page illustrates an array of ADR systems. They are arranged along a spectrum of highest cost (in dollars, time, and emotions) to lowest

115

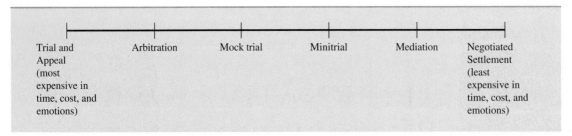

Scale of Alternative Dispute Resolution Systems

cost. Although any given factual situation may cause the items on this spectrum to shift places, this figure presents a generally accepted view of ADR techniques.

It is important to remember two things at the outset of this discussion. First, litigation does not preclude the use of ADR techniques. Indeed, it is very common for disputes to be arbitrated, mediated, or settled through negotiations during the pretrial process discussed in the preceding chapter.

Moreover, disputing parties do not have to begin a lawsuit to use any form of ADR. In this chapter, you will study how ADR systems relate to formal litigation and how they are utilized independently from the litigation process.

The second thing to keep in mind about ADR systems is that their use by disputing parties may be part of a contractual relationship between these parties. For example, it is an effective dispute resolution tool to have the parties' contract specify a preferred ADR system. Disputing parties may agree to use an ADR technique after the dispute arises even if they did not foresee the possibility of needing to use a dispute resolution system at the time of their original agreement.

In this chapter, you will study alternatives to litigation in the following order:

- Negotiated settlements
- Mediations
- Arbitrations
- Other alternatives

We begin with **negotiated settlements** because negotiations are involved throughout litigation or any ADR process.

NEGOTIATED SETTLEMENTS

It is universally acknowledged that both parties to litigation are losers. The winning party in a lawsuit is a loser to the extent of the attorney's fees—which are often substantial. The fact that the loser usually also has to pay court costs is an added incentive to settlement without litigation.

There are also personal reasons to settle controversies. The desire to resolve differences is instinctive for many Americans. Most of us dislike trouble, and many fear going to court. The opinions of others are often a motivating force in encouraging amicable settlements.

Businesses tend to settle disputes with customers for two additional reasons. First, it is simply not good business from a goodwill and public relations standpoint to sue a customer. Second, juries are frequently sympathetic to individuals who have suits against large corporations or defendants who are covered by insur-

Mickey Shears and Naomi Hamilton operate a business that manufactures personal computers. The business name is M&N PCs, Inc. The principal market for M&N computers has been buyers for home use. M&N's reputation is based on assembling a high-quality computer for a relatively low price. M&N's biggest problem has been maintaining a large enough, qualified sales force while keeping the price for its computer below the market average.

William Dalton operates a nationwide chain of discount department stores. This chain is known as Bill's Discount Centers. One year ago, Bill's Discount Centers agreed to buy from M&N a minimum of 250 computers (with specifications stated in the contract) per month for six months. The agreed-upon price of each computer was $1,250.

The relationship between M&N and Bill's worked very well. In the fifth month of this initial contract, Bill's agreed to increase its minimum purchase per month to 750 computers, and Bill's committed to this monthly purchase for a twelve-month period to begin after the sixth month of the original contract. The price per computer was to remain at $1,250.

M&N was delighted with the arrangement since it allowed M&N to concentrate on increasing its production capacity while reducing the costs of maintaining a large, active sales force.

Unlike the success of its initial relationship with M&N, Bill's began receiving complaints from its customers about the lack of quality of M&N's computers. These complaints were traced by Bill's customer service representatives to the newer computers that M&N was assembling under its expanded production program. Despite its knowledge of these quality-related problems, Bill's never informed M&N of its findings.

The complaints continued to become more numerous. During the fifth month of the twelve-month period, Bill's purchased only 350 computers from M&N. When M&N sent an invoice for the 750 computers specified as the monthly minimum, Bill's refused to pay for any computers over the 350 actually purchased. In the second week of the sixth month, Bill's sent M&N written notice that it was canceling the remainder of the sales contract due to declining quality of M&N's computers. M&N offered to reduce the price per computer to $1,050, but Bill's refused to withdraw its termination letter.

M&N wants to sue Bill's for $7,062,500. This figure is based on the shortfalls of 400 computers in the fifth month times $1,250/computer plus 750 computers times 7 months times $1,250/computer. Prior to filing suit, M&N wants to explore the chances for a negotiated settlement in the hope of salvaging a constructive relationship with Bill's.

ance. Juries often decide close questions of liability, as well as size of the verdict, against business organizations because of their presumed ability to pay. As a result, businesses settle many disputes even though they might possibly prevail in litigation.

The process of negotiating has become a major focus of study. We now know that there are certain elements that should be the focus of parties negotiating a possible settlement. To help illustrate two very different styles of negotiation, consider the factual situation in the box above and the sections that follow.

1. POSITION-BASED NEGOTIATIONS

Most people instinctively use a negotiation method referred to as **positional bargaining.** These parties in a dispute state their respective expectations. In the factual situation you just read, Bill's is saying that it owes nothing to M&N. On the other side, M&N is demanding payment of more than $7 million. The difference between these two positions is so wide that it will be difficult to bring these parties into agreement.

Even if Bill's was willing to buy some computers at a revised price and even if M&N agreed to a reduced quantity or selling price, the issue of quality is not being addressed. Does Bill's gain any market advantage in selling an inferior product, albeit at a lower price, to its customers? Clearly not.

If the positions on quantity and price are the only items open for negotiation, Bill's and M&N are unlikely to reach a satisfactory compromise. Hence, the chances of a negotiated settlement through positional bargaining are minimal. Is there a better method of negotiation?

2. INTEREST-BASED NEGOTIATIONS

A better approach to negotiating among disputing parties has been described as **principled interest-based negotiations** in the book *Getting to Yes* by Roger Fisher, William Ury, and Bruce Patton.[1] These authors present seven elements that should become the focus of negotiators. The elements, which are summarized in the table below, will vary in importance depending on the factual situation in dispute and on the "parties individual perspectives?" However, concentrating on these elements can help remove some of the barriers created by position-based negotiations. A quick focus on these elements illustrates how M&N and Bill's can be more productive in their negotiation efforts.

The Seven Elements of Interest-Based Negotiation
• Communication
• Relationship
• Interests
• Options
• Legitimacy
• Alternatives
• Commitment

Communication First, as expressed in the factual situation above, Bill's has not openly explained to M&N the nature of its dissatisfaction. Sharing customer complaints, either in general or with specificity, might help M&N locate a production operations problem. Likewise, M&N does not appear to be informing Bill's of any difficulties it faced as it expanded production capacities. Clear communication between these parties may assist them in becoming joint problem solvers. Without this exchange of information, these parties are likely to continue blaming one another.

Relationship Second, these parties would likely benefit by discussing how each could benefit by continuing their relationship of customer and supplier. Can they solve the current problem and maintain, if not enhance, their future business opportunities together? Maintaining, or even enhancing, the relationship may be possible if these parties focus on effective communications.

---

[1] *Penquin Books, 2d ed., 1991.*

Interests Third, have M&N and Bill's communicated their real interests to each other? Perhaps these interests are not mutually exclusive. For example, Bill's might want to expand its offerings in computing technology to customers. M&N might want to dissolve its sales force and concentrate on production of a variety of computers. These interests, once communicated, may help the parties realize that a continuing relationship is in their mutual best interests.

Options Fourth, M&N and Bill's should brainstorm possible options or solutions to their dispute. This exploration process is best done with the parties agreeing that an option mentioned is not necessarily a proposal for compromise. One attractive option might be for Bill's to agree to buy all the computers M&N can produce and for Bill's to market these computers under its own name. Rather than severing their business relationship, M&N could become the exclusive supplier of store-brand computers. The renaming of these products also can help overcome the "quality problems" customers associate with M&N's computers.

Legitimacy Fifth, legitimacy involves the application of accepted standards to the topic negotiated—rather than having the parties state unsupported propositions. Bill's probably will not be impressed by M&N stating it will improve the quality of its computers. Instead the parties should focus on how quality can be improved and how customers will approve the improvements. Production engineers may help address the former issue while specific test marketing plans may assist in legitimizing the latter.

Alternatives Sixth, alternatives are outcomes that are possible without the agreement of the other party. In essence, alternatives are the thing that parties to a negotiation can do away from the bargaining table. If the parties understand their alternatives to negotiating a settlement and understand the unattractive nature of these alternatives, the desire to negotiate, instead of litigating, is enhanced. M&N, for example, may perceive that bankruptcy is a very likely result if this dispute is not resolved. Bill's, on the other hand, may believe that another supplier is readily available. The desirable result of any negotiation is to agree on an outcome that is better than both parties' alternatives.

Commitment Seventh, any successful negotiation must conclude with the parties making realistic commitments that can be put into practice. Perhaps an initial commitment that assists the overall process of negotiation is to have the parties agree that they will continue to meet and focus on these seven elements. Hopefully, the conclusion of the negotiation will be an agreement between the parties that avoids the expense (dollars, time, and emotions) of litigation. If that commitment is not a settlement, then it might be an agreement to utilize one of the following ADR systems.

The box "Settlement Impacting Corporate Governance" illustrates how parties can reach a negotiated agreement through utilizing creative thinking. Many unanticipated options can become the basis of a workable solution leading to an agreement.

SETTLEMENT IMPACTING CORPORATE GOVERNANCE

By agreeing to change how its corporate directors are elected, Sprint Corporation settled a class-action lawsuit. The suit sought to address how Sprint allocated and supported stock options that favored individuals involved in a proposed merger. Interestingly the merger did not occur, but some Sprint shareholders filed suit.

To settle one class-action lawsuit, Sprint agreed to pay $50 million to shareholders. Rather than focusing on more money to settle a second suit, Sprint agreed its directors would be elected to one-year terms. Previously, Sprint directors served terms lasting three years. Also part of this settlement are increased standards of independence for directors and an increase of two-thirds of the directors meeting these standards of independence.

This settlement illustrates the creativity of using changes in corporate governance as a topic of negotiation and as a means to settle a lawsuit.

Source: Patrick McGeehan, "Sprint Settles Suit with Policy Shift and $50 Million," *The New York Times,* March 20, 2003.

MEDIATION

Today when negotiations between disputing parties begin to fail, the process of mediation is considered as an alternative to litigation. **Mediation** is the process by which a third person, called a **mediator,** attempts to assist disputing parties in resolving their differences. A mediator cannot impose a binding solution on the parties. However, as an unbiased and disinterested third party, a mediator is often able to help the parties bring about an understanding of a dispute and thus avoid litigation of it. Typically, mediators utilize the principles of interest-based negotiations, discussed in the preceding section.

The process of mediation may be utilized by the disputing parties as a result of their agreement to mediate. This agreement may have been made as a part of a contract before a dispute arose. For example, the mediation agreement could be made a part of the culture of the organization in the Business Decision at the beginning of this chapter. On the other hand, parties to a dispute may agree that mediation should be attempted as an alternative to litigating their controversy.

A trial judge can require the disputing parties to submit to the mediation process before a complaint can be litigated formally. There is a growing movement in this court-annexed mediation as one means of controlling the heavy caseload faced by courts. Rules related to court-annexed mediation are local in nature; thus there are wide variations as to the type of cases that courts require to be mediated. Generally, cases involving domestic-relations issues (such as divorce and child custody) and cases involving a dollar amount in dispute below a stated threshold level are examples of those that are subject to court-annexed mediation.

There is no need for judicial review of the mediation process. If mediation is successful in helping the parties resolve their dispute, it is the parties' agreement—not one imposed on them. If parties agree to settle a controversy, they do not have any reason to complain. The settlement was their mutual choice. If mediation is not successful in helping the parties find a solution, they may continue to litigate or utilize another ADR technique.

In the next two sections, you will review the following topics related to mediation:

- Advantages and disadvantages
- Procedures

3. ADVANTAGES/DISADVANTAGES

The basic advantage of mediation over litigation and arbitration is that the disputing parties retain full control over the resolution (or lack thereof) of their controversy. Through retaining this control, the parties can decide how much time and effort to put into the mediation process. The fact that mediation is party driven and does not involve even an informal presentation of evidence makes the process much more efficient than other ADR systems. If parties are making progress toward a settlement, the mediation can be continued and perhaps expanded to involve a possible agreement on other potential disputes. When the mediation is not aiding the parties, any of them can stop the process by simply stating that they will not participate further.

This same aspect of the parties controlling the mediation process may be viewed as a disadvantage rather than as an advantage when compared to other ADR systems. Even in the court-annexed mediations, a party usually satisfies the court's order to mediate by simply showing up. Generally, there is no enforcement mechanism that ensures the parties will mediate in good faith.

An additional disadvantage relates to the selection of the neutral mediator. The parties must be able to agree at least on who will be their mediator. The parties can avoid the need to agree on a mediator by allowing the person or organization that administers the mediation program to select the mediator. If the disputing parties cannot "get together" to select a mediator, the mediation process cannot begin.

Finally, the requirements for training as a mediator are not universally defined. Furthermore, licensing requirements are nonexistent at present. Therefore, anyone can serve as a mediator. The disputing party should be aware of the experience (or lack thereof) of the party chosen as their mediator. The Federal Mediation and Conciliation Service, the American Arbitration Association, and other similar organizations are valuable sources of credible mediators.

4. PROCEDURES

Despite the fact that mediations are informal and controlled by the disputing parties, the odds for a successful mediation occurring increase greatly when the mediator follows some basic procedures. The box below summarizes the typical steps of the mediation process, and a more complete description follows.

First, the mediator usually makes an opening statement. During this statement, mediators should explain the procedures to which they are asking the parties to agree. In essence, the mediator explains much of what you are reading in this section. Also, any "rules"—such as the common courtesy of not interrupting the party speaking—are specified.

Second, all parties are allowed to make a statement about their views of this dispute. These statements are made in the presence of each other and the mediator.

STEPS IN THE MEDIATION PROCESS

1. Mediator's introduction and explanation of mediation
2. Parties' opening statement
3. Parties' exchange (or dialogue or negotiation)
4. Brainstorming possible options (or solutions)
5. The agreement (written and signed)
6. Private sessions or caucuses (These are optional at the mediator's discretion.)

A party's attorney may be the spokesperson; however, it often is more enlightening when the parties speak for themselves.

Third, the mediator attempts to get the parties talking to one another in what some refer to as the dialogue or exchange phase of mediation. Through an exchange based on open communication, the parties "clear the air" and hopefully begin to shift their focus from "the wrongs done in the past" to "how can business be conducted in the future."

Fourth, once the parties concentrate on how to work together or how best to end a relationship, the mutual generation of possible solutions should occur. Brainstorming options that resolve the dispute becomes the purpose of this stage of the mediation process. Skillful mediators assist parties in evaluating the possible solutions. Through productive questioning (some call this reality testing) by the mediator, parties should be able to make informed choices as to the best solution. At this point, the parties hopefully are ready to make a realistic commitment to resolve their dispute and conflict.

Sometimes, the mediator may decide that the process will be more productive if the parties and their attorneys meet with the mediator outside the presence of the other disputant. This private meeting is called a **caucus.** After each side caucuses with the mediator, the mediator may call the parties back together for continued discussions, or the mediator may begin to act as a shuttle diplomat, moving back and forth between the parties who are in separate rooms. Especially during these caucuses, the mediator must win the trust and confidence of each party to the dispute.

Through the good judgment and experience of the mediator, the differences between the parties hopefully will be resolved and a common agreement can be produced. The final step to a successful mediation is the writing of the agreement and the signing of the agreement by the parties.

Arbitration and its Procedures

A much more formal alternative dispute resolution system is called **arbitration.** In arbitration, disputing parties submit their dispute to a neutral third party, called an **arbitrator.** The parties authorize this arbitrator to make a decision that binds these parties and resolves their dispute. The act of referring a matter to arbitration is called **submission.** Submission to arbitration often occurs when the disputing parties agree to use this form of ADR. Such an agreement by the parties is a submission to **voluntary arbitration.** Generally, an agreement to submit an issue to arbitration is irrevocable, and a party that thinks the process is not going well cannot withdraw from the arbitration and resort to litigation. Another form of a submission occurs when a statute or court requires parties to arbitrate. This type of submission results in a **mandatory arbitration.**

After the submission, a hearing is conducted by the arbitrator or arbitrators. Both parties are allowed to present evidence and to argue their own points of view. Then a decision, known as an **award,** is handed down. In most states the arbitrator's award must be in writing. The award is valid as long as it settles the entire controversy and states which party is to pay the other a sum of money.

These topics are discussed in the following sections:

- Submissions
- Arbitrators
- Awards

5. SUBMISSIONS

Submission by contract occurs if the parties enter into an agreement to arbitrate an existing dispute. The arbitration agreement is the submission in this case. In addition, the parties may contractually agree to submit to arbitration all issues that may arise in the future. Submission in these circumstances occurs when a demand to arbitrate is served on the other party. This demand is either a notice that a matter is being referred to the arbitrator agreed upon by the parties or a demand that the matter be referred to arbitration.

Most state statutes authorizing voluntary arbitration require the agreement to arbitrate to be in writing. Since the goal of arbitration is to obtain a quick resolution of disputes, most statutes require submission within a stated time period, usually six months, after the dispute arises.

In the absence of a statute, the rights and duties of the parties to a submission are described and limited by their agreement. Parties that have contracted to arbitrate are not required to arbitrate any matters other than those they previously had agreed to arbitrate. Whether a particular dispute is arbitrable is a question for the court, although the parties may agree to arbitrate additional questions.

The issues submitted to arbitration, as framed in the submission, may be questions of fact, questions of law, or mixed questions of fact and law. They may include the interpretation of the arbitration agreement. Sometimes a dispute arises as to whether the parties have agreed to submit an issue to arbitration. In such a case, one party refuses to arbitrate and the other files suit to compel arbitration. The court hearing the case decides the issue of arbitrability but does not decide the basic issue between the parties. The case that follows explains the role of courts when the issue of arbitrability arises.

AT & T TECH., INC. V. COMMUNICATIONS WORKERS

106 S. CT. 1415 (1986)

A collective bargaining agreement covering telephone equipment installation workers provided for arbitration of differences arising over interpretation of the agreement. Article 9 provided that the employer was free to exercise certain management functions, including the hiring, placement, and termination of employees. Such issues were excluded from the arbitration clause, but Article 20 prescribed the order in which employees would be laid off when lack of work necessitated itself.

The employer laid off seventy-nine installers, and the union filed a grievance claiming that there was no lack of work and, therefore, that the layoffs violated Article 20. The employer refused to submit the grievance to arbitration on the ground that un-

der Article 9 the layoffs were not arbitrable. The union then sought to compel arbitration by filing suit in federal district court. That court found that the union's interpretation of Article 20 was at least "arguable" and that it was for the arbitrator, not the court, to decide whether that interpretation had merit; accordingly, it ordered the petitioner to arbitrate. The court of appeals affirmed. The employer's petition for a writ of certiorari was granted.

WHITE, J.: . . . The issue presented in this case is whether a court asked to order arbitration of a grievance filed under a collective-bargaining agreement must first determine that the parties intended to

[CONTINUED]

arbitrate the dispute, or whether that determination is properly left to the arbitrator.

The principles necessary to decide this case are not new. They were set out by this Court over 25 years ago in a series of cases known as the *Steelworkers Trilogy*. These precepts have served the industrial relations community well, and have led to continued reliance on arbitration, rather than strikes or lockouts, as the preferred method of resolving disputes arising during the term of a collective-bargaining agreement. We see no reason either to question their continuing validity, or to eviscerate their meaning by creating an exception to their general applicability.

The first principle gleaned from the *Trilogy* is that "arbitration is a matter of contract and a party cannot be required to submit to arbitration any dispute which he has not agreed so to submit." This axiom recognizes the fact that arbitrators derive their authority to resolve disputes only because the parties have agreed in advance to submit such grievances to arbitration.

The second rule, which follows inexorably from the first, is that the question of arbitrability— whether a collective-bargaining agreement creates a duty for the parties to arbitrate the particular grievance—is undeniably an issue for judicial determination. Unless the parties clearly and unmistakably provide otherwise, the question of whether the parties agreed to arbitrate is to be decided by the court, not the arbitrator. . . .

The third principle derived from our prior cases is that, in deciding whether the parties have agreed to submit a particular grievance to arbitration, a court is not to rule on the potential merits of the underlying claims. Whether "arguable" or not, indeed even if it appears to the court to be frivolous, the union's claim that the employer has violated the collective-bargaining agreement is to be decided, not by the court asked to order arbitration, but as the parties have agreed, by the arbitrator. The courts, therefore, have no business weighing the merits of the grievance, considering whether there is equity in a particular claim, or determining whether there is particular language in the written instrument which will support the claim. The agreement is to submit all grievances to arbitration, not merely those which the court will deem meritorious.

Finally, where it has been established that where the contract contains an arbitration clause, there is a presumption of arbitrability in the sense that "[a]n order to arbitrate the particular grievance should not be denied unless it may be said with positive assurance that the arbitration clause is not susceptible of an interpretation that covers the asserted dispute. Doubts should be resolved in favor of coverage." Such a presumption is particularly applicable where the clause is as broad as the one employed in this case, which provides for arbitration of "any differences arising with respect to the interpretation of this contract or the performance of any obligation hereunder. . . ."

This presumption of arbitrability for labor disputes recognizes the greater institutional competence of arbitrators in interpreting collective-bargaining agreements, furthers the national labor policy of peaceful resolution of labor and thus best accords with the parties' presumed objectives in pursuing collective bargaining. The willingness of parties to enter into agreements that provide for arbitration of specified disputes would be "drastically reduced," however, if a labor arbitrator had the "power to determine his own jurisdiction. . . ." Were this the applicable rule, an arbitrator would not be constrained to resolve only those disputes that the parties have agreed in advance to settle by arbitration, but instead, would be empowered "to impose obligations outside the contract limited only by his understanding and conscience." This result undercuts the longstanding federal policy of promoting industrial harmony through the use of collective-bargaining agreements, and is antithetical to the function of a collective-bargaining agreement as setting out the rights and duties of the parties.

With these principles in mind, it is evident that the Seventh Circuit erred in ordering the parties to arbitrate the arbitrability question. It is the court's duty to interpret the agreement and to determine whether the parties intended to arbitrate grievances concerning layoffs predicated on a "lack of work" determination by the Company. If the court determines that the agreement so provides, then it is for the arbitrator to determine the relative merits of the parties' substantive interpretations of the agreement. It was for the court, not the arbitrator, to decide in the first instance whether the dispute was to be resolved through arbitration. . . .

[CONTINUED]

The issue in the case is whether, because of express exclusion or other forceful evidence, the dispute over the interpretation of Article 20 of the contract, the lay-off provision, is not subject to the arbitration clause. That issue should have been decided by the District Court and reviewed by the Court of Appeals; it should not have been referred to the arbitrator.

The judgment of the Court of Appeals is vacated, and the case is remanded for proceedings in conformity with this opinion.

It is so ordered.

CASE QUESTIONS

1. How do the provisions of Articles 9 and 20 in the collective bargaining agreement create a conflict between the employer and the union?

2. What three principles (or rules) does the Supreme Court discuss concerning the issue of when a dispute is arbitrable?

3. Why does the Supreme Court conclude that the trial court and the circuit court of appeals were in error?

6. ARBITRATORS

Arbitrators generally are chosen by the disputing parties. A provision in the agreement to arbitrate or in the statute that requires the arbitration describes how the arbitrator is selected. Of concern in the selection process are the expertise of the arbitrator and the number of arbitrators to be chosen.

Expertise   One reason arbitration is frequently preferable to litigation is the use of an expert to resolve the dispute. Appraisers can be used to decide disputes about the value of real estate, medical doctors can be used to decide health care disputes, and academicians can be used to decide issues within their area of expertise.

This use of experts is especially important in labor-management relations. Arbitration is the technique used in collective-bargaining contracts to settle grievances of employees against their employers. Arbitration is able to resolve disputes arising out of labor contracts without resorting to judicial intervention. It is quick and efficient and minimizes disruption in the workplace. Labor arbitration has attracted a large number of experts—both lawyers and academicians.

Arbitration provides for decision making by experts with experience in the particular industry and with knowledge of the customs and practices of the particular work site. Parties often choose arbitrators based on their knowledge of the "common law of the shop." They expect the arbitrator to look beyond strictly legal criteria to other factors that bear on the proper resolution of a dispute. These factors may include the effect upon productivity of a particular result, its consequences to the morale of the shop, and whether tensions will be heightened or diminished. The ablest judge usually does not bring the same experience and competence to bear upon the determination of a grievance, because the judge cannot be as informed as the expert arbitrator.

Number Chosen Another issue relates to the number of arbitrators to hear a dispute. It is common to use one arbitrator who is considered objective and impartial. Any person the disputing parties agree upon can be an arbitrator. There are no licensing requirements an arbitrator must satisfy. However, an arbitrator often is chosen from a list of qualified arbitrators provided by the American Arbitration Association. The disputing parties are not limited to the list unless they have agreed to make their selection from this list.

It is also common to have a panel of three arbitrators. In such cases, each party selects an arbitrator and the two so selected choose a third. It is not surprising that when this procedure is used, allegations of bias are often made by the losing party. Courts generally do not allow such allegations to form a basis for overturning a panel's award unless there is evidence of overt corruption or misconduct in the arbitration proceedings. Since such evidence usually is difficult to obtain, allegations of bias normally do not impact the results of arbitration.

Authority over Certain Matters What arbitrators have authority to decide has been a topic of controversy and litigation. The following case attempts to clarify whose responsibility it is to decide preliminary matters prior to the actual arbitration. You should read this case as a clarification of the *AT & T* case in the preceding section.

HOWSAM V. DEAN WITTER REYNOLDS, INC.

123 S. CT. 588 (2002)

Karen Howsam was an investment client of Dean Witter Reynolds, Inc. Between 1986 and 1994, Howsam bought interests in four limited partnerships. She claims that Dean Witter misrepresented the attributes of these investments. Howsam's claim is subject to the arbitration clause of the Client Service Agreement. To pursue her claim, Howsam chose to use the National Association of Securities Dealers (NASD) arbitration process. The NASD's Uniform Submission Agreement states that no dispute over six years old may be arbitrated. Prior to the arbitration, Dean Witter filed a lawsuit asking the District Court to declare the dispute is more than six years old and thus not eligible for arbitration. The District Judge declined to enjoin the arbitration concluding the arbitrator is authorized to determine the applicable statute of limitations. Dean Witter appealed, and the Tenth Circuit Court

of Appeals reversed. Howsam petitioned for a writ of certiorari, and it was granted.

BREYER, J.: . . . This Court has determined that arbitration is a matter of contract and a party cannot be required to submit to arbitration any dispute which he has not agreed so to submit. Although the Court has also long recognized and enforced a liberal federal policy favoring arbitration agreements, it has made clear that there is an exception to this policy: The question whether the parties have submitted a particular dispute to arbitration, i.e., the "question of arbitrability," is an issue for judicial determination unless the parties clearly and unmistakably provide otherwise. We must decide here whether application of the NASD time limit provision falls into the scope of this last-mentioned interpretive rule.

[CONTINUED]

Linguistically speaking, one might call any potentially dispositive gateway question a "question of arbitrability," for its answer will determine whether the underlying controversy will proceed to arbitration on the merits. The Court's case law, however, makes clear that, for purposes of applying the interpretive rule, the phrase "question of arbitrability" has a far more limited scope. The Court has found the phrase applicable in the kind of narrow circumstance where contracting parties would likely have expected a court to have decided the gateway matter, where they are not likely to have thought that they had agreed that an arbitrator would do so, and, consequently, where reference of the gateway dispute to the court avoids the risk of forcing parties to arbitrate a matter that they may well not have agreed to arbitrate.

Thus, a gateway dispute about whether the parties are bound by a given arbitration clause raises a "question of arbitrability" for a court to decide. Similarly, a disagreement about whether an arbitration clause in a concededly binding contract applies to a particular type of controversy is for the Court.

At the same time the Court has found the phrase "question of arbitrability" not applicable in other kinds of general circumstance where parties would likely expect that an arbitrator would decide the gateway matter. Thus procedural questions which grow out of the dispute and bear on its final disposition are presumptively not for the judge, but for an arbitrator, to decide. So, too, the presumption is that the arbitrator should decide allegations of waiver, delay, or a like defense to arbitrability. . . .

[W]e find that the applicability of the NASD time limit rule is a matter presumptively for the arbitrator, not for the judge. The time limit rule closely resembles the gateway questions that this Court has found not to be "questions of arbitrability." . . .

Moreover, the NASD arbitrators, comparatively more expert about the meaning of their own rule, are comparatively better able to interpret and to apply it. In the absence of any statement to the contrary in the arbitration agreement, it is reasonable to infer that the parties intended the agreement to reflect that understanding. . . .

We consequently conclude that the NASD's time limit rule falls within the class of gateway procedural disputes that do not present what our cases have called "questions of arbitrability." . . .

For these reasons, the judgment of the Tenth Circuit is

Reversed.

CASE QUESTIONS

1. When considering the roles of the judge and the arbitrator, who decides "questions of arbitrability"? Why?

2. How is a "question of arbitrability" distinct from "matters of gateway procedural disputes"?

3. In the Court's opinion, who makes the final decision on the statute of limitations that applies in an arbitration case?

7. AWARDS

Generally an arbitrator's award does not need to set forth findings of fact, conclusions of law, or the reasons for the award. However, a disclosure of findings and the reasons must be given if the applicable statute, arbitration agreement, or submission so requires. When the arbitrator does provide the basis for decision in the form of an opinion or letter, that document becomes a part of the award.

Because the parties themselves, by virtue of the submission, frame the issues to be resolved and define the scope of the arbitrator's powers, the parties are generally bound by the resulting award. A court will make every reasonable presumption in favor of the arbitration award and the arbitrator's acts and proceedings. The U.S. Supreme Court favors a broad scope of the arbitrators' authority. Restrictions on this authority will be allowed only when the disputing parties clearly state such limits.

An arbitrator's award is final on all issues submitted, and it will be enforced by the courts as if it were a judgment of the court. As is discussed in section 12, awards are not subject to judicial review on the merits of the decision. Only when fraud or other clearly inappropriate action by the arbitrator can be shown is a court willing to reverse the award granted in a voluntary arbitration proceeding.

After the award is made by the arbitrator, it is usually filed with the clerk of an appropriate court. If no objections are filed within a statutory period, it becomes final and enforceable, like a judgment.

POPULARITY OF ARBITRATION

Over the past eighty years, arbitration has played an increasingly important role in resolving business disputes. Historically, arbitration has been the most commonly used ADR system.

Arbitration may result when parties to a dispute agree to submit their disagreement to an arbitrator. Parties to a business contract may include an arbitration clause in their agreement in case a dispute arises. Legislation or courts may require particular types of dispute to be arbitrated.

Of particular importance in creating a positive perception and use of arbitration is the Federal Arbitration Act. This law is discussed in more detail in section 9 of this chapter. However, first you will be introduced to some general reasons parties often choose to arbitrate disputes. Sections 10 and 11 discuss specific types of arbitration and how they have contributed to the movement toward increased use of this ADR method. Finally, section 12 discusses the limited role courts exercise when reviewing arbitration procedures and awards.

8. REASONS TO ARBITRATE

The primary reason for the use of arbitration is the laudable goal of providing a relatively quick and inexpensive resolution of disputes. Arbitration not only helps the parties avoid the expense of litigation but also provides a means of avoiding the formalities of the courtroom. Formal pleadings, for example, and other procedural steps such as discovery and the rules of evidence are usually not used in an arbitration hearing.

Arbitration also serves to help ease congested court dockets. A primary function of arbitration is to serve as a substitute for and not a prelude to litigation. It is a private proceeding with no public record available to the press and others. Thus, by keeping their dispute private, adversaries may be more likely to preserve their business relationship.

Arbitration also has the advantage of submitting many disputes to experts for solutions. For example, if the issue involves whether a building has been properly constructed, the matter could be submitted to an architect for resolution. If it involves a technical accounting problem, it could be submitted to a certified public accountant. The Securities and Exchange Commission (SEC) has approved an arrangement whereby investors with complaints against securities dealers must submit them for arbitration to arbitrators assigned by the various stock exchanges and the National Association of Securities Dealers. These arbitrators are selected because they possess the special knowledge required to determine if a customer of a brokerage house has a legitimate complaint.

Arbitration is of special importance in labor relations, where it provides the grievance procedures under collective bargaining contracts. Arbitration is a means for industrial self-government, a system of private law for all problems that may arise in the workplace.

The table "Examples of Contracts with Arbitration Clauses" illustrates the growing importance and widespread use of arbitration as an alternative dispute resolution system.

9. THE FEDERAL ARBITRATION ACT

Prior to the enactment of the Federal Arbitration Act (FAA), our common law system preferred litigation over arbitration as a means of resolving disputes. In 1925, congressional enactment of the FAA began to change this presumed way of dispute resolution. However, it was not until after the revision and reenactment of the FAA in 1947 that courts began to encourage disputing parties to use arbitration instead of litigation. Clearly, the FAA changed public policy perceptions of arbitration and how states can regulate its use. These two impacts of the FAA are discussed now.

Impact on Policy   The FAA covers any arbitration clause in a contract that involves interstate commerce. Under it, courts are "rigorously" to enforce arbitration agreements. A court assumes arbitration was intended unless it can say with positive assurance that the arbitration clause was not intended to include the particular dispute. The federal policy clearly favors arbitration of commercial disputes. The FAA provides that arbitration agreements "shall be valid, irrevocable, and enforceable, save upon such grounds as exist at law or in equity for the revocation of any contract."

The U.S. Supreme Court, through its decisions, gives strong support to the use of arbitration. However, this deference is not absolute. In the following case, the Supreme Court discusses the reasons why arbitration clauses cannot be used to deny employees the right to litigate cases involving statutory protections.

Examples of Contracts with Arbitration Clauses

Stockbroker and client

Commodities broker and customer

Brokerage firm and employee

Attorney* and client

Union-management collective bargaining agreements

Owner-contractor and contractor-subcontractor

Insurance company and insured

Public carrier and shipper of goods

* Most bar associations require lawyers to arbitrate disputes with clients.

WRIGHT V. UNIVERSAL MARITIME SERVICE CORPORATION

119 S. CT. 391 (1998)

Caesar Wright, a longshoreman in Charleston, South Carolina, belonged to the International Long-shoremen's Association. This union assigned Wright work through a hiring hall process. Wright worked for several different companies represented by the South Carolina Stevedores Association (SCSA). The collective bargaining agreement (CBA) between the Longshoremen and the SCSA contained an arbitration clause covering all disputes affecting wages, hours, and other terms and conditions of employment. In 1992, Wright was injured while working, and he received permanent disability benefits. In January 1995, Wright attempted to return to work. When the hiring companies learned that Wright had received disability payments, they refused to hire him. When he inquired of the union about his rights, Wright was told to hire an attorney and sue rather than file for arbitration or grievance. Wright did sue the SCSA and six of its companies. The District Court ruled that Wright must submit his claim to arbitration. On appeal the Fourth Circuit affirmed. The Supreme Court granted certiorari.

SCALIA, J.: This case presents the question whether a general arbitration clause in a collective-bargaining agreement (CBA) requires an employee to use the arbitration procedure for an alleged violation of the Americans with Disabilities Act of 1990 (ADA). . . .

In this case, the Fourth Circuit concluded that the general arbitration provision in the CBA governing Wright's employment was sufficiently broad to en-compass a statutory claim arising under the ADA, and that such a provision was enforceable. The latter conclusion brings into question two lines of our case law. The first is represented by *Alexander v. Gardner-Denver Co.,* 94 S. Ct. 1011 (1974), which held that an employee does not forfeit his right to a judicial forum for claimed discriminatory discharge in violation of Title VII of the Civil Rights Act of 1964, if "he first pursues his grievance to final arbitration under the nondiscrimination clause of a collective-bargaining agreement." In rejecting the argument that the doctrine of election of remedies barred the Title VII lawsuit, we reasoned that a grievance is designed to vindicate a "contractual right" under a CBA, while a lawsuit under Title VII asserts "independent statutory rights accorded by Congress." The statutory cause of action was not waived by the union's agreement to the arbitration provision of the CBA, since "there can be no prospective waiver of an employee's rights under Title VII." We have followed the holding of *Gardner-Denver* in deciding the effect of CBA arbitration upon employee claims under other statutes.

The second line of cases implicated here is represented by *Gilmer v. Interstate/Johnson Lane Corp.,* 111 S. Ct. 1647 (1991), which held that a claim brought under the Age Discrimination in Employment Act of 1967 (ADEA), could be subject to compulsory arbitration pursuant to an arbitration provision in a securities registration form. Relying upon the federal policy favoring arbitration embodied in the Federal Arbitration Act (FAA), we said that "statutory claims may be the subject of an arbitration agreement, enforceable pursuant to the FAA."

. . . The dispute in the present case . . . ultimately concerns not the application or interpretation of any CBA, but the meaning of a federal statute. The cause of action Wright asserts arises not out of contract, but out of the ADA, and is distinct from any right conferred by the collective bargaining agreement. . . . Not only is petitioner's statutory claim not subject to a presumption of arbitrability; we think any CBA requirement to arbitrate it must be particularly clear. . . .

Gardner-Denver at least stands for the proposition that the right to a federal judicial forum is of sufficient importance to be protected against less-than-explicit union waiver in a CBA. The CBA in this case does not meet that standard. Its arbitration clause is very general, providing for arbitration of "matters under dispute," which could be understood to mean matters in dispute under the con-

[CONTINUED]

tract. And the remainder of the contract contains no explicit incorporation of statutory antidiscrimination requirements. . . . The Fourth Circuit relied upon the fact that the equivalently broad arbitration clause in *Gilmer*—applying to "any dispute, claim or controversy"—was held to embrace federal statutory claims. But *Gilmer* involved an individual's waiver of his own rights, rather than a union's waiver of the rights of represented employees—and hence the "clear and unmistakable" standard was not applicable.

Respondents rely upon Clause 15(F) of the CBA, which states that "this Agreement is intended to cover all matters affecting wages, hours, and other terms and conditions of employment." But even if

this could, in isolation, be considered a clear and unmistakable incorporation of employment-discrimination laws (which is doubtful), it is surely deprived of that effect by the provision, later in the same paragraph, that "anything not contained in this Agreement shall not be construed as being part of this Agreement." . . .

We hold that the collective-bargaining agreement in this case does not contain a clear and unmistakable waiver of the covered employees' rights to a judicial forum for federal claims of employment discrimination. . . . The judgment of the Fourth Circuit is vacated, and the case is remanded for further proceedings consistent with this opinion.

It is so ordered.

CASE QUESTIONS

1. What is the statutory claim involved in this case?
2. Why did Caesar Wright choose to sue rather than arbitrate?

3. What are the two differing lines of cases discussed by the Supreme Court?
4. How does the Court resolve the differences in these precedents?

The Supreme Court continues to search for the proper balance between encouraging arbitration and allowing access to the court system. When legislation clearly grants the disputing parties the right to litigate claims, arbitration clauses signed by these parties do not prevent access to the courts. The following box describes a recent case.

DO AGREEMENTS TO ARBITRATE LIMIT THE EEOC'S REMEDIES?

The Equal Employment Opportunity Commission (EEOC) has authority to bring enforcement actions against employers whenever the EEOC believes illegal discrimination has occurred. An employee of Waffle House was discharged from employment because he had a seizure at work. This employee did not pursue the contractual remedy of arbitration; however, he did file a complaint with the EEOC. His complaint alleged Waffle House fired him because of his disability. After investigating the factual situation, the EEOC filed a lawsuit against Waffle House in federal district court. Waffle House sought to have the suit dismissed since the remedy provided by the employment contract was arbitration, and the

employee did not seek arbitration. Waffle House argues that the EEOC takes the place of the employee and therefore cannot avoid the requirement of arbitration.

The Supreme Court reviews the legislative history of the EEOC by examining the Civil Rights Act of 1964, the Equal Employment Opportunity Act of 1972, and the Civil Rights Act of 1991. The Court finds that the EEOC can be a plaintiff in its own right and not simply a representative of an aggrieved employee. Due to the authority given to the EEOC, it can pursue court-ordered victim-specific relief, such as backpay, reinstatement, and damages for violations involving discrimination without first resorting to arbitration.

Source: *Equal Employment Opportunity Commission v. Waffle House, Inc.,* 122 S. Ct. 754 (2002).

Impact on State Laws The federal policy favoring arbitration frequently conflicts with state laws favoring litigation as the means to resolve a dispute. Sometimes a state law specifically provides that designated matters are not to be submitted to arbitration. Are these state laws constitutional when applied to businesses engaged in interstate commerce? The Commerce Clause and the Supremacy Clause of the United States Constitution are often used to set aside such state laws that deny arbitration of certain disputes.

10. STATUTORILY MANDATED ARBITRATION

Another reason why arbitration has become more widespread during the last few decades is because legislation may require disputing parties to submit to arbitration. A growing number of states have adopted statutes that require mandatory arbitration for certain types of disputes. Those whose disputes fall within the boundaries of the mandatory arbitration statute must submit the dispute to arbitration prior to being allowed to litigate. On the basis of studies showing that a dispute requiring three days for resolution before a 12-person jury takes only two to four hours for resolution by an arbitrator, the mandatory arbitration statute is clearly a viable alternative for controlling court congestion.

The arbitrators in the mandatory arbitration process are retired judges and practicing lawyers, usually experienced trial attorneys. A list of eligible arbitrators is maintained by court officials in charge of the mandatory process. Although the parties may agree on using only one arbitrator, mandatory arbitration cases are usually presented to a panel of three. Arbitrators are paid a per-diem fee. The parties involved in the arbitration are responsible for paying these costs.

Types of Cases Mandatory arbitration statutes cover only a few types of cases. A typical statute might apply the procedure to claims exclusively for money of a small amount, such as those for less than $15,000, not including interest and costs. Some statutes require arbitration of specific subject matter, like issues arising out of divorces. In addition, arbitration is required only in those cases in which a party has demanded a jury trial, as it can be assumed that a judge hearing a case is basically as efficient as an arbitrator.

Procedures Mandatory arbitration, while requiring substantially less time than litigation, does not necessarily provide speedy justice. The usual procedure for a claim filed in court that is covered by the mandatory arbitration law is to place the claim in the arbitration track at time of filing. At this time the date and time of hearing is assigned, typically eight months from the date of filing.

Discovery procedures may be used prior to the hearing on arbitration. Since no discovery is permitted after the hearing without permission of the court, an early and thorough degree of preparation is necessary to achieve a full hearing on the merits of the controversy. This preparation also prevents the hearing from being used as an opportunity to discover the adversary's case en route to an eventual trial. Most discovery is by interrogatories rather than by deposition.

The arbitrators have the power to determine the admissibility of evidence and to decide the law and the facts of the case. Rulings on objections to evidence or on other issues that arise during the hearing are made by the arbitrators. States have different rules relating to the admissibility of evidence. In most states the established rules of evidence must be followed by the arbitrators. Several jurisdictions, however, do not require hearings to be conducted according to the established rules of evidence. New Jersey law, for example, provides: "The arbitrator shall admit all relevant evidence and shall not be bound by the rules of evidence." Other states leave to the discretion of the arbitrator the extent to which the rules of evidence apply.

11. VOLUNTARY/CONTRACT-BASED ARBITRATION

Although the statutes that mandate arbitration of certain types of disputes clearly have increased the use of this ADR method, the larger growth in the number of arbitration cases comes from disputing parties agreeing to arbitrate, not litigate. Recall that this agreement may be a part of a contract that anticipated possible disputes, or the agreement may be by disputing parties that wish to avoid all the expenses associated with the litigation process.

To encourage businesspeople to use voluntary arbitration, the goal of an efficient and affordable alternative to litigation must be achieved. When arbitration is as expensive and time-consuming as litigation, the attractiveness of the ADR system declines. Often, an arbitration clause does not specify the cost of the process. The following case describes a situation wherein the courts are asked to decide the impact of not specifying the costs of arbitration.

GREEN TREE FINANCIAL CORP. V. RANDOLPH

121 S. CT. 513 (2000)

Larketta Randolph purchased a mobile home and financed it through the Green Tree Financial Corporation. One condition of this financing arrangement was Randolph having to purchase insurance to protect Green Tree from the expense of repossession should that become necessary. The contract between Green Tree and Randolph provided that any disputes arising from the relationship would be referred to arbitration. Randolph filed a lawsuit in federal district court alleging Truth-in-Lending Act (TILA) and Equal Credit Opportunity Act violations. Green Tree successfully sought to dismiss this suit and to have the court order arbitration. Randolph appealed, and the Eleventh Circuit Court of Appeals found "the arbitration agreement was silent with respect to payment of filing fees, arbitrators' costs, and other arbitration expenses." The Court of Appeals ruled that the arbitration clause was unenforceable since it posed a

risk that Randolph would not be able to afford to protect her interests through arbitration. Green Tree petitioned for a writ of certiorari, and it was granted.

REHNQUIST, C. J.: . . . We . . . turn to the question whether Randolph's agreement to arbitrate is unenforceable because it says nothing about the costs of arbitration, and thus fails to provide her protection from potentially substantial costs of pursuing her federal statutory claims in the arbitral forum. . . . In considering whether respondent's agreement to arbitrate is unenforceable, we are mindful of the FAA's purpose to reverse the longstanding judicial hostility to arbitration agreements and to place arbitration agreements upon the same footing as other contracts.

In light of that purpose, we have recognized that federal statutory claims can be appropriately

[CONTINUED]

resolved through arbitration, and we have enforced agreements to arbitrate that involve such claims. We have likewise rejected generalized attacks on arbitration that rest on suspicion of arbitration as a method of weakening the protections afforded in the substantive law to would-be complainants. These cases demonstrate that even claims arising under a statute designed to further important social policies may be arbitrated because so long as the prospective litigant effectively may vindicate his or her statutory cause of action in the arbitral forum, the statute serves its functions.

In determining whether statutory claims may be arbitrated, we first ask whether the parties agreed to submit their claims to arbitration, and then ask whether Congress has evinced an intention to preclude a waiver of judicial remedies for the statutory rights at issue. In this case, it is undisputed that the parties agreed to arbitrate all claims relating to their contract, including claims involving statutory rights. Nor does Randolph contend that the TILA evinces an intention to preclude a waiver of judicial remedies. She contends instead that the arbitration agreement's silence with respect to costs and fees creates a "risk" that she will be required to bear prohibitive arbitration costs if she pursues her claims in an arbitral forum, and thereby forces her to forgo any claims she may have against petitioners. Therefore, she argues, she is unable to vindicate her statutory rights in arbitration.

It may well be that the existence of large arbitration costs could preclude a litigant such as Randolph from effectively vindicating her federal statutory rights in the arbitral forum. But the record does not show that Randolph will bear such costs if she goes to arbitration. Indeed, it contains hardly any information on the matter. As the Court of Appeals recognized, we lack information about how claimants fare under Green Tree's arbitration clause. The record reveals only the arbitration agreement's silence on the subject, and that fact alone is plainly insufficient to render it unenforceable. The "risk" that Randolph will be saddled with prohibitive costs is too speculative to justify the invalidation of an arbitration agreement.

To invalidate the agreement on that basis would undermine the liberal federal policy favoring arbitration agreements. It would also conflict with our prior holdings that the party resisting arbitration bears the burden of proving that the claims at issue are unsuitable for arbitration. We have held that the party seeking to avoid arbitration bears the burden of establishing that Congress intended to preclude arbitration of the statutory claims at issue. Similarly, we believe that where, as here, a party seeks to invalidate an arbitration agreement on the ground that arbitration would be prohibitively expensive, that party bears the burden of showing the likelihood of incurring such costs. Randolph did not meet that burden. How detailed the showing of prohibitive expense must be before the party seeking arbitration must come forward with contrary evidence is a matter we need not discuss; for in this case neither during discovery nor when the case was presented on the merits was there any timely showing at all on the point. The Court of Appeals therefore erred in deciding that the arbitration agreement's silence with respect to costs and fees rendered it unenforceable.

Reversed.

CASE QUESTIONS

1. Why did Randolph file a lawsuit against Green Tree rather than pursue her claim through arbitration?

2. What is the basis of the Court of Appeals' ruling that the arbitration clause in the Randolph-Green Tree contract is unenforceable?

3. What is the ruling of the Supreme Court with respect to the Court of Appeals' decision? Why did the Court rule that way?

12. JUDICIAL REVIEW

The arbitration process is less time consuming and less costly than litigation only if the parties are limited in seeking judicial review of the arbitrators' awards. From this perspective, voluntary arbitration is a more effective alternative to litigation than mandatory arbitration. The following subsections discuss the extent of judicial review of awards depending on the type of arbitration.

Review of Voluntary/Contract-Based Arbitration Awards Generally, the award resulting from the voluntary arbitration procedure is judged as final. The arbitrator's findings on questions of both fact and law are conclusive. The judicial review of an arbitrator's award is quite restricted and is more limited than the appellate review of a trial court's decision.

Arbitration clauses are liberally interpreted when the issue contested is the scope of the clause. If the scope of an arbitration clause is debatable or reasonably in doubt, the clause is construed in favor of arbitration.

The fact that the arbitrator made erroneous rulings during the hearing, or reached erroneous findings of fact from the evidence, is no ground for setting aside the award because the parties have agreed that he or she should be the judge of the facts. An erroneous view of the law no matter how egregious is binding because the parties have agreed to accept the arbitrator's view of the law. Error of law renders the award void only when it would require the parties to commit a crime or otherwise to violate a positive mandate of the law. Courts do not interfere with an award by examining the merits of the controversy, the sufficiency of the evidence supporting the award, or the reasoning supporting the decision. Were it otherwise, arbitration would fail in its chief purpose: to preclude the need for litigation. Instead of being a substitute for litigation, arbitration would merely be the beginning of litigation. Broad judicial review on the merits would render arbitration wasteful and superfluous.

Judicial review can correct fraudulent or arbitrary actions by an arbitrator. Further, courts of review are sometimes called upon to set aside an award when the decision is allegedly against public policy. In such cases, the reviewing court must establish that an arbitration award is contrary to the public policy which arises from laws and legal precedents. A reviewing court cannot reject an award simply because that court bases public policy on general considerations of presumed public interests. In essence, the scope of review by courts of an arbitrator's award in a voluntary/contract-based arbitration is extremely limited, as discussed in the next box.

Review of Statutorily Mandated Arbitration Although a party may voluntarily consent to almost any restriction upon or deprivation of a right, a similar restriction or deprivation, when compelled by government, must be in accord with procedural and substantive due process of law. Therefore, a higher level of judicial review of an arbitration award is warranted where the arbitration is statutorily mandated.

Laws providing for mandatory arbitration are subject to numerous constitutional challenges. Many courts have generally held that mandatory arbitration statutes that effectively close the courts to the litigants by compelling them to resort to arbitrators for a final and binding determination are void as against public policy and are unconstitutional in that they:

1. Deprive one of property and liberty of contract without due process of law
2. Violate the litigant's Seventh Amendment right to a jury trial and/or the state's constitutional access to courts' provisions

JUDICIAL REVIEW OF ARBITRATOR'S AWARD

Can a judge reject an arbitrator's factual findings and award and substitute a decision by that judge? This is the issue that the Supreme Court resolved in a case involving major league baseball. Steve Garvey sought damages of $3,000,000 after his contract with the San Diego Padres was not extended because of the team's alleged collusion with other teams. This collusion was supposedly in violation of the Major League Baseball Players Association collective bargaining agreement with the various Major League baseball clubs.

Garvey's claim was submitted to arbitration, and the arbitrator denied the claim stating that Garvey had failed to establish proof of the fact that his contract was not extended because of collusion. Garvey sought review at the district court level, and that judge denied Garvey's motion to set aside the arbitrator's award. Garvey appealed to the Ninth Circuit Court of Appeals. This court of appeals reversed the district court's decision, vacated the arbitrator's award, and decided the case on the basis of record established by the arbitrator.

The Supreme Court reversed the decision of the court of appeals. It held when a court finds that the arbitrator made a mistake, that court should vacate the award and remand the matter to the arbitrator for further arbitration proceedings. The court should not resolve the merits of the parties' dispute.

Source: *Major League Baseball Players Association v. Garvey*, 121 S. Ct. 1724 (2001).

3. Result in the unconstitutional delegation of legislative or judicial power in violation of state constitutional separation-of-powers provisions

Mandatory arbitration may be constitutional, however, if fair procedures are provided by the legislature and ultimate judicial review is available. Courts throughout the United States have uniformly upheld mandatory arbitration statutory schemes as against the constitutional challenges previously mentioned where a dissatisfied party can reject the arbitrator's award and seek a ***de novo* judicial review** of that award. *De novo* review means that the court tries the issues anew as if no arbitration occurred.

In mandatory arbitrations, a record of proceedings is required. Also, findings of fact and conclusions of law are essential if there is to be enough judicial review to satisfy due process. Judicial review of mandatory arbitration requires a *de novo* review of the interpretation and application of the law by the arbitrators.

The right to reject the award and to proceed to trial is the sole remedy of a party dissatisfied with the award. In a sense, the award is an intermediate step in resolving the dispute if the trial itself is desired. The right to reject the award exists without regard to the basis for the rejection. Many jurisdictions authorize fee and cost sanctions to be imposed on parties who fail to improve their positions at the trial as compared to the arbitration. It is hoped that the quality of the arbitrators, the integrity of the proceedings, and the fairness of the awards will keep the number of rejections to a minimum.

The failure of a party to be present, either in person or by counsel, at an arbitration constitutes a waiver of the right to reject the award and seek *de novo* judicial review. In essence, a party's lack of participation operates as a consent to the entry by the court of a judgment on the award. Since the procedure of mandatory-court-annexed arbitration is an integral part of the judicial process of dispute resolution, its process must be utilized either to resolve the dispute or as the obligatory step prior to resolution by trial. To allow any party to ignore the arbitration would permit a mockery of this deliberate attempt to achieve an expeditious and less costly resolution of private controversies.

Review under the Federal Arbitration Act If the arbitration is conducted pursuant to state statute, that statute must be consulted to determine what, if any, grounds are available to challenge an award in court. In cases that involve interstate commerce issues, the provisions of the Federal Arbitration Act control.

Section 10 of the Federal Arbitration Act provides that an arbitration award may be vacated or set aside on any one of four grounds:

(a) Where the award was procured by corruption, fraud, or other undue means

(b) Where the arbitrators were obviously partial or corrupt

(c) Where the arbitrators were guilty of misconduct in refusing to postpone the hearing, upon sufficient cause shown or in refusing to hear evidence pertinent and material to the controversy or of any other misbehavior by which the rights of any party have been prejudiced

(d) Where the arbitrators exceeded their powers or so imperfectly executed them that a mutual, final, and definite award upon the subject matter submitted was not made

As set forth in subsection (a), the Federal Arbitration Act provides that an award can be vacated if it can be proved that it was procured by "corruption, fraud, or other undue means." "Undue means" goes beyond the merely inappropriate or inadequate nature of the evidence and refers to some aspect of the arbitrator's decision or decision-making process obtained in some manner that was unfair and beyond the normal process contemplated by the arbitration act. The courts tend to interpret "undue means" in conjunction with the terms "corruption" and "fraud" which precede it, and thus, "undue means" requires some type of bad faith in the procurement of the award.

When the disputing parties each choose an arbitrator and these arbitrators choose a third to make up a three-person panel, the disputing parties may be inclined to charge that the arbitrator chosen by the parties is partial or corrupt. Under subsection (b), the use of "partial or corrupt" in the FAA is interpreted to mean that an arbitrator lacks the ability to consider evidence and to reach a fair conclusion.

Subsection (c) covers arbitral misconduct. The concept of arbitral "misconduct" does not lend itself to a precise definition. Among the actions that have been found to constitute such misconduct on the part of an arbitrator as would warrant vacating an arbitration award are the following:

1. Participation in communications with a party or a witness without the knowledge or consent of the other party

2. Receipt of evidence as to a material fact without notice to a party

3. Holding hearings or conducting deliberations in the absence of a member of an arbitration panel or rendering an award without consulting a panel member

4. Undertaking an independent investigation into a material matter after the close of hearings and without notice to the parties

5. Accepting gifts or other hospitality from a party during the proceedings

An award may likewise be set aside on the basis of procedural error by an arbitration panel if, for instance, the panel arbitrarily denies a reasonable request for postponement of a hearing or commits an egregious evidentiary error, such as refusing to hear material evidence or precluding a party's efforts to develop a full record.

Finally, subsection (d), involving the question of whether the arbitrators exceeded their power, relates to the arbitrability of the underlying dispute. An

arbitrator exceeds his or her powers and authority when he or she attempts to resolve an issue that is not arbitrable because it is outside the scope of the arbitration
agreement. Conversely, if the issues presented to the arbitrators are within the
scope of the arbitration agreement, subsection (d) does not require the court to review the merits of every construction of the contract.

---

concept SUMMARY   *Voluntary versus Mandatory Arbitration*

	Voluntary	**Mandatory Arbitration**
Submission	Based on parties' agreement after dispute arises or on contract clause before dispute arises.	Required by statute.
Procedures	Since process is not tied to a court, it is quick, informal, often with no discovery, and not bound by rules of evidence.	The procedure is associated with a court's supervision; discovery usually is done, and many states require arbitrators to follow the formal rules of evidence.
Review of award	The award is final with no judicial review, unless a party can prove that the arbitrator engaged in fraudulent, arbitrary, or other inappropriate actions.	The court will conduct a *de novo* hearing as if the arbitration process had not occurred.

OTHER ALTERNATIVES

Your study of the preceding material on arbitration hopefully leaves you with the
impression that, although arbitration is more efficient (less time consuming and expensive) than litigation, arbitration often is not a simple process. To avoid even the
costs of arbitration, some disputes can be resolved through other ADR techniques
that utilize aspects of the litigation process. Such techniques are discussed now.

13. COMBINATION OF ADR SYSTEMS

The benefit of flexibility related to mediation allows parties to utilize this process
in conjunction with other dispute resolution systems. For example, in the middle
of heated litigation, parties can agree to mediate just one issue. The resolution of
one issue may help the litigation of the remaining issues proceed in a more efficient manner.

One of the more popular variations has given rise to what some people are calling an additional ADR technique. This variation involves the mediation of a dispute. The parties resolve all the matters of contention that they can and they agree
to arbitrate the unresolved matters. This variation has become known as **Med-Arb.**
The opportunities to use mediation in beneficial ways are limited only by the creativity of the parties involved.

Some laws encourage the parties to be creative in utilizing ADR systems. For
example, the Magnuson-Moss Warranty Act provides that if a business adopts an
informal dispute resolution system to handle complaints about its product warranties, then a customer cannot sue the manufacturer or seller for breach of warranty without first going through the informal procedures. This law does not deny

consumers the right to sue, nor does it compel a compromise solution. It simply allows a manufacturer to require mediation, for instance, before the complaining consumer can litigate.

14. MOCK TRIALS

Recognizing that a jury's function is to determine the facts, attorneys are using a technique called a **mock trial,** in some very significant cases. The attorneys assemble a group of citizens and present their evidence. This group then deliberates and makes findings. This dress rehearsal gives attorneys insight into possible jury reaction to the evidence and points up weaknesses in the case. Sometimes issues are tested without introducing evidence. Lawyers argue the case on the basis of assumed facts to the mock jury for a few hours, and this jury returns a verdict.

The verdicts often cause plaintiffs to take a more realistic view of the damages to which they think they are entitled. This "reality test" helps disputing parties to engage in more meaningful negotiations. Through such negotiations, these parties often settle their dispute without having to go through the formal process of either a trial or an arbitration.

15. MINITRIALS

A **minitrial** is designed to achieve substantial savings in litigation costs and in the time that senior executives have to spend in resolving disputes. The minitrial is designed to turn a lawsuit back into a business problem. In a minitrial, lawyers focus on the central issues. They present an abbreviated case not to a judge or jury, but to top executives of the disputing companies. Following these presentations, the executives meet without their lawyers to negotiate and to seek a settlement. After hearing from both sides, these executives are able to appreciate the merits and risks of their case. It is this balanced perspective that leads to speedy, economical settlements.

The results from minitrials are often quick. The process is confidential, and the results are invariably better than the results of litigation. Since executives know their business objectives and operations, they can consider options that their lawyers—and certainly the judges and juries—cannot. A minitrial can preserve business relationships that are usually destroyed in the acrimony of litigation.

A MINITRIAL'S SUCCESS

An actual minitrial between two companies illustrates the value of the process. Their dispute centered on the interpretation of a contract that was 20 years old. Instead of filing a lawsuit, conducting discovery that would include the production of countless documents, the legal counsels conducted a minitrial. Executives met in a hotel and heard three hours of presentations by both lawyers. Technical experts for each side also participated. Following this presentation, the executives met alone to discuss the dispute. Before dinner, they reached an agreement to settle their dispute.

The attorneys pinpointed the essentials of the dispute, enabling the executives to focus on the basic business interests involved. The executives had a clear understanding of the strengths and weaknesses of their case, and their expertise was productive in reaching a solution. Because the executives had the power to settle, they were able to reach a firm agreement in one day.

Minitrials are successful. They avoid lengthy trials, reduce legal costs, save management time for productive pursuits, and achieve satisfactory settlements. An American Bar Association survey of minitrials showed an 85 percent success rate. Speed, economy, and flexibility were cited as benefits. Even when the negotiators failed to settle immediately, the minitrial process invariably led to a settlement. Today, corporate policy of many large corporations requires the use of ADRs in all major disputes with other corporations.

KEY TERMS

Arbitration 122	Minitrial 139
Arbitrator 122	Mock trial 139
Award 122	Negotiated settlement 116
Caucus 122	Positional bargaining 117
De novo judicial review 136	Principled interest-based negotiations
Mandatory arbitration 122	118
Med-Arb 138	Submission 122
Mediation 120	Voluntary arbitration 122
Mediator 120	

REVIEW QUESTIONS AND PROBLEMS

Negotiated Settlements

1. *Position-Based Negotiations*

   In business disputes, what two items are most likely to dominate a position-based negotiation?

2. *Interest-Based Negotiations*

   (a)   Summarize the seven elements of principled interest-based negotiations.

   (b)   How does focusing on these elements assist the negotiation process?

Mediation

3. *Advantages/Disadvantages*

   (a)   How is mediation fundamentally different from an arbitration?

   (b)   What are some of the advantages and disadvantages of the mediation process?

4. *Procedures*

   What steps usually are followed to ensure an effective mediation? Explain.

Arbitration and its Procedures

5. *Submissions*

   (a)   What is the purpose of a submission in an arbitration?

   (b)   What is the proper role of the courts in determining whether a submission to arbitrate is valid?

6. *Arbitrators*

While conducting an arbitration hearing, an arbitrator allowed laypersons to testify about the cause of injuries to the claimant. The arbitrator awarded dollar damages to be paid to this claimant. May the losing party have this award set aside on the basis that nonexpert testimony was allowed? Why or why not?

7. *Awards*

Generally, what does an arbitrator have to include in the award to make it valid?

Popularity of Arbitration

8. *Reasons to Arbitrate*

List three reasons why arbitration may be a better way to resolve disputes than litigation.

9. *The Federal Arbitration Act*

(a)   A dispute arose between partners. The partnership agreement provided that if the parties were unable to agree on any matter, it would be submitted to arbitration. One partner filed suit asking a court to appoint a receiver for the business. The other insisted on arbitration. How will the dispute be resolved? Why?

(b)   What impact does the FAA have on state laws that prefer the litigation process to arbitration?

10. *Statutorily Mandated Arbitration*

(a)   What is meant by the phrase *statutorily mandated arbitration*?

(b)   Is arbitration required in all cases? Why or why not?

11. *Voluntary/Contract-Based Arbitration*

How is voluntary/contract-based arbitration distinguished from statutorily-mandated arbitration?

12. *Judicial Review*

(a)   Explain why there are different standards of review of arbitration awards depending on whether the arbitration is voluntary or statutorily mandated.

(b)   Barbara and Cole, Inc., disputed the amount of money due as "minimum royalties" under a mineral lease. They submitted the dispute to arbitration, and the arbitrators awarded Barbara $37,214.67. The court held that there was no substantial evidence in the record to support an award of less than the minimum royalty of $75,000 and directed entry of a judgment for that amount. Was it proper for the court to increase the award? Why or why not?

Other Alternatives

13. *Combination of ADR Systems*

Describe how mediation can be used in conjunction with arbitration.

14. *Mock Trials*

What is the benefit to lawyers and parties of conducting a mock trial?

15. *Minitrials*

Describe how a minitrial may assist business executives in the efforts to settle disputes.

TERMINOLOGY REVIEW

For each term in the left-hand column, match the most appropriate description in the right-hand column.

1. Mock trial
2. Voluntary arbitration
3. Caucus
4. *De novo* hearing
5. Submission
6. Interest-based negotiation
7. Mediation
8. Award
9. Minitrial
10. Mandatory arbitration

a. The process involving a neutral third party who attempts to assist the disputing parties but who has no authority to impose a resolution
b. The decision of an arbitrator
c. The meeting between a mediator and only one of the disputing parties
d. The presentation of evidence to a group of citizens with their suggested verdict following
e. The process required when a statute provides for disputing parties to arbitrate
f. To try a case as if for the first time
g. The presentation of a case to business executives as a means of encouraging settlement
h. The contractual agreement of parties to submit any dispute to arbitration
i. A method of bargaining involving emphasis on seven elements
j. The act of referring a dispute to arbitration

BUSINESS DISCUSSION

Your employer, Let's-Get-It-Done, has a history of multiple employee disputes. These disputes range from claims of illegal discrimination to general complaints of worker dissatisfaction with supervisors. You have been assigned the task of changing the organization's culture. Since litigation is the typical method of resolving company disputes, you are considering alternatives to litigation.

What are possible alternative dispute resolution systems (ADRs)?

Should employees be required to sign a contract that an ADR method will be used before any lawsuit is filed against the organization?

THE CONSTITUTION AND BUSINESS

In both your personal and professional lives, you realize how much government at the federal, state, and local levels influences what you can and cannot do. For example, since your business employs more than 15 people, there are numerous federal statutes dictating the physical condition of the workplace, the amount you must pay your employees, the taxes you owe, and the paperwork you must file with regulatory agencies. At the state level, you know you have to obtain certain licenses to conduct business or to engage in recreational activities, such as fishing. And your local government regulates how you can use the land you own.

In light of this multitude of regulatory activity, you ask yourself the following questions:

By what authority do governmental entities impose various regulations?

Is there any limit to the extent such regulations impact our lives?

How can an individual or a business organization challenge the application of regulatory authorities?

I n this chapter, you will study several basic concepts or clauses that are found in the original Constitution. In particular, sections 1 to 7 cover these basic concepts. In latter parts of this chapter, you will study some of our fundamental freedoms as defined in the amendments to the Constitution. Sections 8 to 10 concentrate on aspects of the First Amendment. The Fourteenth Amendment's provisions are the focus of sections 11 to 12.

Through this material you should gain an appreciation of how the federal government's power to regulate business is created and how this power limits the extent of regulation by state and local governments. You will also gain an understanding that even the federal government's authority to regulate is restricted or limited by what we call constitutional protections.

Basic Concepts

The Constitution contains four concepts or clauses that are of great significance to the regulatory environment of business. They are the separation of powers concept, the supremacy clause, the contract clause, and the commerce clause. Each is discussed in the following sections.

1. SEPARATION OF POWERS

Our federal system of government is one in which the powers of government are separated horizontally and vertically. The horizontal division separates the power and functions among three equal branches of government—the legislative, the executive, and the judicial.

The vertical aspect of **separation of powers** is **federalism** or dual federalism. In a federal system there are two levels of government—a federal level and a state and local level. Each has a separate and distinct role to play. The federal government recognizes that it was created by the states and that states have some sovereignty. The Tenth Amendment reserves some powers to the states and to the people. Congress may not impair the ability of state government to function in the federal system. Likewise, state government may not limit the exercise of powers granted by states to the federal government.

2. SUPREMACY CLAUSE

In allocating power between federal and state levels of government, the Constitution makes it clear that the Constitution is supreme under all laws and that federal law is supreme over a state law or local ordinance. Under the **supremacy clause,** courts may be called upon to decide if a state law is invalid because it conflicts with a federal law. They must construe or interpret the two laws to see if they are in conflict. A conflict exists if the state statute would prevent or interfere with the accomplishment and execution of the full purposes and objectives of Congress.

It is immaterial that a state did not intend to frustrate the federal law if the state law in fact does so. For example, an Arizona statute provided for the suspension of licenses of drivers who could not satisfy judgments arising out of auto accidents, even if the driver was bankrupt. The statute was declared unconstitutional since it was in conflict with the federal law on bankruptcy. The purpose of the Bankruptcy Act is to give debtors new opportunity unhampered by the pressure and discouragement of preexisting debt. The challenged state statute hampers the accomplishment and execution of the full purposes and objectives of the Bankruptcy Act enacted by Congress.

Preemption Sometimes a federal law is said to preempt an area of law. If a federal law preempts a subject, then any state law that attempts to regulate the same activity is unconstitutional under the supremacy clause. The concept of **preemption** applies not only to federal statutes but also to the rules and regulations of federal administrative agencies. The following table lists several examples of business-related cases in which the courts have found federal preemption of areas involving business regulations.

The issue of federal preemption can become quite complex. The potential conflict between federal and state or local laws occurs, in part, because of what are

Examples of State Laws Preempted by Federal Law

State or Local Law	Preempted by Federal Law
A city conditions renewal of taxicab franchise on settlement of a labor dispute.	National Labor Relations Act
Municipal zoning ordinance governs size, location, and appearance of satellite dish antennas.	Federal Communications Commission Regulation
A state statute permits indirect purchasers to collect damages for overcharges resulting from price-fixing conspiracies.	Sherman Antitrust Act
A state law authorizes a tort claim by workers that a union has breached its duty to ensure a safe workplace.	Labor-Management Relations Act (Landrum-Griffin)
A state law prohibits repeat violators of labor laws from doing business with the state.	National Labor Relations Act
A state nuisance law purports to cover out-of-state sources of water pollution.	Clean Water Act
State criminal prosecution for aggravated battery is filed against corporate officials because of unsafe workplace conditions.	Occupational Safety and Health Act
State statute prohibits use of the direct molding process to duplicate unpatented boat hulls or knowing sale of hulls so duplicated.	Patent Law

called saving clauses. Very often, a federal law will expressly preempt one area of regulation while allowing state and local regulation in other areas. The following box discusses these points in the context of a recent case.

The following case, which focuses on a product liability lawsuit, further illustrates these technical aspects of preemption under the supremacy clause.

PREEMPTION AND A SAVING CLAUSE

The Employee Retirement Income Security Act (ERISA) passed by Congress in 1974 and signed into law contains a specific preemption provision that it "shall supersede any and all States laws insofar as they may now or hereafter relate to any employee benefit plan." ERISA also contains a saving clause which states "nothing in this subchapter shall be construed to exempt or relieve any person from any law of any State which regulates insurance, banking, or securities."

The Supreme Court attempts to explain these apparently conflicting clauses by recalling the balance of power between the federal and state or local governments. The Court stated the following:

In trying to extrapolate congressional intent in a case like this when congressional language seems simultaneously to preempt everything and hardly anything, we have no choice but to temper the assumption that the ordinary meaning accurately expresses the legislative purpose, with the qualification that the historic police powers of the States are not meant to be superseded by the Federal Act unless that was the clear and manifest purpose of Congress.

In summary, federal preemption is not presumed; it must be clearly and explicitly stated as the intent of Congress or a federal administrative agency.

Source: *Rush Prudential HMO, Inc. v. Moran*, 122 S. Ct. 2151 (2002).

GEIER V. AMERICAN HONDA MOTOR COMPANY, INC.

120 S. CT. 1913 (2000)

BREYER, J.: This case focuses on the 1984 version of a Federal Motor Vehicle Safety Standard promulgated by the Department of Transportation under the authority of the National Traffic and Motor Vehicle Safety Act of 1966. The standard, FMVSS 208, required auto manufacturers to equip some but not all of their 1987 vehicles with passive restraints. We ask whether the Act preempts a state common-law tort action in which the plaintiff claims that the defendant auto manufacturer, who was in compliance with the standard, should nonetheless have equipped a 1987 automobile with airbags. We conclude that the Act, taken together with FMVSS 208, preempts the lawsuit.

In 1992, petitioner Alexis Geier, driving a 1987 Honda Accord, collided with a tree and was seriously injured. The car was equipped with manual shoulder and lap belts which Geier had buckled up at the time. The car was not equipped with airbags or other passive restraint devices.

Geier and her parents . . . sued the car's manufacturer, American Honda Motor Company, Inc. . . . under District of Columbia tort law. They claimed, among other things, that American Honda had designed its car negligently and defectively because it lacked a driver's side airbag. The District Court dismissed the lawsuit. The court noted that FMVSS 208 gave car manufacturers a choice as to whether to install airbags. And the court concluded that petitioners' lawsuit, because it sought to establish a different safety standard—i.e., an airbag requirement—was expressly preempted by a provision of the Act which preempts "any safety standard" that is not identical to a federal safety standard applicable to the same aspect of performance.

The Court of Appeals agreed with the District Court's conclusion. . . .

Several state courts have held . . . that neither the Act's express preemption nor FMVSS 208 preempts a "no airbag" tort suit. All of the Federal Circuit Courts that have considered the question, however, have found preemption. . . . We granted certiorari to resolve these differences. We now hold that this kind of "no airbag" lawsuit conflicts with the objectives of FMVSS 208, a standard authorized by the Act, and is therefore pre-empted by the Act.

In reaching our conclusion, we consider three subsidiary questions. First, does the Act's express preemption provision preempt this lawsuit? We think not. Second, do ordinary preemption principles nonetheless apply? We hold that they do. Third, does this lawsuit actually conflict with FMVSS 208, hence with the Act itself? We hold that it does.

We first ask whether the Safety Act's express preemption provision preempts this tort action. The provision reads as follows:

> "Whenever a Federal motor vehicle safety standard established under this subchapter is in effect, no State or political subdivision of a State shall have any authority either to establish, or to continue in effect, with respect to any motor vehicle or item of motor vehicle equipment[,] any safety standard applicable to the same aspect of performance of such vehicle or item of equipment which is not identical to the Federal standard."

. . . [T]he Act contains another provision, . . . a "saving" clause, says that "compliance with" a federal safety standard "does not exempt any person from any liability under common law." The saving clause assumes that there are some significant number of common-law liability cases to save. . . .

We have . . . said that the saving clause at least removes tort actions from the scope of the express preemption clause. Does it do more? In particular, does it foreclose or limit the operation of ordinary preemption principles insofar as those principles instruct us to read statutes as preempting state laws (including common-law rules) that "actually con-

[CONTINUED]

flict" with the statute or federal standards promulgated thereunder?. . .

We recognize that, when this Court previously considered the preemptive effect of the statute's language, it appeared to leave open the question of how, or the extent to which, the saving clause saves state-law tort actions that conflict with federal regulations promulgated under the Act. We now conclude that the saving clause (like the express preemption provision) does not bar the ordinary working of conflict preemption principles. . . .

The basic question, then, is whether a common-law "no airbag" action like the one before us actually conflicts with FMVSS 208. We hold that it does. . . .

DOT's own contemporaneous explanation of FMVSS 208 makes clear that the 1984 version of FMVSS 208 reflected the following significant considerations. First, buckled up seatbelts are a vital ingredient of automobile safety. Second, despite the enormous and unnecessary risks that a passenger runs by not buckling up manual lap and shoulder belts, more than 80% of front seat passengers would leave their manual seatbelts unbuckled. Third, airbags could make up for the dangers caused by unbuckled manual belts, but they could not make up for them entirely. Fourth, passive restraint systems had their own disadvantages, for example, the dangers associated with, intrusiveness of, and corresponding public dislike for, nondetachable automatic belts. Fifth, airbags brought with them their own special risks to safety, such as the risk of danger to out-of-position occupants (usually children) in small cars. Sixth, airbags were expected to be significantly more expensive than other passive restraint devices, raising the average cost of a vehicle price $320 for full frontal airbags over the cost of a car with manual lap and shoulder seatbelts. And the agency worried that the high replacement cost—estimated to be $800—could lead car owners to refuse to replace them after deployment. Seventh, the public, for reasons of cost, fear, or physical intrusiveness, might resist installation or use of any of the then-available passive restraint devices. . . .

FMVSS 208 reflected these considerations in several ways. Most importantly, that standard deliberately sought variety—a mix of several different passive restraint systems. . . .

The 1984 FMVSS 208 standard also deliberately sought a gradual phase-in of passive restraints. It required the manufacturers to equip only 10% of their car fleet manufactured after September 1, 1986, with passive restraints. It then increased the percentage in three annual stages, up to 100% of the new car fleet for cars manufactured after September 1, 1989. And it explained that the phased-in requirement would allow more time for manufacturers to develop airbags or other, better, safer passive restraint systems. . . .

In sum, the 1984 version of FMVSS 208 "embodies the Secretary's policy judgment that safety would best be promoted if manufacturers installed alternative protection systems in their fleets rather than one particular system in every car." Petitioners' tort suit claims that the manufacturers of the 1987 Honda Accord "had a duty to design, manufacture, distribute and sell a motor vehicle with an effective and safe passive restraint system, including, but not limited to, airbags."

In effect, petitioners' tort action depends upon its claim that manufacturers had a duty to install an airbag when they manufactured the 1987 Honda Accord. Such a state law—i.e., a rule of state tort law imposing such a duty—by its terms would have required manufacturers of all similar cars to install airbags rather than other passive restraint systems, such as automatic belts or passive interiors. It thereby would have presented an obstacle to the variety and mix of devices that the federal regulation sought. It would have required all manufacturers to have installed airbags in respect to the entire District-of-Columbia-related portion of their 1987 new car fleet, even though FMVSS 208 at that time required only that 10% of a manufacturer's nationwide fleet be equipped with any passive restraint device at all. It thereby also would have stood as an obstacle to the gradual passive restraint phase-in that the federal regulation deliberately imposed. In addition, it could have made less likely the adoption of a state mandatory buckle-up law. Because the rule of law for which petitioners contend would have stood "as an obstacle to the accomplishment and execution of" the important means-related federal objectives that we have just discussed, it is preempted. . . .

The judgment of the Court of Appeals is affirmed.

[CONTINUED]

CASE QUESTIONS

1. Under what factual situation and law is Geier suing the American Honda Motor Company?

2. What theory does the American Honda Motor Company use to defend this lawsuit?

3. Why does the Supreme Court conclude that the National Traffic and Motor Vehicle Safety Act's preemption provision prohibit Geier's lawsuit?

4. What is a saving clause and how does it apply in this case?

5. What is the basis for the Supreme Court concluding that Geier's lawsuit is not permissible?

3. CONTRACT CLAUSE

Article I, Section 10, of the Constitution says, "No State shall . . . pass any . . . Law impairing the Obligation of contracts." This is the **contract clause.** It does not apply to the federal government, which does in fact frequently enact laws and adopt regulations that affect existing contracts. For example, the Department of Agriculture from time to time embargoes grain sales to foreign countries, usually as a result of problems in foreign affairs.

The limitation on state action impairing contracts has not been given a literal application. As a result of judicial interpretation, some state laws that affect existing contracts have been approved, especially when the law is passed to deal with a specific emergency situation. On the other hand, this constitutional provision does generally limit alternatives available to state government and prevents the enactment of legislation that changes existing contract rights.

THE COMMERCE CLAUSE

The power of the federal government to regulate business activity is found in the **commerce clause** of the Constitution. Article I, Section 8, states "Congress shall have Power . . . to regulate Commerce with foreign Nations, and among the several States, and with the Indian Tribes."

This simple-sounding clause has been interpreted as creating at least four important areas involving various aspects of the government regulating business. These areas can be summarized by the following headings:

- Regulation of foreign commerce
- Regulation of interstate commerce
- Limitation on state police power
- Limitation on state taxation

The next four sections focus on the impact of the commerce clause on businesses and businesspeople and addresses the questions in the Business Decision at the beginning of this chapter.

4. REGULATION OF FOREIGN COMMERCE

The first part of the commerce clause grants the federal government power to regulate foreign commerce. The power to regulate foreign commerce is vested exclusively in the federal government, and it extends to all aspects of foreign trade. In other words, the power to regulate foreign commerce is total. The federal government can prohibit foreign commerce entirely. In recent years, for example, the federal government has imposed trade embargoes on countries such as Iraq, Bosnia, and Haiti. It can also allow commerce with restrictions.

That the federal power to regulate foreign commerce is exclusive means state and local governments may not regulate such commerce. State and local governments sometimes attempt directly or indirectly to regulate imports or exports to some degree. Such attempts generally are unconstitutional. However, a state may regulate activities that relate to foreign commerce if such activities are conducted entirely within the state's boundaries. For example, the U.S. Supreme Court has upheld a state tax on the leases of cargo containers used in international trade. This decision was based on the tax being fairly apportioned to the use of the cargo containers within the state. Hence, the Court concluded that the state tax did not violate the foreign commerce clause.[1]

5. REGULATION OF INTERSTATE COMMERCE

Among the constitutional clauses that lead to extensive litigation is the phrase in the commerce clause granting the federal government the power to regulate commerce "among the several States." At first this phrase was interpreted to mean only interstate commerce as contrasted with intrastate commerce. Later, in a long series of judicial decisions, the power of the federal government was expanded through interpretation to include not only persons *engaged* in interstate commerce but also activities *affecting* interstate commerce.

The power of Congress over commerce is very broad; it extends to all commerce, be it great or small. Labeling an activity a "local" or "intrastate" activity does not prevent Congress from regulating it under the commerce clause. The power of Congress to regulate commerce "among the several states" extends to those intrastate activities that affect interstate commerce as to make regulation of them appropriate. Regulation is appropriate if it aids interstate commerce. Even activity that is purely intrastate in character may be regulated by Congress, when the activity, combined with like conduct by other similarly situated, substantially affects commerce among states. As a result of various Supreme Court decisions, it is hard to imagine a factual situation involving business transactions that the federal government cannot regulate.

On May 22, 2000, the Supreme Court[2] held that the federal government cannot prosecute a person who burned down a private residence by throwing a Molotov cocktail into the house. The Court reasoned that the private dwelling was not a commercial building and thus was not used "in commerce" or "a commerce-affecting activity." Some commentators report that this case may signal a change in direction regarding the federal government's authority to regulate interstate commerce. We believe that this case will have little or no impact on the extensive scope of the federal government's power to regulate commercial activities under the commerce clause.

---

[1] Itel Containers Int'l Corp. v. Huddleston, *113 S. Ct. 1095 (1993).*
[2] Jones v. U.S., *120 S. Ct. 1904 (2000).*

6. LIMITATION ON STATE POLICE POWER

Whereas the authority of the federal government to regulate business activity comes from the express language of the commerce clause, state and local government[3] authority arises from a concept known as **police powers.** These powers can be summarized as requiring state legislation and regulation to protect the public's health, safety, morals, and general welfare. These words, particularly the last phrase, give state government expansive power to regulate business activities.

These powers are not limitless. For example, there are definite limitations on the state powers over commerce because of the commerce clause. These limitations reflect the **dominant commerce clause concept.**

Three distinct subject areas of government regulation of commerce emerge from Supreme Court decisions. Some areas are exclusively federal, some are said to be exclusively local, and still others are such that regulation of them may be dual.

Exclusively Federal The subject area that is exclusively federal concerns those internal matters where uniformity on a nationwide basis is essential. Any state regulation of such subjects is void whether Congress has expressly regulated the area or not.

A classic example of a regulatory area that needs to be limited to the federal government is the opening and closing of airports. Because airlines need access to airports consistent with their routes, havoc could ensue if local authorities were allowed to set the hours that their airports operate. The regulation of the operating hours of airports is best left to the Federal Aviation Administration so that a coordinated effort is present.

Exclusively Local In theory, those matters that are exclusively within the states' power are intrastate activities that do not have a substantial effect on interstate commerce. As noted in the previous section, it is becoming more and more difficult, if not impossible, to find a subject matter involving business activity that is truly exclusively local in that the activity does not affect interstate commerce.

Dual Regulation Between the two extremes, joint regulation is permissible. This area can be divided into the following three subparts:

- Federal preemption
- Federal regulation but no preemption
- No federal regulation

Federal Preemption. The first subpart concerns those subjects over which the federal government has preempted the field. By express language or by comprehensive regulation, Congress has shown that it intends to exercise exclusive control over the subject matter. When a federal statute preempts a particular area of regulation, any state or local law pertaining to the same subject matter is unconstitutional under the commerce clause and the supremacy clause, and the state regulation is void. The net effect of a law that preempts an area of regula-

---

[3] *To avoid needless repetition, the phrase "state government" is used to refer to both state and local government.*

tion is to make that subject matter of the law exclusively federal. In essence, the commerce clause combines with the supremacy clause to prohibit any state regulation.

No Preemption. The second subpart includes situations in which the federal regulation of a subject matter is not comprehensive enough to preempt the field. Here state regulation is permitted. However, when state law is inconsistent or conflicts irreconcilably with the federal statute, it is unconstitutional and void. **Irreconcilable conflicts** exist when it is not possible for a business to comply with both statutes. If compliance with both is not possible, the state law must fall under the supremacy clause and the commerce clause. If compliance with both is reasonably possible, dual compliance is required. This usually has the effect of forcing business to meet the requirements of the law with the greatest burden. For example, if the state minimum wage is $5.35 per hour and the federal is $5.15, employers would be required to pay $5.35 since the conflict can be reconciled.

The commerce clause also invalidates state laws imposing an **undue burden** on interstate commerce. The commerce clause does not prohibit the imposing of burdens on interstate commerce—only the imposition of *undue* burdens. The states have the authority under the police power to regulate matters of legitimate local concern, even though interstate commerce may be affected. Review the examples in the following box and imagine how the commerce clause is increasingly relevant in cyberspace.

State statutes fall into two categories: those that burden interstate commerce only incidentally and those that affirmatively discriminate against such transactions. For cases in the first category, courts weigh the burdens against the benefits and find undue burdens only if they clearly exceed the local benefits. Cases in the second category are subject to more demanding scrutiny. If a state law either in substance or in practical effect discriminates against interstate commerce, the state must prove not only that the law has a legitimate purpose but also that the purpose cannot be achieved by nondiscriminatory means. If a state law is pure economic protectionism, the courts apply a virtual per se or automatic rule of invalidity.

No Federal Regulation. The third area of possible joint regulation exists where there is no federal law at all. When there is no federal regulation of a subject, state regulation of interstate commerce is permissible, providing, of course, that it does not impose an undue burden on interstate commerce and does not discriminate against interstate commerce in favor of local business.

CYBER LAW *connection*

The commerce clause is being used as a constitutional tool to strike down laws regulating aspects of cyberspace. For example, a California law attempting to prohibit spamming (the sending of unsolicited e-mail messages) was declared unconstitutional. Similarly a Michigan statute that sought protection of children from pornographic materials on the Web was invalidated. In both these situations, courts ruled that persons engaged in interstate commerce faced undue burdens since they would have to either restrict or change what was being sent via the Internet to these particular states. Based on these cases, uniform or federal regulation of the e-commerce may be more practical.

The commerce clause also has been construed as **prohibiting discrimination** against interstate commerce in favor of intrastate commerce. State and local governments frequently attempt by legislation to aid local business in its competition with interstate business. The commerce clause requires that all regulations be the same for local businesses as for businesses engaged in interstate commerce. A state may not place itself in a position of economic isolation from other states. The following case illustrates the interpretation of the commerce clause as it impacts the discriminatory nature of state regulations.

SOUTH CENTRAL BELL TELEPHONE COMPANY V. ALABAMA

119 S. CT. 1180 (1999)

BREYER, J.: The basic question in this case is whether the franchise tax Alabama assesses on foreign corporations violates the Commerce Clause. We conclude that it does.

Alabama requires each corporation doing business in that State to pay a franchise tax based upon the firm's capital. A domestic firm, organized under the laws of Alabama, must pay tax in an amount equal to 1% of the par value of the firm's stock. A foreign firm, organized under the laws of a State other than Alabama, must pay tax in an amount equal to 0.3% of the value of "the actual amount of capital employed" in Alabama. Alabama law grants domestic firms considerable leeway in controlling their own tax base and tax liability, as a firm may set its stock's par value at a level well below its book or market value. Alabama law does not grant a foreign firm similar leeway to control its tax base, however, as the value of the "actual" capital upon which Alabama calculates the foreign franchise tax includes not only the value of capital stock but also other accounting items (e.g., long-term debt, surplus), the value of which depends upon the firm's financial status.

In 1986, the Reynolds Metals Company and three other foreign corporations sued Alabama's tax authorities, seeking a refund of the foreign franchise tax they had paid on the ground that the tax discriminated against foreign corporations. Although the tax favored foreign firms in some respects (granting them a lower tax rate and excluding any capital not

employed in Alabama), that favorable treatment was more than offset by the fact that a domestic firm, unlike a foreign firm, could shrink its tax base significantly simply by setting the par value of its stock at a low level. As a result, Reynolds Metals said, the tax burden borne by foreign corporations was much higher than the burden on domestic corporations, and the tax consequently violated both the Commerce and Equal Protection Clauses.

The Alabama Supreme Court rejected these claims. . . .

While the Alabama courts were considering Reynolds Metals, a different foreign corporation, South Central Bell Telephone Company, brought the lawsuit now before us. Bell asserted the same Commerce Clause and Equal Protection Clause claims as had Reynolds Metals, though in respect to different tax years. Bell initially agreed to hold its suit in abeyance pending the resolution of Reynolds Metal's claims. Then, after the Alabama Supreme Court decided against the taxpayers in Reynolds Metals, Bell went to trial.

The Bell plaintiffs introduced evidence designed to show that the empirical premises that underlay *Reynolds Metals* were wrong: Despite the differences in franchise tax rates, Alabama's franchise tax scheme in practice discriminates substantially against foreign corporations, and the Alabama tax on shares of domestic corporations does not offset the discrimination in the franchise tax. The Alabama trial court

[CONTINUED]

agreed with the Bell plaintiffs that their evidence, taken together with this Court's recent Commerce Clause cases, "clearly and abundantly demonstrates that the franchise tax on foreign corporations discriminates against them for no other reason than the state of their incorporation." But the trial court nonetheless dismissed their claims for a different reason, namely, that given the Alabama Supreme Court's decision in *Reynolds Metals,* the Taxpayer's claims in this case are barred by res judicata.

The Alabama Supreme Court affirmed the trial court by a vote of 5 to 4. . . .

We granted the Bell plaintiffs' petition for certiorari, agreeing to decide (1) whether the Alabama courts' refusal to permit the Bell plaintiffs to raise their constitutional claims because of res judicata "deprived" the Bell plaintiffs "of the due process of law guaranteed by the Fourteenth Amendment," and (2) whether the franchise tax "impermissibly discriminates against interstate commerce, in violation of the Commerce Clause." We decide both questions in favor of the Bell plaintiffs. . . .

[The Supreme Court rejected Alabama's argument that res judicata prevents Bell from litigating its claim of a discriminatory franchise tax.]

Turning to the merits, we conclude that this Court's Commerce Clause precedent requires us to hold Alabama's franchise tax unconstitutional. Alabama law defines a domestic corporation's tax base as including only one item—the par value of capital stock—which the corporation may set at whatever level it chooses. A foreign corporation's tax base, on the other hand, contains many additional balance sheet items that are valued in accordance with generally accepted accounting principles, rather than by arbitrary assignment by the corporation. Accordingly, as the State has admitted, Alabama law gives domestic corporations the ability to reduce their franchise tax liability simply by reducing the par value of their stock, while it denies foreign corporations that same ability. And no one claims that the different tax rates for foreign and domestic corporations offset the difference in the tax base. The tax therefore facially discriminates against interstate commerce and is unconstitutional unless the State can offer a sufficient justification for it. This discrimination is borne out in practice, as the record, undisputed here, shows that the average domestic corporation pays only one-fifth the franchise tax it would pay if it were treated as a foreign corporation.

The State cannot justify this discrimination on the ground that the foreign franchise tax is a "complementary" or "compensatory" tax that offsets the tax burden that the domestic shares tax imposes upon domestic corporations. Our cases hold that a discriminatory tax cannot be upheld as "compensatory" unless the State proves that the special burden that the franchise tax imposes upon foreign corporations is "roughly . . . approximate" to the special burden on domestic corporations, and that the taxes are similar enough "in substance" to serve as "mutually exclusive" proxies for one another.

In this case, however, the relevant tax burdens are not "roughly approximate." And the State has made no effort to persuade this Court otherwise.

Nor are the two tax burdens similar in substance. Alabama imposes its foreign franchise tax upon a foreign firm's decision to do business in the State; Alabama imposes its domestic shares tax upon the ownership of a certain form of property, namely, shares in domestic corporations. No one has explained to us how the one could be seen as a "proxy" for the other. . . .

For these reasons, the decision of the Alabama Supreme Court is reversed, and the case is remanded for further proceedings not inconsistent with this opinion.

Reversed and remanded.

CASE QUESTIONS

1. Why does South Central Bell Telephone Company claim the Alabama franchise tax is discriminatory?

2. What is the basis for the State's original argument that the tax is not discriminatory?

3. Having found that the franchise tax is discriminating against foreign companies, what is the Court's conclusion?

---

concept SUMMARY   *Possible Subjects for Government Regulation*

Exclusively Federal Subjects

- Any state regulatory law is unconstitutional under the supremacy and commerce clauses.

Exclusively Local Subjects

- The impact on state and local government of laws based on the commerce clause is very limited; very few subjects, if any, are exclusively local.

Possible Dual Regulation Subjects

- Federal law preempts the field. The subject matter is considered exclusively federal.

- Federal law does not preempt the field. A state law is unconstitutional if it:
  1. Is in irreconcilable conflict with federal law
  2. Constitutes an undue burden on interstate commerce
  3. Discriminates against interstate commerce in favor of intrastate commerce
- No federal law. A state law is unconstitutional if it:
  1. Constitutes an undue burden on interstate commerce
  2. Discriminates against interstate commerce in favor of intrastate commerce

---

7. LIMITATION ON STATE TAXATION

Taxation is a primary form of regulation. Therefore, taxes imposed by state and local governments are subject to the limitations imposed by the commerce clause. The commerce clause limits property taxes, income taxes, and sales or use taxes levied by state and local governments on interstate commerce. Since taxation distributes the cost of government among those who receive its benefits, interstate commerce is not exempt from state and local taxes. The purpose of the commerce clause is to ensure that a taxpayer engaged in interstate commerce only pays its fair share of state taxes.

To prevent multiple taxation of the same property or income of interstate businesses, taxes are apportioned. **Apportionment** formulas allocate the tax burden of an interstate business among the states entitled to tax it. The commerce clause requires states to use reasonable formulas when more than one state is taxing the same thing.

To justify the tax, there must be sufficient contact, connection, tie, or link between the business and the taxing state. There must be sufficient local activities to justify the tax in a constitutional sense. This connection is called the **nexus.** A business operating in a state directly benefits from its police and fire protection, the use of its roads, and the like. Indirectly, it will be able to recruit employees more easily if they have easy access to good schools, parks, and civic centers. If the state gives anything for which it can reasonably expect payment, then the tax has a sufficient nexus. In cases involving property taxes, the term *taxable situs* is used in place of nexus, but each is concerned with the adequacy of local activities to support the tax.

The concepts of apportionment and nexus become quite complicated in application. The following case illustrates this complexity.

HUNT-WESSON, INC. V. FRANCHISE TAX BOARD OF CALIFORNIA

120 S. CT. 1022 (2000)

BREYER, J.: A State may tax a proportionate share of the income of a nondomiciliary corporation that carries out a particular business both inside and outside that State. The State, however, may not tax income received by a corporation from an unrelated business activity which constitutes a discrete business enterprise. California's rules for taxing its share of a multistate corporation's income authorize a deduction for interest expense. But they permit (with one adjustment) use of that deduction only to the extent that the amount exceeds certain out-of-state income arising from the unrelated business activity of a discrete business enterprise, i.e., income that the State could not otherwise tax. We must decide whether those rules violate the Constitution's Due Process and Commerce Clauses. We conclude that they do.

The legal issue is less complicated than may first appear, as examples will help to show. California, like many other States, uses what is called a "unitary business" income-calculation system for determining its taxable share of a multistate corporation's business income. In effect, that system first determines the corporation's total income from its nationwide business. During the years at issue, it then averaged three ratios—those of the firm's California property, payroll, and sales to total property, payroll, and sales—to make a combined ratio. Finally, it multiplies total income by the combined ratio. The result is "California's share," to which California then applies its corporate income tax. If, for example, an Illinois tin can manufacturer, doing business in California and elsewhere, earns $10 million from its total nationwide tin can sales, and if California's formula determines that the manufacturer does 10% of its business in California, then California will impose its income tax upon 10% of the corporation's tin can income, $1 million.

The income of which California taxes a percentage is constitutionally limited to a corporation's "unitary" income. Unitary income normally includes all income from a corporation's business activities, but excludes income that derives from unrelated business activity which constitutes a discrete business enterprise. As we have said, this later "nonunitary" income normally is not taxable by any State except the corporation's State of domicile (and the states in which the "discrete enterprise" carries out its business).

Any income tax system must have rules for determining the amount of net income to be taxed. California's system, like others, basically does so by asking the corporation to add up its gross income and then deduct costs. One of the costs that California permits the corporation to deduct is interest expense. The statutory language that authorizes that deduction—the language here at issue—contains an important limitation. It says that the amount of "interest deductible" shall be the amount by which "interest expense exceeds interest and dividend income. . . not subject to allocation by formula," i.e., the amount by which the interest expense exceeds the interest and dividends that the nondomiciliary corporation has received from nonunitary business or investment. Suppose the Illinois tin can manufacturer has interest expense of $150,000; and suppose it receives $100,000 in dividend income from a nonunitary New Zealand sheep-farming subsidiary. California's rule authorizes an interest deduction, not of $150,000, but of $50,000, for the deduction is allowed only insofar as the interest expense "exceeds" this other unrelated income. . . .

The question before us then is reasonably straightforward: Does the Constitution permit California to carve out an exception to its interest expense deduction, which it measures by the amount of nonunitary dividend and interest income that the nondomiciliary corporation has received? Petitioner, Hunt-Wesson, is successor in interest to a nondomiciliary corporation. That corporation incurred interest expense during the years at issue. California disallowed the deduction for that expense insofar as the

[CONTINUED]

corporation had received relevant nonunitary dividend and interest income. Hunt-Wesson challenged the constitutional validity of the disallowance. The California Court of Appeal found it constitutional, and the California Supreme Court denied review. We granted certiorari to consider the question.

Relevant precedent makes clear that California's rule violates the Due Process and Commerce Clauses of the Federal Constitution. In *Container Corp. of America v. Franchise Tax Bd.,* 103 S. Ct. 2933 (1983), this Court wrote that the "Due Process and Commerce Clauses . . . do not allow a State to tax income arising out of interstate activities—even on a proportional basis—unless there is a ' "minimal connection" or "nexus" between the interstate activities and the taxing State, and "a rational relationship between the income attributed to the State and the intrastate values of the enterprise." ' " The parties concede that the relevant income here—that which falls within the scope of the statutory phrase "not allocable by formula"—is income that, like the New Zealand sheep farm in our example, by itself bears no "rational relationship" or "nexus" to California. Under our precedent, this "nonunitary" income may not constitutionally be taxed by a State other than the corporation's domicile, unless there is some other connection between the taxing state and the income.

California's statute does not directly impose a tax on nonunitary income. Rather, it simply denies the taxpayer use of a portion of a deduction from unitary income (income like that from tin can manufacture in our example), income which does bear a "rational relationship" or "nexus" to California. . . .

Because California's offset provision is not a reasonable allocation of expense deductions to the income that the expense generates, it constitutes impermissible taxation of income outside its jurisdictional reach. The provision therefore violates the Due Process and Commerce Clauses of the Constitution. The determination of the California Court of Appeals is reversed, and the case remanded for proceedings not inconsistent with this opinion.

Reversed and remanded.

CASE QUESTIONS

1. Describe the basis of Hunt-Wesson's argument that the California limitation on interest deduction was unconstitutional.

2. What is the difference between "unitary" and "nonunitary" income?

3. How can a state government justify its taxation of a business organization that conducts business outside the state imposing this tax?

REGULATION AND BASIC FREEDOMS

The First Amendment to the Constitution of the United States establishes the following basic freedoms:

- Freedom of religion
- Freedom of the press
- Freedom of speech
- Freedom of assembly
- The right to petition the government for a redress of grievances

Usually we do not think of these freedoms in a business context; we think of them as the personal rights of individuals in a free society. There are, however, very important aspects of these freedoms relating to economic opportunity and business activity.

As you study the impact of these basic freedoms on government, keep four important aspects in mind. First, basic constitutional rights are not absolute. Second, the extent of any limitation on a basic constitutional guarantee depends upon the nature of the competing public policy. Cases involving the Bill of Rights almost always require courts to strike a balance either between some goal or policy of society and the constitutional protection involved or between competing constitutional guarantees. For example, such cases may involve conflict between the goal of protecting an individual's or business's reputation and the right of another to speak freely about the reputation. The courts are continually weighing the extent of constitutional protections.

Third, constitutional guarantees exist in order to remove certain issues from the political process and the ballot box. They exist to protect the minority from the majority. Freedom of expression (press and speech) protects the unpopular idea or viewpoint. Freedom of assembly allows groups with ideologies foreign to most of us to meet and express their philosophy. The Bill of Rights protects the "worst" among us even more than it does the "best."

Finally, constitutional rights vary from time to time and may be narrowly interpreted during emergencies such as war or civil strife. Even during peacetime, constitutional principles are constantly reapplied and reexamined.

8. FREEDOM OF RELIGION

The First Amendment states that Congress shall make no law "respecting an establishment of religion" (the **establishment clause**) "or prohibiting the free exercise thereof" (the **free exercise clause**). These clauses guarantee freedom of religion through the separation of church and state.

Most business-related freedom of religion cases involve the free exercise clause. The Supreme Court has held that the denial of unemployment benefits to a worker who refused a position because the job would have required him to work on Sunday violated the free exercise clause of the First Amendment. The constitution requires that the owner of the business either allow the person to have Sunday off or allow the state to pay unemployment compensation and increase the business's taxes.

Freedom of religion has been used to challenge legislation requiring the closing of business establishments on Sunday. Although the motive for such legislation may be, in part, religious, there are also economic reasons for such legislation. As a result, if a law is based on economic considerations, it may be upheld if its classifications are reasonable and in the public interest. However, many such laws have been held invalid as a violation of the First Amendment.

Other examples of freedom of religion cases that concern business are presented in the table on the next page.

9. FREEDOM OF THE PRESS

The publishing business is the only organized private business given explicit constitutional protection. The First Amendment states that "Congress shall make no law . . . abridging the freedom of . . . the press." This guarantee essentially authorizes a private business to provide organized scrutiny of government.

Examples of Freedom of Religion Issues Affecting Business

	Case Decisions Yes	No
Is it constitutional to apply the Fair Labor Standards Act (minimum-wage law) to a nonprofit religious organization?	X	
Is it constitutional to apply the labor laws relating to union elections to parochial school teachers?		X
Is a state law constitutional when it provides Sabbath observers with an absolute and unqualified right not to work on their Sabbath?		X
Is religious belief justification for refusing to participate in the Social Security system?		X
Does the 1964 Civil Rights Act, which obligates employers to make reasonable accommodations of employees' religious beliefs, violate the First Amendment's establishment clause?		X
May a state impose a 6 percent sales tax on religious merchandise sold in the state by religious organizations?	X	
May a state exempt religious periodicals from a sales tax that applies to all other periodicals?		X

Freedom of the press is not absolute. The press is not free to print anything it wants without liability. Rather, freedom of the press is usually construed to prohibit **prior restraints** on publications. If the press publishes that which is illegal or libelous, it has liability for doing so. This liability may be either criminal or civil for damages.

There are many examples of limitations on freedom of the press. For example, courts have allowed the Federal Communications Commission to censor "filthy" words on television. The power of the commission extends to upholding the public's interest in responsible broadcasting.

A major area of litigation involving freedom of the press involves **defamation.** The tort theory known as **libel** is used to recover damages as a result of printed defamation of character. Libel cases compensate individuals for harm inflicted by defamatory printed falsehoods. Since the threat of a libel suit could have a chilling effect on freedom of the press and on the public's rights to information, the law has a different standard for imposing liability when the printed matter concerns an issue of public interest and concern. If the person involved is a public official or figure, a plaintiff seeking damages for emotional distress caused by offensive publications must prove actual **malice** in order to recover. *Actual malice* includes knowledge that the printed statements are false or circumstances showing a reckless disregard for whether they are true or not. If the plaintiff is not a public figure or public official, there is liability for libelous statements without proof of malice.

10. FREEDOM OF SPEECH

Freedom of speech, sometimes referred to as freedom of expression, covers both verbal and written communications. In addition, it covers conduct or actions considered **symbolic speech.** Although freedom of speech is not absolute, it is as close to being absolute as any constitutional guarantee. It exists to protect the minority from the majority. It means freedom to express ideas antagonistic to those of the majority. Freedom of speech exists for thoughts many of us hate and for ideas that may be foreign to us. It means freedom to express the unorthodox, and it recognizes that there is no such thing as a false idea.

The issue of freedom of speech arises in many business situations. The following boxes discuss two common situations that arise when considering the protection and limitation of free speech.

PICKETING AS FREE SPEECH

Cases involving picketing, for example, especially with unions, often are concerned with the issue of free speech. The right to picket peacefully for a lawful purpose is well recognized. A state or local law that prohibits all picketing would be unconstitutional since the act of picketing, itself, is a valuable form of communication. However, a state law that limits picketing or other First Amendment freedoms may be constitutional if:

- The regulation is within the constitutional power of government
- It furthers an important or substantial governmental interest
- It is unrelated to suppression of free expression
- The incidental restriction on First Amendment freedoms is no greater than is essential to further the government's interest

Under these principles, laws that prevent pickets from obstructing traffic and those designed to prevent violence would be constitutional. For example, a Texas statute that prohibits "mass picketing," defined as picketing by more than two persons within 50 feet of any entrance or of one another, does not violate the First Amendment. The Supreme Court has held that a city ordinance prohibiting picketing in front of an individual residence was constitutional. The law was enacted to prevent picketing of the homes of doctors who perform abortions. It did not ban all residential picketing and met the four tests previously noted.

Courts may limit the number of pickets to preserve order and promote safety, but they will not deny pickets the right to express opinions in a picket line. For example, a court order preventing a client from picketing her lawyer was held to be a violation of the First Amendment. Freedom of speech even extends to boycotts of a business for a valid public purpose such as the elimination of discrimination.

OBSCENITY IS NOT PROTECTED: WHAT IS OBSCENE?

Freedom of expression does not protect obscene materials. The community's interest in banning such material outweighs any First Amendment interests. The difficult issues in obscenity cases are defining obscenity and determining whether or not items involved are obscene. A movie, book, or magazine is obscene and subject to state regulation if it violates a three-part test:

- If it, taken as a whole, appeals to a prurient interest in sex

- If it portrays, in a clearly offensive way, sexual conduct as specifically defined by the applicable state law
- If it, taken as a whole, does not have serious literary, artistic, political, or scientific value

In deciding whether allegedly obscene work has "literary, artistic, political, or scientific value," a court must determine not whether an ordinary member of any given community would find serious literary, artistic, political, or scientific value in a work, but whether a reasonable person would find such value in the material taken as a whole.

In some free-speech cases, an individual whose own speech or conduct may not be prohibited is nevertheless permitted to challenge a statute limiting speech because it also threatens other people not before the court. The person is allowed to challenge the statute because others who may desire to engage in legally protected expression may refrain from doing so. They may fear the risk of prosecution, or they may not want to risk having a law declared to be only partially invalid. This is known as the **overbreadth doctrine.** It means that the legislators have gone too far in seeking to achieve a goal.

For example, an airport authority resolution declared the central terminal area "not open for First Amendment activities." The resolution was unconstitutional under the First Amendment overbreadth doctrine. The resolution reached the "universe of expressive activity" and in effect created a "First-Amendment-Free Zone" at the airport. Nearly every person who entered the airport would violate the resolution, since it bars all First Amendment activities, including talking and reading.

FREE SPEECH VERSUS AN INDIVIDUAL'S RIGHT OF PRIVACY

Through wiretapping and electronic surveillance statutes, the federal government and most states make it illegal to intercept and record oral, wire, and electronic conversations. A more complicated issue arises when an illegally obtained conversation involving public issues is broadcast or published by someone who is not involved in the illegal activity. For example, does the Free Speech Clause protect a radio commentator who broadcasts a cell phone conversation when that conversation is illegally recorded but when the commentator is not the party who illegally taped the conversation?

The U.S. Supreme Court holds it would be most unusual to hold "speech by a law-abiding possessor of information can be suppressed in order to deter conduct by a non-law-abiding third party." When the recorded conversation involves public issues (such as the pay of public school teachers), the publication of this public information is protected compared to the interest of individuals to have their conversation remain private.

Source: *Bartnicki v. Vopper,* 121 S. Ct. 1753 (2001).

As you can see, the freedom of speech is cherished as a fundamental right of citizenship. While this right's importance provides significant protection, it sometimes can contradict other critical interests, such as the right of privacy. The box above highlights the balance that courts often seek to find.

Commercial Speech Historically, **commercial speech** was not protected by the First Amendment. However, in the 1970s the Supreme Court began to recognize that free commercial speech was essential to the public's right to know. Therefore, today, freedom of speech protects corporations as well as individuals. The public interests served by freedom of expression protect the listener as well as the speaker. Freedom of expression includes freedom of information or the rights of the public to be informed. Since corporations may add to the public's knowledge and information, they also have the right to free speech. Freedom of speech for corporations may not be as extensive as the right of an individual. However, a government cannot limit commercial speech without a compelling state interest expressed to justify the restriction. State regulatory commissions often seek to limit the activities of public utilities. Such attempts usually run afoul of the First Amendment. The following case explains why and to what extent commercial speech is protected.

SECRETARY OF HEALTH AND HUMAN SERVICES V. WESTERN STATES MEDICAL CENTER

122 S. CT. 1497 (2002)

Drug compounding is a process by which a pharmacist or doctor combines, mixes, or alters ingredients to create a medication tailored to the needs of an individual patient. Compounding is typically used to prepare medications that are not commercially available, such as medication for a patient who is allergic to an ingredient in a mass-produced product. Section 503A of the Food and Drug Administration Modernization Act of 1997 (FDAMA or Act) exempts compounded drugs from the Food and Drug Administration's standard drug approval requirements as long as the pharmacists providing these drugs abide by

[CONTINUED]

several restrictions, most notably refraining from advertising or promoting particular compounded drugs. Pharmacists are not prohibited from advertising the availability of the compounding services, just the existence of specific compounded drugs.

A group of pharmacies specialize in drug compounding. Fearing that the distribution of their promotional materials might result in prosecution under the FDAMA, this group filed a complaint in federal district court seeking to have the prohibition against advertising of compound drugs declared unconstitutional as a violation of the First Amendment's Free Speech Clause. The District Court issued such a declaration, and the Ninth Circuit Court of Appeals affirmed. The Food and Drug Administration (FDA) filed a petition for a writ of certiorari, which was granted.

O'CONNOR, J.: . . . The parties agree that the advertising and soliciting prohibited by the FDAMA constitute commercial speech.

In *Virginia Bd. of Pharmacy v. Virginia Citizens Consumer Council, Inc.,* 96 S. Ct. 1817 (1976), the first case in which we explicitly held that commercial speech receives First Amendment protection, we explained the reasons for this protection: "It is a matter of public interest that [economic] decisions, in the aggregate, be intelligent and well-informed. To this end, the free flow of commercial information is indispensable." Indeed, we recognized that a "particular consumer's interest in the free flow of commercial information . . . may be as keen, if not keener by far, than his interest in the day's most urgent political debate.". . .

Although commercial speech is protected by the First Amendment, not all regulation of such speech is unconstitutional. In *Central Hudson [Gas & Elec. Corp. v. Public Serv. Comm'n of N.Y.,* 100 S. Ct. 2343 (1980)], we articulated a test for determining whether a particular commercial speech regulation is constitutionally permissible. Under that test we ask as a threshold matter whether the commercial speech concerns unlawful activity or is misleading. If so, then the speech is not protected by the First Amendment. If the speech concerns lawful activity and is not misleading, however, we next ask "whether the asserted governmental interest is substantial." If it is, then we "determine whether the regulation directly advances the governmental interest asserted," and, fi-

nally, "whether it is not more extensive than is necessary to serve that interest." Each of these latter three inquiries must be answered in the affirmative for the regulation to be found constitutional. . . .

The Government . . . does not argue that the prohibited advertisements would be about unlawful activity or would be misleading. Instead, the Government argues that the FDAMA satisfies the remaining three prongs of the *Central Hudson* test.

The Government asserts that three substantial interests underlie the FDAMA. The first is an interest in preserving the effectiveness and integrity of the FDA's new drug approval process and the protection of the public health that it provides. The second is an interest in preserving the availability of compounded drugs for those individual patients who, for particularized medical reasons, cannot use commercially available products that have been approved by the FDA. Finally, the Government argues that achieving the proper balance between those two independently compelling but competing interests is itself a substantial governmental interest. . . .

Preserving the effectiveness and integrity of the FDA's new drug approval process is clearly an important governmental interest, and the Government has every reason to want as many drugs as possible to be subject to that approval process. The Government also has an important interest, however, in permitting the continuation of the practice of compounding so that patients with particular needs may obtain medications suited to those needs. And it would not make sense to require compounded drugs created to meet the unique needs of individual patients to undergo the testing required for the new drug approval process. Pharmacists do not make enough money from small-scale compounding to make safety and efficacy testing of their compounded drugs economically feasible, so requiring such testing would force pharmacists to stop providing compounded drugs. Given this, the Government needs to be able to draw a line between small-scale compounding and large-scale drug manufacturing. That line must distinguish compounded drugs produced on such a small scale that they could not undergo safety and efficacy testing from drugs produced and sold on a large enough scale that they could undergo such testing and therefore must do so.

The Government argues that the FDAMA's speech-related provisions . . . directly advance the

[CONTINUED]

governmental interests asserted. Those provisions use advertising as the trigger for requiring FDA approval—essentially, as long as pharmacists do not advertise particular compounded drugs, they may sell compounded drugs without first undergoing safety and efficacy testing and obtaining FDA approval. If they advertise their compounded drugs, however, FDA approval is required. . . .

The Government seems to believe that without advertising it would not be possible to market a drug on a large enough scale to make safety and efficacy testing economically feasible. The Government thus believes that conditioning an exemption from the FDA approval process on refraining from advertising is an ideal way to permit compounding and yet also guarantee that compounding is not conducted on such a scale as to undermine the FDA approval process. Assuming it is true that drugs cannot be marketed on a large scale without advertising, the FDAMA's prohibition on advertising compounded drugs might indeed directly advance the Government's interests. Even assuming that it does, however, the Government has failed to demonstrate that the speech restrictions are not more extensive than is necessary to serve those interests. In previous cases addressing this final prong of the *Central Hudson* test, we have made clear that if the Government could achieve its interests in a manner that does not restrict speech, or that restricts less speech, the Government must do so. . . .

Several non-speech-related means of drawing a line between compounding and large-scale manufacturing might be possible here. First, it seems that the Government could use the very factors the FDA relied on to distinguish compounding from manufacturing. . . . For example, the Government could ban the use of commercial scale manufacturing or testing equipment for compounding drug products. It could prohibit pharmacists from compounding more drugs in anticipation of receiving prescriptions than in re-sponse to prescriptions already received. It could prohibit pharmacists from offering compounded drugs at wholesale to other state-licensed persons or commercial entities for resale. Alternately, it could limit the amount of compounded drugs, either by volume or by numbers of prescriptions, that a given pharmacist or pharmacy sells out of State. Another possibility . . . would be capping the amount of any particular compounded drug, either by drug volume, number of prescriptions, gross revenue, or profit that a pharmacist or pharmacy may make or sell in a given period of time. It might even be sufficient to rely solely on the non-speech-related provisions of the FDAMA, such as the requirement that compounding only be conducted in response to a prescription or a history of receiving a prescription, and the limitation on the percentage of a pharmacy's total sales that out-of-state sales of compounded drugs may represent.

The Government has not offered any reason why these possibilities, alone or in combination, would be insufficient to prevent compounding from occurring on such a scale as to undermine the new drug approval process. Indeed, there is no hint that the Government even considered these or any other alternatives. Nowhere in the legislative history of the FDAMA is there any explanation of why the Government believed forbidding advertising was a necessary as opposed to merely convenient means of achieving its interests. . . . The Government simply has not provided sufficient justification here. If the First Amendment means anything, it means that regulating speech must be a last—not first—resort. Yet here it seems to have been the first strategy the Government thought to try. . . .

Accordingly, we affirm the Court of Appeals' judgment that the speech-related provisions of FDAMA § 503A are unconstitutional.

Affirmed.

CASE QUESTIONS

1. What does the phrase "compounding drugs" mean?
2. Why does the FDAMA allow the practice of compounding drugs while prohibiting the advertising of specific compounds?
3. What is the factual concern and legal basis for certain pharmacists challenging the prohibition of advertising?
4. Why are the *Central Hudson* tests important in determining the outcome of this case?
5. What do the district court, the court of appeals and the Supreme Court decide in this case?

THE FOURTEENTH AMENDMENT

The Fourteenth Amendment to the Constitution states, "No state shall make or enforce any law which shall abridge the privileges or immunities of citizens of the United States; nor shall any state deprive any person of life, liberty or property, without due process of law, nor deny to any person within its jurisdiction the equal protection of the laws." Two of this amendment's provisions are of very special importance to businesspeople—the **due process clause** and the **equal protection clause.**

11. DUE PROCESS OF LAW

The term *due process of law* as used in the Fourteenth Amendment probably arises in more litigation than any other constitutional phrase. It cannot be narrowly defined. The term describes fundamental principles of liberty and justice. Simply stated, due process means "fundamental fairness and decency." It means that *government* may not act in a manner that is arbitrary, capricious, or unreasonable. The clause does not prevent private individuals or corporations, including public utilities, from acting in an arbitrary or unreasonable manner. The due process clause applies only to governmental bodies; it does not apply to the actions of individuals or businesses.

The issues in due process cases are usually divided into questions of **procedural due process** and **substantive due process.** Procedural due process cases often are concerned with whether proper notice has been given and a proper hearing has been conducted. Such cases frequently involve procedures established by statute. However, many cases involve procedures that are not created by statute. For example, the due process clause has been used to challenge the procedure used in the dismissal of a student from a public university. Substantive due process issues arise when property or other rights are directly affected by governmental action. If there is no governmental action involved, due process requirements do not arise. The Supreme Court has ruled that private insurers withholding medical payments, under Pennsylvania's workers' compensation statute, pending a "utilization review" does not amount to governmental action. Hence, the due process requirements of notice and a hearing are not applicable.[4]

In essence, the due process clause can be invoked anytime procedures of government are questioned in litigation. For example, in recent years, the Supreme Court has used the due process clause as its justification for defining the limits for a jury awarding punitive damages to a plaintiff in a civil lawsuit. The following case illustrates this use of the due process clause.

---

[4] American Manufacturers Mutual Insurance Company v. Sullivan, *119 S. Ct. 977 (1999).*

STATE FARM MUTUAL AUTOMOBILE INSURANCE COMPANY V. CAMPBELL

123 S. CT. 1513 (2003)

The Campbells had automobile insurance with State Farm Insurance Company. Following an accident involving the Campbells' car and two others, lawsuits were filed against the Campbells. State Farm told the Campbells that they did not have liability and did not need their own lawyer. These lawsuits resulted in the Campbells being found liable for damages in excess of their insurance policy with State Farm. The Campbells sued State Farm for bad faith and were allowed to introduce examples of State Farm's action from throughout the nation. A jury awarded the Campbells $2.6 million in compensatory damages and $145 million in punitive damages. The trial court reduced the amounts to $1 million and $25 million, respectively. The Campbells and State Farm appealed. The Utah Supreme Court reinstated $145 million in punitive damages. State Farm petitioned for certiorari, which was granted.

KENNEDY, J. . . . We recognized in *Cooper Industries, Inc. v. Leatherman Tool Group, Inc.,* 532 U.S. 424, 149 L. Ed. 2d 674, 121 S. Ct. 1678 (2001), that in our judicial system compensatory and punitive damages, although usually awarded at the same time by the same decisionmaker, serve different purposes. Compensatory damages are intended to redress the concrete loss that the plaintiff has suffered by reason of the defendant's wrongful conduct. By contrast, punitive damages serve a broader function; they are aimed at deterrence and retribution.

While States possess discretion over the imposition of punitive damages, it is well established that there are procedural and substantive constitutional limitations on these awards. The Due Process Clause of the Fourteenth Amendment prohibits the imposition of grossly excessive or arbitrary punishments on a tortfeasor. The reason is that elementary notions of fairness enshrined in our constitutional jurisprudence dictate that a person receive fair notice not only of the conduct that will subject him to punishment, but also of the severity of the penalty that a State may impose. To the extent an award is grossly excessive, it furthers no legitimate purpose and constitutes an arbitrary deprivation of property.

Although these awards serve the same purposes as criminal penalties, defendants subjected to punitive damages in civil cases have not been accorded the protections applicable in a criminal proceeding. This increases our concerns over the imprecise manner in which punitive damages systems are administered. We have admonished that punitive damages pose an acute danger of arbitrary deprivation of property. Jury instructions typically leave the jury with wide discretion in choosing amounts, and the presentation of evidence of a defendant's net worth creates the potential that juries will use their verdicts to express biases against big businesses, particularly those without strong local presences. Our concerns are heightened when the decisionmaker is presented, as we shall discuss, with evidence that has little bearing as to the amount of punitive damages that should be awarded. Vague instructions, or those that merely inform the jury to avoid passion or prejudice, do little to aid the decisionmaker in its task of assigning appropriate weight to evidence that is relevant and evidence that is tangential or only inflammatory.

In light of these concerns, we instructed courts reviewing punitive damages to consider three guideposts: (1) the degree of reprehensibility of the defendant's misconduct; (2) the disparity between the actual or potential harm suffered by the plaintiff and the punitive damages award; and (3) the difference between the punitive damages awarded by the jury and the civil penalties authorized or imposed in comparable cases. We reiterated the importance of these three guideposts . . . and mandated appellate courts to conduct *de novo* review of a trial court's application of them to the jury's award. Exacting appellate review ensures that an award of punitive damages is based upon an application of law, rather than a decisionmaker's caprice.

Under the principles outlined in *BMW of North America, Inc. v. Gore,* this case is neither close nor

[CONTINUED]

difficult. It was error to reinstate the jury's $145 million punitive damages award. We address each guidepost of *Gore* in some detail.

The most important indicium of the reasonableness of a punitive damages award is the degree of reprehensibility of the defendant's conduct. We have instructed courts to determine the reprehensibility of a defendant by considering whether: the harm caused was physical as opposed to economic; the tortious conduct evinced an indifference to or a reckless disregard of the health or safety of others; the target of the conduct had financial vulnerability; the conduct involved repeated actions or was an isolated incident; and the harm was the result of intentional malice, trickery, or deceit, or mere accident. The existence of any one of these factors weighing in favor of a plaintiff may not be sufficient to sustain a punitive damages award; and the absence of all of them renders any award suspect. It should be presumed a plaintiff has been made whole for his injuries by compensatory damages, so punitive damages should only be awarded if the defendant's culpability, after having paid compensatory damages, is so reprehensible as to warrant the imposition of further sanctions to achieve punishment or deterrence.

Applying these factors in the instant case, we must acknowledge that State Farm's handling of the claims against the Campbells merits no praise. The trial court found that State Farm's employees altered the company's records to make Campbell appear less culpable. State Farm disregarded the overwhelming likelihood of liability and the near-certain probability that, by taking the case to trial, a judgment in excess of the policy limits would be awarded. State Farm amplified the harm by at first assuring the Campbells their assets would be safe from any verdict. . . . While we do not suggest there was error in awarding punitive damages based upon State Farm's conduct toward the Campbells, a more modest punishment for this reprehensible conduct could have satisfied the State's legitimate objectives, and the Utah courts should have gone no further.

This case, instead, was used as a platform to expose, and punish, the perceived deficiencies of State Farm's operations throughout the country. The Utah Supreme Court's opinion makes explicit that State Farm was being condemned for its nationwide policies rather than for the conduct directed toward the Campbells. This was, as well, an explicit rationale of the trial court's decision in approving the award, though reduced from $145 million to $25 million. . . .

A State cannot punish a defendant for conduct that may have been lawful where it occurred. Nor, as a general rule, does a State have a legitimate concern in imposing punitive damages to punish a defendant for unlawful acts committed outside of the State's jurisdiction. Any proper adjudication of conduct that occurred outside Utah to other persons would require their inclusion, and, to those parties, the Utah courts, in the usual case, would need to apply the laws of their relevant jurisdiction. . . .

For a more fundamental reason, however, the Utah courts erred in relying upon this and other evidence: The courts awarded punitive damages to punish and deter conduct that bore no relation to the Campbells' harm. A defendant's dissimilar acts, independent from the acts upon which liability was premised, may not serve as the basis for punitive damages. A defendant should be punished for the conduct that harmed the plaintiff, not for being an unsavory individual or business. Due process does not permit courts, in the calculation of punitive damages, to adjudicate the merits of other parties' hypothetical claims against a defendant under the guise of the reprehensibility analysis, but we have no doubt the Utah Supreme Court did that here.

Turning to the second *Gore* guidepost, we have been reluctant to identify concrete constitutional limits on the ratio between harm, or potential harm, to the plaintiff and the punitive damages award. We decline again to impose a bright-line ratio which a punitive damages award cannot exceed. Our jurisprudence and the principles it has now established demonstrate, however, that, in practice, few awards exceeding a single-digit ratio between punitive and compensatory damages, to a significant degree, will satisfy due process. In *Haslip,* in upholding a punitive damages award, we concluded that an award of more than four times the amount of compensatory damages might be close to the line of constitutional impropriety. We cited that 4-to-1 ratio again in *Gore.* The Court further referenced a long legislative history,

[CONTINUED]

dating back over 700 years and going forward to today, providing for sanctions of double, treble, or quadruple damages to deter and punish. While these ratios are not binding, they are instructive. They demonstrate what should be obvious: Single-digit multipliers are more likely to comport with due process, while still achieving the State's goals of deterrence and retribution, than awards with ratios in range of 500 to 1, or, in this case, of 145 to 1. . . .

The . . . premises for the Utah Supreme Court's decision bear no relation to the award's reasonableness or proportionality to the harm. They are, rather, arguments that seek to defend a departure from well-established constraints on punitive damages. While States enjoy considerable discretion in deducing when punitive damages are warranted, each award must comport with the principles set forth in *Gore*. Here the argument that State Farm will be punished in only the rare case, coupled with reference to its assets (which, of course, are what other insured parties in Utah and other States must rely upon for payment of claims) had little to do with the actual harm sustained by the Campbells. The wealth of a defendant cannot justify an otherwise unconstitutional punitive damages award. . . .

The third guidepost in *Gore* is the disparity between the punitive damages award and the civil penalties authorized or imposed in comparable cases. We note that, in the past, we have also looked to criminal penalties that could be imposed. The existence of a criminal penalty does have bearing on the seriousness with which a State views the wrongful action. When used to determine the dollar amount of the award, however, the criminal penalty has less utility. Great care must be taken to avoid use of the civil process to assess criminal penalties that can be imposed only after the heightened protections of a criminal trial have been observed, including, of course, its higher standards of proof. Punitive damages are not a substitute for the criminal process, and the remote possibility of a criminal sanction does not automatically sustain a punitive damages award.

Here, we need not dwell long on this guidepost. The most relevant civil sanction under Utah state law for the wrong done to the Campbells appears to be a $10,000 fine for an act of fraud, an amount dwarfed by the $145 million punitive damages award. The Supreme Court of Utah speculated about the loss of State Farm's business license, the disgorgement of profits, and possible imprisonment, but here again its references were to the broad fraudulent scheme drawn from evidence of out-of-state and dissimilar conduct. This analysis was insufficient to justify the award.

An application of the *Gore* guideposts to the facts of this case, especially in light of the substantial compensatory damages awarded (a portion of which contained a punitive element), likely would justify a punitive damages award at or near the amount of compensatory damages. The punitive award of $145 million, therefore, was neither reasonable nor proportionate to the wrong committed, and it was an irrational and arbitrary deprivation of the property of the defendant. The proper calculation of punitive damages under the principles we have discussed should be resolved, in the first instance, by the Utah courts.

Reversed.

CASE QUESTIONS

1. Describe the factual basis of the lawsuits involved in this case.
2. What were the amounts of the jury's compensatory and punitive damage awards?
3. How were these awards modified by the trial judge and Utah Supreme Court?
4. What are the three key guideposts used by the U.S. Supreme Court in deciding whether a punitive damage award is consistent with the due process clause?
5. Why does the Supreme Court conclude that the $145 million punitive damage award is unconstitutional?

Incorporation Doctrine The due process clause has played a unique role in constitutional development—one that was probably not anticipated at the time of its ratification. This significant role has been to make most of the provisions of the Bill of Rights applicable to the states. The first phrase of the First Amendment begins: "Congress shall make no law." How then are state and local governments prohibited from making such a law? Jurists have used the due process clause of the Fourteenth Amendment to "incorporate" or "carry over" the Bill of Rights and make these constitutional provisions applicable to the states. Starting in 1925, the Supreme Court began applying various portions of the first eight amendments to the states using the due process clause of the Fourteenth Amendment as the reason for this incorporation and application.

The role of the due process doctrine goes well beyond incorporation. For example, the Fifth Amendment contains a due process clause applicable to the federal government. The Fourteenth Amendment contains a due process clause applicable to state and local governments. Due process essentially means the same thing under both amendments. Through the due process clause, all of the constitutionally guaranteed freedoms we discuss in this chapter and in Chapter 10 have been incorporated into the Fourteenth Amendment and are applicable to the state government's regulation of our personal and professional lives.

12. EQUAL PROTECTION

The Fourteenth Amendment's equal protection language is also involved in a great deal of constitutional litigation. No law treats all persons equally; laws draw lines and treat people differently. Therefore, almost any state or local law imaginable can be challenged under the equal protection clause. It is obvious that the equal protection clause does not always deny states the power to treat different persons in different ways. Yet the equal protection clause embodies the ethical idea that law should not treat people differently without a satisfactory reason. In deciding cases using that clause to challenge state and local laws, courts use three distinct approaches. One is the traditional, or **minimum rationality,** approach, and a second is called the **strict scrutiny** approach. Some cases are analyzed as falling in between these approaches. Courts in these cases use the **quasi-strict scrutiny** approach.

As a practical matter, if the traditional (minimum rationality) approach is used, the challenged law and its classifications are usually found *not* to be a violation of equal protection. On the other hand, if the strict scrutiny test is used, the classifications are usually found to be unconstitutional under the equal protection clause.

Minimum Rationality Under the minimum rationality approach, a law creating different classifications will survive an equal protection challenge if it has a *rational* connection to a *permissible* state end. A permissible state end is one not prohibited by another provision of the Constitution. It qualifies as a legitimate goal of government. The classification must have a reasonable basis (not wholly arbitrary), and the courts will assume any statement of facts that can be used to justify the classification. These laws often involve economic issues or social legislation such as welfare laws.

Such laws are presumed to be constitutional because courts recognize that the legislature must draw lines creating distinctions and that such tasks cannot be avoided. Only when no rational basis for the classification exists is it unconstitutional under the equal protection clause. For example, a state law restricting advertising to company-owned trucks was held valid when the rational basis test was applied to it because it is reasonable to assume less advertising on trucks provides for safer roads. Therefore, under this state law, a trucking company could not use the sides of its trucks to carry other companies' ads.

Strict Scrutiny   Under the strict scrutiny test, a classification will be a denial of equal protection unless the classification is necessary to achieve a *compelling* state purpose. It is not enough that a classification be permissible to achieve any state interest; it must be a compelling state objective. To withstand constitutional challenge when this test is used, the law must serve important governmental objectives and the classification must be substantially related to achieving these objectives.

The strict scrutiny test is used if the classification involves either a suspect class or a fundamental constitutional right. A suspect class is one that has such disabilities, has been subjected to such a history of purposeful unequal treatment, or has been placed in such a position of political powerlessness that it commands extraordinary protection from the political process of the majority. For example, classifications directed at race, national origin, and legitimacy of birth are clearly suspect. As a result, the judiciary strictly scrutinizes laws directed at them. Unless the state can prove that its statutory classifications have a compelling state interest as a basis, the classifications will be considered a denial of equal protection. Classifications that are subject to strict judicial scrutiny are presumed to be unconstitutional. The state must convince the court that the classification is fair, reasonable, and necessary to accomplish the objective of legislation that is compelling to a state interest.

The case at the end of Chapter 3 discusses this role of strict scrutiny in analyzing the use of race in college admission policies. The following case focuses on the same analysis in the application of racial consideration in the award of government contracts.

ADARAND CONSTRUCTORS, INC. V. PENA

115 S. CT. 2097 (1995)

O'CONNOR, J.: In 1989, the Central Federal Lands Highway Division (CFLHD), which is part of the United States Department of Transportation (DOT), awarded the prime contract for a highway construction project in Colorado to Mountain Gravel & Construction Company. Mountain Gravel then solicited bids from subcontractors for the guardrail portion of the contract. Adarand, a Colorado-based highway construction company specializing in guardrail work, submitted the low bid. Gonzales Construction Company also submitted a bid.

The prime contract's terms provide that Mountain Gravel would receive additional compensation if it hired subcontractors certified as small businesses controlled by "socially and economically disadvantaged individuals." Gonzales is certified as such a business; Adarand is not. Mountain Gravel awarded the subcontract to Gonzales, despite Adarand's low bid. Federal law requires that a subcontracting clause similar to the one used here must appear in most federal agency contracts, and it also requires the clause to state that "the contractor shall presume that socially and economically disadvantaged individuals include Black Americans, Hispanic Americans, Native Americans, Asian Pacific Americans, and other minorities, or any other individual found

[CONTINUED]

to be disadvantaged by the [Small Business] Administration pursuant to section 8(a) of the Small Business Act." Adarand claims that the presumption set forth in that statute discriminates on the basis of race in violation of the Federal Government's Fifth Amendment obligation not to deny anyone equal protection of the laws. . . .

The contract giving rise to the dispute in this case came about as a result of the Surface Transportation and Uniform Relocation Assistance Act of 1987, a DOT appropriations measure. Section 106(c)(1) of STURAA provides that "not less than 10 percent" of the appropriated funds "shall be expended with small business concerns owned and controlled by socially and economically disadvantaged individuals." STURAA adopts the Small Business Act's definition of "socially and economically disadvantaged individual," including the applicable race-based presumptions, and adds that "women shall be presumed to be socially and economically disadvantaged individuals for purposes of this subsection.". . .

After losing the guardrail subcontract to Gonzales, Adarand filed suit against various federal officials in the United States District Court for the District of Colorado, claiming that the race-based presumptions involved in the use of subcontracting compensation clauses violate Adarand's right to equal protection. The District Court granted the Government's motion for summary judgment. The Court of Appeals for the Tenth Circuit affirmed. It understood our decision in *Fullilove v. Klutznick,* 100 S. Ct. 2758 (1980), to have adopted "a lenient standard, resembling intermediate scrutiny, in assessing" the constitutionality of federal race-based action. Applying that "lenient standard," as further developed in *Metro Broadcasting, Inc. v. FCC,* 110 S. Ct. 2997 (1990), the Court of Appeals upheld the use of subcontractor compensation clauses. We granted certiorari. . . .

In 1978, the Court confronted the question whether race-based governmental action designed to benefit such groups should also be subject to "the most rigid scrutiny." *Regents of Univ. of California v. Bakke,* 98 S. Ct. 2733, involved an equal protection challenge to a state-run medical schools' practice of reserving a number of spaces in its entering class for minority students. The petitioners argued that "strict scrutiny" should apply only to "classifi-

cations that disadvantage 'discrete and insular minorities.' " *Bakke* did not produce an opinion for the Court, but Justice Powell's opinion announcing the Court's judgment rejected the argument. In a passage joined by Justice White, Justice Powell wrote that "the guarantee of equal protection cannot mean one thing when applied to one individual and something else when applied to a person of another color." He concluded that "racial and ethnic distinctions of any sort are inherently suspect and thus call for the most exacting judicial examination.". . .

Two years after *Bakke,* the Court faced another challenge to remedial race-based action, this time involving action undertaken by the Federal Government. In *Fullilove v. Klutznick,* the Court upheld Congress' inclusion of a 10% set-aside for minority-owned businesses in the Public Works Employment Act of 1977. As in *Bakke,* there was no opinion for the Court. Chief Justice Burger, in an opinion joined by Justices White and Powell, observed that "any preference based on racial or ethnic criteria must necessarily receive a most searching examination to make sure that it does not conflict with constitutional guarantees." That opinion, however, "did not adopt, either expressly or implicitly, the formulas of analysis articulated in such cases as [*Bakke*]." It employed instead a two-part test which asked, first, "whether the objectives of the legislation are within the power of Congress," and second, "whether the limited use of racial and ethnic criteria, in the context presented, is a constitutionally permissible means for achieving the congressional objectives." It then upheld the program under that test. . . .

In *Wygant v. Jackson Board of Ed.,* 106 S. Ct. 1842 (1986), the Court considered a Fourteenth Amendment challenge to another form of remedial racial classification. The issue in *Wygant* was whether a school board could adopt race-based preferences in determining which teachers to lay off. Justice Powell's plurality opinion observed that "the level of scrutiny does not change merely because the challenged classification operates against a group that historically has not been subject to governmental discrimination," and stated the two-part inquiry as "whether the layoff provision is supported by a compelling state purpose and whether the means chosen to accomplish that purpose are narrowly tailored." In other words, "racial classifications of any

[CONTINUED]

sort must be subjected to 'strict scrutiny.' " The plurality then concluded that the school board's interest in "providing minority role models for its minority students, as an attempt to alleviate the effects of societal discrimination," was not a compelling interest that could justify the use of a racial classification. It added that "societal discrimination, without more, is too amorphous a basis for imposing a racially classified remedy," and insisted instead that "a public employer . . . must ensure that, before it embarks on an affirmative-action program, it has convincing evidence that remedial action is warranted. That is, it must have sufficient evidence to justify the conclusion that there has been prior discrimination.". . .

The Court's failure to produce a majority opinion in *Bakke, Fullilove,* and *Wygant* left unresolved the proper analysis for remedial race-based governmental action.

The Court resolved the issue, at least in part, in 1989. *Richmond v. J. A. Croson Co.,* 109 S. Ct. 706 (1989), concerned a city's determination that 30% of its contracting work should go to minority-owned businesses. A majority of the Court in *Croson* held that "the standard of review under the Equal Protection Clause is not dependent on the race of those burdened or benefited by a particular classification," and that the single standard of review for racial classifications should be "strict scrutiny." As to the classification before the Court, the plurality agreed that "a state or local subdivision . . . has the authority to eradicate the effects of private discrimination within its own legislative jurisdiction," but the Court thought that the city had not acted with "a 'strong basis in evidence for its conclusion that remedial action was necessary.' " The Court also thought it "obvious that [the] program is not narrowly tailored to remedy the effects of prior discrimination."

With *Croson,* the Court finally agreed that the Fourteenth Amendment requires strict scrutiny of all race-based action by state and local governments. But *Croson* of course had no occasion to declare what standard of review the Fifth Amendment requires for such action taken by the Federal Government. . . .

A year later, however, the Court took a surprising turn. *Metro Broadcasting, Inc. v. FCC* involved a Fifth Amendment challenge to two race-based policies of the Federal Communications Commission. In *Metro Broadcasting,* the Court repudiated the long-held notion that "it would be unthinkable that the same Constitution would impose a lesser duty on the Federal Government" than it does on a State to afford equal protection of the laws. It did so by holding that "benign" federal racial classifications need only satisfy intermediate scrutiny, even though *Croson* had recently concluded that such classifications enacted by a State must satisfy strict scrutiny. "Benign" federal racial classifications, the Court said, "—even if those measures are not *remedial* in the sense of being designed to compensate victims of past governmental or societal discrimination—are constitutionally permissible to the extent that they serve important governmental objectives within the power of Congress and are substantially related to achievement of those objectives.". . .

By adopting intermediate scrutiny as the standard of review for congressionally mandated "benign" racial classifications, *Metro Broadcasting* departed from prior cases in two significant respects. First, it turned its back on *Croson*'s explanation of why strict scrutiny of all governmental racial classifications is essential. . . .

Second, *Metro Broadcasting* squarely rejected one of the three propositions established by the Court's earlier equal protection cases, namely, congruence between the standards applicable to federal and state racial classifications, and in so doing also undermined the other two—skepticism of all racial classifications and consistency of treatment irrespective of the race of the burdened or benefited group. Under *Metro Broadcasting,* certain racial classifications ("benign" ones enacted by the Federal Government) should be treated less skeptically than others; and the race of the benefited group is critical to the determination of which standard of review to apply. *Metro Broadcasting* was thus a significant departure from much of what had come before it.

The three propositions undermined by *Metro Broadcasting* all derive from the basic principle that the Fifth and Fourteenth Amendments to the Constitution protect persons, not groups. It follows from that principle that all governmental action based on race . . . should be subjected to detailed judicial inquiry to ensure that the personal right to equal protection of the laws has not been infringed. These ideas have long been central to this Court's understanding of equal protection, and holding "benign"

[CONTINUED]

state and federal racial classifications to different standards does not square with them. . . . Accordingly, we hold today that all racial classifications, imposed by whatever federal, state, or local governmental actor, must be analyzed by a reviewing court under strict scrutiny. In other words, such classifications are constitutional only if they are narrowly tailored measures that further compelling governmental interests. To the extent that *Metro Broadcasting* is inconsistent with that holding, it is overruled. . . .

Because our decision today alters the playing field in some important respects, we think it best to remand the case to the lower courts for further consideration in light of the principles we have announced. The Court of Appeals, following *Metro Broadcasting and Fullilove,* analyzed the case in terms of intermediate scrutiny. It upheld the challenged statutes and regulations because it found them to be "narrowly tailored to achieve [their] significant governmental purpose of providing subcontracting opportunities for small disadvantaged business enterprises." The Court of Appeals did not

decide the question whether the interests served by the use of subcontractor compensation clauses are properly described as "compelling." It also did not address the question of narrow tailoring in terms of our strict scrutiny cases, by asking, for example, whether there was "any consideration of the use of race-neutral means to increase minority business participation" in government contracting, or whether the program was appropriately limited such that it "will not last longer than the discriminatory effects it is designed to eliminate.". . .

The question whether any of the ways in which the Government uses subcontractor compensation clauses can survive strict scrutiny, and any relevance distinctions such as these may have to that question, should be addressed in the first instance by the lower courts.

Accordingly, the judgment of the Court of Appeals is vacated, and the case is remanded for further proceedings consistent with this opinion.

Vacated and remanded.

CASE QUESTIONS

1. Why was Adarand Constructors, as low bidder on the guardrail subcontract, not awarded the job?

2. What were the holdings of *Bakke, Fullilove,* and *Wygant*? Why did these decisions not resolve the standard of review question?

3. What is the conflict between the opinions in *Croson* and *Metro Broadcasting*?

4. Why is the holding in this case so important? Does this opinion stand for the proposition that affirmative action programs are unconstitutional?

5. Why did the Supreme Court decide not to resolve the issue of which party should be awarded the guardrail subcontract?

Strict judicial scrutiny is applied to a second group of cases involving classifications directed at fundamental rights. If a classification unduly burdens or penalizes the exercise of a constitutional right, it will be stricken unless it is found to be necessary to support a compelling state interest. Among such rights are the right to vote, the right to travel, and the right to appeal. Doubts about such laws result in their being stricken by the courts as a denial of equal protection.

Quasi-Strict Scrutiny Some cases actually fall between the minimum rationality and strict scrutiny approaches. These cases use what is sometimes called quasi-strict scrutiny tests because the classifications are only partially suspect or the rights involved are not quite fundamental. For example, classifications directed at gender are partially suspect. In cases involving classifications based on gender, the courts have taken this position between the two tests or at least have modified the strict scrutiny approach. Such classifications are unconstitutional unless they are *substantially* related to an *important* government objective. This modified version of strict scrutiny has resulted in holdings that find laws to be valid as well as unconstitutional.

Equal protection cases run the whole spectrum of legislative attempts to solve society's problems. For example, courts have used the equal protection clause to require the integration of public schools. In addition, the meaning and application of the equal protection clause have been central issues in cases involving:

- Apportionment of legislative bodies
- Racial segregation in the sale and rental of real estate
- Laws distinguishing between the rights of legitimates and illegitimates
- The makeup of juries
- Voting requirements
- Welfare residency requirements
- Rights of aliens
- The use of property taxes as the means of financing public schools

The next table summarizes the legal approaches courts use when analyzing equal protection cases.

The equal protection clause is the means to the end, or goal, of equality of opportunity. As such, it may be utilized by anyone claiming unequal treatment in any case. At the same time the clause will not prevent states from remedying the effect of past discrimination. As you will study in Chapter 15, courts have upheld laws that provide for preferential treatment of minorities if this remedy is narrowly tailored to serve a compelling governmental interest in eradicating past discrimination against the minority group.

Analysis of Equal Protection

	Minimum Rationality	*Quasi-Strict Scrutiny*	*Strict Scrutiny*
Classifications Must Be	Rationally connected to a permissible or legitimate government objective	Substantially related to an important government interest	Necessary to a compelling state interest
	Presumed Valid	*Quasi-Suspect Classes*	*Suspect Classes*
Examples	Height	Gender	Race
	Weight		National origin
	Age		Legitimacy
	Testing		*Fundamental Rights*
	School desegregation		To vote
	Veteran's preference		To travel
	Marriage		To appeal

KEY TERMS

Apportionment   154
Commerce clause   148
Commercial speech   160
Contract clause   148
Defamation   158
Dominant commerce clause concept
   150
Due process clause   163
Equal protection clause   163
Establishment clause   157
Federalism   144
Free exercise clause   157
Irreconcilable conflicts   151
Libel   158
Malice   158

Minimum rationality   167
Nexus   154
Overbreadth doctrine   159
Police powers   150
Preemption   144
Prior restraints   158
Procedural due process   163
Prohibiting discrimination   152
Quasi-strict scrutiny   167
Separation of powers   144
Strict scrutiny   167
Substantive due process   163
Supremacy clause   144
Symbolic speech   158
Undue burden   151

REVIEW QUESTIONS AND PROBLEMS

Basic Concepts

1. *Separation of Powers*

    Describe the two concepts that (a) balance power within the federal government and (b) provide distinctions in the role of the federal, state, and local governments.

2. *Supremacy Clause*

    In 1916, the federal government passed a law that allows national banks to sell insurance in towns with a population of less than 5,000. In 1974, Florida passed a law prohibiting insurance agents from associating with financial institutions that are owned by or affiliated with a bank holding company. A bank located in a small Florida town is affiliated with a national bank. This bank wants to sell insurance through licensed insurance agents. Can the bank successfully challenge the Florida prohibition as being preempted by the federal law? Explain your reasoning.

3. *Contract Clause*

    (a)   Does this provision of the Constitution apply to the federal government, state government, or both? Explain.

    (b)   Does this provision of the Constitution apply to present contractual relationships, future ones, or both? Explain.

The Commerce Clause

4. *Regulation of Foreign Commerce*

    Why is it important that regulation of international business transactions is reserved exclusively to the federal government?

5. *Regulation of Interstate Commerce*

    What is the legal analysis used by the courts to grant the federal government almost limitless authority to regulate business activity?

6. *Limitation on State Police Powers*

   (a)   Describe the five factual situations wherein the commerce clause might be used to restrict a state or local governmental action. What analysis is used in each situation?

   (b)   A Maine statute imposed a tax on trucks. The tax required owners and operators of foreign-based (out-of-state) trucks using Maine highways to purchase either an annual highway use permit or a one-trip permit. Trucks based in-state were exempt. An out-of-state trucker challenged the constitutionality of the statute. Is this Maine statute constitutional? Why or why not?

7. *Limitation on State Taxation*

   (a)   Define the terms *apportionment* and *nexus.*

   (b)   How are these concepts applied to restrict state government taxation of businesses engaged in interstate commerce?

Regulation and Basic Freedoms

8. *Freedom of Religion*

   Explain the purposes of and distinction between the establishment clause and the free exercise clause.

9. *Freedom of the Press*

   (a)   A promoter of theatrical productions applied to a municipal board (charged with managing a city-leased theater) for a license to stage the play *Hair.* Relying on outside reports that because of nudity the production would not be in the best interests of the community, the board rejected the application. The promoter sought a court order permitting it to use the auditorium. Why should the court allow the production to proceed?

   (b)   What are the distinctions in how the law treats public persons versus private persons with respect to defamation?

10. *Freedom of Speech*

   Silvia, an attorney in Florida, also was a licensed certified public accountant (CPA) and a certified financial planner (CFP). Silvia placed an ad in the yellow pages listing her credentials, including the CPA and CFP designations. The Florida Board of Accountancy reprimanded Silvia for using both the CPA and CFP credentials in an ad essentially emphasizing her legal work. Silvia challenged the board's right to issue this reprimand. What is the legal basis for Silvia's challenge? Explain.

The Fourteenth Amendment

11. *Due Process of Law*

   Explain what is meant by the Incorporation Doctrine and how it was used to expand the impact of the due process clause.

12. *Equal Protection*

   There are three levels of judicial scrutiny under this clause. Describe what these levels are and when they are applicable.

TERMINOLOGY REVIEW

For each term in the left-hand column, match the most appropriate description in the right-hand column.

1. Defamation
2. Libel
3. Prior restraint
4. Federalism
5. Malice
6. Overbreadth doctrine
7. Dominant commerce clause
8. Preemption

a. The separation of governmental functions between the federal and state governments
b. Used to restrict states' police powers from harming interstate business activity
c. The area of law generally meant to protect a person's or organization's reputation
d. The concept of stopping someone from printing material or delivering a speech
e. The principle whereby the federal government reserves for itself the right to regulate certain activities
f. Proof of intent to cause harm
g. The concept that prohibits governments from enforcing laws that are broader than necessary to accomplish a stated purpose
h. A written form of defamation

BUSINESS DISCUSSION

Other retail businesses in the mall in which your sports shoes shop is located have decided to open on Sundays from 12 noon to 6 P.M. You decide to follow suit, but two of your employees refuse to go along, saying it is against their religious beliefs to work on the Sabbath. You terminate their employment. They apply for unemployment compensation, and contend their unemployed status is your fault. If the state grants them benefits, you will be penalized since your unemployment compensation taxes will go up.

Should you contest their claim?

What would be the result if the employees refuse to work on Sunday because of their desire to play golf on that day?

THE PROPERTY
SYSTEM

Colonel Cars, Inc., plans to introduce a new speaker complex in the steering wheels of its automobiles. It believes the change will revolutionize the drivers' music-listening enjoyment. The company is also preparing an advertising campaign around the improved listening experience. Both the new steering-wheel speakers and the ad campaign are carefully kept secrets. But Colonel Cars's vice president for marketing is hired by European Motor Works (EMW) to be the president of its international division. Before Colonel Cars can begin its advertising, EMW comes out with an ad campaign centered on—you guessed it—speakers in the steering wheels of its new model cars.

What is "property"?

Can a company have property in its marketing plans the way you can have property in your car?

Can EMW use Colonel Cars's marketing plans without permission?

As explained in Chapter 1, the legal concept of property is vital to understanding how law provides a foundation for the private market. Property also establishes a central focus, or hub, for grasping the subjects of this book, including contracts, tort laws, and much public law regulation of business. Contracts involve the exchange of what people own (Chapter 8). Tort law permits compensation when one person harms or infringes what belongs to another (Chapter 9). Public law regulation of business helps define and protect the equal right of all to what they own. For instance, antitrust law protects what company A owns from certain competitive harms by company B (Chapter 13), and securities law protects what investors own from misappropriation by corporate agents like managers (Chapter 16).

What is property? In everyday conversation we use *property* interchangeably with things like land or other resources, but it is clear that "property" has some additional meaning. Property indicates legal ownership, that something is recognized by law as being "mine" or "yours." Further, property indicates exclusiveness. You can legally exclude others from things that are yours (i.e., things you own). For example, if you can exclude others from a car that you own, you can do many things with it. You can possess and drive it; you can sell it or give it away; you can rent it out or start a taxi company with it; or you can use it as security for a loan or add it to your car collection. All of these uses of the car, however, are possible because you can legally exclude others from interfering with these uses. As the Supreme Court stated, "The hallmark of a protected property interest is the right to exclude others." [527 U.S. 666, 673 (1999)]

Here is a definition of property that regards it as a legal right rather than a thing or a bunch of things: **Property** *is the legal right to exclude others from resources that are originally possessed or are acquired without force, theft, or fraud.* A "resource" includes anything that someone may need or want. Land, widgets, shares of corporate stock, and the uses of these things are all resources. In a sense, someone's labor or efforts are also resources. "Originally possessed" resources like your capacity for work and health are protected by the property right in that you can legally exclude others from interfering with them or sue others if they harm these resources. For another definition of property see the box "Property as a Bundle of Rights."

The state through its legislatures and courts establishes how property applies to various resources. Sometimes the state does not permit you property in particular resources. You cannot sell human kidneys, although you can give away one of yours. The state recognizes that you have the right to exclude others from your kidney for some purposes but not to sell them. Although a great many legal rules limit the right of property as applied to resources and their uses (which can also be considered resources), prosperous nations in general apply the property right widely to the things that people need or want.

Property law does not function well when it is not adequately enforced. Honest police are needed to deter robbery and theft. Impartial courts are required to settle disputes over who owns what and whether X has wrongfully injured Y's resources. Property becomes not just an exclusionary right but also an entire system, and it is upon this property system of law that business depends.

PROPERTY AS A BUNDLE OF RIGHTS

Many scholars describe property as "a bundle of sticklike rights" that apply to things. Thus, if you have property in land, you have the rights to *possess* it, *control* it, *use* it in various ways, *transfer* it, *gain income* from it, and so forth. Sometimes it is desirable to think of property in this way when deciding whether or not the state has "taken" one's property through regulation under the Fifth Amendment to the Constitution. The Supreme Court has ruled that the state does not have to compensate owners when it has taken only some but not all of the bundle of property rights through regulatory limitations.

For example, regulations in Athens, Georgia, prohibit more than two unrelated people from living in residences zoned for single families. This upsets University of Georgia students who like to rent houses and live in them with three or more unrelated people to the house. It also deprives owners of houses of the right to use their realty to rent to groups of students. But since the owners may still sell their houses and rent them to single families, the city of Athens has not deprived the owners of the entire bundle of property rights and thus need not compensate them.

Rather than regarding property as a bundle of rights, we regard it as a single right, the right to exclude. If owners can legally exclude others from interfering with what they own, they can do what they want with their resources: possess them, control them, use them, or transfer them. The single right of exclusion includes all of the other rights. In explaining the "essence" of property, the right of exclusion conceptualizes it most accurately.

This chapter explores the property system, the problem of limited resources, the connection between property and prosperity, and various ownership rules that apply to different kinds of resources. It focuses on intellectual property, which is a key to appreciating the importance of information resources and of computers, digital programming, and the new issues of property application in the age of the Internet. You should finish this chapter with a deeper knowledge of the central significance of property law to business. Quite simply, it is the necessary foundation for private enterprise in the modern nation.

THE PROPERTY SYSTEM

Arguably the most significant issue for any society is how it orders the relationships among people concerning limited and valued resources, resources needed to survive and flourish. As long as people need or want more resources than they have available to them, society will order how people relate to each other in acquiring and possessing these resources. Such resources include land, food, raw materials, manufactured products, and even some types of information. Human productive effort and creative applications are also limited resources.

1. THE PROBLEM OF LIMITED RESOURCES

In Western political theory, the state (government) comes into being in response to the problem of limited resources. Through law, the state establishes a framework for handling the problem. At least two basic legal frameworks exist. In one framework the state itself, represented by a ruler or legislature, makes the major decisions about the production and distribution of resources. The state takes ownership of resources or acquires them through taxation. It also may direct people in how, when, and where to work, thus assuming rights over the resources people have in themselves, their efforts, and talents. Distribution of resources occurs through state planning.

Communism is one system providing such a framework. The state requires that its citizens produce according to their abilities and share according to the needs of everyone else. The communist state expects people to want to do this, but it legally coerces them when necessary.

A second legal framework that orders how people relate to each other concerning scarce resources is private property. Private property, which we will just call "property," is a system of law under which the state recognizes and enforces an individual's rights to acquire, possess, use, and transfer scarce resources. (As for property other than private property, see the box "The Three Faces of Property.") In the property system, the state does not plan what people should have nor does it acquire and redistribute resources to them. Rather, the people themselves determine how resources are distributed through voluntary exchange, usually for money that they use to acquire other resources they need or want. The role of the state is to recognize legally when people have exclusive property rights in scarce resources and to allow them to enforce their rights through legal institutions like courts.

Probably no society fits entirely into either resource allocation framework. Even the most communist society may allow individuals some right as to how they use their productive efforts, and it usually allows them exclusive control over limited personal possessions and food consumption. On the other hand, societies

THE THREE FACES OF PROPERTY

Legal scholars divide the word "property" into three main usages: private, public, and common. *Private property* protects private persons and allows them to exclude others, including in most instances the state, from interfering with resources that are acquired without force, theft, or fraud. *Public property* refers to the state's right under various circumstances to exclude people from state monuments, buildings, equipment, land, and other public resources.

Common property has two meanings. First, it refers to the right we all have to common resources like the air, rivers, or oceans. However, this meaning is appropriate only to the extent we can legally exclude others from interfering with our usage of these resources, for example, as when anyone who uses a river can sue to prevent or stop its illegal pollution. Second, "common property" sometimes refers to the private ownership by two or more people of a specific resource such as a piece of land.

For studying the legal and regulatory environment of business, private property is most important. It provides the foundation for the conduct of the modern market, and it is often just called "property."

founded on private property law always have legal limitations on how owners can use their resources, prohibiting harm to others and recognizing both some state taxation and regulation over property. The difference in the two frameworks is a matter of degree, and most societies have mixed frameworks for dealing with the reality of limited resources.

However, if the goal of society is to produce more of what people need and want (i.e., to increase the total amount of limited resources), one of the legal frameworks is superior to the other. The available evidence suggests that a property system produces more for a society than a state planning system. And if "freedom" is measured as individual autonomy and the absence of state coercion, then a property system also makes people more free.

For the property system to function most effectively in promoting prosperity, it should be applied according to the rule of law, which means it should be applied generally and equally to everyone. All members of society must have an equal guarantee of exclusive rights to their resources. The following section discusses more specifically how property promotes prosperity.

2. PROPERTY AND PROSPERITY

Property is central to the legal environment of business. It is also central to society's achievement of prosperity. In fact, property creates some of the maximum conditions known for producing and sustaining prosperity. Since property refers to a particular system of laws, rather than to useful resources, it is fair to conclude that certain laws are a major contributing factor to prosperity. Let us examine how property helps generate prosperity.

First, property powerfully promotes *incentive.* By allowing people to keep and benefit from what they produce, property motivates effort in a way that Chapter 1 suggested is very natural to human beings. Whether the activity is growing crops, manufacturing cars, or starting a new cyber business, people will generally expend more effort when they have a protected property in what they produce than when they do not. Likewise, they are willing to produce more when they do not have to spend much of their time defending their homes or other acquisitions from those who may desire to take them. Under conditions where others are likely to take through force, theft, fraud, or even government mandate what people have or produce, there comes a point at which people will simply not work as hard, take as many risks, nor innovate as much. We may debate where that point is (e.g., how much people can be taxed before they slow their efforts), but the fact that property and incentive bear a direct relationship seems beyond debate.

Next, property helps generate prosperity by establishing the conditions necessary for *capital formation,* which refers to that quality of resources that produces new or different resources. For example, property enables people to borrow money at reasonable cost. In the United States most entrepreneurs start businesses by capitalizing the resource they have in their houses. They borrow money, and in a **mortgage** agreement put up their houses to secure the loans.

Lenders are willing to loan money at affordable rates primarily because property law guarantees (1) that a borrower's house is on an identifiable piece of land recognized by the state, (2) that the state recognizes a borrower's claim to the house, and (3) that the state permits lenders to enforce the mortgage agreement through the courts and sell a borrower's house to satisfy the loan if the borrower fails to repay it. The law of property enables entrepreneurs to change the form of their resources from "houses" to "money," so they can start a business. This type of capital formation may seem curiously obvious to business students in the United States. However, as the following box discusses, it is virtually unavailable in the poorer nations of the world due to the absence of adequate property law.

Of course, the relationship of capital formation to property law means more than just mortgages or other collateral-secured loans. Large-scale businesses are capitalized by investors who buy ownership shares. For instance, corporations capitalize by selling stock shares, which are legally recognized property interests in a corporation. This method of capitalization is feasible only because the law recognizes stockholders' property interests in corporations (see Chapter 13). Likewise, securities markets (i.e., markets for stocks, bonds, and other ownership interests in businesses) are not possible without law enforcing the property interests in what these markets sell. Securities markets are vital to capital formation and prosperity in modern nations. Both corporate stock shares and securities markets enable businesses to change a property interest in future profit potential into the money necessary for business operation.

A final contribution property makes to prosperity is to make resources easily divisible. *Divisibility* also relates to capital formation and refers to how property permits resources to be broken into parts and used in many ways while the owner

THE MYSTERY OF CAPITAL

In the book *The Mystery of Capital,* Peruvian economist Hernando de Soto asserts that the reason "why capitalism triumphs in the West but fails everywhere else" is because of the secure system of property law that exists in Western nations. Not new technology, hard work, a superior culture, better management techniques, nor "exploitation" account principally for prosperity in the West, but rather the willingness of lenders in an adequate property system to risk their money to entrepreneurs with business ideas. De Soto's research team estimates that in less-developed countries there exists $9 trillion of "dead capital"—

resources that people possess which they cannot capitalize because the laws in their countries do not adequately guarantee property in these resources, and affordable collateral-secured loans are unavailable. Without the legal recognition of property, many resources may also be difficult to sell since a buyer cannot be sure that the state will recognize and protect a seller's right to transfer the resources. This problem is especially acute with the sale of land and buildings. The lack of an adequate property law system may not account totally for poverty in less-developed countries, but it is arguably the most important contributing factor.

still retains a property interest in each part. Under property law, an owner of a single piece of land can sell part of it outright (change it into money), sell another part of it on credit and hold a mortgage to ensure payment, lease part of it to tenants who pay rent, incorporate part of it and sell shares to investors, and secure a loan against part of it in order to start an e-business. In each of these transactions regarding the single piece of land, the owner retains identifiable and protected property interests. Each transaction is made practically possible because the law of property enables resources to be subdivided as an owner may find advantageous.

This feature of property facilitates the development of resources, which creates new wealth and causes prosperity. The next section further elaborates the divisibility of property.

3. TWO BASIC DIVISIONS OF PROPERTY

The preceding section asserted that the easy divisibility of property contributes to prosperity, and it gave several examples of how property can be divided. This section introduces the two basic legal divisions of property: real property and personal property. **Real property** law applies ownership to land and interests in land such as mining rights or leases. All other types of resources are protected under the law of **personal property.**

Because of the historical importance of land, real property rules are very formal. As Chapter 8 on contracts discusses, agreements transferring interests in land ownership should be written, and many special rules apply to the registration and taxation of land ownership. Land ownership is also known as *real estate* or *realty.*

A particular kind of interest in land is the fixture. A **fixture** is an object of personal property that has become an object of real property (1) by physical annexation (attachment) to the land or its buildings, or (2) whose use has become closely associated with the use to which the land is put. Unless sellers and buyers agree differently when they sell land, the fixtures go with the land to the buyers. Manufacturing equipment is a fixture when it is sold along with a manufacturing plant. Carpeting is a fixture if it is nailed down or glued to the floor. Not being attached to the land, rugs are usually not fixtures. To prevent misunderstandings in land sales, sellers and buyers should identify which things are fixtures and stay with the buyers and which things remain protected under personal property and go with the sellers.

Personal property applies to movable resources, those things that people do not annex to the land. The law divides personal property into rules applying to tangible and intangible resources. *Tangible property* applies to things one can touch, that is, to physical things. Computers, cars, and carrots are such touchable things. The sale of tangible things, also known as "goods," is controlled by the Uniform Commercial Code, a type of contract law explained in the next chapter. Chapter 16 discusses the sale of corporate stock, which is an intangible thing. Real property rules and personal property rules are often different as are rules applying personal property to tangible or intangible things.

ACQUIRING RESOURCES IN A PROPERTY SYSTEM

How do you come to own resources in a property system? In other words how does the right of property to something attach to a specific person? Although you can acquire resources in many ways, including by force (called "robbery"), theft (various forms of stealing), and fraud (intentionally lying and harming others to get what belongs to them), there are only five basic legal ways to become an owner of something in a property system. As you read what follows, consider that **ownership** means the same thing as "property." Both terms refer to the legal right that makes resources exclusive, that makes resources "mine," instead of "yours," or "no one's."

4. ACQUIRING RESOURCES THROUGH EXCHANGE

The most common way of coming to have a property in something is through exchanging resources. For example, when you buy a car, or buy a company, you exchange one form of resources you own (money) for another form of resources (car or company). You are now the legal owner of the car or company. Resources have been switched but property (or ownership) remains. Likewise, when you exchange your services for a paycheck, you become the owner of the paycheck and the money it represents. The employer becomes the owner of your services and what they produce.

The rules under which people exchange resources in a property system are called the rules of **contract.** Contract rules are the subject of Chapter 8, but you should understand now that contract rules make agreements to exchange resources between owners legally binding and enforceable. In particular the rules of contract make it possible for owners to commit legally to future exchange of resources. These rules also make it possible for one owner to sue another if agreements to exchange resources in the future are broken by one of the owners. Further, contract rules allow lawsuits against those who have not adequately performed their agreements. If owner A agrees to sell goods to owner B in 30 days and then does not deliver them, owner B may sue owner A for damages. Likewise, owner B may sue owner A if owner A does deliver the goods, but they turn out to be defective. In addition to damages, contract rules may specify other remedies for contract breach.

It is difficult to overemphasize the importance of contract rules in the property system. Professor Philip Nichols of the Wharton School asserts that observing legally enforceable contracts is the single most significant indicator that a country's economy is ready for international trade. If the right of property is the foundation for the modern private market, the rules of contract are perhaps the keystone of that foundation.

5. ACQUIRING RESOURCES THROUGH POSSESSION

Sometimes you can become an owner of something merely through possession, that is, by physically holding and controlling it. The rule is that the first person to reduce previously unowned things to possession becomes their owner. In Sylacauga, Alabama, a meteorite crashed through the roof of a rented house in 1954 and struck the tenant on the leg, the only recorded instance in history when a meteorite has struck a person. Initially, both the owner of the house and the tenant (owner of the lease) claimed the meteorite, but because the tenant was the first person to reduce it to possession, she acquired the right of property to it. Similarly, ownership is acquired by reducing *abandoned* resources to possession. When an owner abandons a ship at sea, even in the face of a storm, the first person to possess and control the ship becomes its new owner.

When it is not clear who is the first person to reduce previously unowned or abandoned resources to possession, lawsuits may follow. See the box "Barry Bonds Home-Run Ball."

BARRY BONDS HOME-RUN BALL

When Barry Bonds blasted his record-setting 73rd home run ball into the stands of PacBell Park on October 7, 2001, ownership of the ball was abandoned. Unlike in football, where a ball that goes into the stands must be returned, Major League baseball—the association of team owners—deliberately abandons the balls and allows fans to keep them. But who had the right of property in the record-setting ball, Alex Popov who initially appeared to catch it before a wild crowd of fans knocked him to the ground, or Patrick Hayashi who shortly afterward saw the ball rolling free, grabbed it, and stuck it in his pocket?

Popov sued Hayashi, arguing that he was the owner because he had caught and first possessed the ball, which had an estimated value of $1 million. After trial, Judge Kevin McCarthy recognized that the principle of first possession applied to the ball, but did Popov or Hayashi first possess it? The facts were not clear as to whether Popov caught or dropped the ball. The judge stated, "An award of the ball to Mr. Popov would be unfair to Mr. Hayashi. It would be premised on the assumption that Mr. Popov would have caught the ball. That assumption is not supported by the facts. An award of the ball to Mr. Hayashi would unfairly penalize Mr. Popov. It would be based on the assumption that Mr. Popov would have dropped the ball. That conclusion is also unsupported by the facts."

With the facts unclear, Judge McCarthy ruled that it was fairest to divide the ownership of the ball. "The court therefore declares that both plaintiff and defendant have an equal and undivided interest in the ball. . . . In order to effectuate this ruling, the ball must be sold and the proceeds divided equally between the parties." Rather than appeal, Popov and Hayashi agreed they would sell the ball and divide the proceeds.

Things that are *lost* also can acquire a new owner through possession. The finder of a lost item becomes its owner by reducing it to possession and following a statutory procedure, which may require the finder to turn the item over to the police and to advertise it in a local paper for a period of time to allow the original owner to claim it. But at the end of the specified statutory period the finder becomes the new owner.

Finally, you can become an owner of land through **adverse possession.** Adverse possession gives you ownership of land under state statute when the possession is:

- Open and notorious. The possessor must occupy the land in such a way as to put the true owner of the land on notice.
- Actual and exclusive. The possessor must physically occupy the land. However, the building of a fence around the land or construction of a building on it constitutes physical occupation.
- Continuous. Possession must not be interrupted.
- Wrongful. The possessor must not have the owner's permission to be on the land, for example, under a lease.
- For a prescribed period of time. Most states specify an adverse possession of between 10 and 20 years before the possessor becomes the new owner.

The Homestead Act of 1862 illustrates ownership through possession. This act allowed those who lived on certain public land to obtain legal ownership of it by possessing it for five years and making certain improvements. Upward of a half million settlers possessed and then gained title to the 160-acre homesteads under the act.

In parts of the world today, governments are granting ownership of land to "squatters" who possess it without legal right. Studies show that this is one of the best ways to distribute land in poor nations. Squatters become owners and can then capitalize land by selling it or borrowing money and putting up the land as collateral.

Some have criticized the "squatter-to-owner" process because many of the new owners sell their land. However, the process enables poor squatters to raise money for the first time. It is also less violent than a situation where squatting alone occurs, and squatters may have to defend their possession by force. Further, it is more efficient than for the government to specify that the land cannot change ownership. In U.S. history there were numerous instances in which legal title was given to settlers who at first possessed land by squatting. Many of them, too, sold their land after receiving legal title to it.

6. ACQUIRING RESOURCES THROUGH CONFUSION

Ownership through **confusion** arises when *fungible* goods (i.e., goods that are identical) are mixed together. The common example involves grain in a silo when two or more batches of separately owned grain are mixed together. If the confusion occurs by honest mistake or agreement, the owners of the originally separate goods now own a proportional share of the confused goods. Careful records of who owned what grain must be kept since lacking evidence, a court in the case of dispute will assume that everyone claiming the confused mass owns an equal share. If a court determines that the confusion was intentionally wrongful, perhaps done by someone willfully attempting to defraud another, the court will grant ownership of the entire confused mass to the innocent party.

The doctrine of confusion also illustrates the importance of *boundaries* to the concept of property, and it explains one determination of ownership when resource boundaries are not certain. Problems of where boundaries lie are common, however, to various types of resources. Boundaries to the ownership of the water in a creek that crosses your land may be measured by a certain volume of water per minute. Landowners upstream may legally not be able to divert that flow.

Business owners may have a property in certain information like lists of customers, pricing information, and marketing plans. But these forms of information remain protected by property only when their owners take efforts to keep them secret. Their boundaries lie in the efforts that their owners take (see section 13). The owners of music cannot prevent others from hearing their music because sounds have no boundary, but they can exclude others from reproducing the music because such copying defines a boundary for musical ownership (see section 16).

7. ACQUIRING RESOURCES THROUGH ACCESSION

When the owner of an old airplane engine has it restored and has an airplane built around it, the owner of the engine now owns the entire airplane through the doctrine of **accession,** which refers to something "added." Normally, this is not a problem, but suppose a thief steals the engine, repairs it, and builds it into an airplane. A court will likely grant ownership of the entire airplane to the engine's owner.

However, if the builder *accidentally* picked up someone else's engine and builds it into an airplane, a court will probably give ownership of the airplane to the builder, requiring only that the builder adequately compensate the engine's original owner. An exception gives ownership of the entire airplane to the engine's owner if the engine is substantially more valuable than the additions to it. The court may even require the engine's owner to pay for the valuable additions.

The law of accession also explains that when you apply your efforts or ingenuity to any raw materials you own and change their nature into finished products, you own the finished products. Generally, because you own your efforts, you own what they produce, whether it is an airplane, a paycheck (through exchange), or a work of art. Much of the property foundation of the modern private market arises from the right to exclude others legally from what you own and what you add to that.

8. ACQUIRING RESOURCES THROUGH GIFT

In the making of a gift, no mutual exchange of resources occurs. Instead, a *donor* who owns something gives it to a *donee,* who becomes the new owner. The rules of gift specify that the gift does not generally take place until the donor (1) *intends* to make the gift, and (2) *delivers* the gift by physical transfer to the donee. Note that in some instances, a *constructive delivery,* like turning over the keys to a car or the deed to land, constitutes an adequate delivery.

A particular kind of gift is a *testamentary gift,* or one that is made through a will. The rules of such a gift pass ownership not by delivery but upon the death of the donor (called a "testator") and the proving of a valid will that specifies the gift. Some people believe that the purpose of a property system is to stimulate efforts to generate further wealth which benefits society. They argue that permitting people to pass property to vast fortunes through testamentary gifts does not give incentive to those who receive such gifts. What do you think? How would the behavior of owners change during their lifetimes if they could not make testamentary gifts?

9. TYPES OF OWNERSHIP

The law allows division of resource ownership into various types, or degrees. This division is another indication of how sensitive property law is in allowing owners to do exactly what they need and want with their resources: Not all states still use the common law terms that follow, but all states recognize the various aspects of ownership that the terms represent. These terms usually apply to land ownership, but ownership of movable and intangible things can be held practically in the same way.

(1) Fee simple. The bundle of rights and powers of land ownership are called an **estate. Fee simple** represents the maximum estate allowed under law, the owner having the fullest legal rights and powers to possess, use, and transfer the land. The fee simple *absolute* estate has no limitations or conditions attached. The fee simple *defeasible* may have a condition attached to its conveyance (transfer). For example, a seller may convey land to a buyer "as long as it is used for agricultural purposes." If the new owner (buyer) develops the land for other than agricultural purposes, the ownership goes back to the original owner (seller).

(2) Life estate. A **life estate** grants an ownership in land for the lifetime of a specified person. "To Brodie Davis for her life" grants such an estate. Upon Brodie Davis's death the land reverts to the original grantor who is said to keep a *reversion* interest in the land. If the land goes to someone other than the

grantor upon Brodie Davis's death, that person has a *remainder* interest. Reversion and remainder property interests are also called *future* interests as opposed to the life estate, which is a *present* interest. Subject to any attached conditions, all of these estates can be capitalized or transferred. For example, it is possible to borrow upon or sell a future interest.

(3) Leasehold estate. A **leasehold estate** is simply the property right granted to tenants by a landlord. Although it is not common to think of tenants as "owners," they do in a meaningful way have an estate or property. Tenants have a qualified possession, use, and transfer of the land, qualified in that they cannot *waste* the land, which means do something that substantially reduces the value of the land. For an apartment tenant to rip up carpeting and knock holes in the walls would be a waste of the interest in the land. The landlord could terminate the lease and sue the tenant.

Unless prohibited by the lease, the rights owned by tenants can be capitalized by transfer to someone else. Thus, unless prohibited, a tenant who is paying $3,000 per month under a two-year lease of an office can sell the balance of time remaining on the lease at $5,000 per month. Many leases, however, do require that a tenant obtain approval from a landlord, or even of the other tenants, before transferring lease rights.

A landlord may lease land for a *definite duration* of time like two years, or for an *indefinite duration* with rent payable at periodic intervals like monthly, or simply *at will,* which means "for as long as both shall agree." State law generally specifies that the landlord and tenant must give each other written notice of 30 or 60 days in order to terminate a lease that does not run for a definite duration.

(4) Concurrent ownership. Both personal and real property interests can have concurrent owners. That is, more than one person can own the same thing. The ownership is undivided, meaning that no concurrent owner owns a specific piece of the resources that are owned. The shareholders of a corporation are concurrent owners as are the partners of a partnership. In fact, concurrent ownership greatly facilitates almost all forms of modern private enterprise.

Other forms of concurrent ownership include the **joint tenancy** and the **tenancy in common.** In both these forms of ownership, the property interest is undivided, but the tenants in common can own different shares of the resource (e.g., two-thirds and one-third), whereas the joint tenants must have equal ownership shares (e.g., one-half and one-half). On the other hand, joint tenants, but not tenants in common, can have the *right of survivorship.* This right means that if one of the joint tenants dies, the remaining tenant becomes the sole owner of the entire resource. To create a joint tenancy requires special words, such as "convey to X and Y as joint tenants, and not as tenants in common, together with the right of survivorship."

The owners themselves, or the creditors, of a joint tenancy or tenancy in common can usually force the separation of these concurrent ownerships under the doctrine of *partition.*

10. TITLE AND PROPERTY REGISTRATION

Ownership is frequently referred to by the term **title.** Thus, someone who owns something has title to it. When an owner transfers ownership, the owner is said to "pass title." For specific types of resources the law requires that the title be represented by a physical document registered with the state. The title to an automobile is one example of such an ownership document that must be registered with the state. Many states also require the registration of boat titles.

A **deed** is the document of title that transfers ownership of land. The deed contains a precise legal description of the land that specifies the exact location and boundaries according to a mapping or surveying system. Without this description, few buyers or lenders would be willing to risk their money on the land. That exact, accepted boundaries identify land ownership provides the basis for much capital formation.

Even knowing the precise location of the land does not always ensure that there are no problems with the ownership. A lender may have a mortgage claim against the land, or the grantor of a deed may have conveyed the land to more than one person. There are two protections against these problems. First, the kind of deed the buyer receives from the seller can protect the buyer. A *warranty deed* promises the grantee (usually, the buyer) that the grantor (seller) has good ownership and the full power to convey it. The buyer can sue the seller if someone else claims the land. A *special warranty deed* specifies that certain legal claims against the land, like mortgages, exist but guarantees that no other claims exist. A *quit claim deed* makes no guarantees other than that the grantor surrenders all claim against the land. Several other types of deeds may apply in certain states.

Second, buyers and lenders are protected by registration statutes. The law enables buyers to register their deeds to land and lenders to register their mortgage claims against land. Potential buyers or other lenders are thus put on notice regarding the land, and the legal owner or claimant is legally and publicly identified. By going to the county courthouse or other place of record, you can often trace the ownership history of a piece of land for 200 years or more.

11. PRIVATE PROPERTY AND EMINENT DOMAIN

Why does the state recognize private ownership? John Locke thought that property was a natural right which ultimately came from God. Jeremy Bentham argued that Locke's view was "nonsense upon stilts," and maintained that the state instituted property for the "common good." The discussion earlier in this chapter of property and prosperity supports Bentham's view.

The U.S. Constitution does not assume either Locke's view or Bentham's. The Fifth Amendment, however, does recognize the federal government's power of **eminent domain,** the power to take private property for "public use" upon the payment of "just compensation." The eminent domain clause recognizes the existence and importance of private ownership, but allows the government to force private owners, generally of land, to exchange their resources for money in order to build roads or for other public uses.

The exact interpretation of the eminent domain clause is quite controversial. Specifically, when does a *taking* of a private resource occur? It is clear that when the government builds a road through private land, it has "taken" the land. But what if the government merely regulates the land, perhaps for environmental purposes? The following case considers that situation. Try to get from the case a standard for when a taking occurs.

LUCAS V. SOUTH CAROLINA COASTAL COUNCIL

505 U.S. 1003 (1992)

SCALIA, J.: In 1986, petitioner David H. Lucas paid $975,000 for two residential lots on the Isle of Palms in Charleston County, South Carolina, on which he intended to build single-family homes. In 1988, however, the South Carolina Legislature enacted the Beachfront Management Act, which had the direct effect of barring petitioner from erecting any permanent habitable structures on his two parcels.

Lucas promptly filed suit in the South Carolina Court of Common Pleas, contending that the Beachfront Management Act's construction bar effected a taking of his property without just compensation. Lucas did not take issue with the validity of the Act as a lawful exercise of South Carolina's police power, but contended that the Act's complete extinguishment of his property's value entitled him to compensation regardless of whether the legislature had acted in furtherance of legitimate police power objectives. Following a bench trial, the court agreed. Among its factual determinations was the finding that "at the time Lucas purchased the two lots, both were zoned for single-family residential construction and . . . there were no restrictions imposed upon such use of the property by either the State of South Carolina, the County of Charleston, or the Town of the Isle of Palms." The trial court further found that the Beachfront Management Act decreed a permanent ban on construction insofar as Lucas's lots were concerned, and that this prohibition "deprived Lucas of any reasonable economic use of the lots, . . . eliminated the unrestricted right of use, and rendered them valueless." The court thus concluded that Lucas's properties had been "taken" by operation of the Act, and it ordered respondent to pay "just compensation" in the amount of $1,232,387.50.

The Supreme Court of South Carolina reversed. It found dispositive what it described as Lucas's concession "that the Beachfront Management Act [was] properly and validly designed to preserve . . . South Carolina's beaches." Failing an attack on the validity

of the statute as such, the court believed itself bound to accept the "uncontested . . . findings" of the South Carolina Legislature that new construction in the coastal zone—such as petitioner intended—threatened this public resource. The court ruled that when a regulation respecting the use of property is designed "to prevent serious public harm," no compensation is owing under the Takings Clause regardless of the regulation's effect on the property.

Prior to Justice Holmes's exposition in *Pennsylvania Coal Co. v. Mahon,* it was generally thought that the Takings Clause reached only a "direct appropriation" of property, or the functional equivalent of a "practical ouster of [the owner's] possession." Justice Holmes recognized in *Mahon,* however, that if the protection against physical appropriations of private property was to be meaningfully enforced, the government's power to redefine the range of interests included in the ownership of property was necessarily constrained by the Constitution. If, instead, the uses of private property were subject to unbridled, uncompensated qualification under the police power, "the natural tendency of human nature [would be] to extend the qualification more and more until at last private property disappeared." These considerations gave birth in that case to the oft-cited maxim that, "while property may be regulated to a certain extent, if regulation goes too far it will be recognized as a taking."

Nevertheless, our decision in *Mahon* offered little insight into when, and under what circumstances, a given regulation would be seen as going "too far" for purposes of the Fifth Amendment. In 70-odd years of succeeding "regulatory takings" jurisprudence, we have generally eschewed any "set formula" for determining how far is too far, preferring to "engage in . . . essentially ad hoc, factual inquiries." We have, however, described at least two discrete categories of regulatory action as compensable without case-specific inquiry into the public interest advanced in support of the restraint. The

[CONTINUED]

first encompasses regulations that compel the property owner to suffer a physical "invasion" of his property. In general (at least with regard to permanent invasions), no matter how minute the intrusion, and no matter how weighty the public purpose behind it, we have required compensation. For example, in *Loretto v. Teleprompter Manhattan CATV Corp.,* we determined that New York's law requiring landlords to allow television cable companies to emplace cable facilities in their apartment buildings constituted a taking, even though the facilities occupied at most only 1 1/2 cubic feet of the landlord's property.

The second situation in which we have found categorical treatment appropriate is where regulation denies all economically beneficial or productive use of land. As we have said on numerous occasions, the Fifth Amendment is violated when land-use regulation "does not substantially advance legitimate state interests *or denies an owner economically viable use of his land.*"

We have never set forth the justification for this rule. Perhaps it is simply, as Justice Brennan suggested, that total deprivation of beneficial use is, from the landowner's point of view, the equivalent of a physical appropriation. Surely, at least, in the extraordinary circumstance when *no* productive or economically beneficial use of land is permitted, it is less realistic to indulge our usual assumption that the legislature is simply "adjusting the benefits and burdens of economic life," in a manner that secures an "average reciprocity of advantage" to everyone concerned. And the *functional* basis for permitting the government, by regulation, to affect property values without compensation—that "Government hardly could go on if to some extent values incident to property could not be diminished without paying for every such change in the general law," does not apply to the relatively rare situations where the government has deprived a landowner of all economically beneficial uses.

On the other side of the balance, affirmatively supporting a compensation requirement, is the fact that regulations that leave the owner of land without economically beneficial or productive options for its use—typically, as here, by requiring land to be left substantially in its natural state—carry with them a heightened risk that private property is being pressed into some form of public service under the guise of mitigating serious public harm. As Justice Brennan explained: "From the government's point of

view, the benefits flowing to the public from preservation of open space through regulation may be equally great as from creating a wildlife refuge through formal condemnation or increasing electricity production through a dam project that floods private property." The many statutes on the books, both state and federal that provide for the use of eminent domain to impose servitudes on private scenic lands preventing developmental uses, or to acquire such lands altogether, suggest the practical equivalence in this setting of negative regulation and appropriation. We think, in short, that there are good reasons for our frequently expressed belief that when the owner of real property has been called to sacrifice *all* economically beneficial uses in the name of the common good, that is to leave his property economically idle, he has suffered a taking.

Where the state seeks to sustain regulation that deprives land of all economically beneficial use, it may resist compensation only if the logically antecedent inquiry into the nature of the owner's estate shows that the prescribed use interests were not part of his title to begin with. This accords, we think, with our "takings" jurisprudence, which has traditionally been guided by the understandings of our citizens regarding the content of, and the State's power over, the "bundle of rights" that they acquire when they obtain title to property. It seems to us that the property owner necessarily expects the uses of his property to be restricted from time to time, by various measures newly enacted by the State in legitimate exercise of its police powers; "as long recognized some values are enjoyed under an implied limitation and must yield to the police power." And in the case of personal property, by reason of the State's traditionally high degree of control over commercial dealings, he ought to be aware of the possibility that new regulation might even render his property economically worthless (at least if the property's only economically productive use is sale or manufacture for sale). See *Andrus v. Allard* (prohibition on sale of eagle feathers). In the case of land, however, we think the notion pressed by the Council that title is somehow held subject to the "implied limitation" that the State may subsequently eliminate all economically valuable use is inconsistent with the historical compact recorded in the Takings Clause that has become part of our constitutional culture.

Reversed and remanded.

[CONTINUED]

CASE QUESTIONS

1. What did Lucas want to do with his land?

2. Can South Carolina constitutionally limit Lucas from using his land in this way?

3. What are the two standards for determining whether there has been a "taking" of property by the state?

4. Under what circumstances would South Carolina's ban on construction *not* have constituted a taking of Lucas's property?

More recently, the Supreme Court decided *Tahoe-Sierra Preservation Council Inc. v. Tahoe Regional Planning Agency,* 535 U.S. 40 (2002). In this case the Court determined that it was not a taking for the state to prohibit landowners around Lake Tahoe from any construction or the substantial removal of vegetation for a period of 32 months, even though the owners were effectively deprived of all economic value of the land. Can you reconcile the case with the *Lucas* case? The Court in this case noted that the land use ordinance deprived the owners of the economic value of their land for only a limited time, unlike in *Lucas,* where the deprivation of economic value was permanent. Do you agree with this outcome?

12. PROPERTY, THE USE OF RESOURCES, AND THE EQUAL RIGHT OF OTHERS

In law, property is not a *thing.* It is an owner's *right* to exclude others from resources. One of the most important resources is the use owners can make of another resource, for example, a piece of land. Owners can build a house, a shopping mall, or a skyscraper on their land. Or farm it. Or leave it unoccupied. They can take their money and open a computer store with it, or save it for retirement, or invest it in the stock market. All of these ways of using resources come within the legal guarantee of property. Implied in the exclusive rights to private resources is the legal protection to use them in many ways. This quality helps make the marketplace dynamic and responsive to needs and wants.

In an important and meaningful sense, owners also have a property in using their efforts. They have an exclusive right to direct their resource in themselves any way they wish. They can use it to pursue any line of employment, or they can leave the job market and do volunteer work for Meals on Wheels. Or go back to school for an MBA. Or retire on their savings and garden, travel, or watch football.

Having a property right to direct the resources of one's efforts and to be able to exclude others from the further resources one acquires with these efforts is closely related to other concepts like "freedom" and "liberty." The American colonists and the framers of the Constitution certainly thought so. John Dickinson, who helped draft the Constitution, observed that Americans "cannot be happy, without freedom; nor free, without security of property; nor so secure, unless the sole power to dispose of it be lodged within themselves." Revolutionary War diplomat Arthur Lee wrote, "The right of property is the guardian of every other right, and to deprive people of this, is in fact to deprive them of their liberty." In 1768 a colonial American observed, "Liberty and Property are not only join'd in common discourse, but are in their own natures so nearly ally'd [allied], that we cannot be said to possess the one without the other." The early Americans firmly believed they had a property not only in their material possessions but also in liberty, speech, and other rights. In summary, they had an exclusive right to use freely their resource in themselves and the resources produced by their efforts.

Generally speaking, owners are prohibited from using their resources in ways that harm or injure the resources of other owners. As James Madison explained, the concept of property "leaves to everyone else a like advantage." Under the rule of law, a property system protects the equal right of all to their resources, including the resources they have in themselves. Tort law (Chapter 9), criminal law (Chapter 10), and much of the regulatory law discussed throughout this book attempt to prevent owners from using their resources to injure the resources that belong to others. See also the box "The Property System and Corporate Governance."

Two limits on land use that protect the equal right of all land owners is especially relevant to this chapter. They involve the law of nuisance and zoning.

Nuisance   The law limits certain uses of one's land through the doctrine of nuisance. What constitutes a nuisance is somewhat vague, but in most jurisdictions the common law cases have been put in statutory form. Several common elements exist in the law of nuisance in most states. To begin with, there are two types of nuisance: public and private.

A **public nuisance** is one arising from some use of land that causes inconvenience or damage to the public. For example, discharging industrial waste from one's land that kills the fish in a river constitutes a public nuisance since fishing rights are publicly held. Public nuisance claims may be brought only by a public official, not private individuals, unless the latter have suffered some special damage to their property as a result of the public nuisance. Note that many public nuisances can also violate various regulatory laws, such as environmental laws (see Chapter 17).

Any unreasonable use of one's property so as to cause substantial interference with the enjoyment or use of another's land establishes a common law **private nuisance.** The unreasonableness of the interference is measured by a balancing process in which the character, extent, and duration of harm to the plaintiff is weighed against the social utility of the defendant's activity and its appropriateness to its location. Since society needs industrial activity as well as natural tranquility, people must put up with a certain amount of smoke, dust, noise, and polluted water if they live in concentrated areas of industry. But what may be an appropriate industrial use of land in a congested urban area may be a private nuisance if it occurs in a rural or residential location.

Once the plaintiff establishes a substantial and unreasonable interference with the use or enjoyment of his or her property, the court must decide what remedy the plaintiff is entitled to. The court may award damages if the plaintiff has suffered economic loss, but when damages are inadequate the court may also order the defendant to do something, like correct the problem, or else

THE PROPERTY SYSTEM AND CORPORATE GOVERNANCE

Chapter 1 explained why the issues of corporate governance are property issues. The explanation bears reemphasizing.

The property system allows us to enjoy exclusive resources. It protects our resources from the harm of others, but at the same time it limits us from harming the resources of others. Corporate governance illustrates how this property system functions.

In the *specific* sense, corporate governance laws protect the investment resources of corporate owners, or shareholders. These laws define the authority and responsibility of the board of directors, who are elected by the shareholders. The laws also regulate the managers appointed by the board.

In the *broad* sense, corporate governance also includes those laws that protect the resources of others from harm by the corporation. Such laws include antitrust laws, employment discrimination and employee protection laws, environmental protection laws, and a great many antifraud laws.

Sometimes the law does not protect the boundary between what is *mine* and what is *yours.* Sometimes there is disagreement about where proper boundaries lie. Sometimes we have failures of corporate governance. But under a system that permits private resource ownership, corporate governance issues are property issues.

cease the nuisance-creating activity. In determining whether to issue an injunction, the court will take into consideration (1) the relative economic hardship that will be placed upon the parties if such relief is granted, and (2) the public interest in the continuation of the defendant's activity. This balancing of interests required by nuisance law can bring about some unusual remedies. One case involved a large residential development that bordered on an equally big cattle-feeding lot. Over the years the development and the lot had grown together slowly until the odors and the flies from the lot had become greatly offensive to the housing owners. The remedy arising from a nuisance suit ordered the feed-lot to close and transfer its operations and required the housing developer to pay the closing and transfer costs.

Can you see how nuisance law attempts to balance the equal right of all in the property system? It does so by preventing land owners from *unreasonably* interfering with other publicly and privately owned resources. Determining what is unreasonable is an ongoing and controversial process in a property-based legal system.

Zoning Through their exercise of the police powers, states and local governments protect the public health, safety, morals, and general welfare (see Chapter 6). It is under the police powers that a major governmental regulation of land use takes place: zoning. **Zoning ordinances** are generally laws that divide counties or municipalities into use districts designated residential, commercial, or industrial. Zoning limits the use to which land can be put to that specified. For instance, industrial facilities cannot be built in residential districts. Zoning may also specify the height, size, number, and location of buildings that can be built on land. Restricting buildings in a commercial district to no more than eight stories in height is an example. Zoning may additionally impose aesthetic requirements concerning color and exterior design. Zoning boards (or commissions), which are generally agencies of local governments, enforce the zoning ordinances. Owners should always check to determine how zoning limits land use.

An owner can ask a zoning board for a *variance* to allow use of land in a way not permitted under a zoning ordinance. The board is likely to grant a variance only when the owner can prove that the ordinance prevents a reasonable economic return on the land as zoned. Zoning ordinances allow uses of land that existed prior to passage of the ordinances. Such uses are called "nonconforming" uses.

Like nuisance law, zoning regulations are highly controversial because they involve limits on how owners can use their land. The purpose of zoning laws may be to protect the right of all to their lands, but not everyone is going to agree with the limits that zoning laws establish.

INTELLECTUAL PROPERTY

The remainder of this chapter concerns a particular application of property called **intellectual property.** Intellectual property illustrates nicely that property is a legal right rather than a physical thing. Intellectual property applies to allow owners to exclude others from (1) intangible resources like certain secrets that businesses have, (2) the copying of various creative expressions, and (3) the reproducing of inventions and marks that identify the producers of goods and services. Today, many of a business's most valuable resources may be those protected by intellectual property laws.

Intellectual property laws arose out of the common law, but they also reflect constitutional and statutory adoption. Article I, Section 8, of the Constitution grants the power to Congress "[t]o promote the Progress of Science and useful Arts, by securing for limited Times to Authors and Inventors the exclusive Right to their respective Writings and Discoveries." Note that the Constitution identifies the purpose of establishing this "exclusive Right" (property) as "[t]o promote the Progress of Science and useful Arts," which basically means giving incentive to the common good. What Abraham Lincoln said of patent law applies equally to all intellectual property, namely, that property adds "the fuel of interest to the fire of genius."

Keep in mind as you read the following sections on trade secrets, patents, trademarks, and copyrights that they are all applications of the right of property. Do you agree or disagree with the idea that all applications of the right of property are in the common good only when they promote general prosperity and liberty?

13. TRADE SECRET LAW

A 19-year old University of Chicago student posted confidential documents about DirecTV's latest generation of satellite television smart cards to three websites. A former employee of Jasmine Networks, Inc., a San Jose company, downloaded secret materials from Jasmine's computer system and tried to e-mail them as attachments to his personal e-mail accounts. Federal criminal prosecutors arrested them both under the Economic Espionage Act of 1996. The act makes it a crime to steal trade secrets and provides for fines and up to 10 years of imprisonment for individuals and up to a $5 million fine for organizations.

A **trade secret** is any form of information (1) that the owner has taken reasonable measures to keep secret and (2) which has economic value from not being known to the public. A trade secret can be any type of financial, technical, scientific, economic, or engineering information. It may involve customer lists, marketing plans, research results, formulas, and designs, but it is not limited to these things. The taking of trade secrets, often called *misappropriation,* is widespread and costs U.S. businesses $59 billion a year according to the American Society for Industrial Security.

Sometimes those who compete against their former employers misappropriate trade secrets. You may draw upon the general knowledge, skills, and experience you have gained in working for former employers, but it is illegal for you to use trade secrets gained through previous employment. In misappropriating trade secrets, you may commit both a crime and a tort. You risk fine and imprisonment for the crime, and civil damages for the tort. In addition, the owner of a misappropriated trade secret will usually ask the court to enjoin (order) the defendant from using the trade secret in competition against the owner.

Customers or potential customers may sometimes come into contact with your trade secrets when they tour a plant or otherwise pay a visit. On other occasions, you may specifically license a customer to use your trade secret, usually for a limited purpose. As part of reasonably guarding trade secrets, you may wish to have business customers, licensees, and employees sign agreements not to disclose your secrets or use them for unauthorized purposes. Such agreements usually contain stiff damages for improper disclosure.

Cases of trade secret misappropriation are frequently in the news. Recently, a civil jury awarded Avery Dennison Corporation $40 million in damages against a Taiwanese company that had paid an Avery Dennison employee for trade secrets about self-stick adhesives. DuPont has sued competitor Monsanto for obtaining gene-identification trade secrets. DuPont alleges that Monsanto got improper access to the secrets by acquiring Asgrow, a former DuPont business partner. In another case, Global Crossing accused Tyco International of agreeing to help Global build an undersea fiber-optic network, then misappropriating Global's plans and participating in a competing venture. In an increasingly information-rich business environment, greater numbers of trade secret misappropriations can be expected.

Now you understand the Business Decision that begins this chapter. Colonel Cars's marketing plans are trade secrets to which property applies because Colonel Cars can legally exclude others from misappropriating the plans. Although different specific legal rules may apply to the ownership of trade secrets and the ownership of cars, the right of property as the legal right to exclude others is the same in both instances. EMW cannot use Colonel Cars's marketing plans without permission. This Business Decision is based on a trade secrets lawsuit brought by General Motors against Volkswagon, which alleged that a GM marketing vice president had taken hundreds of secret GM documents with him when he left GM to become president of a unit of Volkswagon. Volkswagon settled the case on terms favorable to GM.

14. PATENT LAW

A **patent** is an exclusive right created by statute and recognized by the U.S. Patent and Trademark Office (PTO) for a limited period of time. This property applies to inventions, which are new applications of information. Patent law is very complex, as numerous lawsuits involving patents illustrate, and the settlements and judgment awards for violating, or infringing on, patents can be quite high. In 1999

Genentech agreed to pay the University of California at San Francisco $200 million to settle a patent infringement battle. The university had sued Genentech alleging that Genentech misappropriated patented technology to produce a growth hormone that is one of the company's largest selling products.

Obtaining a Patent   To obtain a patent, an inventor must pay a filing fee and file an application with the PTO. The application must in words and drawings
(1) explain how to make and use the basic invention: (2) show why the invention is different from *prior art,* that is, from all previous and related inventions or state of knowledge, and (3) precisely describe what aspects of the invention (called *claims*) deserve the patent.

The PTO assigns a *patent examiner* to consider the application, and there is usually a great deal of communication between the examiner and the applicant over the adequacy of the application's explanations, the scope of the proposed patent (exactly what the patent applies to), and whether the invention even qualifies at all for a patent. The applicant can amend the application. Since the PTO receives 300 or more patent applications a day, the application process can take several years from start to finish. Note that the patent issuance provides a presumption of a valid property rather than a final determination of one. As the next section discusses, only a court can finally determine patent validity.

Patentable Subject Matter   After a patent is issued, the patent owner may have to defend its property against infringers, those who make, use, or sell the invention without a license from the owner. When the patent owner files a lawsuit, it is common for the alleged infringer to respond by attacking the validity of the patent. If the court finds the patent invalid the alleged infringer will win.

Attacking the "subject matter" of a patent is one common way of testing the validity of a patent. The Patent Statute of 1952 and its amendments identify patentable subject matter as the following:

- Processes
- Machines
- Compositions of matter
- Improvements to processes, machines, or compositions of matter
- Nonfunctional designs of a manufactured article
- Certain plants

Although not unlimited, the subject matter for a potential patent is quite broad. In *Diamond v. Chakrabarty,* 447 U.S. 303 (1980), the Supreme Court ruled that a scientist could patent a genetically modified bacterium which ate hydrocarbons found in oil spills. The Court said, "Congress is free to amend § 101 [the subject matter section of the general patent law] so as to exclude from patent protection organisms produced by genetic engineering. . . . Or it may choose to craft a statute specifically designed for such living things. But until Congress takes such action, the language of § 101 fairly embraces the respondent's invention."

In the following case, the Supreme Court considers whether a modified hybrid plant is patentable subject matter when Congress had earlier passed laws establishing some plant patents, but not the type on appeal.

J.E.M. AG SUPPLY, INC. V. PIONEER HI-BRED INTERNATIONAL, INC.

534 U.S. 124 (2001)

Respondent Pioneer Hi-Bred held patents on hybrid corn seeds. It licensed its corn seeds to petitioner Farm Advantage (the business name of J.E.M. Ag) for use in growing corn, and specifically not for creating new seeds or resale. When petitioner Farm Advantage resold the seed corn, Pioneer sued for patent violation. Farm Advantage argued that the patent was invalid because the hybrid corn was not patentable subject matter. It pointed out that the Plant Patent Act of 1930 (PPA) protected only sexually reproduced plants (those grown without seeds) and that the Plant Variety Protection Act of 1970 (PVPA) gave only limited property protection to seeds that reproduced plants. Because of these specific acts, Farm Advantage claimed that the corn hybrids were not patentable subject matter under §101 of the general patent law.

When the federal district court and the court of appeals ruled for Pioneer, the Supreme Court agreed to hear the case.

THOMAS, J.: . . . The question before us is whether utility patents may be issued for plants pursuant to § 101. The text of § 101 provides:

"Whoever invents or discovers any new and useful process, machine, manufacture, or composition of matter, or any new and useful improvement thereof, may obtain a patent therefor, subject to the conditions and requirements of this title."

As this Court recognized over 20 years ago in *Chakrabarty* the language of § 101 is extremely broad. "In choosing such expansive terms as 'manufacture' and 'composition of matter,' modified by the comprehensive 'any,' Congress plainly contemplated that the patent laws would be given wide scope." This Court thus concluded in *Chakrabarty* that living things were patentable under § 101, and held that a manmade micro-organism fell within the scope of the statute. As Congress recognized, "the relevant distinction was not between living and inanimate things, but between produces of nature, whether living or not, and human-made inventions."

In *Chakrabarty,* the Court also rejected the argument that Congress must expressly authorize protection for new patentable subject matter:

"It is, of course, correct that Congress, not the courts, must define the limits of patentability; but it is equally true that once Congress has spoken it is 'the province and duty of the judicial department to say what the law is.' Congress has performed its constitutional role in defining patentable subject matter in § 101; we perform ours in construing the language Congress has employed. . . . The subject-matter provisions of the patent law have been cast in broad terms to fulfill the constitutional and statutory goal of promoting 'the Progress of Science and the useful Arts' with all that means for the social and economic benefits envisioned by Jefferson."

Petitioners do not allege that Pioneer's patents are invalid for failure to meet the requirements for a utility patent. Nor do they dispute that plants fall within the terms of § 101's broad language that includes "manufacture" or "composition of matter." Rather, petitioners argue that the PPA and PVPA provide the exclusive means of protecting new varieties of plants, and so awarding utility patents for plants upsets the scheme contemplated by Congress.

Petitioners essentially ask us to deny utility patent protection for sexually reproduced plants because it was unforeseen in 1930 that such plants could receive protection under § 101. Denying patent protection under § 101 simply because such coverage was thought technologically infeasible in 1930, however, would be inconsistent with the forward-looking perspective of the utility patent statute. As we noted in *Chakrabarty,* "Congress employed broad general language in drafting § 101 precisely because [new types of] inventions are often unforeseeable."

Second, petitioners maintain that the PPA's limitation to asexually reproduced plants would make no sense if Congress intended § 101 to authorize patents on plant varieties that were sexually reproduced. But this limitation once again merely reflects the reality of plant breeding in 1930. At that time,

[CONTINUED]

the primary means of reproducing bred plants true-to-type was through asexual reproduction. Congress thought that sexual reproduction through seeds was not a stable way to maintain desirable bred characteristics. Thus, it is hardly surprising that plant patents would protect only asexual reproduction, since this was the most reliable type of reproduction for preserving the desirable characteristics of breeding.

By passing the PVPA in 1970, Congress specifically authorized limited patent-like protection for certain sexually reproduced plants. Petitioners therefore argue that this legislation evidences Congress' intent to deny broader § 101 utility patent protection for such plants. Petitioners' argument, however, is unavailing for two reasons. First, nowhere does the PVPA purport to provide the exclusive statutory means of protecting sexually reproduced plants. Second, the PVPA and § 101 can easily be reconciled. Because it is harder to qualify for a utility patent than for a Plant Variety Protection (PVP) certificate, it only makes sense that utility patents would confer a greater scope of protection.

We also note that the PTO [Patent and Trademark Office] has assigned utility patents for plants for at least 16 years and there has been no indication from either Congress or agencies with expertise that such coverage is inconsistent with the PVPA or the PPA. The Board of Patent Appeals and Interferences, which has specific expertise in issues of patent law, relied heavily on this Court's decision in *Chakrabarty* when it interpreted the subject matter of § 101 to include plants. This highly visible decision has led to the issuance of some 1,800 utility patents for plants. Moreover, the PTO, which administers § 101 as well as the PPA, recognizes and regularly issues utility patents for plants. In addition, the Department of Agriculture's Plant Variety Protection Office acknowledges the existence of utility patents for plants.

For these reasons, we hold that newly developed plant breeds fall within the terms of § 101, and that neither the PPA nor the PVPA limits the scope of § 101's coverage. As in *Chakrabarty*, we decline to narrow the reach of § 101 where Congress has given us no indication that it intends this result. Accordingly, we affirm the judgment of the Court of Appeals.

CASE QUESTIONS

1. How does this case differ from *Chakrabarty*?
2. Why does Farm Advantage argue that § 101 does not protect Pioneer's corn?
3. Why does the Supreme Court rule that § 101 does protect Pioneer's corn?
4. Suppose that the Court had agreed with Farm Advantage. What could Pioneer have done in the future to protect its hybrid seed products?

Consider the following. GeneCure Laboratory develops genetically changed human genes that when injected into cancer patients will cure their form of disease. The laboratory can get a 20-year patent on this gene or on a gene that helps people lose weight or change the color of their eyes. But the gene must not be a "naturally" occurring "composition of matter." It must come into existence as an application of human knowledge that, in the words of the Constitution, promotes the "Progress of Science."

Another area of potentially patentable subject matter concerns *business methods,* which are often computer programs that carry out complicated business functions. Historically, business methods like double-entry bookkeeping were considered unpatentable, but they are, after all, a type of "method," and methods are patentable. As the next box discusses, the PTO has begun permitting patents on business methods in recent years.

BUSINESS METHODS AS PATENTABLE SUBJECT MATTER

Mere ideas are not patentable. Nor are mathematical algorithms or formulas like $E = mc^2$ that express truths about the universe. However, the courts have decided that certain computer programs that incorporate mathematical calculations to achieve a method of doing business are indeed patentable subject matter.

An important case is *State Street Bank & Trust Co. v. Signature Financial Group, Inc.,* 149 F.3d 1368 (1998). Signature held a patent on a data processing system that allowed an administrator to monitor and record the financial information flow and make all calculations necessary for maintaining a mutual fund investment partnership. State Street Bank sought to license the patent and when negotiations broke down sued Signature to have the patent invalidated on the basis that it was only a "method of doing business."

On appeal the court wrote: "The Supreme Court has identified three categories of subject matter that are unpatentable, namely 'laws of nature, natural phenomena, and abstract ideas.' Of particular relevance to this case, the Court has held that mathematical algorithms are not patentable subject matter to the extent that they are merely abstract ideas. . . . Today, we hold that the transformation of data, representing discrete dollar amounts, by a machine through a series of mathematical calculations into a final share price, constitutes a practical application of a mathematical algorithm, formula, or calculation, because it produces 'a useful, concrete and tangible result'—a final share price momentarily fixed for recording and reporting purposes and even accepted and relied upon by regulatory authorities and insubsequent trades."

The court of appeals specifically considered whether or not business methods were an exception to statutorily patentable subject matter and concluded: "We take this opportunity to lay this ill-conceived exception to rest." Thus, if business methods meet the other requirements for patentability, they will not be denied a patent because they are inappropriate subject matter for intellectual property. The Supreme Court refused to hear further appeal in this case.

Following the *State Street Bank* case, numerous Internet businesses patented business methods and sued imitators. Amazon.com patented the "one-click" method of ordering over the Internet and obtained a preliminary injunction prohibiting Barnes&Noble.com from implementing a similar ordering system. Priceline.com sued Microsoft over the latter's use of a "reverse auction" method patented by Priceline.com. Concerned that it might be issuing patents for business methods that were not new or unique, the PTO has begun to look more carefully at past practices before issuing business method patents.

Question: If spreadsheets did not exist, and you were the first to patent an algorithm for creating one, could another person create a different program for a spreadsheet or would you own a property in all use of spreadsheets for 20 years? In fact, no one patented spreadsheets as a business method and now they are obvious and unpatentable. But what if you had patented spreadsheets as a useful method of doing business?

Nonobviousness, Novelty, and Usefulness To be patentable, it is not enough for something to be appropriate subject matter. An invention must also have certain characteristics. Namely, it must be nonobvious, novel, and useful. An alleged infringer can always defend against an infringement lawsuit by proving that the patent is invalid because the invention is obvious, previously known, or useless.

The characteristic of *nonobviousness* refers to the ability of an invention to produce surprising or unexpected results, that is, results not anticipated by *prior art* (the previous state of knowledge in the field). The nonobviousness standard is measured in relation to someone who has at least an ordinary understanding in the prior art. For instance, to be patentable a computer hardware invention would need to be nonobvious to an ordinary computer engineer.

Patent litigation over the obviousness of an invention is typically very subjective with each side to the lawsuit producing experts who disagree. Further complicating matters is that obviousness is usually measured from the date the litigation takes place, which can be many years after the application. Ultimately, it is up to the court to determine the state of knowledge existing when the inventor filed the application and whether the invention is nonobvious.

To qualify for a patent, an invention must also possess the characteristic of novelty. *Novelty* indicates that something is new and different from the prior art. The test is met when no single prior element of art meets all of the invention's claims. However, under patent law even if an invention is otherwise new, it fails the novelty test if it has been previously described in a publication or put to public use more than one year before a patent application on it is filed (the *one-year rule*).

Except for patents issued on designs or plants, an invention to be valid must be useful, that is, it must do something. *Usefulness* is also defined as *utility,* and patents that are not plant or design patents are called utility patents. Suppose that Acme Laboratory scientists invent a new chemical compound. Until the compound has a use, say, ridding pets of fleas, Acme will be unable to get a utility patent on it.

Patent Duration and Enforcement As the U.S. Constitution specifies, the property represented by patents runs for limited duration. Statute limits utility patents to 20 years, plant patents to 17 years, and design patents to 14 years. When a patent expires, the invention is in the *public domain,* and others may use it without limitation. Remember that when the patent expires, it is easy to use the invention since the patent application explains exactly how the invention works, including drawings of its construction. The explicit purpose of patent law is to make inventions public following the limited period of legal property right.

For the duration of a patent, the owner can sue those who infringe on it. If successful, the owner can get an injunction prohibiting future infringement, damages, including triple damages for intentional infringement, and an order requiring that any infringing items be destroyed.

15. TRADEMARK LAW

Trademarks constitute a second general form of intellectual property. Like patents they may be registered with the PTO, and also like patents, trademarks are some of the most valuable properties that businesses own. McDonald's golden arches, the Nike "swoosh," Coca-Cola, the Marlboro man, Amazon.com, the Colonel, Exxon, Kodak, Kleenex, the Olympic rings, Rolex, Levi—the list of famous trademarks is almost endless, but always recognizable.

Recognizability or *distinctiveness* is the function of trademarks. In a world cluttered with stimulation, information, and advertising, trademarks pierce through the clutter and let people know that the goods or service represented are "the real thing"—that they come from one source. They are an information property, exclusively distinguishing the reputation and goodwill of a particular business from that of all other businesses. Trademarks protect both businesses and consumers from confusion regarding who makes or provides what. Misappropriation of trademarks is a major business problem, especially in the Cyber Age when often the only point of contact people have with a goods or service provider is a computer monitor screen.

Types of Trademarks Although common law protects trademarks, this chapter focuses on the federal protection given trademarks by the Lanham Act of 1946.

The Lanham Act protects the following marks used to represent a product, service, or organization:

- Trademark—any mark, word, picture, or design that attaches to goods to indicate their source
- Service mark—a mark associated with a service, for example, Monster.com
- Certification mark—a mark used by someone other than the owner to certify the quality, point of origin, or other characteristics of goods or services, for example, the Good Housekeeping Seal of Approval
- Collective mark—a mark representing membership in a certain organization or association, for example, the National Football League logo

For convenience, all of these marks will be referred to as trademarks.

Similar to trademarks, and also protected by the Lanham Act, is *tradedress,* which refers to a colored design or shape associated with a product or service. The red color scheme of Coca-Cola when associated with the general design of Coca-Cola labeling constitutes tradedress. Tradedress protection prevents Coca-Cola competitors from designing a shape that resembles "Coca-Cola" and attaching the characteristic Coke red to the design in such a way as to confuse potential Coke customers about what they are getting. Tradedress also includes distinctive store decorating motifs (e.g., McDonald's) or package shapes and colors.

Trademark Registration Under the Lanham Act, a person must qualify a trademark for registration with the PTO by using it in interstate commerce. Posting the trademark on an Internet website meets this qualification. Alternatively, an intent-to-use application may be filed, followed by an amended application when actual use begins.

To be registerable, a trademark must be distinctive. The PTO will deny registration in the following circumstances:

- If the mark is the same or similar to a mark currently used on similar related goods, for example, a computer company's cherry mark that resembles the apple mark of Apple Computer
- If the mark contains certain prohibited or reserved names or designs, including the U.S. flag, other governmental symbols, immoral names or symbols, the names or likenesses of living persons without their consent, and the names or likenesses of deceased American presidents without the permission of their spouses
- If the mark merely describes a product or service, for example, "Fast Food" for a restaurant franchise
- If the mark is generic and represents a product or service, for example, "Telephone" for a communication company

Note that a mark that is descriptive or generic in one context may be unique and distinctive in another. "Fast Food" used to mark a restaurant franchise is not registerable, but an overnight textbook delivery service could register "Fast Food for the Mind" because the mark easily distinguishes this delivery service from other similar delivery services.

As part of the trademark application process, the PTO places a proposed mark in the *Official Gazette,* which gives existing mark owners notice and allows them to object that the proposed mark is similar to their own. If existing mark owners object to the proposed mark's registration, the PTO holds a hearing to resolve the objection and, possibly, to deny registration. Finally, if the PTO determines the mark acceptable, it registers the mark on the *Principal Register.* This registration provides notice of official trademark status.

Unlike a patent, which specifies a limited property duration, the trademark enjoys a potentially unlimited protection period. But after six years the trademark owner must notify the PTO that the trademark is still in use. Currently, every 10 years the owner must renew the trademark.

The attempt to trademark certain descriptive terms, or a person's name, presents a special problem. Generally, the PTO will not accept a person's name or a descriptive term for protection on the *Principal Register.* However, there is a process by which a name or descriptive term can achieve full trademark status and protection. If it is listed on the PTO's *Supplemental Register* for five years *and* acquires a secondary meaning, it can then be transferred to the *Principal Register* for full protection.

Secondary meaning refers to a public meaning that is different from its meaning as a person's name or as a descriptive term, a public meaning that makes the name or term distinctive. In the public mind, "Ford" now refers to an automobile rather than a person, "Levi" means jeans rather than a family, and "Disney" refers to a specific entertainment company rather than its founder.

Trademark Enforcement Trademark law protects the trademark's owner from having the mark used in an unauthorized way. Manufacturing, distributing, selling, or possessing products (or services) with an unauthorized mark violates the law. The law establishes both civil and criminal trademark violation.

Civil violation of a trademark (or a patent) is termed **infringement.** The violator infringes on the trademark's property right through an unintentional or a willful unauthorized use, misappropriating the goodwill and reputation that the trademark represents and confusing the public about the identity of the user. Remedies for civil infringement include a variety of damages, injunctions, prohibiting future infringement, and orders to destroy infringing products in anyone's possession.

Trademark owners must be vigilant in protecting their marks because if a trademark becomes **generic,** if it loses its distinctiveness, it also loses its status as a protected trademark. A trademark is most likely to become generic (1) when an owner does not defend against unauthorized use and (2) when the public becomes confused as to whether a term refers to a particular products/service or refers to a general class of products/services. Due to concern that its famous trademark not become generic, Coca-Cola seeks to prevent trademark infringement by employees at soda fountains who without comment give customers other colas when asked for a "Coke." Employers are warned to advise employees to specify that another cola will be substituted if Coke is not available.

The band Metallica has sued a variety of defendants for using its trademark: Guerlain for Metallica perfume, Pierre Cardin for a Metallica tuxedo, Victoria's Secret for its Metallica lip liner, and even the Metallika furniture store of Waco, Texas. It is not clear that all of these uses violated trademark precedent. Will there be public confusion between a heavy metal band and a furniture store if the latter sells metal furniture under the name "Metallika"? As the next box illustrates, a number of trademarks have been lost because the public came to think of them as generic terms.

TRADEMARKS LOST DUE TO GENERIC USE

The following generic terms were once trademarks:

Aspirin

Cellophane

Cola

Escalator

Lite Beer

Monopoly (the game)

Refrigerator

Softsoap

Thermos

Zipper

To ensure that its well-known trademark not be lost to generic use, the Xerox Corporation spent millions of dollars advertising to the public that *xerox* is a registered trademark and that the term should not be used as a verb (to "xerox" a copy) or as a noun (a "xerox").

Criminal trademark penalties apply to those who manufacture or traffic in *counterfeit* trademarked products, products such as imitation "Rolex" watches or "Levi" jeans. What makes counterfeiting criminal is the deliberate intent to pass off, or *palm off,* fake products as real by attaching an unauthorized trademark.

To win a trademark infringement lawsuit, a defendant will usually present one of three basic defenses: (1) the mark is not distinctive, (2) there is little chance of the public's being confused by use of a term trademarked by someone else, or (3) the use is a "fair use." In arguing the first defense, the defendant maintains that the mark is descriptive or generic and that the PTO should not have protected it in the first instance. Alternatively, the defendant argues that the mark has become generic since its trademarking and that it now stands for a class of items. Note that a court can declare a mark invalid even if the PTO accepted registration.

The second defense argues that there is little chance of public confusion over two uses of the same mark. For example, the public is not likely confused between the Ford automobile and the Ford Modeling Agency. But the confusion defense does not always work. In 1999 a federal district court jury awarded Trovan, an electronics manufacturer, $143 million against Pfizer for willful trademark infringement in using the trademark "Trovan" on its antibiotic product, which was eventually withdrawn from the market following the deaths of several people who used it.

The third defense raised in trademark infringement lawsuits is that of fair use. *Fair use* of a registered trademark is allowed by the Lanham Act and relates to a discussion, criticism, or parody of the trademark, the product, or its owner, for example in the news media, on the Internet, or in a textbook. The courts have been explicit that the use of a rival's trademark in comparative advertising is also a fair use. You can legally advertise the results of a study that show your product to be superior to a competitor's, even if you mention the competitor's trademarked product by name.

Trademarks and the Internet Cyber technology produces a combination of old and new trademark issues. Two new issues raise some interesting trademark questions.

First, what is the relationship between a website domain name registered with the Internet Corporation for Assigned Names and Numbers and a trademark registered with the Patent and Trademark Office? There have been numerous instances in which people attempt to register domain names containing well-known trademarks that did not belong to them. Generally, it is a violation of trademark law to use another's registered mark in your domain name. Further, the Anticyber-squatting Consumer Protection Act of 1999 provides a remedy of statutory damages and transfer of a *famous* trademark domain name to its owner if it was registered in "bad faith."

Second, does use of someone else's trademark in a metatag constitute illegal infringement? A *metatag* is a key word embedded in the website programming which enables a search engine to guide an Internet search to the website. If you open a website for book sales, you will want the metatag "book sales" in your programming to attract those searching to buy books to your website. Suppose you include the metatags "Amazon" and "Barnes and Noble" in your programming. Now your website will come up for people looking for the two major Internet booksellers. You have appropriated the interest people have in those sellers for your website. Initial court decisions suggest that using the trademarks of others as metatags is infringement.

TRADEMARK DILUTION

In 1995, Congress passed the Federal Trademark Dilution Act. This law prohibits you from using a mark the same as or similar to another's "famous" trademark so as to dilute its significance, reputation, and goodwill. Even if an owner of a famous trademark cannot prove that the public is confused by another's use of a similar mark (called a "junior" mark), the owner of the "senior" famous trademark can still get an injunction prohibiting further use of the junior mark on the basis of **trademark dilution.** The court also has discretion to award the owner the infringer's profits, actual damages, and attorney's fees if the infringer "willfully intended to trade on the owner's reputation or to cause dilution of the famous mark."

In the following case, the Supreme Court examines the kind of evidence needed to prove trademark dilution. Note that Justice Stevens says the lower courts have misinterpreted the federal act under which this case was brought with certain state antidilution laws.

MOSELY V. V SECRET CATALOGUE, INC.

123 SUP. CT. 1115 (2003)

Victor and Cathy Mosely (petitioners) owned and operated a retail store named "Victor's Secret" in Elizabethtown, Kentucky. The store sold a variety of "intimate lingerie" and "adult novelties." Following a tip, the respondent who owns the "Victoria's Secret" trademark demanded that the Moseleys change the store's name or cease operation, claiming that the name "Victor's Secret" for a store selling lingerie was likely to cause confusion with the trademark "Victoria's Secret" and also was likely to "dilute the distinctiveness" of that mark. The petitioners changed the name of their store to "Vic-tor's Little Secret," but the respondent was not satisfied and sued the Moseleys. The federal district court ruled that "Victor's Little Secret" did not violate the respondent's trademark by confusing the public but that "Victor's Little Secret" did violate the Federal Trademark Dilution Act (FTDA) by diluting "Victoria's Secret." The Court of Appeals affirmed and the Supreme Court granted certiorari.

STEVENS, J.: . . . The VICTORIA'S SECRET mark is unquestionably valuable and petitioners have not challenged the conclusion that it qualifies as a "fa-

[CONTINUED]

mous mark" within the meaning of the statute. Moreover, as we understand their submission, petitioners do not contend that the statutory protection is confined to identical uses of famous marks, or that the statute should be construed more narrowly in a case such as this. Even if the legislative history might lend some support to such a contention, it surely is not compelled by the statutory text.

The District Court's decision in this case rested on the conclusion that the name of petitioners' store "tarnished" the reputation of respondents' mark, and the Court of Appeals relied on both "tarnishment" and "blurring" to support its affirmance. Petitioners have not disputed the relevance of tarnishment, presumably because that concept was prominent in litigation brought under state antidilution statutes and because it was mentioned in the legislative history. Whether it is actually embraced by the statutory text, however, is another matter. Indeed, the contrast between the state statutes, which expressly refer to both "injury to business reputation" and to "dilution of the distinctive quality of a trade name or trademark," and the federal statute which refers only to the latter, arguably supports a narrower reading of the FTDA.

The contrast between the state statutes and the federal statute, however, sheds light on the precise question that we must decide. For those statutes, like several provisions in the federal Lanham Act, repeatedly refer to a "likelihood" of harm, rather than to a completed harm. The relevant text of the FTDA provides that "the owner of a famous mark" is entitled to injunctive relief against another person's commercial use of a mark or trade name if that use *causes dilution of the distinctive quality*" of the famous mark. This text unambiguously requires a showing of actual dilution, rather than a likelihood of dilution.

This conclusion is fortified by the definition of the term "dilution" itself. That definition provides:

"The term 'dilution' means the lessening of the capacity of a famous mark to identify and distinguish goods or services, regardless of the presence or absence of—'(1) competition between the owner of the famous mark and other parties,' or '(2) likelihood of confusion, mistake, or deception.' "

The contrast between the initial reference to an actual "lessening of the capacity" of the mark, and the later reference to a "likelihood of confusions, mistake, or deception" in the second caveat that confirms the conclusion that actual dilution must be established.

Of course, that does not mean that the consequences of dilution, such as an actual loss of sales or profits, must also be proved. To the extent that language in the Fourth Circuit's opinion in the *Ringling Bros.* case suggests otherwise, we disagree. We do agree, however, with that court's conclusion that, at least where the marks at issue are not identical, the mere fact that consumers mentally associate the junior user's mark with a famous mark is not sufficient to establish actionable dilution. As the facts of that case demonstrate, such mental association will not necessarily reduce the capacity of the famous mark to identify the goods of its owner, the statutory requirement for dilution under the FTDA. For even though Utah drivers may be reminded of the circus when they see a license plate referring to the "greatest *snow* on earth," it by no means follows that they will associate "the greatest show on earth" with skiing or snow sports, or associate it less strongly or exclusively with the circus. "Blurring" is not a necessary consequence of mental association. (Nor, for that matter, is "tarnishing.")

The record in this case establishes that an army officer who saw the advertisement of the opening of a store named "Victor's Secret" did make the mental association with "Victoria's Secret," but it also shows that he did not therefore form any different impression of the store that his wife and daughter had patronized. There is a complete absence of evidence of any lessening of the capacity of the VICTORIA'S SECRET mark to identify and distinguish goods or services sold in Victoria's Secret stores or advertised in its catalogs. The officer was offended by the ad, but it did not change his conception of Victoria's Secret. His offense was directed entirely at petitioners, not at respondents. Moreover, the expert retained by respondents had nothing to say about the impact of petitioners' name on the strength of respondents' mark.

Noting that consumer surveys and other means of demonstrating actual dilution are expensive and often unreliable, respondents argue that evidence of an actual "lessening of the capacity of a famous mark to identify and distinguish goods or services" may be difficult to obtain. It may well be, however, that

[CONTINUED]

direct evidence of dilution such as consumer surveys will not be necessary if actual dilution can reliably be proven through circumstantial evidence—the obvious case is one where the junior and senior marks are identical. Whatever difficulties of proof may be entailed, they are not an acceptable reason for dispensing with proof of an essential element of a statutory violation. The evidence in the present record is not sufficient to support the summary judgment on the dilution count. The judgment is therefore reversed, and the case is remanded for further proceedings consistent with this opinion.

It is so ordered.

CASE QUESTIONS

1. What is the difference between traditional trademark violation and trademark dilution under the FTDA?

2. What does the Court say is the difference between trademark dilution under statutes and under the FTDA?

3. What resource does the respondent have now in light of the Court's decision?

16. COPYRIGHT LAW

Copyright gives a property a certain creative work that keeps others from reproducing it without the owner's permission. The copyright attaches not to an idea or to facts but to the original *expression* of an idea or facts. Three criteria are necessary for copyright protection to occur:

- A work must be original. It must be created, not copied.
- The work must be fixed in a tangible medium of expression like a book, canvas, compact disc, tape, or computer disk.
- The work must show some creativity. For example, the Supreme Court ruled in *Feist Publications, Inc. v. Rural Telephone Service Co.,* 499 U.S. 340 (1991), that the mere effort and alphabetic arrangement of names that went into a telephone directory's white pages was insufficiently creative to warrant a copyright.

Copyright laws protects authors rather than inventors. An author creates works of a literary, dramatic, musical, graphic, choreographic, audio, or visual nature. Ranging from printed material to photographs to records and motion pictures, these works receive automatic federal protection under the Copyright Act of 1976 from the moment the author creates them. The copyright allows the holder to control the reproduction, display, distribution, and performance of a protected work. The copyright runs for the author's lifetime, plus 70 additional years for all works published after 1977.

Copyright Protection Although copyright protection is automatic, an action for copyright infringement cannot be begun unless the author has properly filed copies of the protected work with the Copyright Office. One who infringes on a copyright cannot be held liable for actual or statutory damages unless a copyright symbol or notice accompanies the protected work. When the author has observed the proper formalities, however, she or he may recover actual or statutory damages, attorney's fees, and any profits the infringer has made. Illegally reproduced copies may also be seized, and willful copyright violations are criminal offenses.

The Copyright Act specifies that a fair use of copyrighted materials is not an infringement of the owner's property. **Fair use** includes copying for "criticism, comment, news reporting, teaching (including multiple copies for classroom use), scholarship, or research." In determining whether a particular use is a fair one, a court will consider

- The purpose and character of the use, including whether such use is for commercial or nonprofit educational purposes
- The nature of the copyrighted work
- The amount and substantiality of the portion used in relation to the copyrighted work as a whole
- The effect of the use upon the potential market for the copyrighted work

The determination of a fair use in light of these factors is made on a case-by-case basis. In the case that follow's, the Supreme Court considers whether one song makes a fair use of a previous song's copyrighted lyrics. The fair use being considered concerns *parody,* a form of expression that criticizes by poking fun at something through exaggeration.

Campbell v. Acuff-Rose Music, Inc.

510 U.S. 569 (1994)

SOUTER, J.: We are called upon to decide whether 2 Live Crew's commercial parody of Roy Orbison's song, "Oh, Pretty Woman," may be a fair use within the meaning of the Copyright Act of 1976.

In 1964, Roy Orbison and William Dees wrote a rock ballad called "Oh, Pretty Woman" and assigned their rights in it to respondent Acuff-Rose Music, Inc. Acuff-Rose registered the song for copyright protection.

Petitioners Luther R. Campbell, Christopher Wongwon, Mark Ross, and David Hobbs are collectively known as 2 Live Crew, a popular rap music group. In 1989, Campbell wrote a song entitled "Pretty Woman," which he later described in an affidavit as intended, "through comical lyrics, to satirize the original work. . . ." 2 Live Crew's manager informed Acuff-Rose that 2 Live Crew had written

a parody of "Oh, Pretty Woman," that they would afford all credit for ownership and authorship of the original song to Acuff-Rose, Dees, and Orbison, and that they were willing to pay a fee for the use they wished to make of it. Enclosed with the letter were a copy of the lyrics and a recording of 2 Live Crew's song. Acuff-Rose's agent refused permission, stating that "I am aware of the success enjoyed by 'The 2 Live Crews', but I must inform you that we cannot permit the use of a parody of 'Oh, Pretty Woman.' " Nonetheless, in June or July 1989, 2 Live Crew released records, cassette tapes, and compact discs of "Pretty Woman" in a collection of songs entitled "As Clean As They Wanna Be." The albums and compact discs identify the authors of "Pretty Woman" as Orbison and Dees and its publisher as Acuff-Rose.

[CONTINUED]

Almost a year later, after nearly a quarter of a million copies of the recording had been sold, Acuff-Rose sued 2 Live Crew and its record company, Luke Skyywalker Records, for copyright infringement. The District Court granted judgment for 2 Live Crew, reasoning that the commercial purpose of 2 Live Crew's song was no bar to fair use; that 2 Live Crew's version was a parody, which "quickly degenerates into a play on words, substituting predictable lyrics with shocking ones" to show "how bland and banal the Orbison song" is; that 2 Live Crew had taken no more than was necessary to "conjure up" the original in order to parody it; and that it was "extremely unlikely that 2 Live Crew's song could adversely affect the market for the original."

The Court of Appeals for the Sixth Circuit reversed and remanded. Although it assumed for the purpose of its opinion that 2 Live Crew's song was a parody of the Orbison original, the Court of Appeals thought the District Court had put too little emphasis on the fact that "every commercial use . . . is presumptively . . . unfair." Next, the Court of Appeals determined that, by "taking the heart of the original and making it the heart of a new work," 2 Live Crew had, qualitatively, taken too much. Finally, after noting that the effect on the potential market for the original (and the market for derivative works) is "undoubtedly the single most important element of fair use," the Court of Appeals faulted the District Court for "refusing to indulge the presumption" that "harm for purposes of the fair use analysis has been established by the presumption attaching to commercial uses." In sum, the court concluded that its "blatantly commercial purpose . . . prevents this parody from being a fair use."

We granted certiorari, to determine whether 2 Live Crew's commercial parody could be a fair use.

It is uncontested here that 2 Live Crew's song would be an infringement of Acuff-Rose's rights in "Oh, Pretty Woman," under the Copyright Act of 1976, but for a finding of fair use through parody. From the infancy of copyright protection, some opportunity for fair use of copyrighted materials has been thought necessary to fulfill copyright's very purpose, "to promote the Progress of Science and useful Arts. . . ." For as Justice Story explained, "in

truth, in literature, in science and in art, there are, and can be, few, if any, things which in an abstract sense, are strictly new and original throughout. Every book in literature, science and art, borrows, and must necessarily borrow, and use much which was well known and used before."

The first factor in a fair use enquiry is "the purpose and character of the use, including whether such use is of a commercial nature or is for non-profit educational purposes." The enquiry here may be guided by looking to whether the use is for criticism, or comment, or news reporting, and the like. The central purpose of this investigation is to see, in Justice Story's words, whether the new work merely "supersede[s] the objects" of the original creation, or instead adds something new, with a further purpose or different character, altering the first with new expression, meaning, or message; it asks, in other words, whether and to what extent the new work is "transformative." Although such transformative use is not absolutely necessary for a finding of fair use, the goal of copyright, to promote science and the arts, is generally furthered by the creation of transformative works. Such works thus lie at the heart of the fair use doctrine's guarantee of breathing space within the confines of copyright, and the more transformative the new work, the less will be the significance of other factors, like commercialism, that may weigh against a finding of fair use.

Here, the District Court held, and the Court of Appeals assumed, that 2 Live Crew's "Pretty Woman" contains parody, commenting on and criticizing the original work, whatever it may have to say about society at large. As the District Court remarked, the words of 2 Live Crew's song copy the original's first line, but then "quickly degenerate into a play on words, substituting predictable lyrics with shocking ones . . . [that] derisively demonstrate how bland and banal the Orbison song seems to them." We think it fair to say that 2 Live Crew's song reasonably could be perceived as commenting on the original or criticizing it, to some degree. 2 Live Crew juxtaposes the romantic musings of a man whose fantasy comes true, with degrading taunts, a bawdy demand for sex, and a sigh of relief from paternal responsibility. The later words can be taken as a comment on the naivete of the original of an ear-

[CONTINUED]

lier day, as a rejection of its sentiment that ignores the ugliness of street life and the debasement that it signifies. It is this joinder of reference and ridicule that marks off the author's choice of parody from the other types of comment and criticism that traditionally have had a claim to fair use protection as transformative works.

The Court of Appeals, however, immediately cut short the enquiry into 2 Live Crew's fair use claim by confining its treatment of the first factor essentially to one relevant fact, the commercial nature of the use. The court then inflated the significance of this fact by applying a presumption that "every commercial use of copyrighted material is presumptively . . . unfair. . . ." In giving virtually dispositive weight to the commercial nature of the parody, the Court of Appeals erred.

The second statutory factor, "the nature of the copyrighted work," calls for recognition that some works are closer to the core of intended copyright protection than others, with one consequence that fair use is more difficult to establish when the former works are copied. We agree with both the District Court and the Court of Appeals that the Orbison original's creative expression for public dissemination falls within the core of the copyright's protective purposes. This fact, however, is not much help in this case, or ever likely to help much in separating the fair use sheep from the infringing goats in a parody case, since parodies almost invariably copy publicly known, expressive works.

The third factor asks whether "the amount and substantiality of the portion used in relation to the copyrighted work as a whole" are reasonable in relation to the purpose of the copying. The District Court considered the song's parodic purpose in finding that 2 Live Crew had not helped themselves overmuch. The Court of Appeals disagreed, stating that "while it may not be inappropriate to find that no more was taken than necessary, the copying was qualitatively substantial. . . . We conclude that taking the heart of the original and making it the heart of a new work was to purloin a substantial portion of the essence of the original."

Suffice it to say here that, as to the lyrics, we fail to see how the copying can be excessive in relation to its parodic purpose, even if the portion taken is the original's "heart." As to the music, we express no opinion whether repetition of the bass riff is excessive copying, and we remand to permit evaluation of the amount taken, in light of the song's parodic purpose and character, its transformative elements, and considerations of the potential for market substitution sketched more fully below.

The fourth fair use factor is "the effect of the use upon the potential market for or value of the copyrighted work." It requires courts to consider not only the extent of market harm caused by the particular actions of the alleged infringer, but also "whether unrestricted and widespread conduct of the sort engaged in by the defendant . . . would result in a substantially adverse impact on the potential market" for the original. The enquiry "must take account not only of harm to the original but also of harm to the market for derivative works."

Although 2 Live Crew submitted uncontroverted affidavits on the question of market harm to the original, neither they, nor Acuff-Rose, introduced evidence or affidavits addressing the likely effect of 2 Live Crew's parodic rap song on the market for a nonparody, rap version of "Oh, Pretty Woman." And while Acuff-Rose would have us find evidence of a rap market in the very facts that 2 Live Crew recorded a rap parody of "Oh, Pretty Woman" and another rap group sought a license to record a rap derivative, there was no evidence that a potential rap market was harmed in any way by 2 Live Crew's parody, rap version.

It was error for the Court of Appeals to conclude that the commercial nature of 2 Live Crew's parody of "Pretty Woman" rendered it presumptively unfair. No such evidentiary presumption is available to address either the first factor, the character and purpose of the use, or the fourth, market harm, in determining whether a transformative use, such as parody, is a fair one. The court also erred in holding that 2 Live Crew had necessarily copied excessively from the Orbison original, considering the parodic purpose of the use. We therefore reverse the judgment of the Court of Appeals and remand the case for further proceedings consistent with this opinion.

Reversed and remanded.

[CONTINUED]

CASE QUESTIONS

1. When 2 Live Crew was willing to pay for the use of "Pretty Woman," why do you think that Acuff-Rose would not grant permission to use the lyrics?

2. Why does copyright law permit someone to make a "fair use" of another's copyrighted material?

3. Why does the Supreme Court decide in this case that 2 Live Crew made a fair use of the song?

Copyright in the Cyber Age Criminal prosecutions and civil lawsuits for "file sharing" copyrighted material over the Internet are growing. One FBI probe of a "warez" website devoted to sharing pirated computer software produced 17 arrests. In 2003 the recording industry sued four university students who maintained websites that facilitated music file sharing, which violates copyright law. The students agreed to pay the industry $12 to $17 thousand each. The film industry as well as the music industry has become more active in pressing civil lawsuits as well as criminal prosecutions for illegal file sharing. However, a district court has ruled that the manufacturers of file-sharing programs did not illegally contribute to (aid and abet) the violation of copyright law since the programs could be used for file sharing of noncopyrighted materials.

Note that the users of file-sharing programs who send or download copyrighted songs and videos are violating copyright law. A 2002 survey by Ipsos Reid showed 52 percent of 12- to 17-year-olds and 44 percent of 18- to 24-year-olds admitted to downloading music files from a file-sharing service, over half of them within the previous 30 days. If you are such a file sharer, do you consider yourself a thief? To explore your own feelings about this, think back to the ethics chapter (Chapter 2). Do you publicly proclaim your file sharing, or do it in secret? Are you proud to tell your families or potential employers about what you are doing?

Some say that intellectual property does not diminish the way that tangible property does when someone misappropriates it. But consider this: Property is a legal right to exclude, not a physical thing, and the object of a property copyright includes the reproduction of music for commercial profit. The market resource *is* diminished for the copyright owner when file sharers misappropriate music. In the early years of the century, the volume of sales for copyrighted music has declined significantly.

Digital Millennium Copyright Act Because copyrighted property is easily misappropriated over the Internet, Congress passed a new law in 1998 that prohibits certain activities leading to copyright violation. The *Digital Millennium Copyright Act* makes illegal the effort to get around devices used by copyright owners to keep their works from being infringed. In particular, the act will be used to prevent the production, marketing, or sales of a product or service designed to get around technological protections of computer software, videos, and compact disks.

The act also restricts the import, distribution, and sales of analog video recorders and camcorders that lack certain features making it difficult to copy copyrighted materials. It further exempts Internet service providers from liability (1) for illegal copies that pass temporarily through their systems and (2) for permanent illegal copies stored in their systems, for example, at a website, if the service provider removes the offending material upon request of a copyright owner. Finally, the act relieves service providers from liability for unintentionally linking to a website that contains infringing materials.

Violations of the act permit civil remedies, including injunction, actual damages, and statutory damages. A court can assess triple damages against a repeat offender. Willful violation for financial gain can also result in up to 10 years imprisonment.

17. PROPERTY: A CONCLUSION AND COMMENT

This chapter has introduced the law of property as it orders society's limited resources. Although many chapter sections have explained the rules making up property law, especially the law of intellectual property, the chapter has also focused on the general importance of the legal property system to private enterprise and society. The key to the most rapid increase of total wealth—the greatest expansion of limited resources—is a property system that applies generally and equally to everyone's resources.

In the modern nation, property law founds the marketplace by establishing an essential framework for the voluntary and certain exchange of identifiable private resources. There is strong reason to think that a prime determinant of wealth in the world today is the presence or absence of an adequate property system under the rule of law. Thus, it is significant that business students appreciate the fundamental role of law in business and the necessity for a strong legal system even when they oppose the wisdom of specific rules or regulations.

Although effective property law may be the foundation for society's material flourishing and the liberty of the individual, it also has another side to it. Property law permits the accumulation of unequal exclusive resources, and as James Madison wrote in *The Federalist:* "The most common and durable source of factions has been the various and unequal distribution of property." A property system functions best when there is a large middle class with adequate resources, or at least a well-educated populace that understands the benefits of property. Otherwise, in a democracy the temptation is great to redistribute resources through taxation, and at some point the motivation to produce additional limited resources diminishes.

The major issues of poverty and prosperity in the Cyber Age and the new millennium involve the understanding of property law's effects on society. To deal knowledgeably with the legal environment of business, students must grasp how law founds the private marketplace.

KEY TERMS

Accession 185	Contract 183
Adverse possession 184	Copyright 206
Confusion 185	Deed 188

REVIEW QUESTIONS AND PROBLEMS

The Property System

1. *The Problem of Limited Resources*

    (a)   According to political theory, why do governments exist?

    (b)   Identify two ways for dealing with the problem of limited resources.

2. *Property and Prosperity*

    Why does a property system produce more of what people want than a system that focuses on state planning?

3. *Two Basic Divisions of Property*

    What is the significance of the distinction between real and personal property? Is manufacturing equipment real or personal property? Or both, according to its context of sale? Explain.

Acquiring Resources in a Property System

4. *Acquiring Resources through Exchange*

    (a)   What are the rules under which people exchange resources in a property system?

    (b)   Explain the functions of contract law in a property system.

5. *Acquiring Resources through Possession*

    (a)   Identify three different ways by which one can become an owner through possession.

    (b)   The Hardwood Timber Company learns that the Pulpwood Paper Company has constructed a fence along an 8-mile disputed boundary with Hardwood. Why might it be important for Hardwood to have a survey conducted to establish the proper boundary? Explain. Suppose the survey shows that Pulpwood's fence encroaches on Hardwood's boundary by nearly 200 feet. Must the fence be torn down? Explain alternatives to tearing down the fence.

    (c)   Discuss the pros and cons of the "squatter-to-owner" process.

6. *Acquiring Resources through Confusion*

    (a)   Explain how someone can become an owner of someone else's fungible goods.

    (b)   Why are boundaries important to the concept of property?

7. *Acquiring Resources through Accession*

Discuss how accession explains much of the property foundation of the private market.

8. *Acquiring Resources through Gift*

(a)   Explain how the law determines when a gift generally takes place.

(b)   What is a testamentary gift? When does such a gift take place?

9. *Types of Ownership*

(a)   What is the difference between the fee simple absolute estate and the fee simple defeasible estate?

(b)   In what sense is a tenant an "owner"?

10. *Title and Property Registration*

(a)   What two other terms mean almost the same thing as "property."

(b)   What is a deed? Explain three different kinds of deeds.

11. *Private Property and Eminent Domain*

(a)   What is eminent domain?

(b)   When does a "taking" occur? What is the significance of a "taking"?

12. *Property, the Use of Resources, and the Equal Right of Others*

(a)   What does it mean to say that we have a property not only in land but also in the uses of land?

(b)   What does it mean to say that the right of property is always limited by the equal right of others?

(c)   Fertilizer, Inc. bought land in the country and constructed a plant that makes fertilizer from stock feedlot wastes. A number of homeowners have sued claiming that the plant's operations produce an awful smell and constitute a nuisance. Discuss.

Intellectual Property

13. *Trade Secret Law*

(a)   Define a trade secret.

(b)   What does it mean to say that a trade secret is "intellectual property"?

14. *Patent Law*

(a)   Why is patent protection limited to 20 years? Discuss.

(b)   Can Dan patent a new musical notation system designed to make it much easier for music students to read music? Discuss.

15. *Trademark Law*

A birth-planning organization published a poster containing a photo of a pregnant Girl Scout and the phrase "Be Prepared." The Boy Scouts of America sued the organization for infringement of its trademarked slogan. Has the organization illegally infringed on the trademark? Discuss.

16. *Copyright Law*

Greg and Sandy are friends at school. He lets her copy his new CDs; she lets him copy hers. Have the students violated copyright law or is this a fair use? Discuss.

17. *Property: A Conclusion and Comment*

Discuss the position that property law and not new technology, better management techniques, careful financial planning, or faster product distribution is the foundation for business prosperity in the modern nation.

TERMINOLOGY REVIEW

For each term in the left-hand column, match the most appropriate description in the right-hand column.

1. Infringement	a. Just compensation
2. Trademark	b. Parody
3. Nuisance	c. Real property
4. Copyright	d. Maximum bundle of ownership rights
5. Eminent domain	e. Metallica
6. Patent	f. Property in expression
7. Fair use	g. Illegal copying
8. Fee simple	h. Unreasonable use of one's land
9. Fixture	i. Twenty years

BUSINESS DISCUSSION

You open Music Plus, an e-business on the Internet. You have software that enables users to exchange music files. Although users do not pay for your service, they are exposed to advertising for which you charge advertisers. Any kind of music file can be exchanged through Music Plus, but in fact 99 percent of the files exchanged come from copyrighted and commercially recorded music.

Can music be property? Explain.

Can you legally use an owner's music without permission?

Can you legally assist another in using an owner's music without permission?

PRINCIPLES OF CONTRACT LAW

You have recently been promoted from the marketing department to become a regional sales manager of Cover-It-Well Carpeting and Floor Covering, Inc. Your company manufactures all types of carpets and other flooring products, such as vinyl and wood laminates. In your new position, you are responsible for 12 salespersons who call on retail stores throughout your assigned region.

As you study the documentation that accompanies the sales transaction, you are uncertain about the answers to a number of legal questions. The typical sales transactions seem to occur when a salesperson calls on a customer in the retail store and when a customer telephones or e-mails an order. Often there is an exchange of documentation, including the customers' orders and your company's confirmation in response. Among your questions are the following:

How can you tell when a contract with the customer exists?

If there is conflicting language in the order form and the sales confirmation, which language controls?

When is the contract considered to be fully performed?

The questions asked in the Business Decision are typical of those arising in business transactions. Answering these and other question related to contracts is a fundamental part of the environment in which people conduct business. Here, at the beginning of this chapter, understanding the basic definition of contracts is essential. Simply stated, a contract involves a **promise** or an exchange of promises. Although the details of contract classifications, terminology, formation, and performance make up the bulk of this chapter, remember at the heart of this topic is a promise or commitment to do or not to do something.

The preceding chapter emphasizes the importance of property as the foundation of our free-enterprise system. The enforcement of contracts is essential in the operation of this property-oriented system. Without contracts and the court systems to enforce contracts, buyers and sellers would not have confidence in exchanging valuable property interests.

Everyday millions of contracts—legally enforceable promises—are created and performed. Businesspeople and consumers make contractual agreements. No other area of the law has been as important as the law of contracts in supporting private enterprise. As you read and study this chapter, keep in mind the role that property and contracts have in making business possible.

Although this chapter focuses on legal issues and contracts, real-life contract problems usually involve business-related and people-related considerations as well as legal rules. The Business Decision illustrates this fact. There are legal considerations about:

1. When communications become a contract
2. Whether a contract is enforceable without being in writing
3. Whether an error in the price excuses your company from having to sell its products at a wrong price

There are also nonlegal business considerations in every contract. If your company tries to get out of the deal the customer believes exists, you risk losing that customer's future business. Although your company may settle a dispute through negotiation rather than litigation, your bargaining power is enhanced when you know the rules of contract law.

BASIC CONCEPTS

1. CONTRACT LAW IN PRIVATE ENTERPRISE

When was the last time you entered into a contract? Was it last month when you signed an apartment or dorm lease? If so, you must be very hungry. This is because one enters a contract when buying a meal or a snack from a vending machine. Actually, most people contract daily for a great variety of goods and services that they purchase or lease. The rules of contract law underlie the private enterprise system at every turn.

A contract need not be a formal, written document, and those who make a contract do not have to use the word *contract* or recognize that they have made a legally enforceable promise. Still, the rules of contract law apply. If the expectations of the parties to a contract are not met, these rules affect legal negotiations and may result in a lawsuit. For instance, contract law says that a restaurant "promises" that its food is fit to eat. Should the restaurant serve a meal that gives the buyer food poisoning, it could be liable for the injury caused by breaking its promise.

Contract law enables private agreements to be legally enforceable. Enforceability of agreements is desirable because it gives people the certainty they need to rely on promises contained in agreements. For instance, a shirt manufacturer in Los Angeles must know that it can rely on the promise of a store in Boston to pay for a thousand specially manufactured shirts. The manufacturer is more likely to agree to sew the shirts if it can enforce payment from the buyer, if necessary, under the law of contracts.

In an important sense, then, the law of contracts is vital for our private enterprise economy. It helps make buyers and sellers willing to do business together. Contract law is not as needed in the economy of the People's Republic of China,

THE CONFIDENTIALITY AGREEMENT

Many companies require employees to sign contractual confidentiality agreements. In these agreements employees promise not to disclose certain things they learn during their employment. Confidentiality agreements are very useful in keeping employees or ex-employees from telling a company's research discoveries, marketing plans, customer lists, and other sensitive information.

Confidentiality agreements are especially important in the tobacco industry. Most medical opinion holds that tobacco is an addictive product that can cause heart and lung disease. What do tobacco industry executives think about these issues? Publicly, the tobacco industry downplays that tobacco is addictive and minimizes tobacco health risks. Discussion within the industry, however, may show concern about the effects of tobacco. Precisely worded confidentiality agreements prohibit tobacco industry employees from revealing documents or discus-

sions at work concerning the risks of tobacco consumption, or even how cigarettes and other tobacco products are made. The tobacco industry can enforce these agreements through court injunctions or damage clauses. Over the years confidentiality agreements have been very useful in keeping industry information out of the hands of those who wish to sue or regulate the industry.

In 1994 a paralegal who worked for a law firm representing a major tobacco company copied and then released many internal company documents that indicated concern within the tobacco industry over the risks of tobacco consumption. *The New York Times,* the *Washington Post,* and other publications carried stories on the contents of these documents. Not long afterward, the tobacco industry began negotiating for a comprehensive settlement to the legal claims arising from tobacco consumption and to the government's regulation of the tobacco industry.

where the state controls many buying and selling relationships. It is also less needed in countries such as Japan, where centuries of tradition regulate business arrangements. But in the United States the law of contracts promotes certainty that agreements will be kept and permits reliance on promises. It encourages the flow of commerce.

Contract law also provides enormous flexibility and precision in business dealings. It provides flexibility in that you can agree (or require agreement) to literally anything that is not illegal or against public policy. It gives precision in that with careful thinking you can make another agree to exactly the requirements that accomplish even a very complex business purpose. The box above provides an example of the precise use of contractual language to accomplish a business purpose.

2. SOURCES OF CONTRACT LAW

Most of the contract law outlined in this chapter is common law. Hopefully, you remember from Chapter 1 that common law comes from judges' decisions. The courts have developed principles controlling contract formation, performance, breach, and remedies in countless cases. This judge-made law affects many types of contracts, including real property, service, employment, and general business contracts.

Another source of contract law is legislation. Various states have enacted the common law as a part of the state statutes. A particularly important example of state-based legislation impacting contract law is the Uniform Commercial Code (UCC). Article 2 of the UCC covers the sale of **goods.** Goods are tangible, movable items of personal property. Every state has adopted this portion of the UCC thereby making state contract law uniform in the area of contracts involving goods. Throughout this chapter, you will study both the common law principles of contracts and the UCC. Remember, this distinction between these two primary sources of contract law relates the UCC to contracts involving goods, and the common law governs other contracts.

Bilateral Contract

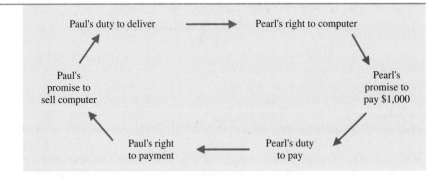

3. CONTRACTUAL CLASSIFICATIONS

We use a number of terms to help classify different types of contracts. Learning these terms will greatly help you understand contract law. This section introduces the following contractual terminology:

- Bilateral and unilateral contracts
- Express and implied-in fact contracts
- Implied-in-law or quasi-contracts

Bilateral and Unilateral Contracts   **Contracts** involve either an exchange of promises by the parties or a promise conditioned on the performance of an act. A **bilateral contract** is an agreement containing mutual promises. For example, suppose Paul promises to sell his laptop computer to Pearl if she promises to pay $1,000 for the equipment. When Pearl makes her promise in response to Paul's, a bilateral contract is formed. This relationship is depicted in the figure "Bilateral Contract." Notice that a bilateral contract involves two promises, two rights, and two duties.

While a bilateral contract involves a promise for a promise, a **unilateral contract** is an agreement with only one promise. The maker of such a promise seeks an action rather than a promise in return. Suppose Pat tells Alex, "I am tired of your idle commitments; when you install my new stereo equipment, I will pay you $200." Here Pat no longer wants Alex's promise to perform. Pat seeks the actual performance. In the figure "Unilateral Contract," notice that there is only one promise, one duty, and one right.

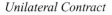

Unilateral Contract

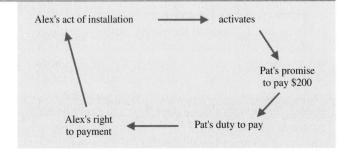

Most business contracts take the bilateral form. Indeed, courts presume a bilateral nature of an agreement whenever there is doubt about the form. Nevertheless, the party making a promise can control the application of many concepts of contract law by understanding the distinction between bilateral and unilateral contracts.

Express and Implied-in-Fact Contracts Many contracts arise from discussions in which parties actually discuss the promised terms of their agreement. These are called **express contracts.** A negotiated purchase of land for construction of a manufacturing plant is an example of an express contract. These are also **implied-in-fact contracts,** which arise from the conduct of the parties rather than from words. For instance, asking a person such as an accountant for professional advice *implies* a promise to pay the going rate for this advice even though you do not make an *express* promise to pay for it.

The case that follows discusses implied-in-fact contracts and illustrates that parties should be cautious when relying on them. As you read this case, ask yourself whether the court could have reached the conclusion that no contract existed. We believe the following case represents an example of an appellate court deferring to the findings of the trial jury. A typical rule of thumb is that expressing one's contractual commitment is better than leaving things unstated.

BENNETT V. EMERSON ELECTRIC COMPANY

2003 U.S. APP. LEXIS 9443 (10TH CIR. 2003)

In 1998 Curtis Bennett contacted Emerson Electric Company about employment. Emerson was planning to implement the "Trailblazer" program. The purpose of this program was to promote RIDGID power tools, as well as other tools manufactured by Emerson and sold by Home Depot, by sending specially equipped tractor-trailer rigs to NASCAR races throughout the nation and to grand openings of Home Depot stores. Emerson's marketing personnel were to accompany the rigs and conduct public demonstrations of the tools to create a "carnival-type" atmosphere. Although the program was initially conceived as a one-year agreement between Emerson and Home Depot, it was renegotiated to three years.

Bennett, who was fifty-six years of age, was interviewed by several Emerson executives for a sales/marketing position in the Trailblazer program. According to Bennett, he informed his interviewers that he was not looking for a short-term position,

but was looking for an opportunity to finish his working career. In response, Dave Pringle, the president of Emerson's tool division, allegedly stated "No problem." Tim Ferry, an Emerson vice-president and general manager, allegedly stated that Emerson had a tentative three-year commitment with Home Depot to market the RIDGID line of power tools. Further, Ferry informed Bennett that it was his intent to keep all Trailblazer employees on board at least for the length of the program.

On November 3, 1998, Emerson sent a letter to Bennett confirming an offer of employment as National NASCAR/Events Manager reporting to Brian Sponsler, VP, Sales & Marketing–Home Depot. The offer letter was silent as to the intended length of his employment. Bennett accepted the offer and began working for Emerson on or about November 15, 1998.

On November 20, 1998, Bennett leased a vehicle in his own name for business use. He chose a three-year lease to coincide with the three-year planned

[CONTINUED]

length of the Trailblazer marketing program. Bennett's understanding was his expenses would be reimbursed by Emerson as a monthly automobile allowance.

Within a month of beginning work, Bennett was reprimanded for exceeding the allowable automobile allowance and per diem for meals. There also were questions regarding expenses, the hiring of support personnel, and personal integrity. Bennett was reprimanded again on January 11, 1999. On February 17, 1999, Bennett's employment was terminated.

Bennett filed suit against Emerson, claiming a breach of an implied contract for the duration of three years. The jury returned a verdict in favor of Bennett in the amount of $236,707.49 on that claim. Emerson filed a post-trial motion for judgment as a matter of law or, in the alternative, for new trial. These motions were denied.

BRISCOE, J.: . . . Emerson contends the district court erred in denying its post-trial motion for judgment as a matter of law. Emerson argues the evidence presented at trial was legally insufficient to support Bennett's claim for breach of implied contract. . . .

We review *de novo* a district court's ruling on a motion for judgment as a matter of law. Judgment as a matter of law is appropriate only if during a trial by jury a party has been fully heard on an issue and there is no legally sufficient evidentiary basis for a reasonable jury to find for that party on that issue. When we review the record, we will not weigh evidence, judge witness credibility, or challenge the factual conclusions of the jury. Instead, we consider the evidence, and any inferences drawn therefrom, in favor of the non-moving party.

As noted, Emerson argues the evidence presented at trial was legally insufficient to establish the existence of an implied-in-fact contract of employment. Emerson asserts that any statements made to Bennett during the interview process were, at most, "general platitudes" or "vague assurances" that did not manifest an intent on the part of Emerson to contract with Bennett. Emerson also points to the following evidence which, in its view, demonstrates there was no contract: (1) there was no mention in Bennett's resume that he was seeking a guaranteed contract of employment; (2) the written offer of employment by Emerson to Bennett did not mention a

specific term of employment; (3) no other Emerson tool division employee had an employment contract; and (4) after his termination, Bennett wrote a letter to the president of Emerson's tool division stating there "was no doubt when [he] accepted the position that it was for a minimum of one year, with the strong possibility of going two additional years without any problem.". . .

According to defendant, there is no legally sufficient evidentiary basis for a reasonable jury to have found in favor of plaintiff on his breach of contract claim. In large part, defendant simply rehashes various arguments. . . . For example, defendant again emphasizes that Dave Pringle, defendant's president, and Tim Ferry denied making the specific representations that plaintiff alleges they made during his initial interviews with defendant. . . . While Pringle and Ferry may have denied making any statements to plaintiff concerning a three-year contract or other term of employment, plaintiff presented evidence to the jury from which it could have reasonably concluded that plaintiff was promised a position with defendant for as long as the Trailblazer program lasted, or a minimum of three years. Plaintiff testified, for example, that he advised Mr. Ferry that he was not looking for a short-term, temporary position and that he wanted an opportunity to finish out [his] working career. According to plaintiff, Mr. Ferry responded that defendant was going to secure a three-year commitment with Home Depot, suggesting that plaintiff would have a job for at least the duration of the Trailblazer program. In any event, despite his subsequent denials, Mr. Ferry testified . . . that it was his intent to keep all Trailblazer employees, including plaintiff, on board at least for the length of the program. Mr. Ferry further testified that he may have conveyed that intent to interviewees, including plaintiff. From this evidence, the jury could reasonably find the existence of a three-year contract.

We find no basis for overturning the district court's conclusions. It is significant to note that Emerson has not specifically challenged the court's conclusions, nor has it attempted to refute the evidence relied on by the court. Instead, Emerson points to evidence that could be construed in its favor. Obviously, that is not sufficient to establish it is entitled to judgment as a matter of law when, as

[CONTINUED]

here, there is evidence in the record that supports the court's conclusions.

Emerson also contends the evidence presented at trial was insufficient to establish a meeting of the minds between Bennett and Emerson regarding all essential terms of the alleged contract. . . . [T]here must be a meeting of the minds on all essential terms to form a binding contract. In our view, the evidence cited by the district court is sufficient to establish such a meeting of the minds. In particular, Ferry's comments to Bennett during the interview process reasonably could have been perceived by the jury as demonstrating assent to a contract of employment for the intended three-year life of the Trailblazer program. . . .

Affirmed.

CASE QUESTIONS

1. What key contractual term is implied from the fact of this situation?

2. Why is the length of the contract at issue in this case?

3. How could the parties have avoided the issue of this contract's duration?

4. What is the role in this case of an implied-in-fact contract as opposed to an express contract?

Implied-in-Law or Quasi-Contracts When one party is unjustly enriched at the expense of another, the law may imply a duty on the first party to pay the second even though there is no contract between the two parties. The doctrine that requires this result is based on a contract **implied in law.** Since there really is no actual contractual agreement, the phrase **quasi-contract** often is used.

If a debtor overpays a creditor $5,000, the debtor can force the creditor to return that amount by suing under quasi-contract. It would be an unjust enrichment to allow the creditor to keep the $5,000. Likewise, when John has paid taxes on land, thinking that he owns it, and Mary comes along with a superior title (ownership) to the land and has John evicted, the remedy of quasi-contract requires that Mary reimburse John for the taxes paid.

Note that quasi-contract is not an answer to every situation in which no contract exists. Over the years, courts have come to apply quasi-contract in a fairly limited number of cases based on unjust enrichment.

4. CONTRACTUAL ENFORCEMENT TERMINOLOGY

Terms used in a contract law related to the enforceability of agreements include *enforceable, unenforceable, valid, void,* and *voidable.*

The ultimate purpose of a contract is the creation of an agreement which courts will order parties to perform or to pay consequences for the failure of performance. When courts uphold the validity of such promises, the resulting agreement is an **enforceable contract.** If a nonperforming party has a justifiable reason for noncompliance with a promise, the result is an **unenforceable contract.** In essence, in this latter situation, a defense exists that denies the legal enforcement of an agreement.

When an agreement is enforceable because all the essential requirements (discussed in sections 7–12) are present, courts refer to a **valid contract.** At the other end of the spectrum, a **void contract** is one that appears to be an agreement but lacks an essential requirement for validity and enforceability. The most typical example of a void contract is an apparent agreement that has an illegal purpose. For example, a business contract that involves the shipment of contraband is void and unenforceable. As described in section 11 in more detail, courts usually refuse to hear arguments of parties to a void contract. Courts simply leave these parties where they are regardless of whether the illegal agreement has been partially or fully performed. Thus, in states where gambling is illegal, a bet on a football game is void. Courts will not enforce the betting agreement and do not care if the losing party has or has not paid off the bet.

A **voidable contract** is an agreement when one party has the right to withdraw from the promise made without incurring any legal liability. One party has the power to end the enforcement of a voidable contract. An interesting aspect of voidable contracts involves the fact that these agreements are enforceable in court until a party with the legal right to do so decides to void the contract, thereby making the agreement unenforceable. Typically this middleground situation arises when a party to the contract lacks capacity or is disadvantaged by specific situations. This existence of voidable contracts is discussed in detail in section 10 below.

5. CONTRACTUAL PERFORMANCE TERMINOLOGY

In addition to issues related to enforcing contracts in court, the topic of parties performing their commitments is vital to contract law. The key terms related to performance are *executed* and *executory.* An **executed contract** is one in which the parties have performed their promises. When the parties have not yet performed their agreement, it is called an **executory contract.**

Since most business contracts are bilateral in nature involving an exchange of promises by the parties, most contracts are executory at some time. For example, if you promise your new employer to begin working next month and that employer promises to pay you at the end of the first month's work, this employment contract is executory from both parties' perspective.

Contracts cover a multitude of situations and these performance terms may be more or less relevant. Suppose you take a grocery item to the cashier and pay for it. The resulting contract is executed at the time of its creation. In fact, there probably was no exchange of spoken promises. The exchange of money for the item results in the performance being the proof of the contract.

In more complicated business transactions, the performance or lack thereof by one party becomes very important in determining the rights and duties under the contracts. A supplier of raw materials may ship its product and await the buyer's payment. The seller's performance is executed while the buyer's performance remains executory. How these terms impact enforceability issues is a part of the discussion in sections 16–17 of this chapter.

6. BREACH OF CONTRACT

A party that does not live up to the obligation of contractual performance is said to breach the contract. There are several remedies or solutions available for a breach of contract. These include the following, as discussed in the next figure.

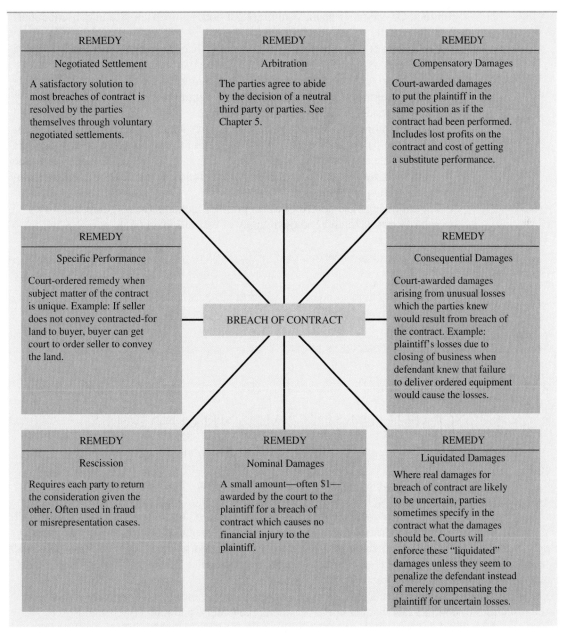

REMEDY	REMEDY	REMEDY
Negotiated Settlement	**Arbitration**	**Compensatory Damages**
A satisfactory solution to most breaches of contract is resolved by the parties themselves through voluntary negotiated settlements.	The parties agree to abide by the decision of a neutral third party or parties. See Chapter 5.	Court-awarded damages to put the plaintiff in the same position as if the contract had been performed. Includes lost profits on the contract and cost of getting a substitute performance.

REMEDY		REMEDY
Specific Performance		**Consequential Damages**
Court-ordered remedy when subject matter of the contract is unique. Example: If seller does not convey contracted-for land to buyer, buyer can get court to order seller to convey the land.	**BREACH OF CONTRACT**	Court-awarded damages arising from unusual losses which the parties knew would result from breach of the contract. Example: plaintiff's losses due to closing of business when defendant knew that failure to deliver ordered equipment would cause the losses.

REMEDY	REMEDY	REMEDY
Rescission	**Nominal Damages**	**Liquidated Damages**
Requires each party to return the consideration given the other. Often used in fraud or misrepresentation cases.	A small amount—often $1—awarded by the court to the plaintiff for a breach of contract which causes no financial injury to the plaintiff.	Where real damages for breach of contract are likely to be uncertain, parties sometimes specify in the contract what the damages should be. Courts will enforce these "liquidated" damages unless they seem to penalize the defendant instead of merely compensating the plaintiff for uncertain losses.

Remedies for Breach of Contract

- Negotiated settlement
- Arbitration
- Various damage awards
- Specific performance
- Rescission

    Note that the various remedies are usually mutually exclusive. For instance, you could not get both specific performance and rescission for the same breach of contract. On the other hand, you might get both compensatory and consequential damages for the same breach of contract.

The victim of a contract breach must **mitigate** damages when possible. To mitigate damages requires the victim to take reasonable steps to reduce them. For example, when a tenant breaches a house lease by moving away before the lease expires, the landlord must mitigate damages by renting the house to another willing and suitable tenant if such a person is available.

At times, money damages are not what a party wants as a remedy. Instead, the nonbreaching party might desire either a return of the value given or an order that the breaching party specifically perform the contractual promise made. The former situation involves the equitable remedy of **rescission** or **restitution.** The latter describes **specific performance.**

The following case describes a complicated factual situation that leads to a breach-of-contract claim and the remedy of restitution.

MOBIL OIL EXPLORATION AND PRODUCING SOUTHEAST, INC. v. UNITED STATES

120 S. CT. 2423 (2000)

BREYER, J.: . . . A description at the outset of the few basic contract law principles applicable to this case will help the reader understand the significance of the complex factual circumstances that follow. When the United States enters into contract relations its rights and duties therein are governed generally by the law applicable to contracts between private individuals. The Restatement of Contracts reflects many of the principles of contract law that are applicable to this case. As set forth in the Restatement of Contracts, the relevant principles specify that, when one party to a contract repudiates that contract, the other party "is entitled to restitution for any benefit that he has conferred on" the repudiating party "by way of part performance or reliance." . . .

In 1981, in return for up-front "bonus" payments to the United States of about $158 million (plus annual rental payments), the companies received 10-year renewable lease contracts with the United States. In these contracts, the United States promised the companies, among other things, that they could explore for oil off the North Carolina coast and develop any oil that they found provided that the companies received exploration and development permissions in accordance with various statutes and regulations to which the lease contracts were made subject.

[The Court reviewed the complex relationship among the Outer Continental Shelf Lands Act (OCSLA), the Coastal Zone Management Act (CZMA), and the Outer Banks Protection Act (OBPA). The OBPA was signed into law on August 18, 1990, two days before the companies submitted their final Exploration Plan. The OBPA prohibited the Secretary of the Interior from approving any Exploration Plan until a new OBPA-created Environmental Sciences Review Panel reported. According to the OBPA, the approval by the Secretary could not occur within 13 months. Prior to the OBPA, the OCSLA required the Secretary of Interior to respond to the Exploration

[CONTINUED]

Plan within 30 days. Due to these legal changes, the Exploration Plan was not approved as anticipated when the lease contracts were signed. In fact, the Plan was finally rejected by the Secretary of Commerce in 1994, four years after it was first submitted.]

In October 1992, . . . petitioners joined a breach-of-contract lawsuit brought in the Court of Federal Claims. On motions for summary judgment, the court found that the United States had broken its contractual promise to follow OCSLA's provisions, in particular the provision requiring Interior to approve an Exploration Plan that satisfied OCSLA's requirements within 30 days of its submission to Interior. The United States thereby repudiated the contracts. And that repudiation entitled the companies to restitution of the up-front cash "bonus" payments it had made.

A panel of the Court of Appeals for the Federal Circuit reversed. . . . The panel held that the Government's refusal to consider the companies' final Exploration Plan was not the "operative cause" of any failure to carry out the contracts' terms because the State's objection to the companies' CZMA "consistency statement" would have prevented the companies from exploring regardless.

We granted certiorari to review the Federal Circuit's decision.

The record makes clear (1) that OCSLA required Interior to approve "within thirty days" a submitted Exploration Plan that satisfies OCSLA's requirements, (2) that Interior told Mobil the companies' submitted Plan met those requirements, (3) that Interior told Mobil it would not approve the companies' submitted Plan for at least 13 months, and likely longer, and (4) that Interior did not approve (or disapprove) the Plan, ever. The Government does not deny that the contracts, made "pursuant to" and "subject to" OCSLA, incorporated OCSLA provisions as promises. The Government further concedes, as it must, that relevant contract law entitles a contracting party to restitution if the other party substantially breached a contract or communicated its intent to do so.

. . . [I]n the Government's view, it did not breach the contracts or communicate its intent to do so; any breach was not substantial; and the companies waived their rights to restitution regardless. . . .

We conclude . . . that the Government violated the contracts. Indeed, as Interior pointed out in its letter to North Carolina, the new statute, OBPA, required Interior to impose the contract-violating delay. It therefore made clear to Interior and to the companies that the United States had to violate the contracts' terms and would continue to do so. . . .

The Government next argues that any violation of the contracts' terms was not significant; hence there was no substantial or material breach that could have amounted to a repudiation. In particular, it says that OCSLA's 30-day approval period does not function as the essence of these agreements. The Court of Claims concluded, however, that timely and fair consideration of a submitted Exploration Plan was a necessary reciprocal obligation, indeed, that any contrary interpretation would render the bargain illusory. We agree. . . .

The Government's modification of the contract-incorporated processes was not technical or insubstantial. It did not announce an approval delay of a few days or weeks, but of 13 months minimum, and likely much longer. The delay turned out to be at least four years. . . .

The upshot is that, under the contracts, the incorporated procedures and standards amounted to a gateway to the companies' enjoyment of all other rights. To significantly narrow that gateway violated material conditions in the contracts. The breach was substantial, depriving the companies of the benefit of their bargain. And the Government's communication of its intent to commit that breach amounted to a repudiation of the contracts. . . .

. . . The oil companies do not seek damages for breach of contract. They seek restitution of their initial payments. Because the Government repudiated the lease contracts, the law entitles the companies to that restitution whether the contracts would, or would not ultimately have produced a financial gain or led them to obtain a definite right to explore. If a lottery operator fails to deliver a purchased ticket, the purchaser can get his money back—whether or not he eventually would have won the lottery. And if one party to a contract, whether oil company or ordinary citizen, advances the other party money, principles of restitution normally require the latter, upon repudiation, to refund that money.

[CONTINUED]

Contract law expresses no view about the wisdom of OBPA. We have examined only that statute's consistency with the promises that the earlier contracts contained. We find that the oil companies gave the United States $158 million in return for a contractual promise to follow the terms of pre-existing statutes and regulations. The new statute prevented the Government from keeping that promise. The breach substantially impaired the value of the contracts. And therefore the Government must give the companies their money back.

For these reasons, the judgment of the Federal Circuit is reversed. We remand the cases for further proceedings consistent with this opinion.

Reversed and remanded.

CASE QUESTIONS

1. What did the oil companies obtain when they were granted 10-year lease contracts?

2. How do legal enactments impact this case?

3. What were the decisions of the lower courts?

4. Why does the Supreme Court find that the U.S. government repudiated the lease contracts?

5. What remedy does the Supreme Court decide is most appropriate to cure the breach of contract?

CONTRACT FORMATION

How a contract is formed is one of the most important issues to understand about contract law. Many agreements are void, and thus unenforceable, because they lack some essential element of contract formation. There are five essential elements of a valid contract, as shown in the figure below.

- Offer
- Acceptance
- Consideration
- Capacity of parties to contract
- A legal purpose

The following sections (7–11) focus on these elements and how they come together to form contracts. Before an agreement can become a legally binding contract, someone must make a specific promise to another and also a specific de-

Elements of a Contract

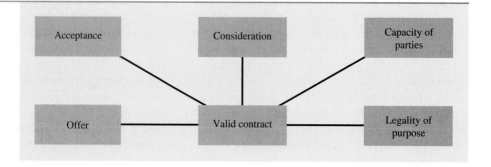

mand of that person. This is the offer. The other person must accept the terms of the offer in the proper way. Both parties must give consideration to the other. Consideration is the promise to give, or the actual giving, of a requested benefit or the incurring of a legal detriment (i.e., doing something one does not have to). Both parties must be of legal age and sound mind, and the purpose of the agreement cannot be illegal or against public policy.

Following the discussion of these requirements of a valid, enforceable contract, the formality of the contract (oral or written form) is the focus of section 12.

7. OFFER TO CONTRACT

An **offer** contains a specific promise and a specific demand. "I will pay $15,000 for the electrical transformer" promises $15,000 and demands a specific product in return. An *offeror* (person making the offer) must intend to make the offer by making a commitment to the offeree (the person to whom the offer is made). Many issues about an offer can and do arise. For example, is the language of the offer clear enough to conclude that a valid contract can result? What if a person makes a statement ("I'll give you $100 for a ride to the mall") intending it as a joke. Is this an offer? Courts answer this question by measuring intent from a reasonable person's perspective. This standard is known as the objective, rather than the subjective, intent of the offeror.

Definition of Terms Under the common law of contracts, contractual terms must be definite and specific. An offer to purchase a house at a "reasonable price" cannot be the basis for a contract because of **indefiniteness.** Most advertisements and catalog price quotes are considered too indefinite to form the basis for a contract unless they are specific about the quality of goods being offered.

However, under the UCC, contracts for the sale of goods can leave open nonquantity terms to be decided at a future time. An agreement for the sale of 500 cameras will bind the parties even though they leave open the price to be decided on delivery in six months. Note that this rule applies only to sales of goods. It does not apply to sales of real estate or services.

Termination of Offer Offers create a legal power in the offeree to bind the offeror in a contract. However, that legal power does not last forever. When an offer *terminates,* the offeree's legal power to bind the offeror ends. Review carefully the box describing various instances when an offer terminates.

When an Offer Terminates

By provision in the offer: "This offer terminates at noon Friday."

By lapse of a reasonable period of time if the offer fails to specify a time: What is "reasonable" depends on the circumstances.

By rejection of the offer: "Thank you, but I do not want the flooring you are offering." A **counteroffer** is also a rejection: "Your offer of $10,000 for the land is too low. I will sell it to you for $12,500."

By revocation of the offer: "I regret to inform you that I am withdrawing my offer."

By destruction of the subject matter: The carpet is destroyed by fire before the offer of their sale has been accepted.

By the offeror's death or insanity: Offeror dies before the offer has been accepted.

By the contractual performance becoming illegal: Congress declares that sales of certain computers to Iraq are illegal. This terminates an offer to sell the computers to an Iraqi trading company.

8. ACCEPTANCE OF OFFER

Acceptance of an offer is necessary to create a valid, enforceable contract. An offer to enter into a bilateral contract is accepted by the offeree's making the required promise. When Toni offers Aaron certain vinyl flooring for $2,500 to be delivered by November 30 on 90-day credit terms, and Aaron accepts, Aaron is promising to pay $2,500 on 90-day credit terms.

Unilateral contracts are accepted by performing a requested act, not by making a promise. A company's offer of a $2,500 reward for information leading to the conviction of anyone vandalizing company property is not accepted by promising to provide the information. Only the act of providing information accepts such an offer.

The language of the offer determines whether acceptance should be a promise resulting in a bilateral contract or an act resulting in a unilateral contract. The rights and duties of the contracting party can turn on the form of the acceptance. The following case illustrates the significant impact of the court's interpretation regarding the method of acceptance.

SHARP ELECTRONICS CORPORATION v. DEUTSCHE FINANCIAL SERVICES CORPORATION

216 F. 3D 388 (4TH CIR. 2000)

NIEMEYER, J.: . . . Deutsche Financial Services Corporation (Deutsche Financial) and Sharp Electronics Corporation (Sharp) signed a financing agreement entitled "Floorplan Repurchase Agreement," which provided that Deutsche Financial would agree from time to time to finance certain transactions between Sharp and its wholesale customers. . . . The agreement was unilateral in that Sharp offered Deutsche Financial inducements . . . to provide financing for ongoing transactions between Sharp and its customers, in this case Montgomery Ward & Co., Incorporated ("Montgomery Ward"), but Deutsche Financial was not obligated to provide any financing. . . .

Only after Deutsche Financial approved a specific request to finance a transaction would it become obligated to complete performance under the terms of the Floorplan Repurchase Agreement by paying the invoice amount of the proposed transaction less agreed-upon finance charges. This obligation to pay, however, was conditioned on (1) Sharp's shipment of the merchandise to Montgomery Ward within 30 days of

Deutsche Financial's approval and (2) Deutsche Financial's receipt of the invoice for the transaction within 10 days after delivery of the merchandise.

Underlying Deutsche Financial's willingness to approve financing under the Floorplan Repurchase Agreement for Montgomery Ward's purchases from Sharp was Deutsche Financial's independently defined role as administrator of a financial "facility" for Montgomery Ward that provided Montgomery Ward with a $100 million line of credit.

Until November 1996, the practice under the Floorplan Repurchase Agreement between Deutsche Financial and Sharp with respect to Montgomery Ward's purchases routinely took the following form: Montgomery Ward would place a purchase order for merchandise with Sharp; Sharp would call Deutsche Financial and request an approval number for the financing of the merchandise; and Deutsche Financial would, if it elected to finance the transaction and if Montgomery Ward had not yet reached its credit limit with Deutsche Financial, orally issue Sharp an approval number. In November 1996, the arrange-

[CONTINUED]

ment changed slightly. Thereafter, Sharp would fax Deutsche Financial its financing request, and Deutsche Financial would fax its approval to Sharp. Sharp would then enter the approval number into its computer system, ship the merchandise to Montgomery Ward, and send the invoice to Deutsche Financial which would pay Sharp.

In early May 1997, in response to its deteriorating financial condition, Montgomery Ward met with its suppliers to discuss its condition and its plans to restructure. As part of these plans, Montgomery Ward announced its intention to transfer the administration of its line of credit from Deutsche Financial to General Electric Capital Corporation, shareholder of Montgomery Ward. Upon the accomplishment of that transfer, Deutsche Financial would no longer be financing any Montgomery Ward purchases, including those from Sharp. . . .

Sharp first received formal notice of a change in Montgomery Ward's financing arrangements on May 22, 1997, when Montgomery Ward faxed it a letter stating: "Effective May 23, 1997, the administrator on the inventory finance facility is being changed from Deutsche Financial Services to GE Capital. Deutsche will not issue approval numbers after May 23, 1997. . . ." On May 23, 1997, Deutsche Financial also faxed a letter to Sharp, which Sharp received at 2:17 P.M., announcing the termination of its financing role and setting deadlines for future transactions in light of that termination. Deutsche Financial's fax, which was entirely consistent with Montgomery Ward's fax, stated in pertinent part:

> Per Montgomery Ward's request, the financing program between [Deutsche Financial and] Montgomery Ward . . . will change administrators on May 23, 1997, 5:00 P.M. CST. [Deutsche Financial] will continue to review your requests for approval numbers until such time, and will continue to administer the Program for any invoices dated May 28, 1997 and earlier. However, any requests for approvals after May 23, 1997 should be processed through General Electric Capital Corporation . . . who will act as the new administrator of the Program.
>
> As [Deutsche Financial] will not administer any invoice dated later than May 28, 1997, [Deutsche Financial] hereby notifies you that [Deutsche Financial] will revoke each approval number which [Deutsche Financial] has issued for inventory which you have not shipped to Montgomery Ward . . . on or before such date.

For purposes of this case, the important change announced by Deutsche Financial in its May 23 fax was the shortened shipping deadline requiring that merchandise be shipped to Montgomery Ward by May 28, rather than within 30 days of financing approval. . . .

Five minutes after Deutsche Financial sent its fax to Sharp's general manager changing the terms under which it would continue to finance transactions, Deutsche Financial faxed Sharp's credit administrator an approval to finance merchandise worth $56,683, for which Sharp had submitted a request for financing approval four days earlier. In this routine fax to Sharp, Deutsche Financial did not make reference to any of the changes transmitted earlier to Sharp's general manager. Less than 30 minutes later, at 2:44 P.M., Sharp's credit administrator submitted a new request to Deutsche Financial to approve financing for almost $2.2 million worth of merchandise that Montgomery Ward had ordered. Later that same day, at 4:05 P.M., Deutsche Financial returned a fax approving the financing of this $2.2 million transaction. Again, Deutsche Financial's approval did not make reference to the changes in the financing arrangement. . . .

On May 28, Sharp shipped Montgomery Ward $945,488 worth of merchandise that had been approved for financing by Deutsche Financial on May 23. The remaining $1.3 million worth of merchandise that had also been approved on May 23 was shipped on May 31, three days after the deadline imposed by Deutsche Financial in its May 23 fax. When Sharp submitted invoices for these two shipments, Deutsche Financial financed the merchandise shipped on May 28 but refused to finance the shipment made on May 31. Because Montgomery Ward later defaulted on its obligation to pay Sharp for the merchandise and subsequently filed for bankruptcy, Sharp was not paid for approximately $1.3 million worth of merchandise.

In January 1998, Sharp filed this diversity-jurisdiction action against Deutsche Financial for breach of the Floorplan Repurchase Agreement. It alleged that it had complied with the agreement and that Deutsche Financial's attempted modification of the agreement on May 23, 1997, was invalid. Sharp demanded more than $1.3 million in damages, the value of the merchandise shipped on May 31, 1997, plus interest and costs.

[CONTINUED]

On Sharp's motion for summary judgment, the district court entered judgment in favor of Sharp in the amount of $1,394,705.11, which included approximately $97,000 of prejudgment interest. In ruling in Sharp's favor, the court concluded that Deutsche Financial had breached the Floorplan Repurchase Agreement with Sharp. . . . This appeal followed. . . .

In contractual terms, the Floorplan Repurchase Agreement was a unilateral promise by Sharp that invited Deutsche Financial's acceptance by performance—i.e., by financing transactions. Traditionally, this type of arrangement is characterized as a unilateral contract, a contract in which the promise is binding only on the promisor. . . .

Until Deutsche Financial accepted Sharp's offer by beginning its performance, i.e., by agreeing to finance a transaction, Sharp could have withdrawn from the arrangement or altered the terms of its offer to Deutsche Financial. And this freedom from obligation continued even after Sharp submitted a request for approval, so long as Deutsche Financial had not given its approval. . . . Deutsche Financial could have demanded different assurances or terms as a condition to future financing. If Sharp refused, Deutsche Financial could have correspondingly refused to finance any transaction and withdrawn from the arrangement. Until Deutsche Financial approved a specific request, either party could cancel the arrangement or condition its participation in future transactions.

When Deutsche Financial approved a transaction for financing, however, it began its performance, thereby accepting Sharp's offer and binding Sharp to the terms of the offer. Deutsche Financial similarly bound itself to complete performance by agreeing to finance the transaction under the terms of the underlying arrangement. . . .

On May 23, 1997, before Deutsche Financial approved any transaction and therefore before it became obligated to do anything under the Floorplan Repurchase Agreement, Deutsche Financial announced that any future financing would be subject to new conditions—pertinently, the requirement of

shipment within 30 days became a requirement of shipment by May 28. Because this May 23 fax controlled Deutsche Financial's future acceptance of Sharp's standing offer (represented by the Floorplan Repurchase Agreement) and because Deutsche Financial purported to condition acceptance of the offer on the condition that its changes be made, the May 23 fax must be treated as a rejection of Sharp's standing offer and as a counteroffer on new terms. . . . The nature of Deutsche Financial's counteroffer included in the May 23 fax was clear. Deutsche Financial was terminating its underlying financing relationship with Montgomery Ward and would no longer approve transactions for financing after May 23. Deutsche Financial further indicated that it would not finance any transaction with an invoice date or shipment date after May 28. In essence, Deutsche Financial was offering to continue for a short time under the underlying Floorplan Repurchase Agreement as long as its new conditions applied, and it was inviting Sharp and Montgomery Ward to submit new transactions for financing subject to those conditions. In contract language, Deutsche Financial extended a counteroffer to Sharp that could be accepted by Sharp's performance—i.e., by Sharp's further submission of financing requests.

Deutsche Financial's May 23 rejection of the standing offer in the Floorplan Repurchase Agreement and its termination of its own power of acceptance occurred upon Sharp's receipt of the counteroffer from Deutsche Financial. . . .

Our determination that Deutsche Financial was not contractually obligated to finance the $1.3 million worth of merchandise, which formed the basis for Sharp's claim, leads to the legal conclusion that, on Sharp's complaint and the undisputed facts of record, Deutsche Financial is entitled to judgment as a matter of law. Accordingly, we vacate the district court's judgment and remand with instructions to enter judgment in favor of Deutsche Financial.

Vacated and remanded with instructions.

[CONTINUED]

CASE QUESTIONS

1. What is the contractual relationship among Sharp, Deutsche Financial, Montgomery Ward, and GE Capital?

2. What company sues and what is the basis for this suit?

3. How did the District Court rule in the lawsuit?

4. What is the impact of the Fourth Circuit Court of Appeals holding that the original contract is unilateral in nature?

5. How does the Fourth Circuit Court of Appeals analyze the May 23 fax from Deutsche Financial to Sharp?

Other issues relating to the importance of acceptance in the formation of a valid contract are discussed under the following headings

Mirror Image Rule For an acceptance to create a binding contract, standard contract law requires that the acceptance must "mirror" the offer, that is, must match it exactly. This is the **mirror image rule.** If the acceptance changes the terms of the offer or adds new terms, it is not really an acceptance. It is a *counteroffer.*

The UCC has changed the mirror image role, especially with regard to merchants contracting for the sale of goods. An acceptance between merchants creates a binding contract even though it proposes new or different terms. The new or different terms become part of the contract unless one of the following takes place:

1. The offer expressly limits acceptance to the original terms.
2. The proposed terms materially (importantly) alter the contract.
3. The offeror rejects the proposed terms.

Silence Not Acceptance In general, an offeree's failure to reject an offer does not imply acceptance. Another way to say this is that silence alone is not acceptance. The offeree has no usual duty to reply to the offer even if the offer states that the offeror will treat silence as acceptance.

There are major exceptions to this rule. For instance, parties may have a contract that specifies that future shipments of goods be made automatically unless the offeree expressly rejects them. Many book- and record-club contracts operate in this manner.

A related doctrine looks at the parties' prior *course of dealing*—the way they have done business in the past. Silence may well imply acceptance if the parties previously dealt with each other by having the buyer take shipments from the seller unless the buyer notified the seller in advance not to ship.

Finally, the UCC says that a contract may arise from the *conduct* of a buyer and seller of goods. Emphasis is placed on how the parties act rather than on a formal offer and acceptance of terms.

Deposited Acceptance Rule When does the acceptance become legally binding on the offeror? Unless the offeror specifies a particular time, the acceptance usually binds the parties when the offeree dispatches it. Since the offeree frequently mails the acceptance, the acceptance becomes binding when it is "deposited" with the postal service—hence the **deposited acceptance rule,** also called the **mailbox rule.**

The importance of the deposited acceptance rule is that the offeror cannot revoke the offer once the offeree has accepted it. An added significance is that an offeror's revocation is not effective until the offeree actually receives it. Thus, a deposited acceptance creates a binding contract even though a revocation is also in the mail.

The next case illustrates the impact of the mailbox rule. Note that the application of the rule in this case focuses on a contractual termination notice rather than an acceptance. The outcome of the rule is significant with respect to the rights and duties of the parties.

UNIVERSITY EMERGENCY MEDICINE FOUNDATION v. RAPIER INVESTMENTS, LTD. AND MEDICAL BUSINESS SYSTEMS, INC.

197 F. 3D 18 (1ST CIR. 1999)

LIPEZ, J.: . . . Emergency Medicine is a non-profit Rhode Island corporation that provides physicians' services to emergency departments at several Rhode Island hospitals. Pursuant to a series of contracts spanning more than ten years, MBS, a subsidiary of Rapier, performed coding, billing, collection and accounts receivable services for Emergency Medicine.

On October 1, 1995, Emergency Medicine and Rapier executed a contract (the "Agreement") calling for MBS to service Emergency Medicine for one year, and further providing that this Agreement shall be automatically extended for additional one (1) year periods ("additional terms") unless and until either party elects to terminate this Agreement as of the end of the initial term or any additional term by giving at least four (4) months written notice that it elects to have this Agreement terminated, without cause. . . . [The Agreement provided that notice of termination must be sent by registered mail to the specified address within the 4-month period.] The only addresses "set forth" in the Agreement are Rapier's principal office, 7 Wells Avenue, Newton, Massachusetts, and Emergency Medicine's principal place of business, 593 Eddy Street, Providence, Rhode Island.

During the contract's first year, neither party terminated, and it automatically renewed for an addi-

tional year, ending September 30, 1997. On Friday, May 30, 1997, Annamarie Monks of Emergency Medicine mailed two letters intended to notify Rapier that Emergency Medicine planned to terminate the Agreement before it renewed for a third year. She sent one letter certified mail to Alan Carr-Locke of Rapier at 1238 Chestnut Street, Newton, Massachusetts. Because the letter was incorrectly addressed, it was returned undelivered on June 10, at which point Emergency Medicine mailed the notice to 7 Wells Avenue, Newton, Massachusetts. She sent the second letter certified mail to JoAnn Barato-Mills of MBS, the employee who had negotiated and signed the Agreement on behalf of Rapier, at her place of business, 20 Altieri Way, Warwick, Rhode Island. Ms. Barato-Mills received the letter the following Monday, June 2, 1997.

In the months following Emergency Medicine's notice of non-renewal, MBS continued to perform services under the Agreement. Meanwhile, Emergency Medicine solicited bids for a new service contract and, although MBS submitted a bid, Emergency Medicine awarded the new contract to a different service provider. MBS then asserted that, because Emergency Medicine's termination notice had been invalid, the Agreement had already extended automat-

[CONTINUED]

ically for an additional year, ending September 30, 1998. Emergency Medicine filed a complaint seeking a declaration that its notice had effectively terminated the Agreement. The parties filed cross-motions for summary judgment on the validity of the termination notice, and the trial court granted judgment in favor of Emergency Medicine. This appeal ensued.

. . . According to Rapier, Emergency Medicine did not fulfill the condition required for termination under the Agreement because it failed to provide Rapier with at least four months written notice. We are asked therefore to evaluate the effectiveness of Emergency Medicine's termination notice pursuant to the contract.

The Agreement expressly conditions a party's right to terminate on that party "giving at least four (4) months written notice" to the other party. Where, as here, such "a condition is required by the agreement of the parties . . . a rule of strict compliance traditionally applies." The Agreement, as extended by renewal for one additional year, was set to expire on September 30, 1997. Counting back exactly four months, the last day on which Emergency Medicine had the power to terminate was May 31, 1997. Although Emergency Medicine mailed notice letters on May 30, these letters were not received until after the notice period had expired. Thus, the timeliness of Emergency Medicine's notice turns on whether notice of termination is effective upon mailing, or upon receipt.

At common law, the default rule—i.e., the rule that governs unless the parties contract for different terms—makes notice effective only upon receipt, not mailing. However, the parties may override the default rule by contract. In particular, the parties may contract to permit notice by mail. If they do, notice becomes effective upon mailing pursuant to the time-honored "mailbox rule."

Here, the Agreement unquestionably authorizes notice by mail. The notice paragraph expressly invites notice "sent by registered or certified mail." This paragraph therefore triggers the "mailbox rule," making notice effective upon mailing. Accordingly, Emergency Medicine's notice letters, mailed on May 30, 1997, took effect on that date, and were timely under the Agreement's four-month notice period, which did not expire until May 31, unless the use of an address other than the one specified in the contract deprived Emergency Medicine of the benefit of the mailbox rule.

. . . [A] party that fails to use the address identified in the contract for mailing notice risks losing the benefit of the mailbox rule. The contract provision at issue in this case, which states that notice of termination may be given effectively by registered or certified mail sent to a particular address, allocated the risk of non-delivery of a notice sent in strict compliance with the contract. That is, if Emergency Medicine chose to give timely notice of termination by registered or certified mail sent to the specified address, and the notice was undelivered because of a failure by the postal service, Emergency Medicine would have still given timely notice of termination despite the non-delivery. If, however, Emergency Medicine directed its otherwise timely notice of termination to the wrong address and there were no delivery, Emergency Medicine would lose the benefit of the mailbox rule. In situations where there is delivery despite the use of a wrong address, and the circumstances indicate that the parties intended the address as merely a collateral term designed to enhance the timely delivery of notice, the continuing availability of the mailbox rule to the sender requires an assessment of the particular facts of the case.

In the case at hand, Emergency Medicine risked losing the benefit of the mailbox rule with respect to both of its improperly addressed May 30 mailings. That risk arguably materialized in the case of the letter mailed to Rapier's Alan Carr-Locke, which was returned undelivered, and finally arrived at Rapier more than 10 days after it was originally sent. However, the letter mailed to MBS's JoAnn Barato-Mills arrived in her hands just one business day after it was mailed (the letter was mailed on Friday and arrived on Monday), within the ordinary time period expected for delivery by mail. Under these circumstances, Emergency Medicine retained the benefit of the mailbox rule despite the improper address, and this second letter placed Rapier on written notice of Emergency Medicine's intent to terminate the Agreement before it automatically renewed for a third year. Therefore, we conclude that Emergency Medicine provided Rapier with four months written notice of its intent to terminate as required under the Agreement.

Affirmed.

[CONTINUED]

CASE QUESTIONS

1. What are the relationships among Emergency Medicine, Rapier, and MBS?

2. What were the specific requirements for the contract's renewal or termination?

3. How and when did Emergency Medicine attempt to give notice of termination?

4. What is the role of the "mailbox rule" in this case?

9. CONSIDERATION

All promises are not enforceable through legal action. There must be some incentive or inducement for a person's promise or it is not binding. The legal mechanism for evaluating the existence of this incentive is **consideration,** the receipt of a legal benefit or the suffering of a legal detriment. Courts will not enforce contractual promises unless they are supported by consideration. Before Robert can enforce a promise made by Peter, Robert must have given consideration that induced Peter to make the promise. In a bilateral contract, each party promises something to the other. The binding promises are the consideration. In a unilateral contract, the consideration of one party is a promise; the consideration of the other party is performance of an act. When it is not clear whether there is consideration to support a promise, a court will often examine a transaction as a whole.

Must Be Bargained For   An important part of consideration is that it must be *bargained for.* Sometimes the parties to an agreement specify an insignificant consideration in return for a great one. For example, a promise of $1 might be made in return for a promise to convey 40 acres of land. In such situations a court must decide whether the party promising to convey the land really bargained for the $1 or merely promised to make a gift. Promises to make gifts are not binding, because no bargained-for consideration supports the promise.

Similarly, *prior consideration* is no consideration. For instance, after many years of working at Acme Co., Bigman retires as vice president for financial planning. The company's board of directors votes him a new car every year "for services rendered." One year later the board rescinds this vote. If Bigman sues for breach of contract, he will lose. He gave no consideration to support the board's promise. The past years of service were not "bargained for" by the company's board when it took its vote. The board merely promised to give an unenforceable gift to Bigman.

Agreement Not to Sue   When reasonable grounds for a lawsuit exist, an agreement not to sue is consideration to support a promise. If First Bank agrees not to sue Maria, who has failed to repay a student loan, in return for the promise of Maria's parents to repay the loan, First Bank has given consideration. It has promised to surrender its legal right to sue Maria.

Likewise, suppose that a consulting firm bills a client $5,000 for 50 hours of work at $100 per hour. The client disputes the bill and contends that the consulting firm worked only 25 hours and should get only $2,500. If the two parties compromise the bill at $3,500 for 35 hours, this agreement binds them both. Each has surrendered the right to have a court determine exactly what amount is owed. Such an agreement and the payment of the $3,500 to resolve a dispute over the amount owed is an **accord and satisfaction.**

Preexisting Obligation   A party to an agreement does not give consideration by promising to do something that he or she is already obligated to do. For example, suppose a warehouse owner contracts to have certain repairs done for $20,000. In the middle of construction, the building contractor demands an additional $5,000 to complete the work. The owner agrees, but when the work is finished, he gives the contractor only $20,000. If the contractor sues, he will lose. The owner's promise to pay an extra $5,000 is not supported by consideration. The contractor is under a *preexisting obligation* to do the work for which the owner promises an additional $5,000.

If the contractor promised to do something he was not already obligated to do, there would be consideration to support the promise of the additional $5,000. Promising to modify the repair plans illustrates such new consideration.

Consideration Not Necessary   The preexisting obligation rule discussed above does not apply to a sale-of-goods contract. The UCC states that parties to a sale-of-goods contract may make binding modifications to it without both parties giving new consideration. In the Business Decision at the beginning of this chapter, if a buyer of carpet agrees to pay your company an additional $5,000 over and above the amount already promised, this buyer is bound, although your company gives only the consideration (carpet) that it is already obligated to give.

Under the UCC, the rules of consideration also do not apply to a **firm offer.** A firm offer exists when a merchant offering goods promises in writing that the offer will not be revoked for a period not to exceed three months. This promise binds the merchant, although the offeree buyer gives no consideration to support it. With offers not involving sales of goods by a merchant, a promise not to revoke an offer must be supported by the offeree's consideration to be binding. Such an arrangement is called an **option.**

An important exception to the rule requiring consideration to support a promise is the doctrine of **promissory estoppel.** This doctrine arises when a promisee justifiably relies on a promisor's promise to his or her economic injury. The promisor must know that the promisee is likely to rely on the promise. Promissory estoppel is increasingly used when the facts of a business relationship do not amount to an express or implied contract.

10. CAPACITY OF PARTIES TO CONTRACT

Capacity refers to a person's ability to be bound by a contract. Courts have traditionally held three classes of persons to lack capacity to be bound by contractual promises:

- Minors (also called "infants")
- Intoxicated persons
- Mentally incompetent persons

Minors   In most states, a *minor* is anyone under age 18. Minors usually cannot be legally bound to contractual promises unless those promises involve *necessaries of life* such as food, clothing, shelter, medical care, and—in some states—education. Even for necessaries, minors often cannot be sued for the contract price, only for a "reasonable" value. In a number of states, courts will hold a minor who has misrepresented his or her age to contractual promises.

A contract into which a minor has entered is voidable at the election of the minor. The minor can *disaffirm* the contract and legally recover any consideration that has been given an adult, even if the minor cannot return the adult's consideration. On the other hand, the adult is bound by the contract unless the minor elects to disaffirm it.

The minor may disaffirm a contract anytime before reaching the age of majority (usually 18) and for a reasonable time after reaching majority. If the minor fails to disaffirm within a reasonable time after reaching majority, the minor is said to *ratify* the contract. Upon ratification, the minor loses the right to disaffirm.

Intoxicated and Mentally Incompetent Persons   Except when a court has judged an adult to be mentally incompetent, she or he does not lose capacity to contract simply because of intoxication or mental impairment. In most cases involving adult capacity to contract, courts measure capacity by whether the adult was capable of understanding the nature and purpose of the contract. Obviously, the more complex a contractual transaction gets, the more likely a court is to decide that an intoxicated or mentally impaired person lacks capacity to contract and has the right to disaffirm the contract. In such factual situations, the contracts are voidable by the intoxicated or mentally impaired person.

Other Situations Involving Voidable Contracts   Contracts based on fraud or misrepresentation are two important examples of voidable contracts. **Fraud** involves an intentional misstatement of a material (important) fact that induces one to rely justifiably to his or her injury. Intentionally calling a zircon a diamond and persuading someone to purchase it on that basis is a fraud. Sometimes failures to disclose a material fact can also be a fraud, as when a landowner sells a buyer land knowing that the buyer wishes to build a home on it and does not disclose that the land is underwater during the rainy season. The defrauded party can withdraw from the contract. **Misrepresentation** is simply a misstatement without intent to mislead. However, a contract entered into through misrepresentation is still voidable by the innocent party.

Other examples of voidable contracts are those induced by duress or undue influence. **Duress** means force or threat of force. The force may be physical or, in some instances, economic. **Undue influence** occurs when one is taken advantage of unfairly through a contract by a party who misuses a position of relationship or legal confidence. Contracts voidable because of undue influence often arise when persons weakened by age or illness are persuaded to enter into a disadvantageous contract.

What happens when each party misunderstands something very basic and material about a contract? Such a situation goes right to the heart of whether there has been a "voluntary" consent to a contract. When there is a **mutual mistake** as to a material fact inducing a contract, rescission is appropriate. The test of materiality is whether the parties would have contracted had they been aware of the mistake. If they would not have contracted, the mistaken fact is material.

There is a difference between a mutual, or bilateral, mistake and a unilateral mistake. A **unilateral mistake** arises when only one of the parties to a contract is wrong about a material fact. Suppose that Royal Carpet Co. bids $8.70 per yard for certain carpet material instead of $7.80 per yard as it had intended. If the seller accepts Royal Carpet's bid, a contract results even though there was a unilateral mistake.

A doctrine similar to mutual mistake is that of **mutual assent.** Mutual assent requires that the "minds" of contracting parties must "meet" before a contract exists. Two parties may sign a piece of paper called a "contract," but if each believes the contract involves something different, there is no mutual assent, no meeting of the minds. There is no real contract.

11. LAWFUL PURPOSE

A basic requirement of a valid contract is *legality of purpose.* A "contract" to murder someone is hardly enforceable in a court of law. Contracts that require commission of a crime or tort or violate accepted standards of behavior (*public policy*) are void. Courts will generally take no action on a void contract, and they will leave the parties to a contract where they have put themselves. The following box gives common examples of illegal contracts.

There are several exceptions to the general rule that courts will take no action on an illegal contract. A contract may have both legal and illegal provisions to it. In such a case, courts will often enforce the legal provisions and refuse to enforce the illegal ones. For instance, a contract providing services or leasing goods sometimes contains a provision excusing the service provider or lessor from liability for negligently caused injury. Courts usually will not enforce this provision but will enforce the rest of the contract.

Often, courts will allow an innocent party to recover payment made to a party who knows (or should know) that a contract is illegal. For example, courts will allow recovery of a payment for professional services made by an innocent person to a person who is unlicensed to provide such services.

In some cases courts may allow a person to recover compensation under quasi-contract for services performed on an illegal contract. Recovery may be allowed when an otherwise qualified professional lets his or her license expire and provides services to a client before renewing the license.

Contracts That Restrain Trade Contracts that restrain trade often are illegal and void. They include contracts to monopolize, to fix prices between competitors, and to divide up markets. Chapter 13 on antitrust law discusses these contracts and their illegality.

EXAMPLES OF ILLEGAL CONTRACTS

Gambling agreements (except where permitted)

Contracts for usurious interest (greater interest than allowed by law)

Professional contracts made by unlicenced persons in which a regulatory statute requires licensing

Contracts that unreasonably restrain trade (see Chapter 13)

Many contracts that attempt to limit negligence liability of a seller of goods or services to the public (called **exculpatory contracts**)

Unconscionable contracts involving a sale of goods under the UCC (usually applied when a difference in bargaining power or education leads a merchant to take unreasonable advantage of a consumer)

Other contracts prohibited by statute or against public policy

Other contracts that restrain trade are important to the efficient operation of business. **Covenants not to compete** are important in protecting employers from having the employees they train leave them and compete against them. They also protect the buyer of a business from having the seller set up a competing business.

However, some covenants not to compete are illegal. Courts will declare such agreements illegal unless they have a valid business purpose, such as to protect the goodwill a business buyer purchases from the seller of the business. Covenants not to compete must also be "reasonable as to time and space." If they restrain competition for too long or in an area too large, the courts will declare them unreasonable and void them as being illegal. Four or five years is generally as long a time as the courts are willing to find reasonable, and even then the length of time must be justified. As to space, the courts will void covenants not to compete any time the area restrained exceeds the area in which the restraining business operates.

12. WRITTEN CONTRACTS

In addition to having five elements required to make a valid, enforceable contract, the issue arises whether the agreement may be orally stated or has to be in writing. Some people have the impression that contracts have to be in writing to be enforceable. In most instances, this is not so. However, it is true that certain contracts must be in writing (or at least evidenced by writing) to be enforceable.

The law requiring that certain contracts be in writing is the **statute of frauds.** Designed to prevent frauds arising from oral contracts, the original English statute is more than 300 years old. Today, every state has its own statute of frauds. Business-related provisions require the following contracts to be in writing:

- Contracts involving an interest in land
- Collateral contracts to pay the debt of another person
- Contracts that cannot be performed within one year
- Sale-of-goods contracts for $500 or more

In some states, the statute of frauds requires that the actual contract between the parties must be in writing. However, most states merely require that the contract be *evidenced* by writing and be signed by the party against whom enforcement is being sought. This requirement means that the party being sued must have signed a note, memorandum, or another written form short of a formal contract that describes with reasonable certainty the terms of the oral agreement. In sales of goods between merchants, the writing need not always be signed by the party sued. Under certain circumstances, it may be signed by the suing party.

Sale of an Interest in Land Sales of interests in land are common contracts covered by the statute of frauds. Although "sales of interests in land" covers a contract to sell land, it includes much more. Interests in land include contracts for mortgages, mining rights, easements (rights to use another's land, such as the right to cross it with electric power wires), and leases of longer than one year. However, a contract to insure land or to erect a building is not an interest in land.

The doctrine of **part performance** creates an exception to the requirement that sales of interests in land must be in writing. When a buyer of land has made valuable improvements in it, or when the buyer is in possession of it and has paid part of the purchase price, even an oral contract to sell is enforceable. The courts will enforce an oral agreement involving land title if the part performance clearly establishes the intent of the parties as buyer and seller. If a court can envision the parties in some other relationship, such as landlord and tenant, the part performance is not sufficient to substitute for a written agreement.

Collateral Promise to Pay Another's Debt   A collateral promise is a secondary or conditional promise. Such a commitment arises when one person, a business shareholder for example, promises to repay the loan of the corporation if and only when that organization does not make payments. This collateral promise usually arises at a time different from the original obligation. Suppose the corporation borrows money from a bank and later finds it is having trouble making payments on time. To avoid the bank calling the entire loan in default, the shareholder may promise to pay if the corporation does not. This promise by the shareholder is of a collateral nature and must be in writing to be enforced by the bank.

To avoid this situation of a collateral promise, banks often require a small business organization to have someone guarantee the performance of its contracts. If a shareholder makes an original promise to be responsible for the corporation's performance, this commitment is not collateral and does not have to be in writing. In essence, in such situations the corporation and the shareholder are considered equally obligated to perform the contract. There is no conditional promise by the shareholder. Although such original promises often are in writing, the law does not require a written agreement.

Cannot Be Performed within One Year   The statute of frauds applies to a contract the parties cannot perform within one year after its making. Courts usually interpret the one-year requirement to mean that the contract must specify a period of performance longer than one year. Thus, an oral contract for services that last 20 months is not enforceable. But an oral contract for services to be completed "by" a date 20 months away is enforceable. The difference is that the latter contract can be performed within one year, even if it actually takes longer than that to perform it.

As interpreted by the courts, the statute of frauds applies only to executory contracts that the parties' cannot perform within a year. Once one of the parties has completed his or her performance for the other, that party can enforce an oral multiyear contract.

EXCEPTIONS TO STATUTE-OF-FRAUDS REQUIREMENT THAT SALE-OF-GOODS CONTRACTS BE IN WRITING

- Contract for goods specially manufactured for the buyer on which the seller had begun performance
- Contract for goods for which payment has been made and accepted or that have been received and accepted
- Contract for goods in which the party being sued admits in court or pleadings that the contract has been made.
- Contract for goods between merchants in which the merchant sued has received a written notice from the other merchant confirming the contract and in which merchant sued does not object to the confirmation within 10 days.

Sale of Goods of $500 or More   Under the UCC, the statute of frauds covers sales of goods of $500 or more. Modifications to such contracts are also included. The box on the preceding page lists exceptions to the writing requirement for sale-of-goods contracts.

Others   In addition to the basic contracts covered by the statute of frauds, other contracts must be in writing in various states. Most states require insurance policies to be written. Several states require written estimates in contracts for automobile repair.

The Parol Evidence Rule   Like the statute of frauds, the **parol evidence rule** influences the form of contracts. This rule states that parties to a complete and final written contract cannot introduce oral evidence in court that changes the intended meaning of the written terms.

The parol evidence rule applies only to evidence of oral agreements made at the time of or prior to the written contract. It does not apply to oral modifications coming after the parties have made the written contract (although the statute of frauds may apply).

Suppose that Chris Consumer wants to testify in court that a merchant of an Ultima washing machine gave him an oral six-month warranty on the machine, even though the $450 written contract specified "no warranties." If the warranty was made after Chris signed the contract, he may testify about its existence. Otherwise, the parol evidence rule prevents him from testifying about an oral agreement that changes the terms of the written contract.

An exception to the parol evidence rule allows evidence of oral agreement that merely explains the meaning of written terms without changing the terms. Also, oral evidence that changes the meaning of written terms can be given if necessary to prevent fraud.

OTHER CONTRACT ISSUES

Once you know how a contract is formed, there are other important contract issues to understand. These issues include interpretation of contracts, assignment of contracts, performance of contracts, and discharge of contracts. Sections 13–17 discuss these issues.

13. INTERPRETATION OF CONTRACTS

If each party is satisfied with the other's performance under a contract, there is no problem with interpreting the contract's terms. But when disagreement about contractual performance exists, interpretation of the terms often becomes necessary. Courts have devised several rules to assist in interpreting contracts.

Common words are given their usual meaning. "A rose is a rose is a rose," said the poet, and a court will interpret this common word to refer to a flower. However, if the word has a particular *trade usage,* courts will give it that meaning. In a contract in the wine trade, the term *rose* would not refer to a flower at all but to a type of wine.

Some words have special legal meanings. A party to a contract had best appreciate that courts give legal terms their legal meaning. The buyer of radios may think that a contractual phrase calling for "delivery to the buyer on November 20" means that the seller will take the radios to the buyer's place of business, but it does not.

Delivery is a legal term referring to the transfer of possession from the seller to the buyer. It does not make the seller responsible for "shipping" the radios to the buyer. Furthermore, the UCC says that when the contract states no place for delivery, the place of delivery is the seller's place of business. The buyer will have to take delivery of the radios at the seller's place of business on November 20. Because some terms have both common and legal meanings, a person should have an attorney examine contracts drawn up by others.

Many businesses today use printed form contracts. Sometimes the parties to one of these printed contracts type or handwrite additional terms. What happens when the typed or handwritten terms contradict the printed terms? What if the printed terms of a contract state "no warranties," but the parties have written in a 90-day warranty? In such a case, courts interpret handwritten terms to control typed terms and typed terms to control printed ones (see Figure below). The written warranty will be enforced since the writing is the best evidence of the parties' true intention.

Another rule is that when only one of the parties drafts (writes) a contract, courts will interpret ambiguous or vague terms against the party that drafts them. Courts often apply this rule to insurance contracts and interpret the policy to give the policyholder the benefit of the doubt when deciding the meaning of a confusing term or phrase.

14. ASSIGNMENT OF CONTRACTS

Contracts often are thought as involving only two parties—the offeror and the offeree. In business, such a view is overly simplistic. Contracts may involve many original parties and sometimes third parties who are not a part of the negotiation resulting in the original contract. This section and the next one discuss how these third parties become involved in the contract's performance.

Electronics, Inc., sells 250 radios on credit at $20 apiece to Radio Land Retail. Electronics then sells its rights under the contract to Manufacturers' Credit Co. When payment is due, can Manufacturers' Credit legally collect the $5,000 owed to Electronics by Radio Land? This transaction is controlled by the law of **assignment,** which is a transfer (generally a sale) of rights under a contract. The figure on the next page shows the transaction and introduces important terminology.

When an assignor assigns rights, he or she makes an implied warranty that the rights are valid. If the assignee is unable to enforce the rights against the obligor

Interpretation of Contract Terms: Handwriting is the Best Evidence of Intention.

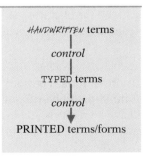

HANDWRITTEN terms

| *control*

TYPED terms

| *control*

PRINTED terms/forms

Assignment

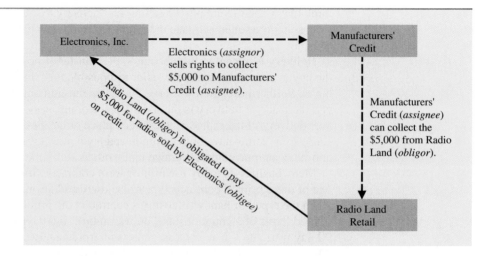

because of illegality, incapacity, or breach of contract, the assignee can sue the assignor. But the assignor does not guarantee that the obligor is able to pay the claim.

Notice of Assignment   When an assignment is made, an assignee should notify the obligor immediately. Otherwise, the obligor may perform for the obligee-assignor. If Radio Land pays Electronics before being notified by Manufacturers' Credit of the assignment, Radio Land cannot be held liable to Manufacturers' Credit.

A dishonest or careless assignor may assign the same contract rights to two different assignees. Notification of the obligor is especially important in this situation. In most states, the law says that the first assignee to notify the obligor has priority no matter which assignee receives the first assignment of rights.

Contracts That Cannot Be Assigned   Although most contracts can be assigned, certain ones cannot. An assignment that increases the burden of performance to the obligor cannot be assigned. For instance, a right to have goods shipped to the buyer's place of business cannot be assigned by an Atlanta buyer to a Miami buyer if a New York seller has to ship the goods to Miami instead of Atlanta. Similarly, a *requirements contract* to supply a retail buyer with all the radios needed cannot be assigned because it depends upon the buyer's personal situation.

Most states regulate the assignment of wages. They limit the amount of wages a wage earner can assign to protect wage earners and their families.

A party to a contract cannot assign (delegate) performance of duties under a contract when performance depends on the character, skill, or training of that party. Otherwise, duties under a contract can be assigned as well as rights.

15. CONTRACTS BENEFITING A THIRD PARTY

The performance of a contract may benefit third persons who are not parties to the contract. Such persons are called **third-party beneficiaries.** In general, persons who are not parties to a contract have no rights to sue to enforce the contract or to get damages for breach of contract. However, a third-party beneficiary can sue if the parties to the contract *intended* to benefit that person.

For instance, if Ajax Co. owes First National Bank $50,000, and if Ajax performs $50,000 of the work for Nadir, Inc., Ajax may contract to have Nadir pay First National $50,000. In this instance, First National is a *creditor beneficiary* of the contract between Ajax and Nadir.

When the performance under a contract is meant as a gift to a third party, that person is a *donee beneficiary.* Donee beneficiaries can sue the party who owes them a performance under a breached contract, but they cannot sue the party who contracted to make them a gift. The beneficiary of a life insurance policy is usually a donee beneficiary.

An *incidental beneficiary* is a third party who unintentionally benefits from a contract. The incidental beneficiary has no rights under a contract. If merchant A contracts to have security service patrol her property—a contract that will likely also protect the other merchants on the block—and if one evening when the service fails to show up merchant B on the block is burglarized, B cannot sue the security service for breach of contract. B is only an incidental beneficiary of the contract between A and the service.

16. PERFORMANCE OF CONTRACTS

At the time parties reach agreement under a contract, the **duty of performance** becomes binding. Each party must perform the consideration promised to the other. Failure to perform breaches the contract.

Conditions Parties often put conditions into a contract that affect its performance. If something must take place in the future before a party has a duty to perform, it is called a **condition precedent.** For example, a building developer may contract to buy certain land "when the city of Euphoria annexes it." The annexation is a condition precedent to the developer's duty to purchase the land.

A **condition subsequent** excuses contractual performance if some future event takes place. A marine insurance policy that terminates shipping loss coverage "if war is declared" contains a condition subsequent.

Under **concurrent conditions** each party's contractual performance is triggered by the other party's tending (offering) performance. In a contract for the purchase of land, the performing obligations of the seller and buyer are concurrent conditions. The significance of a concurrent condition is that a party must offer to perform before legally holding the other party for nonperformance. The land buyer must offer to pay for the land before suing the seller for failing to perform.

The conditions discussed above may be express or implied. **Express conditions** are set forth in the contract. **Implied conditions** do not appear in the contract but are implied by law.

Levels of Performance A party to a contract may not always perfectly perform duties under it. The more complex a contract is, the more difficult it is for a party to complete every aspect of performance. Courts generally recognize three levels of specific performance.

1. COMPLETE PERFORMANCE recognizes that a contracting party has fulfilled every duty required by the contract. Payment of money, for example, is a contractual duty of performance that a party can perform completely. A party that performs completely is entitled to a complete performance by the other party and may sue to enforce this right.

2. SUBSTANTIAL PERFORMANCE represents a less-than-complete performance. A contracting party has honestly attempted to perform but has fallen short. Because of the complexity of building contractors' work, they often are able to reach substantial performance but not complete performance. One who substantially performs is entitled to the price promised by the other less that party's damages.

3. MATERIAL BREACH is a level of performance below what is reasonably acceptable. A party that has materially breached a contract cannot sue the other party for performance and is liable for damages arising from the breach.

Performance of contractual obligations presents parties and courts with legal issues. The resolution of these issues often requires analysis of principles relating to formation as well as performance of contracts. The following case involves a typical business transaction. Notice how the court examines the question of which party made the offer and which one accepted it. The conclusion of this formation issue impacts which party has failed to perform.

VENTURE MEDIA LIMITED PARTNERSHIP V. COLTS PLASTICS COMPANY, INCORPORATED

168 F. 3D 484 (4TH CIR. 1999)

PER CURIAM: . . .Venture sells cosmetic products through direct-response marketing. Colt manufactures and sells plastic containers for cosmetic products.

In 1994, Venture approached Colt seeking to purchase plastic containers for its line of cosmetic products. Meetings were held between representatives of both Colt and Venture. . . . When all of these issues were settled, Venture began placing orders with Colt.

In its business, Colt uses a number of forms including a Quotation/Proposal Form (Proposal Form) and an Invoice Form (Invoice). . . .

Between 1994 and September 1995, Venture ordered from Colt, and Colt manufactured and shipped, plastic containers for Venture's cosmetic products. . . . Venture placed orders with Colt using a purchase order. After manufacturing and shipping the plastic containers requested in the various purchase orders, Colt sent an Invoice to Venture requesting payment. The Invoice stated that payment was "due 30 days from the Invoice date," and "amounts 30 days past due [were] subject" to twelve percent annual interest. This period of time passed with the two companies transacting without incident.

However, in August and early September 1995, Venture felt as if there were problems. The deliveries were arriving late, and Colt refused to increase Venture's line of credit. To resolve these issues, Venture requested a meeting with Colt. At this meeting, Colt assured Venture it would resolve the concerns raised by Venture.

Based on these assurances, on September 21, 1995, Venture sent a purchase order to Colt for plastic containers totaling $339,996.25. The purchase order specified exact quantities, exact prices for each quantity, and the total price. In addition, the purchase order explicitly specified the location where the products should be shipped and stated: "Please notify us immediately if this order cannot be shipped complete on or before 11/03/95." Colt never sent an acknowledgment to Venture but began to manufacture the plastic containers requested in the purchase order.

Between late February and early March 1996, Colt shipped plastic containers aggregating

[CONTINUED]

$47,922.18 to Venture in a series of shipments. Colt also sent Invoices for each shipment to Venture. Venture never paid Colt for these deliveries and did not give notice to Colt of any defects in the delivered goods within the thirty-day period required by the Proposal Form. Colt continued to manufacture plastic containers totaling $122,799.59 after the deadline date for delivery specified in Venture's purchase order. Because of the outstanding balance owed by Venture, Colt never shipped these plastic containers to Venture. Colt sold what it could of these products to third parties, but because these plastic containers were specially manufactured for Venture, they were difficult to sell on the open market. Consequently, Colt continues to hold in its inventory $108,793.84 in plastic containers manufactured for Venture.

On December 30, 1996, Venture filed this suit against Colt in the Circuit Court of Maryland for Baltimore County alleging breach of contract. . . . Colt removed the case to the United States District Court for the District of Maryland based on diversity jurisdiction. Colt filed a counterclaim alleging breach of contract and seeking $47,922.18 plus interest for the plastic containers sent to Venture and $108,793.84 for the plastic containers specially manufactured for, but not sent to Venture.

Both parties moved for summary judgment with respect to all claims. The district court granted Colt's motion for summary judgment, and therefore, entered judgment in favor of Colt on Venture's claims and on Colt's counterclaim. . . . On appeal, Venture contends the district court erred when it granted summary judgment in favor of Colt. . . .

The parties agree that a contract existed for the sale of plastic containers amounting to $339,996.25, but vigorously dispute which terms control the sale. According to Venture, a $339,996.25 contract for plastic containers was formed when it sent its purchase order to Colt and Colt began to manufacture the plastic containers. Venture further maintains that Colt breached the contract by: (1) delivering defective plastic containers; (2) delivering damaged plastic containers; (3) failing to deliver the plastic containers by the agreed upon dates; (4) failing to extend Venture a volume purchase discount; and (5) failing to extend Venture's line of credit. In response, Colt contends that a $339,996.25 contract for plastic containers was formed when Colt sent its

Proposal Form to Venture and Venture sent its purchase order to Colt. According to Colt, Venture breached the contract when it failed to make payment for the plastic containers that were manufactured and delivered to Venture. Colt further maintains that it never breached its contract with Venture because the plain language of the Proposal Form disposes of Venture's breach of contract allegations.

The district court granted summary judgment in favor of Colt on Venture's breach of contract claim, concluding that a contract was formed when Colt sent the Proposal Form to Venture and Venture sent the purchase order for $339,996.25 of plastic containers to Colt. Further, the district court concluded that Venture breached the contract when it failed to make payment for the plastic containers that Colt manufactured and delivered to Venture. Finally, the district court concluded that Colt did not breach its contract with Venture because the plain language of the Proposal Form was dispositive of Venture's breach of contract allegations. . . .

Under Maryland common law, an offer is "a expression by the offeror . . . that something over which he at least assumes to have control shall be done or happen or shall not be done or happen if the conditions stated in the offer are complied with." An offer must be definite and certain. Further, the intention of the parties is one of the primary factors when deciding whether an offer was made. Therefore, the facts and circumstances of each particular case are crucial.

In this case, Colt's Proposal Form was an offer. From 1994 through September 1995, Venture placed purchase orders with Colt for various plastic containers. Throughout this period, Colt sent numerous Proposal Forms to Venture. The Proposal Form explicitly sought acceptance by means of a purchase order. In conformity with this condition, Venture placed all of its orders by means of purchase order. Venture always abided by Colt's terms and never objected to them. Accordingly, we agree with the district court that Colt's Proposal Form was an offer made to Venture.

The Code states that once a certain and definite offer is made, acceptance may be made in any manner that is reasonable. However, an offeror may be particular about the appropriate means of acceptance. Here, Colt's Proposal Form was explicit: the

[CONTINUED]

proposal "may be accepted only by written purchase order." Venture abided by this requirement when it submitted its purchase order on September 21, 1995, accepting Colt's offer, thus creating a binding contract between the two companies under the terms of Colt's Proposal Form.

Having determined that Colt's Proposal Form constituted a valid offer and Venture's purchase order constituted a valid acceptance, thereby creating an enforceable contract, we agree with the district court that the contract's terms are dispositive of Venture's breach of contract claim. Accordingly, for the reasons stated above, the district court appropriately granted summary judgment in favor of Colt on Venture's breach of contract claim.

Turning to Colt's counterclaim for breach of contract, the district court awarded Colt $47,922.18 plus $7,524.50 in interest for the plastic containers Colt manufactured and shipped to Venture. Because Venture accepted the shipment, did not object to the quality, and did not make payment, Colt was entitled to summary judgment on its counterclaim for these damages. Further, because the explicit terms of the Invoices sent to Venture by Colt allow interest at a twelve percent annual rate begin-

ning sixty days after the date the Invoice was due, the district court correctly awarded the sales price and interest to Colt in the total amount of $55,446.68.

Colt is also entitled to damages for the plastic containers that it manufactured specifically for Venture. The aggregate contract price for these plastic containers is $122,799,59. Colt has sold some of these containers on the open market but still has $108,793.84 of the plastic containers manufactured for Venture in its inventory. The district court correctly awarded this amount to Colt.

We conclude that the district court properly granted summary judgment in favor of Colt on Colt's counterclaim for breach of contract. The district court properly awarded Colt: (1) $55,446.68 (sales price and interest) for the plastic containers delivered to Venture; and (2) $108,793.84 for the plastic containers that Colt specially manufactured for Venture and has been unable to sell on the open market. . . .

For the reasons stated herein, the judgment of the district court is

Affirmed.

CASE QUESTIONS

1. In what businesses are Venture and Colt involved?
2. According to the court, who is the offeror and the offeree in this case?
3. What are the actual offer and acceptance in this factual situation?
4. How does the answer to the preceding question impact the conclusion of which party is entitled to a finding in its favor?
5. Which party is liable to the other?

17. DISCHARGE OF CONTRACTS

A party to a contract is **discharged** when the party is released from all further obligation of performance. Of course, complete performance discharges a party to a contract. The next box lists events that create discharge.

Impossibility of Performance One event that discharges a party's obligation of performance deserves special attention. A party is discharged because of **impossibility of performance.**

EVENTS THAT DISCHARGE A PARTY TO A CONTRACT

Occurrence of a condition subsequent

Nonoccurrence of a condition precedent

Material breach by the other party

Legal surrender of the right to enforce performance (**waiver**)

Mutual agreement to rescind

Expiration of the statute of limitations for enforceability

The substitution by agreement of one part for another on a contract (**novation**)

Impossibility of performance

Commercial impracticality

If the subject matter of the contract is destroyed, the contract becomes impossible to perform. When a contract exists for the sale of a building, and the building burns, the seller is discharged from performance. Likewise, when there is a contract for personal services, and the party promising the services becomes ill or dies, the party receives discharge from performances.

The party that promises performance that becomes illegal is also discharged because of impossibility of performance. Mere increased difficulty or reduced profitability, however, does not constitute impossibility of performance.

Commercial Impracticability Under the UCC a party to a sale-of-goods contract receives discharge from performance because of **commercial impracticability.** The *impracticability* standard is not as difficult to meet as the *impossibility* standard. What constitutes impracticability of performance depends upon the circumstances of the situation. For instance, a manufacturer may be discharged from an obligation to make goods for a buyer when the manufacturer's major source of raw materials is unexpectedly interrupted. But if the raw materials are reasonably available from another supplier, the manufacturer may not receive discharge because of impracticability.

18. TRENDS IN CONTRACT LAW

This chapter has given you an appreciation of the influence of contract law on private commercial transactions. To this end, the discussion has centered on the rules of contract law. Legal enforceability of contractual agreements provides an important framework for promoting certainty and efficiency in commercial dealings.

In general, trends in contract law do not affect the basic rules discussed in this chapter. Other chapters in the book develop many of the trends that affect contract law today. They deal with specific types of contracts or the use of contracts in particular situations. Still, several trends not mentioned elsewhere deserve attention here.

Contractual Relationships between Businesses As commercial transactions have grown increasingly complex, courts and legislatures have created more and more exceptions to traditional, fairly inflexible requirements of contract formation. These exceptions reflect an attempt to accommodate law to the actual reality of business dealings. For instance, UCC provisions on modification of contracts without consideration, open-ended contract terms, and contract formation by course of dealing are exceptions to traditional rules.

Similarly, courts have demonstrated greater willingness in recent years to grant damages based on one party's reasonable reliance on another's promises instead of merely on the party's expectations under a formal contract. This development reflects attempts to conform law to actual behavior in a complicated business world.

In seemingly contradictory fashion, the number of court cases focusing on information and performance of contracts has increased significantly over the last 20 years. During the same period, more and more contracting parties do not litigate to enforce breached agreements. Often, parties use arbitration, mediation, and negotiation when business problems arise under contracts. They avoid the time-consuming, expensive, and uncertain litigation process.

Contractual Relationships between Businesses and Employees Most large corporations have employment contracts for top management. Contract negotiation is becoming increasingly important for many executives. These agreements provide complex compensation packages, including golden parachutes and insurance protection from errors in job performance.

Most lower-level workers still do not have express contracts with their employers. Employers may terminate the employment of these workers at will. However, courts in growing numbers have been willing to take statements made by employers in personnel manuals and other documents and sue them as a basis for implying contract rights for employees.

Contractual Relationships between Businesses and Consumers A major trend in contract law has been the passage of many statutes affecting contracts between businesses and consumers. Government has stepped in at both the federal and state levels to protect consumers as they make contracts with businesses.

One development affecting business and consumer contracts has been enactment of "plain English" statutes in several states. These states require that standard business and consumer form contracts be written in a clearly understandable way. Drafters of such contracts must avoid legal expressions not ordinarily comprehended by consumers. More than 30 states have related statutes directed specifically at insurance contracts. A number of federal laws affecting readability also apply to specific types of contracts.

The "Cyber Law Connection" box discusses contractual relationships between businesses and consumers in electronic commerce.

19. CONTRACTUAL ETHICS

In general, ethical concerns are increasingly reflected in how courts decide contractual disputes. Although the traditional rules of contract law are still very important, they cannot always be used to predict what courts will do when one party acts in *bad faith* or violates the *expectations* that another party brings to a business arrangement.

Involved in all lawsuits are not only legal issues but also the ethical values that society holds regarding appropriate business practices. Business persons sometimes argue that jurors do not understand business dealings, and this is likely true. At the same time, however, juries may also be operating from a different set of ethical expectations than a segment of the business community. When this happens, large verdicts against business defendants may surprise the business community.

CYBER LAW *connection*

Principles of contract law are fundamental to conducting business. The new economy of electronic commerce is no different. In a sense, only the factual situation is different; the contractual rules remain the same. For example, envision yourself buying a book in a bookstore. The potential contract involved in this transaction becomes implied as you carry our selection around the store—you are sending the signal that you intend to buy. The actual contract arises when you take the book to the cashier. Whether you view the store as the offeror (the book is being offered for the price listed) or yourself as the offeror (willing to pay a specified price) the contract is formed and performed simultaneously. In essence, the performance (paying and delivery) occur concurrently.

Now envision a similar purchase from an on-line bookseller's website. You complete the information requested and submit your order along with your credit or debit card information. What happens if the seller fails to deliver the item purchased? Is there a breach of contract? Is there any contract at all? What is your remedy? The answers to these questions depend on how the transaction is analyzed. Who is the offeror? If you are, did your offer seek the response of a returned promise to deliver the item ordered (bilateral contract) or the act of actually shipping the item (unilateral, contract). Do you understand the importance of this analysis? If the latter interpretation of your offer applies and the seller does not ship the item, there is no contract. You are entitled to a refund or credit on your card. Assuming that no charge to your card has been processed, then you are not harmed and no remedy is applicable. If your offer sought a commitment (promise) from the seller to ship the item ordered, you will need to determine if the seller made such a promise. Assuming the language of an on-line reply to your order can be read as such a promise, what happens if no delivery is forthcoming?

How do you suppose on-line sellers are describing the nature of the transaction? Read the language of the e-commerce business deal carefully in light of your newly acquired knowledge of contract law principles. E-commerce will continue to utilize and modify the principles of contract law discussed in this chapter. For example, in those transactions that must be evidenced by a signed writing (see section 12 above), the Electronic Signatures in Global and National Commerce Act provides the framework for the written signature to be accomplished electronically.

Eventually, ethical values may provide the basis for legal rules. In contract law the growing use of promissory estoppel and implied contract doctrine shows the willingness of courts to make binding business arrangements that in the past would have been unenforceable without an express contract. It is easy to understand these changes in terms of the good-faith expectations of the parties to business arrangements and in light of society's evolving ethical standards.

KEY TERMS

REVIEW QUESTIONS AND PROBLEMS

Basic Concepts

1. *Contract Law in Private Enterprise*

   Discuss the importance of contract law to the private market system. How does contract law provide flexibility and precision in business dealings?

2. *Sources of Contract Law*

   (a)   What is meant by the common law of contracts?

   (b)   What is the UCC?

3. *Contractual Classifications*

   Why are the following phrases important to the understanding of contract law?

   (a)   Bilateral and unilateral contracts

   (b)   Express and implied-in-fact contracts

   (c)   Implied-in-law (quasi) contracts

4. *Contractual Enforcement Terminology*

   How can someone reasonably say that a voidable contract is both enforceable and unenforceable?

5. *Contractual Performance Terminology*

   Pat hires a tailor to make a suit. The tailor completes all the sewing and now waits for Pat to pick up the suit and pay for it. Is this contractual agreement executed or executory? Explain.

6. *Breach of Contract*

Gustavson contracts with Sanders to buy 51 percent of the stock of Gilmet Corporation. When Sanders breaches the contract, Gustavson sues for specific performance. Is specific performance an appropriate remedy under these circumstances? Explain.

Contract Formation

7. *Offer to Contract*

Condor Equipment Company offers to sell a dough cutting machine to Snappy Jack Biscuits, Inc. The offer states: "This offer expires Friday noon." On Thursday morning, the sale manager for Condor calls the president of Snappy Jack and explains that the machine has been sold to another purchaser. Discuss whether Condor has legally revoked its offer to Snappy Jack.

8. *Acceptance of Offer*

Fielding Bros. offers to ship six furnaces to Central City Heating and Cooling Co. for $4,500 cash. Central City accepts on the condition that Fielding give 120 days' credit. Has a contract resulted? Explain.

9. *Consideration*

Jefferson and Goldberg enter a contract for the sale of five acres of land at $10,000 per acre. Later, Goldberg, the buyer, asks if Jefferson will agree to modify the contract to $9,000 per acre.

(a)   Jefferson agrees. Is Jefferson's promise binding on him?

(b)   Would your answer be different if 5 used cars were being sold instead of 5 acres of land?

10. *Capacity of Parties to Contract*

Describe the circumstances under which an adult lacks the capacity to contract.

11. *Lawful Purpose*

Hunt signs an equipment lease contract with Edwards Rental. The contract contains a clause stating: "Lessor disclaims all liability arising from injuries caused by use of this equipment." Because the equipment has been improperly serviced by Edwards Rental, Hunt is injured while using it. If Hunt sues, will the disclaimer clause likely be enforced? Explain.

12. *Written Contracts*

Elegante Haberdashery telephones an order to Nordic Mills for 500 men's shirts at $15 each. Each shirt will carry the Elegante label and have the Elegante trademark over the pocket. After the shirts are manufactured, Elegante refuses to accept delivery of them and raises the statute of frauds as a defense. Discuss whether this defense applies to these facts.

Other Contract Issues

13. *Interpretation of Contracts*

Gus contracts to buy a used car from Cars Galore, Inc. The printed contract specifies "no warranties." But Gus and the sales manager of Cars handwrite into the contract a 90-day guarantee on the transmission. If the transmission fails after 60 days, is there a warranty protecting Gus? Explain.

14. *Assignment of Contracts*

Franchetti Rifle Distributors assigns a $20,000 claim against Top Gun, Inc., to the Zenith Collection Agency. When Zenith sues Top Gun, Top Gun asserts that it rejected a shipment of rifles from Franchetti out of which the claim arose, because they had defective trigger guards. Explain whether Top Gun can properly assert its defense against plaintiff Zenith.

15. *Contracts Benefiting a Third Party*

    What is the distinction between a creditor beneficiary and an incidental beneficiary? Explain.

16. *Performance of Contracts*

    Ace Contracting constructs an office building for Realty Enterprises. Realty's tenants quickly find a number of minor problems with the plumbing and insulation of the new building. When Realty contacts Ace about bringing its work up to standard, Ace promises to correct the problems, but never does.

    (a)   Can Realty rescind the contract?

    (b)   What are Realty's legal remedies?

17. *Discharge of Contracts*

    A tripling of prices by an illegal cartel of uranium producers caused Westinghouse Electric Corp. to default on uranium delivery contracts to a number of utility companies. The companies sued and Westinghouse settled. If the case had gone to trial, what defense might Westinghouse have raised to excuse its nonperformance under the contracts?

18. *Trends in Contract Law*

    Explain why businesses are increasingly asserting claims for breach of contract and not necessarily using the courts to resolve these claims.

19. *Contractual Ethics*

    When do traditional rules of contract law not adequately predict what a court will decide in a contractual dispute? Discuss.

TERMINOLOGY REVIEW

For each term in the left-hand column, match the most appropriate description in the right-hand column.

1. Accord and satisfaction
2. Assignment
3. Bilateral contract
4. Condition precedent
5. Executory contract
6. Firm offer
7. Material breach
8. Parol evidence rule
9. Quasi-contract
10. Recission
11. Voidable contract

a. A recovery based on unjust enrichment
b. A merchant's written promise to hold open an offer
c. A contract that binds one party but allows the other party to withdraw legally
d. A future uncertain event that must occur before performance is due
e. A failure of contractual performance
f. Settlement and payment of a disputed debt by mutual agreement
g. The doctrine that prohibits use of oral evidence to alter or vary the terms of certain written contracts
h. A contract, the consideration for which is a binding promise given by each party
i. A remedy that requires that each party return what it got from the other
j. A transfer of contractual rights
k. A contract the parties have not yet performed

BUSINESS DISCUSSION

As a new sales representative for Misco Equipment Corporation, you take a customer out to dinner. Before dinner is over, you have shaken hands on a deal to sell the customer nearly a half-million dollars worth of industrial equipment. In writing up the formal contract the next morning, you discover that you misfigured the equipments price. Your error could cost Misco $60,000. You telephone your customer and explain the situation.

> Is the "deal" you made an enforceable contract?
>
> Does the mistake you made permit you to get out of an enforceable contract?
>
> What do you think will happen in this situation?

TORTS IN THE BUSINESS ENVIRONMENT

You manufacture trunk locks and your major account is a large car company. When an important piece of your equipment unexpectedly breaks, you contact Mayfair, Inc., the only manufacturer of such equipment, and contract to replace it. The Mayfair sales representative assures you orally and in writing that the prepaid equipment will arrive by October 1, in time for you to complete your production for the car company. Instead, there is a union strike in the Mayfair trucking division, and the equipment does not arrive until December 1.

By December 1 the car company has made an agreement with another lock manufacturer. You threaten to sue Mayfair for their failure to deliver on time, but Mayfair reminds you of a contract term that relieves them of contractual liability because of "labor difficulties." Then you learn from a former secretary to the Mayfair sales representative that Mayfair knew that its trucking division was likely to strike. In fact the sales representative and the sales vice president had discussed whether or not to tell you of this fact and decided not to out of concern that you would not place your order.

Has Mayfair done anything legally wrong?

Is your legal remedy against Mayfair limited to breach of contract?

Will you be able to get damages from Mayfair other than a refund of your prepayment? Explain.

The word **tort** means "wrong." Legally, a tort is a civil wrong other than a breach of contract. If property is the central legal concept of private enterprise and much of Western civilization, contract concerns transfer of an owner's resources, and tort involves defining when others injure an owner's resources, including the resources of the person. Tort law sets limits on how people can act and use their resources so they do not violate the right others have to their resources. Legal wrongs inflicted on the resources of others may be crimes as well as torts (see Chapter 10), but the law of tort itself is civil rather than criminal. The usual remedy for a tort is dollar damages. Behavior that constitutes a tort is called *tortious* behavior. One who commits a tort is a *tortfeasor.*

255

This chapter divides torts into three main categories: intentional torts, negligence torts, and strict liability torts. Intentional torts involve deliberate actions that cause injury. Negligence torts involve injury following a failure to use reasonable care. Strict liability torts impose legal responsibility for injury even though a liable party neither intentionally nor negligently causes the injury.

Important to torts are the concepts of duty and causation. One is not liable for another's injury unless he or she has a *duty* toward the person injured. And, of course, there is usually no liability for injury unless one has *caused* the injury. We explain these concepts under the discussion of negligence, where they are most relevant.

This chapter also covers the topic of damages. The topic concerns the business community because huge damage awards, frequently against businesses, have become common in recent years. Finally, the chapter explores some alternatives to the current tort system, including workers' compensation.

INTENTIONAL TORTS

An important element in the following torts is *intent,* as we are dealing with intentional torts. **Intent** is usually defined as the desire to bring about certain results. But in some circumstances the meaning is even broader, including not only desired results but also results that are "substantially likely" to result from an action. Recently, employers who knowingly exposed employees to toxic substances without warning them of the dangers have been sued for committing the intentional tort of battery. The employers did not desire their employees' injuries, but these injuries were "substantially likely" to result from the failure to warn.

The following sections explain the basic types of intentional torts. The table "Types of Intentional Torts" lists these torts.

1. ASSAULT AND BATTERY

An **assault** is the placing of another in immediate apprehension for his or her physical safety. "Apprehension" has a broader meaning than "fear." It includes the expectation that one is about to be physically injured. The person who intentionally creates such apprehension in another is guilty of the tort of assault. Many times a battery follows an assault. A **battery** is an illegal touching of another. As used here, "illegal" means that the touching is done without justification and without the consent of the person touched. The touching need not cause injury.

Types of Intentional Torts
Assault and battery
Intentional infliction of mental distress
Invasion of privacy
False imprisonment and malicious prosecution
Trespass
Conversion
Defamation
Fraud
Common law business torts

A store manager who threatens an unpleasant customer with a wrench, for example, is guilty of assault. Actually hitting the customer with the wrench would constitute battery.

2. INTENTIONAL INFLICTION OF MENTAL DISTRESS

Intentional **infliction of mental distress** is a battery to the emotions. It arises from outrageous, intentional conduct that carries a strong probability of causing mental distress to the person at whom it is directed. Usually, one who sues on the basis of an intentional infliction of mental distress must prove that the defendant's outrageous behavior caused not only mental distress but also physical symptoms, such as headaches or sleeplessness.

The most common cases of intentional infliction of mental distress (also called "emotional distress") have concerned employees who have been discriminated against or fired. Many such cases, however, do not involve the type of outrageous conduct necessary for the mental distress tort. In the following case, the court decides whether or not an employer's conduct is outrageous. Pay special attention to the precedent cases the court discusses in its opinion.

VAN STAN V. FANCY COLOURS & COMPANY

125 F. 3D 563 (7TH CIR. 1997)

WOOD, JR., J.: . . . After Fancy Colours & Company ("Fancy Colours") terminated his employment, Michael D. Van Stan ("Van Stan") sued Fancy Colours contending that Fancy Colours' conduct in firing him amounted to intentional infliction of emotional distress. A jury awarded Van Stan damages of $150,000 for intentional infliction of emotional distress. We reverse the entry of judgment against Fancy Colours on the intentional infliction of emotional distress claim.

Under Illinois law, which the parties both agree applies, a plaintiff may recover damages for intentional infliction of emotional distress only if he establishes that (1) the defendant's conduct was extreme and outrageous, (2) the defendant intended to inflict severe emotional distress or knew that there was at least a high probability that his conduct would inflict severe emotional distress, and (3) the defendant's conduct did cause severe emotional distress. Conduct is extreme and outrageous only if "the conduct has been so outrageous in character and so extreme in degree, as to go beyond all possi-

ble bounds of decency. . . ." "Mere insults, indignities, threats, annoyances, petty oppressions, or other trivialities" do not amount to extreme and outrageous conduct, nor does conduct "characterized by malice or a degree of aggravation which would entitle the plaintiff to punitive damages for another tort." Moreover, we judge whether conduct is extreme and outrageous on an objective standard based on all the facts and circumstances of a particular case. Thus, to serve as a basis for recovery, the defendant's conduct must be such that the "recitation of facts to an average member of the community would arouse his resentment against the actor, and lead him to exclaim 'Outrageous!' "

In the employment context, Illinois courts have recognized that personality conflicts and questioning of job performance are "unavoidable aspects of employment" and that "frequently, they produce concern and distress." The courts have reasoned, however, that if such incidents were actionable, nearly all employees would have a cause of action for intentional infliction of emotional distress. Thus,

[CONTINUED]

Illinois courts have limited recovery to cases in which the employer's conduct has been truly egregious. See, e.g., *Pavilon v. Kaferly* . . . (the employer, knowing that the plaintiff was susceptible to emotional distress, offered her money for sexual favors, fired her after she refused, and after he fired her, threatened to kill her, to rape her, and to file a legal action challenging her rights to custody of her child and attempted to disrupt her new employment relationship); *Milton v. Illinois Bell Tel. Co.* . . . (the employer engaged in an extensive course of disciplinary and harassing conduct to coerce the plaintiff to falsify work reports).

In contrast, Illinois courts have denied recovery for distress resulting from recognizably reprehensible conduct which has been linked to an employer's legitimate interest. In *Harris v. First Fed. Sav. & Loan Ass'n of Chicago* an Illinois appellate court held that a plaintiff who alleged that her employer criticized, demoted, and discharged her after she reported allegedly criminal activity to her supervisor did not state a claim because she did not allege that her employer engaged in this course of conduct to coerce her into engaging in illegal activity. While the court characterized the employer's conduct as "reprehensible," the court held that it did not rise to the level of extreme and outrageous conduct because the employer merely acted out of displeasure with the plaintiff's exercise of judgment regarding another employee's conduct.

Recognizing this high threshold, this Court and other federal courts applying Illinois law have denied recovery to plaintiffs who alleged that their employers subjected them to a continuous series of intentionally discriminatory acts. For example, in *Harriston* we held that the plaintiff failed to allege conduct that rose to the level of extreme and outrageous conduct even though she contended that among other things her employer refused to allow her to supervise white subordinates, reprimanded

her for no reason, refused to allow her to participate in a management incentive fund, forced her out of her management position, promised her a promotion she never received, took away from her major accounts and gave her less lucrative accounts in return, excluded her from office activities, monitored her telephone calls with an eavesdropping device and ignored concerns of her health and safety after her personal property was damaged on company property. See also *Briggs v. North Shore Sanitary Dist.* (Allegations that the plaintiff's employer and fellow employees hung a pickaninny doll in her office, subjected her to racial slurs, excluded her from office social activities, placed her on probation, and refused to train her properly did not rise to the level of extreme and outrageous conduct, but allegations that co-workers exposed her to toxic fumes for more than eight hours did).

In this case, Van Stan maintains that viewing the evidence in the light most favorable to him, a reasonable jury could have found that Walters [Van Stan's supervisor,] and other Fancy Colours supervisors knew that Van Stan suffered from a bipolar disorder, that Fancy Colours fired Van Stan because his disorder required him to work less hours, that Walters telephoned Van Stan at home while he was on vacation to inform him that he had been terminated and that after Van Stan requested an explanation, Walters falsely told Van Stan that he was being fired for low productivity. While we do not mean to condone such conduct, we do not believe that this course of conduct was akin to the type of egregious conduct present in *Pavilon* and *Milton,* nor do we believe that it exceeded all possible bounds of decency. Thus, as a matter of law Fancy Colours' conduct did not rise to the level of extreme and outrageous conduct, and Fancy Colours is entitled to a judgment in its favor.

Reversed.

CASE QUESTIONS

1. What was the conduct that plaintiff Van Stan claimed was "extreme and outrageous"?

2. What does the court say about what would happen if more "personality conflicts and questioning of job performance" amounted to intentional infliction of mental and emotional distress?

3. Why is the Illinois case in federal court?

In the business world, other examples of infliction of mental distress come about from the efforts of creditors to extract payment from their debtors. Frequent, abusive, threatening phone calls by creditors might provide the basis for a claim of intentional infliction of mental distress. As torts go, this one is of fairly recent origin. It is a judge-made tort, which furnishes a good example of how the courts are becoming increasingly sensitive to the range of injuries for which compensation is appropriate. In some states, courts have gone so far as to establish liability for carelessly inflicted mental distress, such as the distress of a mother who sees her child negligently run down by a delivery truck.

3. INVASION OF PRIVACY

The tort of **invasion of privacy** is one that is still in the early stages of legal development. As the statutes and court cases recognize it, the tort at present comprises three principal invasions of personal interest. An invasion of any one of these areas of interest is sufficient to trigger liability.

Most commonly, liability will be imposed on a defendant who appropriates the plaintiff's name or likeness for his or her own use. Many advertisers and marketers have been required to pay damages to individuals when pictures of them have been used without authorization to promote products, or when their names and identities have been used without permission for promotional purposes. Before using anyone's picture or name, an advertiser must obtain a proper release from that person to avoid possible liability. Appropriating another's name and identity in order to secure credit is an additional example of this invasion-of-privacy tort.

A second invasion of privacy is the defendant's intrusion upon the plaintiff's physical solitude. Illegal searches or invasions of home or possessions, illegal wiretapping, and persistent and unwanted telephoning can provide the basis for this invasion-of-privacy tort. In one case, a woman even recovered damages against a photographer who entered her sickroom and snapped a picture of her. Employers who enter their employees' homes without permission have also been sued successfully for invasions of privacy. If the invasion of privacy continues, it may be enjoined by the court. Jacqueline Kennedy Onassis sought and obtained an injunction that forbade a certain photographer from getting too close to her and her children. Under this tort, the invasion of physical solitude must be highly objectionable to a reasonable person.

The third invasion of personal interest that gives rise to the invasion-of-privacy tort is the defendant's public disclosure of highly objectionable, private information about the plaintiff. A showing of such facts can be the basis for a cause of action, even if the information is true. Thus, publishing in a newspaper that the plaintiff does not pay his or her debts has been ruled to create liability for the defendant creditor. Communicating the same facts to a credit-reporting agency or the plaintiff's employer usually does not impose liability, however. In these cases, there has been no disclosure to the public in general. Also, the news media are protected under the First Amendment when they publish information about public officials and other public figures.

4. FALSE IMPRISONMENT AND MALICIOUS PROSECUTION

Shoplifting accounts for some $18 billion a year in business losses, almost 1 percent of retail sales. Claims of **false imprisonment** stem most frequently in business from instances of shoplifting. This tort is the intentional unjustified confinement of a non-consenting person. Although most states have statutes that permit merchants or their employees to detain customers suspected of shoplifting, this detention must be a reasonable one. The unnecessary use of force, lack of reasonable suspicion of shoplifting, or an unreasonable length of confinement can cause the merchant to lose the statutory privilege. The improperly detained customer is then able to sue for false imprisonment. Allegations of battery are also usually made if the customer has been touched. Not all false imprisonment lawsuits arise because of shoplifting. In one instance a KPMG employee sued for false imprisonment alleging that his manager blocked a door with a chair during a performance review and caused the employee to have to remain in the room against his will.

The tort of **malicious prosecution** is often called *false arrest.* Malicious prosecution arises from causing someone to be arrested criminally without proper grounds. It occurs, for instance, when the arrest is accomplished simply to harass someone. In Albany, New York, a jury awarded a man $200,000 for malicious prosecution. His zipper had broken, leaving his fly open, and a store security guard had him arrested for indecent exposure even after he explained that he had not noticed the problem.

5. TRESPASS

To enter another's land without consent or to remain there after being asked to leave constitutes the tort of **trespass.** A variation on the trespass tort arises when something (such as particles of pollution) is placed on another's land without consent. Although the usual civil action for trespass asks for an injunction to restrain the trespasser, the action may also ask for damages.

Union pickets walking on company property (in most instances), customers refusing to leave a store after being asked to do so, and unauthorized persons entering restricted areas are all examples of trespass. Note that trespass is often a crime as well as a tort. Intentional wrongdoing is frequently criminal.

6. CONVERSION

Conversion is the wrongful and unlawful exercise of dominion (power) and control over the personal property of another. Conversion deprives the proper owner of lawful rights in the property. The deprivation may be either temporary or permanent, but it must constitute a serious invasion of the owner's rights. Abraham Lincoln once convinced an Illinois court that a defendant's action in riding the plaintiff's horse for 15 miles was not sufficiently serious to be a conversion since the defendant had returned the horse in good condition. The plaintiff had left the horse with the defendant to be stabled and fed.

Conversion arises often in business situations. Stealing property or purchasing stolen property (even innocently) is a conversion. Failing to return properly acquired property at the designated time, delivering property to the wrong party, and destruction and alteration of property are all conversions if the deprivation of ownership rights is serious or long-lasting. Even if she or he intends to return it, one who converts is absolutely liable for any damage done to property. A warehouse operator who improperly transfers stored goods from a designated to a nondesignated warehouse is absolutely liable when a tornado destroys the goods or when a thief steals them.

7. DEFAMATION

Defamation is the publication of untrue statements about another that hold up that individual's character or reputation to contempt and ridicule. "Publication" means that the untruth must be made known to third parties. If defamation is oral, it is called **slander.** Written defamation, or defamation published over radio or television, is termed **libel.**

False accusations of dishonesty or inability to pay debts frequently bring on defamation suits in business relationships. Sometimes, such accusations arise during the course of a takeover attempt by one company of another through an offering to buy stock. In a recent instance, the chairman of one company called the chairman of a rival business "lying, deceitful, and treacherous" and charged that he "violated the standards by which decent men do business." If untrue, these remarks provide a good example of defamation of character. At one major university, a former business professor received a multimillion-dollar settlement following allegations made by university administrators that he had vandalized the new business school. The allegations cost him a deanship at another university. Punitive or punishment damages, as well as actual damages, may be assessed in defamation cases.

Individuals are not the only ones who can sue for defamation. A corporation can also sue for defamation if untrue remarks discredit the way the corporation conducts its business. Untruthfully implying that a company's entire management is dishonest or incompetent defames the corporation.

Because of the First Amendment, special rules regarding defamation apply to the news media. These media are not liable for the defamatory untruths they print about public officials and public figures unless plaintiffs can prove that the untruths were published with "malice" (evil intent, that is, the deliberate intent to injure) or with "reckless disregard for the truth." Public figures are those who have consciously brought themselves to public attention.

Plaintiffs' verdicts in media defamation cases are often overturned by trial or appellate judges. In one instance a Houston investment firm, now defunct, sued the *Wall Street Journal,* claiming that a story published by the newspaper caused the firm to go out of business. Following a huge jury verdict, the trial judge threw out $200 million in damages, ruling that the firm had not proved the newspaper published certain statements with knowledge of their falsity or with reckless disregard for the truth.

Plaintiffs' verdicts in defamation cases are often overturned by appellate courts. Because of the constitutional protection given to speech and the media, appellate judges reexamine trial evidence very closely to determine whether the necessary elements of defamation had been proven.

There are two basic defenses to a claim of defamation. One defense is that the statements made were true. *Truth* is an absolute defense. The second defense is that the statement arose from *privileged communications.* For example, statements made by legislators, judges, attorneys, and those involved in lawsuits are privileged under many circumstances.

Nearly one-third of all defamation suits are currently brought by employees against present and former employers. Often these suits arise when employers give job references on former employees who have been discharged for dishonesty. As a result, many employers will now not give job references or will do no more than verify that former employees did work for them.

8. FRAUD

Business managers must be alert to the intentional tort of **fraud.** A fraud is an intentional misrepresentation of a material fact that is justifiably relied upon by someone to his or her injury. An intentional misrepresentation means a lie. The lie must be of a material fact—an important one. The victim of the fraud must justifiably rely on the misrepresentation and must suffer some injury, usually a loss of money or other resource one owns.

Fraud applies in many different situations. Business frauds often involve the intentional-misrepresentation of property or financial status. Lying about assets or liabilities in order to get credit or a loan is a fraud. Likewise, intentionally misrepresenting that land is free from hazardous waste when the seller knows that toxic chemicals are buried on the land constitutes fraud.

You can also prove fraud by giving evidence that another has harmed you by failing to disclose a material (important) hidden fact. The fraud of failure to disclose arises when the defendant is under a legal duty to disclose a fact, such as when a defendant seller knows that the foundations of a house are weakened by termites and must disclose this to the buyer. Likewise, a defendant who has intentionally concealed an important fact and has induced reliance on it to the plaintiff's injury is liable for fraud.

In the next case, the Supreme Court of Arizona discusses the difference between fraud for failure to disclose and fraud in the concealment.

WELLS FARGO BANK V. ARIZONA LABORERS, TEAMSTERS, AND CEMENT MASONS

38 P. 3D 12 (2002)

J. Fife Symington and his development firm requested funding for a mall construction from the Wells Fargo Bank in Phoenix, Arizona. The bank agreed to offer temporary financing if Symington could secure permanent financing from another source. Symington arranged a loan from various union funds ("the Funds"). Subsequently, Symington defaulted in repaying the Funds, and the Funds sued Wells Fargo, alleging that the bank knew of financial misrepresentations by Symington to the Funds and had actively concealed them from the Funds. The trial court ruled that Wells Fargo had no duty to disclose Symington's true financial condition to the Funds, and the court of appeals affirmed.

Jones, C. J.: . . . Arizona recognizes the tort of fraudulent concealment:

One party to a transaction who by concealment or other action intentionally prevents the other from acquiring material information is subject to the same liability to the other, for pecuniary loss as though he had stated the nonexistence of the matter that the other was thus prevented from discovering.

Where failure to disclose a material fact is calculated to induce a false belief, "the distinction between concealment and affirmative misrepresentation is tenuous." The court of appeals dismissed the Funds' claims for fraudulent concealment on the basis that the Bank's fiduciary and contractual duty was to Symington and not to the Funds. Both the court of appeals and the Bank mistakenly cite *Frazier v. Southwest Savings & Loan Association* for the proposition that concealment was not proven because there was no duty to speak.

[CONTINUED]

In *Frazier,* the court explained that liability for concealment requires knowledge of the false information and action by the defendant that intentionally prevented the plaintiff from finding the truth. The *Frazier* court found concealment unproven, not because there was no duty to disclose, but because there was no evidence from which the jury could have found active concealment.

In Arizona, whether a duty to speak exists at all is determined by reference to all the circumstances of the case. On the issue of duty in a fraudulent concealment claim, we are persuaded by and affirm the reasoning articulated by the court of appeals decision in *King v. O'Rielly Motor Co.*

In *King,* a car buyer sued a car dealer for fraudulently representing that the car the buyer purchased was "as good as new" when in fact the car had been in an accident and, unbeknownst to the buyer, had been repaired by the dealer. The car dealer argued that the dealer could not be liable to the buyer because the dealer was under no duty to disclose. The court stated that, while "*it is often difficult to distinguish misleading representations and fraudulent concealment from mere nondisclosure* and the classification of the act or acts in question must, of course, depend on the facts of each case," it was nevertheless true that "the facts of this case . . . would be supportive of a finding of misleading representation or fraudulent concealment. An Oregon court advanced similar reasoning in *Paul v. Kelley,* concluding that a duty to disclose is not necessary to prevail on a fraudulent concealment claim.

In *Paul,* the seller of real estate knew, before the closing, that he was required to install a storm sewer if a drainage ditch on the property were eliminated. Instead of installing the storm sewer, the sellers simply filled the ditch and sold the property. Buyers of the land sued the sellers when they learned they had to put in an expensive sewer system. The sellers defended on the grounds that they had no affirmative duty to disclose the ditch to the buyers. The court found this argument meritless, stating:

Such a duty is not necessary. . . . An active concealment such as the filling in of the ditch alleged in this case is to be distinguished from a simple nondisclosure. . . . Plaintiff's complaint sets forth facts alleging an active concealment of the drainage ditch and is *sufficient without the assertion of a duty to speak.*

The common law clearly distinguishes between concealment and nondisclosure. The former is characterized by deceptive acts or contrivances intended to hide information, mislead, avoid suspicion, or prevent further inquiry into a material matter. The latter is characterized by mere silence. "Thus, fraudulent concealment—without any misrepresentation or duty to disclose—can constitute common law fraud."

The Funds in the instant case allege the Bank actively strategized to cover up the pending collapse of Symington's financial condition. This allegation fits the definition of concealment, not nondisclosure. Three evidentiary points are clear: the "unjustified and imprudent" loan extensions; the forbearance until one day after the date for the Mercado take-out obligation; and the failure to report Symington's false statements to federal banking authorities. The record reveals evidence of internal bank communications and communication between Symington aides and the Bank. Applying the law, we conclude that the Funds were not required to establish an affirmative duty to speak in order to prove fraudulent concealment. Actions by the Bank which intended to conceal material facts are, if proven, sufficient.

In the final analysis, we reach two conclusions as to the fraudulent concealment claim: there are reasonable inferences from which a jury could find (1) the Bank had knowledge of false information being given the Funds, and (2) the Bank took measures intended to prevent the Funds from learning the truth. These inferences are grounded in fact and are sufficient to take the concealment theory to the jury. The opinion of the court of appeals is vacated, the judgment of the trial court is reversed, and this case is remanded to the trial court for proceedings consistent with this opinion.

CASE QUESTIONS

1. What are three types of fraud?
2. Why was the bank under no duty to disclose Symington's financial condition to the Funds?
3. Give an example to illustrate the difference between knowing a material fact and failing to disclose it and "concealing" the fact.

You should be able now to discuss the Business Decision problem that opens this chapter. Mayfair is liable to you for fraud. The agreement between the sales representative and the vice president not to tell you about likely labor difficulties amounts to a concealment of a material fact, which is the equivalent of a misrepresentation. Whether or not Mayfair is under a duty to disclose labor difficulties, given the contract you signed, is irrelevant. You can get damages amounting to your actual losses plus possible punitive damages upon proof of fraud.

Fraud also can be committed in the hiring process. For instance, courts have found employers liable for misrepresenting to employees about conditions at a business that later affect employment adversely. In one case, former professional football player Phil McConkey received a $10 million award because his employer misrepresented the status of merger talks with another company. McConkey lost his job the year after he was hired when the two companies merged.

Other instances of business fraud can involve misrepresentation about products. The tobacco industry is beginning to lose lawsuits when plaintiffs allege fraud based on the industry's claiming for years that no tobacco consumption harm had been scientifically proved when it knew that such harm had been established. Farmers and growers have received over a billion dollars from DuPont in settlements based on the damage the fungicide Benlate caused various plants. DuPont allegedly committed fraud by concealing that Benlate could cause crop damage even when the company was asked about the possibility.

The previous chapter on contracts discussed fraud as voiding a contract. But fraud is also an intentional tort, and one who is a victim of fraud can sue for damages, including punitive or punishment damages. Fraud is both a common law intentional tort and a type of tort covered in many statutes that prohibit lying to a bank or in various documents that businesses must supply to the government. Note that frauds are sometimes also crimes. Chapter 10 discusses criminal frauds like mail fraud and wire fraud. Today many frauds, as well as other intentional torts, occur on the Internet. See the box "Cyber Law Connection."

 CYBER LAW *connection*

Cyber Torts

A variety of intentional torts take place on the Internet. Defamation occurs when e-mailers place messages on listservs or public chatrooms that hold others up to "public contempt or ridicule." Intentional infliction of mental distress arises, for example, when threats are made via e-mail or websites. A jury in Oregon awarded plaintiffs over $100 million when it found that a website threatened abortion providers. When computer hackers break into company databases, trade secrets are easily misappropriated.

Perhaps the most common intentional cyber-related tort is fraud. The Federal Trade Commission has released a list of such frauds or scams that include a variety of pyramid schemes, fraudulent auctions, deceptive travel offers, sale of unmiraculous "miracle" products, health care rip-offs, phony credit card charges, and work-at-home frauds. There was even a "rebate" check sent to consumers that if cashed gave them new Internet service that could not be canceled. The FTC reports that its enforcement actions against Internet scams have risen steadily in recent years.

Fraud and Corporate Governance Antifraud laws are a major weapon in the enforcement of good corporate governance. Much corporate misgovernance, especially by managers, arises because of misrepresentations of fact about corporate assets or liabilities. These misrepresentations usually induce investors to buy corporate stock shares at higher prices and benefit corporate managers or others inside the corporation who sell their stock. Sometimes a misrepresentation that raises stock price obtains a bonus or other perk for managers or a loan for the corporation. Usually, a misrepresentation amounts to fraud because investors (who become owners) or lenders rely on it to their injury, that is, they lose some or all of their investment.

Many specific laws create civil and criminal liability for the fraud of corporate managers and other corporate agents. Chapter 16 covers the most important of these laws. As you think about fraud, remember that it violates the principle of property. One does not acquire proper ownership by defrauding others of their resources. Fraud does not respect the equal property right of others.

9. COMMON LAW BUSINESS TORTS

The label *business torts* embraces different kinds of torts that involve intentional interference with business relations.

Injurious Falsehood **Injurious falsehood,** sometimes called *trade disparagement,* is a common business tort. It consists of the publication of untrue statements that disparage the business owner's product or its quality. General disparagement of the plaintiff's business may also provide basis for liability. As a cause of action, injurious falsehood is similar to defamation of character. It differs, however, in that it usually applies to a product or business rather than character or reputation. The requirements of proof are also somewhat different. Defamatory remarks are presumed false unless the defendant can prove their truth. But in disparagement cases the plaintiff must establish the falsity of the defendant's statements. The plaintiff must also show actual damages arising from the untrue statements.

As an example of injurious falsehood, consider the potential harm to Procter and Gamble of the assertions that associated its former logo of moon and stars with satanism. The company threatened to sue a number of individuals. In another instance Warnaco sued Calvin Klein, alleging that Klein had made publicly disparaging remarks about how Warnaco made Calvin Klein clothing under license. The lawsuit alleged that Klein "falsely accused [Warnaco] of effectively 'counterfeiting' Calvin Klein apparel."

Intentional Interference with Contractual Relations A second type of business tort is **intentional interference with contractual relations.** Probably the most common example of this tort involves one company raiding another for employees. If employees are under contract to an employer for a period of time, another employer cannot induce them to break their contracts. In a variation on this tort, the brokerage firm PaineWebber Group sued Morgan Stanley Dean Witter & Company over PaineWebber's merger agreement with J. P. Bradford & Company. PaineWebber claimed that Morgan Stanley pursued "a carefully planned, broadbased campaign to raid Bradford personnel and interfere with the merger agreement between PaineWebber and Bradford."

One of the most famous tort cases in history involved interference with a contract of merger. In that case a jury awarded Pennzoil over $10 billion against Texaco for persuading Getty Oil to breach an agreement of merger with Pennzoil. After Texaco filed for bankruptcy, Pennzoil accepted a settlement of around $3 billion.

NEGLIGENCE

The second major area of tort liability involves unreasonable behavior that causes injury. This area of tort is called **negligence.** In the United States more lawsuits allege negligence than any other single cause of action.

Negligence takes place when one who has a duty to act reasonably acts carelessly and causes injury to another. Actually, five separate elements make up negligence, and the following sections discuss these elements. The table "Elements of Negligence" also summarizes them. In business, negligence can occur when employees cause injury to customers or others, when those invited to a business are injured because the business fails to protect them, when products are not carefully manufactured, when services, such as accounting services, are not carefully provided, and in many other situations.

10. DUTY OF CARE

A critical element of the negligence tort is **duty.** Without a duty to another person, one does not owe that person reasonable care. Accidental injuries occur daily for which people other than the victim have no responsibility, legally or otherwise.

Duty usually arises out of a person's conduct or activity. A person doing something has a duty to use reasonable care and skill around others to avoid injuring them. Whether one is driving a car or manufacturing a product, she or he has a duty not to injure others by unreasonable conduct.

Usually, a person has no duty to avoid injuring others through *nonconduct.* There is no general duty requiring a sunbather at the beach to warn a would-be surfer that a great white shark is lurking offshore, even if the sunbather has seen the fin. There is moral responsibility but no legal duty present.

When there is a special relationship between persons, the situation changes. A person in a special relationship to another may have a duty to avoid unreasonable nonconduct. A business renting surfboards at the beach would probably be liable for renting a board to a customer who was attacked by a shark if it knew the shark was nearby and failed to warn the customer. The special business relationship between the two parties creates a duty to take action and makes the business liable for its unreasonable nonconduct.

Elements of Negligence

Existence of a duty of care owed by the defendant to the plaintiff

Unreasonable behavior by the defendant that breaches the duty

Causation in fact

Proximate causation

An actual injury

In recent years, negligence cases against businesses for nonconduct have grown dramatically. Most of these cases have involved failure to protect customers from crimes. The National Crime Prevention Institute estimates that such cases have increased tenfold since the mid-1970s.

One famous case involved the Tailhook scandal. A group of male naval aviators was sexually groping female guests as they walked down the hallway at a Hilton hotel. (Remember that an unconsented-to touching is an intentional tort.) One of the females who was sexually touched sued the Hilton hotel for negligence in knowing of the aviators' behavior and failing to protect her. A jury awarded her a total of $6.7 million against Hilton.

The extent of a business's duty to protect customers is still evolving. Note that in the following case the New Hampshire Supreme Court says that the defendant restaurant has no special relationship to the plaintiff, but still rules that it may have a duty to protect restaurant customers.

IANNELLI V. BURGER KING CORP.

200 N. H. LEXIS 42 (N. H. SUP. CT. 2000)

McHUGH, J.: The plaintiffs, Nicholas and Jodiann Iannelli, individually and on behalf of their three children, brought a negligence action against the defendant, Burger King Corporation, for injuries sustained as a result of an assault at the defendant's restaurant. During the late afternoon or early evening hours of December 26, 1995, the Iannelli family went to the defendant's restaurant for the first time. Upon entering the restaurant, the Iannellis became aware of a group of teenagers consisting of five males and two females, whom they alleged were rowdy, obnoxious, loud, abusive, and using foul language. Some in the group claimed they were "hammered." Initially this group was near the ordering counter talking to an employee whom they appeared to know. The Iannellis alleged that one of the group almost bumped into Nicholas. When that fact was pointed out, the teenager exclaimed, "I don't give an F. That's his F'ing problem."

Nicholas asked his wife and children to sit down in the dining area as he ordered the food. While waiting for the food to be prepared, Nicholas joined his family at their table. The teenagers also moved into the dining area to another table. The obnoxious behavior and foul language allegedly continued. One of the Iannelli children became nervous. Nicholas then walked over to the group intending to ask them to stop swearing. As Nicholas stood two or three feet from the closest of the group, he said, "Guys, hey listen, I have three kids." Whereupon, allegedly unprovoked, one or more of the group assaulted Nicholas by hitting him, knocking him to the ground and striking him in the head with a chair.

The plaintiffs argue that a commercial enterprise such as a restaurant has a general duty to exercise reasonable care toward its patrons, which may include a duty to safeguard against assault when circumstances provide warning signs that the safety of its patrons may be at risk. The most instructive case, given the issues presented, is *Walls v. Oxford Management Co.* In *Walls,* a tenant of an apartment complex alleged that the owner's negligent maintenance of its property allowed her to be subjected to a sexual assault in the parking lot. We held that as a general principle landlords have no duty to protect tenants from criminal attacks. Inasmuch as landlords and tenants have a special relationship that does not exist between a commercial establishment and its guests, it follows that the same general principle of law extends to restaurants and their patrons. We recognized in *Walls,* however, that particular circumstances can give rise to such a duty.

[CONTINUED]

These circumstances include when the opportunity for criminal misconduct is brought about by the actions or inactions of the owner or where overriding foreseeability of such criminal activity exists.

Viewing the evidence in the light most favorable to the plaintiffs, we must decide whether the behavior of the rowdy youths could have created an unreasonable risk of injury to restaurant patrons that was foreseeable to the defendant. If the risk of injury was reasonably foreseeable, then a duty existed. We hold that the teenagers' unruly behavior could reasonably have been anticipated to escalate into acts that would expose patrons to an unreasonable risk of injury. The exact occurrence or precise injuries need not have been foreseen.

Viewed in a light most favorable to the plaintiffs, the evidence could support a finding that the teenagers' obnoxious behavior in the restaurant was open and notorious. Because the group was engaging in a conversation at times with a restaurant employee, it could be found that the defendant was aware of the teenagers' conduct. The near physical contact between one teenager and Nicholas Iannelli at the counter and the indifference expressed by the group member thereafter could be deemed sufficient warning to the restaurant manager of misconduct such that it was incumbent upon him to take affirmative action to reduce the risk of injury. The plaintiffs allege that at least one other restaurant patron expressed disgust with the group's actions prior to the assault. The manager could have warned the group about their behavior or summoned the police if his warnings were not heeded.

In summary, the trial court's ruling that as a matter of law the defendant owed no duty to the plaintiffs to protect them from the assault was error. While as a general principle no such duty exists, here it could be found that the teenagers' behavior in the restaurant created a foreseeable risk of harm that the defendant unreasonably failed to alleviate. Accordingly, we **reverse and remand.**

CASE QUESTIONS

1. Under the decision in this case, when does a duty arise for the defendant restaurant to protect its customers?

2. What does the court suggest that the restaurant manager should have done in this case that would have satisfied the duty?

3. What do you think is the difference in this case between a "special relationship" duty and the duty of the restaurant?

Note that the duty to act reasonably also applies to professional providers, like doctors, lawyers, CPAs, architects, engineers, and others. In most negligence cases, however, the standard of reasonableness is that of a *reasonable person*. In negligence cases involving professionals, the negligence standard applied is that of the *reasonable professional*. The negligence of professionals is called *malpractice*. As the box "Medical Malpractice Crisis" suggests, professional negligence is a controversial area of tort law.

11. UNREASONABLE BEHAVIOR—BREACH OF DUTY

At the core of negligence is the unreasonable behavior that breaches the duty of care that the defendant owes to the plaintiff. The problem is how do we separate reasonable behavior that causes accidental injury from unreasonable behavior that causes injury? Usually a jury determines this issue, but negligence is a mixed question of law and fact. Despite the trend for judges to let juries decide what the

MEDICAL MALPRACTICE CRISIS

Few people would disagree that physicians are extremely unhappy about the rapidly growing insurance premiums they have to pay. Some physicians have gone on strike; others have left the practice of medicine. The exact causes of the situation, however, are difficult to determine. Consider the following and make your own evaluation.

- Some states have capped pain and suffering awards and punitive damages in medical malpractice cases. Insurance premiums have risen almost as rapidly in those states as in states without such caps.
- When adjusted for the inflation in medical costs, the size of average medical malpractice awards has not

grown in the last 10 years. Malpractice payouts by physicians and their insurers accounts for less than 10 percent of health care costs.

- In 2001, only about 5 percent of malpractice payouts amounted to $1 million or more.
- A relatively small number of physicians account for the majority of medical malpractice payouts. Between 1990–2002, 5 percent of physicians accounted for 54 percent of malpractice payouts.
- Between 1997–2001, a study of 17 states shows an increase of 5 percent in the number of malpractice claims filed.

Sources: *Business Week;* Department of Health and Human Services.

standard of reasonable care is, judges also continue to be involved in the definition of negligence. A well-known definition by Judge Learned Hand states that negligence is determined by "the likelihood that the defendant's conduct will injure others, taken with the seriousness of the injury if it happens, and balanced against the interest which he must sacrifice to avoid the risk."

Failure to exercise reasonable care can cost a company substantial sums. In one instance the licensed owner of a National Car Rental agency in Indianapolis was ordered to pay $5.5 million to a man who slipped on the floor and broke his hip. To save overtime pay the rental agency had had its floors mopped during, instead of after, normal working hours. Unaware that someone was mopping the floors behind him, the plaintiff had stepped backwards, slipped, and fallen on the wet floor.

In another case arising from unreasonable behavior, Wal-Mart Stores agreed to pay two young girls a settlement of up to $16 million. A store employee had sold the girls' father a shotgun used to kill their mother in spite of the fact that a federal form filled out by the buyer indicated that he was under a restraining order. Federal law bars those under restraining orders from purchasing guns.

A special type of aggravated negligence is **willful and wanton negligence.** Although this does not reveal intent, it does show an extreme lack of due care. Negligent injuries inflicted by drunk drivers show willful and wanton negligence. The significance of this type of negligence is that the injured plaintiff can recover punitive damages as well as actual damages. For example, following the *Exxon Valdez* oil spill in Alaska, commercial fishers sued Exxon for damage to their livelihoods. A jury awarded substantial actual and punitive damages when it found that Exxon was willful and wanton in allowing the ship captain to be in charge of the ship when they knew he was an alcoholic.

12. CAUSATION IN FACT

Before a person is liable to another for negligent injury, the person's failure to use reasonable care must actually have "caused" the injury. This observation is not so obvious as it first appears. A motorist stops by the roadside to change a tire. Another motorist drives past carelessly and sideswipes the first as he changes the tire. What caused the accident? Was it the inattention of the second motorist or the fact that the first motorist had a flat tire? Did the argument the second motorist had with her boss before getting in the car cause the accident, or was it the decision of the first motorist to visit one more client that afternoon? In a real sense, all these things caused the accident. Chains of causation stretch out infinitely.

Still, in a negligence suit the plaintiff must prove that the defendant actually caused the injury. The courts term this **cause in fact.** In light of the many possible ways to attribute accident causation, how do courts determine if a plaintiff's lack of care, in fact, caused a certain injury? They do so very practically. Courts leave questions of cause in fact almost entirely to juries as long as the evidence reveals that a defendant's alleged carelessness could have been a substantial, material factor in bringing about an injury. Juries then make judgments about whether a defendant's behavior in fact caused the harm.

A particular problem of causation arises where the carelessness of two or more tortfeasors contributes to cause the plaintiff's injury, as when two persons are wrestling over control of the car which strikes the plaintiff. Tort law handles such cases by making each tortfeasor *jointly and severally* liable for the entire judgment. The plaintiff can recover only the amount of the judgment, but she or he may recover it wholly from either of the tortfeasors or get a portion of the judgment from each.

13. PROXIMATE CAUSATION

It is not enough that a plaintiff suing for negligence prove that the defendant caused an injury in fact. The plaintiff also must establish proximate causation. **Proximate cause** is, perhaps, more accurately termed *legal cause.* It represents the proposition that those engaged in activity are legally liable only for the *foreseeable* risk that they cause.

Defining proximate causation in terms of foreseeable risk creates further problems about the meaning of the word "foreseeable." In its application, foreseeability has come to mean that the plaintiff must have been one whom the defendant could reasonably expect to be injured by a negligent act. For example, it is reasonable to expect, thus foreseeable, that a collapsing hotel walkway should injure those on or under it. But many courts would rule as unforeseeable that someone a block away, startled upon hearing the loud crash of the walkway, should trip and stumble into the path of an oncoming car. The court would likely dismiss that person's complaint against the hotel as failing to show proximate causation.

Another application of proximate cause doctrine requires the injury to be caused *directly* by the defendant's negligence. Causes of injury that intervene between the defendant's negligence and the plaintiff's injury can destroy the necessary proximate causation. Some courts, for instance, would hold that it is not foreseeable that an owner's negligence in leaving keys in a parked car should result in an intoxicated thief who steals the car, crashing and injuring another motorist. These courts would dismiss for lack of proximate cause a case brought by the motorist against the car's owner.

14. DEFENSES TO NEGLIGENCE

There are two principal defenses to an allegation of negligence: contributory negligence and assumption of risk. Both these defenses are *affirmative defenses,* which means that the defendant must specifically raise these defenses to take advantage of them. When properly raised and proved, these defenses limit or bar the plaintiff's recovery against the defendant. The defenses are valid even though the defendant has actually been negligent.

Contributory Negligence As originally applied, the **contributory negligence** defense absolutely barred the plaintiff from recovery if the plaintiff's own fault contributed to the injury "in any degree, however slight." The trend today, however, in the great majority of states is to offset the harsh rule of contributory negligence with the doctrine of **comparative responsibility** (also called *comparative negligence* and *comparative fault*). Under comparative principles, the plaintiff's contributory negligence does not bar recovery. It merely compares the plaintiff's fault with the defendant's and reduces the damage award proportionally. For example, a jury determined damages at $3.1 million for an Atlanta plaintiff who was run over and dragged by a bus. But the jury then reduced the damage award by 20 percent ($620,000) on the basis that the plaintiff contributed to his own injury by failing reasonably to look out for his own safety in an area where buses come and go.

Adoption of the comparative negligence principle seems to lead to more frequent and larger awards for plaintiffs. This was the conclusion of a study by the Illinois Insurance Information Service for the year following that state's adoption of comparative negligence.

Assumption of Risk If contributory negligence involves failure to use proper care for one's own safety, the **assumption-of-the-risk** defense arises from the plaintiff's knowing and willing undertaking of an activity made dangerous by the negligence of another. When professional hockey first came to this country, many spectators injured by flying hockey pucks sued and recovered for negligence. But as time went on and spectators came to realize that attending a hockey game meant that one might occasionally be exposed to flying hockey pucks, courts began to allow the defendant owners of hockey teams to assert that injured spectators had assumed the risk of injury from a speeding puck.

Assumption of the risk may be implied from the circumstances, or it can arise from an express agreement. Many businesses attempt to relieve themselves of potential liability by having employees or customers agree contractually not to sue for negligence, that is, to assume the risk. Some of these contractual agreements are legally enforceable, but many will be struck down by the courts as being against public policy, especially where a business possesses a vastly more powerful bargaining position than does its employee or customer.

It is important to a successful assumption-of-the-risk defense that the assumption was voluntary. Entering a hockey arena while knowing the risk of flying pucks is a voluntary assumption of the risk. Courts have often ruled, however, that people who imperil themselves while attempting to rescue their own or others' property from a risk created by the defendant have not assumed the risk voluntarily. A plaintiff who is injured while attempting to save his possessions from a fire negligently caused by the defendant is not subject to the assumption-of-the-risk defense.

---

concept SUMMARY   *Plaintiff v. Defendant in Negligence*

Plaintiff Must Prove:	**Defendant May Prove**
Duty of care owed by defendant to plaintiff	Plaintiff's behavior contributed to injury (contributory negligence)
Unreasonable behavior by defendant is a breach of the duty	Plaintiff assumed risk
Defendant's breach in fact caused injury	
Injury was foreseeable given defendant's actions (proximate causation)	
Injury actually occurred	

STRICT LIABILITY IN TORT

Strict liability is a catchall phrase for the legal responsibility for injury-causing behavior that is neither intentional nor negligent. There are various types of strict liability torts, some of which are more "strict" than others. What ties them together is that they all impose legal liability, regardless of the intent or fault of the defendant. The next sections discuss these torts and tort doctrines.

15. STRICT PRODUCTS LIABILITY

A major type of strict tort liability is **strict products liability,** for the commercial sale of defective products. In most states any retail, wholesale, or manufacturing seller who sells an unreasonably dangerous defective product that causes injury to a user of the product is strictly liable. For example, if a forklift you are using at work malfunctions because of defective brakes and you run off the edge of the loading dock and are injured, you can sue the retailer, wholesaler, and manufacturer of the product for strict liability. The fact that the retailer and wholesaler may have been perfectly careful in selling the product does not matter. They are strictly liable.

Strict products liability applies only to "commercial" sellers, those who normally sell products like the one causing injury, or who place them in the stream of commerce. Included as commercial sellers are the retailer, wholesaler, and manufacturer of a product, but also included are suppliers of defective parts and companies that assemble a defective product. Not included as a commercial seller is your next door neighbor who sells you her defective lawnmower. The neighbor may be negligent, for instance, if she knew of the defect that caused you injury and forgot to warn you about it, but she cannot be held strictly liable.

An important concept in strict products liability is that of "defect." Strict liability only applies to the sale of unreasonably dangerous *defective* products. There are two kinds of defects. **Production defects** arise when products are not manufactured to a manufacturer's own standards. Defective brakes on a new car are a good example of a production defect. Another example involves Weyerhaeuser Company setting aside $82 million to settle claims regarding its hardboard siding, which did not last as long as it was supposed to. **Design defects** occur when a product is manufactured according to the manufacturer's standards, but the product injures a user due to its unsafe design. Lawsuits based on design defects are common but often very controversial. Recent such lawsuits have included one against Ford that claimed Ford should have designed its vans to have a heat-venting system so children accidentally locked in the vans would be safe. Numerous design lawsuits have been filed against gun manufacturers, arguing that guns without trigger locks are defective. Lack of adequate warnings concerning inherently dangerous products can also be considered a design defect. American Home Products recently settled a wrongful death lawsuit for an estimated $10 million. The lawsuit alleged that the company had not adequately warned users of its diet drug about the risks of hypertension, which had been linked to diet-drug use.

In practice, strict products liability is useful in protecting those who suffer personal injury or property damage. It does not protect businesses that have economic losses due to defective products. For instance, a warehouse that loses profits because its defective forklift will not run cannot recover those lost profits under strict products liability. The warehouse would have to sue for breach of contract. However, if the forklift defect causes injury to a worker, the worker can successfully sue the forklift manufacturer for strict products liability.

Under strict products liability, contributory negligence is not a defense but assumption of the risk is. The assumption of the risk defense helped protect tobacco manufacturers from health injury liability for many years. Misuse is another defense that defendants commonly raise in product liability cases. Removing safety guards from equipment is a common basis for the misuse defense. Defendants have also argued that if a product meets some federally required standard, it cannot be considered defective. Most courts, however, have ruled that federal standards only set a minimum requirement for safe design and that meeting federal standards does not automatically keep a manufacturer from being sued for strict products liability.

In recent years some states have changed or modified the rules of products liability. See the box "Tort Reform."

TORT REFORM

The rapid growth of products litigation during the past two decades has brought forth many calls for "tort reform." A number of states have changed their laws to modify the tort doctrines discussed in this section and chapter. At the federal level, comprehensive tort reform has been strongly advocated although it has not passed as of this writing. Some of the tort reforms proposed or passed by the states include:

- Permitting only negligence actions against retailers and wholesalers unless the product manufacturer is insolvent.
- Eliminating strict liability recovery for defective product design.
- Barring products liability claims against sellers if products have been altered or modified by a user.
- Providing for the presumption of reasonableness defense in product design cases in which the product meets the **state-of-the-art;** that is, the prevailing industry standards at the time of product manufacture.
- Creating a **statute of repose** that would specify a period (such as 25 years) following product sale after which plaintiffs would lose their rights to bring suits for product-related injuries.
- Reducing or eliminating punitive damage awards in most product liability cases.

Importantly, note that not all, or even most, of these reforms have been adopted by every state.

16. RESPONDEAT SUPERIOR

Any time an employee is liable for tortious acts in the *scope of employment,* the employer is also liable. This is because of the tort doctrine of **respondeat superior** ("let the master reply").

The reason for respondeat superior is that the employee is advancing the interests of the employer when the tortious act occurs. If the employee were not doing the work, the employer would have to do it. Therefore, the employer is just as liable as the employee when the employee acts tortiously in carrying out the work. In a sense, the employer has set the employee in motion and is responsible for the employee's acts.

Most respondeat superior cases involve employee negligence. Note, however, that the employer is strictly liable once the employee's fault is established. And it does not matter that the employer warned the employee against the tortious behavior. Because Mary's employer told her to be careful while delivering pizzas does not prevent it from being liable when Mary runs a red light and has an accident.

Some respondeat superior cases involve an employee's intentional tort. If a store's service representative strikes a customer during an argument over the return of merchandise, the store will be liable under respondeat superior. But if the argument concerns football instead of the return of merchandise, the store will not be liable. The difference is that the argument over football is not within the scope of employment.

Usually, the only defense the employer has to the strict liability of respondeat superior is that the employee was outside the scope of employment. Sometimes this defense is made using the language **frolic and detour.** An employee who is on a frolic or detour is no longer acting for the employer. If Mary has delivered her employer's pizzas and is driving to see a friend when an accident occurs, the employer is not liable.

An employer who must pay for an employee's tort under respondeat superior may legally sue the employee for reimbursement. In practice, this seldom happens because the employer carries insurance. Occasionally, an insurer who has paid a respondeat superior claim will sue the employee who caused the claim.

17. ULTRAHAZARDOUS ACTIVITY

In most states, the courts impose strict liability in tort for types of activities they call *ultrahazardous.* Transporting and using explosives and poisons fall under this category, as does keeping dangerous wild animals. Injuries caused from artificial storage of large quantities of liquid can also bring strict liability on the one who stores. For an example of the dangers of ultrahazardous activity, see the box "The Great Molasses Flood."

18. OTHER STRICT LIABILITY TORTS

The majority of states impose strict liability upon tavern owners for injuries to third parties caused by their intoxicated patrons. The acts imposing this liability are called **dram shop acts.** Because of the public attention given in recent years to intoxicated drivers, there has been a tremendous increase in dram shop act cases.

Common carriers, transportation companies licensed to serve the public, are also strictly liable for damage to goods being transported by them. Common carriers, however, can limit their liability in certain instances through contractual agreement, and they are not liable for (1) acts of God, such as natural catastrophes; (2) action of an alien enemy; (3) order of public authority, such as authorities of

THE GREAT MOLASSES FLOOD

The Purity Distilling Co. had filled the enormous steel tank on the Boston hillside with two million gallons of molasses to be turned into rum. Unusually warm weather caused the molasses to expand. On January 15, 1919, with sounds like gunfire as the restraining bolts sheared, the tank exploded. A wave of hot molasses 30-feet high raced down the street toward Boston Harbor, faster than people could run, engulfing entire buildings.

Before it subsided, 150 people were injured and 21 drowned. "The dead," reported the *Boston Herald,* "were like candy statues."

It took months to clean up the harbor. It took six years to resolve the 125 lawsuits that followed. The artificial storage of large quantities of liquid can be a sticky matter indeed.

Source: Anthony V. Riccio, *Portrait of an Italian-American Neighborhood* (1998).

one state barring potentially diseased fruit shipments from another state from entering their state; (4) the inherent nature of the goods, such as perishable vegetables; and (5) misconduct of the shipper, such as improper packaging.

DAMAGES

One legal scholar concludes that "the crucial controversy in personal injury torts today" is in the area of damages. This is because the average personal injury award has been increasing at nearly double the rate of inflation. For dramatic examples of the size of awards in some recent cases, examine "Highest Jury Tort Awards of 2002." The size of damage awards is largely determined by juries, but judges also play a role in damages, especially in damage instructions to the jury and in deciding whether to approve substantial damage awards.

19. COMPENSATORY DAMAGES

Most damages awarded in tort cases compensate the plaintiff for injuries suffered. The purpose of damages is to make the plaintiff whole again, at least financially. There are three major types of loss that potentially follow tort injury and are called **compensatory damages.** They are:

- Past and future medical expenses
- Past and future economic loss (including property damage and loss of earning power)
- Past and future pain and suffering

Compensatory damages may also be awarded for loss of limb, loss of consortium (the marriage relationship), and mental distress.

Calculation of damage awards creates significant problems. Juries frequently use state-adopted life expectancy tables and present-value discount tables to help them determine the amount of damages to award. But uncertainty about the life expectancy of injured plaintiffs and the impact of inflation often makes these tables misleading. Also, awarding damages for pain and suffering is an art rather than a science. These awards measure jury sympathy as much as they calculate compensation for any financial loss. The recent dramatic increases in the size of damage awards helps underline the problems in their calculation. One result is that many individuals and businesses are underinsured for major tort liability.

Highest Jury Tort Awards of 2002

Defendant	Event Causing Injury	Jury Award in Millions of Dollars
1. Philip Morris	Cigarettes causing lung cancer	$28,000[a]
2. Courtney Pharmacy	Pharmacist diluted cancer drugs of purchaser	2,200[b]
3. Equitable Resources	Gas explosion in home causes man severe burn	270[c]
4. Ford Motor Co.	Crushed roof in pickup truck rollover killed two	225
5. Philip Morris	Death of woman who smoked low-tar cigarettes	150[d]
6. General Motors	Collapse of passenger compartment in crash causes boy brain damage	122
7. BR Telephony	Plaintiff claimed defendant investment firm drove his company to bankruptcy	97.2[e]
8. St. John's Episcopal Hospital	Malpractice for failure to give proper drugs to baby with cerebral palsy	94.5
9. McCally	Malpractice for failure to diagnose patient's medical condition	91
10. General Motors	Car hit tree after jamming in reverse; injured woman	80

Note how jury awards are often not the final result in a case.

[a] Judge reduced jury award to $28 million.

[b] None of this award appears collectible. The pharmacist defrauded thousands of cancer victims and is serving a 30-year prison term.

[c] After the award, the parties settled for less to avoid appeal.

[d] Judge reduced the award to $100 million, but the defendant is still appealing.

[e] Judge overturned this award and the plaintiff is appealing.

Currently, compensatory damage awards for pain and suffering are very controversial. How do you compensate injured plaintiffs for something like pain which has no market value? Many plaintiffs suffer lifelong pain or the permanent loss of vision, hearing, or mobility. No amount of damages seems large enough to compensate them, yet no amount of damages, however high, will cause their pain and suffering to stop. In 2003, President Bush called for the limitation of tort damages for pain and suffering in a case to $250,000 per person. Do you agree or disagree?

20. PUNITIVE DAMAGES

Compensatory damages are not the only kind of damages. There are also **punitive damages.** By awarding punitive damages, courts or juries punish defendants for committing intentional torts and for negligent behavior considered "gross" or "willful and wanton." The key to the award of punitive damages is the defendant's motive. Usually the motive must be "malicious," "fraudulent," or "evil." Increasingly, punitive damages are also awarded for dangerously negligent conduct that shows a conscious disregard for the interests of others. These damages punish those who commit aggravated torts and act to deter future wrongdoing. Because they make an example out of the defendant, punitive damages are sometimes called *exemplary damages.*

Presently, there is much controversy about how appropriate it is to award punitive damages against corporations for their economic activities. Especially when companies fail to warn of known danger created by their activities, or when cost-benefit decisions are made at the risk of substantial human injury, courts are upholding substantial punitive damage awards against companies. Yet consider that

PUNITIVE DAMAGE GUIDELINES

In 2003 the Supreme Court determined that $145 million in punitive damages in a case was unconstitutional. In *State Farm v. Campbell* (see Chapter 6), the Court decided that the large difference between punitive and compensatory damages violated due process. The Court suggested that a single-digit ratio of punitive to compensatory damages (9/1 or less) would be more constitutionally appropriate than a 145/1 ratio.

State Farm v. Campbell also reaffirmed general punitive damage guidelines from an earlier case. The Court stated in evaluating the appropriateness of punitive damages, that courts should consider:

- "the responsibility of the defendant's conduct (how bad it was),
- the ratio of punitive to actual damages
- how the punitive damages compare with criminal or civil penalties for the same conduct."

Note that juries award punitive damages in only about 2 percent of litigated cases.

---

these damages are a windfall to the injured plaintiff who has already received compensatory damages. And instead of punishing guilty management for wrongdoing, punitive damages may end up punishing innocent shareholders by reducing their dividends.

Many court decisions also overlook a very important consideration about punitive damages. Most companies carry liability insurance policies that reimburse them for "all sums which the insured might become legally obligated to pay." This includes reimbursement for punitive damages. Instead of punishing guilty companies, punitive damages may punish other companies, which have to pay increased insurance premiums, and may punish consumers, who ultimately pay higher prices. As a matter of public policy, several states prohibit insurance from covering punitive damages, but the great majority of states permit such coverage. This fact severely undermines arguments for awarding punitive damages against companies for their economic activities.

Consider also that an award of punitive damages greatly resembles a criminal fine. Yet the defendant who is subject to these criminal-type damages lacks the right to be indicted by a grand jury and cannot assert the right against self-incrimination. In addition, the defendant is subject to a lower standard of proof than in a criminal case. However, defendants in tort suits have challenged awards of punitive damages on a constitutional basis. See the box "Punitive Damage Guidelines."

Finally, note that the United States is the only country in the world where punitive damages are regularly awarded.

ALTERNATIVES TO THE TORT SYSTEM

Of common law origin, the tort system has developed slowly over several centuries. Today, the tort system has come under much criticism because of aspects of its development. The **contingency fee,** which permits a plaintiff to sue without first having to pay an attorney, encourages litigation. Others see litigation as promoted by the fact that even if a plaintiff loses a tort action, the plaintiff does not have to reimburse the defendant's often substantial legal expenses. Apprehension about the easy availability of punitive damages and general concern over the role of the civil jury in handing down large damage awards are also directed at the tort system.

Perhaps the most important problem of the tort system, however, is that it is rarely a cost-effective way of compensating those who are injured by others. For example, the Rand Corporation estimates that only 40 to 60 percent of the insurance dollars paid out due to tort litigation go to injured plaintiffs. Litigation expenses, including legal fees, consume the rest.

There are many alternatives to tort litigation. Arbitration (discussed in Chapter 4) is an important one. No-fault insurance, like that found in many states' automobile liability plans, is another. Workers' compensation acts are a third alternative. Because of their importance to the business community, the next section focuses on this alternative. As you read about workers' compensation, consider if it would be possible to apply some variation of workers' compensation to tort situations that do not involve the employer-employee relationship.

21. WORKERS' COMPENSATION ACTS

Around the turn of the century, the tort system was largely replaced in the workplace by a series of workers' compensation acts. These statutes were enacted at both the state and federal level, and they imposed a type of strict liability on employers for accidental workplace injuries suffered by their employees. The clear purpose of these statues was to remove financial losses of injury from workers and redistribute them onto employers and ultimately onto society.

History **Workers' compensation** laws are state statutes designed to protect employees and their families from the risks of accidental injury, death, or disease resulting from their employment. They were passed because the common law did not give adequate protection to employees from the hazards of their work. At common law, anyone was liable in tort for damages resulting from injuries caused to another as a proximate result of negligence. If an employer acted unreasonably and his or her carelessness was the proximate cause of physical injury suffered by an employee, the latter could sue and recover damages from the employer. However, the common law also provided the employer with the means of escaping this tort liability in most cases through three defenses:

- Assumption of the risk
- Contributory negligence
- The fellow-servant rule

For example, assume that employer E knowingly instructed workers to operate dangerous machinery not equipped with any safety devices, even though it realized injury to them was likely. W, a worker, had his arm mangled when it was caught in the gears of one of these machines. Even though E was negligent in permitting this hazardous condition to persist, if W were aware of the dangers that existed, he would be unable to recover damages because he knowingly *assumed the risk* of his injury. In addition, if the injury were caused by *contributory negligence* of the employee as well as the negligence of the employer, the action was defeated. And if the injury occurred because of the negligence of another employee, the negligent employee, rather than the employer, was liable because of the *fellow-servant rule.*

The English Parliament passed a workers' compensation statute in 1897. Today all states have such legislation, modeled to a greater or lesser degree on the English act. These laws vary a great deal from state to state as to the industries subject to them, the employees they cover, the nature of the injuries or diseases that are compensable, the rates of compensation, and the means of administration. In spite of wide variances in the laws of the states in this area, certain general observations can be made about them.

The System   State workers' compensation statutes provide a system to pay workers or their families if the worker is accidentally killed or injured or incurs an occupational disease while employed. To be compensable, the death, illness, or injury must arise out of and in the course of the employment. Under these acts, the negligence or fault of the employer in causing an on-the-job injury is not an issue. Instead, these laws recognize the fact of life that a certain number of injuries, deaths, and diseases are bound to occur in a modern industrial society as a result of the attempts of businesses and their employees to provide the goods and services demanded by the consuming public.

This view leads to the conclusion that it is fairer for the consuming public to bear the cost of such mishaps rather than to impose it on injured workers. Workers' compensation laws create strict liability for employers of accidentally injured workers. Liability exists regardless of lack of negligence or fault, provided the necessary association between the injuries and the business of the employer is present. The three defenses the employer had at common law are eliminated. The employers, treating the costs of these injuries as part of the costs of production, pass them on to the consumers who created the demand for the product or service being furnished.

Workers' compensation acts give covered employees the right to certain cash payments for their loss of income due to accidental, on-the-job injuries. In the event of a married employee's death, benefits are provided for the surviving spouse and minor children. The amount of such awards usually is subject to a stated maximum and is calculated by using a percentage of the wages of the employee. If the employee suffers permanent, partial disability, most states provide compensation both for injuries that are scheduled in the statute and those that are nonscheduled. As an example of the former, a worker who loses a hand might be awarded 100 weeks of compensation at $95 per week. Besides scheduling specific compensation for certain specific injuries, most acts also provide compensation for nonscheduled ones based upon the earning power the employee lost due to his or her injury. In addition to the above payments, all statutes provide for medical benefits.

In some states, employers have a choice of covering their workers' compensation risk with insurance or of being self-insured (that is, paying all claims directly) if they can demonstrate their capability to do so. Approximately 20 percent of compensation benefits are paid by self-insurers. In other states, employers pay into a state fund used to compensate workers entitled to benefits. In these states, the amounts of the payments are based on the size of the payroll and the experience of the employer in having claims filed against the system by its employees.

Workers' compensation laws are usually administered exclusively by an administrative agency called the industrial commission or board, which has quasi-judicial powers. Of course, the ruling of such boards is subject to review by the courts of the jurisdiction in the same manner as the actions of other administrative agencies.

Tests for Determining Compensation   The tests for determining whether an employer must pay workers' compensation to an employee are simply:

1. Was the injury accidental?
2. Did the injury arise out of and in the course of employment?

Because workers' compensation laws benefit workers, courts interpret them liberally to favor workers.

In recent years, cases have tended to expand employers' liability. For instance, courts have held that heart attacks (as well as other common ailments in which the employee has had either a preexisting disease or a physical condition likely to lead to the disease) are compensable as "accidental injuries." One ruling approved an award to a purchasing agent who became mentally ill because she was exposed to unusual work, stresses, and strains. Her "nerve-racking" job involved a business whose sales grew over sixfold in 10 years. Factors contributing to her "accidental injury" included harsh criticism by her supervisor, long hours of work, and inability to take vacations because of the requirements of her position.

In the following case, the South Carolina Supreme Court gives a broad meaning to the requirement "injury by accident."

PEE v. AUM, INC.

573 S. E. 2D 785 (2002)

MOORE, J.: . . . Respondent (Claimant) was awarded workers' compensation benefits for disability from carpal tunnel syndrome resulting from repetitive trauma to both wrists. Petitioners (Employer) appealed. The circuit court and the Court of Appeals affirmed. The only issue is whether a repetitive trauma injury is compensable under the South Carolina Workers' Compensation Act. We find it is and affirm.

Claimant worked for Employer in various capacities beginning in 1987. Each of her jobs involved the repetitive use of her hands. In the spring of 1995 she began experiencing tingling and numbness in both hands. On April 25, 1995, she was diagnosed with moderately severe carpal tunnel syndrome caused by compression of the median nerve as it passes through the carpal tunnel in the wrist. The evidence is uncontradicted that claimant's injury is work-related.

After surgery in June 1995, Claimant's left wrist improved temporarily but her symptoms returned within six months. Claimant's treating doctor removed her from work beginning April 20, 1996. By May 1996, she had severe carpal tunnel syndrome in her right wrist. Surgery was recommended for her right wrist in October 1996 with no guarantee of relief from her symptoms.

Meanwhile, on July 21, 1996, Claimant filed this action claiming benefits for an on-the-job injury.

Claimant was awarded temporary total benefits continuing until she reaches maximum medical improvement.

The circuit court and the Court of Appeals held a repetitive trauma injury is compensable as an "injury by accident" as provided in the Workers' Compensation Act. Employer contends a repetitive trauma injury does not qualify as an "injury by accident" because the cause of the injury is not unexpected and the injury lacks definiteness of time.

1. Unexpectedness

Employer contends the repetitive event which causes a repetitive trauma injury is not unexpected but is part of the worker's normal work activity. Because the event causing the injury is not unexpected, Employer argues repetitive trauma injury cannot be compensable as an injury by accident.

Under the Act, a claimant is entitled to an "injury by accident arising out of and in the course of employment." In *Layton v. Hammond-Brown-Jennings Co.,* we interpreted for the first time the meaning of "injury by accident" under the newly enacted Workman's Compensation Act. We noted that two lines of cases had evolved in other jurisdictions: some jurisdictions, including North Carolina upon which our Act is modeled, held there must be some unusual or

[CONTINUED]

unlooked-for mishap resulting in injury to constitute an accident; other jurisdictions held no mishap was required for an accident as long as there was an unexpected injury occurring while the employee was performing his usual duties in his customary manner. We chose the latter definition, focusing on the unexpected nature of the injury rather than requiring that the event causing the injury be unexpected. This definition of accident as an unexpected injury has been reiterated in a long line of cases.

As we more recently stated, "in determining whether something constitutes an injury by accident the focus is not on some specific event, but rather on the injury itself." Further, an injury is unexpected if the worker did not intend it or expect it would result from what he was doing. Therefore, if an injury is unexpected from the worker's point of view, it qualifies as an injury by accident. Here, there is no evidence Claimant intended or expected to be injured as a result of her repetitive work activity.

Employer's contention that the cause of the injury must be unexpected is incorrect. Under South Carolina law, if the injury itself is unexpected, it is compensable as an injury by accident.

2. Definiteness of Time

Employer contends the injury resulting from repetitive trauma has no definite time of occurrence and therefore it is not compensable as an injury by accident.

Definiteness of time, while relevant to proving causation, is not required to prove an injury qualifies as an injury by accident. For instance, in *Sturkie v. Ballenger Corp.,* we found the claimant's emphysema, which developed gradually, was caused by repeated exposure to high humidity and dust on the job and was therefore compensable as an injury by accident. Similarly, in *Stokes v. First Nat'l Bank,* we found a psychological disorder which developed over a period of months compensable as an injury by accident.

Further, under the Worker's Compensation Act, a disease, which typically has a gradual onset, is compensable as an injury by accident "when it results naturally and unavoidably from the accident." This provision indicates the legislature intended an accident to be compensable under the Act, even where the effects of the accident develop gradually. The fact that a repetitive trauma injury is disease-like in its gradual onset does not preclude it from coverage as an injury by accident.

Here, is it uncontested that Claimant's carpal tunnel syndrome was caused by her work activities. The lack of a definite time of injury is therefore not dispositive.

Affirmed.

CASE QUESTIONS

1. Why does the employer contend that the injury was not accidental?

2. What is the court's test for whether an injury is accidental?

3. Did the injury arise "out of and in the course of employment"? Explain.

Likewise, the courts have been liberal in upholding awards that have been challenged on the grounds that the injury did not arise "out of and in the course of employment." Courts routinely support compensation awards for almost any accidental injury that employees suffer while traveling for their employers. A Minnesota Supreme Court decision upheld a lower court award of compensation to a bus driver. On a layover during a trip, the driver had been shot accidentally in a tavern parking lot following a night on the town.

Exclusive Remedy Rule Recently, some courts have been liberal in their interpretations of the **exclusive remedy rule.** This rule, which is written into all compensation statutes, states that an employee's sole remedy against an employer for workplace injury or illness shall be workers' compensation. In the past few years, courts in several important jurisdictions have created exceptions to this rule. Note that these exceptions recognize in part that workers' compensation laws do not adequately compensate badly injured workers.

Since workers' compensation laws apply only to accidentally injured workers, the exclusive remedy rule does not protect employers who intentionally injure workers. But the issue arises as to how "intentional" such an injury has to be. What if an employer knowingly exposes employees to a chemical that may cause illness in some employees over a long term?

The Future of State Workers' Compensation Currently, many problems confront the state workers' compensation system. Fifty separate nonuniform acts make up the system. Many acts exclude from coverage groups such as farmworkers, government employees, and employees of small businesses. Many state legislatures have enacted changes in their compensation laws. However, states that have broadened coverage and increased benefits have greatly boosted the cost of doing business within their borders. This discourages new businesses from locating within these states and encourages those already there to move out.

In the last decade, workers' compensation payments have tripled. Many workers exaggerate their injuries to get compensation. At the same time, compensation payments to seriously injured workers are often inadequate, and this has led to attempts to get around the exclusive remedy rule.

As our national economy moves from a manufacturing to a service emphasis, the nature of injuries suffered under workers' compensation programs begins to change. In particular, the number of mental stress claims rises. The National Council on Compensation Insurance states that these claims have increased five-fold in the past few years. Problems of proving (or disproving) mental stress claims bring new concerns for the workers' compensation system.

A major problem concerns slowly developing occupational diseases. Many toxic chemicals cause cancer and other diseases only after workers have been exposed to them over many years. Often it is difficult or impossible for workers or their survivors to recover workers' compensation for such diseases.

One solution to the problems confronting the workers' compensation system would be federal reform. Those advocating such reform have put forth several plans, but Congress has shown little inclination so far to adopt a uniform federal act.

KEY TERMS

Assault 256	Conversion 260
Assumption of risk 271	Defamation 261
Battery 256	Design defect 272
Cause in fact 270	Dram shop act 274
Comparative responsibility 271	Duty 266
Compensatory damages 275	Exclusive remedy rule 282
Contingency fee 277	False imprisonment 259
Contributory negligence 271	Fraud 262

REVIEW QUESTIONS AND PROBLEMS

Intentional Torts

1. *Assault and Battery*

   Under what theory can an employee sue her employer for merely touching her? Explain.

2. *Intentional Infliction of Mental Distress*

   In business the intentional infliction of mental distress tort has most often involved what type of situation?

3. *Invasion of Privacy*

   Explain the three principal invasions of personal interest that make up invasion of privacy.

4. *False Imprisonment and Malicious Prosecution*

   Explain the difference between false imprisonment and malicious prosecution. In what business situation does false imprisonment most frequently arise?

5. *Trespass*

   In recent months, homeowners downwind from International Cement Company have had clouds of cement dust settle on their property. Trees, shrubbery, and flowers have all been killed. The paint on houses has also been affected. Explain what tort cause of action these homeowners might pursue against International.

6. *Conversion*

   Bartley signs a storage contract with Universal Warehouses. The contract specifies that Bartley's household goods will be stored at Universal's midtown storage facility while he is out of the country on business. Later, without contacting Bartley, Universal transfers his goods to a suburban warehouse. Two days after the move, a freak flood wipes out the suburban warehouse and Bartley's goods. Is Universal liable to Bartley? Explain.

7. *Defamation*

   Acme Airlines attempts to get control of Free Fall Airways by making a public offer to buy its stock from shareholders. Free Fall's president, Joan, advises the shareholders in a letter that Acme's president, Richard, is "little better than a crook" and "can't even control his own company." Analyze the potential liability of Free Fall's president for these remarks.

8. *Fraud*

Fraud can be used to void a contract and as a basis for intentional tort. What is the advantage to a plaintiff of suing for the tort of fraud as opposed to using fraud merely as a contractual defense?

Fraud and Corporate Governance

9. *Common Law Business Torts*

You are concerned because several of your employees have recently broken their employment contracts and left town. Investigation reveals that Sly and Company, your competitor in a nearby city, has paid bonuses to your former employees to persuade them to break their contracts. Discuss what legal steps you can take against Sly.

Negligence

10. *Duty of Care*

(a)   Do you have a duty of care to warn a stranger on the street of the potential danger of broken glass ahead?

(b)   Do you have a duty to warn an employee of similar danger at a place of employment? Explain.

11. *Unreasonable Behavior—Breach of Duty*

In litigation who usually determines if the defendant's behavior is unreasonable?

12. *Causation in Fact*

(a)   What does it mean to say that "chains of causation stretch out endlessly"?

(b)   What is the standard used by the judge in instructing the jury about causation?

13. *Proximate Causation*

Explain the difference between proximate causation and causation in fact.

14. *Defenses to Negligence*

A jury finds Lee, the defendant, liable in a tort case. It determines that José, the plaintiff, has suffered $200,000 in damages. The jury also finds that José's own fault contributed 25 percent to his injuries. Under a comparative negligence instruction, what amount of damages will the jury award the plaintiff?

Strict Liability in Tort

15. *Strict Products Liability*

While driving under the influence of alcohol, Joe runs off the road and wrecks his car. As the car turns over, the protruding door latch hits the ground and the door flies open. Joe, who is not wearing his seat belt, is thrown from the car and badly hurt. Joe sues the car manufacturer, asserting that the door latch was defectively designed. Discuss the legal issues raised by these facts.

16. *Respondeat Superior*

Carlos delivers pizza for Mama Mia's Pizza Parlor. One of his employer's rules is that delivery employees are never to violate posted speed limits. While traveling 50 miles per hour in a 30-mile-per-hour speed zone, Carlos negligently crashes into a city bus. Is Mama Mia's liable for the injuries caused by Carlos? Discuss.

17. *Ultrahazardous Activity*

Through no one's fault, a sludge dam of the Phillips Phosphate Company breaks. Millions of gallons of sludge run off into a nearby river that empties into Pico Bay. The fishing industry in the bay area is ruined. Is Phillips Phosphate liable to the fishing industry? Explain.

18. *Other Strict Liability Torts*

Explain when common carriers are not strictly liable for damage to transported goods.

Damages

19. *Compensatory Damages*

Explain the three types of loss that give rise to compensatory damages.

20. *Punitive Damages*

During a business lunch, Bob eats salad dressing that contains almond extract. He is very allergic to nuts and suffers a severe allergic reaction. There are complications and Bob becomes almost totally paralyzed. Because Bob had instructed the restaurant waiter and the chef that he might die if he ate any nuts, he sues the restaurant for negligence. Discuss the types of damages Bob may recover.

Alternatives to the Tort System

21. *Workers' Compensation Acts*

If Corgel fails to wear a hard hat as required by Hammersmith, his employer, and is injured by a falling hammer, can he recover workers' compensation from Hammersmith? Your answer should explain the basis for recovering workers' compensation.

TERMINOLOGY REVIEW

For each term in the left-hand column, match the most appropriate description in the right-hand column.

1. Assumption of risk
2. Comparative negligence
3. Strict liability
4. Defamation
5. Duty
6. Proximate causation
7. Punitive damages
8. Respondeat superior
9. Assault
10. Trespass

a. The liability of an employer for an employee's torts

b. Damages that punish a defendant for wrongdoing

c. Knowingly encountering a dangerous condition caused by another

d. The legal cause of an injury, which is determined by the "foreseeability" test

e. Reduction of plaintiff's damages by the amount by which plaintiff's own carelessness caused the injury

f. Liability without intent or negligence

g. Publication of harmful, untrue statements about another

h. The legal responsibility of a person, which arises out of conduct, to act (or not act) in a certain way toward others

i. The tort of entering another's land without consent

j. The tort of placing someone in apprehension for his or her physical safety.

BUSINESS DISCUSSION

You own University Heights Apartments, a business that rents primarily to students. One evening, your tenant Sharon is attacked by an intruder who forces the lock on the sliding glass door of her ground-floor apartment. Sharon's screams attract the attention of Darryl, your resident manager, who comes to Sharon's aid. Together, he and Sharon drive the intruder off, but not before they both are badly cut by the intruder.

Is the intruder liable for what he has done?

Do you have legal responsibilities to Sharon and Darryl?

What should you consider doing at your apartments?

chapter 10

THE CRIMINAL LAW AND BUSINESS

A drug company applied for the approval of the Food and Drug Administration (FDA) to market a miracle drug that the company believed could cure some cancers. During the period that the application was under consideration the company's stock rose to $65 per share. The president of the company learned that the FDA application was about to be denied. You are a personal friend of the president, and he told you that he believed that the stock will start trading downward. You sell 4,000 shares of stock which you purchased for $10 per share. Your decision appears to be a good one since you made a profit of about $200,000. When questioned about the sale by an investigator from the Securities and Exchange Commission, you state that the sale was because of a preexisting arrangement to sell the shares when the price fell below $60 per share. Following the announcement that the FDA application was denied, the stock went to $7 per share.

> Did you commit a crime when you sold the stock?
>
> Did you commit a crime in your answer to the federal agent?
>
> Were you part of an illegal conspiracy?

This chapter discusses the criminal law as it relates to and impacts business. The primary emphasis is on business as a perpetrator of crimes rather than as a victim. In earlier generations, business school curricula exposed students to very little about the criminal law. Topics such as securities or bankruptcy fraud were mentioned but an understanding of the criminal law and especially white-collar crime was considered not to be important in the education of business students. The business community was considered more likely to be a victim of criminal acts rather than a wrongdoer.

Today an understanding of the importance of the criminal law to the legal environment of business is universally recognized. This change of perception and emphasis is the result of criminal conduct devastating, and even destroying, several significant business entities. Among such business entities were one of the largest accounting firms (Arthur Andersen), a major energy firm (Enron), and a major telecommunications company (WorldCom, which owned MCI).

A crime is a wrong against society. Criminal law provides for the people to punish the wrongdoer. Some crimes, such as murder or rape, are said to be *malum in se* or inherently wrongful. They are universally recognized as wrongful conduct that must be punished by society even though the actual victim may be only one person.

Conduct which is not inherently wrongful may become a crime because a legislative body decides that it is in the interest of society to prohibit certain conduct. By declaring that certain conduct is a crime, legislative bodies seek to protect all of society. An example of such a crime is price fixing by competitors. Price fixing was declared to be a crime in 1890 by the Sherman Antitrust Act. This crime is discussed in Chapter 13.

Crimes often involve acts of violence. Arson which destroys property, burglary, and robbery are examples of violent crimes often committed against businesses, usually by persons unconnected with the business victim. The terrorist attack on the World Trade Center was not only a crime against the owners of the businesses located there and their employees but against humanity as well. That crime damaged almost all local businesses in New York City. In fact, that crime had a significant impact on international businesses, such as airlines, and the economies of countries throughout the world.

Many crimes do not involve acts of violence. They may be committed by strangers to a business but are more likely to be committed by employees of a business. Crimes by employees often have a significant negative impact on a business. Nonviolent crimes by employees on behalf of a business can injure the business as well as significant portions of the economy. Society is often harmed more financially by criminal conduct that injures businesses than by criminal conduct that injures only persons.

Some crimes are said to be **white-collar crimes.** This terminology arose out of a distinction between white-collar and blue-collar workers. The term *white-collar crimes* refers to illegal acts characterized by deceit, concealment, or violations of trust. These crimes are not dependent on the threat of physical force or violence. White-collar crimes are committed to obtain money, property, or services; to avoid the payment or loss of money, property, or services; or to achieve a personal or business advantage. The following box lists examples of white-collar crimes.

EXAMPLES OF WHITE-COLLAR CRIMES

Accounting fraud	Larceny
Bankruptcy fraud	Mail fraud
Bribery	Money laundering
Conspiracy	Obstruction of justice
Forgery	Price fixing
Embezzlement	Racketeering
False statements	Securities fraud
Income tax evasion	Wire fraud

ECONOMIC IMPACT ON CRIMINAL BEHAVIOR

In the first three years of the twenty-first century, the total value of the financial losses to all Americans caused directly and indirectly by white-collar crime is unknown but it is probably in the trillions of dollars. Corporate criminal scandals arising from fraud and obstruction of justice were one the causes of the 2001 economic recession. These crimes contributed significantly to the decreased value of almost every stock that was traded on the public stock exchanges in the first three years of this century. Investment and retirement accounts, such as 401K plans, lost more than half their value. Many stocks selling for $80 to $100 per share became almost worthless.

Although a corporation cannot be put in jail or in a prison, it can be fined. Business organizations can be ordered out of business, which is a type of death sentence. Individuals guilty of a crime can be sent to jail or prison and can be fined. These persons may be banned from certain types of work as well.

As previously noted, white-collar crimes by employees of a business may be committed with the intent to harm the business. Criminal activity also may be done to benefit the business with the intent to harm others, such as competitors or customers. It is estimated that American businesses lose over $100 billion annually as a result of crimes by employees that are intended to harm their employers. Embezzlement, electronic advances to fictitious employees, accepting kickbacks from suppliers in exchange for orders, bid rigging, check forgery, selling trade secrets, falsifying inventories to cover theft, and payment of false invoices, are examples of such crimes by employees. Companies must charge customers higher prices to make up for losses that are due to these white-collar crimes. The box above highlights the recent negative impact of criminal activity on business.

In the last decade of the twentieth century, most business school curriculums included courses in ethics. Almost every major corporation adopted codes of ethics for its employees. Large corporations were known for charitable giving. The Big Four accounting firms endowed chairs for accounting professors at many universities. Yet, what followed was a wave of unimaginable white-collar crime. In this chapter, you will be exposed to conduct which resulted from greed replacing integrity in many businesses. The purpose of this chapter is to help you understand the consequences of white-collar crime so that as an educated person you will not be involved in criminal conduct and will be encouraged to prevent it by others. The table on the next page contains examples of recent white-collar criminal actions.

TERMS AND PROCEDURES

1. CLASSIFICATIONS

There are several ways to classify criminal conduct. Some crimes are violations of federal laws and others violate state laws. We have previously noted that although many crimes involve violence, nonviolent conduct may also be criminal.

Crimes also are classified as **felonies** or **misdemeanors.** This classification is based on the punishment imposed in the event of a conviction. Felonies are punishable by fine or imprisonment in a penitentiary for a period of one year or more, whereas misdemeanors are punishable by a fine or a jail sentence of less than one year.

Executives Charged with White-Collar Crimes		
Company	Executive	Crime
1. HealthSouth	Chief executive officer	Securities fraud—false statements
2. Aurora Foods	Chairman of board	Conspiracy to fix financial statements
3. Cendant Corp.	Chairman of board	Accounting fraud—insider trading
4. Imclone	Chief executive officer	Securites fraud—insider trading
5. Elpaso Corp.	Vice president	False reporting of market information
6. Homestore	Chief financial officer Chief operating officer Director of finance Manager: mergers & acquisitions	Wire fraud
7. Kmart	Vice presidents	Accounting fraud
8. Peregrine Systems, Inc.	Assistant treasurer	Conspiracy to commit bank fraud
9. Quest Comm.	Chief financial officer Senior vice president Sales vice president Assistant controller	Financial fraud
10. TYCO	Chief executive officer Chief financial officer	Financial fraud—larceny
11. Westar Energy	President	Misapplication of bank funds
12. WorldCom	Chief financial officer	False financial statements to bank

In addition, felony cases are commenced by grand jury **indictment,** whereas misdemeanors are usually commenced by the government filing a charge called an **information.** Grand juries are different from petit juries. A grand jury determines if there is sufficient evidence to warrant a trial. A petit jury determines the guilt or innocence of the accused. The role of the grand jury is discussed further in section 3.

2. BASIC CONCEPTS

Criminal conduct involves a combination of act plus intent. Many laws use the word **willfully** to define criminal intent. Willfully means that the act was committed voluntarily and purposely with the specific intent to disobey or to disregard the law.

Some criminal statutes declaring conduct to be criminal use the work **knowingly.** Knowingly means that the criminal act was done voluntarily and was not a mistake or accident. Although knowledge usually cannot be established by demonstrating that the accused was negligent, careless, or foolish, knowledge can be inferred if the accused deliberately blinded himself or herself to the existence of a fact.

A few laws provide that conduct which is reckless is a crime even though the one doing the act does not intend to do harm. Reckless driving is an obvious example of such a crime. Reckless disregard for the truth is often the basis of white-collar criminal conduct.

Criminal cases are brought by public officials such as a United States attorney or a states attorney on behalf of the people. The criminal cases in this chapter will name the "United States" as a party against an individual defendant. Imagine how you would feel if a case was labeled the United States vs. you.

In criminal cases, the defendant has three possible pleas to enter to an indictment charging a violation: *guilty, not guilty,* or ***nolo contendere.*** This last plea, Latin for "no contest," allows sentencing just as if the defendant had pleaded or been found guilty. It has the advantage to a defendant of avoiding the cost of trial and effect of a guilty plea or finding in a subsequent civil suit. Criminal convictions may create prima facie cases for civil damage suits, but this effect can be avoided by the *nolo contendere* plea.

3. THE GRAND JURY

The Fifth Amendment to the U.S. Constitution provides that before anyone can be tried for a capital or otherwise infamous crime, there must be a presentment or an indictment by a grand jury. This protection prevents political trials and unjustified prosecutions by placing a group of citizens between prosecutors and persons accused of major crimes.

A grand jury normally consists of 23 citizens who live within the jurisdiction of the court that would try one accused of a crime. At least 16 persons must be present for the grand jury to hear evidence and vote on cases. For an indictment to be returned, a majority of the grand jury must find that a crime has been committed and that the evidence is sufficient to warrant the accused's standing trial. This determination is **probable cause.**

The grand jury does not attempt to determine if the accused is guilty, only that probable cause exists to believe the accused committed the crime. Since probable cause is the standard for grand jury action, it is not difficult to obtain an indictment. Even an indicted person, however, is entitled to the **presumption of innocence**—to be presumed innocent until found guilty by a petit jury.

Grand juries also serve as an investigative body and occupy a unique role in our criminal justice system. Law enforcement officials such as agents for the Federal Bureau of Investigation, U.S. Customs Service, U.S. Postal Service, and Secret Service often act as arms of federal grand juries investigating possible criminal activities. Persons who are the targets or subjects of investigations may be called before grand juries and may be questioned under oath about possible illegal conduct. In such cases the persons subpoenaed to testify before the grand jury are entitled to invoke their Fifth Amendment privilege against compulsory self-incrimination and refuse to answer questions. Although they are entitled to have the benefit of legal advice, defense counsel is not allowed to accompany a witness before a grand jury. However, counsel may be outside the grand jury room and thus available for consultation whenever a witness desires it.

Grand jurors may also subpoena business records. Witnesses may be called and questioned about documents and records delivered in response to a subpoena. However, grand juries are not authorized to engage in arbitrary fishing expeditions and may not select targets of criminal probes out of malice.

Proper functioning of the grand jury system depends upon the secrecy of the proceedings. This secrecy protects the innocent accused from disclosure of the accusations made against him or her before the grand jury. In judicial proceedings, however, transcripts of grand jury proceedings may be obtained if necessary to avoid possible injustice. For example, a defendant may use a grand jury transcript at a trial to impeach a witness, to refresh the witness's recollection, or to test his or her credibility. The disclosure of a grand jury transcript is appropriate only in those cases where the need for it outweighs the public interest in secrecy, and the burden of demonstrating this balance rests upon a private party seeking disclosure.

4. CONSPIRACIES

It is a separate criminal offense for anyone to conspire or agree with someone else to do something that, if carried out, would be a criminal offense. A **conspiracy** is an agreement or a "kind of partnership" for criminal purposes in which each member becomes the agent or partner of every other member. A formal agreement is not required, and all members of the conspiracy need not plan all of the details of the scheme (see box, below).

The essence of a conspiracy offense is the making of the agreement itself followed by the commission of any overt act. An **overt act** is any transaction or event knowingly committed by a conspirator in an effort to accomplish some object of the conspiracy. Standing alone, the act may be entirely innocent; the context of the conspiracy makes it criminal. For example, driving a car to a bank to pick up a bank robber would constitute an overt act by the driver.

The law on conspiracies is often used to "drag in" defendants who did not actually participate in the commission of an offense. A person may become a coconspirator through participation in routine business meetings if the meetings are followed by illegal conduct. If illegal plans or conduct are in the planning process, it is imperative that persons not wishing to participate in the conspiracy disassociate themselves from the process immediately upon discovery of the illegal scheme.

Circumstantial evidence may prove a conspiracy. A person can be charged with conspiracy even if the individual becomes involved after the conspiracy is stopped and the criminal conduct does not occur. The fact that law enforcement discovers a plot to commit a crime and thwarts it does not prevent prosecution for a conspiracy. The threat of a conspiracy is a public danger beyond the commission of the crime because it is likely that the conspirators will commit more crimes.

A party may be guilty even though one of the coconspirators is acquitted by a jury. In the case which follows, note that the real culprit escaped punishment and his employer did not.

ELEMENTS OF A CONSPIRACY

To convict a person of a conspiracy, it is not necessary for the government to prove the conspirators actually succeeded in accomplishing their intended crime. The evidence must show beyond a reasonable doubt that:

- Two or more persons, in some way or manner, came to a mutual understanding to try to accomplish a common and unlawful plan.
- The defendant willfully became a member of such conspiracy.

- During the existence of the conspiracy, one of the conspirators knowingly committed at least one of the overt acts described in the indictment.
- Such overt act was knowingly committed in an effort to carry out or accomplish some object of the conspiracy.

A person may be convicted of conspiracy even if he or she did not know all the details of the unlawful scheme. If a defendant has an understanding of the unlawful nature of a plan and knowingly and willfully joins in that plan on one occasion, that is sufficient evidence for conviction.

UNITED STATES OF AMERICA
v. HUGHES AIRCRAFT CO., INC

20 F. 3D 974 (9TH CIR. 1994)

PER CURIAM: Hughes Aircraft Co., Inc. ("Hughes") appeals from its conviction and sentence for conspiring to defraud and make false statements to the federal government. . . .

Hughes contracted with the United States to manufacture microelectronic circuits, known as "hybrids," which are used as components in weapons defense systems. The contracts required Hughes to perform a series of tests on each hybrid. As the hybrids made their way through the testing process, they were accompanied by paperwork indicating what tests had been performed, the results of those tests, and the identity of the operator of the testing equipment.

Hughes's former employee, Donald LaRue ("LaRue"), was a supervisor responsible for ensuring the accuracy of the hybrid testing process. LaRue arranged for the paperwork to indicate falsely that all tests had been performed and that each hybrid had passed each test. When LaRue's subordinates called his actions to the attention of LaRue's supervisors, the supervisors did nothing about it. Instead, they responded that LaRue's decisions were his own and were not to be questioned by his subordinates.

Hughes and LaRue were charged with . . . conspiracy to defraud. . . . LaRue was acquitted. . . . Hughes was convicted. . . . Hughes appeals from both its conviction and fine of $3.5 million. . . .

Hughes first argues that it must be acquitted as a matter of law because the same jury that convicted Hughes acquitted its "indispensable co-conspirator," LaRue, of the identical charges on identical evidence. . . .

Inconsistent verdicts can just as easily be the result of jury lenity as a determination of the facts. Thus, the acquittal of all conspirators but one does not necessarily indicate that the jury found no agreement to act. . . . Accordingly, the conviction of one co-conspirator is valid even when all the other co-conspirators are acquitted. . . .

Hughes next argues that it is entitled to a judgment of acquittal because the evidence against it and LaRue was identical, yet one was convicted while the other was acquitted. This argument is predicated on the assumption that LaRue was the sole employee for whose actions Hughes could be found vicariously guilty and that the evidence against each of the two defendants was necessarily identical. However, some of the evidence of conspiracy was offered against Hughes alone. Moreover, as this evidence indicates, the jury could have found Hughes guilty based on the actions or omissions of its supervisors and employees other than LaRue. As Hughes's assumption that the facts against both defendants were identical is erroneous, and no other facts support its argument, we reject this contention.

Hughes's third argument is that the plain language of 18 U.S.C. § 371, which states that if "two or more persons conspire . . . each" may be punished, prevents its conviction because it is legally impossible for a party to conspire with itself. Hughes argues that, because it is vicariously liable for each of its employees, a conspiracy between employees would necessitate a finding that Hughes conspired with itself. We reject this creative construction. The statutory language does not exclude criminal liability for a corporation simply because its employees are the actual conspirators. To rule otherwise would effectively insulate all corporations from liability for conspiracies involving only employees acting on behalf of that corporation. We hold that a corporation may be liable under § 371 for conspiracies entered into by its agents and employees. . . .

Hughes argues that a corporation could only violate 18 U.S.C. § 1001 through the efforts of at least two of its employees due to the supervisory and reporting structure of a corporation. Of course, that is not true: a corporation could be liable under § 1001 for false statements to the government by just one of its employees. A conspiracy arises when more than one of its employees agree to defraud the government.

Moreover, the consequences of government fraud certainly do not rest on the parties themselves rather than society. Government fraud has an adverse effect

[CONTINUED]

on the government treasury, the quality of government projects, and in cases such as this one, the safety of individuals utilizing the government goods purchased.

This argument is rejected.

Affirmed.

CASE QUESTIONS

1. Why do you think that the jury returned a verdict of not guilty for LaRue?

2. What mistake did Hughes management make that resulted in the company being a party to the conspiracy?

3. Why are corporations liable for the conspiracies of its employees?

5. AIDING AND ABETTING

The law recognizes that businesspeople accused of criminal behavior likely did not act alone. Such persons can be assisted by co-workers, subordinates, or individuals outside the business organization. If a person acts under the direction of someone accused of criminal activities, this person might be held responsible for **aiding and abetting** in the commission of the crime. The charge of aiding and abetting is similar to the allegation of participating in a conspiracy. This individual accused of aiding and abetting did not necessarily commit the same criminal acts of others. For example, the accountant who assists the chief financial officer in embezzling funds likely is guilty of aiding and abetting in the actual theft. This accountant also may be guilty of conspiring to steal money.

Indictments often charge persons both with a conspiracy to commit a crime and with aiding and abetting others to do so. These allegations are used to indict persons only minimally involved with the actual substantive crime. To avoid going to trial, many will agree to testify against those more directly involved in return for lesser punishment or even immunity from prosecution. The value to the government of the conspiracy theory and the charge of aiding and abetting should not be underestimated. Corporate officials may be potentially liable for criminal acts committed without their direct involvement.

At the state level, a charge similar to the federal charge of aiding and abetting is that a person is an **accessory** to a crime. A person may be an accessory before the crime is committed. If the person is accused of being involved after the crime is committed, the charge is as an accessory after the fact. A person who assists a perpetrator of a crime in eluding the police would be such an accessory. *Accessories before the crime* assist in preparation for the crime, and they may be punished the same as the person who committed the crime. *Accessories after the fact* are usually subject to specific penalties for their actions as provided for in the laws declaring assistance of criminals to be unlawful.

CONSTITUTIONAL ISSUES

Before covering the elements of some of the more important business-related crimes, an understanding of the constitutional protections afforded persons accused of crimes is essential. These protections are in the Bill of Rights. These first

10 amendments to the Constitution were adopted to overcome the concern that the Constitution granted power to a central government at the expense of the individual citizen. These rights protect not only persons accused of crimes but also businesses from excessive regulation. As you study the Fourth, Fifth, and Sixth Amendments to the Constitution, notice their impact on the regulatory process.

6. THE FOURTH AMENDMENT: ILLEGAL SEARCH AND SEIZURE

The Fourth Amendment protects individuals and corporations from **unreasonable searches and seizures.** It primarily protects persons from unwarranted intrusions on their privacy by requiring the police to obtain a court order called a **search warrant.** As a general rule, the search warrant must be obtained by the police prior to a search of a person, any premises, or other property such as the trunk of an automobile. Before a court will issue a search warrant, the police must offer evidence that a crime has been committed and there is cause to believe that the intended search will assist in its investigation.

To protect police officers, courts have held that officers making an arrest do not need a search warrant to search that person and the immediate area around that person for weapons. Officers are given far more latitude in searching an automobile than in searching a person, a home, or a building. The right to search for evidence also extends to the premises of persons not suspected of criminal conduct. Such premises may include offices of newspapers and attorneys. Electronic surveillance has been held not to violate the Fourth Amendment if used pursuant to a court-authorized order.

Fourth Amendment protection extends to certain civil matters. For example, building inspectors do not have the right to inspect for building code violations without a warrant if the owner of the premises objects. The Securities and Exchange Commission (SEC) cannot use confidential reports obtained in the course of its routine operations to establish a violation of federal law. The Occupational Safety and Health Act (OSHA) inspectors must go to court and obtain a search warrant if an owner of a business objects to an inspection. To obtain this warrant, inspectors must show that the standards for conducting an inspection are satisfied; they do not need to show probable cause that a violation exists.

The protection of the Fourth Amendment provides an expectation of privacy. The Supreme Court has said that warrantless searches of junkyards are constitutional because operators of commercial premises in closely regulated industries have a reduced expectation of privacy. In pervasively regulated industries the privacy interests of the business are weakened and government interests in regulating particular businesses are heightened. Generally, a warrantless inspection of commercial premises may well be reasonable within the meaning of the Fourth Amendment, whereas a warrantless inspection of a private residence is unconstitutional.

Many business operations do not have an **expectation of privacy.** For example, nursing homes that receive Medicaid funds are presumed to have voluntarily consented to warrantless searches. Random surveys for compliance with federal standards should be expected by businesses required to conform to the standards.

Today's increased security at airports and at border crossings do not violate the Fourth Amendment. Neither a warrant, probable cause, nor any level of suspicion is required to search vehicles, persons, or goods arriving in the United States. Presenting oneself at an airport checkpoint is an irrevocable consent to a warrantless search.

Employees of some businesses also do not have Fourth Amendment protection because of public policy. For example, alcohol and drug testing of railroad employees and airline pilots cannot be successfully challenged using the Fourth Amendment.

7. THE FIFTH AMENDMENT: SELF-INCRIMINATION

The Fifth Amendment is best known for its protection against compulsory self-incrimination. When a person giving testimony pleads "the Fifth," he or she is exercising the right to this protection. The privilege against self-incrimination protects an accused from being compelled to testify against himself or herself. The Fifth Amendment does not protect the accused from being compelled to produce real or physical evidence. Fingerprints can be taken, as can voice samples and bodily fluids. In order to be testimonial and protected, an accused's communication must itself, explicitly or implicitly, relate to a factual assertion or disclosure information.

Issues concerning the Fifth Amendment protection as it relates to a business may arise when a businessperson is called to testify about a business matter or is served with a subpoena requiring the production of records. A businessperson may not be called upon to testify against himself or herself in any governmental hearing such as a congressional proceeding. But the protection against compulsory self-incrimination does not protect a businessperson from having to produce, in court, records prepared in the ordinary course of business. Since the production of records does not compel oral testimony, the Fifth Amendment does not prevent the use of written evidence, including documents in the hands either of the accused or of someone else such as an accountant. Of course, corporate officials, union officials, and partners cannot be required to give oral testimony if such testimony may tend to incriminate them. However, these individuals must produce subpoenaed documents. Therefore, business records can be obtained even if they are incriminating.

Obviously a corporation or other collective entity cannot be called upon to testify; only individuals can do so. Therefore, the protection against compulsory self-incrimination does not apply to corporations, including professional corporations and partnerships. These collective entities have no Fifth Amendment right to refuse to submit their books and records in response to a subpoena. The only business protected by the Fifth Amendment privilege against compulsory self-incrimination is a sole proprietorship. A closely held corporation with only one shareholder is not protected. An important legal balancing act is discussed in the following box.

IS THE DOCUMENT PROTECTED BY THE FIFTH AMENDMENT?

An important issue that frequently arises in the Fifth Amendment analysis is whether a particular document belongs to a corporation or to an individual who is the target of the subpoena. As indicated in the text, corporate documents are not protected by the claim of self-incrimination. However, documents owned by an individual may be protected and free from the government's subpoena powers. In resolving this issue of ownership, courts use a balancing approach. Among the factors that courts question are:

1. Who prepared the document?
2. What is the nature of the contents?
3. What is the purpose or use of the document?
4. Who has possession of the document?
5. Who has access to the document?
6. Did the corporation require preparation of the document?
7. Does the document further the business of the corporation?

The answers to these questions help the courts decide whether a businessperson's claim of protection from self-incrimination is meritorious or whether the documents belong to a business organization and are subject to the government's inspection.

8. FIFTH AMENDMENT: DOUBLE JEOPARDY

The Fifth Amendment provides in part that no "person [shall] be subject for the same offense to be twice put in jeopardy of life or limb." This language is known as the **double jeopardy** clause. Courts do not allow individuals to be tried twice by the same governmental entity for the same crime based on the same factual situation. If an illegal activity violates both federal and state laws, double jeopardy does not prohibit two trials, one in federal court and the other in the state court system. Although federal and state governmental prosecutors may cooperate resulting in only one conviction, the double jeopardy clause does not prevent two prosecutions. In its essence, this clause keeps a U.S. district attorney from having a second trial on the same facts if a defendant is found innocent or has the charges dismissed. The same prohibition of a second trial holds true for state prosecutors also.

Sometimes interesting arguments are made under the double jeopardy clause. In the following case, businesspersons attempted to use the double jeopardy clause to prevent criminal prosecution following the imposition of civil penalties for violating various federal laws.

HUDSON v. UNITED STATES

118 S. CT. 488 (1997)

The Government administratively imposed monetary penalties and occupational debarment on petitioners for violation of federal banking statutes, and later criminally indicted them for essentially the same conduct.

Petitioner John Hudson was the chairman and controlling shareholder of the First National Bank of Tipton (Tipton) and the First National Bank of Hammon (Hammon). Petitioner Jack Rackley was president of Tipton and a member of the board of directors of Hammon, and petitioner Larry Baresel was a member of the board of directors of both Tipton and Hammon.

The Office of the Comptroller of the Currency (OCC) concluded that petitioners had used their bank positions to arrange a series of loans to third parties, in violation of various federal banking statutes and regulations. OCC issued a "Notice of Assessment of Civil Money Penalty." The notice alleged that the illegal loans resulted in losses to Tipton and Hammon of almost $900,000 and contributed to the failure of those banks. OCC assessed penalties of $100,000 against Hudson and $50,000 each against both Rackley and Baresel. OCC also

issued a "Notice of Intention to Prohibit Further Participation" against each petitioner.

Petitioners resolved the OCC proceedings against them by each entering into a "Stipulation and Consent Order." These consent orders provided that Hudson, Baresel, and Rackley would pay assessments of $16,500, $15,000, and $12,500 respectively. In addition, each petitioner agreed not to "participate in any manner" in the affairs of any banking institution without the written authorization of the OCC and all other relevant regulatory agencies.

Petitioners subsequently were indicted in the Western District of Oklahoma in a 22-count indictment on charges of conspiracy, misapplication of bank funds, and making false bank entries. The violations charged in the indictment rested on the same lending transactions that formed the basis for the prior administrative actions brought by OCC. Petitioners moved to dismiss the indictment on double jeopardy grounds.

REHNQUIST, J.: We hold that the Double Jeopardy Clause of the Fifth Amendment is not a bar to the

[CONTINUED]

later criminal prosecution because the administrative proceedings were civil, not criminal. . . .

The Double Jeopardy Clause provides that no "person [shall] be subject for the same offense to be twice put in jeopardy of life or limb." We have long recognized that the Double Jeopardy Clause does not prohibit the imposition of punishment. The Clause protects only against the imposition of multiple criminal punishments for the same offense.

Whether a particular punishment is criminal or civil is, at least initially, a matter of statutory construction. A court must first ask whether the legislature, in establishing the penalizing mechanism, indicated either expressly or impliedly a preference for one label or the other. Even in those cases where the legislature has indicated an intention to establish a civil penalty, we have inquired further whether the statutory scheme was so punitive either in purpose or effect as to "transform what was clearly intended as a civil remedy into a criminal penalty."

In making this latter determination, several factors provide useful guideposts, including: (1) whether the sanction involves an affirmative disability or restraint; (2) whether it has historically been regarded as a punishment; (3) whether it comes into play only on a finding of scienter; (4) whether its operation will promote the traditional aims of punishment—retribution and deterrence; (5) whether the behavior to which it applies is already a crime; (6) whether an alternative purpose to which it may rationally be connected is assignable for it; and (7) whether it appears excessive in relation to the alternative purpose assigned. It is important to note, however, that these factors must be considered in relation to the statute on its face, and only the clearest proof will suffice to override legislative intent and transform what has been denominated a civil remedy into a criminal penalty.

Applying traditional double jeopardy principles to the facts of this case, it is clear that the criminal prosecution of these petitioners would not violate the Double Jeopardy Clause. It is evident that Congress intended the OCC money penalties and debarment sanctions to be civil in nature. As for the money penalties, which authorize the imposition of monetary penalties, they expressly provide that such penalties are civil. While the provision authorizing debarment contains no language explicitly denominating the sanction as civil, we think it significant that the authority to issue debarment orders is conferred upon the appropriate federal banking agencies. That such authority was conferred upon administrative agencies is prima facie evidence that Congress intended to provide for a civil sanction.

We find that there is little evidence, much less the clearest proof that we require, suggesting that either OCC money penalties or debarment sanctions are so punitive in form and effect as to render them criminal despite Congress' intent to the contrary.

We recognize that the imposition of both money penalties and debarment sanctions will deter others from emulating petitioners' conduct, a traditional goal of criminal punishment. But the mere presence of this purpose is insufficient to render a sanction criminal, as deterrence may serve civil as well as criminal goals.

In sum, there simply is very little showing, to say nothing of the "clearest proof," that OCC money penalties and debarment sanctions are criminal. The Double Jeopardy Clause is therefore no obstacle to their trial on the pending indictments, and it may proceed.

The judgment of the Court of Appeals for the Tenth Circuit is accordingly **affirmed.**

CASE QUESTIONS

1. What protections against governmental overreaching are provided by the Double Jeopardy Clause?

2. Under which circumstances could a civil penalty be so punitive as to implicate the Double Jeopardy Clause?

3. Why were the money penalties and debarment sanctions insufficient to render the sanctions criminal in nature?

9. THE SIXTH AMENDMENT

The Sixth Amendment, like the Fifth, provides multiple protections in criminal cases. Essentially, its protections give you the right:

- To a speedy and public trial
- To a trial by jury
- To be informed of the charge against you
- To confront your accuser
- To subpoena witnesses in your favor
- To have the assistance of an attorney

The American concept of a jury trial contemplates a jury drawn from a fair cross section of the community. The jury guards against the exercise of arbitrary power by using the common sense judgment of the community as a hedge against the overzealous or mistaken prosecutor. The jury's perspective on facts is used in preference to the professional, or perhaps biased, response of a judge.

Community participation in administering criminal law is not only consistent with our democratic heritage, it is also critical to public confidence in the fairness of the criminal justice system. Therefore, a state may not restrict jury service only to special groups or exclude identifiable segments playing major roles in the community. Likewise, minorities may not be systematically excluded from jury duty, either in the eligibility to serve process or in the actual selection process during a trial. As discussed in Chapter 4, peremptory challenges during *voir dire* examination cannot be used to deny a defendant a jury of one's peers.

The right to a jury trial does not extend to state juvenile court delinquency proceedings because they are not criminal prosecutions. However, juveniles do have the right to counsel, to confront the witnesses against them, and to cross-examine them.

The right to an attorney exists in any cases where incarceration is a possible punishment. It exists at every stage of the proceeding, commencing with an investigation that centers on a person as the accused. Thus, it can be seen that there are many technical aspects to the Sixth Amendment, and numerous cases still arise concerning it. For example, a criminal defendant's right to counsel of his or her choice may be limited in certain situations by the attorney's prior representation of a corporation. By representing the corporation, an attorney may obtain potentially privileged information from employees who later become adverse witnesses against the corporation or individual officers in criminal prosecutions. These potential conflicts of interest also become very complicated when employees provide incriminating information to corporate counsel on the mistaken belief that he or she represents their interests as well as those of the corporation.

To further complicate the issue of representation, a 1994 U.S. Department of Justice rule allows government lawyers to contact workers who are not "high level" in a company without going through the company's legal department. Prosecutors may interview middle managers or line workers about company practices and try to persuade them to blow the whistle on upper management in criminal investigations. Normally, ethical rules would bar an attorney from directly contacting a person who is already represented by counsel. The Justice Department has rejected that rule in the context of corporate counsel primarily on the ground that it would frustrate the development of successful criminal investigations against corporations and corporate officials.

SPECIFIC CRIMES

The following sections consider a number of federal crimes that today are relevant to the conduct of business. They are frequently committed even by small businesses. Many of these crimes result in civil suits against a business for dollar damages as well as criminal prosecutions.

10. ENDANGERING WORKERS

Most of the crimes committed by business are white-collar crimes because they do not involve violence. Businesses are sometimes, however, found guilty of violent crime. A major recent trend in the criminal law is for states to charge corporate officials with crimes such as assault and battery, reckless **endangerment of workers,** and a form of accidental homicide when a worker is injured or killed on the job. These accidents, injuries, and deaths usually occur in manufacturing companies that use extremely dangerous processes. Corporate officials in companies that use mercury, cyanide, or other dangerous chemicals and that do not have adequate safety precautions may face criminal charges when workers are injured or killed as a result of their employment.

When criminal charges are brought in these cases, the defense usually contends that the state criminal laws have been preempted by the federal Occupational Safety and Health Act. While some courts have accepted this argument, most, including such major industrial states as New York, Illinois, and Michigan, have not. On two occasions the Supreme Court has been asked to review the matter and hold that state laws are preempted. It has refused to do so. As a result, in most states company officials can be criminally prosecuted for endangering the health and safety of their employees.

Some states, such as California, have passed specific statutes that require employers to warn employees of life-threatening hazards in the workplace. Failure to do so is a crime. It is likely that additional states will adopt similar legislation in the near future.

11. OBSTRUCTION OF JUSTICE

Congress has enacted several laws designed to protect the proceedings of government. These laws seek to protect legislative proceedings, judicial proceedings, and the proceedings before federal departments or agencies. These laws use the term **obstruction of justice** in a comprehensive manner to encompass all steps and stages from the inception of an investigation to the conclusion of a trial.

The following box contains language of a typical obstruction of justice statute.

SECTION 1505 OF TITLE 18 OF THE U.S. CODE PROVIDES

Whoever corruptly, . . . endeavors to influence, obstruct, or impede . . . the due and proper administration of the law under which any pending proceeding is being had before any department or agency of the United States, or the due and proper exercise of the power of inquiry under which any inquiry or investigation is being had by either House, or any committee of either House or any joint committee of the Congress . . . shall be fined not more than $5,000 or imprisoned not more than five years, or both.

The obstruction of justice statutes are written in general language and are broadly construed. They are drafted with a recognition that there is an unlimited variety of methods by which the proper administration of justice may be impeded or thwarted by the criminally inclined. Such statutes use terms such as "illegal means" and "corrupt endeavor" to define illegal conduct. Any act made with the intent to obstruct either the legislative process or the judicial process may be a crime. The means used to carry out the corrupt intent is not relevant. Otherwise lawful actions can become obstruction of justice if done with corrupt intent. The following box contains examples of activities found to obstruct the administration of justice.

12. FALSE STATEMENT TO A BANK

Borrowers from banks are routinely required to furnish financial statements. These statements intend to supply information to the bank so it can make its decision on the loan request. Financial statements are relied upon by banks even though many of them are not certified as correct by a certified public accountant. It is a federal crime for anyone willfully to make a false statement to a federally insured financial institution. The purpose behind making such falsehoods a crime is to protect banks and attempt to ensure the accuracy of financial information. To prove the crime of a false statement to a bank, the prosecutor must prove beyond a reasonable doubt that the false statement or report was made with the intent to influence the action of the insured financial institution upon an application, advance, commitment, loan, or any change or extension thereof. An *insured bank* is one whose deposits are insured by the Federal Deposit Insurance Corporation. An insured credit union is one whose deposits are insured by the National Credit Union Administration.

A statement or report is *false* when made if it relates to a material fact and is untrue and is then known to be untrue by the person making it. A fact is *material* if it is important to the decision to be made by the officers or employees of the institution involved and has the capacity of influencing them in making that decision. It is not necessary, however, to prove that the institution involved was, in fact, influenced or misled. The gist of the offense is an attempt to influence such an institution by willfully making the false statement or report concerning the matter. The maximum penalty for a violation is two years' imprisonment and a $5,000 fine.

13. FALSE STATEMENT TO A FEDERAL AGENCY

The U.S. Code makes it a federal crime for anyone willfully and knowingly to make a false or fraudulent statement to a department or agency of the United States. The false statement must be related to a material matter, and the defendant

---

EXAMPLES OF OBSTRUCTION OF JUSTICE

1. Filing improper tax liens.
2. Exploiting a special relationship with a judge to obtain a favorable decision.
3. Advising a grand jury witness to take the Fifth Amendment if it is given with a corrupt intent.
4. Testifying falsely before Congress.
5. Instructing an audit staff to destroy documents when an investigation or litigation may be pending.
6. E-mailing a message "time to clean up those files."
7. Hiring a law firm with close political ties to a chairman of a congressional committee to get the congressman to stop an investigation of a corporation.

must have acted willfully and with knowledge of the falsity. It is not necessary to show that the government agency was in fact deceived or misled. The issue of materiality is one of law for the courts. The maximum penalty is five years' imprisonment and a $10,000 fine.

A person may be guilty of a violation without proof that he or she had knowledge that the matter was within the jurisdiction of a federal agency. A businessperson may violate this law by making a false statement to another firm or person with knowledge that the information will be submitted to a government agency. Businesses must take care to avoid puffery or exaggerations in the context of any matter that may come within the jurisdiction of a federal agency.

Due to the sweeping nature of this statute, seven federal appellate courts of appeal had recognized an **exculpatory no** exception for simple denials made in response to government questioning as part of a criminal investigation. This narrow exception protected an individual from prosecution for making a false statement when the person's statement simply denies criminal wrongdoing. The exculpatory no was permitted when a person, in response to governmental questioning, had to choose between three undesirable options: self-incrimination by telling the truth; remaining silent and raising greater suspicions; or denying guilt by making a false statement to the governmental official. Courts permitting this exception believed it balanced the need for protecting the basic functions of government agencies conducting investigations against the Fifth Amendment protection against self-incrimination.

In early 1998, the Supreme Court rejected the exculpatory no exception in the case of *Brogan v. United States,* 118 U.S. 805 (1998). The Court found the exception was not supported by the plain language of the statute and held that the Fifth Amendment does not confer a privilege to lie.

14. LARCENY

Larceny is the unlawful taking of personal property with the intent to deprive the rightful owner of it permanently. Larceny is commonly referred to as theft or stealing. Shoplifting by customers is a common form of larceny. Larceny by violence or threat such as with a gun is **robbery.** Breaking into a building with the intent to commit a felony is **burglary.** The most common felony in burglary cases is larceny.

Larceny by employees of a business is a common white-collar crime. If an employee appropriates funds of his employer to his or her own use, the employee is guilty of embezzlement. Embezzlement is often committed by highly trusted employees with access to cash or to the check-writing process. It is a crime easily committed when there is a lack of internal control over funds. Simple policies such as using cosigned checks, dividing check-writing duties from bank reconciliation duties, and requiring all employees to take vacations can often prevent embezzlement.

Larceny by employees takes many forms. Use of company property such as vehicles or computers without permission is a form of larceny. Padding expense accounts and falsifying time records are also a taking of property and they are a sophisticated form of theft.

Although larceny by rank-and-file employees is important, it pales to insignificance when compared to the larcenies committed by some corporate officers and directors. Larceny at the top-management level of some corporations in recent years

EXAMPLES OF EXECUTIVES STEALING COMPANY ASSETS

The classic case of looting a business involved the founders of a communications company that was publicly held. The father and his two sons were directors and officers of the corporation. The indictment of three officers alleged that:

1. They used $252 million of company funds to pay personal margin calls at brokerage firms.
2. They caused the company to loan $2 billion to other family-owned businesses.
3. The company spent $12 million to build a private golf course.
4. One son used the company jet for an African safari.
5. The company rented a Manhattan apartment for the daughter of one son.

In another case that attracted national attention, a company president was given a no-interest loan of $49 million to buy a 15,000 square foot mansion in Florida. The company not only forgave the loan, it gave him the money to pay the income taxes on the forgiven loan. These matters were not disclosed to the shareholders whose property was clearly stolen in as much as the president used corporate assets as a personal piggy bank.

has involved millions of dollars. In some cases the stealing can only be described as looting the business just as if a mob broke into a store and stole its inventory.

Larceny by directors and officers usually has the appearance of being legal. The business may loan large sums to an officer at little or no interest. If there is no intent to repay the loan and no expectation of repayment, larceny as well as conspiracy to commit larceny has occurred. A company may purchase an airplane or yacht ostensibly for the business. If these are used only by the president for his personal enjoyment, larceny may have been committed. Likewise, if a company buys season tickets for the games of a local professional sports team and the tickets are used only by the officers, a form of larceny occurs. Technically, these examples could be stealing as well as tax fraud because the executive may not report receiving these benefits on the tax returns. The box above provides examples of high-level corporate larceny.

Company lawyers are not immune from prosecution for white-collar crimes. The general counsel for a company helped cover up $600 million looting of the corporation by company executives. He was given a $12 million bonus. He was indicted for grand larceny.

15. FRAUD

The U.S. Code contains several provisions making it criminal to carry out a scheme to defraud. Two of these provisions cover fraud using the mails and interstate wire communication facilities. These provisions are covered in the next section. Another provision makes it a crime for anyone to transport someone or induce someone to travel in interstate commerce for the purpose of executing a scheme to defraud that person of money or property having a value of $5,000 or more. In addition, a federal law outlaws fraud by use of counterfeit access devises, including bank cards, plates, codes, account numbers, or other means of account access to initiate a transfer of funds. The counterfeit or unauthorized access devise used must result in at least $1,000 being fraudulently obtained within a one-year period. An *unauthorized access device* is any access device that is lost, stolen, expired, revoked, canceled, or obtained with intent to defraud.

Chapter 8 on contracts provides the classic definition of **fraud** as part of the discussion of grounds to avoid contract liability. That definition has the following elements:

1. Intention to mislead
2. Misstatement of a material existing fact
3. Justifiable reliance
4. Injury

Fraud in the criminal law usually has the same elements but not always. Some statutes such as mail and wire fraud do not require reliance and injury.

Securities Fraud One of the most important federal laws defining criminal conduct is the Securities Exchange Act of 1934. This act and Rule 10(b)5 of the Securities and Exchange Commission cover fraud in the purchase or sale of a security. The details of this law are discussed in Chapter 16.

Many of the prosecutions are the result of accounting fraud based upon false financial statements. The defendants are corporate officers responsible for the financial statements furnished to the investing public.

Health Care Fraud Another important area of criminal law enforcement against businesses is the health care industry. The Department of Justice has specialized investigative units concentrating on health care fraud. This usually involves false claims under the False Claims Act submitted for payments under government programs.

Prosecuting false claims by large corporations operating several hospitals have resulted in the recoupment of millions of dollars for the federal government. Individual physicians have been prosecuted for false billings to Medicare and Medicaid. For example, a urologist was recently convicted of "upcoding" office visits and billing them as consultations.

Health care fraud investigations are aided by information revealed in "whistleblower" suits brought by former corporate insiders under the federal False Claims Act. The act allows a citizen "relator" who successfully brings a lawsuit that recovers fraudulently obtained federal funds to keep a portion of the recovery as a bounty.

16. MAIL AND WIRE FRAUD

Various provisions of the U.S. Code make it illegal to use either the U.S. Postal Service or electronic means of interstate communication to carry out a scheme to defraud. These provisions provide significant criminal penalties for **mail** or **wire fraud.** The statutory penalties involve fines set by judges and up to 20 years in prison. If mail or wire fraud impacts a financial institution, the fine may be as high as $1,000,000 and imprisonment may be up to 30 years. Each use of the mail or wire communication constitutes a separate violation. Thus, the criminal sanctions can be enormous.

This section of the chapter covers the following three areas:

- A definition of what is a mailing and a use of wire communication
- A presentation on the meaning of a "scheme to defraud"
- A discussion of the legal aspects of fraud

Use of Mail or Wire-Based Communication "To mail" means a communication is sent or received through use of the U.S. Postal Service or any interstate carrier. A "wire transmission" includes the use of radio, television, telephone, Internet, or other wired form of communication. Prosecutors must prove the person accused of mail or wire fraud used the mail or wire communication. However, the government has substantial leeway in proving its case. Courts have held that the use of mail or wire communication can be proven by circumstantial evidence. For example, evidence of business custom and practice may establish the fact a mailing or wire communication occurred. The accused does not have to actually place a letter in the mail or send an e-mail message. Others may do so. The following case illustrates that as long as the mailing is a part of the fraudulent scheme, the accused person does not have to be the party using the mail.

SCHMUCK v. UNITED STATES

109 S. CT. 1443 (1989)

BLACKMUN, J.: In August 1983, petitioner Wayne T. Schmuck, a used-car distributor, was indicted in the United States District Court for the Western District of Wisconsin on 12 counts of mail fraud, in violation of 18 U.S.C. §§ 1341 and 1342.

The alleged fraud was a common and straightforward one. Schmuck purchased used cars, rolled back their odometers, and then sold the automobiles to Wisconsin retail dealers for prices artificially inflated because of the low-mileage readings. These unwitting car dealers, relying on the altered odometer figures, then resold the cars to customers, who in turn paid prices reflecting Schmuck's fraud. To complete the resale of each automobile, the dealer who purchased it from Schmuck would submit a title-application form to the Wisconsin Department of Transportation on behalf of his retail customer. The receipt of a Wisconsin title was a prerequisite for completing the resale; without it, the dealer could not transfer title to the customer and the customer could not obtain Wisconsin tags. The submission of the title-application form supplied the mailing element of each of the alleged mail frauds.

Before trial, Schmuck moved to dismiss the indictment on the ground that the mailings at issue—the submissions of the title-application forms by the automobile dealers—were not in furtherance of the fraudulent scheme and, thus, did not satisfy the

mailing element of the crime of mail fraud. . . . The District Court denied both motions. After trial, the jury returned guilty verdicts on all 12 counts. . . .

We granted certiorari to define further the scope of the mail fraud statute. . . .

The federal mail fraud statute does not purport to reach all frauds, but only those limited instances in which the use of the mails is a part of the execution of the fraud, leaving all other cases to be dealt with by appropriate state law. To be part of the execution of the fraud, however, the use of the mails need not be an essential element of the scheme. It is sufficient for the mailing to be incident to an essential part of the scheme or a step in the plot.

Schmuck . . . argues that mail fraud can be predicated only on a mailing that affirmatively assists the perpetrator in carrying out his fraudulent scheme. The mailing element of the offense, he contends, cannot be satisfied by a mailing, such as those at issue here, that is routine and innocent in and of itself, and that, far from furthering the execution of the fraud, occurs after the fraud has come to fruition, is merely tangentially related to the fraud, and is counterproductive in that it creates a paper trail from which the fraud may be discovered. We disagree both with this characterization of the mailings in the present case and with this description of the applicable law.

[CONTINUED]

We begin by considering the scope of Schmuck's fraudulent scheme. Schmuck was charged with devising and executing a scheme to defraud Wisconsin retail automobile customers who based their decisions to purchase certain automobiles at least in part on the low-mileage readings provided by the tampered odometers. This was a fairly large-scale operation. Evidence at trial indicated that Schmuck had employed a man known only as "Fred" to turn back the odometers on about 150 different cars. Schmuck then marketed these cars to a number of dealers, several of whom he dealt with on a consistent basis over a period of about 15 years. . . . Schmuck's was not a "one-shot" operation in which he sold a single car to an isolated dealer. His was an ongoing fraudulent venture. A rational jury could have concluded that the success of Schmuck's venture depended upon his continued harmonious relations with, and good reputation among, retail dealers, which in turn required the smooth flow of cars from the dealers to their Wisconsin customers.

Under these circumstances, we believe that a rational jury could have found that the title-registration mailings were part of the execution of the fraudulent scheme, a scheme which did not reach fruition until the retail dealers resold the cars and effected transfers of title. Schmuck's scheme would have come to an abrupt halt if the dealers either had lost faith in Schmuck or had not been able to resell the cars obtained from him. These resales and Schmuck's relationships with the retail dealers naturally depended on the successful passage of title among the various parties. Thus, although the registration-form mailings may not have contributed directly to the duping of either the retail dealers or the customers, they were necessary to the passage of title, which in turn was essential to the perpetuation of Schmuck's scheme. As noted earlier, a mailing that is incident to an essential part of the scheme satisfies the mailing element of the mail fraud offense. The mailings here fit this description. . . .

For these reasons, we agree with the Court of Appeals that the mailings in this case satisfy the mailing element of the mail fraud offenses.

Affirmed.

CASE QUESTIONS

1. What was the factual basis of the fraudulent scheme used by Schmuck in this case?
2. How was the mail associated with this factual situation?
3. Why does the Supreme Court conclude that mail fraud existed in this case?

Scheme to Defraud As the preceding case documents, mail and wire fraud covers a wide range of wrongful activities. However, these statutes are not limitless in their scope. Clearly, the prosecutor must establish the presence of a **scheme to defraud.** This phrase includes a plan or program designed to take from a person the intangible right of honest services. In essence, a scheme involves a course of action that deceives others. The box on the next page illustrates a typical wire fraud scheme.

TYPICAL SCHEME TO DEFRAUD

A college student, with access to a university's network, creates a plan to make some "fast" money. This student sends thousands of e-mail messages to university alumni. These messages appear under the university's logo, and a reference to a website is given. This website looks like it is a part of the university's alumni operations. In fact, the site was created by the student and has no connection to the university.

The message and the website offer to sell university sponsored items, such as coffee mugs, clothing, books, furniture, and so on. In fact, the student cashes checks sent in with the orders. At no time does the student intend to furnish the "buyer" with any merchandise.

Legal Aspects of Mail and Wire Fraud A statement or representation is *false* or *fraudulent* if it is known to be untrue or is made with reckless indifference as to its truth or falsity. A statement or representation may also be *false* or *fraudulent* if it constitutes a half truth or effectively conceals a material fact with intent to defraud. A *material fact* is a fact that would be important to a reasonable person in deciding whether to engage or not to engage in a particular transaction.

Intent to defraud means to act knowingly and with the specific intent to deceive someone, ordinarily for the purpose of causing some financial loss to another or bringing about some financial gain to oneself. In many fraud cases the defendant asserts a good-faith defense to the allegations of the indictment. **Good faith** is a complete defense because good faith on the part of a defendant is inconsistent with intent to defraud or willfulness, purposes essential to the charges. A person who expresses an opinion honestly held or a belief honestly entertained does not have fraudulent intent even though the opinion is erroneous or the belief is mistaken. Evidence that establishes only that a person made a mistake in judgment or an error in management or was careless does not establish fraudulent intent.

The burden of proof is not on the defendant to prove good faith or honesty, because he or she has no burden to prove anything. The government must establish beyond a reasonable doubt that the defendant acted with specific intent to defraud. The government does not have to prove actual reliance upon the defendant's misrepresentations. Proof of damage has no application to criminal liability for mail and wire fraud. By prohibiting the "scheme to defraud" rather than the completed fraud, the elements of reliance and damage would clearly be inconsistent with the statutes Congress enacted.

17. BANKRUPTCY CRIMES

Bankruptcy proceedings are conducted in federal courts. To protect the interests of all parties to the proceedings, the U.S. Code makes certain conduct by the debtor and certain conduct by creditors and others a federal crime. These are **bankruptcy crimes.** First, it is a crime for the bankrupt debtor to falsify the information filed in the bankruptcy proceedings. Similarly, it is a crime for anyone to present a false claim in any bankruptcy proceeding.

Any person, including the debtor, in possession of property belonging to the estate of a debtor in bankruptcy, is guilty of a felony if he or she conceals the property from the person charged with control of the property in the bankruptcy proceeding. The law requires that the act of concealment be fraudulent. An act is done fraudulently if done with intent to deceive or cheat any creditor, trustee, or bankruptcy judge. In this context, *conceal* means to secrete, falsify, mutilate, fraudulently transfer, withhold information or knowledge required by law to be made known, or take any action preventing discovery. Since the offense of **concealment** is a continuing one, the acts of concealment may have begun before as well as be committed after the bankruptcy proceeding began.

It is no defense that the concealment may have proved unsuccessful. Even though the property in question is recovered for the debtor's estate, the defendant may still be guilty of concealment. Similarly, it is no defense that there was no demand by any officer of the court or creditor for the property alleged to have been concealed.

18. RACKETEER INFLUENCED AND CORRUPT ORGANIZATIONS ACT (RICO)

The most controversial of the federal criminal laws relating to business is the Racketeer Influenced and Corrupt Organizations Act, commonly known as **RICO.** This law imposes criminal and civil liability upon those businesspersons who engage in certain *prohibited activities* and who engage in interstate commerce. Specifically, liability extends to any person who:

- Uses or invests income from prohibited activities to acquire an interest in or to operate an enterprise
- Acquires or maintains an interest in or control of an enterprise
- Conducts or participates in the conduct of an enterprise while being employed by or associated with it

Each prohibited activity is defined to include, as one necessary element, proof either of a **pattern of racketeering** *activity* or of *collection of unlawful debt.* **Racketeering** is defined in RICO to mean "any act or threat involving" specified state law crimes, any "act" indictable under various specified federal statutes, and certain federal "offenses." As to the term *pattern,* the statute says only that it "requires at least two acts of racketeering activity" within a 10-year period. It is not otherwise defined. The case that follows defined pattern of activity and led to an expansion of RICO cases.

H. J. INC. V. NORTHWESTERN BELL TELEPHONE COMPANY

109 S. CT. 2893 (1989)

Petitioners, H. J. Inc., filed a class action RICO suit for an injunction and triple damages on behalf of customers of the defendant—respondent Northwestern Bell Telephone Company (NBT). It alleged that NBT had bribed the members of the Minnesota Public Utilities Commission (MPUC) to approve rates in excess of a fair and reasonable amount. It had done so by paying for parties, meals, tickets to sporting events, and airline tickets for commissioners.

The lower courts dismissed the complaint because all of the acts alleged had been committed to further a single scheme to influence MPUC commissioners to the detriment of NBT's customers and the law requires a pattern of racketeering activity. They concluded that a pattern of activity requires multiple illegal schemes. Other courts of appeal had reached the opposite conclusion on the meaning of the word "pattern."

[CONTINUED]

As a result, the Supreme Court granted certiorari. The government participated as a friend of the court (amicus curiae), referred to in the opinion as "amici."

BRENNAN, J.: . . . Congress has done nothing . . . to illuminate RICO's key requirement of a pattern of racketeering; and as the plethora of different views expressed by the Courts of Appeals . . . demonstrates, developing a meaningful concept of "pattern" within the existing statutory framework has proved to be no easy task.

It is, nevertheless, a task we must undertake in order to decide this case. Our guides in the endeavor must be the text of the statute and its legislative history. We find no support in those sources for the proposition . . . that predicate acts of racketeering may form a pattern only when they are part of separate illegal schemes. Nor can we agree with those courts that have suggested that a pattern is established merely by proving two predicate acts or with *amici* in this case who argue that the word "pattern" refers only to predicates that are indicative of a perpetrator involved in organized crime or its functional equivalent. In our view, Congress had a more natural and commonsense approach to RICO's pattern element in mind, intending a more stringent requirement than proof simply of two predicates, but also envisioning a concept of sufficient breadth that it might encompass multiple predicates within a single scheme that were related and that amounted to, or threatened the likelihood of, continued criminal activity.

We begin . . . with RICO's text. . . .

Section 1961(5) does indicate that Congress envisioned circumstances in which no more than two predicates would be necessary to establish a pattern of racketeering—otherwise it would have drawn a narrower boundary to RICO liability, requiring proof of a greater number of predicates. But, at the same time, the statement that a pattern requires at least two predicates implies that while two acts are necessary, they may not be sufficient. Section 1961(5) concerns only the minimum *number* of predicates necessary to establish a pattern; and it assumes that there is something to a RICO pattern *beyond* simply the number of predicate acts involved. . . .

The legislative history shows that Congress indeed had a fairly flexible concept of a pattern in mind. A pattern is not formed by "sporadic activity," and a person cannot "be subjected to the sanctions of title IX simply for committing two widely sepa-

rated and isolated criminal offenses." Instead, "[t]he term 'pattern' itself requires the showing of a relationship" between the predicates, and of " 'the threat of continuing activity.' " It is this factor of *continuity plus relationship* which combines to produce a pattern. RICO's legislative history reveals Congress' intent that to prove a pattern of racketeering activity a plaintiff or prosecutor must show that the racketeering predicates are related, *and* that they amount to or pose a threat of continued criminal activity. . . .

RICO's predicate acts or offenses, and the *relationship* these predicates must bear one to another, are distinct requirements. A party alleging a RICO violation may demonstrate continuity over a closed period by proving a series of related predicates extending over a substantial period of time. Predicate acts extending over a few weeks or months and threatening no further criminal conduct do not satisfy this requirement. Congress was concerned in RICO with long-term criminal conduct. Often a RICO action will be brought before continuity can be established in this way. In such cases, liability depends on whether the *threat* of continuity is demonstrated. . . .

Various *amici* urge that RICO's pattern element should be interpreted . . . so that a defendant's racketeering activities form a pattern only if they are characteristic either of organized crime in the traditional sense, or of an organized-crime-type perpetrator, that is, of an association dedicated to the repeated commission of criminal offenses. . . .

Congress' decision not explicitly to limit RICO's broad terms strongly implies that Congress had in mind no such narrow and fixed idea of what constitutes a pattern as that suggested by *amici* here. . . .

The occasion for Congress' action was the perceived need to combat organized crime. But Congress for cogent reasons chose to enact a more general statute, one which, although it had organized crime as its focus, was not limited in application to organized crime. Congress picked out as key to RICO's application broad concepts that might fairly indicate an organized crime connection, but that it fully realized do not either individually or together provide anything approaching a perfect fit with "organized crime." . . .

RICO, with its very generous definition of "racketeering activity," acknowledges the breakdown of the traditional conception of organized crime, and responds to a new situation in which

[CONTINUED]

persons engaged in long-term criminal activity often operate *wholly* within legitimate enterprises. Congress drafted RICO broadly enough to encompass a wide range of criminal activity, taking many different forms and likely to attract a broad array of perpetrators operating in many different ways. We thus decline the invitation to invent a rule that RICO's pattern of racketeering concept requires an allegation and proof of an organized crime nexus. . . .

Petitioners complaint alleges that at different times over the course of at least a 6-year period the non-commissioned respondents gave five members of the MPUC numerous bribes, in several different forms, with the objective—in which they were allegedly successful—of causing these Commissioners to approve unfair and unreasonable rates for Northwestern Bell. RICO defines bribery as a "racketeering activity," so petitioners have alleged multiple predicate acts.

Under the analysis we have set forth above, and consistent with the allegations in their complaint, petitioners may be able to prove that the multiple predicates alleged constitute "a pattern of racketeering activity," in that they satisfy the requirements of relationship and continuity. The acts of bribery alleged are said to be related by a common purpose, to influence Commissioners in carrying out their duties in order to win approval of unfairly and unreasonably high rates for Northwestern Bell. Furthermore, petitioners claim that the racketeering predicates occurred with some frequency over at least a 6-year period, which may be sufficient to satisfy the continuity requirement. Alternatively, a threat of continuity of racketeering activity might be established at trial by showing that the alleged bribes were a regular way of conducting Northwestern Bell's ongoing business, or a regular way of conducting or participating in the conduct of the alleged and ongoing RICO enterprise, the MPUC.

Reversed and remanded.

CASE QUESTIONS

1. What is the purpose behind RICO?
2. What is required to show a pattern of racketeering under RICO?
3. Must racketeering activities be a part of organized crime?

The requirement of a pattern of racketeering activity is not the only issue created by the wording of the RICO statute. The law makes it unlawful for any person employed by or associated with any enterprise to conduct or participate in a violation. Thus, the law foresees two separate entities, a person and a distinct enterprise. An issue arises when a person incorporates and that person is the president and sole shareholder of the corporation. Courts have held in such cases that there are two separate entities and both may have RICO liability.

RICO allegations of fraud must be pled with particularity. A RICO plaintiff must describe the predicate acts of fraud with some specificity and state the time, place, and content of the alleged communications perpetrating the fraud. If there are multiple defendants, the allegations must put each defendant on notice of his alleged participation.

A plaintiff in a civil action is in effect a private attorney general. In filing a complaint, the plaintiff must also allege that the defendant participated in the operation or management of the enterprise and played a part in directing the affairs of the enterprise. Mere employment in an organization is not sufficient to hold someone liable under RICO.

RICO has been used against a variety of defendants by private attorneys general. RICO has encouraged suits against accounting firms, brokerage houses, banks, and other businesses. A recent survey found that less than 10 percent of RICO cases filed involve criminal activity generally associated with organized crime and more than 75 percent of these lawsuits involve allegations of fraud. Because RICO cases constitute almost 10 percent of the caseload in federal courts, the importance of this statute is apparent and its impact on business is significant.

RICO provides drastic remedies. Conviction for a violation of RICO carries severe criminal penalties and forfeitures of illegal proceeds. Upon filing a RICO indictment, the government may seek a temporary restraining order to preserve all forfeitable assets until the trial is completed and judgment entered. A person in a private civil action found to have violated RICO is liable for treble, or triple, damages, costs, and attorneys' fees.

19. CYBER CRIME

One of the most significant trends in the criminal law is the result of the rapid increase of use of the Internet. As the use of the Internet has become a part of everyday business, so also has the opportunity to use the Internet to steal. With billions of dollars flowing through cyberspace, it is not surprising that there are criminals taking advantage of the system. Hackers commit crimes throughout the world that involve millions, if not billions, of dollars.

Electronic theft is not limited to money. Employees have been caught issuing corporate stock to themselves. Trade secrets, personnel records, and customer lists have been stolen by hackers. Company plans are sometimes stolen and sold to competitors. The following box provides some illustrations of how people use the Internet to steal valuable property and information.

Most experts agree that cyber crime is more difficult to detect than crimes that preceded the Internet. Proof based on digital evidence about anonymous persons seldom leads to convictions. There has been an increase in law enforcement agents assigned to combat cyberspace thieves and the training and their education in this area has improved. There are several companies in the security intelligence business that are attempting to help the business community install systems to prevent hacking.

Certain aspects of cyberspace crime should be recognized by managers and shareholders. Electronic crimes are most often committed by employees. Access to confidential information should be limited and carefully controlled. Losses from such crimes are easily hidden in cost of goods sold or in bad debt write-offs. They are usually kept secret for fear of encouraging other criminal acts. Investors typically have little or no knowledge of losses resulting from cyber crime.

EXAMPLES OF INTERNET FRAUD

1. Illegal downloading of music, video, and software
2. Piracy of copyrighted materials
3. Dating services using fictitious persons
4. Websites involving nonexistent banks used to obtain confidential information
5. Fraudulent auctions involving the misrepresentation of products or a lack of intent to deliver the products sold

20. SENTENCING GUIDELINES

Historically, the fate of a person convicted of a crime depended heavily on the judge doing the sentencing. Some judges were lenient, and others were tough. The sentencing of convicted criminals was sometimes described as "judicial roulette." To make the criminal justice system more just and help ensure that similar crimes receive similar sentences, in the late 1980s a federal sentencing commission developed **sentencing guidelines** for federal crimes.

The published guidelines followed a great deal of study and debate. They use a mathematical approach and assign a number to each type of crime and to all attending circumstances. Some numbers are pluses and some are minuses. Multipliers are used for aggravating circumstances, and tables provide a range of sentences. For example, a first-offense armed robbery offender who stole $20,000 would be given a sentence of 46 to 57 months.

The law authorizes judges to depart from the guidelines when they encounter factors not considered by the commission. If a judge intends to impose a sentence in excess of the guidelines, the defendant must be informed in advance of this fact and of the reasons for the departure. In most cases, judges determine the sentence by relying on a probation officer's report. If the report recommends a penalty tougher than the guidelines, the defendant may review the report in advance, argue against the tougher sentence, and challenge the grounds.

The Federal Sentencing Guidelines have been subject to considerable debate and controversy. Many federal judges have been irked at the loss of control in the sentencing phase of the case, and others have criticized the complexity of the guidelines, which are sometimes hard even for the judges to follow.

The U.S. Sentencing Commission, which administers the guidelines, recently reported to Congress that great disparities still persist in sentencing for some federal offenses. Federal prosecutors often pursue money laundering charges in a broad array of cases because the guidelines impose such harsh sentences. For example, a businessperson who fraudulently obtains $20,000 of insurance payments and conducts routine financial transactions with the proceeds may be incarcerated for 8 to 14 months if charged with mail fraud. However, the same defendant would face a jail sentence of 33 to 41 months if charged under the money laundering statute.

Under the guidelines, either party may appeal based upon a claim that the trial judge did not follow the guidelines properly. The following case illustrates that point and how drastically the sentence may change depending upon the amount of fraud involved.

UNITED STATES V. NESENBLATT

171 F. 3D 1227 (9TH CIR. 1999)

BREYER, J.: Steven Nesenblatt pled guilty to one count of conspiracy and three counts of wire fraud, arising out of the $260 million bank fraud scheme. He appeals the district court's four-level enhancement of his sentence for deriving more than one million dollars in gross receipts from his offense.

Nesenblatt and others were indicted in the Central District of California in a 33 count indictment alleging bank fraud, making false statements to obtain bank loans, mail fraud, wire fraud, bank bribery, money laundering, and conspiracy to commit these substantive offenses. The indictment arose out of a

[CONTINUED]

scheme whereby Nesenblatt and his co-conspirators submitted false and misleading information to banks to obtain loans on behalf of Bruce McNall and several of McNall's business entities ("McNall entities"). McNall owned, operated, and controlled numerous entities, including the Los Angeles Kings hockey team; film production and distribution companies; thoroughbred racing and breeding stables; and trading and auction houses which specialized in rare coins, antiquities, and sports memorabilia. By the time the fraud was uncovered, McNall and his entities had obtained over $260 million in bank loans on the basis of false or misleading information.

Nesenblatt served as an attorney, vice chairman, and consultant for various McNall entities, including McNall Sports and Entertainment, a holding company which owned and managed McNall's various business entities. Nesenblatt was paid $500,000 in annual salary. McNall and the McNall entities also paid Nesenblatt an additional $2.3 million in cash, checks, and wire transfers during this same period.

Nesenblatt subsequently pled guilty to conspiracy and three counts of wire fraud pursuant to a plea agreement with the government. At sentencing, the district court found that Nesenblatt's base offense level was six, and then added 18 levels after finding that the amount of loss caused by Nesenblatt's fraud was more than $80 million. The district court also added two levels on the ground that the fraud required more than minimal planning, four levels for Nesenblatt having derived more than one million dollars from an offense that affected a financial institution, and three levels for Nesenblatt's role as a manager or supervisor, resulting in a total offense level of 30. The district court departed downward on several grounds, and imposed a sentence of 13 months imprisonment. Nesenblatt appeals only the four-level enhancement for deriving more than one million dollars from his offense.

We review the district court's interpretation of the Sentencing Guidelines de novo. The district court's factual findings underlying a sentence are reviewed for clear error. [The Sentencing Guidelines] provide a four-level enhancement in a defendant's offense level if the offense "affected a financial institution and the defendant derived more than $1,000,000 in gross receipts from the offense." The Application Note specifies that "gross receipts from the offense" means "gross receipts to the defendant individually,

rather than to all participants," and "includes all property, real or personal, tangible or intangible, which is obtained directly or indirectly as a result of such offense." The district court expressly found that at least one million of the more than three million dollars paid by McNall and McNall entities to Nesenblatt was derived "directly or indirectly" from Nesenblatt's bank fraud offense.

Nesenblatt contends that the district court erred because (1) it did not find that the payments to Nesenblatt were derived from his offense as opposed to legitimate business activities. . . . According to Nesenblatt, the court merely assumed that because a substantial amount of money was obtained by McNall and the McNall entities as a result of the bank fraud, any money which McNall and the McNall entities paid to Nesenblatt was directly or indirectly "derived" from Nesenblatt's offense. He contends that the McNall entities were legitimate businesses producing legitimate revenues, and that if given the opportunity, he could prove that the non-salary payments made to him followed legitimate infusions of revenue into the businesses and therefore the payments were not derived from his offense.

The government asserts that the payments to Nesenblatt were derived from his offense because the fraudulent bank loans kept the McNall entities operating. It contends that the McNall entities were effectively insolvent as of the late 1980s. Therefore, the government argues, although the McNall entities did generate some legitimate income, the $260 million in illegal loans were essential to the entities' continued existence, and the millions of dollars paid to Nesenblatt during this period were at least indirectly derived from his bank fraud offense.

A district court's factual findings underlying application of the Sentencing Guidelines must be made by the preponderance of the evidence. There is ample evidence in the record to support the district court's finding that Nesenblatt derived more than one million dollars from his offense. Nesenblatt does not dispute that during the relevant period he received from McNall or McNall entities approximately $2.3 million in cash, checks and wire transfers in addition to his regular salary. At the trial of Nesenblatt's co-defendant, Mark Eastman, the accountant for the bankruptcy trustee testified that, from sometime prior to 1988 through the present date, McNall and all of his entities were insolvent,

[CONTINUED]

that is, that their liabilities exceeded their assets. Nesenblatt himself testified that virtually all of McNall's businesses were continuously financed almost exclusively through bank loans and that the loans became the primary source of operating funds for McNall and his entities. He testified further that he could not even remember a time when the McNall entities were able to pay all the bills, and that although there were significant revenues "from the businesses in varying degrees at varying times, there were also large gaps all the time, and [the conspirators] came to rely more and more on filling those gaps with bank loans."

In light of the above evidence, it was not clear error for the district court to implicitly find that the McNall entities were able to continue operating only as a result of Nesenblatt and his co-conspirators' repeatedly obtaining fraudulent loan after fraudulent loan. Nor was it clear error for the district court to conclude that any payments the McNall entities made to Nesenblatt were necessarily derived, at least indirectly, from the fraudulently obtained bank loans; without the loans there would not have been any funds available to pay to Nesenblatt.

For the foregoing reasons, Nesenblatt's sentence is **Affirmed.**

CASE QUESTIONS

1. Why do the federal sentencing guidelines exist?
2. Why is the four-level enhancement in Nesenblatt's offense level critical to determining his overall sentence?
3. What standard of review is applied to district court findings underlying application of the sentencing guidelines?

Because corporations cannot be jailed, the sentencing commission has developed special guidelines for sentencing organizations convicted of federal crimes. The emphasis is on monetary penalties. It must be kept in mind, however, that in most criminal cases involving organizations, corporate officers can also be charged. As a result, the guidelines are designed so that the sanctions imposed upon organizations and their agents, taken together, will provide just punishment, adequate deterrence, and incentives for organizations to maintain internal mechanisms for preventing, detecting, and reporting criminal conduct. Punishment and deterrence are goals of the guidelines. The box on the next page summarizes the sentencing guidelines related to organizations.

To illustrate how these guidelines would work, assume that a large corporation committed fraud in selling its product to the federal government. Perhaps the test results on the product were falsely reported. If a high official in the company and some middle managers knew that the test results were falsified and the company had a previous conviction of fraud within ten years, the fine would be $20 to $40 million. However, if the company received good points for cooperation with investigators and had an aggressive internal audit program to detect and prevent fraud, the fine would be only $4 to $8 million. In either case, the court would also order *restitution.* The court may also put the business on probation, preventing it from selling stock and paying dividends, or the court may otherwise be involved in major corporate decisions. This probation provision serves to get and keep the attention of senior management. Management in a company on probation must prevent violations of federal laws by its employees.

GUIDELINES FOR SENTENCING ORGANIZATIONS

1. A court must, whenever practicable, order the organization to remedy any harm caused by the offense. The resources expended to remedy the harm should be viewed not as punishment but rather as a means of making victims whole for the harm caused. This principle is designed to eliminate the need for a tort suit and still allow the court to follow the traditional tort theory of damages.

2. If the organization operated primarily for a criminal purpose or primarily by criminal means, the fine should be high enough to divest the organization of all its assets. If this recommendation is followed, the net result is that the organization is eliminated and the fine becomes a "death penalty."

3. The fine range is based on the seriousness of the offense and the culpability of the organization. The seriousness of the offense generally will be determined by examining the financial gains to the defendant or the financial loss to the victim. These amounts will be applied by use of a guideline offense-level fine table. Culpability generally will be determined by the steps taken by the organization prior to the offense to prevent and detect criminal conduct, the level and extent of involvement in or tolerance of the offense by certain personnel, and the organization's actions after an offense has been committed.

4. Probation will be included in the sentence if needed to ensure that another sanction will be fully implemented or to ensure that steps will be taken within the organization to reduce the likelihood of future criminal conduct.

When these guidelines are followed, some very tough sentences will be imposed on corporations convicted of federal crimes. Criminal conduct will not only not pay; it may also totally destroy a business.

21. TRENDS

The corporate governance scandals in the last few years have resulted in changes and new developments in society's approach to white-collar crime. Congress has enacted important legislation commonly known as the Sarbanes-Oxley Act. That law will be discussed in Chapter 16 on securities regulation.

One of the important trends is to use income tax evasion as the theory to be used against white-collar criminals. This is not a new approach in law enforcement. In the 1930s, Al Capone was considered the most notorious criminal in the United States. Efforts to imprison him failed until the federal government charged him with income tax evasion. That crime was easily proven, and Al Capone died in prison. Because income tax evasion is much easier to prove than crimes such as obstruction of justice, there is a definite trend toward using the tax laws to put greedy corporate executives behind bars.

A second important trend is the government's efforts to obtain proof of illegal conduct by top corporate officials. The trend is to start an investigation of lower-middle-level managers. All of their records including e-mails and memos are subpoenaed by a grand jury or regulatory body such as the Securities and Exchange Commission. If wrongful conduct is found, these lower-level employees are charged with a conspiracy to violate a federal law. Prosecutors then plea bargain with these employees and agree to drop or reduce the charges in exchange for testimony against persons higher in the organizational chart. Prosecutors are able to work their way up to the real target of the investigation—top management.

Criminal investigations not only proceed vertically toward the top of a business organization, they also may proceed horizontally to catch friends and associates who assist in illegal conduct. In one important case, a financier's longtime girlfriend and confidant ended up pleading guilty to money laundering and racketeering.

Separate from the sentencing guidelines, discussed in the preceding section, there are several trends relating to punishment for white-collar crimes. First of all, white-collar criminals in high-profile cases are being treated as common street thugs at the time of their arrest. CEOs have been arrested in their offices, handcuffed and led to jail with TV cameras running. This is sometimes called a perp walk because the perpetrators are paraded before the public.

After an arrest, prosecutors often insist on high sums for bail. Millions of dollars may be required. Prosecutors may object to the source of the bail funds. If the money comes from illegal activity, it should not be used as a "get out of jail card" as if a Monopoly game is being played. For example, a five million dollar bond was required of Enron's chief financial officer who had been charged with fraud. His parents were required to put up their home as part of the security for the bond.

Many criminal cases involve a process known as plea bargaining. A person accused of a crime may offer to plead guilty in return for a reduced punishment. Prosecutors may agree in order to avoid the time and expense of trial or because of weaknesses in the prosecution's case. Another trend is for prosecutors to insist on some prison time when plea bargaining. Automatic probation should not be expected, even by persons with outstanding reputations as law-abiding citizens. For example, a stockbroker who pled guilty to bilking clients was sentenced to seven years in prison. A leading Wall Street stock trader was fined $100 million and served two years in prison. Harsh sentences for white-collar crimes are seen as a strong deterrent to such conduct. The federal laws on sentencing today provide for a maximum of 25 years for fraud.

Finally, criminal punishment often includes the seizure of assets such as bank accounts, luxury homes, yachts, and automobiles. There are laws that provide for forfeiture of illegally obtained assets.

As the result of criminal conduct by business executives, banks have suffered huge losses and many businesses have been forced into bankruptcy. Most major accounting firms have been sued. The accounting profession has been charged with conflicts of interest on the ground that their consulting activity conflicts with the audit function. Brokerage firms have been accused of deceptive practices in their stock recommendations because of conflicts with other aspects of their business. Accounting fraud has shaken investor confidence in the financial statements of publicly held businesses. There is a need to restore confidence that has weakened as the result of criminal prosecutions. Indeed, many persons argue that the prosecutions themselves and the resulting sentences are a part of the process that will restore the public's confidence in honest business practices.

KEY TERMS

Accessory 294	Concealment 308
Aiding and abetting 294	Conspiracy 292
Bankruptcy crime 307	Double jeopardy 297
Burglary 302	Endangerment of workers 300

REVIEW QUESTIONS AND PROBLEMS

Terms and Procedures

1. *Classifications*

   (a)   Why is it important for business persons to have an understanding of the basic principles of criminal law and white-collar crime?

   (b)   What is the difference between felonies and misdemeanors?

2. *Basic Concepts*

   Who are the parties to a criminal case?

3. *The Grand Jury*

   James was indicted by a federal grand jury. During the trial jury's deliberation one juror said, "I think James is guilty or else the grand jury would not have sent us the case." Another juror objected to this statement and said, "The action of the grand jury is irrelevant in our determination of guilt or innocence." Which juror is more accurate about the role of grand juries in our criminal justice system?

4. *Conspiracies*

   Allen, Mary, and Jon agreed to participate in a program to manipulate the values of securities. Allen made several telephone calls to securities brokers in which he delivered false information about a number of companies. Before any further actions were taken, Mary and Jonathan decided to withdraw as active participants in the program. Did Mary and Jon commit any crime? Why?

5. *Aiding and Abetting*

   Susan, a partner in a CPA firm, prepares a federal income tax return knowing that it contains false information. Because the client wants the return prepared in this manner, Susan obtains the taxpayer's signature on the return and files it with the IRS. Has Susan aided and abetted in the commission of a crime? Explain.

Constitutional Issues

6. *Fourth Amendment: Illegal Search and Seizure*

   Burger's junkyard business consists of dismantling automobiles and selling their parts. A New York statute authorized warrantless inspections of automobile junkyards. Police officers entered his junkyard, conducted an inspection, and discovered stolen vehicles and parts. Burger, who was charged with possession of stolen property, moved to suppress the evidence obtained as a result of the inspection. He contends that the administrative inspection statute is unconstitutional when it authorizes warrantless searches. Is he correct? Why or why not?

7. *Fifth Amendment: Self-incrimination*

   Roberts was the president and sole shareholder of a corporation. A federal grand jury issued a subpoena to him in his capacity as president. The subpoena required Roberts to produce corporate records. Roberts moves to quash the subpoena on Fifth Amendment grounds.

   (a)   Must Roberts deliver the records? Why or why not?

   (b)   Could Roberts be required to testify about the documents? Why or why not?

   (c)   If Roberts takes steps to dissolve the corporation, can he then avoid the subpoena? Why or why not?

8. *Fifth Amendment: Double Jeopardy*

   Does the double jeopardy clause apply to civil penalties? Why or why not?

9. *The Sixth Amendment*

   What are the six constitutional rights provided in the Sixth Amendment?

Specific Crimes

10. *Endangering Workers*

    Beth was killed when a trench collapsed. An investigation revealed that the trench was 27 feet deep and without adequate shoring in violation of safety standards. Bob, the president of the firm, is charged with negligent homicide. Is a finding of guilt possible? Why or why not?

11. *Obstruction of Justice*

    Quincy was a successful investment banker specializing in underwriting and merger advice. A federal grand jury was investigating the sales of initial public offerings, and Quincy knew that the grand jury had issued subpoenas seeking information about Quincy's deals. Quincy sent an e-mail to colleagues and encouraged them to "clean up" their files. What crimes, if any, did Quincy commit? If a colleague shredded files, what crimes may have been committed?

12. *False Statements to a Bank*

    Your business is in need of additional working capital. You contact your bank about a loan. A line of credit of $500,000 is tentatively approved pending you furnish audited financial statements. You meet with your auditor who is also a personal friend. Suppose you ask your auditor to add $250,000 as an account receivable. In fact, this asset does not exist. The auditor certifies the financial statements with this phantom asset. You mail the audited financial statements to the bank. What crimes have you committed? What crimes did the auditor commit? What should have been the auditor's response to your request?

13. *False Statement to the Federal Agency*

Adam was hired by a defense contractor for a position that required a clearance for classified material. He failed to disclose a criminal conviction on a Department of Defense personnel security questionnaire, but admitted that he knew there was false information on the form which he signed.

   (a)   Did Adam willfully violate any federal law?

   (b)   If Adam didn't actually realize that the form would be submitted to a federal agency, is that a defense?

14. *Larceny*

Joe, a purchasing agent of ABC Company, entered into a contract to purchase software on behalf of ABC from a software company represented by Harry. The contract stated a price of $10,000 but the actual cost was $8,000. Joe and Harry split the $2,000. What crimes were committed?

15. *Fraud*

Mary lost her billfold which contained credit cards and an ATM access card. She had written her pin number on a piece of paper which was also in the billfold. Al found the billfold. He used the credit cards and ATM card to obtain over $2,500 in goods, services, and cash. Is Al guilty of a federal offense?

16. *Mail and Wire Fraud*

A nursing home brochure represented that there were registered nurses on duty 24–7. That representation was false in that there were no RNs on duty on Sundays. The nursing home used the mails to bill the families of patients. Is the nursing home guilty of mail fraud without proof of any injury?

17. *Bankruptcy Crimes*

Bill was heavily in debt and recently lost his job. Over the years he had collected coins as a hobby. Prior to filing for relief in bankruptcy he gave the coin collection to his son. The coins were not listed as an asset in bankruptcy. Did Bill commit a federal offense?

18. *Racketeer Influenced and Corrupt Organizations Act (RICO)*

Don, a promoter of prize fights, formed a corporation. Don was the sole shareholder, sole director, and president of the corporation. Don was charged with a violation of RICO. Is the requirement of both a person and an enterprise met?

19. *Cyber Crime*

Why is cyber crime difficult to detect and to prosecute successfully?

20. *Sentencing Guidelines*

The U.S. sentencing guidelines apply a mathematical formula to sentencing. How do the guidelines operate?

21. *Trends*

Describe three trends in how criminal law impacts business organizations and businesspeople.

Terminology Review

For each term in the left-hand column, match the most appropriate description in the right-hand column.

1. Grand jury
2. Conspiracy
3. Search warrant
4. Self-incrimination
5. Double jeopardy
6. Trial by jury
7. False statements
8. Exculpatory no
9. RICO
10. Sentencing guidelines

a. Expansive federal law aimed at controlling abusive business practices
b. Sets criminal penalties in federal cases
c. Federal body charged with investigating and enforcing the law
d. Simple denials in response to questioning in criminal investigation
e. Protected by the Fifth Amendment
f. Prevents trial of a person for the same infraction twice
g. Criminal if made to a bank or governmental agency
h. May be issued based upon probable cause
i. An agreement with a criminal purpose
j. Guaranteed by the Sixth Amendment in criminal cases

BUSINESS DISCUSSION

Your business is in need of additional working capital. You contact your bank and a loan of $500,000 is tentatively approved pending a review of your financial statements. The bank loan officer, who is a close personal friend, tells you to make sure that the financial statements "look good" before mailing them to the bank.

Should you juggle the figures to make sure the loan is approved?

Is the bank loan officer a potential grand jury target?

Do you face additional charges by using the mail to return a false financial statement?

chapter 11

CORPORATE GOVERNANCE AND BUSINESS ORGANIZATIONS

How to Operate?

Three years following your graduation with a business degree, you and three classmates began operating a consulting business. Your firm specializes in offering support related to payroll- and account-management computer applications. A potential major client requests that your firm make a proposal for a year-long project. Because of the length of time and financial commitment this project may take, you and your co-workers take time to address the following questions:

Which form of organization is best suited to meet the needs of your business?

What factors do you need to consider to answer the preceding question?

How can you actually accomplish business on such a large scale?

What are the legal concerns related to this potential growth?

The situation posed and questions asked in the Business Decision go to the fundamentals of how business is conducted. At the core of these fundamentals is the concept of corporate governance. As it is discussed in this chapter, the phrase *corporate governance* has at least two meanings. This chapter highlights both of these meanings. First, corporate governance relates to how business organizations are operated, led, or governed. As you study the material in this chapter, continually ask, What governance issues relate to the way business is done within a particular organization? Your search for answers applies equally to all types of business organization. The word *corporate* in the phrase *corporate governance* relates to the combination of people rather than being limited to only the business organization known as a corporation.

The second meaning of corporate governance, which concerns how the law provides regulation of business organizations, also is an important part of this chapter. For the most part, state laws govern the legal entities available to businesspeople through which business is conducted. This chapter addresses both statutory and common law governing business organizations and how these organizations do business. Specifically, this chapter focuses on factors used to select the best organizational form, the various choices of organizations, and agency principles related to the performance of business transactions.

1. FORMS OF BUSINESS ORGANIZATIONS

People conduct business using a number of different organizational forms. The law recognizes three basic forms and several hybrid forms that contain attributes of two or more basic forms. These various forms are listed in the following box and are the subject matter of sections 7 through 12, below.

Before we begin with an explanation of the various factors to consider when selecting the best organizational form for conducting business activities, two terms are important as they relate to the number of owners of a business organization. Some organizations are owned by only a few persons. Such organizations are said to be **closely held.** Family-owned and -operated businesses are common examples of closely held organizations. Other businesses may be owned by hundreds, if not thousands, of persons. These organizations are **publicly held** ones. Examples of publicly held businesses include those whose stock is traded on a public exchange.

You should understand that the decision of selecting an appropriate organizational form usually is limited to those situations involving the few owners of a closely held business. When a business is publicly held by a large number of owners, the form of organization usually is a corporation. The reason for this corporate form being used is that shareholders can transfer their ownership without interfering with the organization's management.

FACTORS TO CONSIDER WHEN SELECTING A BUSINESS'S ORGANIZATIONAL FORM

Significant factors to consider in selecting the best organizational form for a particular business activity include:

- The cost of creating the organization
- The continuity or stability of the organization
- The control of decisions
- The personal liability of the owners
- The taxation of the organization's earnings and its distribution of profits to the owners

In the following sections, each of these factors is defined so that you can more easily apply their meaning in sections 7 through 12.

POSSIBLE FORMS OF BUSINESS ORGANIZATIONS

The three basic forms include:
- Sole proprietorships
- Partnerships
- Corporations

The hybrid forms include:
- Limited partnerships
- S corporations
- Limited liability companies
- Limited liability partnerships

2. CREATION

The word *creation* means the legal steps necessary to form a particular business organization. At times, a businessperson may be concerned with how much it will cost to have each form established. Usually, the cost of creation is not a major factor in considering which form of business organization a person will choose to operate a business. The most significant creation-related issues are how long it will take to create a particular organization and how much paperwork is involved.

3. CONTINUITY

Another factor to consider when selecting the best organizational form for a business activity is the continuity of the organization. How does an organization's existence relate to its owners? By this question the meaning of the word *continuity* becomes associated with the stability or durability of the organization.

The crucial issue with this continuity factor is the method by which a business organization can be dissolved. A **dissolution** is any change in the ownership of an organization that changes the legal existence of the organization. In essence, the questions become: Is the organization easily dissolved? What impact does a dissolution of the organizational form have on the business activity of that organization?

4. MANAGERIAL CONTROL

The factor of control concerns who is managing the business organization. Often this issue is of vital importance to the owners. The egos of businesspeople can cause them to insist on equal voices in management. As you study this factor under each organizational form, keep in mind the difficulties that can arise when a few strong-willed business owners disagree with one another. Usually when people are excited about getting started in a business opportunity, no one takes time to discuss methods of resolving potential deadlocks. The failure to consider how to overcome disputes involving managerial control can cause business activities to suffer and the organization to fail. Therefore, consideration of potential conflict and mechanisms to resolve disputes are essential to consider when selecting a form for a business venture.

5. LIABILITY

When considering the liability factor, you should ask yourself—to what degree is the owner of a business personally liable for the debts of the business organization? Generally, businesspeople want to limit their personal liability. Although there are organizations that appear to accomplish this goal, you will see that such appearances might be misleading when actually conducting business transactions. For this reason, this liability factor is very important and deserves significant consideration as it relates to each of the organizational forms presented below.

6. TAXATION

This factor often is viewed as the most critical when selecting the form of business organization. At issue is: How is the income earned by the business taxed? How is the money distributed to the business owners taxed? Is it possible that owners may have to pay taxes on money that is attributed to them as income but which they have not actually received? The answers to these questions provide much needed guidance when deciding which form of organization is best suited for a business's operation.

People have stated that the double taxation of corporate income should be avoided by selecting a different form of organization. As you will see, there are specific advantages to creating the organizational forms that are "single taxed." However, advantages also exist when an organization is subject to the supposed "double tax."

SELECTING THE BEST ORGANIZATIONAL FORM

The following six sections apply the various factors to consider when deciding which organizational form is best for a particular business activity. Following these sections is a brief discussion on how to make a good decision when selecting the best organizational form.

7. SOLE PROPRIETORSHIPS

When considering the five factors introduced above, it has been said that the **sole proprietorship** has many virtues. However, the use of this business organization is very limited because multiple owners cannot create a proprietorship. Depending on the factual situation presented, greater continuity, less liability, and more flexible tax planning may be required than those afforded by the law of the sole proprietorship.

A sole proprietorship is the easiest and least expensive business organization to create. In essence, the proprietor obtains whatever business licenses are necessary and begins operations. Legally, no formal documentation is needed. The ease of (perhaps the lack of) the steps used to create a proprietorship makes it an attractive alternative when beginning a new business venture. However, as the other factors might dictate, a business might shift away from the proprietorship form as it becomes more successful.

A proprietorship's continuity is tied directly to the will of the proprietor. In essence, the proprietor may dissolve his or her organization at any time by simply changing the organization or terminating the business activity. The fact that the propreitorship's business activity may be more stable than the proprietor's willingness to remain actively involved in the business indicates that the sole proprietorship is a less desirable organizational form. Ownership of a sole proprietorship cannot be transferred.

The sole proprietor is in total control of his or her business's goals and operations. While the proprietor has complete responsibility for the business's success or failure, the owners of all other organizational forms usually share control to some degree. As long as this control issue is carefully thought out, there can be real value in having more than one voice in control of managing a business enterprise.

A sole proprietor is personally obligated for the debt of the proprietorship. Legally speaking, this owner has unlimited liability for the obligations of this type of business organization. The business organization's creditors can seek to hold the proprietor personally liable for 100 percent of the debts that the proprietorship cannot pay. The desire to avoid the potentially high risk of personal liability is an important reason why other organizational forms might be viewed as preferable to the proprietorship.

A sole proprietorship is not taxed as an organization. All the proprietorship's income subject to taxation is attributed to the proprietor. The initial appearance of this tax treatment may appear favorable because the business organization is not taxed. However, the individual proprietor must pay the applicable personal tax rate on the income earned by the proprietorship whether the proprietor actually receives any of the income from the organization or not. If the organization retains its profits for business expansion purposes instead of distributing this money to the proprietor, that owner still must pay taxes on the income made by the proprietorship.

8. PARTNERSHIPS

Whenever two or more people wish to own a business together, a partnership is a possible organizational form. In general, a **partnership** is an agreement between two or more persons to share a common interest in a commercial endeavour and to share profits and losses. The word *persons* in the previous sentence should be interpreted broadly enough to allow business organizations, as well as individuals, to form a partnership. For example, two or more individuals, an individual and a corporation, a partnership and a corporation, or any combination of these entities may agree to create a business organization called a partnership.

Due to the potentially complex relationships established through a partnership, factors to consider when studying the appropriateness of this organizational form are presented under subheadings that correspond to the factors presented above.

Creation When compared to other forms of business organizations (other than the sole proprietorship), a partnership is easily formed. The cost of forming a partnership is relatively minimal. In addition, the creation of a partnership is made easier since it does not need to get permission from each state in which it does business.

The key to a partnership's existence is satisfying the elements of its definition:

1. Two or more persons,
2. A common interest in business, and
3. Sharing profits and losses.

If the parties conduct their affairs in such a way as to meet these definitional elements, a partnership exists regardless of whether the persons involved call themselves partners or not. The following box presents issues related to the existence and naming of a partnership.

Continuity A general partnership is dissolved any time there is a change in the partners. For example, if a partner dies, retires, or otherwise withdraws from the organization, the partnership is dissolved. Likewise, if a person is added as a new

FORMATION AND NAMING OF A PARTNERSHIP

Since the existence of a partnership is based on the partners' agreement, it is possible that this agreement is implied from the conduct or actions of the parties. Partners should never rely on implied agreements. Rather, their agreement should be explicitly stated among the parties and drafted into a formal document. The formal agreement is called the **articles of partnership.**

Since a partnership is created by agreement, the partners select the name of the partnership. This right of se-

lection is subject to two limitations in many states. First, a partnership may not use any word in the name, such as "company," that would imply the existence of a corporation. Second, if the name is other than that of the partners, the partners must give notice as to their actual identity under the state's **assumed-name statute.** Failure to comply with this disclosure requirement may result in the partnership's being denied access to courts, or it may result in criminal actions being brought against those operating under the assumed name.

ANTICIPATING A PARTNERSHIP'S DISSOLUTION—BUY AND SELL AGREEMENTS

To prevent problems that may arise when a partner dies or withdraws from a partnership, the articles of partnership should include a **buy and sell agreement.** This agreement, which should be entered into when the business entity is created, provides for the amount and manner of compensation for the interest of the deceased or withdrawing owner.

Buy and sell agreements frequently use formulas to compute the value of the withdrawing partner's interest and provide for the time and method of payment. In the case of death, the liquidity needed is often provided by the cash proceeds from life insurance taken out on the life of the deceased and made payable to the business or to the surviving partners. Upon payment of the amount required by the buy and sell agreement to the estate of the deceased, the interest of the deceased ends, and all the surviving partners can continue the business.

partner, there is a technical dissolution of the organization. Therefore, it generally is said that the partnership organization is easily dissolved. Even if the partnership agreement provides that the partnership will continue for a stated number of years, any partner still retains the power to dissolve the organization. Although liability may be imposed on the former partner for wrongful dissolution in violation of the agreement, the partnership nevertheless is dissolved.

A dissolution does not necessarily destroy the business of a partnership. Dissolution is not the same thing as terminating an organization's business activity. Termination involves the winding up or liquidating of a business; dissolution simply means the legal form of organization no longer exists. The box above addresses how parties might prevent dissolution from destroying a partnership's business success.

Managerial Control   In a general partnership, unless the agreement provides to the contrary, each partner has an equal voice in the firm's affairs. Partners may agree to divide control in such a way as to make controlling partners and minority partners. The decision of who has what voice in management is of crucial importance to the chances of the business's success and to the welfare of the partners' relationship with each other. The possibility of a deadlock among partners is very real, especially when there are only a few partners and there are an even number of them. Care should be taken to design mechanisms to avoid or at least handle the disputes that will arise when partners share managerial control. A written partnership agreement should provide specific language governing issues of managerial control.

Liability   All partners in a general partnership have unlimited liability for their organization's debts. These partners' personal assets, which are not associated with the partnership, may be claimed by the partnership's creditors. From a creditor's perspective, this personal liability of each partner extends to the organization's entire debt, not just to a pro rata share. These partners are **jointly and severally liable** for the partnership's obligations. For example, assume that a general partnership has three partners and that it owes a creditor $300,000. If it is necessary to collect the debt, this creditor can sue all three partners jointly for the $300,000. As an alternative, the creditor can sue any one partner or any combination of two for the entire $300,000. Among the partners, anyone who has to pay the creditor more than her or his pro rata share of the liability usually can seek contribution from the remaining partners.

Taxation Like proprietorships, partnerships are not a taxable entity. The fact that this type of organization pays no income tax does not mean that the profits of the partnership are free from income tax. A partnership files an information return that allocates to each partner his or her proportionate share of profits or losses from operations, dividend income, capital gains or losses, and other items that would affect the income tax owed by a partner. Partners then report their share of such items on their individual income tax returns, irrespective of whether they have actually received the items.

This aspect of a partnership is an advantage to the partners if the organization suffers a net loss. The pro rata share of this loss is allocated to each partner, and it can be used to reduce these partners' personal taxable income. However, by this same reasoning, a partnership is a disadvantage if the organization retains any profits made by the organization for the purpose of expansion. Suppose a partnership with three equal partners has $30,000 in net income. If the partnership keeps this money, there still is a constructive distribution of $10,000 to each partner for tax purposes. Assuming that these partners are in a 28 percent personal income tax bracket, they each would have to pay $2,800 in taxes even though they actually received nothing from the partnership.

---

concept SUMMARY   ***Advantages and Disadvantages of Partnerships***

The basic law relating to partnerships is found in the Uniform Partnership Act. According to this statute, the partnership form of organization generally has the following advantages:

1. A partnership is easily formed because it is based on a contract among persons.
2. Costs of formation are not significant.
3. Partnerships are not a tax-paying entity.
4. Each partner has an equal voice in management, unless there is a contrary agreement.
5. A partnership may operate in more than one state without obtaining a license to do business.
6. Partnerships generally are subject to less regulation and less governmental supervision than are corporations.

Offsetting these advantages, the following aspects of partnerships have been called disadvantages:

1. For practical reasons, only a limited number of people can be partners.
2. A partnership is dissolved anytime a partner ceases to be a partner, regardless of whether the reason is withdrawal or death.
3. Each partner's liability is unlimited, contrasted with the limited liability of a corporate shareholder.
4. Partners are taxed on their share of the partnership's profits, whether the profits are distributed or not. In other words, partners often are required to pay income tax on money they do not receive.

---

9. CORPORATIONS

The third basic organizational form which might be used to operate a business is the corporation. A **corporation** is an artificial, intangible entity created under the authority of a state's law. A corporation is known as a **domestic corporation** in the state in which it is incorporated. In all other states, this corporation is called a **foreign corporation.** As a creature of state legislative bodies, the corporation is much more complex to create and to operate than other forms of businesses. These legal complexities associated with the corporation are presented above in a structure that parallels the preceding section so that comparisons with partnerships can be easily made.

STEPS IN CREATION OF A CORPORATION

The formal application for a corporate charter is called the **articles of incorporation.** These articles must contain the proposed name of the corporation. So that persons dealing with a business will know that it is a corporation, the law requires that the corporate name include one of the following words or end with an abbreviation of them: "corporation," "company," "incorporated," or "limited." In addition, a corporate name must not be the same as, or deceptively similar to, the name of any domestic corporation or that of a foreign corporation authorized to do business in the state to which the application is made. The corporate name is an asset and an aspect of goodwill. As such, it is legally protected.

In addition to the proposed corporate name, the articles of incorporation usually will include the proposed corporation's period of duration, the purpose for which it is formed, the number of authorized shares, and information about the initial corporate officials.

Once drafted, these papers are sent to the appropriate state official (usually the secretary of state), who approves them and issues a corporate charter. Notice of this incorporation usually has to be advertised in the local newspaper in order to inform the public that a new corporation has been created. The initial board of directors then meets, adopts the corporate bylaws, and approves the sale of stock. At this point, the corporation becomes operational.

Creation   A corporation is created by a state issuing a **charter** upon the application of individuals known as **incorporators.** In comparison with partnerships, corporations are more costly to form. Among the costs of incorporation are filing fees, license fees, franchise taxes, attorneys' fees, and the cost of supplies, such as minute books, corporate seals, and stock certificates. In addition to these costs of creation, there also are annual costs in continuing a corporation's operation. These recurring expenses include annual reporting fees and taxes, the cost of annual shareholders' meetings, and ongoing legal-related expenses. The box above describes the process of incorporation.

If a corporation wishes to conduct business in states other than the state of incorporation, that corporation must be licensed in these foreign states. The process of qualification usually requires payment of license fees and franchise taxes above and beyond those paid during the initial incorporation process. If a corporation fails to qualify in states where it is conducting business, the corporation may be denied access to the courts as a means of enforcing its contracts.

Continuity   In contrast to a partnership, a corporation usually is formed to have perpetual existence. The law treats a corporation's existence as distinct from its owners' status as shareholders. Thus, a shareholder's death or sale of her or his stock does not affect the organizational structure of a corporation. This ability to separate management from ownership is an often cited advantage of the corporation.

Although the sale of stock by a major shareholder or the shareholder's death has no legal impact on the organization's existence, this event may have a very real adverse impact on that corporation's ability to do business. The shareholder may have been the driving force behind the corporation's success. Without this shareholder, the corporation's business may fail.

Managerial Control   In the corporate form of organization, the issue of control is complicated by three groups. First, the **shareholders** elect the members of the board of directors. These **directors** set the objectives or goals of the corporation, and they appoint the officers. These **officers,** such as the president, vice president, secretary, and treasurer, are charged with managing the daily operations of the corporation in an attempt to achieve the stated organizational objectives or goals. Thus, which one of these three groups really controls the corporation?

To answer this question effectively, you must realize that the issue of who controls a corporation varies depending on the size of the ownership base of the organization. In essence, matters of managerial control require us to examine the publicly held corporation as distinct from the closely held corporation.

Publicly Held Corporations. In very large corporations, control by management (a combination of the directors and officers) is maintained with a very small percentage of stock ownership through the use of corporate records and funds to solicit proxies. Technically, a **proxy** is an agent appointed by a shareholder for the purpose of voting the shares. Management can, at corporate expense, solicit the right to vote the stock of shareholders unable to attend the meetings at which the directors of the company are elected. An outsider must either own sufficient stock to elect the directors or must solicit proxies at his or her own expense. The management of a large corporation usually can maintain control with only a small minority of actual stock ownership.

During the first years of this century, we have seen evidence of the negative aspects arising from a few shareholders, who also serve as officers and directors, controlling large, publicly held corporations. The lack of sufficient review and influence from those called "outside directors" contributed to corporate scandals that shocked the public confidence in business and the economy. Chapter 10 contains material on the criminal aspects of these scandals, and Chapter 16 describes the specific violations of securities law. At this point, we want you to appreciate that limiting the role of corporate governance to only a few people can lead to massive fraud. Not having sufficient review, including formal audits, led to the accounting problems described in the following box.

Closely Held Corporations. Unlike the situation with a large, publicly held corporation, one shareholder (or at least a small group of shareholders) may be able to control a closely held corporation. This can result because this individual (or the group) can own an actual majority of the issued shares. This majority can control the election of a board of directors. In fact, the shareholders with the largest amount of stock are often elected to this board of directors. The directors, in turn, elect officers, who again may be the shareholders with the largest interests. In a very real sense, those who own a majority of a closely held corporation can rule with near absolute authority.

Examples of Massive Fraud in Publicly Held Corporations' Financial Documentation	
Company	*Alleged Wrongful Conduct*
WorldCom	Reduced expenses, thereby inflating profits, by $7 billion
Enron	Overstated earnings by $9 billion
Xerox	Overstated profits by $1.4 billion
Reliant	Claimed $6 billion in energy trades that were sham deals
Qwest Communications	Overstated revenues by $950 million

What are the rights of those who do not possess control in a closely held corporation—the so-called minority interest? To a large degree, the owners of the minority interest are subject to the decisions of the majority. The majority may pay themselves salaries that use up profits and may never declare a dividend. However, the minority interest is not without some rights, because the directors and officers stand in a fiduciary relation to the corporation and to the minority shareholders if the corporation is closely held. This relation imposes a duty on directors to act for the best interests of the corporation rather than for themselves individually.

If the majority is acting illegally or oppresses the rights of the minority share-holders, a lawsuit known as a **derivative suit** may be brought by a minority share-holder on behalf of the corporation. Such suits may seek to enjoin the unlawful activity or to collect damages for the corporation. For example, contracts made between the corporation and an interested director or officer may be challenged. If sued, the burden is on the director or officer (who may be the majority share-holder) to prove good faith and inherent fairness in such transactions.

The basic difficulty of owning a minority interest in a closely held corporation arises from the fact that there is no ready market for the stock should the share-holder desire to dispose of it. Of course, if there is a valid buy and sell agreement, then there is a market for the stock. Thus, like with partnerships, buy and sell agreements are absolutely essential in closely held corporations.

Liability The legal ability to separate a corporation's shareholders from its managers means that the owners are liable for the debts of the corporation only to the extent of those shareholders' investment in the cost of the stock. Thus, corporate shareholders are said to have **limited personal liability.**

The generalization that the investors in a corporation have limited liability but those in a partnership have unlimited liability is too broad and needs qualification. To be sure, someone investing in a company listed on the New York Stock Exchange will incur no risk greater than the investment, and the concept of limited liability certainly applies. However, if the company is a small, closely held corporation with limited assets and capital, it will be difficult for it to obtain credit on the strength of its own net worth. As a practical matter, shareholders will usually be required to add their own individual liability as security for borrowing. For example, if the XYZ Company seeks a loan at a local bank, the bank often will require the owners, X, Y, and Z, to personally guarantee repayment of the loan.

This is not to say that shareholders in closely held corporations do not have some degree of limited liability. Shareholders have limited liability for contractlike obligations that are imposed as a matter of law (such as taxes). Liability also is limited when the corporate obligation results from torts committed by company employees while doing company business.

Even in these situations, the mere fact of corporate existence does not mean the shareholders will have liability limited to their investment. When courts find that the corporate organization is being misused, the corporate entity can be disregarded. This has been called **piercing the corporate veil.** When this veil of protection has been pierced, the shareholders are treated like partners who have unlimited liability for their organization's debts.

The **alter-ego theory,** by which the corporate veil can be pierced, may also be used to impose personal liability upon corporate officers, directors, and stockholders. If the corporate entity is disregarded by these officials themselves, so that there is such a unity of ownership and interest that separateness of the corporation has ceased to exist, the alter-ego theory will be followed and the corporate veil will be pierced.

Simply alleging that a person is the sole owner of a corporation engaged in wrongful activity will not result in a piercing of the corporate veil. This conclusion is appropriate when the owner has respect for the existence of the organization. In the following case, notice the Supreme Court's effort to protect the corporate owner, especially since the statute being interpreted seems to limit the liability to the corporate organization.

MEYER v. HOLLEY

123 S. Ct. 824 (2003)

Emma Mary Ellen Holley and David Holley, an interracial couple, tried to purchase a house. Grove Crank, a real estate salesperson, working for Triad, Inc., discriminated against the Holleys and prevented them from buying a home. The Holleys filed two lawsuits. First, the Holleys sued Triad, Inc., and Mr. Crank. Later, the Holleys filed a suit against David Meyer in his capacity as real estate broker, president, and sole owner of Triad, Inc. The Holleys argued that Mr. Meyer was vicariously liable for the discrimination of his salesperson. The District Court combined these suits and dismissed all claims since it held the statute of limitations prevented the claims. The Court further held that Mr. Meyer could not be vicariously responsible for the acts of his salesperson under the Fair Housing Act. The Holleys appealed to the Ninth Circuit Court of Appeals. That court reversed the dismissal. Further, the appellate court held that the Fair Housing Act did permit liability to pass through to a person who had authority to control the salesperson. The court found that Mr. Meyer had such authority, and thus he was vicariously liable.

Mr. Meyer petitioned for a writ of certiorari, which was granted by the Supreme Court

BREYER, J.: . . .The Fair Housing Act itself focuses on prohibited acts. In relevant part the Act forbids any person or other entity whose business includes engaging in residential real estate-related transactions to discriminate, for example, because of

race. It adds that "person" includes, for example, individuals, corporations, partnerships, associations, labor unions, and other organizations. It says nothing about vicarious liablity.

Nonetheless, it is well established that the Act provides for vicarious liability. This Court has noted that an action brought for compensation by a victim of housing discrimination is, in effect, a tort action. And the Court has assumed that, when Congress creates a tort action, it legislates against a legal background of ordinary tort-related vicarious liability rules and consequently intends its legislation to incorporate those rules.

It is well established that traditional vicarious liability rules ordinarily make principals or employers vicariously liable for acts of their agents or employees in the scope of their authority or employment. And in the absence of special circumstances it is the corporation, not its owner or officer, who is the principal or employer, and thus subject to vicarious liability for torts committed by its employees or agents. . . .

The Ninth Circuit held that the Fair Housing Act imposed more extensive vicarious liability—that the Act went well beyond traditional principles. The Court of Appeals held that the Act made corporate owners and officers liable for the unlawful acts of a corporate employee simply on the basis that the owner or officer controlled (or had the right to control) the actions of that employee. We do not agree with the Ninth Circuit that the Act extended traditional vicarious liability rules in this way.

[CONTINUED]

For one thing, Congress said nothing in the statute or in the legislative history about extending vicarious liability in this manner. And Congress' silence, while permitting an inference that Congress intended to apply ordinary background tort principles, cannot show that it intended to apply an unusual modification of those rules. . . .

For another thing, the Department of Housing and Urban Development (HUD), the federal agency primarily charged with the implementation and administration of the statute has specified that ordinary vicarious liability rules apply in this area. And we ordinarily defer to an administering agency's reasonable interpretation of a statute.

A HUD regulation applicable during the relevant time periods for this suit provided that analogous administrative complaints alleging Fair Housing Act violations may be filed

> against any person who directs or controls, or has the right to direct or control, the conduct of another person with respect to any aspect of the sale . . . of dwellings . . . if that other person, acting within the scope of his or her authority as employee or agent of the directing

or controlling person . . . has engaged . . . in a discriminatory housing practice.

. . . Respondents, conceding that traditional vicarious liability rules apply, argue that those principles themselves warrant liability here. For one thing, they say, California law itself creates what amounts, under ordinary common-law principles, to an employer/employee or principal/agent relationship between (a) a corporate officer designated as the broker under a real estate license issued to the corporation, and (b) a corporate employee/salesperson. Insofar as this argument rests solely upon the corporate broker/officer's right to control the employee/salesperson, the Ninth Circuit considered and accepted it. But we must reject it given our determination. . . that the "right to control" is insufficient by itself, under traditional agency principles, to establish a principal/agent or employer/employee relationship. . . .

The judgment of the Court of Appeals is vacated, and the case is remanded for further proceedings consistent with this opinion.

Vacated and remanded.

CASE QUESTIONS

1. What is the relationship of David Meyer to the parties in the various lawsuits filed?

2. On what basis did the District Court and the Ninth Circuit Court of Appeals reach different legal conclusions regarding Meyer's liability for the acts of his salesperson?

3. Did the Supreme Court conclude that vicarious liability could be imposed under the language of the Fair Housing Act?

4. Did the Supreme Court conclude that Meyer could not be held personally liable for his saleperson's discriminatory actions? Why?

Taxation Corporations must pay income taxes on their earnings. The table on the next page sets forth these tax rates. The fact that there is a separate corporate income tax may work as an advantage. For example, if the corporation makes a profit that is to be retained by the corporation to support growth, no income is allocated to the shareholders. These shareholders will not have their personal taxable income increased, as would a partner in a similar situation. In addition, the corporate rate may be lower than the individual rates.

But corporations also have tax disadvantages. Suppose a corporation suffers a loss during a given tax year. The existence of the corporate tax works as a disadvantage, since this loss cannot be distributed to the shareholders in order to reduce

*Corporate Tax Rates**	
Income	Tax Rate
$0–$50,000	15%
$50,000–$75,000	25%
$75,000–$10,000,000	34%
over $10,000,000	35%

In addition to these rates, there are excess taxes when corporate taxable income exceeds $100,000. These taxes increase again if corporate taxable income exceeds $15,000,000.

Source: 26 U.S.C.§ 11.

their personal tax liability. Indeed, a net operating loss to a corporation can be used only to offset corporate income earned in other years. And the allocation of such a loss can be carried back only for 3 years and carried forward for 15 years. (Note: There are many different rules concerning specialized carryover situations. The Internal Revenue Code should be examined prior to relying on the general rule just stated.)

Perhaps a greater disadvantage of the corporate tax occurs when a profit is made and the corporation wishes to pay a dividend to its shareholders. The money used to pay this dividend will have been taxed at the corporate level. It is then taxed again because the shareholder must take the amount of the dividend into his or her own personal income. Although the rate of this second tax is reduced to 15 percent, as a part of a 2003 tax reduction, the existence of the second tax is potentially significant in selecting the best organizational form for a business. This situation has been called the **double tax** on corporate income. A similar situation of double taxation occurs when a corporation is dissolved and its assets are distributed to shareholders as capital gains. Yet, as the discussion next indicates, the double tax may not be as big a disadvantage as it appears at first.

Avoiding Double Taxation. Corporations have employed a variety of techniques for avoiding the double taxation of corporate income. First, reasonable salaries paid to corporate officials may be deducted in computing the taxable income of the business. Thus, in a closely held corporation in which all or most shareholders are officers or employees, this technique may avoid double taxation of substantial portions of income. As might be expected, the Internal Revenue Code disallows a deduction for excessive or unreasonable compensation and treats such payments as dividends. Therefore, the determination of the reasonableness of corporate salaries is often a tax problem in that form of organization.

Second, corporations provide expense accounts for many employees, including shareholder employees. These are used to purchase travel, food, and entertainment. When so used, the employee, to some extent, has compensation that is not taxed. In an attempt to close this tax loophole, the law limits deductions for business meals and entertainment to 50 percent of the cost. Meal expenses and entertainment are deductible only if the expenses are directly related to or associated with the active conduct of a trade or business. For a deduction, business must be discussed directly before, during, or directly after the meal. Additionally, meal expenses are not deductible to the extent the meal is lavish or extravagant. Thus, the use of the expense account to avoid taxation of corporate income is subject to numerous technical rules and limitations.

Third, the capital structure of the corporation may include both common stock and interest-bearing loans from shareholders. For example, assume that a company needs $100,000 cash to go into business. If $100,000 of stock is issued, no expense will be deducted. However, assume that $50,000 worth of stock is purchased by the owners and $50,000 is lent to the company by them at 10 percent interest. In this case, $5,000 interest each year is deductible as an expense of the company and thus subject to only one tax as interest income to the owners. Just as in the case of salaries, the Internal Revenue Code has a counteracting rule relating to corporations that are undercapitalized. If the corporation is undercapitalized, interest payments will be treated as dividends and disallowed as deductible expenses.

The fourth technique for avoiding double taxation, at least in part, is simply not to pay dividends and to accumulate the earnings. The Internal Revenue Service seeks to compel corporations to distribute those profits not needed for a business purpose, such as growth. When a corporation retains earnings in excess of $250,000, there is a presumption that these earnings are being accumulated to avoid a second tax on dividends. If the corporations cannot rebut this presumption, an additional tax of 39.6 percent is imposed.

Fifth, a corporation may elect to file under Subchapter S of the Internal Revenue Code. This election eliminates the corporate tax; this subject is discussed further in section 11 of this chapter.

---

concept SUMMARY   *Advantages and Disadvantages of Corporations*

The usual advantages of the corporate form of organization include the following:

1. This form is the best practical means of bringing together a large number of investors.
2. Control may be held by those with a minority of the investment.
3. Ownership may be divided into many unequal shares.
4. Shareholders' liabilities are limited to their investments.
5. The organization can have perpetual existence.
6. In addition to being owners, shareholders may be employees entitled to benefits such as workers' compensation.

Among the frequently cited disadvantages of the corporate organization are the following:

1. The cost of forming and maintaining a corporation, with its formal procedural requirements, is significant.
2. License fees and franchise taxes often are assessed against corporations but not partnerships.
3. A corporation must be qualified in all states where it is conducting local or intrastate business.
4. Generally, corporations are subject to more governmental regulation at all levels than are other forms of business.
5. Corporate income may be subject to double taxation.

---

10. LIMITED PARTNERSHIPS

A limited partnership basically has all the attributes of a partnership except that one or more of the partners are designated as **limited partners.** This type of partner is not personally responsible for the debts of the business organization. However, these limited partners are not permitted to be involved in the control or operations of the limited partnership. The management is left in the hands of one or more **general partners** who remain personally liable for the organization's debts.

The attributes of a general partnership and a corporation that combine to make the limited partnership an attractive alternative form of business organization are discussed under the subheadings that follow.

Creation   Like a general partnership, a limited partnership is created by agreement. However, as in the case of a corporation, state law requires that the contents of a certificate must be recorded in a public office so that everyone may be fully advised as to the details of the organization. This certificate contains, among other matters, the following information: the name of the partnership, the character of the business, its location, the name and place of residence of each member, those who are to be the general partners and those who are to be the limited partners, the length of time the partnership is to exist, the amount of cash or the agreed value of property to be contributed by each partner, and the share of profit or compensation each limited partner shall receive.

The limited partnership certificate is required to be recorded in the county where the partnership has its principal place of business. An additional copy has to be filed in every community where the partnership conducts business or has an office. Whenever there is a change in the information contained in the filed certificate, a new certificate must be prepared and recorded. If an accurate certificate is not on record and the limited partnership continues its operation, the limited partners become liable as general partners. Substantial compliance with all the technical requirements of the limited partnership law is essential if the limited partners are to be assured of their limited liability.

The terms of the limited partnership agreement control the governance of the organization. These terms should be read carefully and understood by all general and limited partners before the agreement is signed. Failure of the parties to state their agreement clearly may result in a court interpreting the limited partnership agreement.

Continuity   The principles guiding partnerships also apply to limited partnerships if there is a change in the general partners. A limited partner may assign his or her interest to another without dissolving the limited partnership.

Managerial Control   In a limited partnership, the general partners are in control. Limited partners have no right to participate in management. The impact of this relationship on the operations of a limited partnership is discussed in detail in the next subsection.

Liability   The true nature of the limited partnership being a hybrid is in the area of owners' liability. Traditionally, the general partners in a limited partnership have unlimited liability. However, the limited partners are not personally liable for the partnership's debts. These limited partners' liability typically will not exceed the amount of their investments.

Under the Revised Uniform Limited Partnership Act (RULPA), a limited partner's surname may not be used in the partnership's name unless there is a general partner with the same name. If a limited partner's name is used in the firm's name, that partner will become personally liable to unsuspecting creditors.

Limited partners also may not participate in the management of the limited partnership. Under the RULPA, a limited partner who participates in the organization's management becomes liable as a general partner if a third party had knowledge of

ACTIONS BY LIMITED PARTNER

Limited Partners Do Not Lose the Benefit of Limited Personal Liability When Performing the Following:

- Acting as an agent or employee of the partnership
- Consulting with or advising a general partner
- Acting as a guarantor of the partnership's obligations
- Inspecting and copying any of the partnership's financial records
- Demanding true and full information about the partnership whenever circumstances render it just and reasonable

- Receiving a share of the profits or other compensation by way of income
- Approving or disapproving an amendment to the partnership's certificate
- Voting on matters of fundamental importance such as dissolution, sale of assets, or change of the partnership's name
- Having contribution returned upon dissolution

the limited partner's activities. The box above lists actions by a limited partner that do not constitute participation in management.

11. S CORPORATIONS

Beginning in 1958, the federal government permitted shareholders of certain corporations to unanimously elect to have their organization treated like a partnership for income tax purposes. This election is made possible through the language of subchapter S of the Internal Revenue Code. Today, organizations that are subject to this election often are referred to simply as **S corporations.**

The S corporation has all the legal characteristics of the corporation previously discussed in this chapter. The one exception to this similar treatment is that shareholders in the S corporation are responsible for accounting on their individual income tax returns for their respective shares of their organization's profits or losses. In essence, these shareholders can elect to have their business organization treated, for tax purposes, as if it were a partnership. Through this election, the shareholders avoid having a tax assessed on the corporate income itself. Even though the S corporation does not pay any taxes, like a partnership, it must file an information return with the Internal Revenue Service. The following case involves the U.S. Supreme Court deciding whether it is the corporate or shareholder's personal return on which the statute of limitations for challenges is based.

BUFFERD v. COMMISSIONER

113 S. CT. 927 (1993)

WHITE, J.: On his 1979 income tax return, petitioner, a shareholder in a Subchapter S corporation, claimed as "pass-through" items portions of a deduction and a tax credit reported on the corporation's return. The question presented is whether the 3-year period in

which the Internal Revenue Service is permitted to assess petitioner's tax liability runs from the filing date of the individual return or the corporate return. . . .

Subchapter S of the Internal Revenue Code was enacted in 1958 to eliminate tax disadvantages that

[CONTINUED]

might dissuade small businesses from adopting the corporate form and to lessen the tax burden on such businesses. The statute accomplishes these goals by means of a pass-through system under which corporate income, losses, deductions, and credits are attributed to individual shareholders in a manner akin to the tax treatment of partnerships. . . .

Petitioner was treasurer and a shareholder of Compo Financial Services, Inc., an S corporation. On February 1, 1980, Compo filed a return for the tax year of December 26, 1978 to November 30, 1979 as required by § 6037(a) of the Code. On that return, Compo reported a loss deduction and an investment tax credit arising from its partnership interest in a venture known as Printers Associates. Petitioner and his wife filed a joint return for 1979 on April 15, 1980. Their return claimed a pro rata share of the deduction and credit reported by Compo pursuant to the pass-through provisions of Subchapter S.

Code § 6501(a) establishes a generally applicable statute of limitations providing that the Internal Revenue Service may assess tax deficiencies within a 3-year period from the date a return is filed. That limitations period may be extended by written agreement. In March 1983, before three years had passed from the time the joint return was filed, petitioner agreed to extend the period in which deficiencies arising from certain claims on the return could be assessed against him. No extension was obtained from Compo with respect to its return for the 1978–1979 tax year.

In 1987, the Commissioner determined that the loss deduction and credit reported by Compo were erroneous and sent a notice of deficiency to petitioner based on the loss deduction and credit that he had claimed on his return. In the Tax Court, petitioner contended that the Commissioner's claim was time barred because the disallowance was based on an error in Compo's return, for which the 3-year assessment period had lapsed. The Tax Court found for the Commissioner. . . . The Court of Appeals for the Second Circuit affirmed, holding that, where a tax deficiency is assessed against the shareholder, the filing date of the shareholder's return is the relevant date for purposes of § 6501(a). Because another Court of Appeals has a contrary view, we granted certiorari.

. . . We have no doubt that the courts below properly concluded, as the Commissioner argued, that it is the filing of the petitioner's return that triggers the running of the statutory period.

The Commissioner can only determine whether the taxpayer understated his tax obligation and should be assessed a deficiency after examining that taxpayer's return. Plainly, then, "the" return referred to in § 6501 (a) is the return of the taxpayer against whom a deficiency is assessed. Here, the Commissioner sought to assess taxes which petitioner owed under the Code because his return had erroneously reported a loss and credit to which he was not entitled. The fact that the corporation's return erroneously asserted a loss and credit to be passed through to its shareholders is of no consequence. In this case, the errors on the corporate return did not and could not affect the tax liability of the corporation, and hence the Commissioner could only assess a deficiency against the stockholder-taxpayer whose return claimed the benefit of the errors. . . .

We hold that the limitations period within which the Internal Revenue Service must assess the income tax return of an S corporation shareholder runs from the date on which the shareholder's return is filed. The judgment of the Court of Appeals is **affirmed.**

CASE QUESTIONS

1. When was the S corporation's tax return filed?
2. When did Mr. and Mrs. Bufferd file their personal return?
3. When did the IRS assert a challenge claiming that the Bufferds' return contained inaccurate information?
4. What transpired to allow the IRS to claim a challenge beyond the three-year period following the filing of the personal return?
5. Why does the Court conclude that the three-year period of review is based on the shareholder's personal return rather than the S corporation's return?

S corporations cannot have more than 75 shareholders, each of whom must elect to have the corporate income allocated to the shareholders annually in computing their income for tax purposes, whether actually paid out or not. Only individuals are eligible to elect under subchapter S. Therefore, other forms of business organization, such as partnerships, limited partnerships, or corporations, cannot be shareholders in an S corporation.

In addition to the limitations just stated, there are many technical rules of tax law involved in S corporations. However, as a rule of thumb, this method of organization has distinct advantages for a business operating at a loss because the loss is shared and immediately deductible on the returns of the shareholders. It is also advantageous for businesses capable of paying out net profits as earned. In the latter case, the corporate tax is avoided. If net profits must be retained in the business, subchapter S tax treatment is disadvantageous because income tax is paid on earnings not received, and there is a danger of double taxation to the individual because undistributed earnings that have been taxed once are taxed again in the event of the death of a shareholder. Thus, the theoretical advantage of using an S corporation to avoid double taxation of corporate income must be carefully qualified.

12. LIMITED LIABILITY COMPANIES

The **limited liability company** is a relatively new organizational alternative. In 1977, Wyoming was the first state to pass a law permitting the creation of this type of business organization.

In 1988, the Internal Revenue Service ruled that limited liability companies (LLCs) would be treated as nontaxable entities, much like partnerships, for federal income tax purposes. Following this ruling, states rushed to pass legislation authorizing businesspeople to operate their businesses as LLCs. In essence, its owners have more flexibility than with the S corporation while not having to struggle with the complexities of the limited partnership.

A variation of the LLC is known as the **limited liability partnership.** This organization often is used by professionals, such as doctors, lawyers, and accountants. In the true sense of a hybrid, an LLC and an LLP have characteristics of both a partnership and a corporation.

The growing popularity of these forms of business organizations requires a careful examination of the various factors to consider. The focus of the following subheadings is on the LLC.

Creation An LLC is created through filings much like those used when creating a corporation. **Articles of organization** are filed with a state official, usually the secretary of state. Instead of "incorporators," the term **organizers** is used. The name of any LLC must acknowledge the special nature of this organizational form by including the phrase "limited liability company," or "limited company," or some abbreviation, such as "LLC" or "LC." An LLC created in a state other than the one in which it is conducting business is called a foreign LLC. Like a foreign corporation, this LLC must apply to the state to be authorized to transact business legally. An LLC also must file annual reports with the states in which it operates.

Continuity The owners of LLCs are called **members** rather than shareholders or partners. Membership in LLCs is not limited to individuals. Unlike in the

S corporation, a business organization can be an owner in any LLC. The transferability of a member's interest is restricted in the fashion of a partner as opposed to the free transferability of a corporate shareholder. Anytime a member dies or withdraws from the LLC, there is a dissolution of the business organization. However, the business of a dissolved LLC is not necessarily adversely impacted if the remaining members decide to continue business. Either as provided in the articles of organization or by agreement of the remaining members within 90 days of the withdrawing member's disassociation, the business of the LLC may be continued rather than wound up.

Managerial Control   The managerial control of an LLC is vested in its members, unless the articles of organization provide for one or more **managers.** Regardless of whether members or managers control the LLC, a majority of these decision makers decide the direction of the organization. In a few situations enumerated in the state law authorizing LLCs, unanimous consent of the members is required for the organization to make a binding decision. Similarly to partners in a partnership, members of LLCs make contributions of capital. They have equal rights to share in the LLC's profits and losses, unless these members have agreed otherwise. When a member is in the minority with respect to decisions being made on behalf of the LLC, that dissenting member has rights very much like a dissenting shareholder in a corporation. These rights include bringing a derivative lawsuit against the controlling members of the LLC. Ultimately, a dissenting member has the right to sell the membership interest to the other members of the LLC.

Liability   For liability purposes, members do act as agents of their LLC. However, they are not personally liable to third parties. Thus, these members have attributes of both partners and shareholders with respect to liability.

Taxation   Finally, state laws and the IRS recognize LLCs as nontaxable entities. Although the LLC appears to have many advantages, do not forget that careful analysis is needed in every situation to determine whether this type of tax treatment is in the members' best interests.

13. MAKING THE DECISION

There usually is no absolutely right answer to the question, Which organizational form is best for a particular business's operation? Hopefully the preceding sections have presented you with some helpful background material to consider when this important decision is made.

The criteria used to select a form of organization needs to be reviewed periodically. This review should be done in consultation with close advisers such as attorneys, accountants, bankers, and insurers. These people weigh the factors and costs involved and then select the most suitable organizational form for the business's needs at that time. Because this selection process balances advantages against disadvantages, the decision often is to choose the least objectionable form of organization.

As it relates to the Business Decision at the beginning of this chapter, do you have a better understanding of why a new start-up business might select one organizational form and then change its organization as the business grows?

Illustration of the Agency Relationship

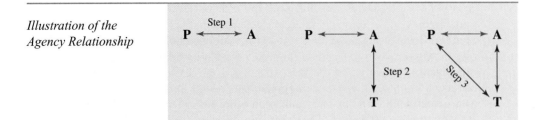

AGENCY PRINCIPLES

Once the organizational form is selected and created, how to conduct business becomes the primary focus. Organizations cannot accomplish anything without the help of individuals, who are referred to as agents. Therefore, practically all business transactions involve agents. The next three sections introduce, illustrate, and discuss general principles of the law of agency.

14. TERMINOLOGY

The application of agency law involves the interaction among three parties. Although individuals usually are these parties, agency relationship can involve business organizations. The figures above illustrate a three-step approach to understanding how the law views the purpose of agency relationship.

First, a **principal** interacts with someone (or some organization) for the purpose of obtaining that second party's assistance. This second party is the **agent.** Second, the agent (on behalf of the principal) interacts with a **third party.** Third, the usual legal purpose of the agent is to create a binding relationship between the principal and third party. Typically, the agent will want Step 3 to involve the understanding that any liability created by Steps 1 and 2 is replaced by the new principal–third party relationship. To accomplish this substitution, the agent must remember to comply with the following duties owed to the principal:

- A duty of loyalty to act for the principal's advantage and not to act to benefit the agent at the principal's expense
- A duty to keep the principal fully informed
- A duty to obey instructions
- A duty to account to the principal for monies handled

In studying the law of agency, keep in mind that the employer/business organization is the principal and the employee is the agent. Whether employee conduct creates liability for the employer is the usual agency issue facing businesses. Such issues may involve either contracts or torts.

15. CONTRACTUAL LIABILITY

For an employee to bind the employer to a contract that the employee negotiates with a third party, the employer must have authorized the employee's actions. Contractual authority can take the following forms:

- Actual authority
- Expressed, written authority

- Implied authority
- Apparent authority

Only when one of these types of authority is present will the principal and the third party become contractually bound.

A simple example may help illustrate the concept of authority. Suppose, as an owner of a restaurant, you hire Alex to be an evening manager. You discover that the restaurant is running low on coffee. You write a note to your friend, Terry, the manager of the local grocery store. In this note, you ask Terry to allow Alex to charge $100 worth of coffee to your restaurant's account at the grocery store. You give this note to Alex with instructions to purchase the coffee and deliver the note to Terry. If Terry allows Alex to charge $100 worth of coffee, is your restaurant liable to pay $100 to the grocery store? The answer is yes, because Alex had **actual authority,** which was expressed in writing.

Now suppose a week later, you send Alex to the same grocery store to buy pound cake and yogurt. This time you call Terry on the phone and ask that Alex be allowed to charge the cost of the cake and yogurt. Once again, your restaurant is contractually liable to pay for this purchase since Alex was actually authorized to contract through your expressed oral statement to Terry.

What if, sometime later, you and your co-owner are out of town and Alex is in charge of the restaurant for the evening. Alex, realizing that the tuna salad is in short supply, goes to Terry's grocery store and charges to the restaurant $60 worth of tuna fish. Upon your return, you find a bill from Terry for this purchase. Legally, do you have to pay it? Again, the answer is yes! This time Alex's actions contractually bind the restaurant to Terry since Alex had **implied authority** to do what was necessary for the restaurant's benefit. This implied authority arises from the position Alex holds as evening manager and by the history of the express authority situations.

Finally, suppose that you terminate Alex's employment. In retaliation, Alex goes to Terry's grocery store and charges a variety of groceries that are consistent with the food your restaurant serves. When you get the bill from Terry, is the restaurant liable? Answer—yes. Even though Alex lacks any actual (expressed or implied) authority, your failure to notify Terry of Alex's termination left Alex with **apparent authority.** Due to the history of Alex representing your restaurant, it is reasonable for Terry to assume that this incident is one more in the series of Alex's properly charging items to the restaurant's account. To prevent this unwanted liability from occurring, you should have let Terry know that Alex is no longer employed. This notice would destroy the existence of apparent authority.

It should be noted that in this last scenario, involving the existence of apparent authority, you would have a claim against Alex for the monies you had to pay Terry. Alex's liability to you arises because Alex breached the duty of loyalty owed to the restaurant.

The basic concepts of agency law apply to the operation of business organizations. Sometimes the law provides technical rules, such as those applicable to how partners can bind their partnership. One such special rule is worthy of mention. A partner in a **trading partnership,** that is, one engaged in the business of buying and selling commodities, has the implied authority to borrow money in the usual course of business and to pledge the credit of the firm. A partner in a **nontrading partnership,** such as an accounting or other service firm, has no implied power to borrow money. In the latter case, such authority must be actual before the firm will be bound.

16. TORT LIABILITY

The legal elements of a tort are discussed in Chapter 9. For the purposes of this brief discussion, accept that a tort is a breach of a duty that causes injury. An agent who causes harm to a third party may create legal liability owed by the principal to that third party. The accomplishment of this vicarious liability depends on whether the agent was acting within the scope of employment when the tort occurred. Details of this type of liability are presented in Chapter 9 under the section heading "Respondeat Superior."

The type of business organization in existence determines the extent of responsibility for agents' torts. In essence, partners are liable for all transactions entered into by any partner in the scope of the partnership business and are similarly liable for any partner's torts committed while she or he is acting in the course of the firm's business. Each partner is in effect both an agent of the partnership and a principal, being capable of creating both contract and tort liability for the firm and for copartners and likewise being responsible for acts of copartners. Generally, shareholders of corporations and members of LLCs are protected from tort liability that exceeds the amount of their investment. The following case involves the Supreme Court analysis of one corporation's potential liability for the acts of another business organization. As you begin reading this case, recall the discussion of piercing the corporate veil in section 9, above.

UNITED STATES V. BESTFOODS

118 S. CT. 1876 (1998)

In a complicated set of facts, the Supreme Court reviews the liability of the parent corporate owners of subsidiaries that operated a chemical manufacturing facility. This facility was originally owned and operated by Ott Chemical Co. (Ott I). It was sold to CPC International, Inc., which reorganized Ott I into a subsidiary. This subsidiary became known as Ott II. Later, the facility was sold to Aerojet-General Corp. Throughout the chemical manufacturing process, toxic wastes were dumped at this facility's location. At issue is whether CPC and Aerojet are liable for the cost of the environmental cleanup under § 107 of the Comprehensive Environmental Response, Compensation, and Liability Act of 1980 (CERCLA).

The District Court found that both the parent corporations were liable. The Sixth Circuit Court of Appeals reversed and found "neither CPC nor Aerojet was liable for controlling the actions of its subsidiaries since the parent and subsidiary corporations maintain separate personalities and the parents did not utilize the subsidiary corporate form to perpetrate fraud or subvert justice." The Supreme Court granted the government's petition for a writ of certiorari.*

SOUTER, J.: It is a general principle of corporate law deeply ingrained in our economic and legal systems that a parent corporation (so called because of control through ownership of another corporation's stock) is not liable for the acts of its subsidiaries. Thus it is hornbook law that "the exercise of the 'control' which stock ownership gives to the stockholders . . . will not create liability beyond the assets of the subsidiary. That 'control' includes the election of directors, the making of by-laws . . . and the doing of all other acts incident to the legal status of stockholders. Nor will a duplication of some or all of the directors or executive officers be fatal." Although this respect for corporate distinctions when the subsidiary is a polluter has been severely criticized in the literature, nothing in CERCLA purports to reject this bedrock principle, and against this ven-

[CONTINUED]

erable common-law backdrop, the congressional silence is audible. The Government has indeed made no claim that a corporate parent is liable as an owner or an operator under § 107 simply because its subsidiary is subject to liability for owning a polluting facility.

But there is an equally fundamental principle of corporate law, applicable to the parent-subsidiary relationship as well as generally, that the corporate veil may be pierced and the shareholder held liable for the corporation's conduct when . . . the corporate form would otherwise be misused to accomplish certain wrongful purposes, most notably fraud. . . . Nothing in CERCLA purports to rewrite this well-settled rule, either. . . . The Court of Appeals was accordingly correct in holding that when (but only when) the corporate veil may be pierced, may a parent corporation be charged with derivative CERCLA liability for its subsidiary's actions.

If the act rested liability entirely on ownership of a polluting facility, this opinion might end here; but CERCLA liability may turn on operation as well as ownership, and nothing in the statute's terms bars a parent corporation from direct liability for its own actions in operating a facility owned by its subsidiary. The fact that a corporate subsidiary happens to own a polluting facility operated by its parent does nothing, then, to displace the rule that the parent corporation is responsible for the wrongs committed by its agents in the course of its business. . . . It is this direct liability that is properly seen as being at issue here.

Under the plain language of the statute, any person who operates a polluting facility is directly liable for the costs of cleaning up the pollution. This is so regardless of whether that person is the facility's owner, the owner's parent corporation or business partner, or even a saboteur who sneaks into the facility at night to discharge its poisons out of malice. If any such act of operating a corporate subsidiary's facility is done on behalf of a parent corporation, the existence of the parent-subsidiary relationship under state corporate law is simply irrelevant to the issue of direct liability.

This much is easy to say; the difficulty comes in defining actions sufficient to constitute direct parental "operation." [The Court studied several definitions of the word *operation* and concluded that]

under CERCLA, an operator is simply someone who directs the workings of, manages, or conducts the affairs of a facility. To sharpen the definition for purposes of CERCLA's concern with environmental contamination, an operator must manage, direct, or conduct operations specifically related to pollution, that is, operations having to do with the leakage or disposal of hazardous waste, or decisions about compliance with environmental regulations. . . .

The question is not whether the parent operates the subsidiary, but rather whether it operates the facility, and that operation is evidenced by participation in the activities of the facility, not the subsidiary. . . .

In imposing direct liability on these grounds, the District Court failed to recognize that it is entirely appropriate for directors of a parent corporation to serve as directors of its subsidiary, and that fact alone may not serve to expose the parent corporation to liability for its subsidiary's acts. . . .

We accordingly agree with the Court of Appeals that a participation-and-control test looking to the parent's supervision over the subsidiary, especially one that assumes that dual officers always act on behalf of the parent, cannot be used to identify operation of a facility resulting in direct parental liability. Nonetheless, a return to the ordinary meaning of the word "operate" in the organizational sense will indicate why we think that the Sixth Circuit stopped short when it confined its examples of direct parental operation to exclusive or joint ventures, and declined to find at least the possibility of direct operation by CPC in this case.

In our enquiry into the meaning Congress presumably had in mind when it used the verb "to operate," we recognized that the statute obviously meant something more than mere mechanical activation of pumps and valves, and must be read to contemplate "operation" as including the exercise of direction over the facility's activities. The Court of Appeals recognized this by indicating that a parent can be held directly liable when the parent operates the facility in the stead of its subsidiary or alongside the subsidiary in some sort of a joint venture. We anticipated a further possibility above, however, when we observed that a dual officer or director might depart so far from the norms of parental influence exercised through dual office-holding as to serve the parent,

[CONTINUED]

even when ostensibly acting on behalf of the subsidiary in operating the facility. Yet another possibility, suggested by the facts of this case, is that an agent of the parent with no hat to wear but the parent's hat might manage or direct activities at the facility.

Identifying such an occurrence calls for line drawing yet again, since the acts of direct operation that give rise to parental liability must necessarily be distinguished from the interference that stems from the normal relationship between parent and subsidiary. Again norms of corporate behaviour (undisturbed by any CERCLA provision) are crucial reference points. . . . The critical question is whether, in degree and detail, actions directed to the facility by an agent of the parent alone are eccentric under accepted norms of parental oversight of a subsidiary's facility.

There is, in fact, some evidence that CPC engaged in just this type and degree of activity at the Muskegon plant. The District Court's opinion speaks of an agent of CPC alone who played a conspicuous part in dealing with the toxic risks emanating from the operation of the plant. G. R. D. Williams worked only for CPC; he was not an employee, officer, or director of Ott II, and thus, his actions were of necessity taken only on behalf of CPC. The District Court found that CPC became directly involved in environmental and regulatory matters through the work of . . . Williams, CPC's govenmental and environmental affairs director. Williams . . . became heavily involved in environmental issues at Ott II. He actively participated in and exerted control over a variety of Ott II environmental matters, and he issued directives regarding Ott II's responses to regulatory inquiries.

We think that these findings are enough to raise an issue of CPC's operation of the facility through Williams's actions, though we would draw no ultimate conclusion from these findings at this point. Not only would we be deciding in the first instance an issue on which the trial and appellate courts did not focus, but the very fact that the District Court did not see the case as we do suggests that there may be still more to be known about Williams's activities. Indeed, even as the factual findings stand, the trial court offered little in the way of concrete detail for its conclusions about Williams's role in Ott II's environmental affairs, and the parties vigorously dispute the extent of Williams's involvement. Prudence thus counsels us to remand, on the theory of direct operation set out here, for reevaluation of Williams's role, and of the role of any other CPC agent who might be said to have had a part in operating the Muskegon facility.

The judgment of the Court of Appeals for the Sixth Circuit is vacated, and the case is remanded with instructions to return it to the District Court for further proceedings consistent with this opinion.

Vacated and remanded.

CASE QUESTIONS

1. What environmental law is the focus of this case?
2. How do the District Court and the Court of Appeals rule?
3. What does the Supreme Court find with respect to the derived or indirect liability of a parent corporation?
4. What does the Supreme Court say about the direct liability of a parent corporation that operates a facility through a subsidiary?
5. Why does the Supreme Court remand this case to the District Court?

KEY TERMS

Actual authority   341
Agent   340
Alter-ego theory   330
Apparent authority   341
Articles of incorporation   328
Articles of organization   328
Articles of partnership   325
Assumed-name statute   325
Buy and sell agreement   326
Charter   328
Closely held   322
Corporation   327
Derivative suit   330
Director   328
Dissolution   323
Domestic corporation   327
Double tax   333
Foreign corporation   327
General partner   334
Implied authority   341
Incorporator   328

Jointly and severally liable   326
Limited liability company   338
Limited liability partnership   338
Limited partner   334
Limited personal liability   330
Manager   339
Member   338
Nontrading partnership   341
Officer   328
Organizer   328
Partnership   325
Piercing the corporate veil   330
Principal   340
Proxy   329
Publicly held   322
S corporation   336
Shareholder   338
Sole proprietorship   324
Third party   340
Trading partnership   341

REVIEW QUESTIONS AND PROBLEMS

1. *Forms of Business Organizations*
   (a)   What are the three traditional business organizations and the four hybrid forms?
   (b)   Explain the distinction between the terms *closely held* and *publicly held.*

Factors to Consider When Selecting a Business's Organizational Form

2. *Creation*
   Relative to other factors discussed in this chapter, how important is the factor of creation?

3. *Continuity*
   Why does dissolution of a business organization not necessarily impact that organization's business activities?

4. *Managerial Control*
   Why should business owners take time to discuss the control each will exert over the organization's activities?

5. *Liability*
   What is meant by the phrase liability of a business organization as compared to the liability of the owners?

6. *Taxation*
   Why is taxation an important element to consider when selecting the appropriate organization for your business activities?

Selecting the Organizational Form

7. *Sole Proprietorships*

   What are the limitations of the sole proprietorship?

8. *Partnerships*

   Terry is the senior partner in an accounting firm. One of Terry's partners performs an audit. The audited firm sues Terry, as the senior partner, for alleged errors in the audit. If Terry is found liable, can Terry sue to collect a pro rata share of this liability from the other partners? Why or why not?

9. *Corporations*

   (a)   Who controls the closely held corporation? Explain.

   (b)   Describe five techniques that a corporation might use to avoid the double taxation of corporate profits.

10. *Limited Partnerships*

    Laura and Gary have formed a limited partnership, with Gary agreeing to be the general partner. This partnership has purchased supplies from Sam. Sam has received a promissory note signed on behalf of the partnership as payment. If the partnership is unable to pay this note, can Sam hold Gary personally liable? Explain.

11. *S Corporations*

    (a)   Although it is technically a corporation, the S corporation has the attributes of which business organization when considering the taxation factor?

    (b)   What is the implication of this treatment if the S corporation has a profitable year but does not distribute dividends to its shareholders?

12. *Limited Liability Companies*

    What is the advantage of this organizational form compared to the S corporation?

13. *Making the Decision*

    Albert and Barbara wish to enter into the business of manufacturing fine furniture. Which form of business organization would you recommend in each of the following situations? Explain each of your answers.

    (a)   Barbara is a furniture expert, but she has no funds. Albert knows nothing about such production, but he is willing to contribute all the money needed to start the business.

    (b)   The furniture-manufacturing process requires more capital than Albert or Barbara can raise together. However, they wish to maintain control of the business.

    (c)   The production process can be very dangerous, and a large tort judgment against the business is foreseeable.

    (d)   Sales will be nationwide.

    (e)   A loss is expected for the first several years.

Agency Principles

14. *Terminology*

    (a)   What are the names given to the three parties typically involved in an agency relationship?

    (b)   Describe the general purpose of the agency relationship.

15. *Contractual Liability*

For several years, Albert acted as a collection agent for Paulette. Recently, Paulette revoked Albert's authority to collect payments from customers. However, neither Paulette nor Albert told any customers of Albert's termination. Yesterday, Theresa, one of Paulette's customers, paid Albert the money owed to Paulette. Albert never gave this money to Paulette. Is Theresa liable to pay Paulette? Why or why not?

16. *Tort Liability*

Tammy was shopping in Save-a-Lot Grocery Store when Stewart, an employee, brushed Tammy's ankle with a grocery cart. A short time later, while still shopping, Tammy told Stewart that he should say "Excuse me," and then people would get out of his way. Stewart then punched Tammy in the face, knocking her to the floor. If Tammy sues Save-a-Lot, what legal issue must be addressed to determine whether Save-a-Lot is liable?

TERMINOLOGY REVIEW

For each term in the left-hand column, match the most appropriate description in the right-hand column.

1. Partnership
2. Sole proprietorship
3. Limited partnership
4. Corporation
5. Limited liability company
6. Buy and sell agreement
7. S corporation
8. Accumulated earnings tax
9. Agent
10. Apparent authority
11. Principal
12. Actual authority

a. A business owned by one person who is personally liable for all loses
b. An artificial being created by a state
c. An individual or business organization that hires employees to "get the job done"
d. Imposed when a corporation fails to justify not paying individuals from earnings
e. Created when shareholders elect to be treated as partners for tax purposes
f. The grant of permission that flows from a principal to an agent, it may be either expressed or implied
g. Created by an agreement between two or more persons who agree to share profits and losses
h. Provides for compensation to a deceased or withdrawing owner of a business in return for that owner's interest
i. The impression a third party has when not notified that an agent has been terminated
j. A relatively new organizational form that combines aspects of partnerships and corporations to provide its members with limited liability
k. The individual or business organization that represents a principal
l. Exists when some partners are treated like shareholders for liability purposes

BUSINESS DISCUSSION

You and two of your college roommates have discussed plans to open a restaurant. You intend to attract college-age students who are health- and fitness-minded to your restaurant. You and your co-owners agree that each will invest equally in terms of time and money. However, in addition to contributions made by each of you, another $700,000 is essential for the restaurant to succeed.

What type of organization is best suited for this business activity?

Who will manage the restaurant during times that you and your co-owners are not present?

What liabilities do you and your co-owners face?

chapter 12

CORPORATE GOVERNANCE AND THE REGULATORY PROCESS

BUSINESS DECISION | *Same-day Delivery or Deception?*

As a manager employed by "Want-It-Now Rapid Delivery Service," you are responsible for pricing the services involving same-day deliveries. Among your primary concerns is the competitive aspects of your business. You have proposed contractual language that states "any package picked up after 10:00 a.m. will be considered as if it is picked up the next business day. Any package delivered before 10:00 p.m. on the day of pick up will be considered to have arrived on that business day. Under the language, a package received at 11:00 a.m. on Tuesday and delivered by 10:00 p.m. on Wednesday is considered, by you, to involve a "same-day delivery." The impact of this language is that a business day lasts for as long as 36 hours; thereby giving a customer the wrong impression of the phrase "same-day delivery."

The Federal Trade Commission (FTC), under its authority to protect the public from unfair or deceptive trade practices, has contacted your company asking questions about the plain meaning of "same-day delivery." In anticipation of a face-to-face meeting with an FTC investigator, you strive to answer these questions.

To what degree does the FTC have authority to question your business practices?

Are your clearly stated contractual provisions unfair or deceptive?

Should you cooperate with this investigator or seek a court order enjoining this investigation?

How do you challenge the FTC's action if a formal complaint is filed against your company?

For years, it seems, the citizens of this country have complained that "there is too much government." Although many people may agree with this sentiment, the recent corporate scandals focus the need for governance of business organizations. Through administrative agencies, the policies of governments, at all levels, result in the regulatory process.

Commentators call the administrative agencies a fourth branch of government. Because of the significant impact these agencies can have on businesses and businesspeople, in this chapter, you will study the following:

- Why our governments have come to rely on the regulatory process
- The basic functions of administrative agencies
- The organization of these agencies
- When courts will review the actions of agencies

ADMINISTRATIVE AGENCIES

The term **administrative agency** is used to describe all the boards, bureaus, commissions, agencies, and organizations that make up the bureaucracy. The process of regulating business through agencies is described as administrative law. The administrative process occurs at all levels of government.

The table on the next page, lists several of the more important federal agencies and briefly describes their functions. Many of these agencies will be discussed in detail in later chapters. For example, the Federal Trade Commission is discussed in Chapter 13, the National Labor Relations Board in Chapter 14, the Equal Employment Opportunity Commission in Chapter 15, the Securities and Exchange Commission in Chapter 16, and the Environmental Protection Agency in Chapter 17.

As you can see from the Business Decision, the activities of the government agencies can have a significant impact on the everyday operations of a business—far more significant, sometimes, than major economic and consumer spending trends or world events. This chapter concerns administrative law—the legal principles relating to regulatory agencies, boards, bureaus, and commissions.

The direct day-to-day legal impact on business of the rules and regulations adopted and enforced by these agencies is probably greater than the impact of the courts or other branches of government. Administrative agencies create and enforce the majority of all laws constituting the legal environment of business. The administrative process at either the state or federal level regulates almost every business activity.

Although we focus on federal agencies in this chapter, keep in mind that state and local governments also have many agencies. For example, state workers' compensation boards hear cases involving industrial accidents and injuries to employees, and most local governments have zoning boards that make recommendations that impact business activities. State governments usually license and regulate intrastate transportation, and state boards usually set rates for local utilities supplying gas and electricity. This chapter discusses the principles and problems generally applicable to the state and local administrative process as well as to the federal. It is clear that the administrative process regulates to a substantial degree almost every aspect of our daily lives.

1. REASONS FOR AGENCIES

There are many reasons why administrative agencies are necessary. Almost every governmental agency exists because of a recognized problem in society and the expectation that the agency may be able to help solve the problem. This section contains a discussion of the following reasons why agencies are the essential part of the regulatory process:

Major Federal Agencies

Name	Functions
Consumer Product Safety Commission (CPSC)	Protects the public against unreasonable risks of injury associated with consumer products
Environmental Protection Agency (EPA)	Administers all laws relating to the environment, including laws on water pollution, air pollution, solid wastes, pesticides, toxic substances, etc.
Federal Aviation Administration (FAA) (part of the Department of Transportation)	Regulates civil aviation to provide safe and efficient use of airspace
Federal Communications Commission (FCC)	Regulates interstate and foreign communications by means of radio, television, wire, cable, and satellite
Federal Energy Regulatory Commission (FERC)	Promotes dependable, affordable energy through sustained competitive markets
Federal Reserve Board (FRB)	Regulates the availability and cost of money and credit; the nation's central bank
Federal Trade Commission (FTC)	Protects the public from anticompetitive behavior and unfair and deceptive business practices
Food and Drug Administration (FDA)	Administers laws to prohibit distribution of adulterated, misbranded, or unsafe food and drugs
Equal Employment Opportunity Commission (EEOC)	Seeks to prevent discrimination in employment based on race, color, religion, sex, or national origin and other unlawful employment practices
National Labor Relations Board (NLRB)	Conducts union certification elections and holds hearings on unfair labor practice complaints
Nuclear Regulatory Commission (NRC)	Licenses and regulates the nuclear energy industry
Occupational Safety and Health Administration (OSHA)	Ensures all workers a safe and healthy work environment
Securities and Exchange Commission (SEC)	Enforces the federal securities laws that regulate sale of securities to the investing public

- To provide specificity
- To provide expertise
- To provide protection
- To provide regulation
- To provide services

Providing Specificity   Legislative branches often cannot legislate in sufficient detail to cover all aspects of many problems. Congress cannot possibly legislate in minute detail, and, as a consequence, it uses more and more general language in stating its regulatory aims and purposes. For example, Congress cannot enact a securities law that covers every possible issue that might arise. Therefore, it delegates to the Securities and Exchange Commission the power to make rules and regulations to fill in the gaps and create the necessary details to make securities laws workable. In many areas an agency develops detailed rules and regulations to carry out a legislative policy.

Also courts cannot handle all disputes and controversies that may arise. For example, each year tens of thousands of industrial accidents cause injury or death to workers. If each of these industrial accidents results in traditional litigation, the courts simply will not have the time or the personnel to handle the multitude of cases. Therefore, workers' compensation boards decide such claims. Likewise, most cases involving alleged discrimination in employment are turned over to agencies for investigation and resolution.

Providing Expertise A reason many agencies are created is to refer a problem or area to experts for solution and management. The Federal Reserve Board (FRB), the Nuclear Regulatory Commission (NRC), and the Food and Drug Administration (FDA) are examples of agencies with expertise beyond that of Congress or the executive branch. The development of sound policies and proper decisions in many areas requires expertise, and thus we tend to resort to administrative agencies for this expertise. Similarly, administrative agencies often provide needed continuity and consistency in the formulation, application, and enforcement of rules and regulations governing business.

Providing Protection Many governmental agencies exist to protect the public, especially from the business community. Business often fails to regulate itself, and the lack of self-regulation is contrary to the public interest. For example, the failure of business to voluntarily refrain from polluting many streams and rivers as well as the air led to the creation of the Environmental Protection Agency (EPA). The sale of worthless securities to the investing public was a major reason for the creation of the Securities and Exchange Commission (SEC). The manufacture and sale of dangerous products led to the creation of the Consumer Product Safety Commission (CPSC). Americans tend to turn to a governmental agency for assistance whenever a business or business practice may injure significant numbers of the general public. A prevailing attitude exists that the government's duty is to protect the public from harm.

Providing Regulation Agencies often replace competition with regulation. When a firm is given monopoly power, it loses its freedom of contract, and a governmental body is given the power to determine the provisions of its contracts. For example, electric utility companies are usually given a monopoly in the geographic area which they serve. A state agency such as a public service commission then has the power to set the rate structure for the utility. Similar agencies regulate transportation and banking because of the difference in bargaining power between the business and the public. Regulation is often a substitute for competition.

Providing Services Many agencies arise simply out of necessity. If we are to have a mail service, a post office is necessary. Welfare programs require government personnel to administer them. Social Security programs necessitate that there be a federal agency to determine eligibility and pay benefits. The mere existence of most government programs automatically creates a new agency or expands the functions of an existing one.

   The following case involves several of the reasons why administrative agencies exist. Indeed, at times regulation by two or more agencies may seem to overlap. In this case, the Supreme Court addresses when one agency preempts another one and when preemption does not occur.

Chao v. Mallard Bay Drilling, Inc.

122 S. Ct. 738 (2002)

Mallard Bay Drilling, Inc., operates a fleet of barges used for oil and gas exploration. On April 9, 1997, one of those barges, "Rig 52," was towed to a location in the territorial waters of Louisiana, where it drilled a well over 2 miles deep. On June 16, 1997, when the crew had nearly completed drilling, an explosion occurred, killing four members of the crew and injuring two others. The Coast Guard investigated this accident and concluded that natural gas leaked from the well into the barge and was ignited by sparks from pumps. The report did not accuse Mallard Bay of violating any Coast Guard regulations and concluded that Rig 52 was an "uninspected vessel" not subject to comprehensive Coast Guard regulations. Following this report, the Occupational Safety and Health Administration (OSHA) cited Mallard Bay with three violations of the Occupational Safety and Health Act of 1970 (Act). Mallard Bay challenged OSHA's jurisdiction to issue citations since Rig 52 was not a "workplace." Mallard Bay also argued that the Act preempts OSHA's jurisdiction since the Coast Guard had authority over vessels, like Rig 52, in nagivable water. The OSHA Administrative Law Judge (ALJ) rejected Mallard Bay's arguments. Mallard Bay appealed to the Fifth Circuit, which reversed this ALJ's decision. OSHA sought review by the Supreme Court, and certiorari was granted.

STEVENS, J.: . . . The Occupational Safety and Health Act imposes on covered employers a duty to provide working conditions that "are free from recognized hazards that are causing or are likely to cause death or serious bodily harm" to their employees, as well as an obligation to comply with safety standards promulgated by the Secretary of Labor. The coverage of the Act does not, however, extend to working conditions that are regulated by other federal agencies. To avoid overlapping regulation, § 4(b)(1) of the Act provides:

> Nothing in this [Act] shall apply to working conditions of employees with respect to which other Federal agencies . . . exercise statutory authority to prescribe or enforce standards or regulations affecting occupational safety and health.

Congress' use of the word "exercise" makes clear that, contrary to respondent's [Mallard Bay's] position, mere possession by another federal agency of unexercised authority to regulate certain working conditions is insufficient to displace OSHA's jurisdiction. Furthermore, another federal agency's minimal exercise of some authority over certain conditions on vessels such as Rig 52 does not result in complete preemption of OSHA jurisdiction, because the statute also makes clear that OSHA is only preempted if the working conditions at issue are the particular ones with respect to which another federal agency has regulated, and if such regulations affect occupational safety or health. To determine whether Coast Guard regulations have preempted OSHA's jurisdiction over the working conditions on Rig 52, it is thus necessary to examine the contours of the Guard's exercise of its statutory authority, not merely the existence of such authority.

Congress has assigned a broad and important mission to the Coast Guard. Its governing statute provides, in part:

> The Coast Guard . . . shall administer laws and promulgate and enforce regulations for the promotion of safety of life and property on and under the high seas and waters subject to the jurisdiction of the United States covering all matters not specifically delegated by law to some other executive department. . . .

Under this provision, the Guard possesses authority to promulgate and enforce regulations promoting the safety of vessels anchored in state navigable waters, such as Rig 52. As mentioned above, however, in defining the Coast Guard's regulatory authority, Congress has divided the universe of vessels into two broad classes: "inspected vessels" and "uninspected vessels." . . .

The parties do not dispute that OSHA's regulations have been preempted with respect to inspected vessels, because the Coast Guard has broad statutory authority to regulate the occupational health and safety of workers aboard inspected vessels, and it has exercised that authority. . . .

[CONTINUED]

Uninspected vessels such as Rig 52, however, present an entirely different regulatory situation. Nearly all of the Coast Guard regulations responsible for displacing OSHA's jurisdiction over inspected vessels do not apply to uninspected vessels like Rig 52. Rather, in the context of uninspected vessels, the Guard's regulatory authority—and exercise thereof—is more limited. With respect to uninspected vessels, the Guard regulates matters related to marine safety, such as fire extinguishers, life preservers, engine flame arrestors, engine ventilation, and emergency locating equipment. Because these general marine safety regulations do not address the occupational safety and health concerns faced by inland drilling operations on uninspected vessels, they do not preempt OSHA's authority under § 4(b)(1) in this case. . . .

In addition to issuing these general marine safety regulations, the Guard has exercised its statutory authority to regulate a number of specific working conditions on certain types of uninspected vessels. For example, the Guard regulates drilling operations that take place on the outer continental shelf. And it is true that some of these more specific regulations would preempt OSHA regulations covering those particular working conditions and vessels. But respondent has not identified any specific Coast Guard regulations that address the types of risk and vessel at issue in this case: namely, dangers from oil-drilling operations on uninspected barges in inland waters. Simply because the Guard has engaged in a limited exercise of its authority to address certain working conditions pertaining to certain classes of uninspected vessels does not mean that all OSHA regulation of all uninspected vessels has been preempted. Because the Guard has neither affirmatively regulated the working conditions at issue in this case, nor asserted comprehensive regulatory jurisdiction over working conditions on uninspected vessels, the Guard has not "exercised" its authority under § 4(b)(1). . . .

Accordingly, the judgment of the Court of Appeals is reversed.

Reversed.

CASE QUESTIONS

1. Why does the Mallard Bay Drilling, Inc., assert that the Occupational Safety and Health Administration lack jurisdiction over Rig 52?

2. Why is § 4(b)(1) of the Occupational Safety and Health Act important to this case?

3. Why is preemption of one agency's authority by another agency's authority important in the conduct of business activities?

4. How does the Supreme Court utilize the phrase *exercise of authority*? Why is this utilization critical to the outcome of this case?

2. FUNCTIONS OF AGENCIES

Administrative agencies tend to possess functions of the other three branches of government, including:

- Rule making
- Adjudicating
- Advising
- Investigating

These functions do not concern all administrative agencies to the same degree. Some agencies are primarily adjudicating bodies, such as industrial commissions

*The Powers of
Administrative
Agencies*

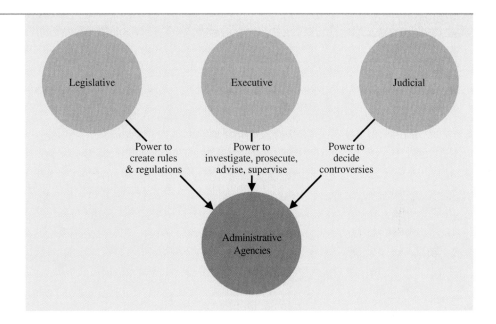

that rule on worker's compensation claims. Others are primarily supervisory, such as the SEC, which oversees the issue and sale of investment securities. To be sure, most agencies perform all these functions to some degree in carrying out their responsibilities. The figure, above, illustrates how these functions have been delegated to these agencies.

Rule Making Agencies exercise their **quasi-legislative** power by issuing rules and regulations that have the force and effect of law. Because of the vast volume of rules and regulations, keeping current challenges many business organizations. By allowing time periods for public comments on proposed regulations, interested parties have an opportunity to be heard on the desirability and legality of the proposals.

Guidelines are also issued by agencies to supplement rules. Guidelines are administrative interpretations of the statutes that an agency is responsible for enforcing. Often, guidelines help businesses determine whether certain practices may or may not be viewed as legal. For example, the Federal Trade Commission and the Justice Department guidelines help businesspeople determine which mergers are legal and which ones are likely to be challenged as illegal.

Rules and regulations may apply to a business practice irrespective of the industry involved, or they may apply only to an industry. For example, Occupational Safety and Health Administrative (OSHA) rules may cover anyone's workplace, or a rule may be drafted so that its coverage is limited to an industry such as drug manufacturing.

While guidelines can be helpful in understanding an agency's policy, these guidelines do not have the same force of law as rules and regulations do.

Adjudicating The **quasi-judicial** function involves both fact-finding and applying law to the facts. If violations of the law are found, sanctions, such as a fine or other penalty, may be imposed. Fines are often quite substantial (see table,

Fines Imposed as Result of Administrative Agencies' Investigations

Company	Violation	Fine	Agency
A combination of the largest broker firms	Misleading stock recommendations and distributing shares of new stock offering to corporate clients	$900 million	SEC
TAP Pharmaceutical Products, Inc.	Encouraging doctors to bill insurers for drugs they received for free	$875 million	FDA through U.S. Justice Dept.
HCA, Inc. (Healthcare Services Facilities)	Improper billing of Medicare	$617 million plus $17.5 million	Social Security Admin. through U.S. Justice Dept. State agencies
Pfizer, Inc.	Overcharging for Lipitor (a drug that reduces cholesterol)	$49 million	U.S. Justice Dept. on behalf of states

above). In addition, an agency may order that a violator stop (cease) the objectionable activity and refrain (desist) from any further similar violations. This type of agency action is called a **cease and desist order.** Violations of a cease and desist order are punishable by fines, which can be as much as $10,000 per day.

Many cases before agencies are settled by agreement before a final decision, just as most lawsuits are settled. Such a settlement results in the issuance of a **consent order,** which requires that the organization or individual accused admit to the jurisdiction of the agency and waive all rights to seek a judicial review. There is no admission that the business has been guilty of a violation of the law, but there is an agreement not to engage in the business activities that were the subject of the complaint. A consent order saves considerable expense and has the same legal force and effect as a final cease and desist order issued after a full hearing.

Advising The advisory function of an administrative agency may be accomplished by making reports to the president or to Congress. For example, an agency may propose new legislation to Congress, or it may inform the attorney general of the need for judicial action due to violations of the law. Agencies also report information to the general public that should be known in the public interest, and they publish advisory opinions. For example, a commission may give advice as to whether a firm's proposed course of action might violate any of the laws that commission administers. Advisory opinions are not as binding as formal rulings, but they do give a business an indication of the view an agency would take if the practice in question were challenged formally. The advisory opinion is a unique device generally not available in the judicial system, as courts deal only with actual cases and controversies.

Investigating One of the major functions of all agencies is to investigate activities and practices that may be illegal. Because of this investigative power, agencies can gather and compile information concerning the organization and business practices of any corporation or industry engaged in commerce to determine whether there has been a violation of any law. In exercising their investigative functions, agencies may use the subpoena power and require reports, examine witnesses under oath, and examine and copy documents, or they may obtain information from other governmental offices. This power of investigation complements the exercise of the agency's other powers, especially the power to adjudicate.

As discussed in Chapter 10, it is a crime to make any false or fraudulent statement in any matter within the jurisdiction of a federal agency. A person may be guilty of a violation without proof that he or she had knowledge that the matter was within the jurisdiction of a federal agency. As a result, information furnished to an agency must be truthful.

3. ORGANIZATION OF AGENCIES

Administrative agencies, boards, or commissions usually consist of five to seven members, one of whom is appointed as chair. Laws creating the regulatory body usually specify that no more than a simple majority of the members (three of the five or four of the seven) may belong to the same political party. Appointments at the federal level require Senate confirmation, and appointees are not permitted to engage in any other business or employment during their terms. They may be removed from office by the president only for inefficiency, neglect of duty, or malfeasance in office.

Regulatory agencies require staffs to carry out their duties. While each agency has its own distinctive organizational structure to meet its responsibilities, most agencies have persons performing certain functions common to all agencies. Because agencies have quasi-legislative and quasi-judicial functions as well as the usual executive ones, the organizational chart of an agency usually embraces the full range of governmental duties. The figure on the next page shows an organizational chart outlining the general functions and duties of administrative agencies.

In General   The chairperson is designated as such at the time of nomination by the president and is the presiding officer at agency meetings. The chairperson usually belongs to the same political party as the president and, while an equal in voting, is somewhat more important than the other agency members because of visibility and the power to appoint staff. For example, the chairman of the Federal Reserve Board is often in the news, while the other board members are relatively unknown.

The secretary is responsible for the minutes of agency meetings and is legal custodian of its records. The secretary usually signs orders and official correspondence and is responsible for publication of all actions in the *Federal Register*. The secretary also coordinates the activities of the agency with others involved in the regulatory process.

The office of **general counsel** is so important in many agencies that the appointment usually requires Senate approval. The general counsel is the chief law officer and legal adviser. He or she represents the agency in court and often makes the decision to file suit or pursue other remedies. The general counsel has significant impact on policy and is often as powerful as a commissioner or board member.

Advisory councils are persons not employed by the agency but interested in its mission. Persons serving on councils are usually selected because of their expertise. For example, the Consumer Product Safety Commission has an advisory council in poison prevention packaging and another on flammable fabrics. These councils provide for interaction between regulators and those being regulated.

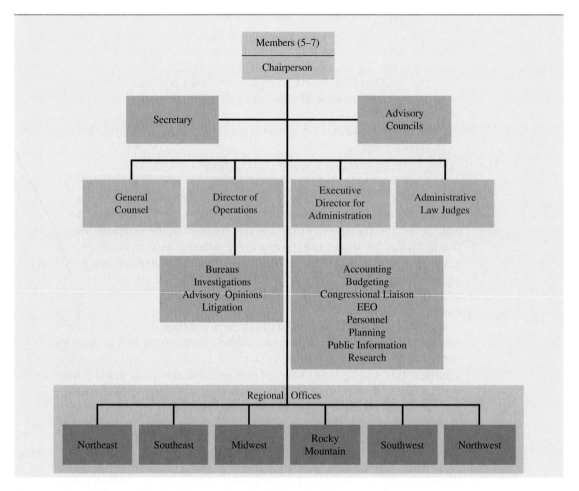

Organizational Chart of Typical Agency, Board, or Commission

The executive director for administration is the chief operating official of an agency and supervises usual administrative functions such as accounting, budgeting, and personnel. Research and planning are usually also supervised by the executive director. Since agencies spend a great deal of time lobbying with Congress, most of them have a legislative liaison, reporting to the executive director for administration.

The duties and suborganization of the director of operations vary greatly from agency to agency. These operating bureaus are assigned specific areas of activity. For example, at the EPA, one group will be concerned with clean air and another with water problems.

Regional offices investigate alleged violations of the law. In addition, they usually have an educational function. Many regional offices have their own administrative law judges and special legal counsel.

Quasi-Judicial Staff **Administrative law judges** perform the adjudicative fact-finding functions. Like other types of judges, administrative law judges are protected from liability for damages based on their decisions. This protection is called **immunity.** Because these administrative law judges must exercise independent judgment on the evidence presented, they must be free from pressures possibly asserted by the parties.

These administrative law judges hear cases of alleged law violations and apply the law to the facts. The members of the agency board or commission hear only appeals from the decisions of the administrative law judges. The judges are organizationally separate from the rest of the agency so that the quasi-judicial function will be performed impartially. Administrative law judges use prior decisions or precedent. In addition, they must follow the procedural rules of the agency as well as its policy directives as shown in the box below.

Historically, administrative law judges and all other personnel involved in a quasi-judicial hearing have been employees of the administrative agency bringing the complaint. Despite their best efforts to serve as neutral adjudicators, administrative law judges have been accused of being biased in favor of their employer (the agency). To reduce the likelihood of this accusation, several states have created an Office of Administrative Hearings. Such an office provides impartial administrative law judges for hearings involving all agencies in the state government. The movement toward this type of office is likely to continue due to the importance of citizens believing that they are treated fairly by governmental agencies.

4. INFLUENCING AGENCY DECISIONS

As discussed in section 2, agencies adopt rules and regulations. Due process of law requires that before a rule or regulation may be adopted by an agency, interested parties must be given notice of the proposed rules and an opportunity to express their views on them. Agencies give public notice of proposed rules and hold public hearings on them.

At public hearings, interested parties are allowed to present evidence in support of, or in opposition to, a proposed rule or regulation. As a result, the best means of influencing a quasi-legislative decision of an administrative agency is to participate in the adoption process.

Agencies are not politically responsible, in the sense that they are elected by the people. However, it is clear that they react, sometimes dramatically, to the force of

PROCEDURES FOLLOWED IN QUASI-JUDICIAL PROCEEDINGS

Quasi-judicial proceedings usually begin with a complaint filed by the agency. The complaint is often the result of an investigation of information received from a consumer or other person affected by business conduct that may be illegal. The complaint contains allegations of fact concerning the alleged illegal conduct. The business or individual accused of some illegality is called the respondent. After the formal complaint is served, the respondent files an answer to the charges and allegations. The case is then assigned to an administrative law judge. At the hearing,

counsels for the agency and the respondent produce evidence to prove or disprove the allegations of fact in the complaint and answer. The judge rules on the admissibility of evidence, rules on motions made by counsel, and renders an initial decision that includes a statement of findings and conclusions, along with reasons for them, as to all material issues of fact and law. The ruling also includes an order the judge deems appropriate in view of the evidence in the record. This order becomes final if not challenged within 30 days after it is filed. On the appeal, the agency, board, or commission reviews the record of the initial decision and has all the powers it could have exercised if it had rendered that decision itself.

public opinion. For example, since 2002, the Securities and Exchange Commission (SEC) consistently garners the media attention as it strives to investigate, adopt rules, and assess fines covering corporate scandals.

Citizens writing letters to agencies to obtain action or a change in policy may be effective. These are probably even more effective if directed to a member of Congress, who in turn asks the agency for an official response or explanation. At various times, an agency may find itself bombarded with official congressional inquiries into its activities. Investigations may result in either budget cutbacks or increases. Just the threat of such a proceeding is often sufficient to cause a review of administrative policy.

Furthermore, each branch of government has some control over the administrative process. The executive branch normally appoints the top officials of an agency with the advice and consent of the legislative branch. In addition, the executive branch makes budget recommendations to the legislature and has veto power over its statutes. The legislature can review and control administrative activity by abolishing the agency, enacting specific legislation contrary to rules adopted by the agency, more explicitly defining limitations on the agency's activities, providing additional procedural requirements for the agency's adjudications, or limiting appropriations of funds to the agency.

Judicial Review of Agency Decisions

What alternatives are available to a person, business, or industry unhappy with either rules and regulations that have been adopted or with the quasi-judicial decisions? What are the powers of courts in reviewing decisions of administrative agencies? What chance does a party upset with an agency's decision have in obtaining a reversal of the decision? How much deference is given to an agency's decisions? Answers to these questions must be clearly understood to appreciate the role of administrative agencies in our system. These answers also help in understanding the Business Decision at the beginning of this chapter.

The following section discusses a requirement that must be satisfied by the parties challenging an agency's rule-making or adjudicating function. Then, in sections 6 through 8, you will see that the issues before a court reviewing an agency's decision vary depending on whether a quasi-legislative or quasi-judicial decision is being reviewed.

5. STANDING TO SUE

Any party seeking the judicial review of any administrative agency's decision must be able to prove *standing to sue*. To establish standing, the challenging party must address two issues.

Reviewability First, is the action or decision of the agency subject to judicial review? Not all administrative decisions are reviewable. The Federal Administrative Procedure Act provides for judicial review except where "(1) statutes preclude judicial review or (2) agency action is committed to agency discretion by law." Few statutes actually preclude judicial review, and preclusion of judicial review by inference is rare. It is most likely to occur when an agency decides not to undertake action to enforce a statute. For example, prison inmates asked the Food and Drug Administration (FDA) to ban the use of lethal injections to carry out the death penalty. It refused to do so. The Supreme Court held that this decision of the FDA was not subject to judicial review.

Aggrieved Party Second, is the plaintiff "an aggrieved party"? Generally the plaintiff must have been harmed by an administrative action or decision to have standing. This aspect of standing was discussed in Chapter 4. It is clear that persons who may suffer economic loss due to an agency's action have standing to sue. Recent decisions have expanded the group of persons with standing to sue to include those who have noneconomic interests, such as First Amendment rights. The box, below, on standing to sue describes why courts give broad meaning to this concept.

6. REVIEW OF RULE MAKING

The rule-making function in the administrative process is essentially legislative in character. Legislatures usually create administrative agencies or quasi-legislative power to the agency. An administrative agency must propose rules and regulations within the confines of its grant of power from the legislature, or a court will find the proposal void.

However, once courts decide that an act of the legislature is constitutional or a rule of an agency is authorized, the courts will not inquire into its wisdom or effectiveness. An unwise or ineffectual law may be corrected by political action at the polls; an unwise rule or regulation adopted by an agency may be corrected by the legislature that gave the agency power to make the rule in the first place.

There are two basic issues in litigation challenging the validity of a rule made by an administrative agency. First, is the delegation valid? Second, has the agency exceeded its authority?

Is Delegation Valid? Delegation of quasi-legislative authority to administrative agencies is subject to two constitutional limitations:

- It must be definite.
- It must be limited.

STANDING TO SUE OR WHO MAY CHALLENGE AN ADMINISTRATIVE POLICY

The Administrative Procedures Act states:

A person suffering legal wrong because of agency action, or adversely affected or aggrieved by agency action within the meaning of a relevant statute, is entitled to judicial review thereof.

Through United States Supreme Court cases, we know that a plaintiff must show a claim within the "zone of in-

terest" protected by the statute under consideration. The plaintiff does not need to prove that the legislative body envisioned protecting this particular plaintiff.

An example of this broad nature of standing to sue is found in the decision of the Supreme Court allowing banks to challenge whether credit unions must limit membership to persons who have a common bond, such as employment with the same company.

Source: *National Credit Union Administration v. First National Bank & Trust Co.,* 118 S. Ct. 927 (1998).

First, delegation of authority must be definite or it will violate due process. Definiteness means that the delegation must be set forth with sufficient clarity so that all concerned, and especially reviewing courts, will be able to determine the extent of the agency's authority. Broad language has been held sufficiently definite to meet this test. For example, the term *unfair methods of competition* is sufficiently definite to meet the requirements of due process and validate the delegation of this authority to the Federal Trade Commission (FTC).

Second, the delegation of authority to an agency from the legislative or executive branch must have limitations. This delegation of authority must provide that the agency's power to act is limited to areas that are certain, even if these areas are not specifically defined. For example, the FTC regulates unfair methods of competition *in or affecting commerce.* Regulations or enforcement activities by the FTC that focus solely on intrastate business are void as being beyond the "limited" authority delegated to that agency. Also, procedural safeguards must exist to control arbitrary administrative action and any administrative abuse of discretionary power.

Just as broad language has been approved as being sufficiently definite for a delegation to be valid under the due process clause since the 1930s, broad standards meet the limited-power test. Today, it is generally agreed that delegations of authority to make rules may involve very broad language. For example, the delegation of authority to make such rules as the "public interest, convenience and necessity may require" is a valid standard.

The general language used in delegating quasi-legislative authority usually involves grants of substantial discretion to an agency. It must be kept in mind that this delegation of discretion is to the agency and not to the judiciary. Therefore, courts cannot interfere with the discretion given to the agency and cannot substitute their judgment for that of the agency. In essence, there is a policy of deference by the judges to the decision of the administrators. This practice of deference further emphasizes why a businessperson's influence on the rule-making process is greater in the administrative process than through appellate procedures (see section 4, above).

The following case illustrates the actual language used by the Supreme Court to express this philosophy of deference. It demonstrates the expansive discretion given to administrative agencies and how slow courts are to substitute their judgment for that of the administrative process.

UNITED STATES POSTAL SERVICE V. GREGORY

122 S. CT. 431 (2001)

Maria Gregory worked for the United States Postal Service overseeing letter carriers on five mail routes and serving as a replacement carrier on those routes. Twice in April and again in August of 1997, Gregory was disciplined. At first, she was given a letter of warning. Next, she was suspended for seven days. The third disciplinary action resulted in a 14-day suspension. Following each of these actions,

Gregory filed grievances. While each of these grievances was pending, the Postal Service terminated Gregory in November following a fourth work-related incident. Because Gregory had served in the Army, she is a "preference eligible" employee covered by the Civil Service Reform Act. This Act allows Gregory to appeal her termination to the Systems Protection Board (Board). Upon review, the Board's

[CONTINUED]

Administrative Law Judge (ALJ) upheld her termination of employment since the Postal Service demonstrated the reasonableness of her dismissal. Gregory sought review of the ALJ's findings by the full Board. While awaiting a decision of the full Board, an arbitrator hearing Gregory's first grievance found in her favor and ordered that the letter of warning be withdrawn. Following this arbitrator's award, the Board refused Gregory's request to review the ALJ's findings. Gregory then petitioned for a review of the Board's decision in the Court of Appeals for the Federal Circuit. This appeals court held that "prior disciplinary actions that are subject to ongoing proceedings may not be used to support" the reasonableness of disciplinary action, such as termination. The court vacated the Board's decision and remanded this case for additional proceedings. The Postal Service petitioned the Supreme Court, and certiorari was granted.

O'CONNOR, J.: . . . The Federal Circuit's statutory review of the substance of Board decisions is limited to determining whether they are unsupported by substantial evidence or are arbitrary, capricious, an abuse of discretion, or otherwise not in accordance with law. . . . [T]he arbitrary and capricious standard is extremely narrow, and allows the Board wide latitude in fulfilling its obligation to review agency disciplinary actions. It is not for the Federal Circuit to substitute its own judgment for that of the Board. The role of judicial review is only to ascertain if the Board has met the minimum standards set forth in the statute. We conclude that the Board need not adopt the Federal Circuit's rule in order to meet these standards. . . .

There is certainly nothing arbitrary about the Board's decision to independently review prior disciplinary violations. Neither the Federal Circuit nor respondent [Gregory] has suggested that the Board has applied this policy inconsistently—indeed, the Board has taken this same approach for 19 years. Nor have they argued that the Board lacks reasons for its approach. Following the Federal Circuit's rule would require the Board either to wait until challenges to disciplinary actions pending in grievance proceedings are completed before rendering its decision, or to ignore altogether the violations being challenged in grievance in determining the reason-

ableness of the penalty. The former may cause undue delay. The latter would, in many cases, effectively preclude agencies from relying on an employee's disciplinary history, which the Federal Circuit itself acknowledged to be an important factor in any disciplinary decision. . . .

Employees covered by the [Civil Service Reform Act] CSRA may elect Board review only for disciplinary actions of a certain seriousness, such as termination, suspension for more than 14 days, or a reduction in grade or pay. For more minor actions, workers may only seek review through negotiated grievance procedures, if they exist. According to [National Treasury Employees Union] NTEU, this scheme deprives the Board of the statutory authority to review minor disciplinary actions like the three that were pending in this case. It is true that the CSRA contemplates that at least some eligible employees (those represented by unions) will have two different forums for challenging disciplinary actions, depending in part on their seriousness. If the Board had attempted to review respondent's first disciplinary action before she was terminated, it would have exceeded its statutory authority. In this case, however, the Board was asked to review respondent's termination, something it clearly has authority to do. Because this termination was based on a series of disciplinary actions, some of which are minor, the Board's authority to review the termination must also include the authority to review each of the prior disciplinary actions to establish the reasonableness of the penalty as a whole.

Independent Board review of disciplinary actions pending in grievance proceedings may at times result in the Board reaching a different conclusion than the arbitrator. It may also result in a terminated employee never reaching a resolution of her grievance at all, because some collective bargaining agreements require unions to withdraw grievances when an employee's termination becomes final before the Board. Rather than being inconsistent with the statutory scheme, however, these possibilities are the result of the parallel structures of review set forth in the CSRA.

Such results are not necessarily unfair. Any employee who appeals a disciplinary action to the Board receives independent Board review. If the Board's mechanism for reviewing prior disciplinary

[CONTINUED]

actions is itself adequate, the review such an employee receives is fair. Although the fairness of the Board's own procedure is not before us, we note that a presumption of regularity attaches to the actions of government agencies, and that some deference to agency disciplinary actions is appropriate.

Although the Board independently reviews prior disciplinary actions pending in grievance, it also has a policy of not relying upon disciplinary actions that have already been overturned in grievance proceedings at the time of Board review. As one of respon-

dent's disciplinary actions was overturned in arbitration before the Board rendered its decision, the Postal Service concedes that a remand to the Federal Circuit is necessary to determine the effect of this reversal on respondent's termination.

The judgment of the United States Court of Appeals for the Federal Circuit is therefore vacated, and the case is remanded for further proceedings consistent with this opinion.

Vacated and remanded.

CASE QUESTIONS

1. Why is it necessary to understand the history of Gregory's employment-related disciplinary events?

2. What are the procedural steps of review this case goes through before reaching the Supreme Court?

3. Why does the Supreme Court decide that courts should defer to the Board's review of an employee's disciplinary history?

4. If the Court declares deference must be given to the Board's review, for what purpose is this case remanded to the Federal Circuit?

Authority Exceeded? Although it is highly unlikely that a court would hold a delegation invalid because of indefiniteness or lack of standards, from time to time courts do find that agencies exceed their authority. Court will hold that an agency exceeds its authority if an analysis of legislative intent confirms the view that the agency has gone beyond that intent, however noble its purpose may be (see box, below).

The following case presents a situation that is important to everyone. Notice how the Supreme Court struggles with the dilemma presented and how the rule of law assists the Court.

THE FCC AND VIDEO DESCRIPTIONS: GOING TOO FAR

Congress authorizes the Federal Communications Commission (FCC) to adopt rules requiring broadcasters to accommodate blind listeners. The FCC issued an order requiring the top four networks to provide each quarter at least 50 hours of programming with audible video descriptions for the blind. Video descriptions involve a narrator explaining the setting, facial expressions, and other descriptions necessary for a blind person to understand the video. When challenged by the networks, this FCC regulation requiring video descriptions was held invalid by a federal court. The court's review of the congressional enactment results in a finding that the FCC was to report to Congress on video descriptions, not issue a rule requiring them.

Source: *Motion Picture Association of America, Inc. v. Federal Communications Commission,* 309 F. 3d 796 (D.C. Cir. 2002)

FOOD AND DRUG ADMINISTRATION V. BROWN & WILLIAMSON TOBACCO CORPORATION

120 S. CT. 1291 (2000)

O'CONNOR, J.: This case involves one of the most troubling public health problems facing our Nation today: the thousands of premature deaths that occur each year because of tobacco use. In 1996, the Food and Drug Administration (FDA), after having expressly disavowed any such authority since its inception, asserted jurisdiction to regulate tobacco products. The FDA concluded that nicotine is a "drug" within the meaning of the Food, Drug, and Cosmetic Act (FDCA or Act), and that cigarettes and smokeless tobacco are "combination products" that deliver nicotine to the body. Pursuant to this authority, it promulgated regulations intended to reduce tobacco consumption among children and adolescents. The agency believed that, because most tobacco consumers begin their use before reaching the age of 18, curbing tobacco use by minors could substantially reduce the prevalence of addiction in future generations and thus the incidence of tobacco-related death and disease.

Regardless of how serious the problem an administrative agency seeks to address, however, it may not exercise its authority in a manner that is inconsistent with the administrative structure that Congress enacted into law. And although agencies are generally entitled to deference in the interpretation of statutes that they administer, a reviewing court, as well as the agency, must give effect to the unambiguously expressed intent of Congress. In this case, we believe that Congress has clearly precluded the FDA from asserting jurisdiction to regulate tobacco products. Such authority is inconsistent with the intent that Congress has expressed in the FDCA's overall regulatory scheme and in the tobacco-specific legislation that it has enacted subsequent to the FDCA. In light of this clear intent, the FDA's assertion of jurisdiction is impermissible.

The FDCA grants the FDA . . . the authority to regulate, among other items, "drugs" and "devices." The Act defines "drug" to include "articles (other than food) intended to affect the structure or any function of the body." It defines "device," in part, as

"an instrument, apparatus, implement, machine, contrivance, . . . or other similar or related article, including any component, part, or accessory, which is . . . intended to affect the structure or any function of the body." The Act also grants the FDA the authority to regulate so-called "combination products," which "constitute a combination of a drug, device, or biologic product." The FDA has construed this provision as giving it the discretion to regulate combination products as drugs, as devices, or as both.

On August 11, 1995, the FDA published a proposed rule concerning the sale of cigarettes and smokeless tobacco to children and adolescents. The rule, which included several restrictions on the sale, distribution, and advertisement of tobacco products, was designed to reduce the availability and attractiveness of tobacco products to young people. A public comment period followed, during which the FDA received over 700,000 submissions, more than "at any other time in its history on any other subject."

On August 28, 1996, the FDA issued a final rule entitled "Regulations Restricting the Sale and Distribution of Cigarettes and Smokeless Tobacco to Protect Children and Adolescents." The FDA determined that nicotine is a "drug" and that cigarettes and smokeless tobacco are "drug delivery devices," and therefore it had jurisdiction under the FDCA to regulate tobacco products. . . .

Based on these findings, the FDA promulgated regulations concerning tobacco products' promotion, labeling, and accessibility to children and adolescents. The access regulations prohibit the sale of cigarettes or smokeless tobacco to persons younger than 18; require retailers to verify through photo identification the age of all purchasers younger than 27; prohibit the sale of cigarettes in quantities smaller than 20; prohibit the distribution of free samples; and prohibit sales through self-service displays and vending machines except in adult-only locations. The promotion regulations require that any print advertising appear in a black-and-white, text-only format unless the publication in which it

[CONTINUED]

appears is read almost exclusively by adults; prohibit outdoor advertising within 1,000 feet of any public playground or school; prohibit the distribution of any promotional items, such as T-shirts or hats, bearing the manufacturer's brand name; and prohibit a manufacturer from sponsoring any athletic, musical, artistic, or other social or cultural event using its brand name. . . .

Respondents, a group of tobacco manufacturers, retailers, and advertisers, filed suit . . . challenging the regulations. They moved for summary judgment on the grounds that the FDA lacked jurisdiction to regulate tobacco products as customarily marketed, the regulations exceeded the FDA's authority, and the advertising restrictions violated the First Amendment. The court held that the FDCA authorizes the FDA to regulate tobacco products as customarily marketed and that the FDA's access and labeling regulations are permissible, but it also found that the agency's advertising and promotion restrictions exceed its authority. . . .

The Court of Appeals for the Fourth Circuit reversed, holding that Congress has not granted the FDA jurisdiction to regulate tobacco products. . . .

We granted the Government's petition for certiorari to determine whether the FDA has authority under the FDCA to regulate tobacco products. . . .

A threshold issue is the appropriate framework for analyzing the FDA's assertion of authority to regulate tobacco products. Because this case involves an administrative agency's construction of a statute that it administers, our analysis is governed by *Chevron U.S.A. Inc. v. Natural Resources Defense Council, Inc.,* 104 S. Ct. 2778 (1984). Under *Chevron,* a reviewing court must first ask "whether Congress has directly spoken to the precise question at issue." If Congress has done so, the inquiry is at an end; the court "must give effect to the unambiguously expressed intent of Congress." But if Congress has not specifically addressed the question, a reviewing court must respect the agency's construction of the statute so long as it is permissible. Such deference is justified because the responsibilities for assessing the wisdom of such policy choices and resolving the struggle between competing views of the public interest are not judicial ones, and because of the agency's greater familiarity with the ever-changing facts and circumstances surrounding the subjects regulated.

In determining whether Congress has specifically addressed the question at issue, a reviewing court should not confine itself to examining a particular statutory provision in isolation. The meaning—or ambiguity—of certain words or phrases may only become evident when placed in context. . . .

Viewing the FDCA as a whole, it is evident that one of the Act's core objectives is to ensure that any product regulated by the FDA is "safe" and "effective" for its intended use. This essential purpose pervades the FDCA. . . .

In its rulemaking proceeding, the FDA quite exhaustively documented that "tobacco products are unsafe," "dangerous," and "cause great pain and suffering from illness." It found that the consumption of tobacco products "presents extraordinary health risks," and that "tobacco use is the single leading cause of preventable death in the United States." It stated that "more than 400,000 people die each year from tobacco-related illnesses, such as cancer, respiratory illnesses, and heart disease, often suffering long and painful deaths," and that "tobacco alone kills more people each year in the United States than acquired immunodeficiency syndrome (AIDS), car accidents, alcohol, homicides, illegal drugs, suicides, and fires, combined." Indeed, the FDA characterized smoking as "a pediatric disease," because "one out of every three young people who become regular smokers . . . will die prematurely as a result."

These findings logically imply that, if tobacco products were "devices" under the FDCA, the FDA would be required to remove them from the market. . . .

Congress, however, has foreclosed the removal of tobacco products from the market. A provision of the United States Code currently in force states that "the marketing of tobacco constitutes one of the greatest basic industries of the United States with ramifying activities which directly affect interstate and foreign commerce at every point, and stable conditions therein are necessary to the general welfare:" 7 U.S.C. § 1311(a). More importantly, Congress has directly addressed the problem

[CONTINUED]

of tobacco and health through legislation on six occasions since 1965. . . . Congress stopped well short of ordering a ban. Instead, it has generally regulated the labeling and advertisement of tobacco products, expressly providing that it is the policy of Congress that "commerce and the national economy may be . . . protected to the maximum extent consistent with" consumers "being adequately informed about any adverse health effects." 15 U.S.C. § 1331. Congress' decisions to regulate labeling and advertising and to adopt the express policy of protecting "commerce and the national economy . . . to the maximum extent" reveal its intent that tobacco products remain on the market. Indeed the collective premise of these statutes is that cigarettes and smokeless tobacco will continue to be sold in the United States. A ban of tobacco products by the FDA would therefore plainly contradict congressional policy. . . .

[O]ur inquiry into whether Congress has directly spoken to the precise question at issue is shaped, at least in some measure, by the nature of the question presented. Deference under *Chevron* to an agency's construction of a statute that it administers is premised on the theory that a statute's ambiguity constitutes an implicit delegation from Congress to the agency to fill in the statutory gaps. In extraordinary cases, however, there may be reason to hesitate before concluding that Congress has intended such an implicit delegation.

This is hardly an ordinary case. Contrary to its representations to Congress since 1914, the FDA has now asserted jurisdiction to regulate an industry constituting a significant portion of the American economy. In fact, the FDA contends that, were it to determine that tobacco products provide no

"reasonable assurance of safety," it would have the authority to ban cigarettes and smokeless tobacco entirely. Owing to its unique place in American history and society, tobacco has its own unique political history. Congress, for better or for worse, has created a distinct regulatory scheme for tobacco products, squarely rejected proposals to give the FDA jurisdiction over tobacco, and repeatedly acted to preclude any agency from exercising significant policymaking authority in the area. Given this history and the breadth of the authority that the FDA has asserted, we are obliged to defer not to the agency's expansive construction of the statute, but to Congress' consistent judgment to deny the FDA this power. . . .

By no means do we question the seriousness of the problem that the FDA has sought to address. The agency has amply demonstrated that tobacco use, particularly among children and adolescents, poses perhaps the single most significant threat to public health in the United States. Nonetheless, no matter how important, conspicuous, and controversial the issue, and regardless of how likely the public is to hold the Executive Branch politically accountable, an administrative agency's power to regulate in the public interest must always be grounded in a valid grant of authority from Congress. . . . Reading the FDCA as a whole, as well as in conjunction with Congress' subsequent tobacco-specific legislation, it is plain that Congress has not given the FDA the authority that it seeks to exercise here. For these reasons, the judgment of the Court of Appeals for the Fourth Circuit is

Affirmed.

CASE QUESTIONS

1. What regulations adopted by the Food and Drug Administration are challenged in this case?

2. Describe the dilemma that the Court discusses regarding its role of determining an agency's authority and deferring to the finding of that agency.

3. What does the Court conclude in this case? Why?

4. If regulation of tobacco is to occur, what has to happen first?

TOBACCO INDUSTRY *insight*

THE FDA AND NICOTINE

The preceding case does not resolve the final role (or lack thereof) that the FDA will play in regulating tobacco. As the litigation process continues and settlements are negotiated, congressional delegation of authority to the FDA continues to be debated. In a proposed national settlement, which was not approved by Congress, the tobacco industry agreed to have the FDA regulate nicotine as an addictive drug by the year 2009. Authority to regulate nicotine, in general, or tobacco products specifically, still could be granted to the FDA.

Recently the Supreme Court addressed the issue of an agency's exceeding authority in the context of balancing the role of the agency against the purpose of federal bankruptcy laws. As the box on the next page illustrates, the Court limits the FCC's authority and treats it like it was any other debtor in a bankruptcy case.

7. REVIEW OF ADJUDICATIONS: PROCEDURAL ASPECTS

Judicial review of agencies' adjudications by its very nature is quite limited. Legislatures have delegated authority to agencies because of their expertise and knowledge, and courts usually exercise restraint and resolve doubtful issues in favor of an agency. For example, courts reviewing administrative interpretations of law do not always decide questions of law for themselves. It is not unusual for a court to accept an administrative interpretation of law as final if it is warranted in the record and has a rational basis in law. Administrative agencies are frequently called upon to interpret the statute governing an agency, and an agency's construction is persuasive to courts.

Administrative agencies develop their own rules of procedure unless mandated otherwise by an act of the legislature. These procedures are far less formal than judicial procedures, because one of the functions of the administrative process is to decide issues expeditiously. To proceed expeditiously usually means, for example, that administrative agencies are not restricted by the strict rules of evidence used by courts. Such agencies cannot ignore all rules, but they can use some leeway. They cannot, for example, refuse to permit any cross-examination or unduly limit it. Because an agency "is frequently the accuser, the prosecutor, the judge and the jury," it must remain alert to observe accepted standards of fairness. Reviewing courts are, therefore, alert to ensure that the true substance of a fair hearing is not denied to a party to an administrative hearing.

The principle that federal administrative agencies should be free to fashion their own rules of procedure and pursue methods of inquiry permitting them to discharge their duties grows out of the view that administrative agencies and administrators will be familiar with the industries they regulate. Thus, they will be in a better position than courts or legislative bodies to design procedural rules adapted to the peculiarities of the industry and the tasks of the agency involved.

In reviewing the procedures of administrative agencies, courts lack the authority to substitute their judgment or their own procedures for those of the

THE FEDERAL COMMUNICATIONS COMMISSION, LICENSES, AND BANKRUPTCY

The Federal Communications Commission (FCC) periodically auctions valuable licenses for broadband personal communications service. NextWave, which is a combination of various business organizations, successfully bid on a number of these licenses totaling more than $4 billion dollars. Following this auction, the FCC agreed to a payment plan by NextWave. To protect itself from nonpayment, the FCC obtained a security interest in NextWave's property, including the licenses it was financing.

Unfortunately, NextWave was unable to make these payments to the FCC, and it filed for bankruptcy. NextWave attempted to work out an alternative payment schedule with the FCC, which refused to cooperate since it claimed it had revoked the licenses awarded to NextWave. In a complicated series of litigation maneuvers, the U.S. Supreme Court is asked to determine whether the FCC has authority to revoke the licenses which are subject to the jurisdiction of the bankruptcy court. The Court concludes that despite its congressionally granted authority to oversee the auction of licenses and payment for them, the FCC is to be treated in the same manner as other creditors in a bankruptcy matter. Therefore, the FCC does not have the authority to revoke the licenses awarded to NextWave. The FCC must proceed as a creditor who holds a valid security interest in collateral.

Source: *Federal Communications Commission v. NextWave Personal Communications, Inc.,* 123 S. Ct. 832 (2003).

agency. Judicial responsibility is limited to ensuring consistency with statutes and compliance with the demands of the Constitution for a fair hearing. The latter responsibility arises from the due process clause. Due process usually requires a hearing by an agency, but on occasion sanctions may be imposed prior to the hearing.

Two doctrines guide courts in the judicial review of agency adjudications:

• Exhaustion of remedies
• Primary jurisdiction

Exhaustion of Remedies   The doctrine of **exhaustion of remedies** is a court-created rule that limits when courts can review administrative decisions. Courts refuse to review administrative actions until a complaining party has exhausted all of the administrative remedies and procedures available to him or her for redress. Judicial review is available only for final actions by an agency. Preliminary orders such as a decision to file a complaint are not reviewable. Otherwise, the administrative system would be denied important opportunities to make a factual record, to exercise its discretion, or to apply its expertise in its decision making. Also, exhaustion allows an agency to discover and correct its own errors, and thus it helps to dispense with any reason for judicial review. Exhaustion clearly should be required in those cases involving an area of the agency's expertise or specialization; it should require no unusual expense. It should also be required when the administrative remedy is just as likely as the judicial one to provide appropriate relief. The doctrine of exhaustion of remedies avoids the premature interruption of the administrative process. In general, it is probably more efficient for that purpose to go forward without interruption (see box on the next page).

Primary Jurisdiction   A doctrine similar to exhaustion of remedies is known as **primary jurisdiction.** *Exhaustion* applies when a claim must go in the first

EXCEPTIONS TO REQUIREMENT OF EXHAUSTION

When there is nothing to be gained from the exhaustion of administrative remedies and when the harm from the continued existence of the administrative ruling is great, the courts have not been reluctant to discard this doctrine. This is especially true when very fundamental constitutional guarantees such as freedom of speech or press are involved or when the administrative remedy is likely to be inadequate. Also, probably no court would insist upon exhaustion when the agency is clearly acting beyond its jurisdiction (because its action is not authorized by statute or the statute authorizing it is unconstitutional) or where it would result in irreparable injury (such as great expense) to the petitioner. Finally, an exception to the doctrine is fraud. If an agency is acting fraudulently, immediate access to the court is appropriate.

instance to an administrative agency alone. *Primary jurisdiction* applies when a claim is originally filed in the courts. It comes into play whenever enforcement of the claim requires the resolution of issues that, under a regulatory scheme, have been placed within the special competence of an administrative body. In such a case, the judicial process is suspended pending referral of such issues to the administrative body for its views. Primary jurisdiction ensures uniformity and consistency in dealing with matters entrusted to an administrative body. The doctrine is invoked when referral to the agency is preferable because of its specialized knowledge or expertise in dealing with the matter in controversy. Statutes such as those guaranteeing equal employment opportunity that create a private remedy for dollar damages sometimes require resort to an administrative agency as a condition precedent to filing suit. Some of these are federal statutes that require referral to state agencies. In these cases, referral must occur, but the right to sue is not limited by the results of the administrative decision.

8. REVIEW OF FACTUAL DETERMINATIONS

When it reviews the findings of fact made by an administrative body, a court presumes them to be correct. A court of review examines the evidence by analyzing the record of the agency's proceedings. It upholds the agency's findings and conclusions on questions of fact if they are supported by substantial evidence in the record. In other words, the record must contain material evidence from which a reasonable person might reach the same conclusion as did the agency. If substantial evidence in support of the decision is present, the court will not disturb the agency's findings, even though the court itself might have reached a different conclusion on the basis of other conflicting evidence also in the record. For example, the determination of credibility of the witnesses who testify in quasi-judicial proceedings is for the agency to determine and not the courts.

The following case provides a further example that courts will not disturb an agency's finding of fact and interpretation of law as long as the court can conclude that there is a reasonable basis for the agency's conclusion.

HOLLY FARMS CORPORATION V. NATIONAL LABOR RELATIONS LABOR BOARD

116 S. CT. 1396 (1996)

GINSBURG, J . . . . Petitioner Holly Farms Corporation, a wholly owned subsidiary of Tyson Foods, Inc., is a vertically integrated poultry producer headquartered in Wilkesboro, North Carolina. Holly Farms' activities encompass numerous poultry operations, including hatcheries, a feed mill, an equipment maintenance center, and a processing plant.

"Broiler" chickens are birds destined for human food markets. Holly Farms hatches broiler chicks at its own hatcheries, and immediately delivers the chicks to the farms of independent contractors. The contractors then raise the birds into full-grown broiler chickens. Holly Farms pays the contract growers for their services, but retains title to the broilers and supplies the food and medicine necessary to their growth.

When the broilers are seven weeks old, Holly Farms sends its live-haul crews to reclaim the birds and ferry them to the processing plant for slaughter. The live-haul crews—which typically comprise nine chicken catchers, one forklift operator, and one live-haul driver—travel in a flat-bed truck from Holly Farms' processing plant to the farms of the independent growers. At the farms, the chicken catchers enter the coops, manually capture the broilers, and load them into cages. The forklift operator lifts the caged chickens onto the bed of the truck, and the live-haul driver returns the truck, with the loaded cases and the crew, to Holly Farms' processing plant. There, the birds are slaughtered and prepared for shipment to retail stores.

In 1989, the Chauffeurs, Teamsters and Helpers, Local 391 (Union), filed a representation petition with the National Labor Relations Board (Board or NLRB), seeking an election in a proposed unit that included live-haul employees working out of Holly Farms' Wilkesboro processing plant. Over Holly Farms' objection, the Board approved the bargaining unit, ruling that the live-haul workers were "employees" protected by the National Labor Relations Act (NLRA or Act), rather than "agricultural laborers" excluded from the Act's coverage. . . . [T]he Board ordered the corporation to bargain with the Union as the representative of the unit.

The United States Court of Appeals for the Fourth Circuit enforced the Board's order. The court held that the Board's classification of the live-haul workers as "employees," rather than "agricultural laborers," rested "on a reasonable interpretation of the Act." . . .

Other Federal Courts of Appeals . . . have held that live-haul workers employed by vertically integrated poultry producers are engaged in "agriculture." We granted certiorari to resolve the division of authority.

The NLRA's protections extend only to workers who qualify as "employees" under § 2(3) of the Act. The term "employee," NLRA § 2(3) states, "[does] not include any individual employed as an agricultural laborer." No definition of "agricultural laborer" appears in the NLRA. But annually since 1946, Congress has instructed, in riders to Appropriations Acts for the Board: "Agricultural laborer," for NLRA § 2(3) purposes, shall derive its meaning from the definition of "agriculture" supplied by §3(f) of the Fair Labor Standards Act of 1938 (FLSA). Section § 3(f) of the FLSA provides:

"Agriculture" includes farming in all its branches and among other things includes the cultivation and tillage of the soil, dairying, the production, cultivation, growing, and harvesting of any agricultural or horticultural commodities . . . , the raising of livestock, bees, furbearing animals, or poultry, and any practices (including any forestry or lumbering operations) performed by a farmer or on a farm as an incident to or in conjunction with such farming operations, including preparation for market, delivery to storage or to market or to carriers for transportation to market.

. . . If a statute's meaning is plain, the Board and reviewing courts must give effect to the unambiguously

[CONTINUED]

expressed intent of Congress. When the legislative prescription is not free from ambiguity, the administrator must choose between conflicting reasonable interpretations. Courts, in turn, must respect the judgment of the agency empowered to apply the law to varying fact patterns, even if the issue with nearly equal reason [might] be resolved one way rather than another. . . .

Holly Farms argues that under the plain language of the statute, the catching and loading of broilers qualifies as work performed "on a farm as an incident to" the raising of poultry. The corporation emphasizes that § 3(f) of the FLSA enumerates "preparation for market" and "delivery to storage or to market" among activities that count as "agriculture." The live-haul employees' work, Holly Farms concludes, thus falls within the domain of the FLSA exemption and, accordingly, enjoys no NLRA protection.

We find Holly Farms' position to be a plausible, but not an inevitable, construction of § 3(f). Hence, we turn to the Board's position, examining only its reasonableness as an interpretation of the governing legislation.

While agreeing that the chicken catchers and forklift operators work "on a farm," the Board contends that their catch and cage work is not incidental to farming operations. Rather, the work is tied to Holly Farms' slaughtering and processing operations, activities that do not constitute "farming" under the statute. . . .

We find the Board's answer reasonable. Once the broilers have grown on the farm for seven weeks, the growers' contractual obligation to raise the birds ends, and the work of the live-haul crew begins. The record reflects minimal overlap between the work of the live-haul crew and the independent growers' raising activities. The growers do not assist the live-haul crews in catching or loading the chickens; their only responsibilities are to move certain equipment from the chicken coops prior to the crews' arrival, and to be present when the crews are on the farms. Nor do the live-haul employees play any role in the growers' performance of their contractual undertakings.

The record, furthermore, supports the Board's conclusion that the live-haul crews' activities were conjoined with Holly Farms' processing operations, rather than with farming. The chicken catchers, forklift operators, and truckdrivers work as a unit. They all work out of the processing plant in Wilkesboro, located three miles from the hatcheries. Crew members begin and end each shift by punching a time-clock at the processing plant and are functionally integrated with other processing-plant employees. . . .

In sum, we find persuasive the Board's conclusion that the collection of broilers for slaughter was an activity serving Holly Farms' processing operations, and not Holly Farms' own or the independent growers' farming operations. Again, we stress that the reviewing court's function is limited. For the Board to prevail, it need not show that its construction is the best way to read the statute; rather, courts must respect the Board's judgment so long as its reading is a reasonable one. Regardless of how we might have resolved the question as an initial matter, the Board's decision here reflects a reasonable interpretation of the law and, therefore, merits our approbation. The judgment of the Court of Appeals is accordingly

Affirmed.

CASE QUESTIONS

1. What is the order of the NLRB from which Holly Farms objects?
2. What are the respective arguments of Holly Farms and the Chauffeurs, Teamsters and Helpers Union with regard to the "employees" in this case?
3. What is the holding of the Fourth Circuit Court of Appeals?
4. How does the Supreme Court rule in this case? Why?

As the preceding case exemplifies, it is apparent that on review, courts do not (1) reweigh the evidence, (2) make independent determinations of fact, or (3) substitute their view of the evidence for that of the agency. However, courts do determine if there is substantial evidence to support the action taken. But in their examination of the evidence, all that is required is evidence sufficient to convince a reasonable mind to a fair degree of certainty. Thus, substantial evidence is that which a reasonable mind might accept as adequate to support the conclusion.

For the courts to exercise their function of limited review, an agency must provide a record that sets forth the reasons and basis for its decision. If this record shows that the agency did not examine all relevant data and that it ignored issues before it, a court may set aside the agency's decision because such a decision is arbitrary and capricious. Agencies cannot assume their decisions. They must be based on evidence, and the record must support the decision.

After reading this section and the preceding ones, do you understand why it is important for businesses to take seriously the procedures within the administrative agency? Remember the FTC investigation in the Business Decision found at the beginning of this chapter. As you have learned, the deference courts give to agencies' decisions make it clear that the manager's chance of winning a judicial reversal of any FTC decision is slight. Thus, the manager must take the FTC investigation and any subsequent administrative hearing very seriously.

---

concept SUMMARY   *Judicial Review of Agency Decisions*

1. Regardless of whether a party is challenging an agency's rule making or adjudication, that party must have standing to sue.

2. To establish standing to sue, the challenger must show the reviewing court that the agency's decision is subject to review and that the challenger is personally affected by the agency's decision.

3. When the decision challenged involves the agency's rule-making function, the court must determine if the agency's authority was validly delegated.

4. If the delegation of authority is definite and limited, the court will decide if the agency has exceeded its authority. If the answer is no, the agency's rule will be upheld.

5. When the decision challenged involves the agency's adjudicatory function, the law requires the challenger to exhaust the available administrative remedies and the court to determine whether an agency should have primary jurisdiction.

6. The factual findings of an agency are presumed to be correct.

7. Courts are not permitted to substitute their personal views for the agency's findings and conclusions if a reasonable person could reach the same result as the agency.

8. An agency's expertise is entitled to great deference and will not be reversed unless it is clearly erroneous.

---

9. EQUAL ACCESS TO JUSTICE ACT

If a business is successful in challenging an administrative agency's decision, that business may be able to collect attorneys' fees. The Equal Access to Justice Act (EAJA) requires the federal government to pay the reasonable attorneys' fees of small businesses, nonprofit groups, and most individuals who can show they were unjustly treated by the federal government. Prior to the enactment of this law, small companies often were reluctant to take on the U.S. government because of litigation costs. The government was at a great advantage because of the number of attorneys and other resources it has. The EAJA enables the "little guy" to fight the bureaucracy. It should be recognized that awards for legal expenses are not available to just anyone. Congress limited eligibility to persons whose net worth does not exceed $1 million and businesses with no more than $5 million net worth and 500 employees. Charitable and religious tax-exempt organizations qualify if they have 500 or fewer employees. The law also grants legal fees only to parties that overcome the government's position in court, administrative proceedings, or a settlement. Even then, the government agency is not required to pay if it can show that its original position was substantially justified.

The word "substantially" means to be justified in substance or in the main, not justified to a high degree. The action must be justified to a degree that could satisfy a reasonable person and must have reasonable basis in both law and fact. For the position of the government to be substantially justified, so that the award of attorney's fees under the Equal Access to Justice Act is not appropriate, the government's position must be more than merely undeserving of sanctions for frivolity.

Under the EAJA, the amount of fees awarded must "be based upon prevailing market rates for the kind of quality of the services furnished, except that . . . fees shall not be awarded in excess of $75 per hour unless the court determines that an increase in the cost of living or a special factor, such as the limited ability of qualified attorneys for the proceedings involved, justifies a higher fee."

CRITICISM OF ADMINISTRATIVE AGENCIES

The independent regulatory agencies and the administrative process face many problems and are subjected to a great deal of criticism. Many of the common criticisms are summarized in the box on the next page. Agencies are often charged with being too vast to be efficient and effective. One of the major criticisms of the fourth branch of government is its high cost.

10. THE COST OF REGULATION

Regulation is a form of taxation. It directly increases the cost of government. But these direct costs of regulation are only a small fraction of the indirect costs. Regulation significantly adds to the cost of doing business, and these costs are passed on to the tax-paying, consuming public. The consumer, for whose protection many regulations are adopted, pays both the direct cost of regulation (in taxes) and the indirect cost (when purchasing products and services).

The existence of a governmental agency usually forces a business subject to the agency's jurisdiction to create a similar bureaucracy within its own organization to deal with the agency. For example, the existence of EEOC has caused most large corporations to designate affirmative action officers. These employees assist their companies in complying with the laws, rules, and regulations enforced by EEOC. Whenever a bureaucracy exists, firms dealing with it must have internal groups with responsibilities that are the mirror image of the agency.

Other costs the public must absorb result from agency regulations that inhibit competition and innovation. Regulation may protect existing companies by creating a barrier to entry into a market. Regulation tends to protect "cozy competition" to the extent that, quite often, the parties that object the most to deregulation are the businesses being regulated.

Perhaps the most disturbing additional cost to the business community is the cost of paperwork. The burden of the paperwork involved in filing applications, returns, reports, and forms is overwhelming and a major cost of doing business.

CRITICISMS OF ADMINISTRATIVE PROCESS

Relating to Personnel

1. Government has difficulty in hiring and retaining the best-qualified people. Salaries are often not competitive, and advancement is often slower than in the private sector. Also, some people are overqualified for their positions.

2. The reward system usually does not make a significant distinction between excellent, mediocre, and poor performances. There are few incentives to improve productivity and job performance.

3. It is very difficult, if not impossible, to discharge unsatisfactory employees. Transfers of employees are easier to accomplish than discharges.

4. The *Peter Principle,* which holds that people are promoted to their level of incompetence, is obviously present in many administrative agencies.

5. Personnel in many top positions are selected for political reasons. They often lack the necessary expertise to run an effective organization.

Relating to Procedures

1. Delay in the decision-making process is quite common. There often is no reason to expedite decisions, and a huge backlog of cases is common in agencies such as EEOC.

2. The administrative process is overwhelmed with paperwork and with meetings.

3. Rules and regulations are often written in complex legal language—"legalese"—which laypeople cannot understand.

4. There is often a lack of enforcement procedures to follow up on actions taken to ensure compliance.

5. The administrative process can be dictatorial; there may be too much discretionary power, often unstructured and unchecked, placed in many bureaucratic hands. Formal as well as informal administrative action can amount to an abuse of power.

Relating to Substance

1. There are so many agencies making rules and regulations directed at the business community that the rules and regulations often overlap and are in conflict.

2. Some agencies are accused of "sweetheart regulations," or favoring the industry or industries they regulate over the public interest. This may arise as a result of the "revolving door" relationship. Regulators are often persons who had former high executive positions in the industries they regulate. The reverse is also true: people in high-paying jobs in certain industries often were regulators of those very industries.

3. Many actions for illegal conduct end only with consent orders. A business accused of a violation agrees not to violate the law in the future without admitting any past violation. Such actions have little deterrent effect on others, and little or no punishment is imposed for illegal conduct.

4. The volume of rules adopted by agencies is beyond the ability of the business community to keep up with and comply with.

5. Enforcement of some laws varies over time.

Historically, there was little or no cost-benefit analysis when new rules and regulations were proposed. Government has tended only to assess the benefits accruing from a cleaner environment, safer products, healthier working conditions, and so on, in deciding to embark upon vast new regulatory programs. The primary focus of policymaking by way of such social regulation has not been on balancing the costs of the programs with their potential benefits. The public, and especially consumers, has frequently been forced to pay for many things it did not want or need in the sense that the cost far exceeded the benefits.

The Problem with Assessing Costs   At first glance, the application of cost-benefit analysis to the administrative process would seem to make sense. However, on closer examination, it is obvious that in many cases it is not possible to weigh the costs against the benefits of regulation.

How do you apply cost-benefit analysis to a rule dealing with human life? How much dollar benefit is to be assigned to a life in measuring it against the cost? Assume that a Department of Transportation rule requiring air bags in all new automobiles sold adds a cost of $800 to each car. Assume also that it saves 50,000 lives per year. Is the cost worth the benefit? Your answer may depend on whether you are one of the 50,000. Cost-benefit analysis becomes ethically awkward when there is an attempt to place a dollar value on things not usually bought and sold, such as life, health, or mobility.

KEY TERMS

Administrative agency 350	General counsel 357
Administrative law judges 358	Immunity 359
Cease and desist order 356	Primary jurisdiction 369
Consent order 356	Quasi-judicial 355
Exhaustion of remedies 369	Quasi-legislative 355

REVIEW QUESTIONS AND PROBLEMS

Administrative Agencies

1. *Reasons for Agencies*

   This chapter discusses five reasons for having administrative agencies. Give an example for each reason.

2. *Functions of Agencies*

   Describe the four possible functions of an administrative agency.

3. *Organization of Agencies*

   (a)   Why is the position of General Counsel of an administrative agency so important?

   (b)   What is the purpose of the administrative law judges within administrative agencies?

4. *Influencing Agency Decisions*

   Suppose that a company is interested in a newly proposed regulation on clean air by the Environmental Protection Agency. What should this company do to provide its input on this EPA regulation?

Judicial Review of Agency Decisions

5. *Standing to Sue*

   What are the two issues that must be considered by courts to determine whether a person has standing to challenge an agency's decision?

6. *Review of Rule Making*

   (a)   Again there are two issues that must be addressed by courts when they review the rule-making (quasi-legislative) functions of agencies. What are these two issues? Explain each.

   (b)   A national bank sought permission from the comptroller of the currency to sell annuities. This permission was granted as "incidental to the business of banking." The Variable Annuity Life Insurance Company filed suit claiming the comptroller should not have granted this permission. What standard of review of this administrative decision should courts apply?

7. *Review of Adjudications: Procedural Aspects*

Plaintiffs purchased state lottery tickets and were winners along with 76 others. The state had advertised that $1,750,000 would be the prize, but it only distributed $744,471. Plaintiff sued the lottery director, alleging fraud in the conduct of the lottery. The state lottery law provides for administrative hearings upon complaints charging violations of the lottery law or of regulations thereunder. It also allows any party adversely affected by a final order of the administrative agency to seek judicial review. Must the plaintiffs exhaust their administrative remedies? Why or why not?

8. *Review of Factual Determinations*

What standard of review do courts use to decide whether to uphold the factual determinations made by an administrative agency?

9. *Equal Access to Justice Act*

A congressman filed an administrative complaint with the Federal Election Commission, alleging various violations of the Federal Election Campaign Act by several different groups that made campaign contributions. Dissatisfied with the progress of the FEC's investigation, he filed suit against the FEC in federal district court, seeking to compel agency action. The court found that the agency action was "arbitrary and capricious." Does this entitle him to an award of attorney's fees under the Equal Access to Justice Act? Why or why not?

Criticism of Administrative Agencies

10. *The Cost of Regulation*

Why has there been so little use of cost-benefit analysis when judging the merits of agencies' actions?

TERMINOLOGY REVIEW

For each agency listed in the left-hand column, match the most appropriate description in the right-hand column:

1. CPSC
2. EPA
3. FCC
4. FTC
5. FDA
6. EEOC
7. NLRB
8. NRC
9. OSHA
10. SEC

a. Protects the public from anticompetitive behavior and unfair and deceptive business practices; a law enforcement agency

b. Licenses and regulates the nuclear energy industry

c. Protects the public against unreasonable risks of injury associated with consumer products

d. Seeks to prevent discrimination in employment based on race, color, religion, sex, or national origin and other unlawful employment practices

e. Regulates interstate and foreign communications by means of radio, television, wire, cable, and satellite

f. Ensures all workers a safe and healthy work environment

g. Enforces the federal securities laws that regulate the sale of securities to the investing public

h. Administers laws to prohibit distribution of adulterated, misbranded, or unsafe food and drugs

i. Conducts union certification elections and holds hearings on unfair labor practice complaints

j. Administers all laws relating to the environment, including laws on water pollution, air pollution, solid wastes, pesticides, toxic substances, etc.

BUSINESS DISCUSSION

You are chief executive officer of a toy manufacturing firm. Your firm has been inspected by officials at OSHA, the federal Occupational Safety and Health Administration, for alleged violations of workplace safety regulations. The evidence presented to the agency was confusing and conflicting. You feel strongly that the company should not be penalized. Nevertheless your firm has been ordered to pay a substantial fine, and an administrative law judge ordered you to make some very expensive modifications in its manufacturing processes.

Should you continue to seek review of your case before the agency's officials?

Should you appeal by filing a lawsuit to reverse the agency's decision?

If you are successful in court, under what circumstances can you recover your attorney's fees?

13

ANTITRUST LAWS— REGULATING COMPETITION

You are feeling very good about your life. This positive feeling is due in large part to your recent promotion to national sales manager of Ever-Present Technologies, Inc. Your company offers full-service consulting and computer sales to manufacturers, especially those in the consumer products areas.

Two weeks into your new responsibilities, you are beginning to lose your good feelings. This change of spirit results from hearing about various activities among your sales personnel. First, you learn one of your new sales representatives has been visiting with a competitor's salesperson about each focusing on particular customers while agreeing not to call on the other's customers. Second, a district manager reports that a large, extremely valuable, customer is asking for a pricing structure that is more favorable than prices offered to any other customer. The district manager expressed concern that your company may lose this customer's business.

> What legal worries do you have about each of these situations?
>
> What type of information should a training/education program for your sales force include?
>
> What are the ramifications if you decide to ignore these situations as you try to return to your "happy" state of mind?

The situations described in this Business Decision illustrate why the topic of this chapter is so important. Your failure to take immediate and significant action to correct the wrongs that may occur could result in your loss of your job. Major fines for you and your company and a prison sentence are not beyond the realm of possibility. The Business Decision also shows that questions of antitrust laws apply equally to small businesses and huge multinational corporations. Even though the dollar figures in the next paragraph are staggering, the details of this chapter will be familiar to businesspeople working for organizations of all sizes.

Six of the ten largest criminal fines throughout the 1990s resulted from domestic and international enforcement of antitrust laws. The largest fine was $500 million. Other major antitrust fines and the relative position in the top 10 were $225 million (#3), $135 million (#4), $110 million (#6), $100 million (#7), and $50 million (#10). These figures clearly document the significance of understanding and complying with the antitrust laws.

1. HISTORICAL DEVELOPMENT

The term *antitrust* is somewhat misleading. Trusts are a legal arrangement used for centuries for such socially desirable purposes as promoting education or caring for spendthrift or incompetent children and for financial and tax planning. A **trust** is a fiduciary relationship concerning property in which one person, known as the **trustee,** holds legal title to property for the benefit of another, known as the **beneficiary.** The trustee has the duty to manage and preserve the property for the use and enjoyment of the beneficiary.

In the last part of the nineteenth century, the trust device was used extensively to gain monopolistic control of several industries. Through it, a group of corporations in the same type of business could unite to eliminate competition among themselves. The trust device allowed all or at least a majority of the stock of several companies to be transferred to a trustee. The trustee then was in a position to control the operations and policy making of all the companies. The trust not only controlled production, but also dominated and divided the market and established price levels. The effect of these concentrations was to destroy the free market—"to restrain trade," as the Sherman Act would put it.

Because the purpose of the laws discussed in this chapter was to "bust" the trusts, these laws became known as the antitrust laws. Today the term is used to describe all laws that intend to promote and regulate competition and make our competitive economic system work. The goal is workable competition and all the benefits that are intended to flow from it.

During its first hundred years, the federal government's role in relation to commerce was that of promoter. The U.S. Constitution itself eliminates trade barriers among the states. In the early and mid-nineteenth century, through its sponsorship of internal improvements such as canals and roads and its support for railroads, the federal government facilitated trade and commerce. But by the end of the nineteenth century business and industrial combinations were so powerful that reformers called on government to break these monopolies and restore healthy competition. The government responded by enacting the **Sherman Act** in 1890.

The goal of the Sherman Act was competition. Competition, these reformers pointed out, tends to keep private markets working in ways that are socially desirable. It encourages an efficient allocation of resources and stimulates efficiency and product innovation. A competitive system that allows easy entry to and withdrawal from the marketplace is consistent with individual freedom and economic opportunity. In 1958, Justice Hugo Black in *Northern Pacific Ry. Co. v. United States* (356 U.S. 1), reflected on the purpose of the Sherman Act when he stated in part:

> The Sherman Act was designed to be a comprehensive charter of economic liberty aimed at preserving free and unfettered competition as the rule of trade. It rests on the premise that the unrestrained interaction of competitive forces will yield the best allocation of our economic resources, the lowest prices, the highest quality and the greatest material progress, while at the same time providing an environment conducive to the preservation of our democratic, political and social institutions.

The Sherman Act still provides the basic framework for the regulation of business and industry. It seeks to preserve competition by prohibiting two types of anticompetitive business behavior:

- Contracts, combinations, and conspiracies in restraint of trade or commerce (see section 2 of this chapter)
- Monopolies and attempts to monopolize (see section 3 of this chapter)

The Sherman Act was general and often ambiguous. It did not define *trust, monopoly,* or *restraint of trade.* It also did not make clear whether it addressed combinations of labor as well as capital.

In 1914 Congress, recognizing that the Sherman Act needed to be more specific, enacted the **Clayton Act** as an amendment to the Sherman Act and later twice amended the Clayton Act (1936, 1950) to clarify its provisions. The Clayton Act declares that certain enumerated practices in interstate commerce are illegal. These are practices that might adversely affect competition but that were not clear violations under the Sherman Act.

In 1914, Congress also passed the **Federal Trade Commission Act.** This act created the Federal Trade Commission (FTC), an independent administrative agency charged with keeping competition free and fair. The FTC enforces the Clayton Act. In addition, it enforces Section 5 of the FTC Act, which prohibits unfair methods of competition and unfair or deceptive acts or practices.

The antitrust laws are enforced by the federal and state governments and by private parties. The federal government's basic enforcement procedures are utilized through the Department of Justice and the Federal Trade Commission (FTC). The Department of Justice alone has the power to bring criminal proceedings, but it shares its civil enforcement powers with the FTC.

State government also plays an important role in the enforcement of antitrust laws. A state attorney general may bring civil suits for damages under the Sherman Act as well as suits for an injunction. In addition, state legislators have enacted antitrust laws that cover both products and services. These laws cover intrastate activities and are designed to prevent loss of competition in local communities.

In addition to these governmental enforcers, private parties may bring civil suits seeking monetary damages or injunction as a means of enforcing the antitrust laws. Section 5 of this chapter and several of the cases present ways that individuals and business organizations help protect the competitive nature of the marketplace.

THE SHERMAN ACT

To fully appreciate the importance that the Sherman Act plays in our legal and regulatory environment of business, you must understand the basic provisions and analysis of the law. The following sections present these basic concepts, as follows:

- Restraint of trade
- Monopoly
- Legal analysis
- Sanctions
- Exemptions

2. RESTRAINT OF TRADE

Section 1 of the Sherman Act prohibits contracts, combinations, and conspiracies in **restraint of trade** or commerce. *Contracts* in restraint of trade usually result from verbal or written agreements; *combinations* usually result from conduct; *conspiracies* are usually established by agreement and followed up by some act carrying out the plan of the conspiracy. An express agreement is not required to create a contract in restraint of trade. Such contracts may be implied. For example, discussion of price with one's competitors together with conscious parallel pricing establishes a violation.

Joint activities by two or more persons may constitute a violation of Section 1. The most common contract in restraint of trade is an agreement among competitors to charge the same price for their products (**price fixing**). Such agreements among producers to set prices in advance rather than allow prices to be set by the operations of a free market are obviously anticompetitive and in restraint of trade. Agreements relating to territories of operation also violate Section 1 of the Sherman Act. So does an attempt to extend the economic power of a patent or copyright to unrelated products or services. These and other examples of Section 1 violations are discussed in sections 7 to 11 of this chapter.

The acceptance of an invitation to participate in a plan that is in restraint of interstate commerce is sufficient to establish an unlawful conspiracy. Circumstantial evidence may be used to prove a conspiracy. For example, the simultaneous price increases by three major cigarette producers at a time of declining sales were admissible evidence to prove a conspiracy without direct proof of communication among them.

Sherman Act cases must satisfy an interstate commerce element. The facts must show that an allegedly illegal activity was either in interstate commerce or had a substantial effect on interstate commerce. The facts need not prove a change in the volume of interstate commerce but only that the activity had a substantial and adverse or not insubstantial effect on interstate commerce. As discussed in Chapter 6, the impact on interstate commerce often is readily apparent.

3. MONOPOLY

Section 2 of the Sherman Act regulates **monopoly** and the attempts to monopolize any part of interstate or foreign commerce. The law establishes the means to break up existing monopolies and to prevent others from developing. It is directed at single firms and does not purport to cover shared monopolies or oligopolies.

Under Section 2 of the Sherman Act, it is a violation for a firm to monopolize, attempt to monopolize, or conspire to monopolize any part of interstate or foreign commerce. Attempts to monopolize cases require proof of intent to destroy competition or achieve monopoly power. This is most difficult to prove, and as a result, there have been few cases concerning attempts to monopolize. A conspiracy to monopolize requires proof of specific intent to monopolize and at least one overt act to accomplish it. Proof of monopoly power or even that it was attainable is not required. This conspiracy theory is usually joined with the allegation of actual monopoly in most cases.

EXAMPLE OF MONOPOLY

The case of *Aspen Skiing Co. v. Aspen Highlands Skiing Corp.** provides an example of the kind of factual situation and legal analysis that leads to a finding of a § 2 violation. In the early years of snow skiing in Aspen, three facilities were operated by three distinct companies. The two parties involved in this case were among these competitors. In addition to offering a daily ski-lift ticket for their own mountain, each competitor sold a multiday, interchangeable, all-Aspen ticket.

Aspen Skiing acquired the third facility and opened a fourth. Eventually, this company sold a multiday ticket that allowed its patrons access to only its facilities. As a result of this action, Aspen Highlands lost a significant share of its business. Ultimately, Aspen Highlands sued Aspen Skiing, alleging that the refusal to sell an all-Aspen ticket was an illegal attempt to monopolize the Aspen Skiing market.

Aspen Skiing argued that it was not in violation of § 2 of the Sherman Act because nothing in this law required it to do business with a competitor. Even though the trial judge agreed with this legal conclusion, the judge instructed the jury that it could find Aspen Skiing in violation of the Sherman Act unless that company persuaded the jury that its conduct was justified by any normal business purpose.

Apparently the jury was not convinced by Aspen Skiing's presentation. The jury rendered a verdict finding Aspen Skiing in violation of § 2 and awarding Aspen Highlands actual damages of $2.5 million. This award was tripled to $7.5 million, and costs and attorneys' fees were added to this amount.

Aspen Skiing was unable to convince either the court of appeals or the United States Supreme Court to reverse this jury verdict. The Supreme Court was particularly influenced by the market studies that showed skiers wanted to have access to the Highlands facilities but refused to ski there due to the lack of an all-area ticket. The Court concluded that the jury was justified in finding that inappropriate motivations to monopolize were behind Aspen Skiing's decision to stop selling the all-area ticket.

*105 S.Ct. 2847 (1985).

Note that in the preceding box the illegal conduct was the failure to cooperate with a competitor. This conduct was designed to eliminate the competitor, and it resulted in liability for triple damages.

Proof of monopoly power alone is not enough. Some monopolies are lawful. If monopoly power is "thrust upon" a firm or if it exists because of a patent or franchise, there is no violation of Section 2 if the firm does not engage in conduct that has the effect or purpose of protecting, enforcing, or extending the monopoly power. The power must have been either acquired or used in ways that go beyond normal, honest industrial business conduct for a violation to exist. To be illegal, the monopoly must have been *deliberatively* acquired or used. A firm is guilty of monopolization when it acquires or maintains monopoly power by a course of deliberate conduct that keeps other firms from entering the market or from expanding their share of it. Deliberativeness is not difficult to prove in most cases.

Conduct that proves deliberativeness may be anything in restraint of trade. For example, predatory conduct would prove deliberativeness. **Predatory conduct** is seeking to advance market share by injuring actual or potential competitors by means other than improved performance. It may be for the purpose of driving out competitors, for keeping them out, or for making them less effective. Pricing policies are frequently examined for proof of predatory conduct. Profit-maximizing pricing; limit pricing, whereby the price is limited to levels that tend to discourage entry; and the practice of price discrimination all may tend to prove monopoly power and predatory conduct. The box on the next page describes the proof needed to document the existence of an illegal monopoly.

PROVING AN ILLEGAL MONOPOLY EXISTS

A firm violates Section 2 if it follows a course of conduct through which it obtained the power to control price or exclude competition. The mere possession of monopoly power is not a violation. There must be proof that the power resulted from a deliberate course of conduct or proof of intent to maintain the power by conduct. Proof of deliberateness is just as essential as is proof of the power to control price to exclude competition.

Section 2 cases require proof of market power—the power to affect the price of the firm's products in the market. Whether such power exists is usually determined by an analysis of the reaction of buyers to price changes by the alleged monopolist seller. Such cases require a definition of the relevant market and a study of the degree of concentration within the market. Barriers to entry are analyzed, and the greater the barriers, the greater the significance of market share. The legal issues in such cases require structural analysis.

In defining the relevant market, the courts examine both product market and geographic market. A relevant market is the smallest one wide enough so that products from outside the geographic area or from other producers in the same area cannot compete with those included in the defined relevant market. In other words, if prices are raised or supply is curtailed within a given area while demand remains constant, will products from other areas or other products from within the area enter the market in enough quantity to force a lower price or increased supply?

Some monopoly cases involve products for which there are few or no substitutes. Other cases involve products for which there are numerous substitutes. For example, aluminum may be considered a product that is generally homogeneous. If a firm has 90 percent of the virgin aluminum market, a violation would be established. However, if a firm had 90 percent of the Danish coffee cake market, the decision is less clear, because numerous products compete with Danish coffee cakes as a breakfast product. The relevant product is often difficult to define because of differences in products, substitute products, product diversification, and even product clusters.

Section 2 cases may involve a variety of proofs and many different forms of economic analysis. The degree of market concentration, barriers to entry, structural features such as market shares of other firms, profit levels, the extent to which prices respond to changes in supply and demand, whether or not a firm discriminates in price between its customers, and the absolute size of the firm are all factors usually considered by courts in monopoly cases. In addition, courts examine the conduct of the firm. How did it achieve its market share? Was it by internal growth or acquisition? Does the firm's current conduct tend to injure competition? These and other issues are important aspects in any finding of the existence of monopoly power.

4. ANALYSIS IN ANTITRUST LAW

As we have seen, the Sherman Act was deliberately vague in expectation that the courts would draw the line between legal and illegal conduct with respect to restraint of trade and monopoly. Courts follow two principles and a middle ground to guide applicability in antitrust law:

- The rule of reason
- Per se illegality
- Quick look

The following discussions illuminate these concepts.

The Rule of Reason   Section 1 of the Sherman Act provides that "*every* contract, combination . . . , or conspiracy in restraint of trade . . . is declared to be illegal." However, the United States Supreme Court has held that Congress did not really mean it when it used the word *every*. For example, if you and I enter into a contract whereby I agree to buy your car, this contract restrains trade. You cannot sell your car to another person without becoming liable to me for a breach of our contract. The Court felt that Congress did not intend our contract to be a violation of the Sherman Act.

The **rule of reason** was announced in *Standard Oil Co. v. United States* (221 U.S. 1 [1911]). The Supreme Court in that case held that contracts or conspiracies in restraint of trade were illegal only if they constituted *undue* or *unreasonable* restraints of trade and that only *unreasonable* attempts to monopolize were covered by the Sherman Act. As a result, acts that the statute prohibits may be removed from the coverage of the law by a finding that they are *reasonable*.

The *test of reasonableness* asks whether challenged contracts or acts are unreasonably restrictive of competitive conditions. Unreasonableness can be based on:

- The nature or character of the contracts
- Surrounding circumstances giving rise to the inference or presumption that the contracts were intended to restrain trade and enhance prices

Under either branch of the test, the inquiry is confined to a consideration of impact on competitive conditions. If an agreement promotes competition, it may be legal. If it suppresses or destroys competition, it is unreasonable and illegal.

For purposes of the rule of reason, Sherman Act violations may be divided into two categories. The first category consists of agreements and practices that are illegal only if they impose an unreasonable restraint upon competitors. The other category consists of agreements or practices that are so plainly anticompetitive and so lacking in any redeeming values that they are conclusively presumed to be illegal without further examination under the rule of reason. These agreements have such a pernicious effect on competition that elaborate inquiry as to the precise harm they may cause or a business excuse for them are unnecessary. They are said to be *illegal per se.* It is not necessary to examine them to see if they are reasonable. They are conclusively presumed to be unreasonable.

Per Se Illegality The concept of **per se illegality** simplifies proof in cases in which it is applied. When an activity is illegal per se, courts are not required to conduct a complicated and prolonged examination of the economic consequences of the activity to determine whether it is unreasonable. If it is illegal per se, proof of the activity is proof of a violation and proof that it is in restraint of trade. It is unreasonable as a matter of law.

The most common example of an agreement that is illegal per se is one that fixes prices. Agreements among competitors to divide up territories or to limit the supply of a commodity are outlawed without proof of any unreasonable effects. Group boycotts are usually held to be illegal per se. In studying antitrust cases, you should note those activities to which the illegal per se concept is applied and those to which the rule of reason is applied. Courts develop this distinction on a case-by-case basis.

Quick Look The courts sometimes use a middleground approach in their legal analysis. Perhaps the facts of a case are not found to involve clearly anticompetitive activities and thus the per se illegal analysis is not applicable. However, the court is comfortable in its belief that the activity tends to be so anticompetitive that it concludes a thorough economic analysis is not necessary. This approach is called the **quick look analysis,** and it is the subject matter of the following case.

CALIFORNIA DENTAL ASSOCIATION V. FEDERAL TRADE COMMISSION

119 S. CT. 1604 (1999)

SOUTER, J.: There are two issues in this case: whether the jurisdiction of the Federal Trade Commission extends to the California Dental Association (CDA), a nonprofit professional association, and whether a "quick look" sufficed to justify finding that certain advertising restrictions adopted by the CDA violated the antitrust laws. . . .

The dentists who belong to the CDA through these associations agree to abide by a Code of Ethics (Code) including the following § 10:

> Although any dentist may advertise, no dentist shall advertise or solicit patients in any form of communication in a manner that is false or misleading in any material respect. In order to properly serve the public, dentists should represent themselves in a manner that contributes to the esteem of the public. Dentists should not misrepresent their training and competence in any way that would be false or misleading in any material respect.

. . . Responsibility for enforcing the Code rests in the first instance with the local dental societies, to which applicants for CDA membership must submit copies of their own advertisements and those of their employers or referral services to assure compliance with the Code. The local societies also actively seek information about potential Code violations by applicants or CDA members. Applicants who refuse to withdraw or revise objectionable advertisements may be denied membership; and members who, after a hearing, remain similarly recalcitrant are subject to censure, suspension, or expulsion from the CDA.

The Commission brought a complaint against the CDA, alleging that it applied its guidelines so as to restrict truthful, nondeceptive advertising, and so violated § 5 of the FTC Act. The complaint alleged that the CDA had unreasonably restricted two types of advertising: price advertising, particularly discounted fees, and advertising relating to the quality of dental services. An Administrative Law Judge (ALJ) held the Commission to have jurisdiction over the CDA. . . . He found that, although there had been no proof that the CDA exerted market power, no

such proof was required to establish an antitrust violation . . . since the CDA had unreasonably prevented members and potential members from using truthful, nondeceptive advertising, all to the detriment of both dentists and consumers of dental services. He accordingly found a violation of § 5 of the FTC Act.

The Commission adopted the factual findings of the ALJ except for his conclusion that the CDA lacked market power, with which the Commission disagreed. The Commission treated the CDA's restrictions on discount advertising as illegal per se. In the alternative, the Commission held the price advertising (as well as the nonprice) restrictions to be violations of the Sherman and FTC Acts under an abbreviated rule-of-reason analysis. . . .

The Court of Appeals for the Ninth Circuit affirmed, sustaining the Commission's assertion of jurisdiction over the CDA and its ultimate conclusion on the merits. The court thought it error for the Commission to have applied per se analysis to the price advertising restrictions, finding analysis under the rule of reason required for all the restrictions. But the Court of Appeals went on to explain that the Commission had properly applied an abbreviated, or 'quick look,' rule of reason analysis designed for restraints that are not per se unlawful but are sufficiently anticompetitive on their face that they do not require a full-blown rule of reason inquiry. . . .

We granted certiorari to resolve conflicts among the Circuits on the Commission's jurisdiction over a nonprofit professional association and the occasions for abbreviated rule of reason analysis. We now vacate the judgment of the Court of Appeals and remand. . . .

[The Supreme Court agreed that the FTC Act gives the Commission jurisdiction over a nonprofit organization which has the commercial purpose to benefit its members.] The logic and purpose of the FTC Act comport with this result. The FTC Act directs the Commission to "prevent" the broad set of

[CONTINUED]

entities under its jurisdiction "from using unfair methods of competition in or affecting commerce and unfair or deceptive acts or practices in or affecting commerce." Nonprofit entities organized on behalf of for-profit members have the same capacity and derivatively, at least, the same incentives as for-profit organizations to engage in unfair methods of competition or unfair and deceptive acts. . . .

We therefore conclude that the Commission had jurisdiction to pursue the claim here, and turn to the question whether the Court of Appeals devoted sufficient analysis to sustain the claim that the advertising restrictions promulgated by the CDA violated the FTC Act. . . .

The case before us . . . fails to present a situation in which the likelihood of anticompetitive effects is comparably obvious. . . . [I]t seems to us that the CDA's advertising restrictions might plausibly be thought to have a net procompetitive effect, or possibly no effect at all on competition. The restrictions on both discount and nondiscount advertising are, at least on their face, designed to avoid false or deceptive advertising in a market characterized by striking disparities between the information available to the professional and the patient. In a market for professional services, in which advertising is relatively rare and the comparability of service packages not easily established, the difficulty for customers or potential competitors to get and verify information about the price and availability of services magnifies the dangers to competition associated with misleading advertising. What is more, the quality of professional services tends to resist either calibration or monitoring by individual patients or clients, partly because of the specialized knowledge required to evaluate the services, and partly because of the difficulty in determining whether, and the degree to which, an outcome is attributable to the quality of services . . . or to something else. . . . Patients' attachments to particular professionals, the rationality of which is difficult to assess, complicate the picture even further. The existence of such significant challenges to informed decision making by the customer for professional services immediately suggests that advertising restrictions arguably protecting patients from misleading or irrelevant

advertising call for more than cursory treatment as obviously comparable to classic horizontal agreements to limit output or price competition. . . .

Saying here that the Court of Appeals's conclusion at least required a more extended examination of the possible factual underpinnings than it received is not, of course, necessarily to call for the fullest market analysis. Although we have said that a challenge to a naked restraint on price and output need not be supported by a detailed market analysis in order to require some competitive justification, it does not follow that every case attacking a less obviously anticompetitive restraint (like this one) is a candidate for plenary market examination. The truth is that our categories of analysis of anticompetitive effect are less fixed than terms like "per se," "quick look," and "rule of reason" tend to make them appear. We have recognized, for example, that there is often no bright line separating per se from rule of reason analysis, since considerable inquiry into market conditions may be required before the application of any so-called "per se" condemnation is justified. Whether the ultimate finding is the product of a presumption or actual market analysis, the essential inquiry remains the same—whether or not the challenged restraint enhances competition. . . . As the circumstances here demonstrate, there is generally no categorical line to be drawn between restraints that give rise to an intuitively obvious inference of anticompetitive effect and those that call for more detailed treatment. . . . The object is to see whether the experience of the market has been so clear, or necessarily will be, that a confident conclusion about the principal tendency of a restriction will follow from a quick (or at least quicker) look, in place of a more sedulous one. And of course what we see may vary over time, if rule of reason analyses in case after case reach identical conclusions. For now, at least, a less quick look was required for the initial assessment of the tendency of these professional advertising restrictions. Because the Court of Appeals did not scrutinize the assumption of relative anticompetitive tendencies, we vacate the judgment and remand the case for a fuller consideration of the issue.

Reversed and remanded.

[CONTINUED]

CASE QUESTIONS

1. What is the basis of the FTC claiming to have jurisdiction over the California Dental Association, a nonprofit organization?

2. What is meant by the phrases: "rule of reason," "per se illegality," and "quick look analysis"?

3. What were the conclusions of the FTC and the Circuit Court of Appeals?

4. How does the Supreme Court decide this case? What is the reasoning for this decision?

5. SANCTIONS

The Sherman Act as amended by the Clayton Act recognizes four separate legal sanctions:

1. Violations may be subject to criminal fines and imprisonment.
2. Violations may be enjoined by the courts.
3. Injured parties may collect **triple damages.**
4. Any property owned in violation of Section 1 of the Sherman Act that is being transported from one state to another is subject to a seizure by and forfeiture to the United States.

The first sanction is criminal punishment. Crimes under the Sherman Act are felonies. An individual found guilty may be fined up to $350,000 and imprisoned up to three years. A corporation found guilty may be fined up to $10 million for each offense.

The second sanction of the Sherman Act empowers courts to grant injunctions, at the request of the government or a private party, that will prevent and restrain violations or continued violations of its provisions. An injunction may prevent anticompetitive behavior, or it may even force a breakup of a corporation.

The injunction is frequently used when the success of a criminal prosecution is doubtful. It takes less proof to enjoin an activity (*preponderance of the evidence*) than it does to convict of a crime (*beyond a reasonable doubt*). There have been cases involving this remedy even after an acquittal in a criminal case. In effect, the court ordered the defendant not to do something it had been found innocent of doing.

The third sanction affords relief to persons, including governments, injured by another's violations of the Sherman Act. Section 4 of the Clayton Act authorizes such victims in a civil action to collect three times the damages they have suffered plus court costs and reasonable attorneys' fees. Normally, the objective of awarding money damages to individuals in a private lawsuit is to place them in the position they would have enjoyed, as nearly as this can be done with money, had their rights not been invaded. The triple-damage provisions of the antitrust laws, however, employ the remedy of damages to punish a defendant for a wrongful act in addition to compensating the plaintiff for actual injury. Today it is perhaps the most important sanction for an antitrust violation, because it allows one's competitors as well as injured members of the general public to enforce the law. Legislation also allows both federal and state governments to file a suit for triple damages.

Successful triple-damage suits may impose financial burdens on violators far in excess of any fine that could be imposed as a result of a criminal prosecution. This significant liability may be far in excess of the damages caused by any one defendant, because the liability of defendants is based on tort law and is said to be *joint and several.* For example, assume that 10 companies in an industry conspire to fix prices and that the total damages caused by the conspiracy equal $100 million. Also, assume that nine of the defendants settle out of court for $25 million. The remaining defendant, if the case is lost, would owe $275 million (3 × 100 − 25). The Supreme Court has held that there is no right of contribution by the losing party against those that settled prior to the final judgment.

There is a significant relationship between the criminal antitrust prosecution and the civil suit for triple damages. If the defendant in a criminal antitrust suit is convicted or pleads guilty, the plaintiff in the related triple damages suit is greatly aided. This result arises from the criminal case's prima facie evidence that an antitrust violation occurred. The cost of the investigation and preparation needed to prove the existence of an antitrust violation is usually substantial. Using the defendant's criminal conviction or guilty plea as proof of the wrong allows the civil plaintiff to concentrate on proving damages, which are then tripled by the court. This automatic proof deriving from the criminal case can be avoided if the defendant enters a plea of *nolo contendere* (no contest) in the criminal case. Because this plea technically is interpreted as avoiding a conviction, the civil plaintiff is left with the burden of proving the antitrust violation.

concept SUMMARY   *Antitrust Sanctions*

1. Four sanctions are recognized by the antitrust laws:
   a. Federal criminal penalties
   b. Injunctions ordered by the courts
   c. Triple damages payable to an injured party
   d. Seizure and forfeiture of property owned in restraint of trade if such property is transported between states
2. The federal criminal penalties are, for an individual, up to a $350,000 fine plus up to three years in prison, and for a corporation, up to $10 million in fines.

3. An injunction may prevent anticompetitive behavior
4. Under the triple-damage sanctions, a defendant cannot seek contribution from other wrongdoers.
5. To avoid the impact of a guilty plea or a conviction on a pending civil antitrust suit, the criminally accused defendant often pleads *nolo contendere* (no contest).

6. EXEMPTIONS

Certain businesses may be exempt from the Sherman Act because of a statute or as the result of a judicial decision. Among activities and businesses for which there are statutory exemptions are insurance companies; farmers' cooperatives; shipping, milk marketing, and investment companies. Activities required by state law are exempt. In addition, normal activities of labor unions are exempt.

These exemptions are narrowly construed and do not mean that every activity of a firm is necessarily exempted simply because most activities are exempted. For example, an agreement between an insurance company and a pharmaceutical organization that regulates the price of prescription drugs given to policyholders of the insurance company is not exempt—it was not the business of insurance involved in this transaction. It is the business of insurance that is exempt and not the business of insurance companies. Likewise, a labor union would forfeit its exemption when it agrees with one set of employers to impose a certain wage scale on other employers' bargaining units. It is only the usual and legitimate union activity that is exempt. In Chapter 14, we discuss how a union must deal directly with the company involved in the labor dispute. Therefore, the arrangement in the example above is beyond the normal and proper activities of a union and not protected from antitrust claims.

In a 1943 case known as *Parker v. Brown,* the Supreme Court created a **state action exemption** to the Sherman Act. This state action exemption, referred to as the **Parker v. Brown doctrine,** is based on the reasoning that the Sherman Act does not apply to state government. When a state acts in its sovereign capacity, it is immune from federal antitrust scrutiny. For example, an unsuccessful candidate for admittance to the Arizona bar alleged a conspiracy by the bar examiners in violation of the Sherman Act. He contended that the grading scale was dictated by the number of new attorneys desired rather than by the level of competition and answers on the exam. The courts held that this activity was exempt from the Sherman Act. The grading of bar examinations is, in reality, conduct of the Arizona Supreme Court and thus exempt. Action by the courts is just as immune as actions by the legislature.

Another exemption from the Sherman Act extends to concerted efforts to lobby government officials, regardless of the anticompetitive purposes of the lobbying effort. The doctrine, known as the **Noerr-Pennington doctrine** is based on the First Amendment. For example, Budget Rent-A-Car filed suit against Hertz and National Rent-A-Car because the defendants lobbied officials at three state-owned airports to limit the number of car-rental operations. This lobbying was ruled exempt from the Sherman Act under the First Amendment right to petition government for a redress of grievances and recognition of the value of the free flow of information.

TYPES OF CASES

As the courts deal with potential violations of the Sherman Act, the types of cases typically heard can be divided into price fixing, territorial agreements, and concerted activities. Each of these is discussed in the following sections. A further word regarding price fixing is necessary before you start the examination of these types of cases. The philosophy expressed in the Sherman Act believes a competitive marketplace requires that prices be set by the operation of free markets. No competitor should have the economic power to set prices. Since price is an essential element of competition, the legal analysis used in price fixing cases is hotly debated regardless of the form of pricing agreements: horizontal, vertical, or indirect.

7. HORIZONTAL PRICE FIXING

Horizontal price fixing is an agreement between competitors to fix prices. The term *price fixing* means more than setting a price. For example, if partners set the price of their goods or service, they have engaged in a form of price fixing but not the type envisioned by the Sherman Act. The price fixing covered by the Sherman Act is that which threatens free competition.

It is no defense to a charge of price fixing that the prices fixed are fair or reasonable. It also is no defense that price fixing is engaged in by small competitors to allow them to compete with larger competitors. The per se rule makes price fixing illegal whether the parties to it have control of the market or not and whether or not they are trying to raise or lower the market price. It is just as illegal to fix a low price as it is to fix a high price. Maximum-price agreements are just as illegal as minimum-price agreements.

Historically, the Sherman Act was thought to apply only to the sale of goods. Price fixing in the service sector was commonly engaged in by professional persons such as architects, lawyers, and physicians. Persons performing services argued they were not engaged in trade or commerce and thus they were not covered by the Sherman Act. They also contended there was a "learned profession" exception to the Sherman Act.

In the mid-1970s, the Supreme Court rejected these arguments and held that the Sherman Act covers services, including those performed by the learned professions such as attorneys-at-law. Today, it is just as illegal to fix the price of services as it is to fix the price of goods.

Some professional groups have attempted to avoid restrictions on price fixing through the use of ethical standards. Although such ethical standards are not illegal per se, they are nevertheless anticompetitive and a violation of the Sherman Act. Others have attempted to determine the price of services indirectly by using formulas and relative-value scales. For example, some medical organizations have determined that a given medical procedure would be allocated a relative value on a scale of 1 to 10. Open-heart surgery might be labeled a 9 and an appendectomy a 3. All members of the profession would then use these values in determining professional fees. Such attempts have been uniformly held to be illegal.

The table on the next page presents examples of horizontal price-fixing cases. The companies and industries involved demonstrate the pervasiveness of Sherman Act violations.

8. VERTICAL PRICE FIXING

Attempts by manufacturers to control the ultimate retail price for their products is known as **vertical price fixing** or **resale price maintenance.** Such efforts result in part from the desire to maintain a high-quality product image, the assumption being that a relatively high price suggests a relatively high quality. These efforts are also based on a desire to maintain adequate channels of distribution. If one retailer is selling a product at prices significantly below those of other retailers, there is a strong likelihood that the other retailers will not continue to carry the product.

Although most resale price-maintenance schemes run afoul of the Sherman Act, it is possible for a manufacturer to control the resale price of its products. The primary method of legally controlling the retail price is for a manufacturer simply to announce its prices and refuse to deal with those who fail to comply. Under what is commonly referred to as the **Colgate doctrine,** the Supreme Court recognizes that such independent action by a manufacturer is not a per se violation of the Sherman Act. Resale price maintenance is legal only if there is no coercion or pressure other than the announced policy and its implementation. If the manufacturer sits down with the distributor or retailer and gets an agreement that the parties will comply, then there is a violation of Section 1 of the Sherman Act.

Examples of Horizontal Price-Fixing Cases

Business	Type of Case	Sherman Act Violation	Case Result
Archer Daniels Midland Company and others	Criminal and civil	Fixed prices on citric acid	$70 million fine and $35 million civil settlement
Mrs. Baird's Bakery	Criminal and civil	Fixed prices on baked goods	$10 million fine and $18 million settlement
President of Pepsi-Cola Bottling Co.	Criminal	Agreed with Coca-Cola bottler to stop discounts to retailers	4 months in jail, $45,000 fine, 3 years' probation, community service
Southland Corp. and Borden Inc.	Criminal and civil	Rigged bids for dairy products sold to Florida school-milk programs	$8 million combined fine and $2.5 million in civil claims
American Institute of Architects	Civil, injunction	Discouraged competitive bidding, discount fees, and free services	Consent decree that practices would cease plus $50,000 in costs
Fireman's Fund Home Insurance Co., Liberty Mutual Insurance, and Traveler's Corp.	Civil, class action, triple damages	Boycotted Minnesota law requiring workers' compensation rates to be established by competition	$34 million settlement
Kanzaki Specialty Papers Inc. and Mitsubishi Corp.	Criminal	Fixed prices on thermal fax paper	$6.3 million settlement
Delta, United, USAir, American, TWA, and Northwest Airlines	Civil	Use of computerized clearinghouse to fix airfares	$458 million settlement involving the issuance of coupons for future air travel

Whether or not vertical price fixing should be illegal per se has been a matter of debate among economists and politicians. There is a possibility that a vertical restraint imposed by a single manufacturer or wholesaler may stimulate interbrand competition as it reduces intrabrand competition. This debate produced the following case, in which the Supreme Court announces that the rule of reason is the correct analysis when determining the legality of vertical price-fixing situations. The review of previous antitrust cases and analyses make up an important part of this case.

STATE OIL COMPANY V. KHAN

118 S. CT. 275 (1997)

O'CONNOR, J.: . . . Respondents, Barkat U. Khan and his corporation, entered into an agreement with petitioner, State Oil Company, to lease and operate a gas station and convenience store owned by State Oil. The agreement provided that respondents would obtain the station's gasoline supply from State Oil at a price equal to a suggested retail price set by State Oil, less a margin of 3.25 cents per gallon. Under the agreement, respondents could charge any amount for gasoline sold to the station's customers, but if the price charged was higher than State Oil's suggested retail price, the excess was to be rebated to State Oil. Respondents could sell gasoline for less than State Oil's suggested retail price, but any such decrease would reduce their 3.25 cents-per-gallon margin.

[CONTINUED]

About a year after respondents began operating the gas station, they fell behind in lease payments. State Oil then gave notice of its intent to terminate the agreement and commenced a state court proceeding to evict respondents. . . .

Respondents sued State Oil . . . alleging . . . that State Oil had engaged in price fixing in violation of § 1 of the Sherman Act by preventing respondents from raising or lowering retail gas prices.

The District Court found that the allegations in the complaint did not state a per se violation of the Sherman Act because they did not establish the sort of "manifestly anticompetitive implications or pernicious effect on competition" that would justify per se prohibition of State Oil's conduct. The District Court held that respondents had not shown that a difference in gasoline pricing would have increased the station's sales; nor had they shown that State Oil had market power or that its pricing provisions affected competition in a relevant market. Accordingly, the District Court entered summary judgment for State Oil on respondents' Sherman Act claim.

The Court of Appeals . . . reversed. The court first noted that the agreement between respondents and State Oil did indeed fix maximum gasoline prices by making it "worthless" for respondents to exceed the suggested retail prices. After reviewing legal and economic aspects of price fixing, the court concluded that State Oil's pricing scheme was a per se antitrust violation under *Albrecht v. Herald Co.* . . .

We granted certiorari to consider two questions, whether State Oil's conduct constitutes a per se violation of the Sherman Act and whether respondents are entitled to recover damages based on that conduct.

Although the Sherman Act, by its terms, prohibits every agreement "in restraint of trade," this Court has long recognized that Congress intended to outlaw only unreasonable restraints. As a consequence, most antitrust claims are analyzed under a "rule of reason," according to which the finder of fact must decide whether the questioned practice imposes an unreasonable restraint on competition, taking into account a variety of factors, including specific information about the relevant business, its condition before and after the restraint was imposed, and the restraint's history, nature, and effect.

Some types of restraints, however, have such predictable and pernicious anticompetitive effect, and such limited potential for procompetitive benefit, that they are deemed unlawful per se. Per se treatment is appropriate once experience with a particular kind of restraint enables the Court to predict with confidence that the rule of reason will condemn it. Thus, we have expressed reluctance to adopt per se rules with regard to restraints imposed in the context of business relationships where the economic impact of certain practices is not immediately obvious.

A review of this Court's decisions leading up to and beyond *Albrecht* is relevant to our assessment of the continuing validity of the per se rule established in *Albrecht.* Beginning with *Dr. Miles Medical Co. v. John D. Park & Sons Co.,* the Court recognized the illegality of agreements under which manufacturers or suppliers set the minimum resale prices to be charged by their distributors. By 1940, the Court broadly declared all business combinations "formed for the purpose and with the effect of raising, depressing, fixing, pegging, or stabilizing the price of a commodity in interstate or foreign commerce" illegal per se. *United States v. Socony-Vacuum Oil Co.* Accordingly, the Court condemned an agreement between two affiliated liquor distillers to limit the maximum price charged by retailers in *Kiefer-Stewart Co. v. Joseph E. Seagram & Sons, Inc.,* noting that agreements to fix maximum prices, "no less than those to fix minimum prices, cripple the freedom of traders and thereby restrain their ability to sell in accordance with their own judgment."

In subsequent cases, the Court's attention turned to arrangements through which suppliers imposed restrictions on dealers with respect to matters other than resale price. In *White Motor Co. v. United States,* the Court considered the validity of a manufacturer's assignment of exclusive territories to its distributors and dealers. The Court determined that too little was known about the competitive impact of such vertical limitations to warrant treating them as per se unlawful. Four years later, in *United States v. Arnold, Schwinn & Co.,* the Court reconsidered the status of exclusive dealer territories and held that, upon the transfer of title to goods to a distributor, a supplier's imposition of territorial restrictions on the distributor was "so obviously destructive of competition" as to constitute a per se violation of the Sherman Act. In *Schwinn,* the Court acknowledged that some vertical restrictions, such as the conferral of territorial rights or franchises, could have procompetitive benefits by allowing smaller enterprises to

[CONTINUED]

compete, and that such restrictions might avert vertical integration in the distribution process. The Court drew the line, however, at permitting manufacturers to control product marketing once dominion over the goods had passed to dealers.

Albrecht, decided the following Term, involved a newspaper publisher who had granted exclusive territories to independent carriers subject to their adherence to a maximum price on resale of the newspapers to the public. Influenced by its decisions in *Socony-Vacuum, Kiefer-Stewart,* and *Schwinn,* the Court concluded that it was per se unlawful for the publisher to fix the maximum resale price of its newspapers. The Court acknowledged that "maximum and minimum price fixing may have different consequences in many situations," but nonetheless condemned maximum price fixing for substituting the perhaps erroneous judgment of a seller for the forces of the competitive market. . . .

Nine years later, in *Continental T. V., Inc. v. GTE Sylvania, Inc.,* the Court overruled *Schwinn,* thereby rejecting application of a per se rule in the context of vertical nonprice restrictions. The Court acknowledged the principle of stare decisis, but explained that the need for clarification in the law justified reconsideration of *Schwinn:*

> Since its announcement, *Schwinn* has been the subject of continuing controversy and confusion, both in the scholarly journals and in the federal courts. The great weight of scholarly opinion has been critical of the decision, and a number of the federal courts confronted with analogous vertical restrictions have sought to limit its reach. In our view, the experience of the past 10 years should be brought to bear on this subject of considerable commercial importance.

. . . In *GTE Sylvania,* the Court declined to comment on *Albrecht'*s per se treatment of vertical maximum price restrictions, noting that the issue "in-

volved significantly different questions of analysis and policy." Subsequent decisions of the Court, however, have hinted that the analytical underpinnings of *Albrecht* were substantially weakened by *GTE Sylvania.* We noted . . . that vertical restraints are generally more defensible than horizontal restraints. . . . [D]ecisions such as *GTE Sylvania* recognize the possibility that a vertical restraint imposed by a single manufacturer or wholesaler may stimulate interbrand competition even as it reduces intrabrand competition . . . .

Albrecht reflected the Court's fear that maximum price fixing could be used to disguise arrangements to fix minimum prices, which remain illegal per se. Although we have acknowledged the possibility that maximum pricing might mask minimum pricing, we believe that such conduct—as with the other concerns articulated in *Albrecht*—can be appropriately recognized and punished under the rule of reason . . . .

In overruling *Albrecht,* we of course do not hold that all vertical maximum price fixing is per se lawful. Instead, vertical maximum price fixing, like the majority of commercial arrangements subject to the antitrust laws, should be evaluated under the rule of reason. In our view, rule-of-reason analysis will effectively identify those situations in which vertical maximum price fixing amounts to anticompetitive conduct.

There remains the question whether respondents are entitled to recover damages based on State Oil's conduct. . . . Under the circumstances, the matter should be reviewed by the Court of Appeals in the first instance. We therefore vacate the judgment of the Court of Appeals and remand the case for further proceedings consistent with this opinion.

Vacate and remand.

CASE QUESTIONS

1. How did State Oil Company impose a maximum pricing policy on its retail station?

2. Why does the Court find the rule of reason analysis sufficient to regulate anticompetitive aspects of vertical maximum price fixing?

3. What impact does this decision have on the analysis used to judge the legality of vertical minimum price fixing? On horizontal price fixing?

9. INDIRECT PRICE FIXING

The ingenuity of businesspersons produces numerous attempts to fix prices by indirect means. Such attempts to control prices take a variety of forms and appear in diverse circumstances. Some arise out of a desire to protect a channel of distribution or a marketing system. Others result from attempts to keep marginal competitors in business to avoid becoming a monopoly.

In one case, indirect price fixing took the form of an exchange of price information. Economic theory was used to support the assumption that prices would be more unstable and lower if the information had not been exchanged. This case established that conduct directed at price stabilization is per se anticompetitive. The warning to business and industry is clear: Cooperation and cozy relationships between competitors may be illegal.

---

concept SUMMARY   *Price Fixing*

1. Horizontal price fixing in the sales of goods or services is illegal per se.

2. It is just as illegal for competitors to fix a low price as it is a high price.

3. Professionals and service providers cannot legally conspire to fix prices.

4. Ethical standards cannot be used to fix prices.

5. Attempts by manufacturers to control the ultimate sale of their product (vertical price fixing) is analyzed under the rule of reason.

6. The Colgate doctrine is an exception in vertical price-fixing cases. It allows a manufacturer to select its customers and to refuse to deal with those who fail to follow its suggested prices.

7. The mere exchange of price information among competitors may constitute a Sherman Act violation.

---

10. TERRITORIAL AGREEMENTS

Territorial agreements restrain trade by allocating geographical areas among competitors. They may be either horizontal or vertical. Competing businesses may enter into a **horizontal territorial agreement** for the purpose of giving each an exclusive territory. For example, if all Chevrolet dealers in a state agree to allocate to each an exclusive territory, a horizontal arrangement would exist. This agreement is illegal per se under the Sherman Act. This is true even if the arrangement is made with a third party. For example, an agreement among competing cable television operators to divide the market in Houston, Texas, was found to be a per se violation even though the agreement required city council approval.

A **vertical territorial agreement** is one between a manufacturer and a dealer or distributor. It assigns the dealer or distributor an exclusive territory, and the manufacturer agrees not to sell to other dealers or distributors in that territory in exchange for an agreement by the dealer that it will not operate outside the area assigned. Such agreements are usually part of a franchise or license agreement. These vertical arrangements are not per se violations; they are subject to the rule of reason.

11. CONCERTED ACTIVITIES

Many antitrust cases involve agreements or conduct by competitors that have anticompetitive effects. Competitors sometimes attempt to share some activities or join together in the performance of a function. These are known as **concerted activities.**

Concerted activities are often beneficial to society even though they reduce competition. For example, joint research efforts to find a cure for cancer or to find substitutes for gasoline would seem to provide significant benefits to society. A sharing of technology may be beneficial also. Joint efforts in other areas may reduce costs and improve efficiency, with direct benefit to the public.

Congress has recognized the need to encourage cooperation among competitors. For example, in 1984, the National Cooperative Research Act was enacted. In 1990, Congress created an exception to the Sherman Act so that television industry officials could discuss the development of joint guidelines to limit the depiction of violence on television.

Again, in 1993, Congress made it easier for U.S. companies to engage in joint production ventures. The National Cooperative Production Amendments Act does not protect joint production ventures from all possibilities of antitrust violations. Rather, this law provides protection to activities described in the box, below. Despite these exceptions to the Sherman Act that permit specific joint activities, you should always remain aware that concerted activities among competitors can lead to the severe sanctions discussed in section 5.

THE CLAYTON ACT

12. INTRODUCTION

By 1914, it was obvious that the Sherman Act of 1890 had not accomplished its intended purpose. Practices that reduced competition were commonplace. In order to improve the antitrust laws, Congress in 1914 enacted the Clayton Act and the Federal Trade Commission Act. The Clayton Act is more specific than the Sherman Act in declaring certain enumerated practices in commerce illegal. These were practices that might adversely affect competition but were not themselves contracts, combinations, or conspiracies in restraint of trade; such practices did not go far enough to constitute actual monopolization or attempts to monopolize. Further, the enumerated practices did not have to actually injure competition to be wrongful; they were outlawed if their effect **may substantially lessen competition or tends to create a monopoly.** Thus, the burden of proving a violation was eased. The Clayton Act made it possible to attack in their incipiency many practices which, if continued, eventually could destroy competition or create a monopoly. The idea was to remedy these matters before full harm was done.

BASIC PROVISIONS OF NATIONAL COOPERATIVE PRODUCTION AMENDMENT ACT

- Joint production ventures will be subject to the rule of reason analysis rather than the per se illegality standard.

- A joint production venture must notify the Justice Department and the FTC of its plans to engage in joint activities.

- In a private civil antitrust action brought against the joint production venture, the plaintiff can be awarded only actual damages plus costs. The joint production venture will not be subject to triple damages.

Violations of the original Clayton Act were not crimes, and the act contained no sanction for forfeiture of property. However, it did provide that the Justice Department might obtain injunctions to prevent violations. Individuals or organizations injured by a violation could obtain injunctive relief on their own behalf. In addition, they were given the right to collect three times the damages suffered plus court costs and reasonable attorney's fees.

The following three sections of this chapter focus on three important provisions of the Clayton Act. As you study this material, ask yourself what business practices occur today that may violate the Clayton Act.

13. PRICE DISCRIMINATION

Section 2 of the Clayton Act as originally adopted in 1914 made it unlawful for a seller to discriminate in the price that is charged to different purchasers of commodities when the effect may be to lessen competition substantially or to tend to create a monopoly in any line of commerce. Discrimination in price on account of differences in the grade, quality, or quantity of the commodity sold, or that makes only due allowance for differences in the cost of selling or transportation was not illegal.

In the 1920s and early 1930s, various techniques such as large-volume purchases with quantity discounts were used by big retailers, especially chain stores, to obtain more favorable prices than those available to smaller competitors. In addition to obtaining quantity discounts, some large businesses created subsidiary corporations that received brokerage allowances as wholesalers. Another method used by big buyers to obtain price advantages was to demand and obtain larger promotional allowances than were given to smaller buyers. The prevalence of these practices led to the enactment in 1936 of the **Robinson-Patman amendment** to Section 2 of the Clayton Act. This statute attempted to eliminate the advantage that a large buyer could secure over a small buyer solely because of the larger buyer's quantity-purchasing ability.

The Robinson-Patman amendment attempts to ensure equality of price to all customers of a seller of commodities for resale. The law protects a single competitor who is victimized by price discrimination. It is a violation both to knowingly give and to receive the benefits of such discrimination. Therefore, the law applies to both sellers and buyers. It is just as illegal to receive the benefit of price discrimination as it is to give a lower price to one of two buyers.

The Robinson-Patman amendment extends only to transactions in interstate commerce; it does not extend to transactions that affect only intrastate commerce. In addition, the law is applicable only to the sale of goods; it does not cover contracts that involve the sale of services or the sale of advertising such as television time.

The Robinson-Patman amendment gives the Federal Trade Commission (FTC) jurisdiction and authority to regulate quantity discounts. It also prohibits certain hidden or indirect discriminations by sellers in favor of certain buyers. Section 2(c) prohibits an unearned brokerage commission related to a sale of goods. For example, it is unlawful to pay or to receive a commission or discount on sales or purchases except for actual services rendered. Section 2(d) outlaws granting promotional allowances or payments on goods bought for resale unless such allowances are available to all competing customers. For example, a manufacturer who gives a retailer a right to purchase three items for the price of two as part of a special promotion must give the same right to all competitors in the market. Section 2(e) prohibits giving promotional facilities or services on goods bought for resale unless they are made available to all competing customers.

The Robinson-Patman amendment makes it a crime for a seller to sell either at lower prices in one geographic area than elsewhere in the United States to eliminate competition or a competitor, or at unreasonably low prices to drive out a competitor. This statute declared **predatory pricing** to be illegal.

Predatory pricing is pricing below marginal cost by a company willing and able to sustain losses for a prolonged period to drive out competition. (It is assumed that the price will later be increased when the competition or competitor is destroyed.) Predatory pricing also involves charging higher prices on some products to subsidize below-cost sales of other products or cutting prices below cost on a product in just one area to wipe out a small local competitor.

The following case illustrates the complexity of the Robinson-Patman amendment.

TEXACO INC. V. HASBROUCK

110 S. CT. 2535 (1990)

Texaco sold gasoline directly to 12 independent Texaco retailers at retail tank wagon (RTW) prices. It also sold gasoline to two wholesale distributors (Gull and Dompier), who in turn supplied stations competing with the Texaco stations. The sales price to Gull and Dompier was 3¢ and 6¢ per gallon less than the RTW price. As a result, the sales at Texaco stations dropped dramatically.

The Texaco retailers filed suit against Texaco alleging a violation of Section 2(a) of the Robinson-Patman amendment. Texaco contended that the price differential was a legitimate functional discount. The lower courts awarded plaintiffs $449,900 actual damages, and Texaco was granted a writ of certiorari.

STEVENS, J.: . . . It is appropriate to begin our consideration of the legal status of functional discounts by examining the language of the Act. Section 2(a) provides in part:

It shall be unlawful for any person engaged in commerce, in the course of such commerce, either directly or indirectly, to discriminate in price between different purchasers of commodities of like grade and quality, where either or any of the purchases involved in such

discrimination are in commerce, where such commodities are sold for use, consumption, or resale within the United States or any Territory thereof or the District of Columbia or any insular possession or other place under the jurisdiction of the United States, and where the effect of such discrimination may be substantially to lessen competition or tend to create a monopoly in any line of commerce, or to injure, destroy, or prevent competition with any person who either grants or knowingly receives the benefit of such discrimination, or with customers of either of them. . . .

The Act contains no express reference to functional discounts. It does contain two affirmative defenses that provide protection for two categories of discounts—those that are justified by savings in the seller's cost of manufacture, delivery or sale, and those that represent a good faith response to the equally low prices of a competitor. As the case comes to us, neither of those defenses is available to Texaco.

In order to establish a violation of the Act, respondents had the burden of proving four facts: (1) that Texaco's sales to Gull and Dompier were made in interstate commerce; (2) that the gasoline sold to them was of the same grade and quality as that sold to respondents; (3) that Texaco discriminated in price as between Gull and Dompier on the one hand and re-

[CONTINUED]

spondents on the other; and (4) that the discrimination had a prohibited effect on competition. . . .

Texaco argues that although it charged different prices, it did not "discriminate in price" within the meaning of the Act, and that, at least to the extent that Gull and Dompier acted as wholesalers, the price differentials did not injure competition.

Texaco's first argument would create a blanket exemption for all functional discounts. Indeed, carried to its logical conclusion, it would exempt all price differentials except those given to competing purchasers.

Since we have already decided that a price discrimination within the meaning of Section 2(a) "is merely a price difference," we must reject Texaco's first argument.

In *FTC v. Morton Salt Co.,* 334 U.S. 37, 46–47 (1948), we held that an injury to competition may be inferred from evidence that some purchasers had to pay their supplier "substantially more for their goods than their competitors had to pay." Texaco . . . argues that this presumption should not apply to differences between prices charged to wholesalers and those charged to retailers. Moreover, they argue that it would be inconsistent with fundamental antitrust policies to construe the Act as requiring a seller to control his customers' resale prices. The seller should not be held liable for the independent pricing decisions of his customers. . . .

A supplier need not satisfy the rigorous requirements of the cost justification defense in order to prove that a particular functional discount is reasonable and accordingly did not cause any substantial lessening of competition between a wholesaler's customers and the supplier's direct customers. The record in this case, however, adequately supports the finding that Texaco violated the Act.

The hypothetical predicate for the . . . entire discussion of functional discounts is a price differential "that merely accords due recognition and reimbursement for actual marketing functions." Such a discount is not illegal. In this case, however, . . . there was no substantial evidence indicating that the discounts to Gull and Dompier constituted a reasonable reimbursement for the value to Texaco of their actual marketing functions. Indeed, Dompier was separately compensated for its hauling function, and neither Gull nor Dompier maintained any significant storage facilities. . . .

The longstanding principle that functional discounts provide no safe harbor from the Act is . . . evident from the practice of the Federal Trade Commission, which has, while permitting legitimate functional discounts, proceeded against those discounts which appeared to be subterfuges to avoid the Act's restrictions. . . .

The evidence indicates . . . that Texaco affirmatively encouraged Dompier to expand its retail business and that Texaco was fully informed about the persistent and marketwide consequences of its own pricing policies. Indeed, its own executives recognized that the dramatic impact on the market was almost entirely attributable to the magnitude of the distributor discount and the hauling allowance. . . . The special facts of this case . . . make it peculiarly difficult for Texaco to claim that it is being held liable for the independent pricing decisions of Gull or Dompier.

. . . The competitive injury component of a Robinson-Patman Act violation is not limited to the injury to competition between the favored and the disfavored purchaser; it also encompasses the injury to competition between their customers. This conclusion is compelled by the statutory language, which specifically encompasses not only the adverse effect of price discrimination on persons who either grant or knowingly receive the benefit of such discrimination, but also on "customers of either of them." Such indirect competitive effects surely may not be presumed automatically in every functional discount setting, and, indeed, one would expect that most functional discounts will be legitimate discounts which do not cause harm to competition. At the least, a functional discount that constitutes a reasonable reimbursement for the purchasers' actual marketing functions will not violate the Act. When a functional discount is legitimate, the inference of injury to competition . . . will simply not arise. Yet it is also true that not every functional discount is entitled to a judgment of legitimacy, and that it will sometimes be possible to produce evidence showing that a particular functional discount caused a price discrimination of the sort the Act prohibits. When such anticompetitive effects are proved—as we believe they were in this case—they are covered by the Act. . . .

Affirmed.

[CONTINUED]

CASE QUESTIONS

1. What four factual elements must be proven by the plaintiff-respondents to establish a Section 2 Robinson-Patman violation?

2. What were the holdings of the lower courts?

3. What is Texaco's argument for charging different prices to its customers?

4. Why does the Court reject Texaco's argument?

The Robinson-Patman amendment recognizes certain exceptions or defenses:

- Sellers may select their own customers in good-faith transactions and not in restraint of trade.
- Price changes may be made in response to changing conditions, such as actual or imminent deterioration of perishable goods, obsolescence of seasonal goods, distress sales under court process, or sales in good faith in discontinuance of business in the goods concerned (changing conditions defense).
- Price differentials based on differences in the cost of manufacture, sale, or delivery of commodities are permitted (**cost justification defense**).
- A seller in good faith may meet the equally low price of a competitor (**good-faith meeting-of-competition defense**).

---

concept SUMMARY   *Robinson-Patman Amendment*

1. It is a violation to sell the same goods to competing buyers for resale at different prices.

2. The law also is violated by a buyer that knowingly receives a lower price.

3. The law does not apply to transactions wholly in intrastate commerce or to transactions that do not involve goods.

4. Price discrimination may result from quantity discounts, unearned brokerage allowances, or promotional allowances.

5. Functional discounts must be based on legitimate marketing functions actually performed.

6. It is a crime for a seller to sell at low prices in an attempt to drive out a competitor.

7. Plaintiffs must prove actual injury to collect triple damages for Robinson-Patman violations.

8. The good-faith meeting-of-competition defense is available to both the seller and the buyer.

---

14. SPECIAL ARRANGEMENTS

Section 3 of the Clayton Act limits the use of certain types of contractual arrangements involving goods when the impact of these contracts may substantially lessen competition or tends to create a monopoly. These special arrangements include sales contracts that tie one product with another, contracts that contain reciprocal arrangements in which each party is a buyer and a seller, and provisions foreclosing buying or selling with others.

A **tying contract** is one in which a product is sold or leased only on the condition that the buyer or lessee purchase a different product or service from the seller or lessor. A common form of tying arrangement is known as **full-line forcing.** In full-line forcing, the buyer or lessee is compelled to take a complete product line from the seller. Under these arrangements, the buyer cannot purchase only one product of the line. A typical illegal agreement is one in which a clothing manufacturer requires a retailer to carry the manufacturer's full line of articles in order to sell a popular line of shirts.

A **reciprocal dealing** arrangement exists when two parties face each other as both buyer and seller. One party offers to buy the other's goods but only if the second party buys other goods from the first party. For example, suppose that company A is a manufacturer of microprocessor chips for personal computers. Further assume that company B manufactures personal computers. A reciprocal dealing occurs if B agrees to buy processor chips only if A agrees to buy a specified number of B's computers for use in A's offices.

An **exclusive dealing** contract contains a provision that one party or the other (buyer or seller) will deal only with the other party. For example a seller of tomatoes agrees to sell only to Campbell Soup. A buyer of coal may agree to purchase only from a certain coal company. Such agreements tend to foreclose a portion of the market from competitors.

A similar arrangement is known as a **requirements contract.** In a requirements contract, a buyer agrees to purchase all of its needs of a given contract from the seller during a certain period of time. The buyer may be a manufacturer who needs the raw materials or parts agreed to be supplied, or it may be a retailer who needs goods for resale. In effect, the buyer is agreeing not to purchase any of the products from competitors of the seller.

Franchise contracts often require that the franchisee purchase all of its equipment and inventory from the franchiser as a condition of the agreement. These provisions are commonly inserted because of the value of the franchiser's trademark and the desire for quality control to protect it. For example, Baskin-Robbins ice cream may require its franchisees to purchase all of their ice cream from Baskin-Robbins. The legitimate purpose is to maintain the image of the franchise and the product. Customers expect the same ice cream from every retail operation. Such agreements, while anticompetitive, are legal because the legitimate purpose outweighs the anticompetitive aspects.

However, a franchiser is not able to license its trademark in such a manner that it can coerce franchisees to give up all alternate supply sources, because such agreements are unreasonable restraints of trade. The quality-control aspect is not present for items such as packaging materials and food items in which special ingredients or secret formulas are not involved; thus, the purpose of the "exclusive source of supply" proviso is only to limit competition. Franchise agreements are not per se violations; they are subject to the rule of reason.

Exclusive contracts and requirements contracts are less likely to harm competition than are tying contracts. Such contracts may add competition by eliminating uncertainties and the expense of repeated contracts. However, the courts tend to give per se violation treatment to exclusive contracts if they substantially affect commerce.

15. ILLEGAL MERGERS AND ACQUISITIONS

Section 7 of the Clayton Act makes certain mergers and acquisitions illegal. **Mergers** are usually classified as horizontal, market extension, vertical, or conglomerate. A **horizontal merger** usually combines two businesses in the same field or industry. The acquired and acquiring companies have competed with each other, and the merger reduces the number of competitors and leads to greater concentration in the industry. A **market extension merger** describes an acquisition in which the acquiring company extends its markets. This market extension may be either in new products (**product extension**) or in new areas (**geographic extension**). For example, if a brewery that did not operate in New England acquired a New England brewery, it would have accomplished a geographic market extension merger.

A **vertical merger** brings together one company that is the customer of the other in one of the lines of commerce in which the other is a supplier. Such a combination ordinarily removes or has the potential to remove the merged customer from the market as far as other suppliers are concerned. It also may remove a source of supply if the acquiring company is a customer of the acquired one. A **conglomerate merger** is one in which the businesses involved neither compete nor are related as customer and supplier in any given line of commerce. Some analysts consider product extension and geographic extension mergers to be conglomerate ones with many characteristics of horizontal ones. In any event, there is a great deal of similarity in the legal principles applied to market extension and to conglomerate mergers.

As originally enacted in 1914, the Clayton Act prohibited only horizontal mergers through the acquisition of stock of one competing company by another. A merger between competitors could be accomplished and was permitted through one acquiring the assets of the other. In 1950, Congress passed the **Celler-Kefauver amendment,** which substantially broadened the coverage of Section 7. First, this amendment plugged the stock-versus-assets loophole. After 1950, the acquisition of assets was also covered by Section 7. Second, the Celler-Kefauver amendment prohibited all acquisitions in which the effect lessened competition substantially in any line of commerce in any section of the country. Thus, the amendment added vertical and conglomerate mergers to the coverage of Section 7. In 1980, Congress expanded coverage by including not only businesses engaged in interstate commerce but also businesses engaged in activities that affect commerce. It also substituted the word "person" for "corporation" so as to include partnerships and sole proprietorships.

The Federal Trade Commission Act — Unfair Competition

As previously noted, the Federal Trade Commission (FTC) enforces the Clayton Act. The FTC also enforces Section 5 of the Federal Trade Commission Act, which made "unfair methods of competition" in commerce unlawful. The **Wheeler-Lea amendment** in 1938 added that "unfair or deceptive acts or practices in commerce" are also unlawful under Section 5.

16. ENFORCEMENT

The FTC has broad, sweeping powers and a mandate to determine what methods, acts, or practices in commerce constitute unfair competition. The original Section 5 of the Federal Trade Commission Act outlawed unfair methods of competition in commerce and directed the FTC to prevent the use of such, but it offered no definition of the specific practices that were unfair. The term *unfair methods of competition* was designed by Congress as a flexible concept, the exact meaning of which could evolve on a case-by-case basis. It can apply to a variety of unrelated activities. It is generally up to the FTC to determine what business conduct is "unfair." Great deference is given to the FTC's opinion as to what constitutes a violation and to the remedies it proposes to correct anticompetitive behavior.

To decide whether challenged business conduct is "unfair" as a method of competition or as a commercial practice, the FTC asks three major questions if there is no deception or antitrust violation involved:

1. Does the conduct injure consumers significantly?
2. Does the conduct offend an established public policy? (Conduct may offend public policy even though not previously unlawful.)
3. Is the conduct oppressive, unscrupulous, immoral, or unethical?

Answering any one of these questions affirmatively could lead to a finding of unfairness. The Supreme Court has declared that the FTC can operate "like a court of equity" in considering "public values" to establish what is unfair under Section 5.

Business conduct in violation of any provision of the antitrust laws may also be ruled illegal under Section 5. However, the purpose of Section 5 was to establish that anticompetitive acts or practices that *fall short* of transgressing the Sherman or Clayton Act may be restrained by the FTC as being "unfair methods of competition." If a business practice is such that it is doubtful that the evidence is sufficient to prove a Sherman or Clayton Act violation, the FTC may nevertheless proceed and find the business practice is unfair. The following case is an example of how Section 5 is used as an enforcement tool in conjunction with and independent from the Sherman Act and Clayton Act provisions.

TOYS "R" US, INC. V. FEDERAL TRADE COMMISSION

221 F. 3D 928 (7TH CIR. 2000)

WOOD, J. . . . The [Federal Trade] Commission concluded that [Toys "R" Us] TRU had acted as the coordinator of a horizontal agreement among a number of toy manufacturers. The agreements took the form of a network of vertical agreements between TRU and the individual manufacturers, in each of which the manufacturer promised to restrict the distribution of its products to low-priced warehouse club stores, on the condition that other manufacturers would do the same. This practice, the Commission found, violated § 5 of the Federal Trade Commission Act. . . .

TRU is a giant in the toy retailing industry. The Commission found that it sells approximately 20% of all the toys sold in the United States, and that in some metropolitan areas its share of toy sales ranges between 35% and 49%. The variety of toys it sells is staggering: over the course of a year, it offers about 11,000 individual toy items, far more than any of its competitors. As one might suspect from these figures alone, TRU is a critical outlet for toy manufacturers. It buys about 30% of the large, traditional toy companies' total output and it is usually their most important customer. . . .

[CONTINUED]

Toys are sold in a number of different kinds of stores. At the high end are traditional toy stores and department stores, both of which typically sell toys for 40 to 50% above their cost. Next are the specialized discount stores—a category virtually monopolized by TRU today—that sell at an average 30% mark-up. General discounters like Wal-Mart, K-Mart, and Target are next, with a 22% mark-up and last are the stores that are the focus of this case, the warehouse clubs like Costco and Pace. The clubs sell toys at a slender mark-up of 9% or so. . . .

What happened in this case, according to the Commission, was fairly simple. For a long time, TRU had enjoyed a strong position at the low price end for toy sales, because its only competition came from traditional toy stores who could not or did not wish to meet its prices, or from general discounters like Wal-Mart or K-Mart, which could not offer anything like the variety of items TRU had and whose prices were not too far off TRU's mark.

The advent of the warehouse clubs changed all that. They were a retail innovation of the late 1970s: the first one opened in 1976, and by 1992 there were some 600 individual club stores around the country. Rather than earning all of their money from their mark-up on products, the clubs sell only to their members, and they charge a modest annual membership fee, often about $30. As the word "warehouse" in the name suggests, the clubs emphasize price competition over service amenities. Nevertheless, the Commission found that the clubs seek to offer name-brand merchandise, including toys. During the late 1980s and early 1990s, warehouse clubs selected and purchased from the toy manufacturers' full array of products, just like everyone else. . . .

To the extent this strategy was successful, however, TRU did not welcome it. By 1989, its senior executives were concerned that the clubs were a threat to TRU's low-price image and, more importantly, to its profits. A little legwork revealed that as of that year the clubs carried approximately 120–240 items in direct competition with TRU, priced as much as 25 to 30% below TRU's own price levels.

TRU put its President of Merchandising, a Mr. Goddu, to work to see what could be done. The re-sponse Goddu and other TRU executives formulated to beat back the challenge from the clubs began with TRU's decision to contact some of its suppliers, including toy manufacturing heavyweights Mattel, Hasbro, and Fisher Price. At the Toy Fair in 1992 (a major event at which the next Christmas season's orders are placed), Goddu informed the manufacturers of a new TRU policy, which was reflected in a memo of January 29, 1992. The policy set forth the following conditions and privileges for TRU:

- The clubs could have no new or promoted product unless they carried the entire line.
- All specials and exclusives to be sold to the clubs had to be shown first to TRU to see if TRU wanted the item.
- Old and basic product had to be in special packs.
- Clearance and closeout items were permissible provided that TRU was given the first opportunity to buy the product.
- There would be no discussion about prices.

TRU was careful to meet individually with each of its suppliers to explain its new policy. Afterwards, it then asked each one what it intended to do. Negotiations between TRU and the manufacturers followed, as a result of which each manufacturer eventually agreed that it would sell to the clubs only highly differentiated products (either unique individual items or combo packs) that were not offered to anything but a club (and thus of course not to TRU). As the Commission put it, "through its announced policy and the related agreements discussed below, TRU sought to eliminate the competitive threat the clubs posed by denying them merchandise, forcing the clubs' customers to buy products they did not want, and frustrating customers' ability to make direct price comparisons of club prices and TRU prices."

The agreements between TRU and the various manufacturers were, of course, vertical agreements, because they ran individually from the supplier/manufacturer to the purchaser/retailer. The Commission found that TRU reached about 10 of these agreements. After the agreements were concluded, TRU then supervised and enforced each toy company's compliance with its commitment.

[CONTINUED]

But TRU was not content to stop with vertical agreements. Instead, the Commission found, it decided to go further. It worked for over a year and a half to put the vertical agreements in place, but "the biggest hindrance TRU had to overcome was the major toy companies' reluctance to give up a new, fast-growing, and profitable channel of distribution." The manufacturers were also concerned that any of their rivals who broke ranks and sold to the clubs might gain sales at their expense, given the widespread and increasing popularity of the club format. To address this problem, the Commission found, TRU orchestrated a horizontal agreement among its key suppliers to boycott the clubs. The evidence on which the Commission relied showed that, at a minimum, Mattel, Hasbro, Fisher Price, Tyco, Little Tikes, Today's Kids, and Tiger Electronics agreed to join in the boycott on the condition that their competitors would do the same. . . .

Once the special warehouse club policy (or, in the Commission's more pejorative language, boycott) was underway, TRU served as the central clearinghouse for complaints about breaches in the agreement. . . .

Based on this record, the Commission drew three central conclusions of law: (1) the TRU-led manufacturer boycott of the warehouse clubs was illegal per se . . . ;(2) the boycott was illegal under a full rule of reason analysis because its anticompetitive effects clearly outweighed any possible business justification; and (3) the vertical agreements between TRU and the individual toy manufacturers, entered into . . . with clear anticompetitive effect, violate

section 1 of the Sherman Act. These antitrust violations in turn were enough to prove a violation of FTC Act § 5. . . .

We have found that this case satisfies the criteria the [U.S. Supreme] Court used . . . for condemnation without an extensive inquiry into market power and economic pros and cons: (1) the boycotting firm has cut off access to a supply, facility or market necessary for the boycotted firm (i.e. the clubs) to compete; (2) the boycotting firm possesses a "dominant" position in the market (where "dominant" is an undefined term, but plainly chosen to stand for something different from antitrust's term of art "monopoly"); and (3) the boycott . . . cannot be justified by plausible arguments that it was designed to enhance overall efficiency. . . .

The Commission found here that, however TRU's market power as a toy retailer was measured, it was clear that its boycott was having an effect in the market. It was remarkably successful in causing the 10 major toy manufacturers to reduce output of toys to the warehouse clubs, and that reduction in output protected TRU from having to lower its prices to meet the clubs' price levels. . . . Proof that this is what TRU was doing is sufficient proof of actual anticompetitive effects that no more elaborate market analysis was necessary. . . .

We conclude that the Commission's decision is supported by substantial evidence on the record, and that its . . . decree falls within the broad discretion it has been granted under the FTC Act. The decision is hereby

Affirmed.

CASE QUESTIONS

1. Why was Toys "R" Us so concerned about warehouse clubs as compared to toy stores and discount outlets?

2. What action did Toys "R" Us take to address its competitive concerns with warehouse clubs?

3. What is the basis for the FTC finding that these actions violated § 5 of the FTC Act?

4. How did Toys "R" Us justify its appeal of this FTC finding?

5. What was the decision of the Court of Appeals?

17. PREVENTION

The primary function of the FTC is to prevent illegal business practices rather than punish violations. It prevents wrongful actions by the use of cease and desist orders. To prevent unfair competition, the FTC issues trade regulation rules that deal with business practices in an industry plus FTC guidelines on particular practices.

The FTC also periodically issues trade practice rules and guides, sometimes referred to as industry guides. These rules are the FTC's informal opinion of legal requirements applicable to a particular industry's practices. Although compliance with the rules is voluntary, they provide the basis for the informal and simultaneous abandonment by industry members of practices thought to be unlawful. For example, the FTC has said the American Medical Association must allow doctors to advertise. FTC guidelines are administrative interpretations of the statutes the commission enforces, and they provide guidance to both FTC staff and business-people evaluating the legality of certain practices. Guidelines deal with specific practices and may cut across industry lines.

KEY TERMS

REVIEW QUESTIONS AND PROBLEMS

1. *Historical Development*
   (a)   The Sherman Act, as amended by the Clayton Act, seeks to preserve competition by declaring two types of anticompetitive behavior to be illegal. Describe these two behaviors.
   (b)   Through what agencies does the federal government enforce the antitrust laws?
   (c)   What role do state attorneys generally play in antitrust enforcement?
   (d)   Can individuals or business organizations enforce antitrust laws?

The Sherman Act

2. *Restraint of Trade*

   All of the orthodontists in your community at their annual holiday party agreed to charge the parents of each child patient a nonrefundable fee of $200 prior to beginning any treatment. They also agreed that the charge for an orthodontia procedure would not be less than $2,000. Are these agreements in violation of the Sherman Act? Explain.

3. *Monopoly*

   The Justice Department filed a civil suit claiming Grinnell corporation had a monopoly in the operation of central station hazard-detecting devices. These security devices are used to prevent burglary and to detect fires. They involve electronic notification of the police and fire departments at a central location. Grinnell, through three separate subsidiaries, controlled 87 percent of that business. It argues that it faces competition from other modes of protection from burglary, and therefore it does not have monopoly power. What argument does the Justice Department have to make to prove its claim that Grinnell is operating an illegal monopoly?

4. *Analysis in Antitrust Law*
   (a)   Why is it important for courts to use the rule of reason analysis when considering actions allegedly in violation of the Sherman Act?
   (b)   What is the significance of the per se analysis under the rule of reason?

5. *Sanctions*
   (a)   Name the four sanctions used to enforce the Sherman Act.
   (b)   What is the relationship between the criminal sanction and suits for triple damages?
   (c)   What is the impact of the *nolo contendere* plea?

6. *Exemptions*

   The operators of adult bookstores got together and each agreed to contribute $1,000 to a fund for use in lobbying the city council to repeal an ordinance which made the sale of sexually explicit publications a crime. If the operators are charged with violating the antitrust laws, what will be the likely defense? Explain.

Types of Cases

7. *Horizontal Price Fixing*

   The members of a real estate brokers' multiple listing service voted to raise their commission rate from 6 to 7 percent. The bylaws of the association provided for expulsion of any member charging less than the agreed-upon commission. If broker Hillary continues to charge 6 percent, can she be expelled legally? Why or why not?

8. *Vertical Price Fixing*

   (a)   Describe the situations when a supplier can legally fix the minimum price that a customer must charge to its buyers.

   (b)   What analysis do courts use when judging the legality of a vertical price-fixing plan? Why is this legal analysis the appropriate one to use?

9. *Indirect Price Fixing*

   Assume that all manufacturers of computer chips entered into an agreement whereby each agreed to exchange information as to the most recent price charged or quoted to a consumer. Is this agreement a violation of the Sherman Act? Why or why not?

10. *Territorial Agreements*

    (a)   Are franchise agreements which allocate an exclusive territory to the franchisee always illegal? Explain.

    (b)   Give an example of a product where intrabrand competition is as important as interbrand competition.

11. *Concerted Activities*

    In response to public pressure, all of the manufacturers of chewing tobacco agree not to advertise on radio or television. The resultant savings is used to reduce the price of the product to consumers. Furthermore, the use of chewing tobacco by teenagers is reduced dramatically. Is the agreement legal? Explain.

The Clayton Act

12. *Introduction*

    (a)   Name the sanctions that can be imposed against a violator of the Clayton Act.

    (b)   What is the significance of the word "incipiency" in Clayton Act enforcement?

13. *Price Discrimination*

    You are the sales representative for a manufacturer of insulation. A customer that accounts for approximately one-third of your sales suddenly asks for a discount because of the volume of its purchases. You are politely told that a refusal will cause the customer to take its business to another manufacturer. Your income is solely from commissions on sales, which are calculated on gross profit margins.

    (a)   If you agree to a discount, have you broken any law?

    (b)   If you have violated a law, what are the potential consequences?

    (c)   If you give the same discount to all customers, would your actions be illegal? Explain.

14. *Special Arrangements*

    (a)   An ice-cream franchiser requires its franchisees to purchase all ice cream, cones and syrups from the franchiser. Does this contract violate the antitrust laws? Why or why not?

    (b)   Would your answer be the same if the contract also required the franchisees to purchase all of its paper products and cleaning supplies, such as napkins, from the franchiser? Explain.

15. *Illegal Mergers and Acquisitions*

The government challenged the acquisition by Procter & Gamble (P&G) of Clorox. Clorox was the leading manufacturer of liquid bleach at the time of the acquisition, accounting for 48 percent of the national sales. It was the only firm selling nationally, and the top two firms accounted for 65 percent of national sales. P&G is a large, diversified manufacturer of household products, with its primary activity being in the area of soaps, detergents, and cleaners. P&G accounted for 54 percent of all packaged detergent sales, and the top three firms accounted for 50 percent of the market. P&G is among the nation's leading advertiser. What is the basis for the government's challenge to this acquisition? Explain.

The Federal Trade Commission—Unfair Competition

16. *Enforcement*

A group of lawyers in private practices who regularly acted as court-appointed counsel for indigent defendants in District of Columbia criminal cases agreed at a meeting of the Superior Court Trial Lawyers Association (SCTLA) to stop providing such representation until the District increased group members' compensation. The boycott had a severe impact on the District's criminal justice system, and the District government capitulated to the lawyers' demands. After the lawyers returned to work, the FTC filed a complaint against SCTLA and four of its officers, alleging that they had entered into a conspiracy to fix prices and to conduct a boycott that constituted unfair methods of competition in violation of Section 5 of the FTC Act. Does the FTC have the authority to bring a Section 5 case against these lawyers? Explain.

17. *Prevention*

    (a)   The FTC has responsibility for preventing unfair methods of competition and unfair and deceptive business practices. Describe three examples of business activities that could be declared unlawful by the FTC pursuant to these powers.

    (b)   Does the FTC have to prove that these examples involve violations of the Sherman or Clayton Acts to be successful in establishing an unfair method of competition or an unfair or deceptive business practice? Explain.

TERMINOLOGY REVIEW

For each term in the left-hand column, match the most appropriate description in the right-hand column.

1. Rule of reason
2. Per se illegality
3. Triple damages
4. State action exemption
5. Noerr-Pennington doctrine
6. Horizontal price fixing
7. Resale price maintenance
8. Robinson-Patman
9. Tying contract
10. Horizontal merger
11. Vertical merger
12. Conglomerate merger
13. Celler-Kefauver

a. A merger that combines two businesses that formerly competed with each other in a particular line of commerce

b. When a commodity is sold or leased for use only on condition that the buyer or lessee purchase certain additional products or services from the seller or lessor

c. A rule that states that contracts or conspiracies are illegal only if they constitute an undue or unreasonable restraint of trade or if they unreasonably attempt to monopolize

d. An exemption from the antitrust laws that covers concerted efforts to lobby governmental bodies

e. The analysis used when an activity is inherently anticompetitive

f. An agreement among competitors to charge the same price for goods or services

g. A powerful sanction imposed against those that violate antitrust laws in order to make an example of the wrongdoer while providing a financial incentive to the wronged party to act as an enforcer

h. A type of vertical price fixing that may be legal under the Colgate doctrine

i. An exception to the antitrust laws that protects activities mandated by state law

j. The 1950 amendment to the Clayton Act that broadens the scope of Section 7, thereby making more mergers illegal

k. The 1936 amendment to the Clayton Act that broadens the scope of Section 2, thereby making illegal price discrimination more common

l. A merger in which the businesses that are combined neither compete nor are related as customer and supplier in any given line of commerce

m. A merger that brings together a customer and supplier

Monopoly Worries?

Following graduation from college, you become the marketing manager for a company that owns and operates one of the three ski slopes in a well-known resort. Prior to your employment each company that owns and operates a slope sold lift passes to their slope and sold an all-area pass that could be used on all three slopes. Your company has obtained the right to develop a fourth ski slope. As a part of the planning process, the president of your company asks you to investigate the wisdom of discontinuing your company's sale of the all-area pass and to begin offering the sale of the company-owned two-slope pass.

> Do you have any concerns about this proposal?
>
> What issues, including factual findings, should you pursue?

Best Customer Prices

You are the sales manager for a building materials manufacturer. A customer that accounts for approximately one-third of your sales suddenly asks for a discount because of the volume of its purchases. You are politely told that a refusal will cause the customer to take its business elsewhere. Times are not so good that you can easily refuse.

> Are you in trouble no matter what you do?
>
> If you agree, have you broken any law?
>
> If you have violated a law, what are the potential consequences?

14

EMPLOYMENT AND LABOR LAWS

In your role as president of Hi-Tech Printing, Inc., you supervise more than 250 employees. The jobs of these employees range from executive management, to office staff, to graphic designers and computer programmers, to printing press operators, to loading dock manual laborers, to truck drivers. This past year has been a difficult one because you have discovered at least one of your employees improperly shared customers' secrets with others. The information shared was obtained from documents your company printed for the customer. To prevent similar incidents, you announced a policy of monitoring all employees' phone calls and e-mail messages. As a result of what some employees feel is an invasion of their workplace privacy, they have begun discussions with the Machinist Union about organizing your employees.

Are there legal limits which relate to monitoring employees' activities?

Can you prohibit employees from attempts to organize the workplace?

Is it possible to prevent the Machinist Union from talking with all your employees?

Are there any advantages in having only one union with which you are required to bargain? What precaution must be taken in dealing with a particular union?

Throughout the twentieth century, the United States government passed laws, issued executive orders, and promulgated regulations designed to influence the employment relationship. There are literally hundreds of examples of how laws have impacted the employer and employee. This chapter and the next one focus on two of the most important policy initiatives of the federal government in the employment setting—(1) the union-management relationship and (2) employment discrimination.

Having these two topics as our primary concentration does not mean that the other laws and regulations related to employment are unimportant. A listing of some of the major laws and the purpose of each appears in the following table. As

Summary of Major Federal Employment Laws	
Law	*Purpose*
Fair Labor Standards Act	• Provides restrictions on child labor
	• Provides hourly minimum wage and maximum number of hours before overtime is owed
Social Security Act	• Provides unemployment compensation
	• Provides disability benefits
Employment Retirement Income Security Act	• Provides requirements for private pension plans
Occupational Safety and Health Act	• Provides standards for safe and healthy working environment
Electronic Communications Privacy Act	• Provides standards to protect privacy
Railway Labor Act, Norris LaGuardia Act, Wagner Act, Taft-Hartley Act, and Landrum-Griffin Act	• Provide national policy for governing the union-management relationship
Civil Rights Acts, Equal Employment Opportunity Act, Pregnancy Discrimination Act, Americans with Disabilities Act, Age Discrimination in Employment Act	• Provide national policy governing employment discrimination

current and future business managers, a working knowledge of all of these laws is vital to your success. This chapter presents a brief discussion of some "hot" employment topics followed by labor laws. Employment discrimination is discussed in the next chapter. This chapter also illustrates how legal policies are developed over a period of time as lawmakers strive to meet the societal needs they perceive.

CURRENT TRENDS AND ISSUES

Before we address labor laws, other employment topics merit a close examination. The following three sections discuss legal issues involving the federal Fair Labor Standards Act, the employment-at-will doctrine, and employees' privacy rights. A fourth section raises some questions concerning how the business manager should handle an employee's complaint prior to taking any action relating to the employee.

1. MINIMUM WAGES AND MAXIMUM HOURS

The federal government regulates wages and hours through the **Fair Labor Standards Act (FLSA).** Originally enacted in 1938, amendments to the FLSA have kept it up to date. Since September 1, 1997, the federal minimum wage has been $5.15 per hour. Today, the maximum amount of time per week that an employer can require an employee to work before overtime is due is 40 hours. The FLSA requires that overtime be at least one and one-half times the hourly rate of the employee's compensation. For example, if an employee earned $7.00 per hour, the overtime must be at least $10.50 per hour. Of course, contractual agreements (or state law) may require a higher compensation rate for overtime.

Provisions in the FLSA permit an employer to allow employees to take time off from work instead of paying overtime. The following case addresses the issue of whether an employer can require that employees take time off rather than receive overtime compensation.

CHRISTENSEN V. HARRIS COUNTY

120 S. CT. 1655 (2000)

THOMAS, J.: Under the Fair Labor Standards Act of 1938 (FLSA), States and their political subdivisions may compensate their employees for overtime by granting them compensatory time or "comp time," which entitles them to take time off work with full pay. . . .

The FLSA generally provides that hourly employees who work in excess of 40 hours per week must be compensated for the excess hours at a rate not less than 1 1/2 times their regular hourly wage. Although this requirement did not initially apply to public-sector employers, Congress amended the FLSA to subject States and their political subdivisions to its constraints. . . .

[A]mendments permit States and their political subdivisions to compensate employees for overtime by granting them compensatory time at a rate of 1 1/2 hours for every hour worked. To provide this form of compensation, the employer must arrive at an agreement or understanding with employees that compensatory time will be granted instead of cash compensation.

. . . The FLSA also caps the number of compensatory time hours that an employee may accrue. After an employee reaches that maximum, the employer must pay cash compensation for additional overtime hours worked. In addition, the FLSA permits the employer at any time to cancel or "cash out" accrued compensatory time hours by paying the employee cash compensation for unused compensatory time. And the FLSA entitles the employee to cash payment for any accrued compensatory time remaining upon the termination of employment.

Petitioners are 127 deputy sheriffs employed by respondents Harris County, Texas, and its sheriff, Tommy B. Thomas (collectively, Harris County). It is undisputed that each of the petitioners individually agreed to accept compensatory time, in lieu of cash, as compensation for overtime.

As petitioners accumulated compensatory time, Harris County became concerned that it lacked the resources to pay monetary compensation to employees who worked overtime after reaching the statutory cap on compensatory time accrual and to employees who left their jobs with sizable reserves of accrued time. As a result, the county began looking for a way to reduce accumulated compensatory time. . . .

Harris County implemented a policy under which the employee's supervisor sets a maximum number of compensatory hours that may be accumulated. When an employee's stock of hours approaches that maximum, the employee is advised of the maximum and is asked to take steps to reduce accumulated compensatory time. If the employee does not do so voluntarily, a supervisor may order the employee to use his compensatory time at specified times.

Petitioners sued, claiming that the county's policy violates the FLSA because § 207(o)(5)—which requires that an employer reasonably accommodate employee requests to use compensatory time—provides the exclusive means of utilizing accrued time in the absence of an agreement or understanding permitting some other method. The District Court agreed, granting summary judgment for petitioners and entering a declaratory judgment that the county's policy violated the FLSA. The Court of Appeals for the Fifth Circuit reversed, holding that the FLSA did not speak to the issue and thus did not prohibit the county from implementing its compensatory time policy. . . . We granted certiorari because the Courts of Appeals are divided on the issue.

Both parties, and the United States as amicus curiae, concede that nothing in the FLSA expressly prohibits a State or subdivision thereof from compelling employees to utilize accrued compensatory time. Petitioners and the United States, however, contend that the FLSA implicitly prohibits such a practice in the absence of an agreement or understanding authorizing compelled use. Title *29 U.S.C. § 207(o)(5)* provides:

An employee . . .

(A) who has accrued compensatory time off . . ., and

(B) who has requested the use of such compensatory time,

shall be permitted by the employee's employer to use such time within a reasonable period after making the request if the use of the compensatory time does not unduly disrupt the operations of the public agency.

[CONTINUED]

. . . [V]iewed in the context of the overall statutory scheme, § 207(o)(5) is better read not as setting forth the exclusive method by which compensatory time can be used, but as setting up a safeguard to ensure that an employee will receive timely compensation for working overtime. Section 207(o)(5) guarantees that, at the very minimum, an employee will get to use his compensatory time (i.e., take time off work with full pay) unless doing so would disrupt the employer's operations. . . .

[W]e think the better reading of § 207(o)(5) is that it imposes a restriction upon an employer's efforts to prohibit the use of compensatory time when employees request to do so; that provision says nothing about restricting an employer's efforts to require employees to use compensatory time. Because the statute is silent on this issue and because Harris County's policy is entirely compatible with § 207(o)(5), petitioners cannot prove that Harris County has violated § 207.

Our interpretation of § 207(o)(5)—one that does not prohibit employers from forcing employees to use compensatory time—finds support in two other features of the FLSA. First, employers remain free under the FLSA to decrease the number of hours that employees work. An employer may tell the employee to take off an afternoon, a day, or even an entire week. Second, the FLSA explicitly permits an employer to cash out accumulated compensatory time by paying the employee his regular hourly wage for each hour accrued. Thus, under the FLSA an employer is free to require an employee to take time off work, and an employer is also free to use the money it would have paid in wages to cash out accrued compensatory time. The compelled use of compensatory time challenged in this case merely involves doing both of these steps at once. It would make little sense to interpret § 207(o)(5) to make the combination of the two steps unlawful when each independently is lawful. . . .

The judgment of the Court of Appeals is

Affirmed.

CASE QUESTIONS

1. Why are the employees of the Harris County sheriff's office suing?

2. What were the rulings by the District Court and the Fifth Circuit Court of Appeals?

3. What is the explanation for the difference in the two lower court decisions?

4. How does the Supreme Court rule with respect to the employer's right to require the employee to take time off instead of paying overtime compensation?

2. LIMITATIONS ON EMPLOYMENT AT WILL

Historically, unless employees contracted for a definite period of employment (such as for one year), employers were able to discharge them without cause at any time. This is called the **employment-at-will** doctrine.

During the 1930s, employers began to lose this absolute right to discharge employees whenever they desired. The Labor-Management Relations Act prohibited employers from firing employees for union activities. Now, many federal laws limit employers in their right to terminate employees, even at-will employees (see box on the next page). Some states also prohibit employers by statute from discharging employees for certain reasons, such as for refusing to take lie detector examinations.

Federal Statutes Limiting Employment-at-Will Doctrine

Statute	Limitation on Employee Discharge
Labor-Management Relations Act	Prohibits discharge for union activity or for filing charges under the act
Fair Labor Standards Act	Forbids discharge for exercising rights guaranteed by minimum-wage and overtime provisions of the act
Occupational Safety and Health Act	Prohibits discharge for exercising rights under the act
Civil Rights Act	Makes illegal discharge based on race, sex, color, religion, or national origin
Age Discrimination in Employment Act	Forbids age-based discharge of employees over age 40
Employee Retirement Income Security Act	Prohibits discharge to prevent employees from getting vested pension rights
Clean Air Act	Prevents discharge of employees who cooperate in proceedings against an employer for violation of the act
Clean Water Act	Prevents discharge of employees who cooperate in proceedings against an employer for violation of the act
Consumer Credit Protection Act	Prohibits discharge of employees due to garnishment of wages for any one indebtedness
Judiciary and Judicial Procedure Act	Forbids discharge of employees for service on federal grand or petit juries

Courts, too, have begun limiting the at-will doctrine. Under contract theory, several courts have stated that at-will employment contracts (which are not written and are little more than an agreement to pay for work performed) contain an implied promise of good faith and fair dealing by the employer. This promise, implied by law, can be broken in certain cases by unjustified dismissal of employees.

Other courts have ruled that the employer's publication of a personnel handbook can change the nature of at-will employment. They have held the employer liable for breach of contract for discharging an employee in violation of statements made in the handbook about discharge procedures.

Many contract and tort exceptions to employment at will have involved one of three types of employer behavior:

- Discharge of employee for performance of an important public obligation, such as jury duty
- Discharge of employee for reporting employer's alleged violations of law (whistle-blowing)
- Discharge of employee for exercising statutory rights

Most of the cases that limit at-will employment state that the employer has violated *public policy*. What does it mean to say that an employer has violated public policy? Is it a court's way of saying that most people no longer support the employer's right to do what it did?

Limitations on discrimination and employment at will evidence a growing concern for the rights of employees in their jobs and may suggest a trend that could lead to some type of broad, legally guaranteed job security. In recent years, unions have also increasingly focused on job-security issues in their bargaining with employers.

3. WORKERS' PRIVACY

Individual privacy is such an important part of individual freedom that both legal and ethical questions regarding privacy are bound to multiply in the computer age. While debate continues concerning the need for further federal privacy legislation, many states have passed their own privacy-related statutes. Several states guarantee workers access to their job personnel files and restrict disclosure of personal information to third parties.

Concerns for individual privacy also contributed to passage of the Electronic Communications Privacy Act of 1986 and the 1988 Employee Polygraph Protection Act. Under this latter federal law, private employers generally are forbidden from using lie detector tests while screening job applicants. Current employees may not be tested randomly but may be tested as a result of a specific incident or activity that causes economic injury or loss to an employer's business. The act permits private security companies to test job applicants and allows companies that manufacture or sell controlled substances to test both job applicants and current employees. The Labor Department may seek fines of up to $10,000 against employers who violate the act. Employees are also authorized to sue employers for violating the act.

Another important privacy concern involves drug testing. At present there is no uniform law regarding the drug testing of employees. Many private companies conduct such testing. However, some states have placed some limits on a private company's right to test for drugs.

Public employees are protected from some drug testing by the Fourth Amendment's prohibition against *unreasonable* searches. However, exactly when drug tests are unreasonable is subject to much debate in the courts. In general, public employees may be tested when there is a proper suspicion that employees are using illegal drugs that impair working ability or violate employment rules. Courts have also upheld drug testing as part of required annual medical exams.

The following case combines aspects of the at-will doctrine and workers' expectations of privacy. The case illustrates that the expectation of privacy regarding e-mail communication is very limited.

GARRITY V. JOHN HANCOCK MUTUAL LIFE INSURANCE COMPANY

2002 U.S. DIST. LEXIS 8343 (D. MASS. 2002)

ZOBEL, D. J.: Plaintiffs Nancy Garrity ("Mrs. Garrity") and Joanne Clark ("Ms. Clark") were employees of John Hancock Mutual Life Insurance Company ("John Hancock") for twelve and two years, respectively, until their termination in July of 1999. According to the defendant, plaintiffs regularly received on their office computers, sexually explicit e-mails from internet joke sites and other third parties, including Mrs. Garrity's husband, Arthur Garrity ("Mr. Garrity"), which they then sent to coworkers. These facts are undisputed: A fellow employee complained after receiving one such e-mail. Hancock promptly commenced an investigation of plaintiffs' e-mail folders, as well as the folders of those with whom they e-mailed on a regular basis. Based upon the information gleaned from this investigation, Hancock determined that plaintiffs had violated its E-Mail Policy, which states, in relevant part:

- Messages that are defamatory, abusive, obscene, profane, sexually oriented, threatening or racially offensive are prohibited.

[CONTINUED]

- The inappropriate use of E-mail is in violation of company policy and may be subject (sic) to disciplinary action, up to and including termination of employment.

- All information stored, transmitted, received, or contained in the company's E-mail systems is the property of John Hancock. It is not company policy to intentionally inspect E-mail usage. However, there may be business or legal situations that necessitate company review of E-mail messages and other documents.

- Company management reserves the right to access all E-mail files.

During plaintiffs' employment, defendant periodically reminded its employees that it was their responsibility to know and understand the e-mail policy. In addition, defendant warned them of several incidents in which employees were disciplined for violations. Plaintiffs assert that the e-mail policy is almost impossible to locate on Hancock's intranet system, and even harder to decipher. In addition, they contend that the reminders sent by defendant during plaintiffs' employment did not accurately communicate its e-mail policy. . . . [P]laintiffs assert that Hancock led them to believe that these personal e-mails could be kept private with the use of personal passwords and e-mail folders. Their complaint sets forth claims based on invasion of privacy . . . and defamation. Defendant filed a Motion for Summary Judgment on all counts.

Plaintiffs' opposition states that "it is uncontested . . . that Ms. Garrity, Mr. Garrity and Ms. Clark believed that the personal e-mail correspondence they sent and received was private." While that may be true, the relevant inquiry is whether the expectation of privacy was reasonable. Any reasonable expectation on the part of plaintiffs is belied by the record and plaintiffs' own statements. According to deposition testimony, Mrs. Garrity and Ms. Clark assumed that the recipients of their messages might forward them to others. Likewise, Mr. Garrity testified that the e-mails he sent to his wife would eventually be sent to third parties. . . .

Both Mrs. Garrity and Ms. Clark admit that they knew defendant had the ability to look at e-mail on the company's intranet system, and knew they had to be careful about sending e-mails. Nevertheless, they claim that their e-mails were private because the company had instructed them on how to create passwords and personal e-mail folders. . . .

Even if plaintiffs had a reasonable expectation of privacy in their work e-mail, defendant's legitimate business interest in protecting its employees from harassment in the workplace would likely trump plaintiffs' privacy interests. . . . Therefore, once defendant received a complaint about the plaintiffs' sexually explicit e-mails, it was required by law to commence an investigation. . . .

The last count asserts that two Hancock supervisors defamed plaintiffs by telling former coworkers, and Hancock employees in other departments, that plaintiffs were terminated for sending and receiving "sexually lewd, harassing [and] defamatory" and "sexually explicit" e-mails. Even if the statements made by defendant met the required elements of a defamation claim, defendant is entitled to a conditional privilege which insulates it from liability for these statements. The privilege protects an employer's statements of opinion and facts, and statements that an employer reasonably believes to be true. It also extends to information which may turn out not to be true concerning an employee when the publication is reasonably necessary to serve the employer's legitimate interest in the fitness of an employee to perform his or her job. In order to defeat the employer's conditional privilege, the employee bears the burden of proving that the employer abused the privilege by recklessly publishing the defamatory facts. Plaintiffs have not done so here. Rather, plaintiffs simply state that "no legitimate business purpose was served by disseminating these statements among such a large group of employees." To the contrary, all Hancock employees are subject to its e-mail policy. Therefore, defendant had an obvious legitimate business purpose, as to all employees, if it so chose—to warn them and thereby prevent any recurrence of the events that led to this lawsuit. **Accordingly, defendant's motion for summary judgment is allowed. Judgment may be entered for defendant.**

[CONTINUED]

CASE QUESTIONS

1. What is the factual basis that caused John Hancock Company to terminate the employment of Mrs. Garrity and Ms. Clark?

2. What argument did these employees make as a basis for retaining their jobs?

3. What was the district judge ruling with respect to the rights of these employees and this employer?

Having read this section, do you have a clear understanding of how you should answer the first question under the Business Decision at the beginning of this chapter?

4. EMPLOYEE LAWSUITS

Despite the presence of many examples of the employer violating an employment law, most employers strive to obey the law. They still risk lawsuits, however, including many brought by unsatisfactory employees who have been disciplined, denied promotion, or discharged. How can employers protect themselves from unjustified employee lawsuits?

One important protection against unjustified employee lawsuits is an established system of adequate documentation. Sometimes called the **paper fortress,** this documentation consists of job descriptions, personnel manuals, and employee personnel files.

Before handing anyone an employment application, the employer should insist that the potential candidate carefully study a job description. A well-written job description will help potential applicants eliminate themselves from job situations for which they lack interest or qualification, thus preventing employers from having to dismiss them later and risking lawsuits.

Once a new employee is hired, the employer should give the employee a personnel manual. This manual should include information about employee benefits and should also outline work rules and job requirements. The employer should go over the manual with the employee and answer any questions. Clear identification of employer expectations and policies helps provide a defense against employee lawsuits if subsequent discipline or discharge of the employee becomes necessary. The employer should ask that the employee sign a form indicating receipt of the manual and an understanding of the employer's explanation of its contents.

The employer should enter this form, with all other documentation relevant to an employee's work history, into the employee's personnel file. Regular written evaluations of employee performance should also be entered into the personnel file. A chronological record of unsatisfactory work performance is a very useful defense against unjustified lawsuits following discipline, denial of promotion, or discharge.

Another piece of documentation that helps justify employer decisions is the written warning. Anytime an employee breaks a work rule or performs unsatisfactorily, the employer should issue the employee a written warning and place a duplicate in the personnel file. The warning should explain specifically what work rule the employee violated. In addition, employers should either have an employee sign that he or she has received a written warning or else note in the personnel file that the employee has received a copy of it. The employer should also give the employee the opportunity to place a letter of explanation in the personnel file.

Laws discussed in this chapter and the next one should not prevent employers from discharging unsatisfactory employees. In an actual termination conversation, however, the employer should provide the employee with specific reasons for discharge, taken from the personnel file. Detailed documentation is vital in successfully responding to unjustified employee lawsuits. Even better is to prevent them in the first place through the development, enforcement, and review of company policies that promote legal compliance.

LABOR-MANAGEMENT RELATIONSHIP

The goal of labor law is successful **collective bargaining,** the process by which labor and management negotiate and reach agreements on matters of importance to both. Such matters include wages to be paid workers, hours to be worked, and other terms and conditions of employment. Collective bargaining can be successful only if the bargaining power of the parties is equal. Most laws regulating labor-management relations seek to equalize this bargaining power. As a result, some laws add to the bargaining position of labor and others add to that of management.

The major federal laws that govern labor-management relations are highlighted in the table on the next page. As you read, keep in mind that this chapter is a historical review of when, why, and how the federal government has created laws regulating the labor-management relationship.

5. LAWS BEFORE 1935

During the time prior to 1935, Congress viewed the labor-management relationship as being unbalanced. In a series of laws that are thought of as being prolabor, Congress attempted to correct the perceived inequities. It did so by passing the following:

- The Clayton Act
- The Railway Labor Act
- The Norris-LaGuardia Act

The Clayton Act The first federal statute of any importance to the labor movement is the **Clayton Act** of 1914, which was passed principally to strengthen the antitrust laws. Between 1890 (when the Sherman Antitrust Act was passed) and 1914, labor unions were weak in their ability to represent employees. At least one reason for the relative strength enjoyed by management was the fact that it could and did argue that employees acting together were restraining trade illegally under the Sherman Act.

The Clayton Act stated that antitrust laws regulating anticompetitive contracts did not apply to labor unions or their members in lawfully carrying out their legitimate activities. This exemption covered only *legitimate* union practices. Although the Clayton Act exempted employees from the claim that they were restraining trade through unionization, this law did not expressly grant employees

Federal Laws Governing Labor-Management Relations

Year	Statute	Major Provisions
1914	Clayton Act	1. Exempted union activity from the antitrust laws
1926	Railway Labor Act	1. Governs collective bargaining for railroads and airlines
		2. Created the National Mediation Board to conduct union elections and mediate differences between employers and unions
1932	Norris-LaGuardia Act	1. Outlawed yellow-dog contracts
		2. Prohibited federal courts from enjoining lawful union activities, including picketing and strikes
1935	Wagner Act (National Labor Relations Act)	1. Created the National Labor Relations Board (NLRB)
		2. Authorized the NLRB to conduct union certification elections
		3. Outlawed certain conduct by management as unfair to labor (five unfair labor practices)
		4. Authorized the NLRB to hold hearings on unfair labor practices and correct wrongs resulting from them
1947	Taft-Hartley Act (Labor-Management Relations Act)	1. Outlawed certain conduct by unions as six unfair labor practices
		2. Provided for an 80-day cooling-off period in strikes that imperil national health or safety
		3. Allowed states to enact right-to-work laws
		4. Created the Federal Mediation and Conciliation Service to assist in settlement of labor disputes.
1959	Landrum-Griffin Act (Labor-Management Reporting and Disclosure Act, LMRDA)	1. Created a Bill of Rights for union members
		2. Requires reports to the secretary of labor
		3. Added to the list of unfair labor practices

the protected right to join a union. Therefore, the Clayton Act did not balance the bargaining power between labor and management. The latter group remained the stronger one.

The Railway Labor Act Among the first industries to unionize were the railroads. In 1926, Congress enacted the **Railway Labor Act** to encourage collective bargaining in the railroad industry. The goal was to resolve labor disputes that might otherwise disrupt transportation and result in violence. The act was later extended to airlines; today it applies to both air and rail transportation. It established the three-member **National Mediation Board,** which must designate the bargaining representative for any given bargaining unit of employees in the railway or air transport industries. The board generally does this by holding representation elections. (See the box "How the Railway Labor Act Works.")

The Railway Labor Act has played a vitally important role in balancing the labor-management relationship in the transportation industries. However, due to this act's limited application, the management of businesses outside the transportation industry generally continued to have superior bargaining power following 1926.

The Norris-LaGuardia Act Because of management's superior bargaining power, prior to 1932 management often made it a condition of employment that employees agree not to join a labor union. Such agreements became known as **yellow-dog contracts** on the basis that any employee who would forsake the right

HOW THE RAILWAY LABOR ACT WORKS

When the parties to a dispute over proposed contract terms in the transportation industry cannot reach an agreement concerning rates of pay or working conditions, the National Mediation Board must attempt mediation of their differences. If mediation does not resolve their differences, the board encourages voluntary arbitration. If the parties refuse arbitration and the dispute is likely to disrupt interstate commerce substantially, the board informs the president, who then appoints a special emergency board. This emergency board lacks judicial power, but it encourages the parties to reach an agreement by investigating the dispute and publishing its findings of fact and recommendations for settlement. During the investigation, which lasts 30 days, and for an additional 30 days after the report is issued, business is conducted without interruption. The parties, however, have no duty to comply with the special board's proposals. Thus, if no new collective bargaining agreement is reached after the 60-day period, lockouts by management and strikes by workers become legal.

to join fellow employees in unionization was a cowardly scoundrel (yellow dog). Passed in 1932, the **Norris-LaGuardia Act** made yellow-dog contracts illegal. In essence, management no longer could explicitly deny an employee the right to unionize.

Seeking injunctions to stop concerted activities had remained an important tool of management in fighting the growth of labor unions. The Norris-LaGuardia Act listed specific acts of persons and organizations participating in labor disputes that were not subject to federal court injunctions. These are summarized in the box, below.

Although the Norris-LaGuardia Act greatly restricts the use of injunctions in labor disputes, it does not prohibit them altogether. An injunction may be issued to enjoin illegal strikes, such as ones by public employees. In addition, a party seeking an injunction in a labor dispute must meet the test of a stringent, clean-hands rule. No restraining order will be granted to any person who fails to comply with any obligation imposed by law or who fails to make every reasonable effort to settle the dispute.

The Norris-LaGuardia Act restricts the use of federal court injunctions in labor disputes; it does not limit the jurisdiction of state courts in issuing them. The Supreme Court has upheld the jurisdiction of a state court to enjoin a union's work stoppage and picketing in violation of a no-strike clause in its collective bargaining agreement. Due to these limitations and economic conditions that existed in the labor market in 1932, the Norris-LaGuardia Act did not substantially strengthen the organized labor movement.

FEDERAL COURTS CANNOT ENJOIN

- Striking or quitting work
- Belonging to a labor organization
- Paying strike or unemployment benefits to participants in a labor dispute
- Publicizing the existence of a labor dispute or the facts related to it (including picketing)
- Assembling peaceably to promote interests in a labor dispute
- Agreeing with others or advising or causing them to do any of the above acts without fraud or violence

The Wagner Act

The labor movement received its greatest stimulus for growth with the enactment in 1935 of the National Labor Relations Act, known as the **Wagner Act.** Perhaps most significantly, Congress explicitly affirmed labor's right to organize and to bargain collectively. Recognizing that a major cause of industrial strife was the inequality of bargaining power between employees and employers, Section 7 of the act states:

> Employees shall have the right to self-organization, to form, join, or assist labor organizations, to bargain collectively through representatives of their own choosing, and to engage in concerted activities for the purpose of collective bargaining or other mutual aid or protection.

This provision clearly means that your response to the second question in the Business Decision box must be "no."

In addition to this Section 7 right to unionize, the Wagner Act contains several other key provisions, as summarized in the following box.

6. THE NATIONAL LABOR RELATIONS BOARD

Established by the Wagner Act, the **National Labor Relations Board (NLRB)** operates as an independent agency of the U.S. government. This section discusses the organizational structure of the NLRB, its jurisdiction, and its quasi-judicial function. The following section examines the NLRB's authority to certify unions as the collective bargaining representative of employees. After this introduction to the NLRB, the remainder of the chapter will illustrate the significant role this agency plays in balancing the labor-management relationship.

NLRB Organization The NLRB consists of five members, appointed by the president with the advice and consent of the Senate, who serve staggered terms of five years each. In addition, there is a general counsel of the board who supervises board investigations and serves as prosecutor in cases before the board. The general counsel supervises operations of the NLRB so that the board itself may perform its quasi-judicial function of deciding unfair labor practice cases free of bias. Administrative law judges are responsible for the initial conduct of hearings in unfair labor practice cases.

The general counsel also is responsible for conducting representation elections. In addition, the general counsel is responsible for seeking court orders requiring compliance with the board's orders and represents the board in miscellaneous litigation. The board determines policy questions, such as what types of employers

CONGRESSIONAL ACTIONS THROUGH THE WAGNER ACT

- Creating the National Labor Relations Board (NLRB) to administer the act
- Providing employees the right to select a union to act as their collective bargaining agent
- Outlawing certain conduct by employers that generally has the effect of either preventing the organization of employees or emasculating their unions where they do exist; these forbidden acts are called *unfair labor practices*
- Authorizing the NLRB to conduct hearings on unfair labor practice allegations and, if unfair practices are found to exist, to take corrective action including issuing cease and desist orders and awarding dollar damages to unions and employees

PERSONNEL EXEMPT FROM NLRB

- Employees of federal and state governments
- Employees of political subdivisions of the states
- Persons subject to the Railway Labor Act

- Independent contractors
- Individuals employed as agricultural laborers or domestic servants in a home
- Individuals employed by their spouse or parent

and groups of employees are covered by the labor law. Recall the *Holly Farms* case in Chapter 12 and how courts are bound to defer to the rulings of the NLRB as long as the board members reach a reasonable result. That case helps illustrate the extensive authority and power of NLRB.

Jurisdiction Congress gave the NLRB jurisdiction over any business "affecting commerce." Employers and employees listed in the box above are, however, specifically exempt from NLRB jurisdiction.

The NLRB has never been able to exercise fully the powers given it because of budget and time constraints. It has limited its own jurisdiction to businesses of a certain size (the box, below, lists these businesses). As a result of this policy, federal laws do not cover many small employers, which are subject to applicable state law on labor relations and common law principles. Of course the board may decide to take jurisdiction over any business that affects interstate commerce.

Quasi-Judicial Authority In sections 8, 13, and 14 of this chapter, you will study the various unfair labor practices. Congress has granted the NLRB the authority to conduct the quasi-judicial hearings that are required to investigate and to enforce sanctions if these unfair labor practices occur.

This authority is extensive in that NLRB has discretion to order whatever action is necessary to correct the unlawful practice. However, as the box on the next page illustrates, there are limits to the NLRB's authority to order remedial actions.

NLRB ASSUMES JURISDICTION OVER THE FOLLOWING

- Nonretail operations with an annual outflow or inflow across state lines of at least $50,000
- Retail enterprises with a gross volume of $500,000 or more a year
- Enterprises operating office buildings if the gross revenues are at least $100,000 per year
- Transportation enterprises furnishing interstate services
- Local transit systems with an annual gross volume of $250,000
- Newspapers that subscribe to interstate news services, publish nationally syndicated features, or advertise nationally sold products and have a minimum annual gross volume of $250,000
- Communication enterprises that operate radio or television stations or telephone or telegraph services with a gross volume of $100,000 or more per year
- Local public utilities with an annual gross volume of $250,000 per year or an outflow or inflow of goods or services across state lines of $50,000 or more per year
- Hotel and motel enterprises that serve transient guests and gross at least $500,000 in revenues per year
- All enterprises whose operations have a substantial impact on national defense
- Nonprofit hospitals
- Private universities and colleges

LIMITATION OF NLRB'S REMEDIES

After presenting documents that verified his legal status to work in the United States, Jose Castro was hired by Hoffman Plastic Compounds, Inc. Castro participated in a union-organizing campaign at the Hoffman facility where he worked. Hoffman laid off Castro and others engaged in this organizing effort. When it was presented with this factual situation, the National Labor Relations Board (NLRB) ordered Hoffman to reinstate Castro (and the other employees) with backpay. During a compliance hearing before an NLRB administrative law judge (ALJ), Castro acknowledged that he did not have the proper paperwork to be a legal alien eligible to work. In essence, Castro admitted that he has used another person's birth

certificate to get a driver's license and social security number. Because of these admissions, the ALJ concluded that the NLRB could not award Castro reinstatement and backpay. Castro appealed to the full board which reversed the ALJ and awarded backpay. Hoffman sought review by the Court of Appeals for the D.C. Circuit. This court upheld the NLRB's award of backpay.

Upon further review, the U.S. Supreme Court reversed the NLRB's decision. It concluded that backpay awarded to illegal aliens would "encourage the successful evasion of apprehension by immigration authorities, condone prior violations of the immigration laws, and encourage future violations."

Source: *Hoffman Plastic Compounds, Inc. v. NLRB*, 122 S. Ct. 1275 (2002).

7. CERTIFICATION OF UNIONS

An employer may voluntarily recognize that its workers desire to have a certain labor union represent them. The employer is free to agree to bargain with the union as the collective bargaining representative of the employees. In actuality, such voluntary recognition occurs in relatively few situations. More common is the NLRB's certification of a union as the bargaining agent for a group of employees. This certification process is the result of an election or occurs through authorization cards. These certification processes are discussed in the next two subsections.

Unionization Elections Elections are by secret ballot and are supervised by the NLRB. The board decides what unit of employees is appropriate for purposes of collective bargaining and therefore which employees are entitled to vote in the election. It may select the total employer unit, craft unit, plant unit, or any subdivision of the plant.

Obviously, how the board exercises its discretion in this regard may be crucial to the outcome of a given election. If all 100 workers at one plant operated by an employer desire to organize but 400 out of 500 at another of the employer's plants do not, designation of the total employees as the one appropriate bargaining unit would ensure that both plants would remain nonunion. The following case involves the Court's discussion of how the NLRB allocates the burden of proving who is and is not an employee eligible to vote.

NLRB v. KENTUCKY RIVER COMMUNITY CARE, INC.

121 S. CT. 1861 (2001)

Kentucky River Community Care, Inc. (employer) operates a facility for patients suffering from mental retardation and illness. This facility is called Caney

Creek, and 110 employees and about 12 managerial and supervisory personnel work at this facility. In 1997, the Kentucky State District Council of Car-

[CONTINUED]

penters (union) petitioned the National Labor Relations Board (NLRB) for certification to represent all 110 eligible employees at Caney Creek. At this certification hearing, the employer objected to the inclusion of six registered nurses in the proposed bargaining unit since these nurses are supervisors. The NLRB's Regional Director placed on the employer the burden of proving the supervisory stature of these nurses. Further, the Regional Director found that the employer did not carry this burden. Therefore, the nurses were included in the Caney Creek bargaining unit. The union won the certification election and was certified as the bargaining representative of all Caney Creek employees. Following further procedural maneuvers, the employer sought review of these decisions before the Sixth Circuit Court of Appeals. This court held that the NLRB was mistaken to place the burden of proving supervisory status on the employer. The court ruled that the NLRB's General Counsel should have this burden of proof. Because of this conclusion, the certification was set aside as was the order declaring the union to be the bargaining representative of the Caney Creek employees. The NLRB petitioned the Supreme Court for a writ of certiorari, which was granted.

SCALIA, J.: . . . The [National Labor Relations] Act expressly defines the term "supervisor" in § 2(11), which provides:

> The term "supervisor" means any individual having authority, in the interest of the employer, to hire, transfer, suspend, lay off, recall, promote, discharge, assign, reward, or discipline other employees, or responsibly to direct them, or to adjust their grievances, or effectively to recommend such action, if in connection with the foregoing the exercise of such authority is not of a merely routine or clerical nature, but requires the use of independent judgment.

The Act does not, however, expressly allocate the burden of proving or disproving a challenged employee's supervisory status. The Board therefore has filled the statutory gap with the consistent rule that the burden is borne by the party claiming that the employee is a supervisor. For example, when the General Counsel seeks to attribute the conduct of certain employees to the employer by virtue of their supervisory status, this rule dictates that he bear the burden of proving supervisory status. Or, when a union challenges certain ballots cast in a representation election on the basis that they were cast by supervisors, the union bears the burden.

The Board argues that the Court of Appeals for the Sixth Circuit erred in not deferring to its resolution of the statutory ambiguity, and we agree. The Board's rule is supported by the general rule of statutory construction that the burden of proving justification or exemption under a special exception to the prohibitions of a statute generally rests on one who claims its benefits. . . . In addition, it is easier to prove an employee's authority to exercise 1 of the 12 listed supervisory functions than to disprove an employee's authority to exercise any of those functions, and practicality therefore favors placing the burden on the party asserting supervisory status. We find that the Board's rule for allocating the burden of proof is reasonable and consistent with the Act, and we therefore defer to it.

[The Supreme Court then concluded that the Sixth Circuit Court of Appeals ruling was a proper application of the law (in this case the NLRB's General Counsel has the burden of proving supervisory status) even if the court's statement that such burden is always on the General Counsel is incorrect.]

Affirmed.

CASE QUESTIONS

1. What procedural steps did the parties go through to have the union certified as the employees' bargaining representative?

2. Why is the issue of supervisory personnel so important in the labor-management relationship?

3. What is the difference between the ruling of the NLRB, the Sixth Circuit, and the Supreme Court with respect to the burden of proving supervisory status?

The NLRB conducts elections upon receipt of a petition signed by at least 30 percent of the employees. In addition, an employer may file a petition for selection of an initial representative. An employer may also file a petition for an election to invalidate certification of an incumbent union. It must show that it doubts, in good faith, the continued support of the union by a majority of the employees. Petitions are used to obtain votes to certify a union or to rescind a union's authority. After any valid election has been conducted by the NLRB, another is not permitted for one year, regardless of whether the union wins or loses the certification vote. Also, an election is not allowed within the term of a collective bargaining agreement or three years after it has been signed, whichever period is shorter.

Unionization through Cards   A union seeking to represent employees may solicit cards from them indicating their willingness for the union to represent them. An employer may then recognize the union as the bargaining agent for its employees if the cards are signed by a majority of the employees. An employer, however, is not required to recognize the union based on a majority card showing and always has the option to insist on an election. However, once an employer recognizes the union—no matter how informally—the employer is bound by the recognition and loses the right to seek an election.

Cards also may substitute for an election if certain conditions are met. The NLRB may issue a bargaining order based on such cards if the cards are unequivocal and clearly indicate that the employee signing the card is authorizing the union to represent him or her. The general counsel of the NLRB is not required to prove that the employees read or understood the cards. If a card states on its face that it authorizes collective bargaining, it will be counted for that purpose unless there is clear proof that the employee was told that it would not be used for that purpose.

8. UNFAIR LABOR PRACTICES BY MANAGEMENT

Remember that Congress desired to strengthen the bargaining power of labor unions when it passed the Wagner Act in 1935. A principal means of accomplishing this goal was through the creation of five unfair labor practices by management. These practices, as summarized in the following box, are now illegal.

Conduct may be, and often is, a violation of more than one of the listed unfair labor practices. Indeed, most violations constitute interference with the right to engage in concerted activity (the first category). For example, retaliation against a union leader for filing charges would constitute a violation of both the first and fourth categories.

UNFAIR LABOR PRACTICES BY MANAGEMENT

1. Interference with efforts of employees to form, join, or assist labor organizations or to engage in concerted activities for mutual aid or protection

2. Domination of a labor organization or contribution of financial or other support to it

3. Discrimination in hiring or tenure of employees for reason of union affiliation

4. Discrimination against employees for filing charges or giving testimony under the act

5. Refusal to bargain collectively in good faith with a duly designated representative of the employees

This section of the chapter attempts to introduce you to these unfair labor practices under the following headings:

- Interfering
- Dominating a labor organization
- Discriminating based on union affiliation
- Discriminating as a result of NLRB proceedings
- Refusing to bargain in good faith

Interfering with Unionization   The first unfair labor practice has two distinct parts. First, it is unfair for an employer to interfere with the efforts of employees to form, join, or assist labor organizations. The second part covers interfering with "concerted activities for mutual aid or protection." This violation does not have to involve a union; the act protects any group of employees acting for their mutual aid and protection.

The first part of this unfair labor practice by management is a catchall intended to guarantee the right of employees to organize and join unions. It clearly prohibits "scare" tactics such as threats by employers to fire those involved in organizing employees or threats to cut back on employee benefits if employees succeed in unionizing. In addition, less obvious activities are outlawed, such as requiring job applicants to state on a questionnaire whether they would cross a picket line in a strike. An employer cannot engage in any conduct calculated to erode employee support for the union.

Interference with unionization may take the form of a carrot as well as a stick. The conferring of benefits by an employer may be an unfair labor practice. In one case, the employer reminded its employees two weeks before a representation election that the company had just instituted a "floating holiday" that employees could take on their birthdays. The union lost the election, but it was set aside by the NLRB. It was an unfair labor practice for the employer to engage in conduct immediately favorable to employees. The conduct interfered with the freedom of choice for or against unionization.

The following case illustrates how an unfair labor practice allegation arises. Note that the issue of a union's status as a certified bargaining agent becomes intertwined with management's duty to refrain from interfering with an employee's right to engage in union activity.

ALLENTOWN MACK SALES AND SERVICE, INC. v. NATIONAL LABOR RELATIONS BOARD

118 S. Ct. 818 (1998)

SCALIA, J.: Under longstanding precedent of the National Labor Relations Board, an employer who believes that an incumbent union no longer enjoys the support of a majority of its employees has three options: to request a formal, Board-supervised election, to withdraw recognition from the union and refuse to bargain, or to conduct an internal poll of employee support for the union. The Board has held that the latter two are unfair labor practices unless the employer can show that it had a "good faith reasonable doubt"

[CONTINUED]

about the union's majority support. We must decide whether the Board's standard for employer polling is rational and consistent with the National Labor Relations Act, and whether the Board's factual determinations in this case are supported by substantial evidence in the record.

Mack Trucks, Inc., had a factory branch in Allentown, Pennsylvania, whose service and parts employees were represented by Local Lodge 724 of the International Association of Machinists and Aerospace Workers, AFL-CIO. Mack notified its Allentown managers in May of 1990 that it intended to sell the branch, and several of those managers formed Allentown Mack Sales, Inc., the petitioner here, which purchased the assets of the business on December 20, 1990, and began to operate it as an independent dealership. From December 21, 1990, to January 1, 1991, Allentown hired 32 of the original 45 Mack employees.

During the period before and immediately after the sale, a number of Mack employees made statements to the prospective owners of Allentown Mack Sales suggesting that the incumbent union had lost support among employees in the bargaining unit. In job interviews, eight employees made statements indicating, or at least arguably indicating, that they personally no longer supported the union. In addition, Ron Mohr, a member of the union's bargaining committee and shop steward for the Mack Trucks service department, told an Allentown manager that it was his feeling that the employees did not want a union, and that "with a new company, if a vote was taken, the Union would lose." And Kermit Bloch, who worked for Mack Trucks as a mechanic on the night shift, told a manager that the entire night shift (then 5 or 6 employees) did not want the union.

On January 2, 1991, Local Lodge 724 asked Allentown Mack Sales to recognize it as the employees' collective-bargaining representative, and to begin negotiations for a contract. The new employer rejected that request by letter dated January 25, claiming a "good faith doubt as to support of the Union among the employees." The letter also announced that Allentown had "arranged for an independent poll by secret ballot of its hourly employees to be conducted under guidelines prescribed by the National Labor Relations Board." The poll, supervised by a Roman Catholic priest, was conducted on

February 8, 1991; the union lost 19 to 13. Shortly thereafter, the union filed an unfair-labor-practice charge with the Board.

The Administrative Law Judge (ALJ) concluded that Allentown was a successor employer to Mack Trucks, Inc., and therefore inherited Mack's bargaining obligation and a presumption of continuing majority support for the union. The ALJ held that Allentown's poll . . . violated § § 8(a)(1) and 8 (a)(5) of the National Labor Relations Act (Act) because Allentown did not have an "objective reasonable doubt" about the majority status of the union. The Board adopted the ALJ's findings, . . . agreed with his conclusion, . . . [and] ordered Allentown to recognize and bargain with Local 724.

On review in the Court of Appeals for the District of Columbia Circuit, Allentown challenged both the facial rationality of the Board's test for employer polling and the Board's application of that standard to the facts of this case. The court enforced the Board's bargaining order. . . . We granted certiorari.

Allentown challenges the Board's decision in this case on several grounds. First, it contends that because the Board's "reasonable doubt" standard for employer polls is the same as its standard for unilateral withdrawal of recognition and for employer initiation of a Board-supervised election (a so-called "Representation Management," or "RM" election), the Board irrationally permits employers to poll only when it would be unnecessary and legally pointless to do so. Second, Allentown argues that the record evidence clearly demonstrates that it had a good-faith reasonable doubt about the union's claim to majority support. Finally, it asserts that the Board has abandoned the "reasonable doubt" prong of its polling standard, and recognizes an employer's "reasonable doubt" only if a majority of the unit employees renounce the union. . . . Allentown argues that it is irrational to require the same factual showing to justify a poll as to justify an outright withdrawal of recognition, because that leaves the employer with no legal incentive to poll. Under the Board's framework, the results of a poll can never supply an otherwise lacking "good faith reasonable doubt" necessary to justify a withdrawal of recognition, since the employer must already have that same reasonable doubt before he is permitted to conduct a poll. . . . While the Board's adoption of a unitary standard for

[CONTINUED]

polling, RM elections, and withdrawals of recognition is in some respects a puzzling policy, we do not find it so irrational as to be "arbitrary [or] capricious" within the meaning of the Administrative Procedure Act. The Board believes that employer polling is potentially "disruptive" to established bargaining relationships and "unsettling" to employees, and so has chosen to limit severely the circumstances under which it may be conducted. The unitary standard reflects the Board's apparent conclusion that polling should be tolerated only when the employer might otherwise simply withdraw recognition and refuse to bargain. . . .

If it would be rational for the Board to set the polling standard either higher or lower than the threshold for an RM election, then surely it is not irrational for the Board to split the difference.

The Board held Allentown guilty of an unfair labor practice in its conduct of the polling because it had not demonstrated that it held a reasonable doubt, based on objective considerations, that the Union continued to enjoy the support of a majority of the bargaining unit employees. We must decide whether that conclusion is supported by substantial evidence on the record as a whole. Put differently, we must decide whether on this record it would have been possible for a reasonable jury to reach the Board's conclusion. . . .

[The Court reviewed the facts and determined that the evidence supported the petitioner's doubt that the majority of its employees supported the union.] We conclude that the Board's "reasonable doubt" test for employer polls is facially rational and consistent with the Act. But the Board's factual finding that Allentown Mack Sales lacked such a doubt is not supported by substantial evidence on the record as a whole. The judgment of the Court of Appeals for the D. C. Circuit is therefore reversed, and the case is remanded with instructions to deny enforcement.

Reversed and remanded.

CASE QUESTIONS

1. What event occurred that allowed the representation of employees by a union to be called into question?
2. What were the findings and order by the NLRB?
3. What issues were presented to the Supreme Court?
4. Why does the Court agree with the NLRB about a unitary standard of "reasonable doubt" for refusing to bargain, polling employees, and requesting a decertification election?
5. How does the Court differ with the NLRB in this case?
6. Do you agree with the Court analyses and conclusions?

With Concerted Activities. The term **concerted activity** is given a liberal interpretation in order to create a climate that encourages unionization, collective bargaining, and all that may flow therefrom. For example, some employees refused to work after a heated grievance meeting. They followed their supervisors onto the workroom floor and continued to argue loudly until they were ordered a second time to resume work. The employer issued letters of reprimand alleging insubordination. This was an unfair labor practice. The employees were engaged in a protected activity. The protection of employee conduct at grievance meetings is extended to a brief cooling-off period following an employer's termination of such a meeting. Protection of employees' participation in the meetings themselves would be seriously threatened if the employer could at any point call an immediate halt to the operation of the law simply by declaring the meeting ended.

The concerted-activity concept is quite extensive. In one case, an employer was investigating theft by employees. One employee asked that a union representative be present during her interview. She was refused. The Supreme Court held that the employee had a right to representation when there was a perceived threat to her employment security. The presence of a representative assures other employees in the bargaining unit that they, too, can obtain aid and protection if they wish when there appears to be a threat to their job security. Refusing the assistance at the interview was an unfair labor practice. In addition, the right to engage in concerted activity has been expanded to cover the actions of a sole employee under certain circumstances. If an employee has a grievance that may affect other workers, that employee has rights protected by the concerted-activity language of this unfair labor practice, even though no other worker participates in the activity.

Dominating a Labor Organization The second unfair labor practice prohibits the domination of a labor organization by employers or their contribution of financial or other support to any union. Under the Wagner Act, any organization of employees must be completely independent of their employers. In the case of a controversy between competing unions, employers must remain strictly neutral. It is an unfair labor practice for the employer to support a union by giving it a meeting place, providing refreshments for union meetings, permitting the union to use the employer's telephone, secretary, or copying machine, or allowing the union to keep cafeteria or vending-machine profits. This unfair labor practice in the context of the Business Decision, at the beginning of the chapter, requires you to be very careful in treating the one or more unions representing your employees.

Discriminating Based on Union Affiliation Under the third unfair labor practice, an employer may neither discharge nor refuse to hire an employee to either encourage or discourage membership in any labor organization. Nor may the employer discriminate regarding any term or condition of employment for such purposes. The law does not oblige an employer to favor union members in hiring employees. It also does not restrict him or her in the normal exercise of any employer's right to select or discharge employees. However, the employer may not abuse that right by discriminatory action based on union membership or activities that encourage or discourage membership in a labor organization. For example, the Supreme Court has held that an employer who reports the possible existence of illegal aliens to the Immigration and Naturalization Service engages in an unfair labor practice when that report is closely associated with the employees' approval of a labor union as their bargaining agent.

A company may not go partially out of business because some of its employees have organized, nor may it temporarily close that portion of its business that has unionized. If a company closes one plant because a union is voted in, such action discourages union activity at other plants. Partial closings to "chill" unionism are unfair labor practices.

Discriminating as a Result of NLRB Proceedings Under the fourth unfair labor practice, employees are protected from being discharged or from other reprisals by their employers because they have sought to enforce their rights under the Wagner Act by filing charges or giving testimony in NLRB proceedings. This protection prevents the NLRB's channels of information from being dried up by employer intimidation of complainants and witnesses. An employer cannot refuse to hire a prospective employee because charges have been filed by him or her.

The main defense of any employer accused of reprisal is that he or she discharged or discriminated against the employee for some reason other than filing charges or giving testimony. Most often such cases boil down to trying to prove what motivated the company in pursuing its course of action. If the company can convince the NLRB that the employee was discharged because of misconduct, low production, personnel cutbacks necessitated by economic conditions, or other legitimate considerations, the company will be exonerated. Otherwise, it will be found guilty of this unfair labor practice.

Refusing to Bargain in Good Faith The fifth unfair labor practice occurs when management refuses to bargain with the collective bargaining representative of its employees. The Wagner Act did not define the phrase "to bargain collectively." Judicial decisions have added the concept of *good faith* to bargaining. To comply with the requirement that they bargain collectively in good faith, employers must approach the bargaining table with fair and open minds and a sincere intent to find a basis of agreement. Refusing to meet at reasonable times with representatives of the other party, refusing to reduce agreements to writing, and designating persons with no authority to negotiate as representatives at meetings are examples of this unfair labor practice.

The employer's duty to bargain collectively includes a duty to provide relevant information needed by a union for the proper performance of its duties as the employees' bargaining representative. For example, data about job-related safety and health must be furnished so that the union can safeguard its members' health and safety.

A more fundamental issue inherent in the requirement that parties bargain collectively is: "About what?" Must the employer bargain with the union about all subjects and all management decisions in which the union or the employees are interested? Are there subjects and issues upon which management is allowed to act alone?

In answering these questions, the law divides issues into two categories—**compulsory bargaining issues** and **voluntary bargaining issues.** Compulsory, or mandatory, bargaining issues are those concerned with wages, hours, and other terms and conditions of employment. Although the parties may voluntarily consider other issues, the refusal by either to bargain in good faith on such other permissive matters is not an unfair labor practice.

Classifying an issue as *compulsory* or *voluntary* is done on a case-by-case basis. For example, questions relating to fringe benefits are compulsory bargaining issues because they are "wages." The NLRB and the courts are called on to decide whether management and labor must bargain with each other on a multitude of issues. The box on the next page illustrates one example.

A party to labor negotiations may present a demand relating to a nonmandatory bargaining issue as long as this issue does not have to be resolved before the parties can resolve mandatory bargaining issues. Tying a voluntary bargaining issue to a compulsory bargaining issue results in a failure to bargain in good faith and is in effect an unfair labor practice.

Courts tend to defer to the special expertise of the NLRB in classifying collective bargaining subjects, especially in the area of "terms or conditions of employment." The courts have affirmed board rulings holding that issues such as union dues checkoff, health and accident insurance, safety rules, merit pay increases, incentive pay plans, Christmas and other bonuses, stock purchase plans, pensions,

IS BARGAINING REQUIRED?

Employees of the Ford Motor Company belong to the United Auto Workers. Ford provides in-plant cafeterias and vending machines as two ways to ensure its employees with food services. An independent caterer managed both the cafeterias and vending machines. This caterer informed Ford that the increased costs associated with these food services required food prices to go up. When Ford notified the union representative of these food cost increases, the union requested bargaining be held over the food prices and services.

Ford refused to bargain, and the union filed a charge with the NLRB alleging Ford's refusal to bargain in good faith, which is an unfair labor practice. The NLRB concluded that in-plant food and related services are "other terms and conditions of employment." Therefore, Ford must negotiate with the union over this compulsory bargaining issue. The Supreme Court's review of these facts results in the NLRB's ruling being affirmed.

Source: *Ford Motor Company v. NLRB,* 99 S. Ct. 1842 (1979).

paid vacations and holidays, the privilege of hunting on a reserved portion of a paper company's forest preserve, proposals for effective arbitration and grievance procedures, and no-strike and no-lockout clauses are compulsory bargaining issues.

Remember that neither the employer nor the union is required to make concessions to the other concerning a mandatory subject of bargaining. The law only demands that each negotiate such matters in good faith with the other before making a decision and taking unilateral action. If the parties fail to reach an agreement after discussing these problems, each may take steps that are against the wishes and best interests of the other party. For example, the employer may refuse to grant a wage increase requested by the union, and the union is free to strike.

THE TAFT-HARTLEY ACT

The Wagner Act opened the door for the rapid growth of the union movement. From 1935 to the end of World War II, the strength and influence of unions grew substantially. Where, prior to the Wagner Act, employers had the greater advantage in bargaining power, by 1946 many persons felt the pendulum had shifted and that unions, with their ability to call nationwide, crippling strikes, had the better bargaining position. To balance the scale, the Labor-Management Relations Act (the **Taft-Hartley Act**) was enacted in 1947 to amend the Wagner Act.

The purposes of the Taft-Hartley Act are to ensure the free flow of commerce by eliminating union practices that burden commerce and to provide procedures for avoiding disputes that jeopardize the public health, safety, or interest. It recognizes that both parties to collective bargaining need protection from wrongful interference by the other and that employees sometimes need protection from the union itself. Finally, it sought to protect the public interest in major labor disputes. Congress authorized the creation of the Federal Mediation and Conciliation Service to help achieve the goals of the Taft-Hartley Act. Members of this service are available to assist the parties in settling labor disputes. (See the box "Major Provisions of Taft-Hartley Act.")

9. EIGHTY-DAY COOLING-OFF PERIOD

Somewhat like the 60-day period provided under the Railway Labor Act, the Taft-Hartley Act provides for an *80-day cooling-off period* following certain procedures. This provision's intent is to limit the adverse impact of the nationwide

MAJOR PROVISIONS OF TAFT-HARTLEY ACT

In its attempt to balance the bargaining power between labor unions and management, the Taft-Hartley Act:

- Provides for an *80-day cooling-off period* in strikes that imperil the nation's health or safety
- Reinforces the employer's freedom of speech in labor-management relations

- Outlaws the *closed-shop* concept but permits *union shops* in the absence of a state *right-to-know* law
- Permits suits by union members for breach of contract against unions
- Creates six unfair labor practices by unions

strikes by steelworkers, mineworkers, autoworkers, and longshoremen than can paralyze the economy. When a threatened or actual strike or lockout affecting an entire industry or substantial part thereof will, if permitted to occur or to continue, imperil the national health or safety, the 80-day period may be enforced. The procedure starts with the president recognizing the emergency and appointing a board of inquiry to obtain facts about the threatened or actual strike or lockout. The board studies the situation and reports back to the president. If the board finds that the national health or safety is indeed affected by the strike, then the president, through the attorney general, goes to the federal court for an injunction ordering the union to suspend the strike (or the company to suspend the lockout) for 80 days.

During the 80-day period, the Federal Mediation and Conciliation Service works with the labor-management parties to try to achieve an agreement. If during this time the reconciliation effort fails, the presidential board holds new hearings and receives the company's final offer. The union members are then allowed to vote on this final proposal by the company. If they vote for the new proposal, the dispute is over and work continues as usual. If they vote against the proposal, the workers may again be called out on strike. At this point, the strike may continue indefinitely until the disagreement causing it is resolved by collective bargaining or unless there is additional legislation by Congress to solve the problem.

Experience has shown that disputes are settled during the 80-day period. The injunction provided for in the Taft-Hartley Act may not be used for all strikes and lockouts. This injunction is limited to *national emergency* strikes and lockouts, those that involve national defense or key industries or have a substantial effect on the economy.

10. FREE SPEECH

Employers had complained that the Wagner Act violated their right of free speech. Statements by management had been used as the basis of finding an employer guilty of unfair labor practices. To meet this objection, Congress, in Taft-Hartley, added the following provision:

> 8(c) The expressing of any views, argument, or opinion, or the dissemination thereof, whether in written, printed, graphic, or visual form, shall not constitute or be evidence of an unfair labor practice under any of the provisions of this Act, if such expression contains no threat of reprisal or force or promise of benefit.

This provision gives employers limited free speech, at best. It is difficult to make statements that cannot be construed as a threat or a promise. For example, if an employer predicts dire economic events as a result of unionization, such may be an illegal threat if the employer has it within his or her power to make the prediction come true. Whether particular language is coercive or not often depends on the analysis of the total background of facts and circumstances in which it was uttered. To be forbidden, the statements of an employer need not be proved to have been coercive in fact but only to have had a reasonable tendency to intimidate employees under the circumstances.

An employer's threats to withdraw existing benefits if employees unionize is not speech protected by Section 8(c). However, mere predictions and prophecies are protected. For example, in one case an employer's speeches and handbills during the union's organizational campaign stated its intention to fight the union in every legal way possible and to "deal hard" with the union at arm's length if it were voted in. The employer also warned that employees could be permanently replaced if the union called an economic strike. This language was held to fall within the protection of Section 8(c). The right of free speech guaranteed by the Taft-Hartley Act applies to labor unions as well as employers. However, there is a rule prohibiting either side from making election speeches on company time to massed assemblies of employees within 24 hours before an election.

11. UNION SHOP—MEMBERSHIPS AND FEES

The Wagner Act's strong support of unionization gave unintended bargaining power to unions with respect to an employer's hiring practices. In many bargaining situations, the union became so strong that it successfully insisted on management hiring only union members. In essence, to apply for a prospective job, a person would have to join the union. These situations became known as **closed shops.**

One of the major changes brought about by the Taft-Hartley Act was outlawing of the closed shop. This act still permitted the **union shop.** In a union shop contract, which also is known as a **union security clause,** the employer agrees that after an employee has been hired that employee must join the union as a condition of continued employment. Under the Taft-Hartley Act, such a requirement may not be imposed until the thirtieth day after employment begins.

Through a series of cases, the Supreme Court has clarified the limited mandatory relationship created by the inclusion of the union security clause in a contract. This type of relationship requires that the union members pay reasonable membership fees and dues (see the box, below). In turn, the union can use these fees and dues only for collective bargaining, contract administration, and grievance activities.

One of the sections of the Taft-Hartley Act most distasteful to unions is 14(b), which outlaws the union shop in states that have adopted a right-to-work law. **Right-to-work laws** prohibit agreements requiring membership in a labor organization as a condition of continued employment of a person who was not in the union when hired. Approximately 20 states have right-to-work laws today. Workers in these states who do not belong to a union may not be required to pay repre-

USE OF DUES COLLECTED THROUGH THE UNION SHOP

Fees and dues from "members" required to join the union cannot be used for political purposes. The Supreme Court has clarified the law related to union security clauses. It is not a breach of the union's duty of fair representation if that union negotiates and obtains a union security clause as part of the bargaining agreement. The union does not have to inform a new mandatory member of the limitation of the dues and fees received. The union simply must use the funds for the court-restricted purposes.

Source: *Marquez v. Screen Actors Guild, Inc.,* 119 S. Ct. 292 (1998).

sentation fees to the union that represents the employees. However, such workers are subject to the terms of the collective bargaining agreement, and the union must handle their grievances, if any, with management.

12. SUITS AGAINST UNIONS

Section 301 of the Taft-Hartley Act provides that suits for breach of a contract between an employer and a labor organization can be filed in the federal district courts without regard to the amount in question. A labor organization is responsible for the acts of its agents and may sue or be sued. Any money judgment against it is enforceable only against its assets and not against any individual member. Moreover, individuals cannot be sued for actions such as violating no-strike provisions of a collective bargaining contract.

In addition, members may sue their union and recover the money damages they suffer because of an illegal strike. If a union activity is both an unfair labor practice and a breach of a collective bargaining agreement, the NLRB's authority is not exclusive and does not destroy the jurisdiction of courts under Section 301 of the Taft-Hartley Act.

Many suits against unions are by members alleging a breach of the duty of fair representation. Since workers cannot bargain individually when represented by a union, the union has an implied duty of fair representation to act reasonably, with honesty of purpose, and in good faith. The union must represent all the employees in the bargaining unit, including those who are nonunion, impartially and without hostile discrimination.

The duty of fair representation applies not only to the *negotiation* of a collective bargaining agreement but also to the *administration* of the agreement. Unions must fairly represent employers in disputes with the employer regarding the *interpretation* and *application* of the terms of an existing contract.

An employee may file suit against the union and its representatives for damages resulting from breach of their duty of fair representation in processing his or her grievance against the employer. A union may not process a grievance in an arbitrary, indifferent, or careless manner.

Finally, a union member may sue a local union for failing to enforce the international union's constitution and bylaws. Thus, Section 301 of the Taft-Hartley Act authorizes an employer to sue a union for breach of contract as well as employees to sue to enforce either the union-management collective bargaining agreement or a union contract with a member.

UNFAIR LABOR PRACTICES BY UNIONS AS ENACTED IN THE TAFT-HARTLEY ACT

1. Restraining or coercing an employee to join a union or an employer in selecting representatives to bargain with the union

2. Causing or attempting to cause the employer to discriminate against an employee who is not a union member unless there is a legal union shop agreement in effect

3. Refusing to bargain with the employer if it is the NLRB-designated representative of the employees

4. Striking, picketing, or engaging in secondary boycotts for illegal purposes

5. Charging new members excessive or discriminatory initiation fees when there is a union-shop agreement

6. Causing an employer to pay for work not performed (featherbedding)

13. UNFAIR LABOR PRACTICES BY UNIONS

Perhaps more than with any other provision of the Taft-Hartley Act, Congress attempted to balance the bargaining power in the labor-management relationship by enacting six unfair labor practices by unions. These balance the unfair labor practices by management in the Wagner Act, as discussed in section 8. The preceding box lists the unfair labor practices by unions as passed in 1947.

Three of these illegal practices can be presented in a summary fashion due to the preceding discussions in this chapter or because they have very little impact today. The third unfair labor practice by unions is complementary to the fifth unfair labor practice by management. In essence, Congress requires unions to bargain in good faith as is required of management. The fifth unfair labor practice by unions simply means that unions cannot take advantage of the union-shop agreement by charging unreasonable dues or fees when members and nonmembers are obligated to pay them. Today, the sixth unfair labor practice, involving *featherbedding,* or payment for work not actually performed, is of less importance than when it was enacted in 1947.

The remaining unfair labor practices by unions are presented under the following headings:

- Restraining or coercing an employee into joining a union
- Causing an employer to discriminate against a nonunion member
- Striking or picketing for illegal purposes or engaging in secondary boycotts

Restraining or Coercing an Employee into Joining a Union This unfair labor practice includes misconduct by unions directed toward employees. The law makes it illegal for a union to restrain or coerce employees in the exercise of their rights to bargain collectively, just as it is an unfair labor practice by employers to interfere with the same rights. Employees also are guaranteed the right to *refrain* from union activities unless they are required to join the union by a legal union shop agreement.

Causing an Employer to Discriminate against a Nonunion Member If a legal union shop agreement is in effect, a labor organization may insist that the employer observe its terms. But even when a legal union shop contract is in effect, the law prohibits a union from attempting to cause an employer to discriminate against an employee who has been denied membership or had his or her membership terminated for some reason other than failure to pay the dues and initiation fees uniformly required of all members. And even if an employee is a member, the union may not cause the employer to discriminate against him or her for not following union rules. This prohibition prevents the use of the union shop as a means of intimidating employees who were at odds with union officials over their policies.

Striking or Picketing for Illegal Purposes or Engaging in Secondary Boycotts Jurisdictional strikes are unfair labor practices. A **jurisdictional strike** is used to force an employer to assign work to employees in one craft union rather than another. Since the dispute is between the two unions and not with the employer, the law requires that such disputes be submitted to the NLRB by the unions.

EXAMPLE OF SECONDARY BOYCOTT

An example of illegal secondary activity occurs when a union induces the employees of an employer to strike or engage in a concerted refusal to use, handle, or work on any goods or to perform any service to force the employer to stop doing business with some third person. For example, assume that a supplier (like a bakery) has a workforce that is nonunionized. A customer (i.e., a grocery store) has employees who belong to a union. This union would like to be the bargaining representative for the supplier's employees. It would be an illegal secondary boycott for this union to have its members either strike or picket the grocery store in the hope that the grocery store would discontinue its buying from this bakery. The union must deal directly with the bakery.

It is also an unfair labor practice for a union to threaten or to coerce by picketing, for example, an employer to recognize or bargain with one union if another one has been certified as the representative of its employees.

It is an unfair labor practice for a union to threaten, coerce, or restrain a third person not party to a labor dispute for the purpose of causing that third person to exert pressure on the company involved in the labor dispute. This law requires that strikes and picketing be directed at the employer with which the union actually has a labor dispute. The box above describes how the law protects neutral parties from serious economic injury or even ruin.

14. AMENDMENTS

Congressional hearings in the 1950s uncovered widespread corruption, violence, and lack of democratic procedures in some labor unions. As a result, Congress passed the **Landrum-Griffin Act,** or Labor-Management Reporting and Disclosure Act (LMRDA), in 1959. Its provisions constitute a "bill of rights" for union members and provide for union reform. Also in this act, Congress included some amendments to the unfair labor practices by management and unions.

In essence, in its continuing attempt to balance the bargaining power in the labor-management relationship, Congress added one unfair labor practice by management and two by unions.

Agreeing to Engage in a Secondary Boycott You should recall from your reading in the preceding section that unions cannot engage in secondary boycotts. Technically, nothing in that unfair labor practice, as enacted in the Taft-Hartley Act, prohibited a union and an employer from agreeing to engage in a secondary boycott. The original restriction applied only to the unilateral acts of the union. The Landrum-Griffin Act clarified the concern over secondary boycotts by prohibiting a union-management agreement that would adversely impact a neutral third party.

It is also an unfair labor practice for both the employer involved and the union to enter into a **hot-cargo contract.** A hot-cargo contract is one in which an employer voluntarily agrees with a union that the employees should not be required by their employer to handle or work on goods or materials going to or coming from an employer designated by the union as "unfair." Such goods are said to be hot cargo. These clauses were common in trucking and construction labor contracts. The law thus forbids an employer and a labor organization to make an agreement under which the employer agrees to stop doing business with any other employer.

Picketing When Not Certified In certain cases it is illegal for unions to force an employer to recognize or bargain with the union if it is not currently certified as the duly authorized collective bargaining representative. The purpose is to reinforce the effectiveness of the election procedures employed by the NLRB by outlawing certain tactics used by unions backed by only a minority of the employees of a particular employer. Thus, picketing to force an employer to recognize an uncertified union is an unfair labor practice in the following cases:

1. When the employer has lawfully recognized another union as the collective bargaining representative of its employees
2. When a valid representation election has been conducted by the NLRB within the past 12 months
3. When picketing has been conducted for an unreasonable time, in excess of 30 days, without a petition for a representation election being filed with the NLRB

Including these amendments to the Landrum-Griffin Act, the law on unfair labor practices is summarized in the following box.

---

concept SUMMARY   *Unfair Labor Practices*

By Management

1. Interfering with unionization and concerted activities by employees
2. Dominating a union or contributing to it, financially or otherwise
3. Discriminating in hiring or tenure of employees on the basis of union affiliation
4. Discriminating against employees who seek to enforce their Wagner Act rights
5. Refusing to bargain collectively in good faith
6. Agreeing with a labor organization to engage in a secondary boycott

By Unions

1. Restraining or coercing an employee to join a union
2. Causing an employer to discriminate against a nonunion member
3. Refusing to bargain collectively in good faith
4. Striking, picketing, or engaging in secondary boycotts for illegal purposes
5. Charging excessive or discriminatory fees
6. Causing an employer to pay for work not performed
7. Picketing to force an employer to recognize or bargain with an uncertified union
8. Agreeing with an employer to engage in a secondary boycott

---

KEY TERMS

REVIEW QUESTIONS AND PROBLEMS

Current Trends and Issues

1. *Minimum Wages and Maximum Hours*

    (a)   What federal law establishes the minimum wage and the hours in a work week?

    (b)   What is the minimum wage and what is considered the maximum work week?

    (c)   What is required regarding overtime compensation or time off?

2. *Limitations on Employment at Will*

    Terry was hired as an assistant manager by the Assurance Manufacturing Company. There was no specific time period related to Terry's employment. During Terry's first day at work, the personnel director of Assurance gave Terry a copy of the employee's handbook. In this handbook, Assurance stated that no employee would be terminated without a justifiable explanation. Five months after beginning work at Assurance, Terry was notified that after an additional two weeks there would be no further job for Terry at Assurance. When Terry asked why this termination was occurring, the personnel director told Terry, "Under state law no reason for termination has to be given. In essence, you are an employee only for as long as Assurance desires." What is the best argument Terry can make that the employment-at-will doctrine is not applicable in this situation? Explain.

3. *Workers' Privacy*

    Discuss three examples of how an employer may invade an employee's privacy at the workplace.

4. *Employee Lawsuits*

    (a)   What is meant by the phrase "paper fortress"?

    (b)   How does maintaining a paper fortress aid the employer when the employee claims unfair treatment?

Labor-Management Relationship

5. *Laws before 1935*

    (a)   What is the specific purpose of (1) the Clayton Act, (2) the Railway Labor Act, and (3) the Norris-LaGuardia Act?

    (b)   Why did these laws not increase laborers' bargaining power to the degree that is considered equal to management's bargaining power?

The Wagner Act

6. *National Labor Relations Board*

    Describe the nature and limitations of the NLRB's jurisdiction.

7. *Certification of Unions*

    The NLRB conducted a certification election, and the union won by a vote of 22–20. Management refused to bargain with this union. The reason for this refusal to recognize the union as the employees' bargaining agent was that the union had used "recognition slips" as a means of indicating the employees' support for the union. Several employees testified that they signed these slips to avoid the payment of the initiation fee. Further, at least a few employees indicated that they thought they had to vote for the union since they had signed a recognition slip. Should the NLRB set aside this election of the union? Explain.

8. *Unfair Labor Practices by Management*
   (a)   List the five unfair labor practices created by the Wagner Act.
   (b)   Describe a situation for each of these unfair labor practices.

Taft-Hartley Act

9. *Eighty-Day Cooling-Off Period*
   (a)   Under what circumstances is the president authorized to order parties in a labor dispute back to work for 80 days?
   (b)   Describe the procedures that must be followed to invoke this cooling-off period.

10. *Free Speech*

The personnel director of your company has been asked to talk with the employees about the benefits and detriments of voting for or against the union in an upcoming certification election. What should this director keep in mind about the Free Speech Clause in the Taft-Hartley Act? Explain.

11. *Union Shop—Memberships and Fees*

Pat lives in a state that has enacted a right-to-work law. The company that employs her has recognized the United Clerical Workers (UCW) as the bargaining representative of its workers. The union has sought to collect union dues or their equivalent from Pat. Is she required to pay them? Why or why not?

12. *Suits against Unions*

Ed is discharged for allegedly stealing property from his employer. He asks his union to have him reinstated because his discharge violates the collective bargaining agreement in force. However, the union does not investigate the incident until it is too late to file a request for arbitration under the collective bargaining agreement. Assuming that Ed is innocent of the charges, does he have any rights against the union? Explain.

13. *Unfair Labor Practices by Unions*
   (a)   List the six unfair labor practices created by the Taft-Hartley Act.
   (b)   Describe a situation for each of these unfair labor practices.

14. *Amendments*
   (a)   What were two basic purposes for Congress passing the Landrum-Griffin Act?
   (b)   What are the two additional unfair labor practices added by this law?

STATUTORY IDENTIFICATION

Identify the federal statute that accomplished each of the following:

1. Exempted union activity from the antitrust laws
2. Created the National Labor Relations Board (NLRB)
3. Allowed states to enact right-to-work laws
4. Outlawed certain conduct by management as unfair to labor (unfair labor practices)
5. Governed collective bargaining for railroads and airlines
6. Prohibited federal courts from enjoining lawful union activities, including picketing and strikes

7. Established a bill of rights for union members
8. Provided for an 80-day cooling-off period in strikes that imperil national health or safety
9. Outlawed yellow-dog contracts
10. Created the Federal Mediation and Conciliation Service

BUSINESS DISCUSSION

For years, your small electronics company has given all its employees one week's pay and a turkey each Christmas. But now a recession is eroding profitability and the company is operating at a significant loss, so you consider canceling the Christmas presents for this year. The employees have just voted for union representation, and the extra pay and turkeys are not mentioned in the collective bargaining agreement.

Is a Christmas gift still purely a management decision?

Are you in trouble if you cancel the turkeys?

What is the union's role in the decision?

chapter

15

DISCRIMINATION IN EMPLOYMENT

Delivery Quik, Inc., delivers packages to small retail stores from a central distribution point in a major metropolitan area. Drivers both load and unload their packages, some of which weigh close to 100 pounds. Although equipment helps the drivers in their tasks, there is still considerable lifting necessary. Delivery Quik has a policy that drivers must stand at least 6 feet tall and weigh no less than 180 pounds. All drivers must retire at age 45 and have at least a high school education.

> Does the height, weight, age, and education policy discriminate illegally?
>
> How would you change the policy?
>
> If your customers prefer male drivers, does their preference mean that the company can hire only males as drivers?

"Trouble Quik" illustrates several discrimination issues in today's employment environment. First, it shows that even policies that apply neutrally to everyone on height and weight may discriminate against job applicants on the basis of sex, race, or national origin. Second, it emphasizes why a hiring policy should carefully target specific requirements like strength and job skills, rather than general qualities like age, education, height, and weight. Last, it suggests that customer preference for the race, sex, color, religion, national origin, age, or lack of disability of employees cannot form the basis for a legal hiring policy. As you read this chapter, look for more complete answers for the questions in "Trouble Quik."

Laws prohibiting discrimination exist at both the federal and state levels. In the opening sections of the chapter we focus on antidiscrimination laws at the federal level. The Civil Rights Act of 1964 (including its 1991 amendments) is the principal such law. It prohibits certain discrimination based on race, sex, color, religion, and national origin. Other antidiscrimination laws covered are the Equal Pay Act, the Civil Rights Act of 1866 (called Section 1981), the Age Discrimination in Employment Act, and the Americans with Disabilities Act. The chapter concludes with a discussion of trends in employment discrimination litigation and a section on employment discrimination, corporate governance, and the broad sense of property.

THE CIVIL RIGHTS ACT OF 1964

"That all men are created equal" was one of the "self-evident" truths recognized by the Founding Fathers in the Declaration of Independence. However, equality among all our citizens clearly has been an ideal rather than a fact. The Constitution itself recognizes slavery by saying that slaves should count as "three fifths of all other Persons" for determining population in House of Representatives elections. And of course, that all *men* are created equal says nothing about women, who did not even get a constitutionally guaranteed right to vote until 1920.

Nowhere have effects of inequality and discrimination been felt more acutely than in the area of job opportunity. Historically, common law permitted employers to hire and fire virtually at will, unless restrained by contract or statute. Under this system, white males came to dominate the job market in their ability to gain employment and their salaries and wages.

Although the Civil Rights Act of 1866 contains a provision that plaintiffs now widely use in employment discrimination cases, such use is recent. Passage of labor law in the 1920s and 1930s marks the first significant federal limitation on the relatively unrestricted right of employers to hire and fire. Then, in connection with the war effort, President Franklin D. Roosevelt issued executive orders in 1941 and 1943 requiring a clause prohibiting racial discrimination in all federal contracts with private contractors. Subsequent executive orders in the 1950s established committees to investigate complaints of racial discrimination against such contractors. Affirmative action requirements on federal contracts followed from executive orders of the 1960s.

The most important statute eliminating discriminatory employment practices, however, is the federal Civil Rights Act of 1964, as amended by the Equal Employment Opportunity Act of 1972 and the Civil Rights Act of 1991.

1. GENERAL PROVISIONS

The provisions of Title VII of the Civil Rights Act of 1964 apply to employers with 15 or more employees. They also cover labor unions and certain others (see box, below). The major purpose of these laws is to eliminate job discrimination based on race, color, religion, sex, or national origin. Discrimination for any of these reasons is a violation of the law, except that employers, employment agencies, and labor unions can discriminate on the basis of religion, sex, or national origin where these are **bona fide occupational qualifications (BFOQs)** reasonably necessary to normal business operations. Title VII also permits discrimination if it results unintentionally from a seniority or merit system.

EMPLOYERS AND OTHERS COVERED BY TITLE VII	Employment agencies
	State and local governments
Private employers with 15 or more employees	Public and private educational institutions
Labor unions with 15 or more members	Federal government (in most instances)

The types of employer action in which discrimination is prohibited include:

- Discharge
- Refusal to hire
- Compensation
- Terms, conditions, or privileges of employment

Employment *agencies* are prohibited from either *failing to refer* or from *actually referring* an individual for employment on the basis of race, color, religion, sex, or national origin. This prohibition differs from the law binding *employers,* where it is unlawful only to fail or refuse to hire on discriminatory grounds—the affirmative act of hiring for a discriminatory reason is apparently not illegal. For example, assume that a contractor with a government contract seeks a qualified African American engineer and requests an employment agency to refer one. The agency complies with the request. Unless a white applicant was discriminated against, the employer likely did not break the law; but the employment agency, by referring on the basis of color, unquestionably *did* violate Title VII.

Employers, unions, and employment agencies are prohibited from discriminating against an employee, applicant, or union member because he or she has made a charge, testified, or participated in an investigation or hearing under the act or otherwise opposed any unlawful practice.

Note that regarding general hiring, referrals, advertising, and admissions to training or apprenticeship programs, Title VII allows discrimination only on the basis of religion, sex, or national origin and only where these considerations are bona fide occupational qualifications. For example, it is legal for a Baptist church to refuse to engage a Lutheran minister. EEOC guidelines on sex discrimination consider sex to be a bona fide occupational qualification, for example, where it is necessary for authenticity or genuineness in hiring an actor or actress. The omission of *race* and *color* from this exception must mean that Congress does not feel these two factors are ever bona fide occupational qualifications.

Additional exemptions exist with respect to laws creating preferential treatment for veterans and hiring based on professionally developed ability tests that are not designed or intended to be used to discriminate. Such tests must bear a relationship to the job for which they are administered, however.

Recent Awards or Settlements in Discrimination Cases

Defendant	Plaintiffs	Award or Settlement
California Public Employees Retirement System	Older employees	$250 million
Dial Corp.	Females	$10 million
Lucky Stores, Inc.	Females	$107 million
Mitsubishi Motors	Females	$34 million
Northwest Airlines	Females	$52.5 million
Publix Super Markets	Females	$81.5 million
Shoney's, Inc.	African Americans	$132.5 million
Texaco, Inc.	African Americans	$176 million

1994–2000 Median Award in Employment Discrimination	
Cases by Category	
Category	*Award*
Age	$268,926
Disability	175,001
Race	120,951
Sex	100,000
Discrimination, overall	150,000

Source: Jury Verdict Research.

2. ENFORCEMENT PROCEDURES

The Civil Rights Act of 1964 created the Equal Employment Opportunity Commission (EEOC). This agency has the primary responsibility of enforcing the provisions of the act. The EEOC is composed of five members, not more than three of whom may be members of the same political party. They are appointed by the president, with the advice and consent of the Senate, and serve a five-year term. In the course of its investigations, the EEOC has broad authority to hold hearings, obtain evidence, and subpoena and examine witnesses under oath.

Under the Equal Employment Opportunity Act of 1972, the EEOC can file a civil suit in federal district court and represent a person charging a violation of the act. However, it must first exhaust efforts to settle the claim. Remedies that may be obtained in such an action include reinstatement with back pay for the victim of an illegal discrimination and injunctions against future violations of the act by the defendant. Since discrimination complaints can take years to litigate and may involve large employee classes, the size of awards and settlements is sometimes many millions of dollars. (See "Recent Awards.") Although the median award in employment discrimination cases is much less, plaintiffs won 67 percent of jury cases in 2000, up from 50 percent in 1994.

In 1991 Congress amended the Civil Rights Act to allow the recovery of compensatory and punitive damages of up to $300,000 per person. These damages are in addition to other remedies such as job reinstatement and back pay. Compensatory damages include damages for the pain and suffering of discrimination. Punitive damages are appropriate whenever discrimination occurs with "malice or with reckless or callous indifference to the federally protected rights of others." Very important, the 1991 amendments allow compensatory and punitive damages *only* when employers are guilty of *intentional* discrimination.

In enacting Title VII of the Civil Rights Act of 1964, Congress made it clear that it did not intend to preempt states' fair employment laws. Where state agencies begin discrimination proceedings, the EEOC must wait 60 days before it starts action. Furthermore, if a state law provides relief to a discrimination charge, the EEOC must notify the appropriate state officials and wait 60 days before continuing action.

An employee must file charges of illegal discrimination with the EEOC within 180 days after the unlawful practice occurred. If the employee first filed in a timely fashion with a state fair employment practices commission, the law extends the time for filing with the EEOC to 300 days. In 2002, employees and job applicants filed 84,442 complaints with the EEOC.

To win a Title VII civil action, a plaintiff must initially show that actions taken by the employer were likely based on an illegally discriminatory basis, such as race. Generally, the plaintiff must prove either disparate (unequal) treatment or disparate impact. In proving **disparate treatment,** the plaintiff must convince the court that the employer *intentionally* discriminated against the plaintiff. If discrimination is a motivating factor, an employer's practice is illegal even though other factors (such as customer preference) also contributed.

In a **disparate impact** case the plaintiff must prove that the employer's policies had a discriminatory effect on a group protected by Title VII. The employer can defeat the plaintiff's claim by proving the **business necessity defense.** This defense requires that the employer prove that the policies used are job related and based on business necessity. However, the plaintiff can still establish a violation by showing that other policies would serve the legitimate interests of business necessity without having undesirable discriminatory effects.

Before the 1991 Civil Rights Act amendments, employees or the EEOC sometimes claimed that proving racial or gender statistical imbalances in a workforce established illegal discrimination. They claimed that such imbalances showed illegal discrimination, much like disparate impact discrimination, even in the absence of proof of an employer's discriminatory intent. However, the 1991 amendments state that the showing of a statistically imbalanced workforce is not enough *in itself* to establish a violation of Title VII.

3. DISCRIMINATION ON THE BASIS OF RACE OR COLOR

The integration of African Americans into the mainstream of American society is the primary objective of the Civil Rights Act of 1964. Title VII, which deals with employment practices, is the key legal regulation for achieving this goal. Without equal employment opportunities, African Americans can hardly enjoy other guaranteed rights, such as access to public accommodations.

Title VII prohibits discriminatory employment practices based on race or color that involve *recruiting, hiring,* and *promotion* of employees. Of course, intentional discrimination in these matters is illegal, but, as previously stated, policies with disparate impact are also forbidden. Such discrimination arises from an employer's policies or practices that apply equally to everyone but that discriminate in greater proportion against minorities and have no relation to job qualification. The next box gives examples of disparate impact on race. Often at issue in disparate impact cases is whether a discriminatory policy or practice relates to job qualification. Courts require proof, not mere assertion, of job relatedness before upholding an employer's discriminatory personnel test or other practice.

The law also prohibits discrimination in *employment conditions* and *benefits.* EEOC decisions have found such practices as the following to be violations:

- Permitting racial insults in the work situation
- Maintaining all-white or all-black crews for no demonstrable reasons
- Providing better housing for whites than blacks
- Granting higher average Christmas bonuses to whites than blacks for reasons that were not persuasive to the Commission

EXAMPLES OF DISPARATE IMPACT ON RACE

Denying employment to unwed mothers when minorities have a higher rate of illegitimate births than whites

Refusing to hire people because of poor credit rating when minorities are disproportionately affected

Refusing to hire people with arrest records when minorities have higher arrest rates than whites

Giving hiring priority to relatives of present employees when minorities are underrepresented in the workforce

Using discriminatory personnel tests that have no substantial relation to job qualification

It is important to appreciate that Title VII prohibits employment discrimination against members of all races. In one recent case, a federal court jury awarded a white senior air traffic official $500,000 in damages against the Federal Aviation Administration. The official charged the FAA had demoted him and replaced him with an African American following complaints that blacks were underrepresented in senior management levels. Note that this case did not involve affirmative action (see section 10).

4. DISCRIMINATION ON THE BASIS OF NATIONAL ORIGIN

Title VII's prohibition against national origin discrimination protects various ethnic groups in the workplace. In a recent case, the court ruled that Title VII had been violated when a bakery employee of Iranian descent was called "Ayatollah" in the workplace by the assistant manager and other employees. After he complained, he was fired.

Discrimination concerning the speaking of a native language frequently causes national-origin lawsuits under Title VII. For instance, courts have ruled illegal an employer's rule against speaking Spanish during work hours when the employer could not show a business need to understand all conversations between Hispanic employees. On the other hand, some courts have held that if jobs require contact with the public, a requirement that employees speak some English *may* be a bona fide occupational qualification.

Direct foreign investment in the United States has doubled and redoubled in recent years. This increasing investment has presented some unusual issues of employment discrimination law. For instance, many commercial treaties with foreign countries give foreign companies operating in the United States the right to hire executive-level employees "of their choice." Does this mean that foreign companies in the United States can discriminate as to their managerial employees on a basis forbidden under Title VII? In 1982, the Supreme Court partially resolved this issue by ruling that the civil rights laws applied to a Japanese company that did business through a subsidiary incorporated in this country.

5. DISCRIMINATION ON THE BASIS OF RELIGION

Note that religious corporations, associations, or societies can discriminate in all their employment practices on the basis of religion, but not on the basis of race, color, sex, or national origin. Other employers cannot discriminate on the basis of religion in employment practices, and they must make **reasonable accommodation** to the religious needs of their employees if it does not result in undue hardship to them.

In one case the Supreme Court let stand a lower court ruling that employees cannot be required to pay union dues if they have religious objections to unions. The case determined that a union violated Title VII by forcing a company to fire a Seventh Day Adventist who did not comply with a collective bargaining agreement term that all employees must pay union dues. The union argued unsuccessfully that it had made reasonable accommodation to the worker's religious beliefs by offering to give any dues paid by him to charity. However, in another case the Supreme Court ruled that a company rightfully fired an employee who refused to work on Saturdays due to religious belief. The Court said that the company did not have to burden other employees by making them work Saturdays.

A growing source of religious discrimination lawsuits concerns employees who for religious reasons refuse to perform some task required by the employer. For example, in one case a vegetarian bus driver refused to distribute hamburger coupons on his bus, asserting religious beliefs. When his employer fired him, he sued. The parties settled the case for $50,000. Note that even if an employer wins such a lawsuit, it can cost the employer $100,000 or more to defend itself. Since 1990, Title VII complaints filed annually with the EEOC on the basis of religious discrimination have more than doubled. Between 2001 and 2002 alone, EEOC religious discrimination filings rose 21 percent.

Since the 9/11 bombings, religious discrimination against Muslim employees has risen steeply. In 2003 the EEOC settled a complaint by four Muslim machine operators against Stockton Steel of California for $1.1 million. The four operators claimed they were given the worst jobs, ridiculed during their prayers, and called names like "camel jockey" and "raghead."

6. DISCRIMINATION ON THE BASIS OF SEX

Historically, states have enacted many laws designed supposedly to protect women. For example, many states by statute have prohibited the employment of women in certain occupations such as those that require lifting heavy objects. Others have barred women from working during the night or more than a given number of hours per week or day. A federal district court held that a California state law that required rest periods for women only was in violation of Title VII. Some statutes prohibit employing women for a specified time after childbirth. Under EEOC guidelines, such statutes are not a defense to a charge of illegal sex discrimination and do not provide an employer with a bona fide occupational qualification in hiring standards. Other EEOC guidelines forbid employers:

- To classify jobs as male or female
- To advertise in help-wanted columns that are designated male or female, unless sex is a bona fide job qualification

Similarly, employers may not have separate male and female seniority lists.

The next box gives examples of prohibited acts of sex discrimination under Title VII.

Whether sex is a bona fide occupational qualification (and discrimination is thus legal) has been raised in several cases. The courts have tended to consider this exception narrowly. In the following instances involving hiring policy, *no* bona fide occupational qualification was found to exist:

- A rule requiring airline stewardesses, but not stewards, to be single
- A policy of hiring only females as flight cabin attendants

Examples of Illegal Sex Discrimination	
Type of Business	*Violation*
Radio station	Refusing to hire a female newscaster because "news coming from a woman sounds like gossip"
Bank	Allowing males but not females to smoke at their desks
Utility company	Allowing women to retire at age 50 but requiring men to wait until age 55
International business	Failing to promote women to overseas positions because foreign clients were reluctant to do business with women
Hospital	Firing a pregnant X-ray technician for health reasons instead of giving her a leave of absence
Manufacturing firm	Failing to stop repeated, offensive sexual flirtations by some of its employees

- A rule against hiring females with preschool-age children, but not against hiring males with such children
- A telephone company policy against hiring females as switchers because of the alleged heavy lifting involved on the job

In the telephone company case, the court held that for a bona fide occupational qualification to exist, there must be "reasonable cause to believe, that is, a factual basis for believing, that all or substantially all women would be unable to perform safely and efficiently the duties of the job involved." The Supreme Court has indicated that for such a qualification to exist, sex must be provably relevant to job performance.

Sexual Harassment A common type of illegal sex discrimination in the workplace is **sexual harassment.** The typical sexual harassment case involves a plaintiff who has been promised benefits or threatened with loss if she or he does not give sexual favors to an employment supervisor. Such a case is also called a "quid pro quo" (this for that) case. Under Title VII and agency law, an employer is liable for this sex discrimination.

Another type of sexual harassment is the **hostile work environment,** one in which coworkers make offensive sexual comments or propositions, engage in suggestive touching, show nude pictures, or draw sexual graffiti. In 1986 the Supreme Court in *Meritor Savings Bank v. Vinson* ruled that Title VII prohibits "an offensive or hostile working environment," even when no economic loss occurs. By so ruling, the Court acknowledged that the work environment itself is a condition of employment covered by Title VII. Now you should understand why it is so important for the employer in The Business Decision at the beginning of this chapter to act promptly to correct the hostile environment.

In 1993 the Supreme Court again addressed the hostile work environment issue. Specifically, the Court was asked to determine whether, before a person could sue under Title VII, a hostile work environment had "to seriously affect [his or her] psychological well-being" or "cause injury." In *Harris v. Forklift Systems, Inc.*, the Court ruled that illegal sexual harassment goes beyond that which causes "injury." It includes any harassment reasonably perceived as "hostile and abusive."

In 1998 the Supreme Court confronted the issue of whether Title VII covered harassment of an employee by other employees of the same sex as seen in the following case.

ONCALE V. SUNDOWNER OFFSHORE SERVICES, INC.

118 S. Ct. 998 (1998)

SCALIA, J.: In late October 1991, Joseph Oncale was working for respondent Sundowner Offshore Services on a Chevron U.S.A., Inc., oil platform in the Gulf of Mexico. He was employed as a roustabout on an eight-man crew which included respondents John Lyons, Danny Pippen, and Brandon Johnson. Lyons, the crane operator, and Pippen, the driller, had supervisory authority. On several occasions, Oncale was forcibly subjected to sex-related, humiliating actions against him by Lyons, Pippen and Johnson in the presence of the rest of the crew. Pippen and Lyons also physically assaulted Oncale in a sexual manner, and Lyons threatened him with rape.

Oncale's complaints to supervisory personnel produced no remedial action; in fact, the company's Safety Compliance Clerk, Valent Hohen, told Oncale that Lyons and Pippen "picked [on] him all the time too," and called him a name suggesting homosexuality. Oncale eventually quit—asking that his pink slip reflect that he "voluntarily left due to sexual harassment and verbal abuse." When asked at his deposition why he left Sundowner, Oncale stated "I felt that if I didn't leave my job, that I would be raped or forced to have sex."

Title VII of the Civil Rights Act of 1964 provides, in relevant part, that "it shall be an unlawful employment practice for an employer . . . to discriminate against any individual with respect to his compensation, terms, conditions, or privileges of employment, because of such individual's race, color, religion, sex, or national origin." We have held that this not only covers "terms" and "conditions" in the narrow contractual sense, but "evinces a congressional intent to strike at the entire spectrum of disparate treatment of men and women in employment."

Title VII's prohibition of discrimination "because of . . . sex" protects men as well as women, and in the related context of racial discrimination in the workplace we have rejected any conclusive presumption that an employer will not discriminate against members of his own race. If our precedents leave any doubt on the question, we hold today that nothing in Title VII necessarily bars a claim of discrimination "because of . . . sex" merely because the plaintiff and the defendant (or the person charged with acting on behalf of the defendant) are of the same sex.

Courts have had little trouble with that principle in cases where an employee claims to have been passed over for a job or promotion. But when the issue arises in the context of a "hostile environment" sexual harassment claim, the state and federal courts have taken a bewildering variety of stances. Some, like the Fifth Circuit in this case, have held that same-sex sexual harassment claims are never cognizable under Title VII. Other decisions say that such claims are actionable only if the plaintiff can prove that the harasser is homosexual (and thus presumably motivated by sexual desire). Still others suggest that workplace harassment that is sexual in content is always actionable, regardless of the harasser's sex, sexual orientation, or motivation.

Courts and juries have found the inference of discrimination easy to draw in most male–female sexual harassment situations, because the challenged conduct typically involves explicit or implicit proposals of sexual activity; it is reasonable to assume those proposals would not have been made to someone of the same sex. The same chain of inference would be available to a plaintiff alleging same-sex

[CONTINUED]

harassment, if there were credible evidence that the harasser was homosexual. But harassing conduct need not be motivated by sexual desire to support an inference of discrimination on the basis of sex. A trier of fact might reasonably find such discrimination, for example, if a female victim is harassed in such sex-specific and derogatory terms by another woman as to make it clear that the harasser is motivated by general hostility to the presence of women in the workplace. A same-sex harassment plaintiff may also, of course, offer direct comparative evidence about how the alleged harasser treated members of both sexes in a mixed-sex workplace. Whatever evidentiary route the plaintiff chooses to follow, he or she must always prove that the conduct at issue was not merely tinged with offensive sexual connotations, but actually constituted "discrimination . . . because of . . . sex."

And there is another requirement that prevents Title VII from expanding into a general civility code: As we emphasized in *Meritor* and *Harris,* the statute does not reach genuine but innocuous differences in the ways men and women routinely interact with members of the same sex and of the opposite sex. The prohibition of harassment on the basis of sex requires neither asexuality nor androgyny in the workplace; it forbids only behavior so objectively offensive as to alter the "conditions" of the victim's employment. "Conduct that is not severe or pervasive enough to create an objectively hostile or abusive work environment—an environment that a reasonable person would find hostile or abusive—is beyond Title VII's purview." We have always regarded that requirement as crucial, and as sufficient to ensure that courts and juries do not mistake ordinary socializing in the workplace—such as male-on-male horseplay or intersexual flirtation—for discriminatory "conditions of employment."

We have emphasized, moreover, that the objective severity of harassment should be judged from the perspective of a reasonable person in the plaintiff's position, considering "all the circumstances." In same-sex (as in all) harassment cases, that inquiry requires careful consideration of the social context in which particular behavior occurs and is experienced by its target. A professional football player's working environment is not severely or pervasively abusive, for example, if the coach smacks him on the buttocks as he heads onto the field—even if the same behavior would reasonably be experienced as abusive by the coach's secretary (male or female) back at the office. The real social impact of workplace behavior often depends on a constellation of surrounding circumstances, expectations, and relationships which are not fully captured by a simple recitation of the words used or the physical acts performed. Common sense, and an appropriate sensitivity to social context, will enable courts and juries to distinguish between simple teasing or roughhousing among members of the same sex, and conduct which a reasonable person in the plaintiff's position would find severely hostile or abusive.

Because we conclude that sex discrimination consisting of same-sex sexual harassment is actionable under Title VII, the judgment of the Court of Appeals for the Fifth Circuit is reversed, and the case is remanded for further proceedings consistent with this opinion.

Reversed and remanded.

CASE QUESTIONS

1. Before the decision in this case, what had the lower courts decided about whether same-sex harassment could violate Title VII?

2. Did the Court determine that the harassment of Oncale violated Title VII? Explain.

3. Does flirting violate Title VII? Explain.

Is an employer always liable when fellow employees create a hostile environment based on gender? The answer is no. Courts have ruled that an employer is liable to a plaintiff employee for a hostile working environment created by fellow employees only when the employer knows of the problem and fails to take prompt and reasonable steps to correct it, such as by moving the harassers away from the plaintiff employee.

What is the precise legal standard under which an employer can defend itself from a hostile environment claim? In *Faragher v. City of Boca Raton,* 524 U.S. 775 (1998), the Supreme Court decided a case involving hostile environment discrimination by an employee's supervisor. The Court stated that an employer was liable under Title VII for a supervisor's actions. However, the employer can defend itself by proving "(a) that the employer exercised reasonable care to prevent and correct promptly any sexually harassing behavior, and (b) that the plaintiff employee unreasonably failed to take advantage of any preventive or corrective opportunities provided by the employer or to avoid harm otherwise."

Recently, in *National Railroad Passenger Corporation v. Morgan,* 122 S. Ct. 2061 (2002), the Supreme Court ruled that a hostile, harassing environment was a single employment practice. This decision is important because Title VII says that an employer is liable for discriminatory practices only if an employee files a complaint concerning them with the EEOC within 180 days of their happening (within 300 days if the employee has first filed with a state fair employment practices commission). Employers are liable for acts that occurred before 180 days of EEOC filing if they are part of a single hostile environment that continued within the 180-day period.

Pregnancy Discrimination Act The Pregnancy Discrimination Act amended the Civil Rights Act in 1978. Under it, employers can no longer discriminate against women workers who become pregnant or give birth. Thus, employers with health or disability plans must cover pregnancy, childbirth, and related medical conditions in the same manner as other conditions are covered. The law covers unmarried as well as married pregnant women. It also states that an employer cannot force a pregnant woman to stop working until her baby is born, provided she is still capable of performing her duties properly. And the employer cannot specify how long a leave of absence must be taken after childbirth. Coverage for abortion is not required by the statute unless an employee carries to term and her life is endangered or she develops medical complications because of an abortion. If a woman undergoes an abortion, though, all other benefits provided for employees, such as sick leave, must be provided to her.

Note that sex discrimination applies to discrimination against men as well as women. For example, under the Pregnancy Discrimination Act the Supreme Court ruled unlawful an employer's health insurance plan that covered the pregnancies of female employees but did not cover the pregnancies of male employees' wives.

Equal Pay Act Historically, employers have paid female employees less than males, even when they held the same jobs. However, females also tended to fill lower-paying job categories, a trend that continues today. A look at some of the figures regarding male-female employment and pay will be illuminating (see next box).

U.S. GENDER EMPLOYMENT FIGURES
FOR 2002

Men outnumber women in workforce 53 to 47%

Women working full time earn 77.5% of what men do. In 1993 the figure was 77.1%.

Women fill 46% of management positions, up from around 33% in 1983.

Almost 16% of full-time working men earn at least $75,000 a year; 6% of full-time women do.

20% of men working full time earn between $50,000 and $75,000; 12% of full-time women do.

In Spain, Denmark, and Australia, women earn roughly 90% of what men do.

Source: Bureau of Labor Statistics, Census Bureau.

Federal legislation prohibits sex discrimination in employment compensation under both Title VII and the Equal Pay Act of 1963. Administered by the EEOC, the Equal Pay Act prohibits an employer from discriminating on the basis of sex in the payment of wages for equal work performed. For jobs to be equal, they must require "equal skill, effort, and responsibility" and must be performed "under similar working conditions." Discrimination is allowed if it arises from a seniority system, a merit system, a piecework production system, or any factor other than sex.

The focus of Equal Pay Act cases is whether the male and female jobs being compared involve "equal" work. Courts have recognized that *equal* does not mean *identical;* it means *substantially* equal. Thus, courts have ruled "equal" the work of male barbers and female beauticians and of male tailors and female seamstresses. Differences in male and female job descriptions will not totally protect employers against charges of equal-pay infractions. The courts have held that "substantially equal" work done on different machines would require the employer to compensate male and female employees equally.

In 1983, the Supreme Court ruled that discriminatory male and female pay differences can also be illegal under Title VII. In *County of Washington v. Gunther,* the Court decided that plaintiffs can use evidence of such pay differences to help prove intentional sex discrimination, even when the work performed is not substantially equal. Relying on the *Gunther* case, at least one lower court has held that women must be paid equally with men who perform comparable work. A federal district court ruled that the state of Washington discriminated against secretaries (mostly women) by paying them less than maintenance and other personnel (mostly men). However, the **comparable worth** theory is highly controversial, and other courts have not agreed with the theory.

Sexual Orientation Discrimination The courts have not interpreted Title VII to prohibit discrimination against employees based on their sexual orientation, or whether they are gay, lesbian, bisexual, or heterosexual. Instead, the courts have defined the word *sex* in Title VII to refer only to gender, to whether someone is female or male. A quarter of the states, however, and numerous cities do forbid discrimination based on sexual orientation, and Congress could amend Title VII to protect employees from such discrimination. Already, thousands of companies ranging from American Express, Coca-Cola, and Chase Manhattan Bank to Ford, General Motors, and Daimler Chrysler, have begun offering domestic partner benefits to all employees without regard to sexual orientation, which illustrates the decline of one type of gender-orientation discrimination concerning terms of employment. See the box "Transgender Discrimination."

TRANSGENDER DISCRIMINATION

Increasingly, antidiscrimination laws also protect employees following transgender medical procedures, that is, when males have become females, or vice versa. Several states, including Minnesota, New Mexico, and Rhode Island, prohibit transgender discrimination. Dozens of cities, like New York, Boston, and Philadelphia protect transgenders from workplace discrimination. Internationally, Great Britain and Germany offer the same protection.

EMPLOYMENT PRACTICES THAT MAY BE CHALLENGED

In studying the Civil Rights Act, it is useful to consider several specific employment practices that employees or job applicants may challenge as discriminatory. These practices include:

- Setting testing and educational requirements
- Having height and weight requirements for physical labor
- Maintaining appearance requirements
- Practicing affirmative action
- Using seniority systems

The following sections take a close look at these practices.

7. QUESTIONNAIRES, INTERVIEWS, TESTING, AND EDUCATIONAL REQUIREMENTS

Employers have used a number of tools to help them find the right person for the right job. Among these tools are questionnaires, interviews, references, minimum educational requirements (such as a high school diploma), and personnel tests. However, employers must be extremely careful not to use tools that illegally discriminate. For example, Rent-A-Center, a Dallas-based appliance-rental company, agreed to pay more than $2 million in damages to more than 1,200 job applicants and employees who were asked questions about their sex lives and religious views in a 500-item true-false questionnaire. Plaintiffs claimed the questionnaire was used to discriminate illegally on the basis of gender and religion and that it violated their privacy.

Interviews can also discriminate illegally, and personnel interviewers must be well trained. One study indicated that interviewers can be biased even if they are not aware of it. The study showed that the interviewers tended to select males over females for sales positions because the interviewers *subconsciously* related sales success with height, and males are on the average taller than females. References may not be so reliable, either. A previous employer's letter may reflect personal biases against an applicant that were not related to job performance.

At the other extreme, an employer may give a poor employee a top recommendation because of sympathy or fear of a lawsuit in case the letter is somehow obtained by the employee. Advocates of personnel tests in the selection process feel they are very valuable in weeding out the wrong persons for a job and picking the right ones. They believe reliance on test results eliminates biases that interviewers or former employers who give references may have.

Tests, however, can have a *disparate impact* on job applicants, discriminating on the basis of race, sex, color, religion, or national origin. Setting educational standards such as requiring a high school diploma for employment can also have a disparate impact. To avoid discrimination challenges, employers must make sure that all testing and educational requirements are job related and necessary for the business.

In the past, some employers have "race normed" employment tests. *Race norming* is the practice of setting two different cutoff test scores for employment based on race or one of the other Title VII categories. For example, on a race-normed test, the minimum score for employment of white job applicants might be set at 75 out of 100. For minority applicants, the minimum score might be set at 65. *The Civil Rights Act amendments of 1991 specifically prohibit the race norming of employment tests.*

8. HEIGHT AND WEIGHT REQUIREMENTS

Minimum or maximum height or weight job requirements apply equally to all job applicants, but if they have the effect of screening out applicants on the basis of race, national origin, or sex, the employer must demonstrate that such requirements are validly related to the ability to perform the work in question. For example, maximum size standards would be permissible, even if they favored women over men, if the available work space were too small to permit large persons to perform the duties of the job properly. Most size requirements have dictated minimum heights or weights, often based on a stereotyped assumption that a certain amount of strength that smaller persons might not have probably was necessary for the work. In one case, a 5-foot, 5-inch, 130-pound Hispanic won a suit against a police department on the basis that the department's 5-foot, 8-inch minimum height requirement discriminated against Hispanics, who often are shorter than that standard. He was later hired when he passed the department's physical agility examination, which included dragging a 150-pound body 75 feet and scaling a 6-foot wall.

9. APPEARANCE REQUIREMENTS

Employers often have set grooming standards for their employees. Those regulating hair length of males or prohibiting beards or mustaches have been among the most common. Undoubtedly, motivation for these rules stems from the feeling of the employer that the image it projects to the public through its employees will be adversely affected if their appearance is not "proper." It is unclear whether appearance requirements are legal or illegal, since there have been rulings both ways. However, in 2000 the EEOC filed a lawsuit in Atlanta against FedEx Corporation for firing a bearded delivery driver who refused to shave in violation of a company policy that permitted beards only when medically necessary. The driver's Islamic beliefs required males to wear beards, and the lawsuit alleged that FedEx's policy constituted religious discrimination.

In another case, a black employee argued that he was wrongfully fired for breaking a company rule prohibiting beards. Dermatologists testified that the plaintiff had a condition called "razor bumps" (which occurs when the tightly curled facial hairs of black men become ingrown from shaving) and that the only known cure was for him not to shave. Although the federal appeals court found that the plaintiff was prejudiced by the employer's regulation, it held in favor of the company, ruling that its *slight racial impact* was justified by the *business necessity* it served. A conflicting opinion in still another case upheld an employee's right to wear a beard because of razor bumps.

10. AFFIRMATIVE ACTION PROGRAMS AND REVERSE DISCRIMINATION

Since the 1940s, a series of presidential executive orders have promoted nondiscrimination and **affirmative action** by employers who contract with the federal government. The authority for these orders rests with the president's executive power to control the granting of federal contracts. As a condition to obtaining such contracts, employers must agree contractually to take affirmative action to avoid unlawful discrimination in recruitment, employment, promotion, training, rate of compensation, and layoff of workers.

The affirmative action requirement means that federally contracting employers must actively recruit members of minority groups being underused in the workforce. That is, employers must hire members of these groups when there are fewer minority workers in a given job category than one could reasonably expect, considering their availability. In many instances, employers must develop written affirmative action plans and set goals and timetables for bringing minority (or female) workforces up to their percentages in the available labor pool.

The Labor Department administers executive orders through its Office of Federal Contract Compliance Programs (OFCCP). The OFCCP can terminate federal contracts with employers who do not comply with its guidelines and can make them ineligible for any future federal business. For instance, it required Uniroyal, Inc., to give its female employees an estimated $18 million in back pay to compensate for past employment discrimination. The alternative was elimination of $36 million of existing federal contracts and ineligibility for future federal business.

The Labor Department has eased OFCCP regulations on 75 percent of the firms that do business with the federal government. Firms with fewer than 250 employees and federal contracts of under $1 million no longer must prepare written affirmative action plans for hiring women and minorities. The OFCCP has also begun to limit its use of back pay awards to specific individuals who can show an actual loss due to violation of OFCCP guidelines.

Not all affirmative action programs are imposed on employers by the government. Many employers have adopted programs voluntarily or through collective bargaining agreements with unions. These affirmative action programs have sometimes subjected employers to charges of **reverse discrimination** when minorities or women with lower qualifications or less seniority than white males are given preference in employment or training. Even though such programs are intended to remedy the effects of present or past discrimination or other barriers to equal employment opportunity, white males have argued that the law does not permit employers to discriminate against *them* on the basis of race or sex any more than it allows discrimination against minorities or women.

In *United Steelworkers of America v. Weber,* the Supreme Court ruled legal under Title VII a voluntary affirmative action plan between an employer and a union. The plan required that at least 50 percent of certain new work trainees be black. The Court noted that the plan did not require that white employees be fired or excluded altogether from advancement. It was only a temporary measure to eliminate actual racial imbalance in the workforce.

Note the difference between taking affirmative action and setting a "quota." Affirmative action is taken to help correct historic workforce imbalances and usually has target goals that are pursued for a limited time. On the other hand, quotas set rigid standards for various groups, such as that 50 percent of the workforce must be female. The 1991 Civil Rights Act amendments prohibit the setting of quotas in employment.

The EEOC has issued guidelines intended to protect employers who set up affirmative action plans. These guidelines indicate that Title VII is not violated if an employer determines that there is a reasonable basis for concluding that such a plan is appropriate and the employer takes *reasonable* affirmative action. For example, if an employer discovers that it has a job category where one might expect to find more women and minorities employed than are actually in its workforce, the employer has a reasonable basis for affirmative action.

In 1995 the Supreme Court decided *Adarand Constructors, Inc. v. Pena.* The Court emphasized in this important case that government-imposed affirmative action plans are subject to *strict judicial scrutiny* under equal protection guaranteed by the Fifth and Fourteenth Amendments. To be constitutional, such plans must now be supported by a *compelling interest.* The *Adarand* decision will make it constitutionally difficult to justify some government-imposed affirmative action plans. Much litigation has followed that tests the constitutionality of various plans.

In 1996, California voters approved the controversial Proposition 209. In relevant part it says that "the state shall not discriminate against, or grant preferential treatment to, any individual or group on the basis of race, sex, color, ethnicity, or national origin in the operation of public employment, public education, or public contracting." The Supreme Court refused to hear an appeal from a lower court decision that upheld Proposition 209 against constitutional challenge and the assertion it violated federal civil rights law. Although Proposition 209 *does not* affect private employer affirmative action plans required by federal law, it does illustrate the current opposition that many Americans have to affirmative action. Polls show that almost three-fourths of the general population disapproves of affirmative action. Nearly 50 percent of African Americans also oppose it.

11. SENIORITY SYSTEMS

Seniority systems give priority to those employees who have worked longer for a particular employer or in a particular line of employment of the employer. Employers may institute seniority systems on their own, but in a union shop they are usually the result of collective bargaining. Their terms are spelled out in the agreement between the company and the union. Seniority systems often determine the calculation of vacation, pension, and other fringe benefits. They also control many employment decisions such as the order in which employees may choose shifts or qualify for promotions or transfers to different jobs. They also are used to select the persons to be laid off when an employer is reducing its labor force. As a result of seniority, the last hired are usually the first fired. Decisions based on seniority have been challenged in recent years as violating the laws relating to equal employment opportunity. Challenges often arose when recently hired members of minority groups were laid off during periods of economic downturn. Firms with successful affirmative action programs often lost most of their minority employees.

Section 703(h) of the Civil Rights Act of 1964 provides that, in spite of other provisions in the act, it is not an unlawful employment practice for an employer to apply different employment standards under a bona fide (good-faith) seniority system if the differences are not the result of an *intention* to discriminate. In *Memphis Fire Dept. v. Stotts* the Supreme Court ruled that discrimination resulting from application of a seniority system was lawful even when it affected minorities hired or promoted by affirmative action.

OTHER STATUTES AND DISCRIMINATION IN EMPLOYMENT

Although the Civil Rights Act of 1964 is the most widely used antidiscrimination statute, there are other important antidiscrimination laws. They include the Civil Rights Act of 1866, the Age Discrimination in Employment Act, the Americans with Disabilities Act, and various state and local laws. The following sections examine these laws.

12. CIVIL RIGHTS ACT OF 1866

An important federal law that complements Title VII of the 1964 Civil Rights Act is the Civil Rights Act of 1866. One provision of that act, known as **Section 1981,** provides that "all persons . . . shall have the same right to make and enforce contracts . . . as enjoyed by white citizens." Since union memberships and employment relationships involve contracts, Section 1981 bans racial discrimination in these areas.

The courts have interpreted Section 1981 as giving a private plaintiff most of the same protections against racial discrimination that the 1964 Civil Rights Act provides. In addition, there are at least two advantages to the plaintiff who files a suit based on Section 1981. First, there are no procedural requirements for bringing such a suit, whereas there are a number of fairly complex requirements plaintiffs must follow before bringing a private suit under Title VII. For instance, before a plaintiff can file a lawsuit against an employer, the plaintiff must file charges of discrimination with the EEOC and have that agency fail to bring an action against the employer. By using Section 1981, a plaintiff can immediately sue an employer in federal court without first going through the EEOC.

A second advantage to Section 1981 is that under it the courts can award unlimited compensatory and punitive damages. There are no capped limits as there are under Title VII. As a practical matter, parties alleging racial discrimination usually sue under both Section 1981 and Title VII.

Note that Section 1981 does not cover discrimination based on sex, religion, national origin, age, or handicap. As interpreted by the courts, this section applies only to *racial* discrimination. However, what is race? The Supreme Court has held that being of Arabic or Jewish ancestry constitutes "race" as protected by Section 1981. The Court stated that when the law was passed in the nineteenth century, the concept of race was much broader than it is today. Race then included the descendants of a particular "family, tribe, people, or nation." Has the Court opened the door for a white job applicant to sue a black employer for discrimination under Section 1981?

In *Patterson v. McLean,* the Supreme Court interpreted Section 1981 to apply only to the actual hiring or firing of employees based on race. Under this interpretation, Section 1981 did not offer protection against discrimination such as a hostile working environment. But the Civil Rights Act amendments of 1991 redefined Section 1981 to include protection against discrimination in "enjoyment of all benefits, privileges, terms and conditions of the contractual relationship." Thus Section 1981 now also protects against hostile environment discrimination.

13. DISCRIMINATION ON THE BASIS OF AGE

Neither the Civil Rights Act nor the Equal Employment Opportunity Act forbids discrimination based on age. However, the Age Discrimination in Employment Act (ADEA) does. It prohibits employment discrimination against employees ages 40 and older, and it prohibits the mandatory retirement of these employees. Only bona fide executives and high policymakers of private companies can be forced into early retirement. The ADEA also invalidates retirement plans and labor contracts that violate the act.

What kind of evidence is necessary to sustain a plaintiff's claim based on age discrimination? In the following case the Supreme Court decides whether an employer's general discriminatory comments to an employee support a claim of disparate treatment (intentional discrimination) when in the specific context of an employee's firing no such comments are made.

REEVES v. SANDERSON PLUMBING PRODUCTS, INC.

120 S. CT. 2097 (2000)

The petitioner Roger Reeves, age 57, was one of two employees fired by respondent Sanderson Plumbing following an audit of the department which he supervised. Reeves sued Sanderson Plumbing, claiming age discrimination and asserting that alleged errors and misrepresentations shown by the audit were merely a "pretext" for his firing, and Reeves asserted that Powe Chesnut, the director of manufacturing and husband of the company president, was behind the firing and had made numerous age-related remarks to him. The jury returned a verdict and damages in favor of Reeves. On appeal the court of appeals reversed, stating that the trial court should have decided as a matter of law in favor of the company. The court of appeals noted that Chesnut did not make his discriminatory comments in the context of Reeves' termination, that two other managers had also recommended firing Reeves, and that others in Reeves' job category who were his age were not fired. Reeves then petitioned the U.S. Supreme Court and certiorari was granted.

O'Connor, J.: [I]t is apparent that respondent was not entitled to judgment as a matter of law. In this case, in addition to establishing a prima facie case of discrimination and creating a jury issue as to the falsity of the employer's explanation, petitioner introduced additional evidence that Chesnut was motivated by age-based animus and was principally responsible for petitioner's firing. Petitioner testified that Chesnut had told him that he "was so old [he] must have come over on the Mayflower" and, on one occasion when petitioner was having difficulty starting a machine, that he "was too damn old to do [his] job." According to petitioner, Chesnut would regularly "cuss at me and shake his finger in my face." Oswalt [another employee], roughly 24 years younger than petitioner, corroborated that there was an "obvious difference" in how Chesnut treated them. He stated that, although he and Chesnut "had [their] differences," "it was nothing compared to the way [Chesnut] treated Roger." Oswalt explained that Chesnut "tolerated quite a bit" from him even though he "defied" Chesnut "quite often," but that Chesnut treated petitioner "in a manner, as you would . . . treat . . . a child when . . . you're angry with [him]." Petitioner also demonstrated that, according to company records, he and Oswalt had nearly identical rates of productivity in 1993. Yet respondent conducted an efficiency study of only the

[CONTINUED]

regular line, supervised by petitioner, and placed only petitioner on probation. Chesnut conducted that efficiency study and, after having testified to the contrary on direct examination, acknowledged on cross-examination that he had recommended that petitioner be placed on probation following the study.

Further, petitioner introduced evidence that Chesnut was the actual decisionmaker behind his firing. Chesnut was married to Sanderson, who made the formal decision to discharge petitioner. Although Sanderson testified that she fired petitioner because he had "intentionally falsified company pay records," respondent only introduced evidence concerning the inaccuracy of the records, not their falsification. A 1994 letter authored by Chesnut indicated that he berated other company directors, who were supposedly his co-equals, about how to do their jobs. Moreover, Oswalt testified that all of respondent's employees feared Chesnut, and that Chesnut had exercised "absolute power" within the company for "as long as [he] can remember."

In holding that the record contained insufficient evidence to sustain the jury's verdict, the Court of Appeals misapplied the standard of review. . . . Again, the court disregarded critical evidence favorable to petitioner—namely, the evidence supporting petitioner's prima facie case and undermining respondent's nondiscriminatory explanation. The court also failed to draw all reasonable inferences in favor of petitioner. For instance, while acknowledging "the potentially damning nature" of Chesnut's age-related comments, the court discounted them on the ground that they "were not made in the direct context of Reeve's termination." And the court discredited petitioner's evidence that Chesnut was the actual decisionmaker by giving weight to the fact that there was "no evidence to suggest that any of the other decision makers were motivated by age." Moreover, the other

evidence on which the court relied—that Caldwell and Oswalt were also cited for poor recordkeeping, and that respondent employed many managers over age 50—although relevant, is certainly not dispositive. In concluding that these circumstances so overwhelmed the evidence favoring petitioner that no rational trier of fact could have found that petitioner was fired because of his age, the Court of Appeals impermissibly substituted its judgment concerning the weight of the evidence for the jury's.

The ultimate question in every employment discrimination case involving a claim of disparate treatment is whether the plaintiff was the victim of intentional discrimination. Given the evidence in the record supporting petitioner, we see no reason to subject the parties to an additional round of litigation before the Court of Appeals rather than to resolve the matter here. The District Court plainly informed the jury that petitioner was required to show "by a preponderance of the evidence that his age was a determining and motivating factor in the decision of [respondent] to terminate him." The court instructed the jury that, to show that respondent's explanation was a pretext for discrimination, petitioner had to demonstrate "1, that the stated reasons were not the real reasons for [petitioner's] discharge; *and* 2, that age discrimination was the real reason for [petitioner's] discharge." Given that petitioner established a prima facie case of discrimination, introduced enough evidence for the jury to reject respondent's explanation, and produced additional evidence of age-based animus, there was sufficient evidence for the jury to find that respondent had intentionally discriminated. The District Court was therefore correct to submit the case to the jury, and the Court of Appeals erred in overturning its verdict.

For these reasons, the judgment of the Court of Appeals is reversed. **Reversed.**

CASE QUESTIONS

1. Why did the petitioner argue he had been fired? Why did the respondent argue he had been fired?

2. What does it mean for a judge to decide an issue like discrimination "as a matter of law"?

3. In light of this case, explain why managers must not make discriminatory comments to employees.

In one case American Home Products had to pay a former employee $1.9 million for age discrimination when he proved that at the company, according to his lawyer, "once you reach 65, you're out." In another case, a 54-year-old administrative assistant successfully sued Quantum Chemical Corporation after being replaced by a younger employee and being told she was "chronologically challenged."

An important area of age discrimination litigation exists when age is a bona fide occupational qualification. It is recognized that as people grow older, their physical strength, agility, reflexes, hearing, and vision tend to diminish in quality. However, this generally provides no legal reason for discriminating against older persons as a class. Although courts will uphold job-related physical requirements if they apply on a case-by-case basis, they frequently find as illegal those policies that prohibit the hiring of persons beyond a maximum age or that establish a maximum age beyond which employees are forced to retire for physical reasons. Thus, one court ruled that a mandatory retirement age of 65 was illegally discriminatory as applied to the job of district fire chief. To the contrary, another court ruled that the airlines could impose a maximum age for hiring a new pilot in light of a Federal Aviation Administration–mandated retirement age for pilots.

Courts have disagreed on whether remedies for violation of the act include, in addition to reinstatement and wages lost, damages for the psychological trauma of being fired or forced to resign illegally. One federal district court awarded $200,000 to a victim of age discrimination who was an inventor and scientist, for the psychological and physical effects suffered from being forced into early retirement at age 60. Also awarded were out-of-pocket costs of $60,000 and attorneys' fees of $65,000. Note that *willful* violations of the act entitle discrimination victims to *double damages*.

Since the 1978 amendments to the act, age discrimination claims have grown rapidly. In recent years, they have more than doubled in number.

14. DISCRIMINATION ON THE BASIS OF DISABILITIES

According to a Harris poll, two-thirds of all disabled Americans between the ages of 16 and 64 are not working, even though most of them want to work. To help those with disabilities get work, Congress in 1990 passed the Americans with Disabilities Act (ADA). Major provisions of this act prohibit employment discrimination against the disabled.

To prevent disability discrimination in general, the ADA prohibits employers from requiring a preemployment medical examination or asking questions about a job applicant's medical history. Only after a job offer has been given can the employer condition employment on an employee's passing a job-related medical exam or on the employee's responses to job-related medical questions.

The ADA prohibits employer discrimination against job applicants or employees based on (1) their having a disability, (2) their having had a disability in the past, or (3) their being regarded as having a disability. Under the ADA **disability** is defined as "any physical or mental impairment that substantially limits one or more of an individual's major life activities." "Physical and mental impairment" includes physical disorders or conditions, disease, disfigurement, amputation affecting a vital body system, psychological disorders, mental retardation, mental illness, and learning disabilities. "Major life activities" include the ability to perform manual tasks, walk, see, hear, speak, learn, breathe, care for oneself, or work.

Not included by the ADA as protected disabilities are homosexuality, sexual behavior disorders, compulsive gambling, kleptomania, and disorders resulting from *current* drug or alcohol use. The emphasis on current drug or alcohol use means that employees who have successfully recovered or are successfully recovering from drug or alcohol disabilities are protected from employment discrimination.

What about people with acquired immunodeficiency syndrome (AIDS)? Does having it make an employee disabled under the ADA? The answer to this question is yes. Although those who test positive for the AIDS virus may not initially have any obvious physical or mental disability, they are disabled in the sense that others' fear of them can interfere with their ability to work, which is a major life activity.

The ADA prohibits employers of 15 or more employees (also unions with 15 or more members and employment agencies) from discriminating against the qualified disabled with respect to hiring, advancement, termination, compensation, training, or other terms, conditions, or privileges of employment. **Qualified disabled** are defined as those with a disability who, with or without reasonable accommodation, can perform the essential functions of a particular job position.

The ADA does not require employers to hire the unqualified disabled, but they must make reasonable accommodation so disabled employees can succeed in the workplace. **Reasonable accommodation** is the process of adjusting a job or work environment to fit the needs of disabled employees. It may include:

- Making the work facilities accessible and usable to disabled employees
- Restructuring jobs or modifying work schedules
- Purchasing or modifying necessary equipment for use by the disabled
- Providing appropriate training materials or assistance modified to fit the needs of disabled employees

In the case that follows, the Supreme Court decides whether a requested accommodation that conflicts with seniority rules is "reasonable." Note that seniority rules may give employees preference in promotions and in getting or keeping various jobs on the basis of how long they have worked for an employer.

U.S. AIRWAYS, INC. V. BARNETT

122 S. CT. 1516 (2002)

Robert Barnett (respondent), a cargo handler for U.S. Airways (petitioner), injured his back and became disabled. He transferred to a less physically demanding job in the mailroom. When his new job later became open to "employee bidding" under the U.S. Airways' seniority system and other employees senior to him planned to bid on his job, he requested "accommodation." He wanted to keep his job without allowing senior employees to get it from him by bidding on it. When U.S. Airways refused this accommodation, Barnett sued under the ADA. The district court ruled for U.S. Airways, but the court of appeals reversed. The Supreme Court granted certiorari.

BREYER, J.: The question in the present case focuses on the relationship between seniority systems and the plaintiff's need to show that an "accommodation" seems reasonable. . . . We must assume that the plaintiff, an employee, is an "individual with a disability." He has requested assignment to a mailroom position as a "reasonable accommodation." We also assume that normally such a request would be reasonable within the meaning of the statute, were it not for one circumstance, namely, that the assignment would violate the rules of a seniority system. Does that circumstance mean that the proposed accommodation is not a "reasonable" one?

[CONTINUED]

In our view, the answer to this question ordinarily is "yes." The statute does not require proof on a case-by-case basis that a seniority system should prevail. That is because it would not be reasonable in the run of cases that the assignment in question trump the rules of a seniority system. To the contrary, it will ordinarily be unreasonable for the assignment to prevail.

For one thing, the typical seniority system provides important employee benefits by creating, and fulfilling, employee expectations of fair, uniform treatment. These benefits include "job security and an opportunity for steady and predictable advancement based on objective standards." They include "an element of due process," limiting "unfairness in personal decisions." And they consequently encourage employees to invest in the employing company, accepting "less than their value to the firm early in their careers" in return for greater benefits in later years.

Most important for present purposes, to require the typical employer to show more than the existence of a seniority system might well undermine the employees' expectations of consistent, uniform treatment—expectations upon which the seniority system's benefits depend. That is because such a rule would substitute a complex case-specific "accommodation" decision made by management for the more uniform, impersonal operation of seniority rules. Such management decisionmaking, with its inevitable discretionary elements, would involve a matter of the greatest importance to employees, namely, layoffs; it would take place outside, as well as inside, the confines of a court case; and it might well take place fairly often. We can find nothing in the statute that suggests Congress intended to undermine seniority systems in this way. And we consequently conclude that the employer's showing of violation of the rules of a seniority system is by itself ordinarily sufficient.

The plaintiff (here the employee) nonetheless remains free to show that special circumstances warrant a finding that, despite the presence of a seniority system (which the ADA may not trump in the run of cases), the requested "accommodation" is "reasonable" on the particular facts. That is because special circumstances might alter the important expectations described above. The plaintiff might show, for example, that the employer, having retained the right to change the seniority system unilaterally, exercises that right fairly frequently, reducing employee expectations that the system will be followed—to the point where one more departure, needed to accommodate an individual with a disability, will not likely make a difference. The plaintiff might show that the system already contains exceptions such that, in the circumstances, one further exception is unlikely to matter. We do not mean these examples to exhaust the kinds of showings that a plaintiff might make. But we do mean to say that the plaintiff must bear the burden of showing special circumstances that make an exception from the seniority system reasonable in the particular case. And to do so, the plaintiff must explain why, in the particular case, an exception to the employer's seniority policy can constitute a "reasonable accommodation" even though in the ordinary case it cannot.

In its question presented, U.S. Airways asked us whether the ADA requires an employer to assign a disabled employee to a particular position even though another employee is entitled to that position under the employer's "established seniority system." We answer that *ordinarily* the ADA does not require that assignment. Hence, a showing that the assignment would violate the rules of a seniority system warrants summary judgment for the employer—unless there is more. The plaintiff must present evidence of that "more," namely, special circumstances surrounding the particular case that demonstrate the assignment is nonetheless reasonable.

We vacate the Court of Appeals' judgment and remand the case for further proceedings consistent with this opinion.

It is so ordered.

CASE QUESTIONS

1. What does the employee request the employer to do?

2. Why does the employer deny the accommodation request?

3. Does the Supreme Court decide that a seniority system "trumps" an accommodation request? Explain.

concept SUMMARY   *Illegal Employment Practices*

Unless bona fide occupational qualifications or business necessity can be proved, federal law prohibits recruiting, hiring, promoting, and other employment practices that involve disparate treatment or produce a disparate impact on the basis of:

Race or color

National origin

Religion

Sex

Test scores and educational requirements

Height and weight

Appearance

Age

Disabilities

Note that an employer need make only reasonable accommodation for disabled employees. The employer can plead *undue hardship,* defined as "an action requiring significant difficulty or expense," as a reason for not accommodating the needs of disabled employees. The ADA specifies that in evaluating undue hardship, the cost of the accommodation, the resources of the employer, the size of the employer, and the nature of the employer's business be considered.

Businesses must reasonably accommodate not only *employees* for their disabilities under the ADA but also customers and others who use public facilities such as hotels, restaurants, theaters, schools (even private ones), most places of entertainment, offices providing services, and other establishments doing business with the public. The Supreme Court ruled that the Professional Golf Association had to accommodate golfer Casey Martin, who suffered a walking disability because of a circulatory disorder, by allowing him to use a golf cart in PGA tournaments. The Court held (1) that PGA tournaments were open to any member of the public who paid a qualifying fee and participated successfully in a qualifying tournament and (2) that accommodating Casey Martin by allowing him to use a golf cart while other golfers walked a tournament course did not "fundamentally alter the nature" of PGA tournament events.

Remedies under the ADA are basically the same remedies available under the Civil Rights Act, including hiring, reinstatement, back pay, injunctive relief, and compensatory and punitive damages. As with the Civil Rights Act, compensatory and punitive damages are not available for policies that merely have disparate impact. They are available for intentional discrimination and for other employer actions such as failing to make reasonable accommodation for known job applicant or employee disabilities.

The ADA replaces the Rehabilitation Act of 1973 as the primary federal law protecting the disabled. However, the Rehabilitation Act, which applies only to employers doing business with the government under a federal contract for $2,500 or more, still requires that such employers have a qualified affirmative action program for hiring and promoting the disabled.

15. DISCRIMINATION IN GETTING AND KEEPING HEALTH INSURANCE

Since July 1, 1997, a new act prohibits group health plans and health insurance issuers from discriminating against employees based on certain factors. The Health Insurance Portability and Accountability Act (HIPAA) forbids group plans and issuers from excluding an employee from insurance coverage or requiring different premiums based on the employee's health status, medical condition or history, genetic information, or disability.

The act primarily prevents discrimination against individual employees in small businesses. Before the act, individual employees with an illness like cancer or a genetic condition like sickle cell anemia were sometimes denied coverage in a new health plan. The small size of the plan deterred insurers from covering individual employees whose medical condition might produce large claims. The act denies insurers the right to discriminate on this basis. It also guarantees that insured employees who leave their old employer and join a new employer are not denied health insurance. As of this writing, the exact meanings of many HIPAA provisions are still unclear.

Note, however, that the act only applies to prevent discrimination in group health insurance plans. It does not apply to individuals who purchase individual health insurance. Congress is considering legislation to extend HIPAA's antidiscrimination provisions to individual insurance. Behind HIPAA and proposals for new legislation is the concern that new forms of genetic testing will allow insurers and employers to identify and discriminate against individuals who may in the future develop certain medical conditions.

16. OTHER FEDERAL LEGISLATION

Other federal legislation dealing with employment discrimination includes the National Labor Relations Act of 1936. The National Labor Relations Board has ruled that appeals to racial prejudice in a collective bargaining representation election constitute an unfair labor practice. The NLRB has also revoked the certification of unions that practice discriminatory admission or representation policies. Additionally, employers have an obligation to bargain with certified unions over matters of employment discrimination. Such matters are considered "terms and conditions of employment" and are thus mandatory bargaining issues. Note that the reverse discrimination issue in the Weber case (p. 459) arose because of an affirmative action plan in a collective bargaining contract.

Finally, various other federal agencies may prohibit discriminatory employment practices under their authorizing statutes. The Federal Communications Commission, for example, has prohibited employment discrimination by its licensees (radio and TV stations) and has required the submission of affirmative action plans as a condition of license renewal.

17. STATE ANTIDISCRIMINATION LAWS

Federal laws concerning equal employment opportunity specifically permit state laws imposing additional duties and liabilities. In recent years, fair employment practices legislation has been introduced and passed by many state legislatures. When the federal Equal Employment Opportunity Act became effective, 40 states had such laws, but their provisions varied considerably. A typical state act makes it an unfair employment practice for any employer to refuse to hire or otherwise discriminate against any individual because of his or her race, color, religion, national origin, or ancestry. If employment agencies or labor organizations discriminate against an individual in any way because of one of these reasons, they are also guilty of an unfair employment practice. State acts usually set up an administrative body, generally known as the Fair Employment Practices Commission, which has the power to make rules and regulations and hear and decide charges of violations filed by complainants.

State antidiscrimination laws sometimes protect categories of persons not protected by federal law. For example, some protect persons from employment discrimination based on weight. Others protect persons from discrimination based on sexual preference.

As indicated in Chapter 9 on torts, discrimination plaintiffs can also sue employers under various state common law causes of action, like negligence, assault, battery, intentional infliction of mental distress, and defamation. Under common law, plaintiffs can usually receive unlimited compensatory and punitive damages, and greater numbers of plaintiffs seem to be suing under common law. In Las Vegas a jury awarded over $5 million against the Hilton Hotel and in favor of a plaintiff who had been sexually groped at an aviators' Tailhook convention. The jury determined that the hotel had been negligent in failing to provide adequate security.

18. TRENDS IN EMPLOYMENT DISCRIMINATION AND LITIGATION

Several current trends in employment discrimination and litigation will require close attention from managers in the coming years. These trends highlight the fact that the workforce is increasingly diverse and that new managers must be alert to the full impact of antidiscrimination laws. They also show the effects of new technology (see the box, below).

Surge in Private Lawsuits Private lawsuits alleging discrimination in employment surged in recent years, more than tripling. Several factors account for the rapid increase. The 1991 revision of the Civil Rights Act to support punitive and compensatory damages has encouraged employees to sue their employers. The passage of the Americans with Disabilities Act has led to a new area of discrimination lawsuits, and some 50 million Americans, according to a conservative estimate, may legally qualify as disabled. Finally, as the large generation of baby boomers ages in the workforce, more lawsuits arise under the Age Discrimination in Employment Act. In the new century, these trends continue, making it ever more important for business managers to understand the law prohibiting discrimination in employment.

Discrimination Based on Genetic Testing With the success of the Human Genome Project comes not only the likelihood of important medical advances but also the real possibility that employers may use genetic testing to screen

---

 **CYBER LAW** *connection*

Discrimination by E-Mail

Recently, more and more complaints about discriminatory company e-mail have surfaced. Racist and sexist jokes passed generally through a company's e-mail system can create a hostile work environment prohibited under Title VII. Employees at Chevron Corporation, Citibank, R. R. Donnelley & Sons Company, and Morgan Stanley & Company have all sued their employers at least in part because of discriminatory e-mail messages.

Managers must note that legal issues of employee privacy and constitutional free speech do not apply to situations of company e-mail use. Employees should be alerted that computer hard drives store e-mail where plaintiffs in discrimination lawsuits can recover it. Companies should develop formal policies regarding acceptable e-mail use in order to protect themselves. They must also take prompt action against discriminatory e-mail messages and those employees who send them.

employees for genetic conditions. The possibility raises moral issues, but it presents legal issues as well. Will Congress pass legislation forbidding employers from using genetic testing to discriminate against employees? In 2000, President Clinton signed an executive order barring discrimination against federal employees based on genetic information.

A number of states already prohibit employers from using genetic tests to evaluate employees, but often the laws regulate discrimination against employees with only a specific genetic disease. Some companies claim that they need to test employees for genetic susceptibility to certain chemicals that they are exposed to in the workplace. Almost certainly, the scientific ability to test for genetic conditions will grow tremendously in the near future. With it will come pressure for new antidiscrimination regulation.

Arbitration in Employment Discrimination Disputes Arbitration is usually cheaper, quicker, and less public than litigation. Accustomed to using arbitration clauses in contracts with customers and suppliers, many employers also have begun placing arbitration clauses in employment contracts and personnel handbooks. These clauses require arbitration in employment discrimination disputes and with other employment controversies.

The Federal Arbitration Act (see Chapter 5) prefers arbitration over litigation, but that act may not apply to certain employment contracts. The EEOC has issued a policy statement concluding that "agreements that mandate binding arbitration of discrimination claims as a condition of employment are contrary to the fundamental principles" of antidiscrimination laws.

However, without specifically discussing the EEOC's policy statement the Supreme Court has upheld arbitration clauses in certain employment discrimination cases (see box, below).

Congress may ultimately decide whether binding arbitration as a condition of working for an employer is an acceptable part of the employment contract. In the meantime, employers who wish to have employment disputes, including discrimination disputes, arbitrated should consider the following:

- Paying employees separately from the employment contract to sign arbitration agreements
- Ensuring that arbitration agreements allow for the same range of remedies contained in the antidiscrimination laws

CIRCUIT CITY'S ARBITRATION PROVISION

In *Circuit City Stores, Inc. v. Adams,* 532 U.S. 105 (2001), the Supreme Court decided that the Federal Arbitration Act did not prohibit enforceability of the following arbitration provision, which an employee had signed in his job application.

I agree that I will settle any and all previously unasserted claims, disputes or controversies arising out of or relating to my application or candidacy for employment, employment and/or cessa-

tion of employment with Circuit City, *exclusively* by final and binding *arbitration* before a neutral arbitrator. By way of example only, such claims include claims under federal, state, and local statutory or common law, such as the Age Discrimination in Employment Act, Title VII of the Civil Rights Act of 1964, as amended, including the amendments of the Civil Rights Act of 1991, the Americans with Disabilities Act, the law of contract and the law of tort.

- Allowing limited discovery in arbitration, which traditionally has no discovery process
- Permitting employees to participate in selecting neutral, knowledgeable professional arbitrators instead of using an industry arbitration panel

These steps should go far toward eliminating many of the objections to the arbitration of employment discrimination disputes.

Proper arbitration agreements should continue to be part of the business response to discrimination in employment disputes. Interestingly, at least one study has found that employees alleging discrimination win more often before arbitration panels than before juries and in only two-thirds of the time.

Insuring against Employment Discrimination Claims Employers commonly insure against many potential liabilities. However, the general liability policies carried by many businesses, which cover bodily injury and property damage, often do not insure against intentional torts. Intent is a key element in many employment discrimination claims. In addition, general policies may not cover the back pay or damages for mental anguish that many discrimination plaintiffs seek. As a result, employers are beginning to ask for and get employment practices liability insurance, a type of insurance aimed specifically at discrimination claims.

Even with the availability of the new insurance, not all types of employment discrimination can be insured against in every state. States like New York and California do not permit companies to insure against "intentional acts." Disparate treatment discrimination is an example of such an act. Similarly, some states do not permit companies to insure against punitive damages that can arise in intentional violations of Title VII. Managers should also be aware that what the new policies cover and what they exclude vary widely.

19. EMPLOYMENT DISCRIMINATION, CORPORATE GOVERNANCE, AND PROPERTY

In law we often find that words have both specific and broad meanings. Specifically, corporate governance means the regulation of the relationship between the directors and managers who run a corporation and the shareholders who own it. More broadly, corporate governance refers to the general public regulation of businesses, the very biggest of which are corporations. In this sense the regulation of the employer-employee relationship through nondiscrimination laws also deserves the name *corporate governance.*

Property, too, has a specific and a broader meaning. As James Madison wrote: "Property . . . in its particular application means that 'dominion which one . . . claims and exercises over the external things of the world. . . . In its larger and juster meaning, it embraces everything to which a man may attach a value and have a right. . . ." In this "larger and juster meaning," property applies to whether the employer has a right to discriminate or whether the employee/job applicant has the right not to be discriminated against.

Previously, one of the uses employers could make of their businesses was to discriminate against job applicants and employees on the basis of race, sex, color, religion, national origin, age, and disability. They could exclude others from interfering with the exercise of this right, and in the broad Madisonian sense this right was a property right. With Title VII and other antidiscrimination laws, the property right shifted. The law took the property right away from the employer and reassigned it to job applicants and employees. Under the law, these people now possess an exclusionary right not to have employers discriminate against them in the employment relationship. In the Madisonian sense, the right to enforce nondiscrimination is a property right.

In Chapters 1 and 7, you learned that the state determines through legislatures and courts how property applies and that this exclusionary right produces the maximum potential for resource development. Resources represent not only physical things but the conditions for human action. Thus, if society wishes to produce the maximum potential for employment discrimination, it should recognize business owners as having property in the action of discrimination. But if society wishes to produce more nondiscrimination in employment, it should recognize nondiscrimination as the object of property and institute appropriate enforcement laws. With the institution of nondiscrimination laws, society has taken this latter step.

Thinking of nondiscrimination as the object of a property right may be confusing at first. But in the broad Madisonian sense, it certainly is an application of property. It is a form of corporate governance as well, part of the regulatory environment of business. Are all rights really applications of the property right? James Madison argued so in his article entitled "Property," which appeared in the *National Gazette* on March 29, 1792. In other writings he also maintained that the state must be very reluctant to change an application of the right of property. From our perspective in this book, we believe that the right of property should shift only when society wants to produce more of something on one side and less of something on the other. Do you agree?

KEY TERMS

Affirmative action 459	Hostile work environment 452
Bona fide occupational qualifications (BFOQs) 446	Qualified disabled 465
	Reasonable accommodation 450, 465
Business necessity defense 449	Reverse discrimination 459
Comparable worth 456	Section 1981 461
Disability 464	Seniority system 460
Disparate impact 449	Sexual harassment 452
Disparate treatment 449	

REVIEW QUESTIONS AND PROBLEMS

The Civil Rights Act of 1964

1. *General Provisions*

   Martel, a competent male secretary to the president of ICU, was fired because the new president of the company believed it is more appropriate to have a female secretary.

   (a)   Has a violation of the law occurred?

   (b)   Assume that a violation of the law has occurred and Martel decided to take an extended vacation after he was fired. Upon his return seven months later, Martel filed suit in federal district court against ICU, charging illegal discrimination under the Civil Rights Act of 1964. What remedies will be available to him under the act?

2. *Enforcement Procedures*

   Muscles-Are-You, Inc., a bodybuilding spa targeted primarily toward male body builders, refused to hire a woman for the position of executive director. The spa's management stated that the executive director must have a "macho" image to relate well with the spa's customers. Discuss whether it is likely that the spa has violated Title VII.

3. *Discrimination on the Basis of Race or Color*

   Does Title VII prohibit employment discrimination against members of all races? Explain.

4. *Discrimination on the Basis of National Origin*

   Ace Tennis Co. hires only employees who speak English. Does this policy illegally discriminate against Hispanic job applicants who speak only Spanish? Discuss.

5. *Discrimination on the Basis of Religion*

   Ortega, an employee of ABC, Inc., recently joined a church that forbids working on Saturdays, Sundays, and Mondays. Ortega requested that his employer change his work schedule from eight-hour days, Monday through Friday, to ten-hour days, Tuesday through Friday. Ortega's request was refused because the employer is in operation only eight hours per day, five days a week. After a month during which Ortega failed to work on Mondays, he was fired. The employer stated that "only a full-time employee would be acceptable" for Ortega's position. What are Ortega's legal rights, if any?

6. *Discrimination on the Basis of Sex*

   A male supervisor at Star Company made repeated offensive sexual remarks to female employees. The employees complained to higher management, which ignored the complaints. If the company does not discharge or otherwise penalize the employee, has it violated Title VII? Discuss.

Employment Practices That May Be Challenged

7. *Questionnaires, Interviews, Testing, and Educational Requirements*

   Jennings Company, which manufactures sophisticated electronic equipment, hires its assembly employees on the basis of applicants' scores on a standardized mathematics aptitude test. It has been shown that those who score higher on the test almost always perform better on the job. However, it has also been demonstrated that the use of the test in hiring employees has the effect of excluding African Americans and other minority groups. Is this practice of the Jennings Company prohibited by the Civil Rights Act of 1964?

8. *Height and Weight Requirements*

   (a) An employer hires job applicants to wait tables in the Executive Heights Restaurant only if they are over 6 feet tall. Does this policy likely violate Title VII? Explain.

   (b) If a class of job applicants under 6 feet sues the employer, will it likely get compensatory and punitive damages? Explain.

9. *Appearance Requirements*

   Silicon Products requires all male employees to wear their hair "off the collar." Does this policy violate Title VII? Discuss.

10. *Affirmative Action Programs and Reverse Discrimination*

    Kartel, Inc., found that historically African Americans had been significantly underrepresented in its workforce. It decided to remedy the situation and place African Americans in 50 percent of all new job openings. Discuss the legality of Kartel's action.

11. *Seniority Systems*

    Are seniority systems in the workplace legal under Title VII if in fact they discriminate on the basis of gender or race? Explain.

Other Statutes and Discrimination in Employment

12. *Civil Rights Act of 1866*

    When is it an advantage for a plaintiff to use Section 1981 as the basis for discrimination litigation as contrasted with using Title VII?

13. *Discrimination on the Basis of Age*

    Cantrell, the controller of Xylec's, Inc., was forced to retire at age 58 due to a general company policy. Although Cantrell has a company pension of $50,000 per year, she believes that her lifestyle will soon be hampered due to inflation, since the pension provides for no cost-of-living increases. What are Cantrell's rights, if any?

14. *Discrimination on the Basis of Disabilities*

    Ralph is a systems analyst for the Silicon Corporation, a major defense contractor. When Ralph's coworkers learn that he has AIDS, six of them quit work immediately. Fearing that additional resignations will delay production, the company discharges Ralph. Discuss whether or not the company acted legally.

15. *Discrimination in Getting and Keeping Health Insurance*

    Why does Title VII not apply to preventing discrimination in the getting and keeping of health insurance?

16. *Other Federal Legislation*

    Do employers have an obligation to negotiate with groups of employees over issues of discrimination? Explain.

17. *State Antidiscrimination Laws*

    Explain how state antidiscrimination laws protect workers in situations where federal laws do not.

18. *Trends in Employment Discrimination and Litigation*

    Can arbitration agreements be used to keep employees from litigating discrimination issues? Discuss.

19. *Employment Discrimination, Corporate Governance, and Property*

    If the state is depriving employers of property by taking away their right to discriminate, why does the state not have to pay "just compensation" to employers under the takings clause of the Fifth Amendment to the Constitution?

TERMINOLOGY REVIEW

For each term in the left-hand column, match the most appropriate description in the right-hand column:

1. Affirmative action
2. Seniority system
3. Reverse discrimination
4. Disparate impact
5. BFOQs
6. Section 1981

a. Selection of employees for hire or promotion in a pattern significantly different from that of racial minorities or women available in the pool of job applicants
b. Job-related employment characteristics based on sex or religion
c. Taking active steps to seek out and employ groups traditionally underrepresented in the workforce
d. A system to give priority to those employees who have worked longer for a particular employer
e. Prohibits contractual discrimination based on race
f. Employment discrimination against white males

BUSINESS DISCUSSION

When Maria Suarez got her new job, she was happy. As an oil rigger, she would make enough money to support herself and her two children. But after a week of working with a primarily male crew, her happiness was gone. Her co-workers were the reason. At first the men made unwelcome comments about her body. Then sexual graffiti mentioning her name appeared. When she came to work one morning a nude female picture was pinned to one of the rigs. Her name had been scrawled across the bottom. Maria complained to the crew foreman, who referred her to the site manager. "Let's ignore it for a while," he told Maria. "It's just good fun. The men are testing you. You've got to fit in."

What are Maria's legal rights in this situation?

What would you do if you were the site manager?

Do you think Maria should just try to "fit in"?

16

SECURITIES REGULATIONS

You and a former classmate started a computer software company five years ago. Originally, the two of you were the owners and only employees. The foundation of your company was your combined expertise in creating custom-designed applications addressing the human resource needs of your clients. As your company grew, you added programmers that now allow your business to provide a greater array of computer applications. You and your co-owner decide to raise capital by making a public offering of stock. In preparation for going public, you visit with several of your most valuable clients about investing in your company.

What concerns should you have regarding these conversations?

Is there anything about your expectations of the company's future performance you must or must not share?

Chapter 11 examines how business activities can be organized. That chapter focuses on how the concept of corporate governance relates to the creation and management of business organizations. One way to view this chapter is as a continuation of the topics presented in Chapter 11. The phrase corporate governance as used in this chapter relates to government regulation of the ownership of business organizations. Indeed, of all the topics covered in this text, enforcement and revisions of securities regulations are the principle means used by the federal and state government to create and restore investor confidence following scandals involving Enron, WorldCom, Tyco, Vivendi, Adelphia, HealthSouth, and other major corporations.

The Business Decision provides just one factual situation requiring business managers and owners to pay careful attention to securities regulations. A clear understanding of these legal issues is essential if managers are to avoid the liability, both civil and criminal, discussed in this chapter. This chapter also acquaints investors with the laws designed to protect them.

As you study this chapter, remember that the regulation of securities began as part of the program to help the United States overcome the great depression of the early 1930s. You should also realize that these securities laws are designed to give potential investors sufficient information so that they can make intelligent investment decisions based on factual information rather than on other less certain criteria. Although federal securities laws are now more than 70 years old, their application is at the heart of corporate governance during the first years of the twenty-first century.

INTRODUCTION

The following sections examine the broad legal meaning given to the word "security." In addition, federal and state securities laws are discussed. Such laws at the federal level regulate the sale of securities in interstate commerce as well as the operation of national securities exchanges. These sections should give you an understanding of two major federal securities laws—the Securities Act of 1933 and the Securities Exchange Act of 1934—and significant recent legislation such as the Sarbanes-Oxley Act. The following table provides an overview of the major provisions of the laws discussed in this chapter.

Laws Regulating Securities Transactions

Statute	*Summary of Major Provisions*
Securities Act of 1933	Disclosure law governing initial sale of securities to public
	Defines the term "security"
	Creates liability for false or misleading registration statement (Section 11)
	Creates liability for failure to file a registration statement (Section 12[1])
	Creates liability for false or misleading prospectus (Section 12[2])
	Creates liability for fraudulent communications used in the offer of sales of securities (Section 17[a])
Securities Exchange Act of 1934	Created Securities and Exchange Commission
	Governs exchanges of securities beyond the initial sale
	Creates liability for fraudulent manipulation of securities' value (Section 10[b])
	Creates liability for short-swing profits made by insiders (Section 16)
	Creates liability for false or misleading filings with the SEC (Section 18)
	Creates liability for fraudulent transactions related to tender offers (Section 14[e])
Insider Trading and Securities Fraud Enforcement Act of 1988	Provides for recovery of triple damages in civil actions against user of nonpublic information
	Increases criminal sanctions for use of nonpublic information
Securities Enforcement Remedies Act of 1990	Increases civil fines for violations of securities laws
	Prohibits an individual's service as an officer or director
Sarbanes-Oxley Act of 2002	Increases budgetary support to Securities and Exchange Commission
	Creates Public Company Accounting Oversight Board
	Changes membership requirements of corporate audit committees
	Requires CEOs to certify financial statements
	Increases criminal penalties for fraud and false statements
State blue sky laws	Impose another level of securities regulations beyond federal laws
	Govern intrastate securities transactions not regulated by federal laws

1. WHAT IS A SECURITY?

Because the objective of securities laws is to protect uninformed people from investing their money without sufficient information, the term **security** has a very broad definition. Indeed, the federal securities laws provide the following definition:

> "Security" means any note, stock, treasury stock, bond, debenture, evidence of indebtedness, certificate of interest or participation in any profit-sharing agreement, collateral-trust certificate, preorganization certificate or subscription, transferable share, investment contract, voting-trust certificate, certificate of deposit for a security, fractional undivided interest in oil, gas, or other mineral rights, or in general, any interest or instrument commonly known as a "security," or any certificate of interest or participation in, temporary or interim certificate for receipt for, guarantee of, or warrant or right to subscribe to or purchase, any of the foregoing.[1]

As this definition indicates, the word "security" includes much more than corporation stock. Historically, the Supreme Court has held that a security exists when one person invests money and looks to others to manage the money for profit. On the basis of this statement, courts seek positive answers to the following three questions when determining whether a person has purchased a security:

1. Is the investment in a common business activity?
2. Is the investment based on a reasonable expectation of profits?
3. Will these profits be earned through the efforts of someone other than the investor?

If the answer to all three questions is yes, then a security is involved regardless of the form it takes. This analysis permits courts to hold that the sale of oil well interests, orange trees in an orchard, a condominium unit, and interests in a limited partnership are all securities.

2. SECURITIES AND EXCHANGE COMMISSION

The **Securities and Exchange Commission (SEC)** is an administrative agency created in 1934 that is responsible for administering the federal securities laws. The SEC consists of five commissioners appointed by the president for five-year terms. In addition to these commissioners, the SEC employs staff personnel such as lawyers, accountants, security analysts, security examiners, and others.

The SEC has both quasi-legislative and quasi-judicial powers. Under its quasi-legislative power, it has adopted rules and regulations relating to financial and other information that must be furnished to the Commission. Other rules prescribe information that must be given to potential investors. The SEC also regulates the various stock exchanges, utility holding companies, investment trusts, and investment advisers. Under its quasi-judicial power, the SEC also is involved in a variety of investigations. The box on the next page highlights recent actions by the SEC.

THE SECURITIES ACT OF 1933: GOING PUBLIC

The **Securities Act of 1933** is a disclosure law with respect to the initial sale of securities to the public. This law makes it illegal to use the mails or any other means of interstate communication or transportation to sell securities without disclosing

---

[1] *15 U.S.C.A. § 77b(1). This definition is a part of the 1933 Securities Act. It is virtually identical to the definition of security found in the 1934 Securities Exchange Act.*

THE SECURITIES AND EXCHANGE
COMMISSION IN THE HEADLINES

The SEC's involvement in addressing the massive corporate fraud revealed through accounting and auditing irregularities has resulted in some staggering fines. For example, in 2003, WorldCom, while under the protection of the bankruptcy court, settled all claims with the SEC by agreeing to pay a fine of $500,000,000. Also in 2003, the SEC settled claims with the 10 largest securities brokerage firms for a combined total of approximately $1.4 billion. These firms agreed to resolve allegations they participated in inappropriate dealings during the 1990s

stock market mania. These 10 firms paid $487.5 million in fines. They created a pool of $387.5 million from which their customers can make claims. Finally, these firms agreed to pay $432.5 million to support financial research that will be available free of charge to their customers, and $80 million to support investor education programs.

As a part of the federal government's response to corporate scandals, the powers and responsibilities of the SEC were enhanced through the passage of the Sarbanes-Oxley Act of 2002. This law is the subject matter of section 12, below.

certain financial information to potential investors. The following sections discuss several aspects of the act in detail, including who is regulated, what documents are required, when criminal and civil liability exist, and what defenses are available. As you read, remember that this law applies only to the initial sale of the security. Subsequent transfers of securities are governed by the Securities Exchange Act of 1934, discussed in sections 7 through 11.

In essence, the 1933 Securities Act requires the disclosure of information to the potential investor or other interested party. The information given must not be untrue or even misleading. If this information is not accurate, liability is imposed upon those responsible.

The act recognizes three sanctions for violations:

- Criminal punishment
- Civil liability, which may be imposed in favor of injured parties in certain cases
- Equitable remedy of an injunction

Proof of an intentional violation usually is required before criminal or civil sanctions are imposed. Proof of negligence will, however, support an injunction.

3. PARTIES REGULATED

The Securities Act of 1933 regulates anyone who is involved with or who promotes the initial sale of securities. The persons typically subject to the 1933 act are listed in the following box.

PARTIES WHO MUST COMPLY WITH THE
DISCLOSURE REQUIREMENTS OF THE
SECURITIES ACT OF 1933

- Issuers
- Underwriters
- Controlling persons
- Sellers

An **issuer** is the individual or business organization offering a security for sale to the public. An **underwriter** is anyone who participates in the original distribution of securities by selling such securities for the issuer or by guaranteeing their sale. Often securities brokerage firms or investment bankers act as underwriters with respect to a particular transaction. A **controlling person** is one who controls or is controlled by the issuer, such as a major stockholder of a corporation. Finally, a **seller** is anyone who contracts with a purchaser or who is a motivating influence that causes the purchase transaction to occur.

In the Business Decision at the beginning of this chapter, you, your co-owner, and your business organization must understand the requirements of the 1933 Securities Act. Your organization clearly is an issuer. You and your co-owner clearly are controlling persons. Whether you also are an underwriter or seller or both will depend on the factual situation and relationships you create with other individuals or firms to promote and sell stock in your organization.

4. DOCUMENTS INVOLVED

In regulating the initial sales of securities, the Securities Act of 1933 is viewed as a disclosure law. In essence, this law requires that securities subject to its provisions be registered prior to any sale and that a prospectus be furnished to any potential investor prior to any sale being consummated. Thus, an issuer of securities who complies with the federal law must prepare:

- A registration statement
- A prospectus

Registration Statement   In an attempt to accomplish its purpose of disclosure, the Securities Act of 1933 contains detailed provisions relating to the registration of securities. These provisions require that a **registration statement** be filed with the SEC. The statement includes a detailed disclosure of financial information about the issuer and the controlling individuals involved in the offering of securities for sale to the public.

With respect to the filing of the registration statement, the law describes selling activities permitted at the various stages of the registration process. This procedure and its time frame are a primary reason why you and your co-owner described in the Business Decision cannot begin business immediately. You must comply with the periods mentioned in the following box and discussed below.

During the **prefiling period,** it is legal for the issuer of a security to engage in preliminary negotiations and agreements with underwriters. It is illegal to sell a covered security during this period. Offers to sell and offers to buy securities also are prohibited during this prefiling period.

| THE THREE DISTINCT PERIODS DURING THE REGISTRATION PROCESS | • The prefiling period
• The waiting period
• The posteffective period |

After the registration statement is filed, a **waiting period** commences. This period typically lasts 20 days. During this time, the SEC staff investigates the accuracy of the registration statement to determine whether the sale of the securities should be permitted. During the waiting period, it is still illegal to sell a security subject to the act. However, it is not illegal to solicit a buyer or receive offers to buy. Since contracts to sell are still illegal, offers cannot be accepted during the waiting period. However, during these waiting periods, sellers may solicit offers for later acceptance.

Many solicitations during the waiting period are made in advertisements called **tombstone ads.** These ads are brief announcements identifying the security and stating its price, by whom orders will be executed, and from whom a prospectus may be obtained. Almost every issue of *The Wall Street Journal* contains such ads. Solicitations may also be made during the waiting period by use of a statistical summary, a summary prospectus, or a preliminary prospectus. These techniques allow dissemination of the facts that are to be ultimately disclosed in the formal prospectus.

A registration becomes effective at the expiration of the waiting period, 20 days after it is filed, unless the SEC gives notice that it is not in proper form or unless the SEC accelerates the effective date. Any amendment filed without the commission's consent starts the 20-day period running again. The end of the waiting period is the beginning of the **posteffective period.** During this period, contracts to buy and sell securities are finalized.

Prospectus During the posteffective period, securities may be sold. A **prospectus** must be furnished to any interested investor, and it must conform to the statutory requirements. Like the registration statement, the prospectus contains financial information related to the issuer and controlling persons. Indeed, the prospectus contains the same essential information contained in the registration statement. The prospectus supplies the investor with sufficient facts (including financial information) so that he or she can make an intelligent investment decision. The SEC has adopted rules relating to the detailed requirements of the prospectus. The major requirements are detailed facts about the issuer and financial statements, including balance sheets and statements of operations of the issuer.

Theoretically, any security may be sold under the act, provided the law and the rules and regulations enacted under it are followed. The law does not prohibit the sale of worthless securities. An investor may "foolishly" invest his or her money, and a person may legally sell the blue sky if the statutory requirements are met. In fact, the prospectus must contain the following in capital letters and boldface type:

> **THESE SECURITIES HAVE NOT BEEN APPROVED OR DISAPPROVED BY THE SECURITIES AND EXCHANGE COMMISSION NOR HAS THE COMMISSION PASSED UPON THE ACCURACY OR ADEQUACY OF THIS PROSPECTUS. ANY REPRESENTATION TO THE CONTRARY IS A CRIMINAL OFFENSE.**

5. LIABILITY

Under the federal Securities Act of 1933, both civil and criminal liability may be imposed for violations. Criminal liability results from a willful violation of the act or fraud in *any* offer or sale of securities. Fraud also occurs when any material fact is omitted, causing a statement to be misleading. The penalty is a fine of up to $10,000 or five years in prison or both.

Three sections of the Securities Act of 1933 directly apply to civil liability of parties involved in issuing securities:

- Section 11 deals with registration statements.
- Section 12 relates to prospectuses and oral and written communication.
- Section 17 concerns fraudulent interstate transactions.

Section 11: Registration Statement The civil liability provision dealing with registration statements imposes liability on the following persons in favor of purchasers of securities:

1. Every person who signed the registration statement
2. Every director of the corporation or partner in the partnership issuing the security
3. Every person who, with his or her consent, is named in the registration statement as about to become a director or partner
4. Every accountant, engineer, or appraiser who assists in the preparation of the registration statement or its certification
5. Every underwriter

These persons are liable if the registration statement:

- Contains untrue statements of material facts
- Omits material facts required by statute or regulation
- Omits information that if not given makes the facts stated misleading

This last situation describes the factual situation of a statement containing a half-truth, which has the net effect of being misleading. The test of accuracy and materiality is as of the date the registration statement becomes effective.

A plaintiff-purchaser need not prove reliance on the registration statement in order to recover the amount of an investment, but proof of actual knowledge of the falsity by the purchaser is a defense. Knowledge of the falsity by a defendant need not be proved, but reliance on an expert such as an accountant is a defense. For example, a director may defend a suit on the basis of a false financial statement by showing reliance on a certified public accountant. This reliance exception logically does not apply to the issuer. Because the issuer provides information to the expert, the issuer should not be allowed to rely on the expert's use of the inaccurate information.

Section 12: Prospectus and Other Communications This section of the 1933 act is divided into two parts. While Section 11 creates liability for those responsible for a false or misleading registration statement, the first subsection of Section 12 imposes liability on those who offer or sell securities that are not registered with the SEC. This liability exists regardless of the intent or conduct of those who fail to comply with the registration requirements. Thus, liability traditionally has been imposed against violators even though they lacked any wrongful intent.

In the following case, the Supreme Court approved the defendant's argument that the plaintiff was equally responsible for the failure to register the securities sold. This case appears to be a movement away from traditional strict liability for failure to file the required registration statement.

PINTER V. DAHL

108 S. CT. 2063 (1988)

BLACKMUN, J.: The question presented by this case . . . [is] whether the common-law *in pari delicto* defense is available in a private action brought under § 12(1) of the Securities Act of 1933 for the rescission of the sale of unregistered securities. . . .

The controversy arises out of the sale prior to 1982 of unregistered securities (fractional undivided interests in oil and gas leases) by petitioner Billy J. "B. J." Pinter to respondents Maurice Dahl and Dahl's friends, family, and business associates. Pinter is an oil and gas producer in Texas and Oklahoma, and a registered securities dealer in Texas. Dahl is a California real estate broker and investor, who, at the time of his dealings with Pinter, was a veteran of two unsuccessful oil and gas ventures. . . . Pinter located leases in Oklahoma, and Dahl toured the properties, often without Pinter, in order to talk to others and get a feel for the properties. Upon examining the geology, drilling logs, and production history assembled by Pinter, Dahl concluded, in the words of the District Court, that "there was no way to lose."

After investing approximately $310,000 in the properties, Dahl told the other respondents about the venture. Except for Dahl and respondent Grantham, none of the respondents spoke to or met Pinter or toured the properties. Because of Dahl's involvement in the venture, each of the other respondents decided to invest about $7,500.

Dahl assisted his fellow investors in completing the subscription-agreement form prepared by Pinter. Each letter-contract signed by the purchaser stated that the participating interests were being sold without the benefit of registration under the Securities Act. . . .

When the venture failed and their interests proved to be worthless, respondents brought suit against Pinter . . . seeking rescission under § 12(1) of the Securities Act for the unlawful sale of unregistered securities.

In a counterclaim, Pinter alleged that Dahl, by means of fraudulent misrepresentations and concealment of facts, induced Pinter to sell and deliver the securities. Pinter averred that Dahl falsely assured Pinter that he would provide other qualified, sophisticated, and knowledgeable investors with all the information necessary for evaluation of the investment. Dahl allegedly agreed to raise the funds for the venture from those investors, with the understanding that Pinter would simply be the "operator" of the wells. Pinter also asserted, on the basis of the same factual allegations, that Dahl's suit was barred by the equitable defenses of estoppel and *in pari delicto.*

The District Court, after a bench trial, granted judgment for respondent-investors. . . . A divided panel of the Court of Appeals for the Fifth Circuit affirmed. The court . . . held that Dahl's involvement in the sales to the other respondents did not give Pinter an *in pari delicto* defense to Dahl's recovery. The court concluded that the defense is not available in an action under § 12(1) because that section creates "a strict liability offense" rather than liability based on intentional misconduct. . . .

Because of the importance of the issues involved to the administration of the federal securities laws, we granted certiorari.

The equitable defense of *in pari delicto,* which literally means "in equal fault," is rooted in the common-law notion that a plaintiff's recovery may be barred by his own wrongful conduct. Traditionally, the defense was limited to situations where the plaintiff bore at least substantially equal responsibility for his injury and where the parties' culpability arose out of the same illegal act. . . .

We feel that the Court of Appeals' notion that the *in pari delicto* defense should not be allowed in actions involving strict liability offenses is without support in history or logic. The doctrine traditionally has been applied in any action based on conduct that "transgresses statutory prohibitions." . . .

Our task . . . is to determine whether . . . recognition of the defense is proper in a suit for rescission brought under § 12(1) of the Securities Act. All parties in this case, as well as the Commission, maintain that the defense should be available. We agree, but find it necessary to circumscribe the scope of its application.

[CONTINUED]

. . . [A] defendant cannot escape liability unless, as a direct result of the plaintiff's own actions, the plaintiff bears at least substantially equal responsibility for the underlying illegality. The plaintiff must be an active, voluntary participant in the unlawful activity that is the subject of the suit. . . . Unless the degrees of fault are essentially indistinguishable or the plaintiff's responsibility is clearly greater, the *in pari delicto* defense should not be allowed, and the plaintiff should be compensated. . . .

In our view, where the § 12(1) plaintiff is primarily an investor, precluding suit would interfere significantly with effective enforcement of the securities laws and frustrate the primary objective of the Securities Act. The commission, too, takes this position. Because the Act is specifically designed to protect investors, even where a plaintiff actively participates in the distribution of unregistered securities, his suit should not be barred where his promotional efforts are incidental to his role as an investor. Thus, the *in pari delicto* defense may defeat recovery in a § 12(1) action only where the plaintiff's role in the offering or sale of nonexempted, unregistered securities is more as a promoter than as an investor. . . .

Given the record in this case, we cannot ascertain whether Pinter may successfully assert an *in pari delicto* defense against Dahl's § 12(1) claim. The District Court's findings in this case are not adequate to determine whether Dahl bears at least substantially equal responsibility for the failure to register the oil and gas interests or to distribute the securities in a manner that conformed with the statutory exemption and whether he was primarily a promoter of the offering. The findings indicate, on the one hand, that Dahl may have participated in initiating the entire investment, and that he loaned money to Pinter and solicited his associates' participation in the venture, but, on the other hand, that Dahl invested substantially more money than the other investor-respondents, expected and received no commission for his endeavors, and drafted none of the offering documents. Furthermore, the District Court made no findings as to who was responsible for the failure to register or for the manner in which the offering was conducted. Those findings will be made on the remand of this case for further proceedings. . . .

The judgment of the Court of Appeals is vacated, and the case is remanded for further proceedings consistent with this opinion.

Vacated and remanded.

CASE QUESTIONS

1. What is the relationship between Pinter and Dahl in this investment scenario?

2. Why and on what basis are the investors suing Pinter?

3. What is Pinter's argument for claiming the *in pari delicto* defense?

4. Why can't the Supreme Court make a final and determinative decision about the rights and duties of the parties in this case?

The second subsection of Section 12 imposes liability on sellers who use a prospectus or make communications (by mail, telephone, or other instrumentalities of interstate commerce) that contain an untrue statement of material facts required to be stated or necessary to make statements not misleading. As under Section 11, the plaintiff does not have to prove reliance on the false or misleading prospectus or communication. Nor does the plaintiff have to establish that the defendant intended the deception.

Purchasers of such securities may sue for their actual damages. If the purchaser still owns the securities and he or she can prove a direct contractual relationship with the seller, the remedy of rescission and a refund of the purchase price is also available.

Section 17: Fraudulent Transactions   This provision concerning fraudulent interstate transactions prohibits the use of any instrument of interstate communication in the offer or sale of any securities when the result is:

1. To defraud
2. To obtain money or property by means of an untrue or misleading statement
3. To engage in a business transaction or practice that may operate to defraud or deceive a purchaser

The requirement that a defendant-seller must act with the intent (**scienter**) to deceive or mislead in order to prove a Section 17 violation has caused much controversy over the years. The Supreme Court has resolved this issue by holding that a plaintiff must prove the defendant's intent to violate 1, above. However, no proof of the defendant's intent is required to find a violation of 2 or 3. The Court's decision is limited to when the plaintiff is seeking an injunction, because Section 17 does not explicitly provide for the private remedy of monetary damages.

6. DEFENSES

The Securities Act of 1933 recognized several defenses that may be used to avoid civil liability. Among the most important defenses are:

- Materiality
- The statute of limitations
- Due diligence

Materiality   A defendant in a case involving the 1933 act might argue that the false or misleading information is not *material* and thus should not have had an impact on the purchaser's decision-making process. Determining whether or not a particular fact is material depends on the facts and the parties involved.

The SEC and the courts have attempted to define materiality. The term "material" describes the kinds of information that an average prudent investor would want to have so that he or she can make an intelligent, informed decision whether or not to buy the security. A material fact is one that if correctly stated or disclosed would have deterred or tended to deter the average prudent investor from purchasing the securities in question. The term does not cover minor inaccuracies or errors in matters of no interest to investors. Facts that tend to deter a person from purchasing a security are those that have an important bearing upon the nature or condition of the issuing corporation or its business.

Statute of Limitations   The statute of limitations is a defense for both civil and criminal liability. The basic period is one year. The one year does not start to run until the discovery of the untrue statement or omission. Or it does not start to run until the time such discovery would have been made with reasonable diligence. In no event may a suit be brought more than three years after the sale.

A defense similar to the statute of limitations is also provided. The 1933 act provides that if the person acquiring the security does so after the issuer has made generally available an earnings statement covering at least 12 months after the effective date of the registration statement, then this person must prove actual reliance on the registration statement.

Due Diligence   A very important defense for experts such as accountants is the **due diligence defense.**

To establish this defense, the expert must prove that a reasonable investigation of the financial statements of the issuer and controlling persons was conducted. As the result of this investigation, an expert exercising due diligence must prove that there was no reason to believe any of the information in the registration statement or prospectus was false or misleading.

In determining whether or not an expert, such as an accountant, has made a reasonable investigation, the law provides that the standard of *reasonableness* is that required of a prudent person in the management of his or her own property. The burden of proof of this defense is on the expert, and the test is as of the time the registration statement became effective. The due diligence defense, in effect, requires proof that a party was not guilty of fraud or negligence.

concept SUMMARY   *Liability under the Securities Act of 1933*

Section 11

Purpose: Creates liability for false or misleading registration statements

Plaintiff's case: Not required to prove defendant's intent to deceive or plaintiff's reliance on documents

Defendant's defenses: Proof of no false or misleading information; proof that plaintiff knew of false or misleading nature of information; except for issuers, proof of reliance on an expert (attorney or accountant)

Section 12

Purpose: (1) Creates liability for failing to file a required registration statement; (2) creates liability for false or misleading prospectus

Plaintiff's case: Not required to prove defendant's intent to deceive or plaintiff's reliance on documents

Defendant's defenses: For (1), *in pari delicto,* plaintiff equally at fault for failing to file a registration statement; for (2), same as Section 11 defenses

Section 17

Purpose: In an interstate transaction, it is unlawful to (1) employ any device, scheme, or artifice of fraud; (2) obtain money or property by untrue statement or omission of material fact; (3) engage in events that operate or would operate as fraud or deceit

Plaintiff's case: For (1), required to prove defendant's intent to deceive; for (2) and (3), not required to prove intent to deceive

Defendant's defenses: For (1), proof of no intent to deceive and proof of good faith; for (2), proof of no material misstatement or omission; for (3), proof of no involvement in unlawful activities

Criminal Liability

$10,000 fine or 5 years in prison or both

SECURITIES EXCHANGE ACT OF 1934: BEING PUBLIC

Whereas the Securities Act of 1933 deals with original offerings of securities, the **Securities Exchange Act of 1934** regulates transfers of securities after the initial sale. The 1934 act, which created the Securities and Exchange Commission, also deals with regulation of securities exchanges, brokers, and dealers in securities.

The Securities Exchange Act makes it illegal to sell a security on a national exchange unless a registration is effective for the security. Registration under the 1934 act differs from registration under the 1933 act. Registration under the 1934 act requires filing prescribed forms with the applicable stock exchange and the SEC.

Provisions relating to stockbrokers and dealers prohibit the use of the mails or any other instrumentality of interstate commerce to sell securities unless the broker or the dealer is registered. The language is sufficiently broad to cover attempted sales as well as actual sales. Brokers and dealers must keep detailed records of their activities and file annual reports with the SEC.

The SEC requires that issuers of registered securities file periodic reports as well as report significant developments that would affect the value of the security. For example, the SEC requires companies to disclose foreign payoffs or bribes to obtain or retain foreign business operations. Businesses must disclose their minority hiring practices and other social data that may be of public concern. Business has been forced by the SEC to submit certain shareholder proposals to all shareholders as a part of proxy solicitation. When a new pension law was enacted, the SEC required that financial reports disclose the law's impact on the reporting business. The SEC's activity concerning information corporations must furnish to the investing public is almost limitless. As a result, SEC regulations are of paramount significance to all persons concerned with the financial aspects of business. This area of regulation directly affects the accounting profession. Since the SEC regulates financial statements, it frequently decides issues of proper accounting and auditing theory and practices.

The following sections examine how the Securities Exchange Act of 1934 affects the businessperson, the accountant, the lawyer, the broker, and the investor. These sections cover some fundamental concepts of this law, such as civil liability in general and insider transactions in particular, as well as criminal violations and penalties under the 1934 act.

7. SECTION 10(B) AND RULE 10B-5

Most of the litigation under the Securities and Exchange Act of 1934 is brought under Section 10(b) of the act and Rule 10b-5 promulgated by the SEC pursuant to the act. Section 10(b) and Rule 10b-5 declare that it is unlawful to use the mails or any instrumentality of interstate commerce or any national securities exchange to defraud *any person* in connection with the *purchase or sale* of any security. The actual language of this section and rule are contained in the box on the next page.

Courts have interpreted Section 10(b) and Rule 10b-5 as implicitly providing a private cause of action for the benefit of defrauded investors. Because this private action is recognized by the courts as being implicit, rather than explicitly created by Congress, several legal issues have been resolved on a case-by-case basis. Perhaps because of this judicially created confusion, common issues regarding litigation under Section 10(b) and Rule 10b-5 include the following:

- Who is liable?
- What can be recovered by the plaintiff, and does the defendant have the right to seek contribution from third parties?
- When is information material to the transaction?

LANGUAGE OF SECTION 10(B) OF THE 1934 ACT AND SEC'S RULE 10B-5

Section 10(b) states:

It shall be unlawful for any person, directly or indirectly, by the use of any means or instrumentality of interstate commerce or of the mails, or of any facility of any national securities exchange—

(b) To use or employ, in connection with the purchase or sale of any security registered on a national securities exchange or any security not so registered, any manipulative or deceptive device or contrivance in contravention of such rules and regulations as the [SEC] may prescribe.

Rule 10b-5, adopted by the SEC in 1942, states:

It shall be unlawful for any person, directly or indirectly, by the use of any means or instrumentality of interstate commerce, or of the mails or of any facility of any national securities exchange,

(a) To employ any device, scheme, or artifice to defraud,

(b) To make any untrue statement of a material fact or to omit to state a material fact necessary in order to make the statements made, in the light of the circumstances under which they were made, not misleading, or

(c) To engage in any act, practice, or course of business which operates or would operate as a fraud or deceit upon any person, in connection with the purchase or sale of any security.

Persons Liable Section 10(b) and Rule 10b-5 may be invoked against any person who indulges in fraudulent practices in the purchase or sale of securities. In actual practice, defendants in such cases tend to fall into four general categories:

- Insiders
- Broker-dealers
- Corporations whose stock is purchased or sold by plaintiffs
- Those, such as accountants, who aid and abet or conspire with a party who falls into one of the first three categories

In addition to these four groups, the statute and its rule require that those standing in a fiduciary relationship disclose all material facts before entering into transactions. This means that an officer, a director, or a controlling shareholder has a duty to disclose all material facts. Failure to do so is a violation and, in effect, fraudulent. Privity of contract is not required for a violation, and lack of privity of contract is no defense.

Liability under Rule 10b-5 may be imposed on an accountant even though he or she performs only an unaudited write-up. An accountant is liable for errors in financial statements contained in a prospectus or other filed report even though unaudited if there are errors he or she knew or should have known. Even when performing an unaudited write-up, an accountant must undertake at least a minimal investigation into the figures supplied to him or her and cannot disregard suspicious circumstances.

One issue that has been the subject matter of many court decisions is the applicable statute of limitations for a private Section 10(b) cause of action. Congress resolved this controversy by enacting legislation in December 1991. This legislation provides that the statute of limitations applicable to private actions under Section 10(b) "shall be the limitation period provided by the laws applicable in the jurisdiction" where the case arises. In essence, there is no federal statute of limitations for private actions under Section 10(b) of the 1934 act.

A more recent issue concerning who is liable under Section 10(b) and Rule 10b-5 relates to the meaning of the phrase "in connection with" the sale of a security. Notice in the following case how the Supreme Court gives a broad interpretation to protect the investor.

SEC v. ZANDFORD

122 S. Ct. 1899 (2002)

In 1987, William Wood, who is an elderly man in poor health, opened an investment account for himself and his mentally retarded daughter. Mr. Wood placed $419,255 in this account. Mr. Wood entrusted Charles Zandford, a securities broker, to exercise his discretion in managing these funds. Mr. Wood completed documentation stating the investment objective for the funds in this account were "safety of principal and income." Over a period of four years, Zandford withdrew funds from the Wood account and transferred it to accounts he controlled. In 1991, when Mr. Wood died, there was no money left in the original account.

Zandford was charged with and convicted of 13 counts of wire fraud. He was sentenced to 52 months in prison and ordered to pay $10,800 in restitution. The SEC then filed this civil complaint alleging violations of § 10(b) of the Securities Exchange Act of 1934 and Rule 10b-5. The SEC sought a court order requiring Zandford to pay $343,000 in damages to Mr. Wood's estate. The District Court entered a summary judgment in favor of the SEC on the basis of the criminal conviction establishing the facts of a § 10(b) violation. The Fourth Circuit Court of Appeals reversed and dismissed the civil complaint since it found that the conviction did not necessarily establish that Zandford's fraud was "in connection with" the sale of a security.

The SEC's petition for a writ of certiorari was granted so that the Supreme Court could construe the meaning of "in connection with the purchase or sale of any security" as it applies in this case.

STEVENS, J.: . . . Section 10(b) of the Securities Exchange Act makes it "unlawful for any person . . . to use or employ, in connection with the pur-

chase or sale of any security . . . , any manipulative or deceptive device or contrivance in contravention of such rules and regulations as the [SEC] may prescribe." Rule 10b-5, which implements this provision, forbids the use, "in connection with the purchase or sale of any security," of "any device, scheme, or artifice to defraud" or any other "act, practice, or course of business" that "operates . . . as a fraud or deceit." Among Congress' objectives in passing the Act was to insure honest securities markets and thereby promote investor confidence after the market crash of 1929. More generally, Congress sought to substitute a philosophy of full disclosure for the philosophy of caveat emptor and thus to achieve a high standard of business ethics in the securities industry.

. . . In its role enforcing the Act, the SEC has consistently adopted a broad reading of the phrase "in connection with the purchase or sale of any security." It has maintained that a broker who accepts payment for securities that he never intends to deliver, or who sells customer securities with intent to misappropriate the proceeds, violates § 10(b) and Rule 10b-5. This interpretation of the ambiguous text of § 10(b), in the context of formal adjudication, is entitled to deference if it is reasonable. For the reasons set forth below, we think it is. While the statute must not be construed so broadly as to convert every common-law fraud that happens to involve securities into a violation of § 10(b), neither the SEC nor this Court has ever held that there must be a misrepresentation about the value of a particular security in order to run afoul of the Act.

The SEC claims respondent engaged in a fraudulent scheme in which he made sales of his cus-

[CONTINUED]

tomer's securities for his own benefit. Respondent submits that the sales themselves were perfectly lawful and that the subsequent misappropriation of the proceeds, though fraudulent, is not properly viewed as having the requisite connection with the sales; in his view, the alleged scheme is not materially different from a simple theft of cash or securities in an investment account. We disagree.

According to the complaint, respondent "engaged in a scheme to defraud" the Woods beginning in 1988, shortly after they opened their account, and that scheme continued throughout the 2-year period during which respondent made a series of transactions that enabled him to convert the proceeds of the sales of the Woods' securities to his own use. The securities sales and respondent's fraudulent practices were not independent events. This is not a case in which, after a lawful transaction had been consummated, a broker decided to steal the proceeds and did so. Nor is it a case in which a thief simply invested the proceeds of a routine conversion in the stock market. Rather, respondent's fraud coincided with the sales themselves.

Taking the allegations in the complaint as true, each sale was made to further respondent's fraudulent scheme; each was deceptive because it was neither authorized by, nor disclosed to, the Woods. With regard to the sales of shares in the Woods' mutual fund, respondent initiated these transactions by writing a check to himself from that account, knowing that redeeming the check would require the sale of securities. Indeed, each time respondent exercised his power of disposition for his own benefit, that conduct, without more, was a fraud. In the aggregate, the sales are properly viewed as a course of business that operated as a fraud or deceit on a stockbroker's customer.

. . . [T]he Woods were injured as investors through respondent's deceptions, which deprived them of any compensation for the sale of their valuable securities. They were duped into believing respondent would conservatively invest their assets in the stock market and that any transactions made on their behalf would be for their benefit for the safety of principal and income. The fact that respondent misappropriated the proceeds of the sales provides persuasive evidence that he had violated § 10(b) when he made the sales, but misappropriation is not an essential element of the offense. . . .

Not only does such a fraud prevent investors from trusting that their brokers are executing transactions for their benefit, but it undermines the value of a discretionary account like that held by the Woods. The benefit of a discretionary account is that it enables individuals, like the Woods, who lack the time, capacity, or know-how to supervise investment decisions, to delegate authority to a broker who will make decisions in their best interests without prior approval. If such individuals cannot rely on a broker to exercise that discretion for their benefit, then the account loses its added value. Moreover, any distinction between omissions and misrepresentations is illusory in the context of a broker who has a fiduciary duty to her clients. . . .

[T]he SEC complaint describes a fraudulent scheme in which the securities transactions and breaches of fiduciary duty coincide. Those breaches were therefore "in connection with" securities sales within the meaning of § 10(b). Accordingly, the judgment of the Court of Appeals is reversed, and the case is remanded for further proceedings consistent with this opinion.

Reversed and remanded.

CASE QUESTIONS

1. What type of investment account did Mr. Wood open?

2. What was the stated investment strategy applicable to this account?

3. What argument did the securities dealer make in seeking to have the civil complaint dismissed?

4. What does the Supreme Court conclude with respect to the language "in connection with the purchase or sale of any security"?

Damages A plaintiff in a suit under Rule 10b-5 must prove damages. The damages of a defrauded purchaser are actual out-of-pocket losses or the excess of what was paid over the value of what was received. Courts in a few cases have used the *benefit of the bargain* measure of damages and awarded the buyer the difference between what he or she paid and what the security was represented to be worth. A buyer's damages are measured at the time of purchase.

Computation of a defrauded seller's damages is more difficult. A defrauding purchaser usually benefits from an increase in the value of the securities, while the plaintiff seller loses this increase. Courts do not allow defrauding buyers to keep these increases in value. Therefore, the measure of the seller's damages is the difference between the fair value of all that the seller received and the fair value of what he or she would have received had there been no fraud, except where the defendant received more than the seller's loss. In this latter case, the seller is entitled to the defendant's profit. As a result, defendants lose all profits flowing from the fraudulent conduct.

Plaintiffs under Rule 10b-5 are also entitled to consequential damages. These include lost dividends, brokerage fees, and taxes. In addition, courts may order payment of interest on the funds. Punitive damages are not permitted as they are in cases of common law fraud based on state laws. This distinction results from the language of the 1934 act, which limits recoveries to actual damages.

The issue of whether a defendant who is liable under Section 10(b) can seek contribution from third parties was not resolved until 1993. In the following case, the Supreme Court concludes that a right of contribution does exist in Section 10(b) private actions.

MUSICK, PEELER & GARRETT v. WAUSAU INS.

113 S. Ct. 2085 (1993)

KENNEDY, J.: Where there is joint responsibility for tortious conduct, the question often arises whether those who compensate the injured party may seek contribution from other joint tortfeasors who have paid no damages or paid less than their fair share. In this case we must determine whether defendants in a suit based on an implied private right of action under § 10(b) of the Securities Exchange Act of 1934 and Rule 10b-5 of the Securities and Exchange Commission (a 10b-5 action) may seek contribution from joint tortfeasors. Without addressing the merits of the claim for contribution in this case, we hold that defendants in a 10b-5 action have a right to seek contribution as a matter of federal law.

Cousins Home Furnishings, Inc. made a public offering of its stock in December 1983. The stock purchasers later brought a class action against Cousins, its parent company, various officers and directors of Cousins, and two lead underwriters. The plaintiffs alleged the stock offering was misleading in material respects in violation of §§ 11 and 12 of the Securities Act of 1933, § 10(b) of the Securities Exchange Act of 1934, and certain state laws. The named defendants settled with the plaintiffs for $13.5 million. Respondents, who insured most of the named defendants, funded $13 million of the settlement. Subrogated to the rights of their insureds, respondents brought this lawsuit seeking contribution from petitioners, who were the attorneys and accountants involved in the public offering. Respondents' complaint alleged these professionals had joint responsibility for the securities violations and were liable for contribution under

[CONTINUED]

various theories, including a right to contribution based on the 10b-5 action central to the complaint in the original class suit. . . .

Some three months after the Court of Appeals ruled in favor of respondents, the United States Court of Appeals for the Eighth Circuit created a conflict on the basic issue whether defendants in a 10b-5 action have a right to contribution. . . . Petitioners requested that we resolve the conflict among the Circuits. We granted their petition for a writ of certiorari on the sole question presented: "Whether federal courts may imply a private right to contribution in Section 10(b) of the Securities Exchange Act of 1934 and Rule 10b-5 of the Securities & Exchange Commission." . . .

The parties have devoted considerable portions of their briefs to debating whether a rule of contribution or of no contribution is more efficient or more equitable. . . . Our task is not to assess the relative merits of the competing rules, but rather to attempt to infer how the 1934 Congress would have addressed the issue had the 10b-5 action been included as an express provision in the 1934 Act. . . .

Inquiring about what a given Congress might have done, though not a promising venture as a general proposition, does in this case yield an answer we find convincing. . . . [T]wo sections of the 1934 Act, §§ 9 and 18 that, as we have noted, are close in structure, purpose and intent to the 10b-5 action. Each confers an explicit right of action in favor of private parties and, in so doing, discloses a congressional intent regarding the definition and apportionment of liability among private parties. . . . [T]hese express causes of action are of particular significance in determining how Congress would have resolved the question of contribution had it provided for a private cause of action under § 10(b). . . . §§ 9 and 18 are instructive because both target the precise dangers that are the focus of § 10(b), and the intent motivating all three sections is the same—"to deter fraud and manipulative practices in the securities market, and to ensure full disclosure of information material to investment decisions." . . .

Sections 9 and 18 contain nearly identical express provisions for a right to contribution, each permitting a defendant to "recover contribution as in cases of contract from any person who, if joined in the original suit, would have been liable to make the same payment." These were forward-looking provisions at the time. The course of tort law in this century has been to reverse the old rule against contribution, but this movement has been confined in large part to actions in negligence. The express contribution provisions in §§ 9 and 18 were, and still are, cited as important precedents because they permit contribution for intentional torts. We think that these explicit provisions for contribution are an important, not an inconsequential, feature of the federal securities laws and that consistency requires us to adopt a like contribution rule for the right of action existing under Rule 10b-5. Given the identity of purpose behind §§ 9, 10(b) and 18, and similarity in their operation, we find no ground for ruling that allowing contribution in 10b-5 actions will frustrate the purposes of the statutory section from which it is derived. . . .

Absent any showing that the implied § 10(b) liability structure or the 1934 Act as a whole will be frustrated by finding a right to contribution paralleling the right to contribution in analogous express liability provisions, our task is complete and our resolution clear: Those charged with liability in a 10b-5 action have a right to contribution against other parties who have joint responsibility for the violation.

The judgment of the Court of Appeals is **affirmed.**

CASE QUESTIONS

1. What is the factual basis for Wausau Insurance Company's making a claim of contribution against the attorneys and accountants in this case?

2. What is the argument by these professionals (petitioners) that they are not liable?

3. How does the Supreme Court determine the congressional intent related to the implicit Section 10(b) private cause of action?

Materiality Section 10(b) and Rule 10b-5 are usually referred to as the *antifraud provisions* of the act. A plaintiff seeking damages under the provisions must establish the existence of a material misrepresentation or omission made in connection with the purchase or sale of a security and the culpable state of mind of the defendant. Materiality under the 1934 act is the same as materiality under the 1933 act. However, liability under Rule 10b-5 requires proof of the defendant's intent to deceive. Proof of the defendant's simple negligence is not enough to establish liability. The plaintiff also must establish that the defendant's practice is manipulative and not merely corporate mismanagement.

The concept of fraud under Section 10(b) encompasses not only untrue statements of material facts but also the failure to state material facts necessary to prevent statements actually made from being misleading. In other words, a half-truth that misleads is fraudulent. Finally, failure to correct a misleading impression left by statements already made, or silence where there is a duty to speak, gives rise to a violation of Rule 10b-5 because it is a form of aiding and abetting the deception. Although there is no general duty on the part of all persons with knowledge of improper activities to report them, a duty to disclose may arise from the fact of a special relationship or set of circumstances, such as an accountant certifying financial statements.

One of the most difficult issues concerning materiality arises in preliminary merger negotiations. What should management respond when asked about merger possibilities? Should management reveal information about merger possibilities even when the likelihood of an actual merger is very slight? The Supreme Court uses an objective-person case-by-case analysis to determine whether information about potential mergers is material and thus required to be disclosed. The Court said, "materiality depends on the significance the reasonable investor would place on the withheld or misrepresented information."

8. INSIDER TRANSACTIONS

Section 16, one of the most important provisions of the Securities Exchange Act of 1934, concerns insider transactions. An **insider** is any person who:

- Owns more than 10 percent of any security
- Is a director or an officer of the issuer of the security

In early 1991, the SEC adopted new rules under Section 16. These rules define an officer for insider trading purposes as the executive officers, accounting officers, chief financial officers, and controllers. The SEC also examines the individual investor's function within the company rather than the title of the position held.

Section 16 and SEC regulations require that insiders file, at the time of the registration or within 10 days after becoming an insider, a statement of the amount of such issues of which they are the owners. The regulations also require filing within 10 days after the close of each calendar month thereafter if there has been any change in such ownership during such month (indicating the change). There are exemptions to the insider rules for executors or administrators of estates. Odd-lot dealers are also generally exempt.

The reason for prohibiting insiders from trading for profit is to prevent the use of information that is available to an insider but not to the general public. Because the SEC cannot determine for certain when nonpublic information is improperly used, Section 16 creates a presumption that any profit made within a six-month time period is illegal. These profits are referred to as **short-swing profits.** Thus, if a director, officer, or principal owner realizes profits on the purchase and sale of a security within a six-month period, the profits legally belong to the company or to the investor who purchased it from or sold it to an insider, resulting in the insider's profit and the investor's loss. The order of the purchase and sale is immaterial. The profit is calculated on the lowest price in and highest price out during any six-month period. Unlike the required proof of intent to deceive under Section 10(b), the short-swing profits rule of Section 16 does not depend on any misuse of information. In other words, short-swing profits by insiders, regardless of the insiders' states of mind, are absolutely prohibited.

While the SEC enforces the requirements of Section 16 that insiders file certain documents, the SEC does not enforce the provision that prohibits insiders from engaging in short-swing profits. This provision of Section 16 is enforced by civil actions filed by the issuer of the security or by a person who owns a security of the issuer.

9. NONPUBLIC INFORMATION

The SEC's concern for trading based on nonpublic information goes beyond the Section 16 ban on short-swing profits. Indeed, a person who is not technically an insider but who trades securities without disclosing nonpublic information may violate Section 10(b) and Rule 10b-5. The SEC takes the position that the profit obtained as the result of a trader's silence concerning information that is not freely available to everyone is a manipulation or deception prohibited by Section 10(b) and Rule 10b-5. In essence, the users of nonpublic information are treated like insiders if they can be classified as tippees.

A **tippee** is a person who learns of nonpublic information from an insider. In essence, a tippee is viewed as a temporary insider. A tippee is liable for the use of nonpublic information because an insider should not be allowed to do indirectly what he or she cannot do directly. In other words, a tippee is liable for trading or passing on information that is nonpublic.

The use of nonpublic information for financial gain has not been prohibited entirely. For example, in one case, a financial printer had been hired to print corporate takeover bids. An employee of the printer was able to deduce the identities of both the acquiring companies and the companies targeted for takeover. Without disclosing the knowledge about the prospective takeover bids, the employee purchased stock in the target companies and then sold it for a profit immediately after the takeover attempts were made public. He was indicted and convicted for having violated Section 10(b) and Rule 10b-5. The Supreme Court reversed, holding that the defendant had no duty to reveal the nonpublic information, since he was not in a fiduciary position with respect to either the acquiring or the acquired company.

In another case the U.S. Supreme Court further narrowed a tippee's liability. The Court ruled that a tippee becomes liable under Section 10(b) only if the tipper breaches a fiduciary duty to the business organization or fellow shareholders. Therefore, if the tipper communicated nonpublic information for reasons other than personal gain, neither the tipper nor the tippee could be liable for a securities violation.

These two Supreme Court cases have made it more difficult for the SEC to control the use of nonpublic information. However, the SEC has successfully argued that a person should be considered to be a temporary insider if that person conveys nonpublic information that was to have been kept confidential. This philosophy has become known as the **misappropriation theory** of insider trading. The following case approves the misappropriation theory.

UNITED STATES V. O'HAGAN

117 S. CT. 2199 (1997)

GINSBURG, J.: . . . Respondent James Herman O'Hagan was a partner in the law firm of Dorsey & Whitney in Minneapolis, Minnesota. In July 1988, Grand Metropolitan PLC (Grand Met), a company based in London, England, retained Dorsey & Whitney as local counsel to represent Grand Met regarding a potential tender offer for the common stock of the Pillsbury Company, headquartered in Minneapolis. Both Grand Met and Dorsey & Whitney took precautions to protect the confidentiality of Grand Met's tender offer plans. O'Hagan did no work on the Grand Met representation. Dorsey & Whitney withdrew from representing Grand Met on September 9, 1988. Less than a month later, on October 4, 1988, Grand Met publicly announced its tender offer for Pillsbury stock.

On August 18, 1988, while Dorsey & Whitney was still representing Grand Met, O'Hagan began purchasing call options for Pillsbury stock. Each option gave him the right to purchase 100 shares of Pillsbury stock by a specified date in September 1988. Later in August and in September, O'Hagan made additional purchases of Pillsbury call options. By the end of September, he owned 2,500 unexpired Pillsbury options. . . . O'Hagan also purchased, in September 1988, some 5,000 shares of Pillsbury common stock, at a price just under $39 per share. When Grand Met announced its tender offer in October, the price of Pillsbury stock rose to nearly $60 per share. O'Hagan then sold his Pillsbury call options and common stock, making a profit of more than $4.3 million.

The Securities and Exchange Commission (SEC or Commission) initiated an investigation into O'Hagan's transactions, culminating in a 57-count indictment. The indictment alleged that O'Hagan de-

frauded his law firm and its client, Grand Met, by using for his own trading purposes material, nonpublic information regarding Grand Met's planned tender offer. . . .

A divided panel of the Court of Appeals for the Eighth Circuit reversed all of O'Hagan's convictions. Liability under § 10(b) and Rule 10b-5, the Eighth Circuit held, may not be grounded on the "misappropriation theory" of securities fraud on which the prosecution relied. . . .

Decisions of the Courts of Appeals are in conflict on the propriety of the misappropriation theory under § 10(b) and Rule. . . . We granted certiorari and now reverse the Eighth Circuit's judgment. . . .

In pertinent part, § 10(b) of the Exchange Act provides:

> It shall be unlawful for any person, directly or indirectly, by the use of any means or instrumentality of interstate commerce or of the mails, or of any facility of any national securities exchange— . . .
>
> (b) To use or employ, in connection with the purchase or sale of any security registered on a national securities exchange or any security not so registered, any manipulative or deceptive device or contrivance in contravention of such rules and regulations as the [Securities and Exchange] Commission may prescribe as necessary or appropriate in the public interest or for the protection of investors.

The statute thus proscribes (1) using any deceptive device (2) in connection with the purchase or sale of securities, in contravention of rules prescribed by the Commission. The provision, as written, does not confine its coverage to deception of a purchaser or seller of securities; rather, the statute reaches any deceptive device used in connection with the purchase or sale of any security.

[CONTINUED]

Pursuant to its § 10(b) rulemaking authority, the Commission has adopted Rule 10b-5, which, as relevant here, provides:

> It shall be unlawful for any person, directly or indirectly, by the use of any means or instrumentality of interstate commerce, or of the mails or of any facility of any national securities exchange,
>
> (a) To employ any device, scheme, or artifice to defraud, [or] . . .
>
> (c) To engage in any act, practice, or course of business which operates or would operate as a fraud or deceit upon any person, in connection with the purchase or sale of any security.

. . . Under the "traditional" or "classical theory" of insider trading liability, § 10(b) and Rule 10b-5 are violated when a corporate insider trades in the securities of his corporation on the basis of material, nonpublic information. . . .

The "misappropriation theory" holds that a person commits fraud "in connection with" a securities transaction, and thereby violates § 10(b) and Rule 10b-5, when he misappropriates confidential information for securities trading purposes, in breach of a duty owed to the source of the information. Under this theory, a fiduciary's undisclosed, self-serving use of a principal's information to purchase or sell securities, in breach of a duty of loyalty and confidentiality, defrauds the principal of the exclusive use of that information. In lieu of premising liability on a fiduciary relationship between company insider and purchaser or seller of the company's stock, the misappropriation theory premises liability on a fiduciary-turned-trader's deception of those who entrusted him with access to confidential information.

The two theories are complementary, each addressing efforts to capitalize on nonpublic information through the purchase or sale of securities. The classical theory targets a corporate insider's breach of duty to shareholders with whom the insider transacts; the misappropriation theory outlaws trading on the basis of nonpublic information by a corporate "outsider" in breach of a duty owed not to a trading party, but to the source of the information. The misappropriation theory is thus designed to protect the integrity of the securities markets against abuses by outsiders to a corporation who have access to confidential information that will affect the corporation's security price when revealed, but who owe no fiduciary or other duty to that corporation's shareholders.

In this case, the indictment alleged that O'Hagan, in breach of a duty of trust and confidence he owed to his law firm, Dorsey & Whitney, and to its client, Grand Met, traded on the basis of nonpublic information regarding Grand Met's planned tender offer for Pillsbury common stock. This conduct, the Government charged, constituted a fraudulent device in connection with the purchase and sale of securities.

We agree with the Government that misappropriation, as just defined, satisfies § 10(b)'s requirement that chargeable conduct involve a "deceptive device or contrivance" used "in connection with" the purchase or sale of securities. We observe, first, that misappropriators, as the Government describes them, deal in deception. A fiduciary who "[pretends] loyalty to the principal while secretly converting the principal's information for personal gain," "dupes" or defrauds the principal. . . .

Deception through nondisclosure is central to the theory of liability for which the Government seeks recognition. As counsel for the Government stated in explanation of the theory at oral argument: "To satisfy the common law rule that a trustee may not use the property that [has] been entrusted [to] him, there would have to be consent. To satisfy the requirement of the Securities Act that there be no deception, there would only have to be disclosure." . . .

[F]ull disclosure forecloses liability under the misappropriation theory: Because the deception essential to the misappropriation theory involves feigning fidelity to the source of information, if the fiduciary discloses to the source that he plans to trade on the nonpublic information, there is no "deceptive device" and thus no § 10(b) violation—although the fiduciary-turned-trader may remain liable under state law for breach of a duty of loyalty.

We turn next to the § 10(b) requirement that the misappropriator's deceptive use of information be "in connection with the purchase or sale of [a] security." This element is satisfied because the fiduciary's fraud is consummated, not when the fiduciary gains the confidential information, but when, without disclosure to his principal, he uses the information to purchase or sell securities. The securities transaction and the breach of duty thus coincide.

[CONTINUED]

This is so even though the person or entity defrauded is not the other party to the trade; but is, instead, the source of the nonpublic information. A misappropriator who trades on the basis of material, nonpublic information, in short, gains his advantageous market position through deception; he deceives the source of the information and simultaneously harms members of the investing public.

The misappropriation theory targets information of a sort that misappropriators ordinarily capitalize upon to gain no-risk profits through the purchase or sale of securities. . . .

The misappropriation theory comports with § 10(b)'s language, which requires deception "in connection with the purchase or sale of any security," not deception of an identifiable purchaser or seller. The theory is also well-turned to an animating purpose of the Exchange Act: to insure honest securities markets and thereby promote investor confidence. Although informational disparity is inevitable in the securities markets, investors likely would hesitate to venture their capital in a market where trading based on misappropriated nonpublic information is unchecked by law. An investor's informational disadvantage vis-a-vis a misappropriator with material, nonpublic information stems from contrivance, not luck; it is a disadvantage that cannot be overcome with research or skill.

In sum, considering the inhibiting impact on market participation of trading on misappropriated information, and the congressional purposes underlying § 10(b), it makes scant sense to hold a lawyer like O'Hagan a § 10(b) violator if he works for a law firm representing the target of a tender offer, but not if he works for a law firm representing the bidder. The text of the statute requires no such result. The misappropriation at issue here was properly made the subject of a § 10(b) charge because it meets the statutory requirement that there be "deceptive" conduct "in connection with" securities transactions. . . .

. . . [T]he misappropriation theory, as we have examined and explained it in this opinion, is both consistent with the statute and with our precedent. Vital to our decision that criminal liability may be sustained under the misappropriation theory, we emphasize, are two sturdy safeguards Congress has provided regarding scienter. To establish a criminal violation of Rule 10b-5, the Government must prove that a person "willfully" violated the provision. Furthermore, a defendant may not be imprisoned for violating Rule 10b-5 if he proves that he had no knowledge of the rule. . . .

The Eighth Circuit erred in holding that the misappropriation theory is inconsistent with § 10(b). The Court of Appeals may address on remand O'Hagan's other challenges to his convictions under § 10(b) and Rule 10b-5. . . .

Reversed and remanded.

CASE QUESTIONS

1. What was O'Hagan accused of doing that was illegal?
2. What is the theory that the SEC argues is the basis of O'Hagan's wrongdoing?
3. How did the trial court and the appellate court rule in this case?
4. What reasons did the Supreme Court give for finding that the misappropriation theory is appropriate?
5. According to the Supreme Court, when and against whom did the misappropriation occur?

The SEC continues to focus its enforcement efforts on the misuse of nonpublic information at all levels of transactions. The SEC's efforts are aided by the fact that the civil penalty for gaining illegal profits with nonpublic information is three times the profits gained. In addition, controlling persons who fail to prevent these violations by employees may be civilly liable for the greater amount of triple damages or S1,000,000.

The penalties were increased to their current levels by the Insider Trading and Securities Fraud Enforcement Act of 1988. This law also provides that suits alleging the illegal use of nonpublic information may be filed within a five-year period after the wrongful transaction. This period, being substantially longer than the one year/three years limitation periods for other federal securities violations, illustrates the emphasis Congress has placed on preventing trading on nonpublic information.

10. ADDITIONAL CIVIL LIABILITY

In 1990, Congress expressed its concern for enforcement of the securities laws. In that year, the Securities Enforcement Remedies Act became law. This legislation provides that civil fines of up to $500,000 per organization and $100,000 per individual may be imposed and collected by the courts. In addition, an individual found to have violated the securities laws may be prohibited by the court from serving as an officer or director of a business organization. These fines and this prohibition from service can be utilized, at the judge's discretion, when a party in a civil case is found to have violated the securities laws. There does not have to be any proof of a criminal violation for these fines to be imposed.

Furthermore, Section 18 of the Securities Exchange Act of 1934 imposes liability on a theory of fraud on any person who shall make or cause to be made any false and misleading statements of material fact in any application, report, or document filed under the act. This liability favors both purchasers and sellers. A plaintiff must prove that the defendant knowingly made a false statement, that plaintiff relied on the false or misleading statement, and that plaintiff suffered damage.

Two distinctions between this section of the 1934 act and Sections 11 and 12 of the 1933 act are noteworthy. First, the requirement that an intent to deceive be proven under Section 18 means that the defendant's good faith is a defense. Good faith exists when a person acts without knowledge that the statement is false and misleading. In other words, freedom from fraud is a defense under an action based on Section 18. There is no liability under this section for simple negligence. Second, the plaintiff in a Section 18 case must prove reliance on the false or misleading filing. The simple fact that the filing is inaccurate is not sufficient. In a Section 11 or 12 case under the 1933 act, the plaintiff does not have to establish reliance.

11. CRIMINAL LIABILITY

The 1934 act provides for criminal sanctions for willful violations of its provisions or the rules adopted under it. Liability is imposed for false material statements in applications, reports, documents, and registration statements. In response to the corporate scandals occurring during the beginning of the twenty-first century, Congress in 2002 increased the criminal penalties for violating the Securities Exchange Act of 1934. An individual found guilty of filing false or misleading documents with the SEC may be fined up to $5,000,000 and imprisoned for up to 20 years. A business organization found guilty of filing with the SEC false or misleading documents may be subject to a fine up to $25,000,000. An individual guilty of securities fraud may face a prison sentence of up to 25 years. These increased sanctions emphasize the seriousness with which all businesspeople must treat compliance with securities regulations.

Failure to file the required reports and documents makes the issuer subject to a $100 forfeiture per day. A person cannot be convicted if he or she proves that he or she has no knowledge of a rule or regulation, but, of course, lack of knowledge of a statute is no defense.

Criminal liability is an important consideration for officers and directors as well as for accountants. Accountants have been found guilty of a crime for failure to disclose important facts to shareholder-investors. Compliance with generally accepted accounting principles is not an absolute defense. The critical issue in such cases is whether the financial statements as a whole fairly present the financial condition of the company and whether they accurately report operations for the covered periods. If they do not, the second issue is whether the accountant acted in good faith. Compliance with generally accepted accounting principles is evidence of good faith, but such evidence is not necessarily conclusive. Lack of criminal intent is the defense usually asserted by accountants charged with a crime. They usually admit mistakes or even negligence but deny any criminal wrongdoing. Proof of motive is not required.

As with issues of civil liability, most cases involving potential criminal liability are litigated under Section 10(b) and Rule 10b-5.

---

concept SUMMARY **Securities Exchange Act of 1934**

Section 10(b)

Purpose: Creates liability for use of mail or any instrumentality of interstate commerce to defraud any person in connection with the purchase or sale of any security

Plaintiff's case: Proof of defendant's intent to deceive through use of false information or nondisclosure of truthful information; plaintiff's reliance on fraudulent documents; and damages

Defendant's defenses: No actual fraud was involved; only aided or abetted fraud; information was not material

Civil liability: person in violation of § 10(b) is liable for actual damages, court costs, and reasonable attorney fees

Section 16(b)

Purpose: Creates strict liability for any insider making a profit on issuer's securities during any six-month period

Plaintiff's case: Proof of the short-swing nature of the profitable transaction

Defendant's defenses: Proof of no short-swing transaction; good faith (lack of intent) is no defense

Civil fines: Up to three times the illegal profits; ban from service as director or officer

Section 18

Purpose: Imposes liability for fraudulently filing false or misleading documents with the SEC or any exchange

Plaintiff's case: Proof of defendant's intent to make false or misleading documents filed; plaintiff's reliance on documents filed; and damages

Defendant's defenses: Freedom from fraud; good faith—no intent to defraud; no reliance by plaintiff on documents filed

Criminal Liability

For securities fraud: up to 25 years in prison

For false or misleading documents filed: $5,000,000 fine or 20 years in prison or both per individual; $25,000,000 fine per organization

For trading on nonpublic information: $1 million fine or 10 years in prison or both per individual; $10 million fine per organization

---

RECENT DEVELOPMENTS IN AND CONSIDERATIONS BEYOND THE FEDERAL SECURITIES LAWS

In addition to understanding the historical nature of federal securities laws discussed in the previous sections, every person dealing with the issuance of securities should be familiar with recent developments and the applicable state's securities regulations. Federal statutes do not preempt states from imposing dual regulations. For example, although a securities transaction might be in full compliance with the federal requirements, the intrastate aspects of the transaction are governed by the state. Furthermore, a business or individual exempt from the application of the federal laws may still have to comply with state regulations. Before examining state securities regulations, a review of recent legislative developments is presented.

12. SARBANES-OXLEY ACT OF 2002

The major corporate scandals that adversely impacted the securities markets during the first years of this new century were met with a significant federal legislative response. In 2002, Congress passed and President George W. Bush signed the **Sarbanes-Oxley Act.** This law attempted to address some of the perceived needs for change in the area of regulating securities. In particular, the impact of the Sarbanes-Oxley Act is summarized in the box below.

Some commentators believe the Sarbanes-Oxley Act is a major piece of legislation helping to correct some inadequacies that exist. Others have commented that this legislation is more likely to address perceptions rather than substance. The real impact of this recent enactment will have to be evaluated over the next few years.

A quick review of the Sarbanes-Oxley Act may help you understand why its impact is uncertain. First, the call to increase the SEC's budget met resistance from the White House as President Bush proposed an increase in the SEC's 2003 budget to $568 million. Congress had suggested a budget of $776 million. There is little doubt that the SEC budget will grow, but clearly the legislative and executive branches have different visions as to the most appropriate size or amount.

Second, the Public Company Accounting Oversight Board is a five-member panel appointed by the SEC commissioners. Thus, this board reports to the SEC as opposed to having its own standing as an administrative agency. The controversy over this appointment process resulted in the SEC chairman resigning followed by the resignation of the first chairman of the new board.

Third, the requirement that members of the corporate audit committee be independent of that organization's management is seen as a positive step in ensuring serious and thorough review of the financial condition of business organizations. This aspect of the Sarbanes-Oxley Act is combined with the requirement that CEOs certify financial statements. How this fourth element of the law will change the oversight exhibited by CEOs and other key members of management teams remains to be fully developed.

Finally, the significant increases in criminal penalties have been discussed previously in the chapter. In particular, you might want to reread the preceding section.

SARBANES-OXLEY ACT OF 2002

- Increases the SEC budget significantly
- Creates the Public Company Accounting Oversight Board
- Requires that members of corporate audit committees must be independent
- Mandates that CEOs certify financial statements
- Increases in criminal penalties

13. STATE BLUE SKY LAWS

Throughout their history, state regulations regarding securities laws commonly have been referred to as **blue sky laws**—probably because they were intended to protect the potential investor from buying "a piece of the attractive blue sky" (worthless or risky securities) without financial and other information about what was being purchased. The blue sky laws can apply to securities subject to federal laws as well as to those securities exempt from the federal statutes. It is clearly established that the federal laws do not preempt the existence of state blue sky laws. Due to their broad application, any person associated with issuing or thereafter transferring securities should survey the blue sky laws passed by the various states.

Although the existence of federal securities laws has influenced state legislatures, enactment of blue sky laws has not been uniform. Indeed, states typically have enacted laws that contain provisions similar to the antifraud provisions, the registration of securities provisions, the registration of securities brokers and dealers provisions, or a combination of these provisions of the federal laws. To bring some similarity to the various blue sky laws, the Uniform Securities Act was proposed for adoption by all states beginning in 1956. Since that time, the Uniform Securities Act has been the model for blue sky laws. A majority of states have used the uniform proposal as a guideline when enacting or amending their blue sky laws.

Registration Requirements Despite the trend toward uniformity, state laws still vary a great deal in their methods of regulating both the distribution of securities and the practices of the securities industry within each state. For example, state regulations concerning the requirements of registering securities vary widely. Some states require *registration by notification,* other states require *registration by qualification.* Registration by notification allows issuers to offer securities for sale automatically after a stated time period expires unless the administrative agency takes action to prevent the offering. This is very similar to the registration process under the Securities Act of 1933. Registration by qualification usually requires a more detailed disclosure by the issuer. Under this type of regulation, a security cannot be offered for sale until the administrative agency grants the issuer a license or certificate to sell securities.

In an attempt to resolve some of this conflict over the registration procedure, the drafters of the Uniform Securities Act may have compounded the problem. This act adopts the registration by notification process for an issuer who has demonstrated stability and performance. Registration by qualification is required by those issuers who do not have a proven record and who are not subject to the Securities Act of 1933. In addition, the Uniform Securities Act created a third procedure—*registration by coordination.* For those issuers of securities who must register with the SEC, duplicate documents are filed with the state's administrative agency. Unless a state official objects, the state registration becomes effective automatically when the federal registration statement is deemed effective.

Exemptions To further compound the confusion about blue sky laws, various exemptions of the securities or transactions have been adopted by the states. Four basic exemptions from blue sky laws have been identified. Every state likely has enacted at least one and perhaps a combination of these exemptions. Among these common four are the exemption:

1. For an isolated transaction
2. For an offer or sale to a limited number of offerees or purchasers within a stated time period

3. For a private offering
4. For a sale if the number of holders after the sale does not exceed a specified number

The second type of exemption probably is the most common exemption, because it is part of the Uniform Securities Act. Nevertheless, states vary on whether the exemption applies to offerees or to purchasers. There also is great variation on the maximum number of such offerees or purchasers involved. That number likely ranges between 5 and 35, depending on the applicable blue sky law. The time period for the offers or purchases, as the case may be, also may vary; however, 12 months seems to be the most common period.

Usually the applicable time limitation is worded to read, for example, "*any* 12-month time period." In essence, this language means that each day starts a new time period running. For example, assume a security is exempt from blue sky registration requirements if the issuer sells (or offers to sell) securities to no more than 35 investors during any 12-month period. Furthermore, assume the following transactions occur, with each investor being a different person or entity:

• On February 1, 2003, issuer sells to 5 investors.
• On June 1, 2003, issuer sells to 10 investors.
• On September 1, 2003, issuer sells to 10 investors.
• On December 1, 2003, issuer sells to 5 investors.
• On March 1, 2004, issuer sells to 5 investors.
• On May 1, 2004, issuer sells to 10 investors.

Only 30 investors are involved during the 12-month period following February 1, 2003. However, 40 investors are purchasers during the 12 months following June 1, 2003. Therefore, this security and the transactions involved are not exempt from the blue sky law. Civil as well as criminal liability may result for failure to comply with applicable legal regulations.

Although blue sky laws may cause confusion because of their variation, ignorance of the state legal requirements is no defense. This confusion is aggravated when the businessperson considers the further applicability of federal securities laws. To diminish this confusion, any person involved in the issuance or subsequent transfer of securities should consult with lawyers and accountants as well as other experts who have a working knowledge of securities regulations.

KEY TERMS

Blue sky laws   502
Controlling person   481
Due diligence defense   487
Insider   494
Issuer   481
Misappropriation theory   496
Posteffective period   482
Prefiling period   481
Prospectus   482
Registration statement   481
Sarbanes-Oxley Act of 2002   501
Scienter   486

Securities Act of 1933   479
Securities and Exchange Commission (SEC)   479
Securities Exchange Act of 1934   487
Security   479
Seller   481
Short-swing profits   495
Tippee   495
Tombstone ad   482
Underwriter   481
Waiting period   482

REVIEW QUESTIONS AND PROBLEMS

Introduction

1. *What Is a Security?*

   W. J. Howey Company and Howey-in-the-Hills Service, Inc., are Florida corporations under common control and management. Howey Company offers to sell to the public its orange grove, tree by tree. Howey-in-the-Hills Service, Inc., offers these buyers a contract wherein the appropriate care, harvesting, and marketing of the oranges would be provided. Most of the buyers who sign the service contracts are nonresidents of Florida who have very little knowledge or skill needed to care for and harvest the oranges. These buyers are attracted by the expectation of profits. Is a sale of orange trees by the Howey Company and a sale of services by Howey-in-the-Hills Service, Inc., a sale of a security? Why or why not?

2. *Securities and Exchange Commission*

   (a) When was this administrative agency created?

   (b) What types of regulatory authorities does the SEC have at its disposal?

The Securities Act of 1933: Going Public

3. *Parties Regulated*

   Who are the four types of parties governed by the 1933 Securities Act?

4. *Documents Involved*

   (a) What are the two important documents required by the Securities Act of 1933?

   (b) Under the provisions of the federal Securities Act of 1933, there are three important time periods concerning when securities may be sold or offered for sale. Name and describe these three time periods.

5. *Liability*

   To secure a loan, Rubin pledges stock that he represents as being marketable and worth approximately $1.7 million. In fact, the stock is nonmarketable and practically worthless. He is charged with violating the Securities Act of 1933. He claims that because no sale occurred, he is not guilty. Is he correct? Why or why not?

6. *Defenses*

   What are three defenses that might be used by a party charged with violating the Securities Act of 1933?

Securities Exchange Act of 1934: Being Public

7. *Section 10(b) and Rule 10b-5*

   (a) Section 10(b) of the Securities Exchange Act of 1934 and Rule 10b-5 are of fundamental importance in the law of securities regulations. What is the main purpose of this section and rule?

   (b) Do you suppose that an oral promise made and not performed can be the basis of arguing a party is guilty of defrauding another under § 10(b) and Rule 10b-5?

8. *Insider Transactions*

   Donna, a corporate director, sold 100 shares of stock in her corporation on June 1, 2003. The selling price was $10.50 a share. Two months later, after the corporation had announced substantial losses for the second quarter of the year, Donna purchased 100 shares of the corporation's stock for $7.25 a share. Are there any problems with Donna's sale and purchase? Explain.

9. *Nonpublic Information*

Eric Ethan, president of Inside-Outside Sports Equipment Company, has access to information which is not available to the general investor. What standard should Eric Ethan apply in deciding whether this information is so material as to prevent him from investing in his company prior to the information's public release?

10. *Additional Civil Liability*

What is the purpose of Section 18 of the Securities Exchange Act of 1934?

11. *Criminal Liability*

What are the dollar amounts related to fines and what are the number of years related to prison terms for those that violate the Securities Act of 1934?

Recent Developments in and Considerations beyond Federal Securities Laws

12. *Sarbanes-Oxley Act of 2002*

What are five provisions of this recent legislation designed to reduce fraudulent securities transactions?

13. *State Blue Sky Laws*

Why is it important for businesspeople to understand the role of state blue sky laws in addition to federal securities regulations?

TERMINOLOGY REVIEW

Identify the terms in the left-hand column by matching each with the appropriate statement in the right-hand column.

1. Registration statement
2. Prospectus
3. Tombstone ad
4. Insider
5. Issuer
6. Controlling person
7. Underwriter
8. Seller

a. An advertisement made during the waiting period that announces the security, its price, by whom orders will be executed, and from whom a prospectus may be obtained

b. A participant in the distribution of a security who guarantees the sale of an issue

c. The individual or business organization that offers a security for sale

d. The document that contains financial and other information and must be filed with the SEC prior to any sale of a security

e. A party who controls or is controlled by the issuer

f. A person who owns more than 10 percent of a security of an issuer or who is a director or an officer of an issuer

g. Any person who contracts with a purchaser or who exerts a substantial role that causes a purchase transaction to occur

h. A document or pamphlet that includes the essential information contained in the registration statement; filed with the SEC and made available to potential investors

BUSINESS DISCUSSION

Two former roommates from college contact you about an opportunity to make big money. Their idea is to start a business to market a new video game system (the computer science major developed the software, the engineer created the hardware). They estimate it will take $5 to $10 million to begin production, and they want to raise money by selling shares in the company to investors. They think their product is superior, and they are aware of the time factor. They want to get started as soon as possible. Your field of expertise is securities marketing.

Can the three of you just begin advertising for investors?

What steps must be followed to comply with the law?

How much time is needed before potential investors can be approached legally?

ENVIRONMENTAL LAWS AND POLLUTION CONTROL

You are senior project manager for Superior Paper, Inc., a paper processing company with plants in several states. Recently, you have been given responsibility for overseeing the construction of a new plant in High Top, Tennessee, on the edge of the Talladega National Forest. You must also secure a lease from the U.S. Department of Interior to harvest timber on federal land. Although many residents welcome the new jobs your company will create, others have moved into the area for its natural beauty and are mounting a campaign to keep out new development.

> What environmental laws will apply to the new plant construction?
>
> What environmental law will have to be followed as you seek to get the national forest lease?
>
> What steps should you take to maintain good community relations?

Environmental regulation remains the single most expensive area of government's regulation of the business community. Over the next decade, industry will spend several hundred billion dollars on pollution control. The primary reason for environmental regulation is concern over the effects of human population growth and the impacts of human technology. Almost daily we hear of threats to the environment arising from human behavior. Destruction of the rain forests, extinction of animal and plant species, depletion of the ozone layer, and the greenhouse effect are only some of the current environmental concerns.

Environmental and pollution-control laws govern regulation on three levels:

- Government's regulation of itself
- Government's regulation of business
- Suits by private individuals

CATEGORIES OF ENVIRONMENTAL AND POLLUTION-CONTROL LAWS

Government's Regulation of Itself

National Environmental Policy Act

State environmental policy acts

Government's Regulation of Business

Clean Air Act

Clean Water Act

Pesticide Control Acts

Solid Waste Disposal Act

Toxic Substances Control Act

Resource Conservation and Recovery Act

Other federal, state, and local statutes

Suits by Private Individuals

Citizen enforcement provisions of various statutes

Public and private nuisance

Trespass

Negligence

Strict liability for ultrahazardous activity

The box, above, illustrates this breakdown.

This chapter examines environmental and pollution-control laws by looking first at federal environmental policy and then at specific laws aimed at reducing specific kinds of pollution. The emphasis is on the compliance these laws force on business and industry. The final section of the chapter looks at the rights and liabilities of private individuals under environmental law.

Administering environmental laws at the federal level is the Environmental Protection Agency (EPA). Since many of the laws provide for joint federal-state enforcement, the states also have strong environmental agencies. Policies are set at the federal level, and the states devise plans to implement them. States, and even local governments, also enforce their own laws that affect the environment and control pollution. For a summary of federal environmental laws, see the table on the next page.

GOVERNMENT'S REGULATION OF ITSELF

The modern environmental movement began in the 1960s. As it gained momentum, it generated political pressure that forced government to reassess its role in environmental issues.

1. THE NATIONAL ENVIRONMENTAL POLICY ACT

The way the government considers the environmental impact of its decision making greatly interests the business community. For instance, the federal government pays private enterprise almost $100 billion annually to conduct studies, prepare reports, and carry out projects. In addition, the federal government is by far the nation's largest landholder, controlling one-third of the entire area of the United States. Private enterprise must rely on governmental agencies to issue permits and licenses to explore and mine for minerals, graze cattle, cut timber, or conduct other business activities on government property. Thus, any congressional legislation that influences the decision making concerning federal funding or license granting also affects business. Such legislation is the **National Environmental Policy Act (NEPA).**

Year	Statute	Summary of Major Provisions
1969	National Environmental Policy Act	1. Establishes broad policy goals 2. Imposes specific duties on all federal agencies 3. Sets up Council on Environmental Quality

Air

Year	Statute	Summary of Major Provisions
1970	Clean Air Act	1. Directs the EPA to establish air quality standards and timetables 2. Directs states to establish implementation plans 3. Permits required record keeping and inspection 4. Establishes civil and criminal penalties and fines
1990	Clean Air Act amendments	1. Require certain cities to reduce emissions through tougher standards 2. Require certain industries to use *best available technology* to reduce emissions 3. Require cuts in utility power plant emissions 4. Permit utilities to engage in emissions reduction banking and trading

Water

Year	Statute	Summary of Major Provisions
1972	Clean Water Act	1. Sets goals and timetables to eliminate water pollution 2. Establishes means of enforcement through permits and criminal penalties
1972	Marine Protection, Research, and Sanctuaries Act	1. Requires permit for discharge or dumping various materials into the seas
1974	Safe Drinking Water Act	1. Directs the EPA to set maximum drinking water contaminant levels for chemicals, pesticides, and microbiological pollutants

Pesticides

Year	Statute	Summary of Major Provisions
1972	Federal Environmental Pesticide Control Act	1. Requires registration and labeling of agricultural pesticides 2. Regulates application of pesticides
1973	Federal Insecticide, Fungicide, and Rodenticide Act	1. Requires registration and labeling of agricultural pesticides

Waste Disposal/Cleanup

Year	Statute	Summary of Major Provisions
1965	Solid Waste Disposal Act	1. Promotes research 2. Provides technical and financial assistance to the states
1976	Resource Conservation and Recovery Act	1. Requires a generator to determine whether its wastes are hazardous 2. Requires such wastes to be properly transported to an EPA-licensed disposal facility 3. Prescribes record keeping requirements 4. Assesses penalties for noncompliance
1976	Toxic Substances Control Act	1. Requires advance notice of manufacture and analysis of new chemical substances that present a *substantial risk* of injury to health or the environment
1980	Comprehensive Environmental Response and Liability Act	1. Establishes Superfund for environmental cleanup of dangerous hazardous wastes 2. Requires notification of unauthorized release of hazardous substances 3. Permits assessment of punitive damages for noncompliance

The NEPA became effective in 1970. It imposes specific "action-forcing" requirements on federal agencies. The most important requirement demands that all federal agencies prepare an **environmental impact statement (EIS)** prior to taking certain actions. An EIS must be included "in every recommendation or report on proposals for legislation and other major federal actions significantly affecting the quality of the human environment." This EIS is a "detailed statement" that

Components of the Environmental Impact Statement

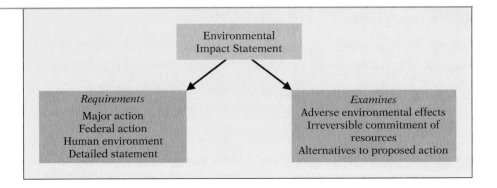

estimates the environmental impact of the proposed action. Any discussion of such action and its impact must contain information on adverse environmental effects that cannot be avoided, any irreversible use of resources necessary, and available alternatives to the action (see the box above).

There have been hundreds of cases that interpret the EIS requirements. In the following case, the Supreme Court decides whether psychological fear caused by the risk of accident at a nuclear power plant is an "environmental effect."

METROPOLITAN EDISON COMPANY v. PEOPLE AGAINST NUCLEAR ENERGY

103 S. CT. 1556 (1983)

Metropolitan Edison Company decided to reopen its TMI-1 plant at Three Mile Island, Pennsylvania, after it had been shut down when a serious accident damaged the reactor. People Against Nuclear Energy (PANE), an association of Three Mile Island-area residents, sued, claiming that the Nuclear Regulatory Commission failed to consider the psychological harm that reopening the plant and exposing the community to the risk of a nuclear accident might cause.

REHNQUIST, J.: Section 102(C) of NEPA directs all federal agencies to "include in every recommendation or report on proposals for legislation and other major Federal actions significantly affecting the quality of the human environment, a detailed statement by the responsible official on—(i) the environmental impact of the proposed action, [and] (ii) any adverse environmental effects which cannot be avoided should the proposal be implemented. . . ."

To paraphrase the statutory language in light of the facts of this case, where an agency action significantly affects the quality of the human environment, the agency must evaluate the "environmental impact" and any unavoidable adverse environmental effects of its proposal. The theme of section 102 is sounded by the adjective "environmental": NEPA does not require the agency to assess the impact or effect of its proposed action, but only the impact or effect on the environment. If we were to seize the word "environmental" out of its context and give it the broadest possible definition, the words "adverse environmental effects" might embrace virtually any consequence of a governmental action that someone thought "adverse." But we think the context of the statute shows that Congress was talking about the physical environment— the world around us, so to speak. NEPA was designed to promote human welfare by alerting governmental actors to the effect of their proposed actions on the physical environment. . . .

[CONTINUED]

Our understanding of the congressional concerns that led to the enactment of NEPA suggests that the terms "environmental effect" and "environmental impact" in section 102 be read to include a requirement of a reasonably close causal relationship between a change in the physical environment and the effect at issue. The issue before us, then, is how to give content to this requirement. This is a question of first impression in this Court.

The federal action that affects the environment in this case is permitting renewed operation of TMI-1. The direct effects on the environment of this action include release of low-level radiation, increased fog in the Harrisburg area (caused by operation of the plant's cooling towers), and the release of warm water into the Susquehanna River. The NCR has considered each of these effects in its EIS, and again in the EIA. Another effect of renewed operation is a risk of a nuclear accident. The NRC has also considered this effect.

PANE argues that the psychological health damage it alleges "will flow directly from the risk of [a nuclear] accident." But a risk of an accident is not an effect on the physical environment. A risk is, by definition, unrealized in the physical world. In a causal chain from renewed operation of TMI-1 to psychological health damage, the element of risk and its perception by PANE's members are necessary middle links. We believe that the element of risk lengthens the causal chain beyond the reach of NEPA.

Risk is a pervasive element of modern life; to say more would belabor the obvious. Many of the risks we face are generated by modern technology, which brings both the possibility of major accidents and opportunities for tremendous achievements. Medical experts apparently agree that risk can generate stress in human beings, which in turn may rise to the level of serious health damage. For this reason among many others, the question whether the gains from any technological advance are worth its attendant risks may be an important public policy issue. Nonetheless, it is quite different from the question whether the same gains are worth a given level of alteration of our physical environment or depletion of our natural resources. The latter question rather than the former is the central concern of NEPA.

Time and resources are simply too limited for us to believe that Congress intended to extend NEPA as far as the Court of Appeals has taken it. The scope of the agency's inquiries must remain manageable if NEPA's goal of "ensur[ing] a fully informed and well considered decision," is to be accomplished.

If contentions of psychological health damage caused by risk were cognizable under NEPA, agencies would, at the very least, be obliged to expend considerable resources developing psychiatric expertise that is not otherwise relevant to their congressionally assigned functions. The available resources may be spread so thin that agencies are unable adequately to pursue protection of the physical environment and natural resources. As we said in another context "[w]e cannot attribute to Congress the intention to . . . open the door to such obvious incongruities and undesirable possibilities." . . . **Reversed.**

CASE QUESTIONS

1. Why did PANE members want the Nuclear Regulatory Commission to consider "psychological harm" in the EIS?

2. What did the Supreme Court define the statutory language "adverse environmental effects" to mean?

3. Did the Supreme Court think that the risk of nuclear accident was itself an "adverse environmental effect"? Explain.

Several regulatory guidelines have made the EIS more useful. One guideline directs federal agencies to engage in **scoping.** Scoping requires that even before preparing an EIS, agencies must designate which environmental issues of a contemplated action are most significant. It encourages impact statements to focus on more substantial environmental concerns and reduce the attention devoted to trivial issues. It also allows other agencies and interested parties to participate in the scoping process. Scoping helps ensure that formal impact statements will address matters regarded as most important.

Another guideline directs that EISs be "clear, to the point, and written in plain English." This requirement deters the use of technical jargon and helps those reading impact statements to understand them. The Council on Environmental Quality (CEQ) has also limited the length of impact statements, which once ran to more than 1,000 pages, to 150 pages, except in unusual circumstances.

2. EVALUATION OF ENVIRONMENTAL IMPACT STATEMENTS

Importantly, NEPA does not require that federal agencies follow the conclusions of an EIS. However, as a practical political matter, agencies are not likely to proceed with a project when an EIS concludes that the environmental costs outweigh the benefits. EISs have been responsible for the abandonment or delay of many federal projects.

Some critics point out that the present process fails to consider the economic injury caused by abandoning or delaying projects. They also contend that those preparing EISs are forced to consider far too many alternatives to proposed federal action without regard to their economic reasonableness. Other critics maintain that most impact statements are too descriptive and not sufficiently analytical. They fear that the EIS is "a document of compliance rather than a decision-making tool." A final general criticism of the EIS process notes the limits of its usefulness. As follow-ups on some EISs have shown, environmental factors are often so complex that projections concerning environmental effects amount to little more than guesswork.

Although the NEPA applies only to federal actions, many states have enacted similar legislation to assist their decision making. Many interpretive problems found on the national level are also encountered at the state level. In addition, as the states frequently lack the resources and expertise of the federal government, state EISs are often even less helpful in evaluating complex environmental factors than are those prepared by federal agencies.

GOVERNMENT'S REGULATION OF BUSINESS

In the past 25 years, the federal government has enacted a series of laws regulating the impact of private enterprise on the environment. More and more companies are hiring environmental managers to deal with environmental compliance issues. This trend reflects the continuing importance of government regulation in this area. Congress may fine-tune environmental acts, but the national commitment to a cleaner environment is here to stay. As the CEO of a large chemical company observed about environmental concern, "Sometimes you find that the public has spoken, and you get on with it."

3. THE ENVIRONMENTAL PROTECTION AGENCY

One of the first steps taken at the federal level in response to concerns about the environment was the establishment of the **Environmental Protection Agency (EPA)** in 1970. At the federal level, the EPA coordinates public control of private action as it affects the environment.

Today, the EPA is a large agency with a number of major responsibilities (see the box, below). Most important, it administers federal laws that concern pollution of the air and water, solid waste and toxic substance disposal, pesticide regulation, and radiation. The following sections examine these laws.

4. AIR POLLUTION

In 1257, Queen Eleanor of England was driven from Nottingham Castle because of harsh smoke from the numerous coal fires in London. Coal had come into widespread use in England during this time, following the cutting of forests for fuel and agricultural purposes. By 1307, a royal order prohibited coal burning in London's kilns under punishment of "grievous ransoms." This early attempt at controlling air pollution does not appear, however, to have been very effective. As recently as the London smog of 1952, four thousand people died of air pollution-related causes, including coal smoke.

In the United States the key federal legislation for controlling air pollution is the Clean Air Act.

Clean Air Act and Amendments The **Clean Air Act** directs the EPA administrator to establish air quality standards and to see that these standards are achieved according to a definite timetable. The administrator has set primary and secondary air quality standards for particulates, carbon monoxide, sulfur dioxide, nitrogen dioxide, hydrocarbons, and lead. **Primary air quality standards** are those necessary to protect public health. **Secondary air quality standards** guard the public from other adverse air pollution effects such as injury to property, vegetation, and climate and damage to aesthetic values. In most instances, primary and secondary air quality standards are identical.

Government regulation of private action under the Clean Air Act is a joint federal and state effort. The EPA sets national ambient (outside) air quality standards, and the states devise implementation plans, which the EPA must approve, to carry them out. The states thus bear principal responsibility for enforcing the Clean Air Act, with the EPA providing standard-setting, coordinating, and supervisory functions. However, the EPA may also participate in enforcement. The administrator

RESPONSIBILITIES OF THE EPA

Conducts research on the harmful impact of pollution

Gathers information about present pollution problems

Assists states and local governments in controlling pollution through grants, technical advice, and other means

Advises the CEQ about new policies needed for protection of the environment

Administers federal pollution laws

can require the operator of any air pollution source to keep such records and perform such monitoring or sampling as the EPA thinks appropriate. In addition, the EPA has the right to inspect these records and data. Various criminal and civil penalties and fines back up the Clean Air Act. In addition, industries that do not obey cleanup orders face payment to the EPA; payment amounts to the economic savings they realize from their failure to install and operate proper antipollution equipment.

In setting air quality standards, does the EPA have to consider the costs to business? In the following case, several trucking associations raise the issue of cost/benefit analysis involving ozone and particulate matter standards.

WHITMAN V. AMERICAN TRUCKING ASSOCIATIONS, INC.

531 U.S. 457 (2001)

The EPA set revised national ambient air quality standards (NAAQS) for ozone and particulate matter. Several trucking associations (respondents) challenged the standards adopted under Section (§) 109(b)(1) of the Clean Air Act (CAA), arguing that the standards failed to take implementation costs adequately into account. The Supreme Court agreed to decide this issue.

SCALIA, J.: . . . Section 109(b)(1) instructs the EPA to set primary ambient air quality standards "the attainment and maintenance of which . . . are requisite to protect the public health" with "an adequate margin of safety." Were it not for the hundreds of pages of briefing respondents submitted on the issue, one would have thought it fairly clear that this text does not permit the EPA to consider costs in setting the standards. The language, as one scholar has noted, "is absolute." The EPA, "based on" the information about health effects contained in the technical "criteria" documents is to identify the maximum airborne concentration of a pollutant that the public health can tolerate, decrease the concentration to provide an "adequate" margin of safety, and set the standard at that level. Nowhere are the costs of achieving such a standard made part of that initial calculation.

Against this most natural of readings, respondents make a lengthy, spirited, but ultimately unsuccessful attack. They begin with the object of § 109(b)(1)'s focus, the "public health." When the term first appeared in federal clean air legislation—in the Act of July 14, 1955, which expressed "recognition of the dangers to the public health" from air pollution—its ordinary meaning was "the health of the community." Respondents argue, however, that § 109(b)(1), as added by the Clean Air Amendments of 1970, meant to use the term's secondary meaning: "the ways and means of conserving the health of the members of a community, as by preventive medicine, organized care of the sick, etc."

Words that can have more than one meaning are given content, however, by their surroundings, and in the context of § 109(b)(1) this second definition makes no sense. Congress could not have meant to instruct the Administrator to set NAAQS at a level "requisite to protect the art and science dealing with the protection and improvement of community health." We therefore revert to the primary definition of the term: the health of the public.

Even so, respondents argue, many more factors than air pollution affect public health. In particular, the economic cost of implementing a very stringent standard might produce health losses sufficient to

[CONTINUED]

offset the health gains achieved in cleaning the air—for example, by closing down whole industries and thereby impoverishing the workers and consumers dependent upon those industries. That is unquestionably true, and Congress was unquestionably aware of it. Thus, . . . Section 110(f)(1) of the CAA permitted the Administrator to waive the compliance deadline for stationary sources if sufficient control measures were simply unavailable and "the continued operation of such sources is *essential . . . to the public health* or welfare." Other provisions explicitly permitted or required economic costs to be taken into account in implementing the air quality standards. Section 111(b)(1)(B), for example, commanded the Administrator to set "standards of performance" for certain new sources of emissions that as specified in § 111(a)(1) were to "reflect the degree of emission limitation achievable through the application of the best system of emission reduction which (taking into account the cost of achieving such reduction) the Administrator determines has been adequately demonstrated." Section 202(a)(2) prescribed that emissions standards for automobiles could take effect only "after such period as the Administrator finds necessary to permit the development and application of the requisite technology,

giving appropriate consideration to the cost of compliance within such period." Subsequent amendments to the CAA have added many more provisions directing, in explicit language, that the Administrator consider costs in performing various duties. We have therefore refused to find implicit in ambiguous sections of the CAA an authorization to consider costs that has elsewhere, and so often, been expressly granted.

Accordingly, to prevail in their present challenge, respondents must show a commitment of authority to the EPA to consider costs in setting NAAQS under § 109(b)(1). And because § 109(b)(1) and the NAAQS for which it provides are the engine that drives nearly all of Title I of the CAA, that commitment must be a clear one. Congress, we have held, does not alter the fundamental details of a regulatory scheme in vague terms or ancillary provisions—it does not, one might say, hide elephants in mouseholes. The text of § 109(b), interpreted in its statutory and historical context and with appreciation for its importance to the CAA as a whole, unambiguously bars cost considerations from the NAAQS-setting process, and thus ends the matter for us as well as the EPA. We therefore affirm the judgment of the Court of Appeals on this point.

Case Questions

1. In § 109(b)(1) what is the safety requirement the EPA must observe in setting primary ambient air quality standards? What does "ambient" mean?

2. How do the respondents argue that § 109(b)(1) requires consideration of economic costs in setting primary ambient air quality standards?

3. What does the Supreme Court say about whether or not § 109(b)(1) permits the EPA to consider cost in setting primary ambient air quality standards?

In 1990, Congress passed significant amendments to the Clean Air Act. These amendments have added billions of dollars annually to the cost of complying with environmental regulations. In cities that did not meet clean air standards, businesses were required to install new pollution control equipment, and tailpipe emissions for cars and trucks were reduced. A pilot program in California has introduced alternative fuel cars, and cleaner gasoline blends are now sold in specific cities with the worst pollution problems.

Since many cities currently do not meet existing Clean Air Act standards, the amendments force businesses in these areas to install new pollution-control equipment to cut emissions. Tailpipe emissions for cars and trucks must be reduced, and companies must phase in alternative fuel vehicles for their fleets of vehicles. A pilot program for California will introduce up to 300,000 alternative fuel cars. The amendments also required sale of cleaner gasoline blends in cities with the worst pollution problems. The goal of all these requirements is to cut pollution by 3 percent per year until air quality standards are met. The states have prepared blueprints for meeting these goals.

Expressing concern about airborne toxic chemicals, the 1990 amendments require industry to use the "best available technology" on plants to reduce emissions of 189 toxics by 90 percent. Significantly, the plants covered include bakeries and dry cleaning businesses as well as chemical companies. The EPA must also study how to reduce toxic emissions from vehicles and fuels.

To control the sulfur dioxide that contributes to acid rain, the Clean Air Act amendments require cuts in utility power plant emissions. Nationwide sulfur dioxide emissions must be reduced by 10 million tons. The law imposes a nationwide cap on emissions. Reducing these emissions will mean that utilities will burn less soft coal. Miners put out of work because of this may qualify for extra weeks of unemployment pay.

Air Pollution Sources   For control purposes, the Clean Air Act amendments divide air pollution sources into two categories: *stationary source* and *mobile source* (transportation). Under the state implementation plans, major stationary polluters, such as steel mills and utilities, must reduce their emissions to a level sufficient to bring down air pollution to meet primary and secondary standards. Polluters must follow timetables and schedules in complying with these requirements. To achieve designated standards, they must install a variety of control devices, including wet collectors (scrubbers), filter collectors, tall stacks, electrostatic precipitators, and afterburners. New stationary pollution sources, or modified ones, must install the best system of emission reduction that has been adequately demonstrated. Under the act's provision, citizens are granted standing to enforce compliance with these standards.

The act requires both stationary and mobile sources to meet a timetable of air pollution standards for which control technology may not exist at the time. This *technology-forcing* aspect of the act is unique to the history of governmental regulation of business, yet it has been upheld by the Supreme Court. In large part due to technology forcing, new automobiles today emit less than 1 percent as much pollution per mile as cars of 25 years ago.

Technology forcing does not always succeed. It is neither always possible nor always feasible to force new technological developments. In recognizing this fact, the Clean Air Act allows the EPA in many instances to grant *compliance waivers* and *variances* from its standards.

5. CLEAN AIR ACT TRENDS

As originally implemented, the Clean Air Act did not try to promote efficient pollution. For instance, if an area's air could tolerate a million tons of pollution per year, the authorities made no attempt to identify those who could make the best productive use of air pollution. Likewise, when a business was permitted to pollute a certain annual amount, the act specified the allowable pollution from each smokestack or other polluting source within the business instead of letting the business arrange its total allowable pollution in the most efficient way.

In the past few years, the EPA has moved to make its regulatory practices more economically efficient. All new pollution control rules are now subjected to cost-benefit analysis. The EPA has also developed specific policies to achieve air pollution control in an economically efficient manner.

Traditionally, the EPA has regulated each individual pollution emission **point source** (such as a smokestack) within an industrial plant or complex. Increasingly, however, the EPA is encouraging the states, through their implementation plans, to adopt an approach called the **bubble concept.** Under the bubble concept, each plant complex is treated as if it were encased in a bubble. Instead of each pollution point source being licensed for a limited amount of pollution emission, the pollution of the plant complex as a whole is the focus of regulation. Businesses may suggest their own plans for cleaning up multiple sources of pollution within the entire complex as long as the total pollution emitted does not exceed certain limits. This approach permits flexibility in curtailing pollution and provides businesses with economic incentives to discover new methods of control. The Supreme Court has upheld the EPA's authority to approve the bubble concept even in states where pollution exceeds air quality standards.

Emissions Reduction Banking A number of states have developed EPA-approved plans for **emissions reduction banking.** Under such plans, businesses can cut pollution beyond what the law requires and "bank" these reductions for their own future use or to sell to other companies as emission offsets. Eventually, we may be headed for a *marketable rights* approach to pollution control, under which the right to discharge a certain pollutant would be auctioned off to the highest bidder. This approach would promote efficiency by offering to those who have the greatest need for pollution rights the opportunity to obtain them by bidding highest for them. Under the 1990 Clean Air Act amendments, Congress specifically allows utility companies to engage in emissions reduction banking and trading. Since 1992 the Chicago Board of Trade has run an auction in pollution credits given by the EPA to the nation's 110 most polluting utility plants.

According to the EPA, emissions trading accounts significantly for the fact that electric utilities today emit a quarter fewer tons of sulfur dioxide than they did in 1980 while producing 41 percent more electricity. The General Accounting Office figures that emissions trading saves the utility industry $3 billion a year over previous pollution-enforcement approaches. The EPA estimates that for every $1 billion of sulfur dioxide reduction there is a $50 billion saving in health costs. As the following box discusses, emissions reduction banking and trading is rapidly growing and extending beyond the Clean Air Act.

Prevention of Significant Deterioration Another important policy of the Clean Air Act is the **prevention of significant deterioration.** Under this policy, pollution emission is controlled, even in areas where the air is cleaner than prevailing primary and secondary air quality standards require. In some of these areas, the EPA permits construction of new pollution emission sources according to a strictly limited scheme. In other areas, it allows no new pollution emission at all. Critics of this policy argue that it prevents industry from moving into southern and western states, where air quality is cleaner than standards require.

BEYOND THE CLEAN AIR ACT

The Clean Air Act does not regulate greenhouse gases (GHG) like carbon dioxide, methane, nitrous oxide, hydrofluorocarbons, perfluorocarbons, and sulfur hexafluoride that heat and change the world's climate. Anticipating future regulation, however, U.S. companies are beginning to trade in GHG emissions.

In 2003 the Chicago Climate Exchange began operation. This program for trading GHG marks the first time that major U.S. companies have begun to take voluntary property-based market steps to cut emissions linked to global warming.

Great Britain and Denmark already have GHG emissions trading markets. The European Union has issued plans to begin full-scale trading by 2005. These markets are based on the principle of **cap and trade.** The government issues a limited number of pollution permits, effectively capping total GHG pollution. Companies then trade the permits. Whoever can reduce emissions can sell the unused amount of a permit. The government may slowly reduce the number of outstanding permits.

One of the most controversial issues involving the Clean Air Act concerns the delay and red tape caused by the *permitting process.* Before a business can construct new pollution emission sources, it must obtain the necessary environmental permits from the appropriate state agency. Today, the estimated time needed to acquire the necessary permits to build a coal-fired electric-generating plant is 5 to 10 years. This is nearly twice the length of time it took in the early 1970s. The formalities of the permitting process, the lack of flexibility in state implementation plans, the requirement that even minor variations in state implementation plans be approved by the EPA—all these factors contribute to delay. Both the EPA and Congress are considering ways to streamline the permitting process.

The EPA is experimenting with allowing states to issue "smart permits" to air polluters. Under these permits, polluters can engage in "a family of alternative operating scenarios" (i.e., engage in new operations) without the expensive delay of obtaining new permits as the EPA previously required. Some environmental groups oppose smart-permitting as failing to allow communities a time period to determine if new operations really meet clean air standards.

The EPA has also grown increasingly concerned about indoor air pollution. Paints, cleaning products, furniture polishes, gas furnaces, and stoves all emit pollutants that can be harmful to human health. Radioactive radon seeping into homes and buildings from the ground has now been recognized as a major health hazard. Some studies have found that indoor levels of certain pollutants far exceed outdoor levels, whether at work or at home. Although the Clean Air Act does not currently apply to indoor pollution, its application may be extended in the future. (See the box "Tobacco Industry Insight.")

In spite of the controversy generated by the Clean Air Act, evidence indicates that the overall air quality in the United States is steadily improving. The 16,000 quarts of air we each breathe daily are cleaner and healthier in most places than they were a decade ago. Yet an estimated 80 million persons in the United States still breathe air that violates one or more primary air quality standards. Note, also, that air pollution is an international problem and that not all countries of the world have, or can afford, our air quality standards. Air pollution is especially severe in developing nations of the world, which are striving to reach our standard of living.

Significantly, the EPA does not regulate indoor air pollution under the Clean Air Act although OSHA could regulate it as to the workplace. Numerous major businesses already ban workplace smoking. Many local governments also regulate or prohibit indoor smoking in public buildings.

TOBACCO INDUSTRY *insight*

INDOOR POLLUTION

The Environmental Protection Agency ranks indoor air pollution as one of the five top pollution problems. Although tobacco smoke is only one type of indoor air pollutant, it may be the most significant. Since 1993, the EPA has classified tobacco smoke as a "Group A" carcinogen and estimates that secondhand smoke kills 3,000 people annually from lung cancer alone. The California EPA concludes that secondhand smoke is responsible for as many as 62,000 deaths from heart disease, 2,700 deaths from Sudden Infant Death Syndrome, and 2,600 new asthma cases annually. Tobacco companies have challenged the research on which these conclusions are based.

6. WATER POLLUTION

Business enterprise is a major source of water pollution in the United States. Almost one-half of all water used in this country is for cooling and condensing purposes in connection with industrial activities. The resulting discharge into our rivers and lakes sometimes takes the form of heated water, called thermal effluents. In addition to thermal effluents, industry also discharges chemical and other effluents into the nation's waterways.

The principal federal law regulating water pollution is the **Clean Water Act,** passed by Congress in 1972. As with the Clean Air Act, the Clean Water Act is administered primarily by the states in accordance with EPA standards. If the states do not fulfill their responsibilities, however, the federal government, through the EPA, can step in and enforce the law. The Clean Water Act applies to all navigable waterways, intrastate as well as interstate. As to what is "navigable," consider the following case.

SOLID WASTE AGENCY v. UNITED STATES ARMY CORPS OF ENGINEERS

531 U.S. 159 (2001)

Several towns in northern Illinois (petitioner) chose as a solid waste disposal site an abandoned sand and gravel pit. The site had several ponds on it, some permanent and some seasonal. The petitioner applied for a landfill permit from the Army Corps of Engineers (respondent) to drain and fill the ponds. Under its authority from the Clean Water Act to regulate "navigable waters" (§ 404a), the respondent denied the permit, relying on its interpretation of § 404(a) called the "Migratory Bird Rule." The respondent stated that to fill these ponds would unduly
harm various migratory waterfowl. The petitioner sued, but both the federal district court and the court of appeals upheld the respondent's authority to refuse to issue the permit. The Supreme Court granted certiorari.

REHNQUIST, C. J.: . . . Section 404(a) of the Clean Water Act (CWA) grants the Corps authority to issue permits "for the discharge of dredged or fill material into the navigable waters at specified disposal sites." The term "navigable waters" is defined under the

[CONTINUED]

Act as "the waters of the United States, including the territorial seas." The Corps has issued regulations defining the term "waters of the United States" to include

> waters such as intrastate lakes, rivers, streams (including intermittent streams), mudflats, sandflats, wetlands, sloughs, prairie potholes, wet meadows, playa lakes, or natural ponds, the use, degradation or destruction of which could affect interstate or foreign commerce. . . .

In 1986, in an attempt to "clarify" the reach of its jurisdiction, the Corps stated that § 404(a) extends to intrastate waters:

a. Which are or would be used as habitat by birds protected by Migratory Bird Treaties; or

b. Which are or would be used as habitat by other migratory birds which cross state lines; or

c. Which are or would be used as habitat for endangered species; or

d. Used to irrigate crops sold in interstate commerce.

This interpretation has been dubbed the "Migratory Bird Rule."

This is not the first time we have been called upon to evaluate the meaning of § 404(a). In *United States v. Riverside Bayview Homes, Inc.,* we held that the Corps has § 404(a) jurisdiction over wetlands that actually abutted on a navigable waterway. In so doing, we noted that the term "navigable" is of "limited import" and that Congress evidenced its intent to "regulate at least some waters that would not be deemed 'navigable' under the classical understanding of that term." But our holding was based in large measure upon Congress' unequivocal acquiescence to, and approval of, the Corps' regulations interpreting the CWA to cover wetlands adjacent to navigable waters. We found that Congress' concern for the protection of water quality and aquatic ecosystems indicated its intent to regulate wetlands "inseparably bound up with the 'waters' of the United States."

We decline respondents' invitation to take what they see as the next step after *Riverside Bayview Homes:* holding that isolated ponds, some only seasonal, wholly located within two Illinois counties, fall under § 404(a)'s definition of "navigable waters" because they serve as habitat for migratory birds. As counsel for respondents conceded at oral argument, such a ruling would assume that "the use of the word navigable in the statute . . . does not have any independent significance." We cannot agree that Congress' separate definitional use of the phrase "waters of the United States" constitutes a basis for reading the term "navigable waters" out of the statute. We said in *Riverside Bayview Homes* that the word "navigable" in the statute was of "limited effect" and went on to hold that § 404(a) extended to nonnavigable wetlands adjacent to open waters. But it is one thing to give a word limited effect and quite another to give it no effect whatever. The term "navigable" has at least the import of showing us what Congress had in mind as its authority for enacting the CWA: its traditional jurisdiction over waters that were or had been navigable in fact or which could reasonably be so made.

We hold that the Corps' regulations as clarified and applied to petitioner's fill site pursuant to the "Migratory Bird Rule," exceeds the authority granted to respondents under § 404(a) of the CWA. The judgment of the Court of Appeals for the Seventh Circuit is therefore

Reversed.

CASE QUESTIONS

1. Why did the Illinois towns have to apply to the Army Corps of Engineers for a permit to create their solid waste disposal site?

2. Section 404(a) applies only to "navigable" waters. How does the Corps argue that § 404(a) applies to these small ponds?

3. Think back to Chapter 6. Does Congress have authority under the commerce clause to regulate these ponds? Why does the Supreme Court not resolve this case by saying that it would be unconstitutional for Congress to regulate small ponds because they do not have a "substantial impact on interstate commerce"?

Goals and Enforcement The Clean Water Act sets goals to eliminate water pollution. Principally, these goals are to make the nation's waterways safe for swimming and other recreational use and clean enough for the protection of fish, shellfish, and wildlife. The law sets strict deadlines and strong enforcement provisions, which must be followed by industry, municipalities, and other water polluters. Enforcement of the Clean Water Act revolves around its permit discharge system. Without being subject to criminal penalties, no polluter can discharge pollutants from any *point source* (such as a pipe) without a permit, and municipal as well as industrial dischargers must obtain permits. The EPA has issued guidelines for state permit programs and has approved those programs that meet the guidelines.

Since the Clean Water Act applies to "navigable waterways," the criminal penalties of the act cover only the unpermitted point-source pollution of navigable waterways. However, the penalties under the Clean Water Act can still be substantial. In 2000, Koch Industries agreed to pay a $30 million fine to settle lawsuits involving oil spills from its pipelines and oil facilities in six states.

Under the Clean Water Act, industries adopt a two-step sequence for cleanup of industrial wastes discharged into rivers and streams. The first step requires polluters to install *best practicable technology (BPT).* The second demands installation of *best available technology (BAT).* Various timetables apply in achieving these steps, according to the type of pollutant being discharged. In 1984, the EPA announced application of the bubble concept to water pollution in the steel industry.

In addition to the Clean Water Act, the EPA administers two other acts related to water pollution control. One, the Marine Protection, Research, and Sanctuaries Act of 1972, requires a permit system for the discharge or dumping of various material into the seas. The other is the Safe Drinking Water Act of 1974, which has forced the EPA to set maximum drinking water contaminant levels for certain organic and inorganic chemicals, pesticides, and microbiological pollutants.

The Clean Water Act and other current statutes do not reach one important type of water pollution: *non–point source pollution,* which comes from runoffs into streams and rivers. These runoffs often contain agricultural fertilizers and pesticides as well as oil and lead compounds from streets and highways. Congress has authorized $400 million for the National Non–Point Source Pollution Program to study the problem. One response to non–point source pollution came in 2000 when the EPA issued a rule requiring the states to impose antipollution standards for about twenty thousand bodies of water. The rule requires states to set standards within five years for the total "maximum daily load" of pollutants in a body of water. This standard would apply to pollutants from nonpoint sources as well as point sources. However, as of this writing Congress was requiring the EPA to conduct further studies of the rule's impact before the rule could be implemented.

7. ENDANGERED SPECIES ACT

Every day entire species of animals and plants die off. As with the dinosaurs, sometimes great catastrophes like comet impacts cause species to become extinct. Gradual climate changes and competition from other species also can kill off animals and plants. However, in modern times, human activity has caused the vast majority of species extinctions. Air and water pollution, the clearing of land for agriculture, the development of water resources, hunting and fishing, and a growing human population all potentially threaten other species.

In 1973 Congress passed the Endangered Species Act (ESA), the world's toughest law protecting animals and plants and, perhaps, the country's most controversial environmental standard. Under the act the Secretary of the Interior can list any species as "endangered," that is, "in danger of extinction throughout all or a significant portion of its range," except for certain insect pests. ("Threatened" species are also protected.) In determining the factors of endangerment, the secretary must consider the destruction of habitat, disease or predation, commercial and recreational activity, and "other natural or manmade factors." Within a year of listing an endangered species, the secretary is required to define the "critical habitat" of the species which is the area with the biological or physical features necessary to species survival. The Fish and Wildlife Services and the National Marine Fisheries Services administer the ESA for the Department of Interior.

Although no federal agency can authorize, fund, or carry out any action that is likely to jeopardize an endangered species, the ESA's application to private business activity has caused the greater debate in recent years. Section 9 of the act prohibits any person from transporting or trading in any endangered species of fish or wildlife (a separate section applies to plants) or from "taking any such species within the United States" or "upon the high seas." *Taking* a species is defined as "harass, harm, pursue, hunt, shoot, wound, kill, trap, capture, or collect, or attempt to engage in any such conduct."

The Secretary of the Interior has further defined the "harm" of taking to mean any act that actually kills or injures wildlife, including harming habitat or essential behavior patterns. Thus, neither private businesses nor individuals can harm the habitats of endangered species. As the following case illustrates, defining the word *harm* to include adverse changes in wildlife habitat has been the subject of much litigation.

Babbit v. Sweet Home Chapter
of Communities for a Greater Oregon

515 U.S. 687 (1995)

Small landowners, logging companies, and families dependent on the forest products industry in the Pacific Northwest and in the Southeast sued the Secretary of the Interior. They challenged the validity of the Secretary's regulation defining the word harm in the Endangered Species Act (ESA) to include habitat modification and degradation. They alleged that application of the "harm" regulation to the red-cockaded woodpecker and the northern spotted owl had injured them economically. When the Court of Appeals ruled that the Secretary's regulation was invalid, the Secretary petitioned the Supreme Court to hear the case.

STEVENS, J.: . . . The Endangered Species Act of 1973 (ESA or Act) contains a variety of protections designed to save from extinction species that the Secretary of the Interior designates as endangered or threatened. Section 9 of the Act makes it unlawful for any person to "take" any endangered or threatened species. The Secretary has promulgated a regulation that defines the statute's prohibition on takings to include "significant habitat modification or degradation where it actually kills or injures wildlife." This case presents the question whether the Secretary exceeded his authority under the Act by promulgating that regulation.

[CONTINUED]

The text of the Act provides three reasons for concluding that the Secretary's interpretation is reasonable. First, an ordinary understanding of the word "harm" supports it. The dictionary definition of the verb form of "harm" is "to cause hurt or damage to: injure." In the context of the ESA, that definition naturally encompasses habitat modification that results in actual injury or death to members of an endangered or threatened species.

Respondents [landowners, companies, and employees] argue that the Secretary should have limited the purview of "harm" to direct applications of force against protected species, but the dictionary definition does not include the word "directly" or suggest in any way that only direct or willful action that leads to injury constitutes "harm." Moreover, unless the statutory term "harm" encompasses indirect as well as direct injuries, the word has no meaning that does not duplicate the meaning of other words that §3 uses to define "take." A reluctance to treat statutory terms as surplusage supports the reasonableness of the Secretary's interpretation.

Second, the broad purpose of the ESA supports the Secretary's decision to extend protection against activities that cause the precise harms Congress enacted the statute to avoid. In *TVA v. Hill,* we described the Act as "the most comprehensive legislation for the preservation of endangered species ever enacted by any nation." Whereas predecessor statutes enacted in 1966 and 1969 had not contained any sweeping prohibition against the taking of endangered species except on federal lands, the 1973 Act applied to all land in the United States and to the Nation's territorial seas. As stated in §2 of the Act, among its central purposes is "to provide a means whereby the ecosystems upon which endangered species and threatened species depend may be conserved. . . ."

Respondents advance strong arguments that activities that cause minimal or unforeseeable harm will not violate the Act as construed in the "harm" regulation. But they ask us to invalidate the Secretary's understanding of "harm" in every circumstance, even when an actor knows that an activity, such as draining a pond, would actually result in the extinction of a listed species by destroying its habitat. Given Congress's clear expression of the ESA's broad purpose to protect endangered and threatened wildlife, the Secretary's definition of "harm" is reasonable.

Third, the fact that Congress in 1982 authorized the Secretary to issue permits for takings that §9 would otherwise prohibit, "if such taking is incidental to, and not the purpose of, the carrying out of an otherwise lawful activity," strongly suggests that Congress understood §9 to prohibit indirect as well as deliberate takings. The permit process requires the applicant to prepare a "conservation plan" that specifies how he intends to "minimize and mitigate" the "impact" of his activity on endangered and threatened species, making clear that Congress had in mind foreseeable rather than merely accidental effects on listed species. No one could seriously request an "incidental" taking permit to avert §9 liability for direct, deliberate action against a member of an endangered or threatened species, but respondents would read "harm" so narrowly that the permit procedure would have little more than that absurd purpose. "When Congress acts to amend a statute, we presume it intends its amendment to have real and substantial effect." Congress's addition to the §10 permit provision supports the Secretary's conclusion that activities not intended to harm an endangered species, such as habitat modifications, may constitute unlawful takings under the ESA unless the Secretary permits them.

The Court of Appeals made three errors in asserting that "harm" must refer to a direct application of force because the words around it do. First, the court's premise was flawed. Several of the words that accompany "harm" in the §3 definition of "take," especially "harass," "pursue," "wound," and "kill," refer to actions or effects that do not require direct applications of force. Second, to the extent the court read a requirement of intent or purpose into the words used to define "take," it ignored §9's express provision that a "knowing" action is enough to violate the Act. Third, the statutory context of "harm" suggests that Congress meant that term to serve a particular function in the ESA, consistent with but distinct from the functions of the other verbs used to define "take." The Secretary's interpretation of "harm" to include indirectly injuring endangered animals through habitat modification permissibly interprets "harm" to have "a character of its own not to be submerged by its association."

[CONTINUED]

When it enacted the ESA, Congress delegated broad administrative and interpretive power to the Secretary. The task of defining and listing endangered and threatened species requires an expertise and attention to detail that exceeds the normal province of Congress. Fashioning appropriate standards for issuing permits under §10 for takings that would otherwise violate §9 necessarily requires the exercise of broad discretion. The proper interpretation of a term such as "harm" involves a complex policy choice. When Congress has entrusted the Secretary with broad discretion, we are especially reluctant to substitute our views of wise policy for his. In this case, that reluctance accords with our conclusion, based on the text, structure, and legislative history of the ESA, that the Secretary reasonably construed the intent of Congress when he defined "harm," to include "significant habitat modification or degradation that actually kills or injures wildlife." The judgment of the Court of Appeals is **reversed.**

CASE QUESTIONS

1. How did the Secretary's regulation economically affect the landowners, companies, and families of employees?
2. What is the issue that the Supreme Court is deciding in this case?
3. What argument do the respondents make that the Secretary exceeded his authority?
4. What arguments does the Supreme Court use in deciding that the Secretary's regulation is valid?

Note that the ESA does not permit courts or regulators to take economic factors into consideration in applying its provisions. There has been much criticism of the act, and amendments to it have been proposed to Congress. Congress has established a review board that can grant exemptions to the ESA for certain important federal projects. However, the exemptions do not apply to private activities.

8. PESTICIDE CONTROL

Pests, especially insects and mice, destroy over 10 percent of all crops grown in the United States, causing several billion dollars of damage annually. In many underdeveloped countries, however, a much greater percentage of total crop production is lost to pests, as high as 40 to 50 percent in countries such as India. Perhaps the principal reason for our lower rate of crop loss is that the United States uses more pesticides per acre than any other country.

The widespread, continual application of pesticides creates environmental problems, however. Not only is it dangerous to wildlife, particularly birds and fish, but it is also harmful to humans and may eventually threaten our agricultural capacity itself. Rapidly breeding pests gradually become immune to the application of pesticides, and researchers may not always be able to invent new poisons to kill them.

Nationwide, nearly half of the farmers responding to one poll expressed increasing concern about their own safety when using pesticides. In 1992 a National Cancer Institute report concluded that farm families suffer from elevated rates of seven types of cancer, including leukemia, with pesticides suspected as a leading cause.

Federal regulation of pesticides is accomplished primarily through two statutes: the **Federal Insecticide, Fungicide, and Rodenticide Act of 1947,** as amended, and the **Federal Environmental Pesticide Control Act of 1972 (FEPCA).** Both statutes require the registration and labeling of agricultural pesticides, although FEPCA coverage extends to the application of pesticides as well.

Under the acts, the administrator of the EPA is directed to register those pesticides that are properly labeled, meet the claims made as to their effectiveness, and will not have *unreasonable adverse effects on the environment,* which is defined as "any unreasonable risk to man or the environment, taking into account the economic, social, and environmental costs and benefits of the use of any pesticide." In addition to its authority to request registration of pesticides, the EPA classifies pesticides for either general use or restricted use. In the latter category, the EPA may impose further restrictions that require application only by a trained applicator or with the approval of a trained consultant. Today, the EPA requires that employers train agricultural workers in pesticide safety, post safety information, and place warning signs to keep workers out of freshly sprayed fields.

The EPA has a variety of enforcement powers to ensure that pesticide goals are met, including the power to deny or suspend registration. In the 1980s, the EPA used this power and banned several pesticides suspected of causing cancer. In 2000 the EPA used its authority to halt the manufacture of household products containing the pesticide chlorpyrifos sold under the trade names Dursban and Lorsban. The EPA determined that the pesticide was more harmful to humans, particularly children, than had been thought previously.

The EPA also defines what a pesticide can and cannot be used for and may seek penalties against violators. For example, the EPA sought criminal charges against several quail-hunting clubs in Florida and Georgia that improperly used the pesticide Furadan to kill predators that ate quail eggs.

Pesticide control has been attacked by both affected businesses and the environmental movement itself. Pesticide manufacturers complain that the lengthy, expensive testing procedures required by the FEPCA registration process delay useful pesticides from reaching the market and inhibit new research. On the other hand, many in the environmental movement contend that our country's pesticide control policy is hypocritical in that the FEPCA does not apply to pesticides U.S. manufacturers ship to foreign countries. Companies can sell overseas what they cannot sell in this country.

9. SOLID WASTE

Pollution problems cannot always be neatly categorized. For instance, solid waste disposal processes often create pollution in several environmentally related forms. When solid waste is burned, it can cause air pollution and violate the Clean Air Act. When dumped into rivers, streams, and lakes, solid waste can pollute the water beyond amounts permitted under the Clean Water Act. Machinery used in solid waste disposal can also be subject to the regulation of the Noise Control Act.

By all accounts, solid waste pollution problems during the last 25 years have grown as pollution has risen and the country has become more affluent and productive. Currently, total solid wastes produced yearly in the United States exceed 5 billion tons, or almost 25 tons for every individual. Half this amount is agricultural waste, another third is mineral waste, and the remainder is industrial, institutional, and residential waste. Some wastes are toxic and hazardous, while others stink or attract pests. All present disposal problems of significant proportion.

Landfills represent the primary disposal sites for most household and much business solid wastes. The figure, below, illustrates the composition of solid wastes in the typical landfill. According to Bill Rathje, professor of anthropology at the University of Arizona, paper is the biggest solid waste category in landfills. And paper, which in 1970 constituted 35 percent of landfill volume, today constitutes 50 percent. By contrast, disposable diapers take up less than 1 percent of landfill volume. Polystyrene foam, such as thermal cups, also takes up less than 1 percent of landfill volume.

The **Solid Waste Disposal Act** passed in 1965 represents the primary federal effort in solid waste control. Congress recognized in this act that the main responsibility for nontoxic waste management rests with regional, state, and local management and limited the federal role in this area. Under this act, the federal role in nontoxic waste management is limited mainly to promoting research and providing technical and financial assistance to the states.

In responding to solid waste disposal problems, state and local governments have taken a variety of approaches. These include developing sanitary landfills, requiring that solid waste be separated into categories that facilitate disposal and recycling, and granting tax breaks for industries using recycled materials. A report by the Council of State Governments noted that thousands of cities and towns recycle solid wastes, usually in the form of household trash-separation requirements.

One recycling success story involves tires. The Scrap Tire Management Council estimates that two-thirds of the nearly 300 million tires discarded annually end up in dozens of retail and industrial products. Companies use recycled tires in indoor flooring, fuel alternatives, playground surfaces, and automobile parts. General Motors, for example, uses recycled rubber in 35 parts along the production line.

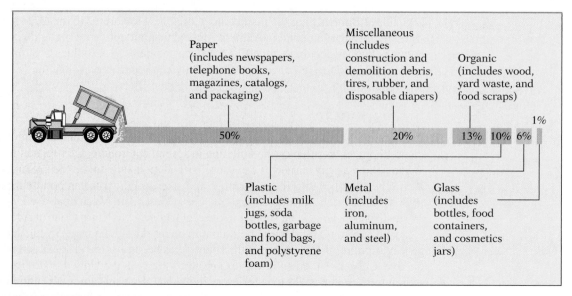

Composition of a Typical Landfill by Volume

10. TOXIC AND HAZARDOUS SUBSTANCES

According to the opinion research organization Yankelovich, Skelly and White, the control of toxic and hazardous chemicals "ranks first" on the public's list of where the government's regulation of industry is needed. In the last several years, regulation of such chemicals has been expanding rapidly. We can divide public control of private action in this area into three categories:

- Regulation of the use of toxic chemicals
- Regulation of toxic and hazardous waste disposal
- Regulation of toxic and hazardous waste cleanup

Toxic Substances Control Act Even as the Clean Air and Clean Water Acts are slowly beginning to diminish many types of air and water pollution, attention is being drawn to another environmental problem that is potentially the most serious of all: toxic substances. Hardly a day passes without the news media reporting some new instance of alleged threat to human health and well-being from one or another of the chemical substances so important to manufacturing, farming, mining, and other aspects of modern life.

Threats to human welfare from toxic substances are not new to history. Some scholars have suggested that poisoning from lead water pipes and drinking vessels may have depleted the ranks of the ruling class of ancient Rome and thus contributed to the downfall of the Roman Empire. More recently, some think that the "mad hatters" of the nineteenth-century fur and felt trades likely suffered brain disorders from inhaling the vapors of mercury used in their crafts. Today, however, the problem of toxic substances in the environment is more widespread. More than 70,000 industrial and agricultural chemical compounds are in commercial use, and new chemicals, a significant percentage of which are toxic, are being introduced into the marketplace at the rate of more than 1,000 substances annually.

To meet the special environmental problems posed by the use of toxic chemicals, Congress in 1976 enacted the **Toxic Substances Control Act (TSCA).** Prior to passage of the TSCA, there was no coordinated effort to evaluate effects of these chemical compounds. Some of these compounds are beneficial to society and present no threat to the environment. Some, however, are both toxic and nondegradable, a fact that in the past has been uncovered only after these compounds were introduced into wide use and became important to manufacturing and farming. The primary purpose of the TSCA is to force an early evaluation of suspect chemicals before they become economically important.

The EPA collects information under TSCA sections that require manufacturers and distributors to report to the EPA any information they possess that indicates a chemical substance presents a *substantial risk* of injury to health or to the environment. The TSCA further demands that the EPA be given advance notice before the manufacture of new chemical substances or the processing of any substance for a significant new use. Based on the results of its review, the EPA can take action to stop or limit introduction of new chemicals if they threaten human health or the environment with unreasonable risks.

The law also authorizes the EPA to require manufacturers to test their chemicals for possible harmful effects. Since not all the 70,000 chemicals in commerce can be tested all at once, the EPA has developed a priority scheme for selecting substances for testing based on whether or not the chemicals cause cancer, birth defects, or gene mutations. Today, only a small fraction of the total chemicals in production use have been safety tested.

In view of the beneficial role that many chemical substances play in all aspects of production and consumption, Congress directed the EPA through the TSCA to consider the economic and social impact, as well as the environmental one, of its decisions. In this respect the TSCA is unlike the Clean Air Act, which requires that certain pollution standards be met without regard for economic factors.

Resource Conservation and Recovery Act   The congressional Office of Technology Assessment reports that more than a ton of hazardous waste per citizen is dumped annually into the nation's environment. A major environmental problem has been how to ensure that the generators of toxic wastes dispose of them safely. In the past, there have been instances where even some otherwise responsible companies have placed highly toxic wastes in the hands of less-than-reputable disposal contractors.

To help ensure proper handling and disposal of hazardous and toxic wastes, Congress in 1976 amended the Solid Waste Disposal Act by the **Resource Conservation and Recovery Act (RCRA).** Under the RCRA, a generator of wastes has two primary obligations:

- To determine whether its wastes qualify as hazardous under RCRA
- To see that such wastes are properly transported to a disposal facility that has an EPA permit or license

The EPA lists a number of hazardous wastes, and a generator can determine if a non-listed waste is hazardous in terms of several chemical characteristics specified by the EPA. The RCRA accomplishes proper disposal of hazardous wastes through the **manifest system.** This system requires a generator to prepare a manifest document that designates a licensed facility for disposal purposes. The generator then gives copies of the manifest to the transporter of the waste. After receiving hazardous wastes, the disposal facility must return a copy of the manifest to the generator. In this fashion, the generator knows the waste has received proper disposal.

Failure to receive this manifest copy from the disposal facility within certain time limits requires the generator to notify the EPA. Under RCRA, the EPA has various investigatory powers. The act also prescribes various record-keeping requirements and assesses penalties for failure to comply with its provisions. The penalties include criminal fines and imprisonment. Between 1983 and 1990 the Department of Justice (at the request of the EPA) brought criminal charges against 253 individuals and corporations under the RCRA.

As amended in 1986, the RCRA is moving the handling of toxic wastes away from burial on land to treatments that destroy or permanently detoxify wastes. Today, RCRA requirements cost business an estimated $20 billion annually.

The Superfund   After passage of the TSCA and RCRA in 1976, regulation of toxic and hazardous substances was still incomplete. These acts did not deal with problems of the cleanup costs of unsafe hazardous waste dumps or spills, which are often substantial. Many abandoned dump sites date back as far as the nineteenth century. Even current owners of unsafe dump sites are frequently financially incapable of cleaning up hazardous wastes. Nor are transporters and others who cause spills or unauthorized discharges of hazardous wastes.

In 1980, Congress created the **Comprehensive Environmental Response, Compensation, and Liability Act (CERCLA)** to address these problems. Known as the **Superfund,** this act has allotted billions of dollars for environmental cleanup of dangerous hazardous wastes.

The act requires anyone who releases unauthorized amounts of hazardous substances into the environment to notify the government. Whether it is notified or not, the government has the power to order those responsible to clean up such releases. Refusal to obey can lead to a suit for reimbursement for any cleanup monies spent from the Superfund plus punitive damages of up to triple the cleanup costs. The government can also recover damages for injury done to natural resources. To date, the biggest Superfund case involved Shell Oil and the U.S. Army. These parties agreed to clean up a site outside Denver. Total costs may exceed $1 billion.

The Superfund imposes strict liability on those responsible for unauthorized discharges of hazardous wastes. No negligence need be proved. Responsible parties have liability when there is a release or threatened release of a hazardous substance that causes response costs. Responsible parties include (1) those who currently or formerly operate or own waste disposal sites, (2) those who arrange for disposal of wastes, and (3) those who transport wastes. Liability includes the costs of **remediation,** which are basically the costs of restoring land to its previous condition.

In the next case, the Supreme Court grapples with who might be an "operator" of a hazardous waste facility. Note that CERCLA itself gives no help in defining the terms *operator* and *owner.*

UNITED STATES V. BESTFOODS

524 U.S. 51 (1998)

The United States sued CPC International, Inc., under CERCLA to recover the costs of hazardous industrial waste generated by the now defunct Ott Chemical Co. (Ott II). Ott II had been a wholly owned subsidiary of CPC, its parent corporation. The federal district court ruled that CPC was an "operator" of the hazardous waste facility that Ott II owned. The court of appeals reversed, and the Supreme Court granted certiorari.

SOUTER, J.: The United States brought this action for the costs of cleaning up industrial waste generated by a chemical plant. The issue before us, under the Comprehensive Environmental Response, Com-

pensation, and Liability Act of 1980 (CERCLA) is whether a parent corporation that actively participated in, and exercised control over, the operations of a subsidiary may, without more, be held liable as an operator of a polluting facility owned or operated by the subsidiary. We answer no, unless the corporate veil may be pierced. But a corporate parent that actively participated in, and exercised control over, the operations of the facility itself may be held directly liable in its own right as an operator of the facility.

In 1980, CERCLA was enacted in response to the serious environmental and health risks posed by industrial pollution. If it satisfies certain statutory

[CONTINUED]

conditions, the United States may, for instance, use the "Hazardous Substance Superfund" to finance cleanup efforts, which it may then replenish by suits brought under the Act against, among others, "any person who at the time of disposal of any hazardous substance owned or operated any facility." So, those actually "responsible for any damage, environmental harm, or injury from chemical poisons [may be tagged with] the cost of their actions." The term "person" is defined in CERCLA to include corporations and other business organizations, and the term "facility" enjoys a broad and detailed definition as well. The phrase "owner or operator" is defined only by tautology, however, as "any person owning or operating" a facility, and it is this bit of circularity that prompts our review.

It is a general principle of corporate law deeply "ingrained in our economic and legal systems" that a parent corporation (so-called because of control through ownership of another corporation's stock) is not liable for the acts of its subsidiaries. Thus it is hornbook law that "the exercise of the 'control' which stock ownership gives to the stockholders . . . will not create liability beyond the assets of the subsidiary. That 'control' includes the election of directors, the making of by-laws . . . and the doing of all other acts incident to the legal status of stockholders. Nor will a duplication of some or all of the directors or executive officers be fatal." Although this respect for corporate distinctions when the subsidiary is a polluter has been severely criticized in the literature, nothing in CERCLA purports to reject this bedrock principle, and against this venerable common-law backdrop, the congressional silence is audible. The Government has indeed made no claim that a corporate parent is liable as an owner or an operator simply because its subsidiary is subject to liability for owning or operating a polluting facility.

[However, under] the plain language of the statute, any person who operates a polluting facility is directly liable for the costs of cleaning up the pollution. This is so regardless of whether that person is the facility's owner, the owner's parent corporation or business partner, or even a saboteur who sneaks into the facility at night to discharge its poisons out of malice. If any such act of operating a corporate subsidiary's facility is done on behalf of a parent corporation, the existence of the parent-subsidiary relationship under state corporate law is simply irrelevant to the issue of direct liability.

This much is easy to say; the difficulty comes in defining actions sufficient to constitute direct parental "operation." Here of course we may again rue the uselessness of CERCLA's definition of a facility's "operator" as "any person . . . operating" the facility, which leaves us to do the best we can to give the term its "ordinary or natural meaning." In a mechanical sense, to "operate" ordinarily means "to control the functioning of; run: *operate a business*." So, under CERCLA, an operator is simply someone who directs the workings of, manages, or conducts the affairs of a facility. To sharpen the definition for purposes of CERCLA's concern with environmental contamination, an operator must manage, direct, or conduct operations specifically related to pollution, that is, operations having to do with the leakage or disposal of hazardous waste, or decisions about compliance with environmental regulations.

In our inquiry into the meaning Congress presumably had in mind when it used the verb "to operate," we recognized that the statute obviously meant something more than mere mechanical activation of pumps and valves, and must be read to contemplate "operation" as including the exercise of direction over the facility's activities. The Court of Appeals recognized this by indicating that a parent can be held directly liable when the parent operates the facility in the stead of its subsidiary or alongside the subsidiary in some sort of a joint venture. We anticipated a further possibility above, however, when we observed that a dual officer or director might depart so far from the norms of parental influence exercised through dual office-holding as to serve the parent, even when ostensibly acting on behalf of the subsidiary in operating the facility. Yet another possibility, suggested by the fact of this case, is that an agent of the parent with no hat to wear but the parent's hat might manage or direct activities at the facility.

There is, in fact, some evidence that CPC engaged in just this type and degree of activity at the Muskegon plant. The District Court's opinion speaks of an agent of CPC alone who played a conspicuous part in dealing with the toxic risks emanating from

[CONTINUED]

the operation of the plant. G. R. D. Williams worked only for CPC; he was not an employee, officer, or director of Ott II, and thus, his actions were of necessity taken only on behalf of CPC. The District Court found that "CPC became directly involved in environmental and regulatory matters through the work of . . . Williams, CPC's governmental and environmental affairs director. Williams . . . became heavily involved in environmental issues at Ott II." He "actively participated in and exerted control over a variety of Ott II environmental matters," and he "issued directives regarding Ott II's responses to regulatory inquiries."

We think that these findings are enough to raise an issue of CPC's operation of the facility through William's actions. . . . The judgment of the Court of Appeals for the Sixth Circuit is vacated, and the case is remanded with instructions to return it to the District Court for further proceedings consistent with this opinion. **It is so ordered.**

CASE QUESTIONS

1. Explain why CERCLA is not helpful in defining *operator* and *owner*.

2. Under ordinary circumstances, what is the liability of the shareholder of a parent corporation for the CERCLA cleanup of its subsidiary?

3. In this case did the Supreme Court determine that the parent was responsible for the cleanup of its subsidiary's hazardous waste facility? Explain.

Superfund law has caused land purchasers to be very careful in buying land that may contain hazardous wastes. The law makes current as well as former landowners liable for hazardous wastes. The purchaser may escape liability by proving that it is innocent of knowledge of the wastes and has used *due diligence* in checking the land for toxic hazards. But exercising due diligence can be both costly and difficult to prove. Fortunately, the Superfund permits a land purchaser to sue a land seller if the purchaser incurs response costs due to hazardous wastes left by the seller.

Banks and other lenders who take out a security interest (such as a mortgage) in land that turns out to be contaminated and subject to the Superfund are not liable responsible parties. However, if a lender exerts control over a borrower's contaminated land, or assumes ownership of it, the lender will become a responsible party. Many lenders have become very wary about loaning money to borrowers who wish to put up as security land that may be contaminated.

As responsible parties engage in Superfund-required cleanup, they try to pass on the costs to others, often their insurers. In the future insurers may specifically refuse to cover pollution risks in their policies. Some courts, however, have interpreted existing policies to cover waste-cleanup costs as insured-against *damages* arising from an *occurrence,* which includes an *accidental* discharge of pollutants.

The business community has proposed various reforms to the Superfund law. Possible reforms include:

- Prorating liability for companies in Superfund litigation that agree to pay their share of cleanup costs

SUPERFUND IN DECLINE?

Consider the following statistics:

- 646 U.S. toxic waste sites identified by the EPA remained to be cleaned up as of 2003.
- The total number of completed Superfund cleanups in 2001 and 2002 fell 41 percent compared with the annual average in the preceding eight years.

- The $1.3 billion budgeted by Congress for Superfund cleanup in 2003 represented a 36 percent reduction in real dollars from the 1992 level.
- Penalties assessed under the Superfund against toxic waste polluters is down 41 percent in 2001 and 2002 compared with the annual average in the preceding eight years. Cleanup costs recovered from polluters has declined 13 percent.

- Exempting companies from liability when they have contributed very small amounts of waste at a dump site
- Permitting dump site cleanups that meet health and safety standards, rather than requiring that the land be returned to a pristine state

Finally, take note that both the Clean Air Act and the Clean Water Act also contain provisions related to government suits to recover costs for the cleanup of toxic chemicals. Suits under the Superfund and other acts may be a major area of litigation in coming years. The U.S. Office of Technology Assessment estimates that it will require as much as $500 billion during the next 50 years to clean up the nation's hazardous waste sites. However, after 2000 the pace of cleanups has begun to decline. (See box, above.)

Radiation In 1979, the nuclear power plant accident at the Three Mile Island installation in Pennsylvania and subsequent evacuation of thousands of nearby residents focused the nation's attention on the potential hazards of radiation pollution. Although no single piece of legislation comprehensively controls radiation pollution and no one agency is responsible for administering legislation in this technologically complex area, overall responsibility for such control rests with the Nuclear Regulatory Commission. The EPA, however, does have general authority to conduct testing and provide technical assistance in the area of radiation pollution control. In addition, the Clean Air Act and the Clean Water Act also contain sections applicable to radiation discharges into the air and water.

SUITS BY PRIVATE INDIVIDUALS

Achieving environmental goals requires coordinated strategy and implementation. As private citizens, individuals and groups of individuals lack both the power and foresight necessary to control pollution on a broad scale. There is a role, however, for the private control of private action in two principal areas:

- Citizen enforcement provisions
- Tort law

The following sections examine suits by private individuals that relate to environmental concerns.

---

concept SUMMARY   *An Environmental Alphabet*

Environmental and pollution control legislation seems especially given to acronyms. Here's a key.

BAT: best available technology

BPT: best practicable technology

CEQ: Council on Environmental Quality

CERCLA: Comprehensive Environmental Response, Compensation, and Liability Act

EIS: environmental impact statement

EPA: Environmental Protection Agency

FEPCA: Federal Environmental Pesticide Control Act

NEPA: National Environmental Policy Act

RCRA: Resource Conservation and Recovery Act

TSCA: Toxic Substances Control Act

---

11. CITIZEN ENFORCEMENT

Most of the environmental laws, such as the Clean Air and Water Acts, contain *citizen enforcement* provisions, which grant private citizens and groups the standing to sue to challenge failures to comply with the environmental laws. In many instances, private citizens can sue polluters directly to force them to cease violating the law. Private citizens also have standing to sue public agencies (for example, the EPA) to require them to adopt regulations or implement enforcement against private polluters that the environmental laws require.

12. TORT THEORIES

A second area of private control of private action lies in tort law and its state codifications. When pollution directly injures private citizens, they may sue offending polluters under various theories of tort law. Thus, the traditional deterrence of tort law contributes to private control of private action. This section further develops tort law's role in pollution control.

Examination of tort law and pollution control reveals little understanding of the interdependence between ourselves and our environment. Instead, tort theories, as they have been applied to environmental problems, focus on the action of one person (or business) as it injures the health or interferes with the property rights of another. In other words, tort law attacks the pollution problem by using the established theories of nuisance, trespass, negligence, and strict liability.

Nuisance   The principal tort theory used in pollution control has been that of **nuisance.** The law relating to nuisance is somewhat vague, but in most jurisdictions the common law has been put into statutory form. Several common elements exist in the law of nuisance in most states. To begin with, there are two types of nuisances: public and private.

A *public nuisance* arises from an act that causes inconvenience or damage to the public in the exercise of rights common to everyone. In the environmental area, air, water, and noise pollution can all constitute a public nuisance if they affect common rights. More specifically, industrial waste discharge that kills the fish in a stream may be held a public nuisance, since fishing rights are commonly possessed by the public. Public nuisance actions may be brought only by a public official, not private individuals, unless the latter have suffered some special damage to their persons or property as a result of the public nuisance.

Any unreasonable use of one's property that causes substantial interference with the enjoyment or use of another's land establishes a common law *private nuisance.* The unreasonableness of the interference is measured by a balancing process in which the character, extent, and duration of harm to the plaintiff are weighed against the social utility of the defendant's activity and its appropriateness to its location. Since society needs industrial activity as well as natural tranquillity, people must put up with a certain amount of smoke, dust, noise, and polluted water if they live in concentrated areas of industry. But what may be an appropriate industrial use of land in a congested urban area may be a private nuisance if it occurs in a rural or residential location.

Note that the proving of nuisance does not demand that a property owner be found negligent. An unreasonable *use* of one's land does not mean that one's *conduct* is unreasonable.

Other Tort Doctrines   Private plaintiffs in pollution cases frequently allege the applicability of tort doctrines other than that of nuisance. These doctrines, however, do overlap that of nuisance, which is really a field of tort liability rather than a type of conduct.

One such doctrine is that of *trespass.* A defendant is liable for trespass if, without right, she or he intentionally enters land in possession of another or causes something to do so. The entrance is considered intentional if the defendant knew that it was substantially certain to result from her or his conduct. Thus, airborne particles that fall on a plaintiff's property can constitute a trespass. In recent years, many courts have merged the theories of nuisance and trespass to such an extent that before plaintiffs can recover for a particle trespass, they must prove that the harm done to them exceeds the social utility of the defendant's enterprise.

Negligence doctrine is sometimes used by private plaintiffs in environmental pollution cases. The basis for the negligence tort lies in the defendant's breach of his or her duty to use ordinary and reasonable care toward the plaintiff, which *proximately* (foreseeably) causes the plaintiff injury. A factory's failure to use available pollution-control equipment may be evidence of its failure to employ *reasonable care.*

Finally, some courts recognize the applicability in pollution cases of *strict liability* tort doctrine. This tort liability arises when the defendant injures the plaintiff's person or property by voluntarily engaging in ultrahazardous activity that necessarily involves a risk of serious harm that cannot be eliminated through the exercise of the utmost care. No finding of *fault,* or *failure of reasonable care,* on the defendant's part is necessary. This doctrine has been employed in situations involving the use of poisons, such as in crop dusting and certain industrial work, the storage and use of explosives, and the storage of water in large quantities in a dangerous place.

Increasing numbers of private plaintiffs are suing companies for pollution-related harm. In one case, residents in northeast Denver, Colorado, sued Asarco, Inc., for environmental property damage caused by its smelter. Asarco settled the suit for $35 million. Not all pollution, however, comes from smokestacks. In agricultural states like Iowa and North Carolina, tort suits arise because of pollution from agricultural production. For example, plaintiffs have sued because of brain damage alleged to be caused by hydrogen sulfide, a by-product of waste from pork production.

TRENDS IN ENVIRONMENTAL REGULATION

A *Wall Street Journal*/NBC News survey suggests strong nationwide support for environment cleanup. A 61 percent majority favored more government regulation of the environment. Only 6 percent thought there should be less environmental regulation.

Public and business awareness of environmental issues has significantly increased. At the World Economic Forum, 650 business and government leaders ranked the environment as the greatest challenge facing business. Yet in a recent poll only 36 percent of Americans responded that business is doing an adequate job of keeping the environment clean.

13. AREAS OF ENVIRONMENTAL CONCERN

Researchers almost daily report new instances of how industry and technology affect life on our planet. For every allegation of pollution-caused environmental harm, however, countertheories maintain that the harm is not as significant as alleged or argue that the harm arises from causes unrelated to industrial pollution. Lack of unanimous scientific opinion on many environmental issues underscores their great complexity. It also reveals a key controversy at the heart of environmental regulation: *How much certainty of harm is required to justify regulatory intervention?*

Loss of Natural Ecosystems A report signed by 1,575 scientists, including 100 Nobel Prize winners, warned of the effects of worldwide destruction to natural ecosystems, the cutting of rainforests being the most widely publicized destruction. The report concluded: "If not checked, many of our current practices put at serious risk the future that we wish for human society and the plant and animal kingdoms, and may so alter the living world that it will be unable to sustain life in the manner that we know." At risk in the next 30 years are up to 20 percent of the planet's species of animals and plants.

Ozone In 1990, 59 countries agreed to stop producing certain chemicals that destroy the earth's protective *ozone layer.* The agreement required participating countries to stop production of chlorofluorocarbons and halons by the year 2000. Destruction of the ozone layer could lead to hundreds of thousands of cases of cataracts and skin cancer in humans plus unknown serious damage to animals and plants.

Research has recently identified other chemicals that may be at work in destroying the ozone layer, including methane and bromine compounds.

Greenhouse Effect Overshadowing even ozone destruction as a future pollution concern are increasing atmospheric concentrations of carbon dioxide. The National Academy of Sciences notes that global carbon dioxide levels have increased 6 percent since 1960. The increase is due largely to the burning of fossil fuels such as oil and coal.

Higher carbon dioxide levels will likely lead to warmer global temperatures, the so-called *greenhouse effect.* The last decade has had many of the warmest years on record, and atmospheric scientists believe the rise in global carbon dioxide levels was the cause. Changing climatic patterns and rising sea levels are possible results. In 1997 delegates from 150 nations reached a treaty to reduce emission of various greenhouse gases such as carbon dioxide. Under the Kyoto Protocol the industrialized nations, including the United States, will lower greenhouse gas emission to 7 or 8 percent below 1990 levels. The reductions will be achieved between 2008 and 2012.

However, the United States Senate has not ratified the treaty, a step necessary for it to become law in this country. The reduction in the burning of fossil fuels—coal and oil—necessary to lower greenhouse gas levels might seriously impact the economy. Business production might also relocate in developing countries, which the treaty does not require to reduce greenhouse gas emission.

The United States represents only 5 percent of the world's population, yet it consumes more than 20 percent of the world's energy production, much of it in fossil fuels. Can we reduce our disproportionate production of greenhouse gases without dramatically lowering our standard of living? Is it fair or necessary for us to hold back our standard of living while developing countries use cheap fossil fuels as their own economies grow? These questions are hotly debated. Only one conclusion is clearcut. We possess immense technological power today to change the environment for better and for worse, both intentionally and inadvertently.

Population Growth The world's population continues to grow. According to a Johns Hopkins University study, if human fertility rates do not drop to roughly two children per woman—merely replacing people who die—the world's population will rise to eight billion by 2025 from its current level of five and a half billion. Concerns about pollution, climate change, and even food production are magnified by population growth, yet birth control raises controversial cultural and religious issues. As a business student, you must be aware of and appreciate the significance of population growth because during your career the social and environmental problems associated with such growth will have to be addressed.

14. CORPORATE GOVERNANCE AND THE ENVIRONMENT

Concerned about the environment, some investors are turning to corporate governance as a way to make polluting industries more environmentally sensitive. Boards of directors legally control the activities of corporations, but shareholders who own these businesses elect the boards of directors. Increasingly, shareholders are presenting resolutions at the annual meetings of corporations to encourage or require the directors and managers of major polluting industries to analyze and report on certain environmental issues.

For instance, in 2003 shareholders filed resolutions with 28 companies in the United States and Canada on issues concerning global warming. These resolutions promoted increased investment in renewable resources and expressed concern over reports from the United Nations and Europe that by 2050 climate changes from global warming may cost the world $300 billion annually. Some resolutions asked boards of directors to submit reports detailing the financial risks of their companies resulting from past and future pollution emissions.

The number of shareholders voting for these resolutions ranged from 18 to over 30 percent. None of the companies adopted the resolutions but percentages of support showed rapid rise in some instances. According to one public interest research group, shareholder support for global warming resolutions went from 18 to more than 25 percent between 2002 and 2003 in two dozen major companies where resolutions were presented. At a shareholder meeting of Chevron Texaco, a global warming resolution that received only 9.6 percent of the shareholders' vote in 2001 got 32 percent support in 2003.

15. PRIVATE PROPERTY AND THE ENVIRONMENT

Considering the human impact on the natural world, does the existence of exclusive private ownership of resources help or hurt the environment? Theory and practice suggest that improper use of common resources causes more environmental problems than does improper use of private resources. Garrett Hardin called this the "tragedy of the commons." People tend to misuse and waste resources that are common to all, like air, water, and public land. They are more careful with their own private resources. Destruction of the world's rain forests is occurring mainly on public or unowned lands. Overall, then, private ownership contributes to a wiser, less wasteful use of resources than do other ways of using resources.

However, exceptions to the general rule do occur. For instance, species of plants and animals that have little immediate market value suffer even on private land. And some companies dump toxic substances that will be hazardous for generations even on their own land. Some landowners have challenged environmental regulation and zoning as a governmental "taking" of private property without "just compensation," which the Fifth Amendment expressly prohibits. The Supreme Court has ruled that land regulation is not a taking that must be compensated as long as an owner is allowed a "reasonable" use of the land. If a law like the Endangered Species Act is applied to prohibit any building on a piece of land, has there been a "taking"? What do you think?

Remember that "property" includes the concept of the equal right of others. In a strong property system, owners cannot use their land or other resources in ways that harm the resources of others, including the resource that others have in their health. The problem is how does the law define "the equal right of others"? Traditional tort law simply does not deal well with pollution harms that occur over long distances or across many years. It is too difficult to prove that the pollution caused the harm. So the government steps in and sets pollution limits that are themselves controversial.

Note that the emissions trading approach to pollution management is a property approach. Granting private owners an exclusive right to sell a quantity of pollution emission to a buyer is the essence of the exclusionary right of property. The world is heading toward increased emissions trading. Imagine in the future that an international treaty sets acceptable emission levels for greenhouse gases and companies worldwide bid for permits to engage in such pollution. What if everyone on earth were considered to own an equal right to engage in greenhouse pollution and proceeds from the emissions auction were distributed to the countries of the world on a population proportional basis?

KEY TERMS

Bubble concept   517
Cap and trade   518
Clean Air Act   513
Clean Water Act   519

Comprehensive Environmental
   Response, Compensation, and
   Liability Act (CERCLA)   529
Emissions reduction banking   517

REVIEW QUESTIONS AND PROBLEMS

Government's Regulations of Itself

1. *The National Environmental Policy Act*

   (a) Your firm has been hired to build a large government facility near a residential neighborhood. A committee of residents has been formed to oppose the building. You have been asked to assist in writing the EIS. What factors must your EIS take into consideration?

   (b) The Avila Timber Company has asked for and been granted permission by the Department of Interior to cut 40 acres of timber from the 10,000-acre Oconee National Forest. Prior to the actual logging, a local environmental group files suit in federal district court, contending that the Department of Interior has not filed an EIS. Can the group challenge the department's action? Analyze whether an EIS should be filed in light of the facts given.

2. *Evaluation of Environmental Impact Statements*

   Outline criticisms of the EIS process. Why are state EISs often less helpful in evaluating complex environmental factors than are those prepared by federal agencies?

Government's Regulation of Business

3. *The Environmental Protection Agency*

   Explain the function of the EPA.

4. *Air Pollution*

   The Akins Corporation wishes to build a new smelting facility in Owens County, an area where air pollution exceeds primary air quality standards.

   (a) What legal difficulties may Akins face?

   (b) What solutions might you suggest for these difficulties?

5. *Clean Air Act Trends*

   (a) What is the difference between an individual point-source approach and a bubble-policy approach to dealing with factory pollution?

(b)   For the factory owner, what are the advantages of employing the bubble concept?

6. *Water Pollution*

Explain the concept of "navigable waterway" and how it is related to the Clean Water Act.

7. *Endangered Species Act*

How does the ESA apply to private businesses? Explain.

8. *Pesticide Control*

Before beginning the manufacture of a new pesticide, what process must a company follow under the pesticide-control acts?

9. *Solid Waste*

(a)   Who has the primary responsibility for nontoxic solid waste disposal?

(b)   Describe the role of the Solid Waste Disposal Act in waste disposal.

10. *Toxic and Hazardous Substances*

(a)   As a manufacturer of paints, you need to dispose of certain production by-products that are highly toxic. Discuss the process the law requires you to follow in disposing of these products.

(b)   An abandoned radioactive waste site is discovered by local authorities. The waste came from a company that manufactured radium watch faces and is now out of business. Who will pay to clean up these radioactive wastes? Discuss.

Suits by Private Individuals

11. *Citizen Enforcement*

Explain the standing to sue doctrine as it applies to the citizen enforcement of federal pollution laws.

12. *Tort Theories*

Several years ago, the Spul Chemical Corporation built a new plant near your neighborhood. About once a month clouds of odorous mist have passed across your property, your children have complained of skin rashes, and you have heard that the water table has been contaminated with toxic chemicals. You and your neighbors are fearful of health hazards from the plant, and the neighborhood property values have dropped significantly. Explain possible tort causes of action you may have against the chemical company.

Trends in Environmental Regulation

13. *Emerging Areas of Environmental Concern*

Give examples of why a key controversy at the heart of environmental regulation concerns how much certainty of harm is required to justify regulatory intervention.

14. *Corporate Governance and the Environment*

How have shareholder groups tried to make environmental concerns relevant to corporate governance?

15. *Private Property and the Environment*

Explain what it means to say that "emissions trading has propertitized pollution."

TERMINOLOGY REVIEW

For each term in the left-hand column match the most appropriate description in the right-hand column.

1. EIS
2. Point source
3. Prevention of significant deterioration
4. Superfund
5. Nuisance
6. Bubble concept
7. Manifest system
8. Primary air quality standards

a. An unreasonable use of one's land that interferes with the use or enjoyment of another's land
b. Treating several point sources at a plant as one source
c. A process that must be followed by federal agencies before undertaking major actions that significantly affect the environment
d. A smokestack, pipe, or other opening that discharges pollution
e. The Comprehensive Environmental Response, Compensation, and Liability Act
f. The tracking process for toxic waste disposal
g. Air pollution levels necessary to protect human health
h. The policy of preventing additional pollution in certain areas that have cleaner air than required by primary standards

BUSINESS DISCUSSION

International Paint Company wants to sell a large tract of land with several facilities on it to U.S. Parts, Inc. As acquisitions manager for U.S. Parts, what do you need to know before buying this land, other than that International Paint has good ownership, that your company needs the site, and that the price is right?

Why might you need to know the environmental condition of the land?

What steps might you want to take before buying the land?

INTERNATIONAL LAW

XYZ Company is a U.S. firm that makes communication software used in a variety of consumer goods manufactured and sold in the United States. XYZ recently learned that one of the manufacturing firms it supplies, ABC Company, is exporting finished goods to a country where U.S. goods and component parts are prohibited because of numerous conflicts with the U.S. government.

> Does XYZ have any moral or legal responsibility in this case?
>
> How should XYZ protect itself under these circumstances?
>
> Should American business practices be impacted by conflicts between governments?

As American business faces an increasingly competitive global market, some understanding of the legal issues raised by international business transactions is essential. The stability needed for economic growth around the world can be achieved only by nations demonstrating their respect for the rule of law. Law is fundamental to business in the United States and throughout the globe. The protection of property rights, through the law of contracts, is critical for governing the intense competition for business in the global market. Nations enter into treaties and agreements with other countries that govern competition and the way goods and technology are sold from one country to the next. Every country is interested in developing rules that make its products and services more competitive in the global market. The rule of law and a respect for property rights does not mean businesses may do as they please. Nation-states and corporations are protected by a mutual respect for property rights.

Who engages in international business? The players are diverse and the results affect virtually every corner of the world. National economies rely upon their ability to export products and services abroad to create jobs and economic growth at home.

The United States continues to run a huge trade deficit because it buys more than it sells abroad as demonstrated in the table, below. The total trade deficit in goods and services rose to $470 billion in 2002 from $164 billion in 1998. Bilateral trade deficits with most of our major trading partners continue to widen sharply. This chapter focuses on issues important to management decision making by examining the methods and risks of transacting international business. This chapter also considers the role and impact of international organizations and agreements on business and the effect of foreign competition on American business at home.

INTERNATIONAL LAW AND ORGANIZATIONS

As you explore international legal transactions as a business manager please remember that, unfortunately, international law does not consist of a cohesive body of uniform principles. Nonetheless, international law can be found in a variety of sources from U.S. domestic law to the law of other countries to international agreements and treaties and even in customary international principles found in the general practice of civilized nations.

In the famous case of *The Paquette Habana* (175 U.S. 677 [1900]), the Supreme Court held that "[i]nternational law is part of our law, and must be ascertained and administered by the courts of justice of appropriate jurisdiction as often as questions of right depending upon it are duly presented for their determination."

1. SOURCES OF INTERNATIONAL LAW

How does one go about finding the principles or rules of international law that apply to a particular contract or dispute? Generally, international law is classified as either **public international law** or **private international law.** Public international law examines relationships between nations and uses rules that are binding on all countries in the international community. Private international law, which is of principal concern to the business manager, examines relationships created by commercial transactions and utilizes international agreements and the individual laws of nations to resolve business disputes.

2002 U.S. Trade Deficit

U.S. Imports	Worldwide Deficit	U.S. Imports
$971 billion	$436 billion	$1.407 trillion

Top Five Countries with Which the United States Has a Trade Deficit

China	$103 billion
Japan	70 billion
Canada	50 billion
Mexico	37 billion
Germany	36 billion

Source: U.S. Department of Commerce.

Public International Law   Article 38 of the Statute of the **International Court of Justice (ICJ)** is the traditional place for ascertaining what is public international law. However, in contrast to what you learned in Chapter 1 regarding U.S. cases, the decisions made by the ICJ, the World Court, do not create binding rules of law or precedent in future cases.

The ICJ is the judicial branch of the United Nations and sits at The Hague in the Netherlands. It consists of 15 judges representing all of the world's major legal systems. The judges are elected by the U.N. General Assembly and the Security Council after having been nominated by national groups, not governments. No more than one judge may be a national of any country.

The ICJ has not been a major force in settling disputes since it began functioning in 1946. The ICJ renders, on average, only one contested decision per year and one advisory opinion every two years. There has been widespread reluctance to resort to the ICJ as a forum for resolving international disputes for several reasons. First, only countries have access to the Court. Private parties or corporations may not directly present claims before the Court. No device exists under U.S. law by which a firm or individual can compel the U.S. government to press a claim on its behalf before the ICJ. Furthermore, only countries that have submitted to the Court's jurisdiction may be parties, since there is no compulsory process for forcing a country to come before the Court. A country may choose to accept the Court's jurisdiction only when the use of the Court may suit its own interests. Moreover, the ICJ has no enforcement authority and must rely on diplomacy or economic sanctions against countries that breach international law. For these reasons, infractions of international law often are settled through diplomacy or arbitration, rather than by the presentation of formal charges to the ICJ.

Of course, deciding whether international law has been violated is often a very difficult question. Article 38 sets forth the following order of importance for determining what is international law in a given case:

> The Court, whose function is to decide in accordance with international law such disputes as are submitted to it, shall apply:
>
> a. *International Conventions,* whether general or particular, establishing rules expressly recognized by the contesting states;
>
> b. *International Custom,* as evidence of a general practice accepted as law;
>
> c. *The General Principles of Law* recognized by civilized nations;
>
> d. *Judicial Decisions and the Teachings of the Most Highly Qualified Publicists* of various nations, as subsidiary means for the determination of rules of law.

International Conventions are similar to legislation or statutes and represent formal agreements between nations. International Custom describes common legal practices followed by nations in working with each other over a long period of time. General Principles of Law may be found in national rules common to the countries in a dispute. Finally, Judicial Decisions and Teachings, although not binding, may be used for guidance in resolving a dispute.

Private International Law   Private international law is represented by the laws of individual nations and the multilateral agreements developed between nations to provide mutual understanding and some degree of continuity to international business transactions. Even in purely domestic business deals, the law is rarely predictable or certain. When different national laws, languages, practices, and cultures are added to the transaction, the situation can become very unstable for international business.

International commerce is seldom uncomplicated, and a single business transaction often involves several firms with operations in different nations. For example, in a contract dispute among a German manufacturer, an American wholesaler, and a Canadian retailer, which nation's law controls the transaction may be crucial for determining the outcome of the case. Moreover, determining the proper forum for the case (which nation's court may hear the case) can be difficult.

2. INTERNATIONAL ORGANIZATIONS AND AGREEMENTS AFFECTING TRADE

Several international organizations and agreements play important roles in the development of political, economic, and legal rules for the conduct of international business. They include the United Nations, the World Trade Organization, and the Convention on the International Sale of Goods.

United Nations   The **United Nations** was established after World War II and has grown in size from 51 founding nations at that time to almost every nation in the world today. The Charter of the United Nations sets forth as its primary goal "to save succeeding generations from the scourge of war" and to that end authorizes "collective measures for the prevention and removal of threats to the peace, and for the suppression of acts of aggression or other breaches of the peace."

The General Assembly is composed of every nation represented in the United Nations and permits each country to cast one vote. The real power in the United Nations rests in the Security Council, which is composed of 15 member states. The council has the power to authorize military action and to sever diplomatic relations with other nations. The five permanent members of the Council (United States, Russia, China, France, and United Kingdom) have veto power over any action proposed in the Council. France and Russia used the threat of a veto in 2003 to force the United States to go forward with the war in Iraq without clear United Nations' authority. While the United States contended that its authority for war came from previously passed UN resolutions regarding Iraq, the U.S. government clearly was perturbed by the veto threat. The failure of the United Nations to dictate the resolution of the U.S.-Iraq conflict created serious questions about the future authority and role of the United Nations in international conflicts.

A number of organizations affiliated with the United Nations have authority over activities that directly affect international business. The United Nations Commission on International Trade Law (UNCITRAL) was created in 1966 in an effort to develop standardized commercial practices and agreements. One of the documents drafted by the UNCITRAL is the Convention on the International Sale of Goods. UNCITRAL has no authority to force any country to adopt any of the con-

HUMAN RIGHTS AND CORPORATE SOCIAL RESPONSIBILITY

There is a growing movement to hold multinational corporations liable in U.S. courts for alleged human rights violations around the world. Recent cases involve allegations against a large energy company in the murder and torture of villagers in Indonesia, against a food processing company in Guatemala in torture and kidnapping, against an oil company in Myanmar claiming slavelike working conditions, and against a bottler engaging in antiunion violence.

ventions or agreements that it proposes. The United Nations Conference on Trade and Development (UNCTAD) was created in 1964 to deal with international trade reform and the redistribution of income through trading with developing countries. The UNCTAD has drafted both the Transfer of Technology Code and the Restrictive Business Practices Code, which have gone largely ignored by most nations.

At the Bretton Woods Conference of 1944, two important agencies were also created under the auspices of the United Nations. The International Monetary Fund (IMF) encourages international trade by maintaining stable foreign exchange rates and works closely with commercial banks to promote orderly exchange policies with members. The World Bank promotes economic development in poor countries by making loans to finance necessary development projects and programs.

World Trade Organization Every nation has the right to establish its own trading policies and has its own national interests at stake when dealing with other nations. Ultimately, after years of economic conflict, many countries concluded that their own interests could be served best by liberalizing trade through reduced tariffs and free markets. The **General Agreement on Tariffs and Trade (GATT)** was originally signed by 23 countries after World War II and represented the determination of a war-weary world to open trade and end the protection of domestic industries. Since GATT was created in 1948, it has undergone eight major revisions, including the 1994 Uruguay Round, which culminated in the creation of the **World Trade Organization (WTO)** as an umbrella organization to regulate world trade. The 1994 agreement was signed by 125 countries.

The WTO is an international organization which, as its primary purpose, seeks to resolve trade disputes between member nations. The WTO administers the GATT but does not have the authority to regulate world trade in any manner it desires. The WTO expects nations to avoid unilateral trade wars and rely on GATT dispute settlement procedures to avert conflict. At the heart of the 1994 Uruguay Round are several enduring GATT principles: (1) nondiscrimination (treating all member countries equally with respect to trade); (2) national treatment (countries not favoring their domestic products over imported products); and (3) elimination of trade barriers (reducing tariffs and other restrictions in foreign products). (See the box, below.)

Under the WTO, existing tariffs were reduced and the agreement also extended GATT rules to new areas such as agricultural products and service industries. The WTO further restricts tariffs on textiles, apparel, and forest products. It also requires countries to upgrade their intellectual property laws to protect patents and copyrights and to guard against the piracy of items such as computer software and videotapes. The largest and most powerful trading nations in the world comply with the WTO rulings, and the WTO can sanction nations that ignore its rulings.

However, warning signs that the WTO is in trouble have emerged. The United States, for example, began criticizing the lack of appreciation for competition and antitrust enforcement in WTO rulings. Part of the U.S. frustration arose out of a

BENEFITS OF THE WTO

1. The WTO helps promote peace.
2. Disputes are handled constructively.
3. Free trade reduces the cost of living.
4. Trade stimulates economic growth.
5. WTO encourages good government.

THE WTO AND THE ENVIRONMENT

The WTO troubles many environmental groups that believe the WTO's ability to sanction a violating country has undercut U.S. environmental policies that impact free trade. For example, an earlier 1994 GATT panel found that U.S. embargoes on imports of tuna caught by nations that use purse seine nets were inconsistent with the free-trade provisions in GATT. Although the United States imposed these embargoes because these types of nets often will injure dolphins, the panel held that the United States may not distinguish between "environmentally friendly" products and those produced in ecologically damaging ways.

In 2003, the U.S. National Oceanic and Atmospheric Administration (NOAA) ruled that imported tuna can be sold to Americans as "dolphin safe," even when fishers set huge nets around dolphins in order to catch fish known to swim near them.

NOAA said that current fishing practices kill an estimated 2,000 dolphins a year, but it ruled that those deaths are not a "significant" impact on the animal populations. Environmentalists and animal-rights groups attacked the standard and claimed that "dolphin-deadly" tuna will be sold in the United States misleadingly labeled as "dolphin safe" tuna.

highly publicized case against Japan in which the WTO rejected the U.S. claim that Japanese business practices favored Fuji over Kodak film products. Several U.S. trade experts also criticized the WTO for its inability to gather and collect evidence and for weakening U.S. sovereignty and control over its own trading practices. Many European countries, along with the United States, also are worried that the WTO rules will undermine their ability to compete in many emerging markets such as Asia.

The difficulties encountered at recent WTO meetings with televised scenes of thousands of protesters demonstrating against globalization provided evidence of the growing tensions between developed and developing economies. There remain many positive reasons to support the WTO. However, the concerns about globalization and the WTO certainly have stalled progress. The WTO's latest round of negotiations seeks to cut tariffs and overhaul the dispute settlement system. However, the negotiations are behind schedule, and the future remains murky and uncertain. (See box on the next page.)

Convention on the International Sale of Goods The **Convention on the International Sale of Goods (CISG)** outlines standard international practices for the sale of goods. It took several years to develop, and it represents many compromises among nations that follow a variety of practices in the area of contracts. It became effective in 1988 and has been adopted by the United States and most of the other countries that engage in large quantities of international trade. The CISG represents the cumulative work of over 60 nations and international groups. It has become widely accepted around the globe.

The CISG applies to contracts for the commercial sale of goods (consumer sales for personal, family, or household use are excluded) between parties whose businesses are located in different nations, provided that those nations have adopted the convention. If a commercial seller or buyer in the United States, for example, contracts for the sale of goods with a company located in another country that also has adopted the CISG, the convention and not the U.S. Uniform Commercial Code (UCC) applies to the transaction.

Under the CISG, a significant degree of freedom is provided for the individual parties in an international contract. The parties may negotiate contract terms as

IS GLOBALIZATION AND INTERNATIONAL TRADE TOO RISKY?

Globalization, through increased international trade and development, was supposed to bring nations and cultures around the world together. Has it? Financial crises, emerging diseases, and international terrorism have adversely impacted the desires of some businesses to reach out to new markets. Business insecurity and uncertainty about future global events have caused many companies to focus on avoiding risks rather than expanding markets. Can peace and stability be restored to provide businesses with adequate protection from the risks associated with international business transactions?

Nations also have backed away from globalization at any cost. Struggling through poor economic growth since 2000, wealthy nations have been unwilling to make the concessions necessary for new international trade agreements. In recent times, some nations have gone the other way to erect new barriers to international trade. At the same time, poorer nations have become more demanding as they seek new trade agreements that allow them to benefit more equally from globalization. Everyone, from states to business firms, is questioning the benefits of globalization.

they deem fit for their business practices and may, if desired, even opt out of the CISG entirely. One of the most interesting provisions in the CISG includes a rule that contracts for the sale of goods need not be in writing. The CISG also provides that in contract negotiations an acceptance that contains new provisions that do not materially alter the terms of the offer becomes part of the contract, unless the offeror promptly objects to the change. The CISG also sets forth the fundamental elements that will materially alter a contract such as price, payment, quality, and quantity of the goods, place and time of delivery of goods, provisions related to one party's liability to the other, and methods for settling disputes. Since international transactions typically involve sophisticated parties, the CISG also makes it easier to disclaim warranties on goods than under traditional U.S. law. Of course, the CISG does not resolve all areas of contract law and parties are still subject to local laws and customs making international agreements complex and tricky to negotiate.

3. THE EUROPEAN UNION

Probably the single most significant development affecting international business was the original action by six European countries in 1957 to achieve economic unity by signing the Treaty of Rome, which created the European Community. Now known as the **European Union (EU),** it quickly grew to include 15 member countries: Austria, Belgium, Denmark, Finland, France, Germany, Greece, Ireland, Italy, Luxembourg, the Netherlands, Portugal, Spain, Sweden, and the United Kingdom. The combined gross domestic product (GDP) of the top five European countries is very significant when compared to that of either Japan or the United States.

The past 15 years have provided remarkable development for the modern Europe. In 1987, the member states passed the Single European Act, which required each country by 1992 to complete many reforms necessary to reach the goal of a unified internal market. The 1987 act mandated the removal of many physical, technical, and tax barriers to the free movement of persons, goods, services, and capital. In 1992, the leaders of the EU member nations signed a far-reaching agreement, known as the Maastricht Treaty, designed to create a more federal system of government and further political and economic union within the EU. The

Maastricht Treaty, which took effect in late 1993, created common foreign and defense policies, established a joint central bank, and required member countries to reduce government deficits and to initiate a single currency. The single currency (euro) is now the unit of exchange in 11 EU countries. Moreover, under the treaty, trade barriers between member states essentially are being eliminated under a system similar to the trading policy between states in the United States.

The Nice Summit, which was held in 2000, brought 15 national leaders together to contemplate the next chapter in the European Union. The summit was convened to lay the groundwork for admitting 12 additional countries to the EU, 9 of them under communist control several years ago. In 2002, Ireland became the last of the 15 EU members to approve the Nice Accord to admit the 12 new members. The first 10 of those 12 countries joined in 2004: Hungary, Poland, the Czech Republic, Slovenia, Latvia, Lithuania, Slovakia, Estonia, Malta, and Cyprus. Bulgaria and Romania are expected to enter the EU by 2007, if they complete economic and political reforms.

The major institutions of the EU are the Council of Ministers, the Commission, the Parliament, and the Court of Justice. The Council is composed of one representative from each member state. Its purpose is to coordinate the policies of the member states in a variety of areas from economics to foreign affairs. The Commission consists of individuals who represent the will of the entire Union rather than specific national concerns. Much of the executive functions of the EU are carried out by the Commission as it seeks to forge a single identity. The Parliament is comprised of elected representatives from each member state and is divided into political factions that often create coalitions across national borders. Finally, the Court of Justice serves the role of deciding the nature and parameters of EU law. Justices are appointed by the Council, and each member nation has a justice seated on the Court.

4. THE NORTH AMERICAN FREE TRADE AGREEMENT

With passage in 1993 of the **North American Free Trade Agreement (NAFTA),** the United States, Mexico, and Canada set in motion increased trade and foreign investment, and unlimited opportunities for economic growth in one of the fastest-growing regions of the world. At the core of NAFTA is free trade with the reduction and eventual elimination of tariffs and other barriers to business between the three countries. NAFTA also provides for a dispute settlement mechanism that

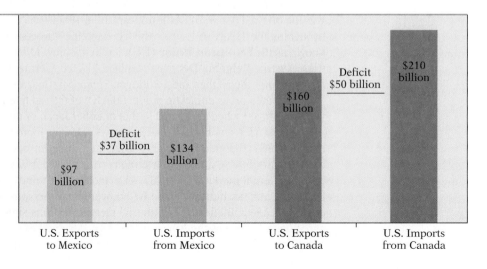

U.S. Balance of Trade with Mexico and Canada, 2002

makes it easier to resolve trade disputes between the three countries. Based upon concerns that cheap labor and poor environmental controls might cause U.S. firms to relocate to Mexico, side agreements also were reached to improve labor rights and environmental protection in Mexico.

Since its enactment, NAFTA has expanded shipments of U.S. goods to Mexico and Canada as well as Mexican and Canadian exports to the United States. As the figure on the preceding page demonstrates, the balance of trade favors Mexico and Canada. Mexico and Canada are among the top trading partners with which the United States has a trade deficit.

---

concept SUMMARY   *International Law and Organizations*

1. International law is classified as either public or private.
2. The International Court of Justice is the traditional place for determining public international law.
3. The World Trade Organization regulates world trade.
4. The Convention on the International Sale of Goods governs international practices for the sale of goods.
5. The European Union has evolved into the most important economic force in Europe.
6. The North American Free Trade Agreement has substantially expanded trade with Mexico and Canada.

METHODS OF TRANSACTING INTERNATIONAL BUSINESS

A U.S. business that wants to engage in international trade is presented with an almost limitless array of possibilities. Choosing a method of doing business in foreign countries not only requires understanding the factors normally involved in selecting an organization and operating a business domestically but also demands an appreciation of the international trade perspective. Depending upon the country, type of export, and amount of export involved in a particular transaction, international trade may involve direct foreign sales, licensing agreements, franchise agreements, or direct foreign investment.

5. FOREIGN SALES

The most common approach for a manufacturer to use when trying to penetrate foreign markets is to sell goods directly to buyers located in other countries. However, with foreign sales, increased uncertainty over the ability to enforce the buyer's promise to pay for goods often requires that more complex arrangements for payment be made than with the usual domestic sale. International sales involve many risky legal issues. Commonly, an **irrevocable letter of credit** is used to ensure payment. Transactions using such a letter involve, in addition to a seller and buyer, an *issuing bank* in the buyer's country. The buyer obtains a commitment from the bank to advance (pay) a specified amount (i.e., the price of the goods) upon receipt, from the carrier, of a **bill of lading,** stating that the goods have been shipped. The issuing bank's commitment to pay is given, not to the seller directly, but to a *confirming bank* located in the United States from which the seller obtains payment. The confirming bank forwards the bill of lading to the issuing bank in order to obtain reimbursement of the funds that have been paid to the seller. The issuing bank releases the bill of lading to the buyer after it has been paid, and with the bill of lading the buyer is able to obtain the goods from the carrier. Use of a letter of credit in the transaction thus reduces the uncertainties involved. The buyer need not pay the seller for goods prior to shipment, and the seller can obtain payment for the goods immediately upon shipment.

There is no room in documentary transactions for substantial performance. All of the duties and responsibilities of parties must be evaluated based upon the documents tendered, and these documents must comply strictly with the letter of credit. The tradition and purpose of the letter of credit in international transactions is demonstrated by the following case, where the issue of notice became the central issue for the court.

VOEST-ALPINE TRADING USA V. BANK OF CHINA

288 F. 3D 262 (5TH CIR. 2002)

Jiangyin Foreign Trade Corporation ("JFTC"), a Chinese company, agreed to purchase 1,000 metric tons of styrene monomer from Voest-Alpine Trading USA Corporation ("Voest-Alpine"), an American company. At Voest-Alpine's insistence, JFTC obtained a letter of credit from the Bank of China for the purchase price of $1.2 million. The letter of credit provided for payment to Voest-Alpine after it delivered the monomer and presented several designated documents to the Bank of China. By the time Voest-Alpine was ready to ship its product, the market price of styrene monomer had dropped significantly from the original contract price. JFTC asked for a price concession, but Voest-Alpine refused. After shipping the monomer to JFTC, Voest-Alpine presented the documents specified in the letter of credit to Texas Commerce Bank ("TCB"), which would forward the documents to the Bank of China. TCB noted several discrepancies between what Voest-Alpine presented and what the letter of credit required. Because it did not believe any of the discrepancies would warrant refusal to pay, Voest-Alpine instructed TCB to present the documents to the Bank of China "on approval," meaning that JFTC would be asked to waive the problems.

The Bank of China received the documents. The bank notified TCB that the documents contained several discrepancies and that it would contact JFTC about acceptance. On August 15, 1995, TCB, acting on behalf of Voest-Alpine, responded that the

alleged discrepancies were not adequate grounds for dishonoring the letter of credit and demanded payment. On August 19, the Bank of China reiterated its position that the documents were insufficient and stated: "Now the discrepant documents may have us refuse to take up the documents according to article 14(B) of UCP 500." JFTC refused to waive the discrepancies, and the Bank of China returned the documents to TCB on September 18, 1995.

CLEMENT, J.: Voest-Alpine filed the instant action for payment on the letter of credit.

The Bank of China's primary contention on appeal is that the district court erroneously concluded that the bank failed to provide proper notice of refusal to Voest-Alpine. In order to reject payment on a letter of credit, an issuing bank must give notice of refusal to the beneficiary no later than the close of the seventh banking day following the day of receipt of the [presentation] documents. If the Bank of China did not provide timely notice, it must honor the letter of credit despite any questions as to Voest-Alpine's compliance.

The Bank of China received Voest-Alpine's documents on August 9. Since August 12 and 13 were Chinese banking holidays, the deadline for giving notice of dishonor was August 18. The Bank of China's only communication before the deadline was its telex of August 11. Accordingly, the issue is whether that telex provided notice of refusal. The bank's August 11 telex stated:

[CONTINUED]

Upon checking documents, we note the following discrepancy:

1. Late presentation.
2. Beneficiary's name is differ (*sic*) from L/C.
3. B/L should be presented in three originals (*sic*) i/o duplicate, triplicate.
4. Inv. P/L. and cert. Of origin not showing "original."
5. The date of surver (*sic*) report later than B/L date.
6. Wrong L/C no. in fax copy.
7. Wrong destination in cert. Of origin and beneficiary's cert.

We are contacting the applicant for acceptance of the relative discrepancy. Holding documents at your risk and disposal.

The district court found that the telex failed to provide notice of refusal because (1) the bank did not explicitly state that it was rejecting the documents; (2) the bank's statement that it would contact JFTC about accepting the documents despite the discrepancies holds open the possibility of acceptance upon waiver and indicates that the Bank of China has not refused the documents; and (3) the Bank of China did not even mention refusal until its August 19 telex in which it wrote: "Now the discrepant documents may have us refuse to take up the documents according to article 14(B) of UCP 500." In light of these circumstances, the district court concluded that the August 11 telex was merely a status report, the bank would not reject the documents until after it consulted JFTC, and the bank did not raise the possibility of refusing payment on the letter of credit until August 19. Accordingly, the district court held that the Bank of China forfeited its right to refuse the documents and was obligated to pay Voest-Alpine.

We find ample evidence supporting the district court's decision. The court's determination that the August 11 telex did not reject the letter of credit is based primarily on the Bank of China's offer to obtain waiver from JFTC. The offer to solicit a waiver, the district court reasoned, suggests that the documents had not in fact been refused but might be accepted after consultation with JFTC. In reaching this conclusion, the district court relied heavily on the testimony of Voest-Alpine's expert witness on international standard banking practices. [The expert] testified that the bank's telex would have given adequate notice had it not contained the waiver clause. The waiver clause, he explained, deviated from the norm and introduced an ambiguity that converted what might otherwise have been a notice of refusal into nothing more than a status report. Faced with this evidence, the district court correctly decided that the Bank of China noted discrepancies in the documents, and, instead of rejecting the letter of credit outright, contacted JFTC for waiver.

Viewed in the context of standard international banking practices, the Bank of China's notice of refusal was clearly deficient. The bank failed to use the standard language for refusal, failed to comply with generally accepted trade usages, and created ambiguity by offering to contact JFTC about waiver, thus leaving open the possibility that the allegedly discrepant documents might have been accepted at a future date. Accordingly, the district court properly found that the August 11 telex was not an adequate notice of refusal. Since we agree with the district court that the bank failed to provide timely notice, we need not reach the question of whether the alleged discrepancies warranted refusal.

The Bank of China failed to provide Voest-Alpine with adequate notice that it was refusing payment on the letter of credit. Without a valid excuse for nonpayment, the bank is liable for the full amount of the letter of credit and for Voest-Alpine's legal fees. Accordingly, we affirm the judgment of the district court.

Affirmed.

CASE QUESTIONS

1. Why is the issue of "timely notice" so important in the case?

2. What is the primary importance of a letter of credit?

3. Why did the court rule against Bank of China?

6. LICENSES OR FRANCHISES

In appropriate circumstances, a domestic firm may choose to grant a foreign firm the means to produce and sell its product. The typical method for controlling these transfers of information is the **license** or **franchise** contract. In this manner, intangible property rights, such as patents, copyrights, trademarks, or manufacturing processes, are transferred in exchange for royalties in the foreign country. A licensing arrangement allows the international business to enter a foreign market without any direct foreign investment. Licensing often is used as a transitional technique for firms expanding international operations since the risks are greater than with foreign sales but considerably less than with direct foreign investment. Licensing and franchise agreements also must follow the local laws where they operate.

Licensing technology or the sale of a product to a foreign firm is a way to expand the company's market without the need for substantial capital. The foreign firm may agree to this arrangement because it lacks sufficient research and development capability or the management skills or marketing strategies to promote the product alone. Of course, as with all international trade agreements, there is some level of risk. The licensor must take care to restrict the use of the product or technology to agreed-upon geographic areas and must take adequate steps to protect the confidential information that is licensed to the foreign firm so that third parties cannot exploit it.

7. DIRECT FOREIGN INVESTMENT

As a business increases its level of international trade, it may find that creation of a **foreign subsidiary** is necessary. Most countries will permit a foreign firm to conduct business only if a national (individual or firm) of the host country is designated as its legal representative. Since this designation may create difficulties in control and result in unnecessary expense, the usual practice for multinational corporations is to create a foreign subsidiary in the host country. The form of subsidiary most closely resembling a U.S. corporation is known as a *société anonyme (S.A.)* or, in German-speaking countries, an *Aktiengesellschaft (AG)*. Other forms of subsidiaries may also exist that have characteristics of limited liability of the owners and fewer formalities in their creation and operation.

Creation of a foreign subsidiary may pose considerable risk to the domestic parent firm by subjecting it to foreign laws and the jurisdiction of foreign courts. The industrial accident in Bhopal, India, where hundreds of people were killed and thousands injured as a result of toxic gas leaks from a chemical plant, resulted in lawsuits against both the Indian subsidiary corporation and Union Carbide, the parent firm in the United States. Union Carbide agreed to pay more than $450 million to settle outstanding claims and compensate the victims of the disaster.

In many instances, however, the only legal or political means a firm has to invest directly in a foreign country is to engage in a **joint venture** with an entity from that host country. A host country's participant may be a private enterprise or, especially in developing countries, a government agency or government-owned corporation. Many foreign countries favor joint ventures because they allow local individuals and firms to participate in the benefits of economic growth and decrease the risk of foreign domination of local industry.

E-COMMERCE *connection*

INTERNATIONAL LAW AND THE INTERNET

International legal uncertainty concerning Internet operations has weakened e-commerce's early promise of borderless trade around the world. Many online merchants refuse to sell their products outside their home countries for fear over copyright enforcement, products liability claims, and libel protection. The most ambitious effort to date for resolving this crisis is the Hague Conference on Private International Law. In 2003, delegates from more than 60 countries were working on an e-commerce treaty that would make rulings by a court in one country enforceable in all other countries that sign the treaty. However, whether there is the political will to cede sovereignty over to other nations remains unclear.

Many of the developing countries require that the local partner have majority equity control of the venture and also insist on joint ventures with government participation.

RISKS INVOLVED IN INTERNATIONAL TRADE

Because international trade means dealing with different legal systems, cultures, and ways of doing business, there are a number of risks involved. Among them are expropriation and nationalization, export controls, pressures for bribes, and ill will resulting from U.S. antitrust laws.

8. EXPROPRIATION AND NATIONALIZATION

If a domestic firm is involved in a foreign country to the extent of locating assets there (whether through branches, subsidiaries, joint ventures, or otherwise), it may be subject to the ultimate legal and political risk of international business activity—expropriation. **Expropriation,** as used in the context of international law, is the seizure of foreign-owned property by a government. When the owners are not fairly compensated, the expropriation is also considered to be a *confiscation* of property. Usually, the expropriating government also assumes ownership of the property, so the process includes **nationalization** as well. In the United States, the counterpart of expropriation is called the *power of eminent domain.*

This power of a government to take private property is regarded as inherent; yet it is subject to restraints upon its exercise. The U.S. Constitution (as well as the constitutions and laws of most nations) prohibits the government from seizing private property except for "public purposes" and upon the payment of "just compensation."

However, the extent of such protection varies widely. Treaties (or other agreements) between the United States and other countries provide additional protection against uncompensated takings of property. It is customary for international law to recognize the right of governments to expropriate the property of foreigners only when accompanied by "prompt, adequate and effective compensation." This so-called "modern traditional theory" is accepted by most nations as the international standard and requires full compensation to the investor including fair market value as a going concern.

9. EXPORT CONTROLS

Another risk involved in doing business abroad is **export controls** placed on the sale of U.S. strategic products and technology abroad. Controlling the export of such items has been the cornerstone of Western policy since the conclusion of World War II. Most of the attention was focused on preventing the acquisition of technology by the former Soviet Union and its allies. However, since the end of the Cold War the policy rationale behind export controls has been drawn into question, with many Western countries contending they should be eliminated to increase trading opportunities with Russia, China, Eastern Europe, and the Middle East. Indeed, the Coordinating Committee for Multilateral Export Controls (COCOM), an organization created by the major western nations (including the United States, Europe, and Japan) to control exports, came to an end in 1994.

Since that time, a new organization supported by 33 countries, known as the Wassanaar Arrangement, has come into existence to help control the spread of both military and dual-use technology to unstable areas of the world. Participating nations seek, through their national policies, to ensure that transfer of conventional arms and strategic goods and technologies do not destabilize regional and international security. The 2002 plenary meeting of the Wassanaar Arrangement, held in Vienna, resulted in several significant initiatives to combat terrorism. The member countries agreed on several measures aimed at intensifying cooperation to prevent terrorist groups and individuals from acquiring arms and strategic goods and technologies.

The U.S. export control system currently is regulated by the Department of State and the Department of Commerce under authority provided by the Export Administration Act and the Arms Export Control Act. The Department of Defense also plays a key role in determining the technology to be controlled as does the U.S. Customs Service in the enforcement of the controls. Significant criminal and administrative sanctions may be imposed upon corporations and individuals convicted of violating the law.

In 2003, two leading American aerospace companies, Hughes Electronics and Boeing Satellite Systems, paid a record $32 million in penalties to settle charges in connection with 123 alleged violations of export control laws in connection with the transfer of rocket and satellite data to China. Preventing weapons proliferation requires vigorous enforcement of export controls of this nature.

In 2000, the U.S. government extended the Export Administration Act and raised the penalties for violators. The export control agenda for the twenty-first century remains focused on maintaining national security and reducing the proliferation of weapons, while also facilitating U.S. competitiveness in the global economy.

However, the future of the U.S. system remains in doubt with many proposals pending in Congress to reform and limit the current export control system. Over the past several years, these controls have become an extremely controversial topic in the international business community. Export controls make successful business deals more difficult because foreign buyers may be reluctant to trade with a U.S. firm due to the red tape involved in obtaining governmental approval as compared with Europe or Japan.

The following case illustrates the complexity and international intrigue that often accompany export controls.

UNITED STATES V. REYES

270 F. 3D 1158 (7TH CIR. 2001)

COFFEY, J.: The Arms Export Control Act (AECA), and its attendant regulations, the International Traffic in Arms Regulations, authorize the President of the United States to regulate and control the exportation of military and defense products through a licensing system administered by the State Department's Office of Defense Trade Controls. A license must be obtained before the export of any products or items designated as "defense articles" on the United States Munitions List. Federal regulations also state that it is the policy of the United States to deny requests for licenses to export defense articles at any given time destined for certain specified countries, including Iran. This prohibition includes the exportation of any goods to any person in a third country undertaken with knowledge or reason to know that such goods . . . are intended specifically for supply, transshipment, or reexportation, directly or indirectly, to Iran or the Government of Iran.

The defendant, Randy Reyes, was employed by Siraj International ("Siraj"), a middleman/broker of aviation component parts. Shortly after Reyes was hired by Siraj, he made contact with a customer named Texam Holding, Ltd., located in Geneva, Switzerland, and operated by Mehrad Banimostafavi (a/k/a Michael Bani). Reyes maintained Texam as his own client and handled virtually all transactions between Siraj and Texam.

At approximately the same time that Reyes made contact with Texam, another Milwaukee-area aircraft parts broker named International Aircraft Support Group (IASG) likewise began receiving orders from Texam. In January of 1997, Tina Bembenek (co-owner of IASG) received a purchase order from Texam requesting engine parts for an F-111 military aircraft, which in turn served to raise Bembenek's suspicion, for she was cognizant of the fact that only Iran and Australia flew the F-111. Bembenek called Bani (Texam) and inquired as to the end-user of the F-111 parts. According to Bembenek's testimony at trial, Bani told her that the parts were destined for Singapore. When confronted with Bembenek's statement that only Iran and Australia fly the F-111, Bani replied, "Let's send them to Australia."

In February, 1997, Bembenek was in Switzerland on unrelated business and arranged a meeting with Bani in Geneva. During this meeting Bani disclosed to Bembenek that he was an Iranian citizen living in Switzerland engaged in procuring military aircraft parts for Iran and at this time he provided Bembenek with a list of American companies with whom he did business. The list included Siraj International.

Upon Bembenek's return to the United States, she advised the U.S. Customs Service ("Customs") that Texam was acting as a front for Iran's procurement of military aircraft components. Thereafter Customs initiated an investigation into Texam and Bembenek agreed to assist in the investigation with the placing and receiving of telephone calls (recorded) with Bani and Reyes. In a recorded phone call to Reyes, Bembenek informed him that she had received correspondence from Bani stating that Texam intended to ship military aircraft parts purchased from her company (IASG) to Iran. Reyes responded, "Oh-oh, double no-no," indicating that he knew that sales of military equipment to Iran were prohibited by federal law. Reyes further displayed his knowledge of the law as he informed Bembenek at that time that all of his Siraj sale documents included a written stipulation that parts sold to Texam were destined for Texam's stock, and he suggested to Bembenek that she might make use of the same "stipulation" to protect herself, stating "the only thing I can suggest is . . . stipulate on your orders that this is going to your stock there in Geneva. . . ."

Approximately three weeks after this conversation with Bembenek, Reyes shipped a number of "junction covers" and fuel flometer brackets to Texam in Geneva, Switzerland without first having obtained the required licensing permits from the State Department. These aircraft parts were

[CONTINUED]

contained on the Munitions List since they were designed for exclusive use on TF-30 military aircraft engines, which are used on F-111, A-7, and F-14 military aircraft. This shipment from Milwaukee to Switzerland was seized by U.S. Customs officials at JFK airport. About the same time, Milwaukee U.S. Customs agents executed a search warrant at Siraj's Oak Creek, Wisconsin offices and seized a number of documents relating to Siraj's business dealings with Texam. The Customs Agents also found numerous documents in Reyes' office at Siraj, including but not limited to pamphlets detailing the State Department's registration and licensing process containing Reyes' handwritten notes, a partially completed draft of Siraj's registrant application containing Reyes' handwriting, and a copy of the Munitions List. Contemporaneous with the Siraj raid, Special Customs Agent John Heyer interviewed Reyes while on the premises, and during the interview Reyes admitted that Texam was his client, that he was aware that the shipment of aircraft parts destined to Iran was prohibited by federal law, and when questioned, further stated that Bani had informed him that the ultimate user of the airplane parts was either the Swiss Red Cross or Texam's stock. Contrary to his recorded telephone conversation with Bembenek, Reyes falsely stated to Heyer the he had never heard from any source that Texam supplied aircraft parts to Iran, and that he would not have exported any aircraft parts to Texam had he any reason to suspect that the parts were destined for Iran.

Upon the completion of the investigation, a grand jury returned a five-count indictment against Reyes with conspiracy to violate the AECA and IEEPA by exporting Munitions List aircraft component parts from the United States destined for Iran without the necessary government licenses. The jury returned guilty verdicts against Reyes.

At trial, the prosecution submitted a mountain of evidence to establish that Reyes was aware of his legal duty not to export Munitions List articles to Iran or any foreign country without a license. This evidence included expert testimony establishing that the aircraft parts Reyes attempted to export were designed exclusively for use on a TF-30 military aircraft engine (which is used on F-111 and F-14 military aircraft), as well as many documents (several with Reyes' handwritten notes on them) seized from Reyes' private office, that helped to establish Reyes' knowledge of the Munitions List and the law restricting exports of items on that list. The evidence also included the tape-recorded phone conversation between Reyes and Bembenek in which Reyes explicitly acknowledges both the illegality of shipping to Iran without a license and his awareness of the fact that Texam was shipping the parts it ordered to Iran. This combination of direct and circumstantial evidence was overwhelming and obviously more than sufficient to convict Reyes.

Reyes' obvious disregard for his known legal duties in attempting to export items on the Munitions List without a license, provided more than sufficient grounds for the jury's finding of a willful violation of the AECA.

The judgment and sentence of the district court are **affirmed.**

CASE QUESTIONS

1. What steps must a U.S. exporter follow in order to send goods abroad? Should these controls on business exist? Why or why not?

2. What evidence did the government offer to show that Reyes was aware of his legal responsibility?

3. Why is the U.S. system so fragmented among various government agencies (i.e., the State Department, Commerce Department, Defense Department, and Customs Service)? Would it make sense to centralize the responsibility for export controls in one government agency?

10. PRESSURES FOR BRIBES

Following widespread disclosure of scandalous payments by domestic firms to officials of foreign government, Congress enacted the **Foreign Corrupt Practices Act (FCPA)** in 1977. The law is designed to stop bribery of foreign officials and to prohibit U.S. citizens and companies from making payments to foreign officials whose duties are not "essentially ministerial or clerical" for the purpose of obtaining business.

This statute has two principal requirements:

1. Financial records and accounts must be kept "which, in reasonable detail, accurately and fairly reflect the transactions and dispositions of assets" of the business.
2. The business must "devise and maintain a system of internal accounting controls sufficient to provide reasonable assurances" that transactions are being carried out in accordance with management's authorization.

These provisions are intended to correct the previously widespread practice of accounting for bribes as commission payments, payments for services, or other normal business expenses and then illegally deducting the payments on income tax returns.

Many legal observers criticized the FCPA for creating a significantly chilling effect on U.S. companies seeking business in many developing countries where under-the-table payments to government officials are an accepted practice. Indeed, many civil servants in other nations are expected to supplement their salaries in this manner. The U.S. prohibition of such payments is perceived as an attempt to impose U.S. standards of morality in other parts of the world, and it has caused resentment and discrimination against U.S. businesses. Moreover, the FCPA puts U.S. firms at a competitive disadvantage with businesses in other countries that are not operating under similar constraints. According to a 1997 study, U.S. exporters are least likely to pay bribes, whereas companies from Belgium, France, and Italy are the most likely. The existence of the FCPA probably accounts for the difference.

As a result of intensive lobbying by the U.S. business community, Congress amended the FCPA in 1988 in an effort to eliminate ambiguity and uncertainty over what constitutes improper conduct. Although the law still prohibits bribery and corruption, the amendments establish clearer standards for firms to follow in overseas operations. The amendments limit criminal liability for violations of accounting standards to those who "knowingly" circumvent accounting controls or falsify records of corporate payments and transactions. The amendments also clarify the level of detail required in such record keeping and should improve compliance by businesses and enforcement by the government. Moreover, under the new

THE FOREIGN CORRUPT PRACTICES ACT

Legal or Permissible Payments

1. Any payments permitted under the written laws of a foreign country
2. Travel expenses of a foreign official for purpose of seeing demonstration of product
3. "Grease" payments to foreign customs officials to speed goods through customs
4. Other small payments for "routine" government action such as obtaining visas, work permits, or police protection

law otherwise prohibited payments to foreign officials may be defended if they were legal under the written laws of the host country or if they cover "reasonable and bona fide" expenses associated with the promotion of the product and the completion of the contract. The box on the preceding page illustrates the types of payments that are legal under the FCPA.

Under the 1988 amendments, criminal penalties for companies violating the FCPA have been increased to a maximum of $2 million and individuals may be fined up to $100,000 and/or five years in prison. Although bribes were "outlawed" with the passage of the Foreign Corrupt Practices Act, a new type of payment called "offsets" has taken their place in the international world of business. Offsets, which are legal and rarely talked about, can be any form of aid, such as, direct investments, agreements to help countries export their goods, or pacts to use more foreign components or transfer subassembly jobs overseas. Statistics show that more than 120 countries require offsets in military sales. From 1993 to 1998, American contractors provided $21 billion in aid to foreign countries under 279 agreements. Officially, the federal government discourages the practice of offsets.

11. CONFLICTS WITH U.S. ANTITRUST LAWS

The U.S. antitrust laws, discussed in detail in Chapter 13, represent our nation's legal commitment to free markets and international competition. Perhaps no other aspect of our legal system has generated as much recent controversy and ill will abroad as the extraterritorial application of our antitrust laws to conduct occurring beyond the borders of the United States. To protect the welfare of the U.S. consumer, however, the government's enforcement efforts must sometimes reach foreign defendants as a means of ensuring open and free markets. (See box, below.)

The Department of Justice and the Federal Trade Commission have issued guidelines delineating the U.S. government's policy on enforcement of federal antitrust law in the international arena. The guidelines provide that anticompetitive conduct, regardless of where such conduct occurs in the world or the nationality of the parties involved, may be prosecuted if it affects U.S. domestic or foreign commerce. The guidelines also provide that imports intended for sale in the United States by definition affect the U.S. market directly and will, therefore, invariably be subject to control. For example, suppose two foreign firms organize a cartel, produce a product abroad, and agree to fix the price of the finished product sold to the United States. Under the guidelines, this type of conduct is subject to prosecution because the transaction will affect U.S. commerce. Anticompetitive conduct

ANTITRUST PROBLEMS AND INTERNATIONAL BUSINESS

Antitrust laws have taken on international issues in recent years in a variety of ways. Of course, U.S. antitrust laws may be applied to foreign commerce, under the Foreign Trade Antitrust Improvements Act (FTAIA), where the action has a "direct, substantial, and reasonably foreseeable effect" on U.S. commerce. The European Commission can impose penalties on U.S. firms who engage in anticompetitive conduct within the European Union. The commission recently investigated Microsoft and General Electric with respect to such antitrust issues.

CORPORATE GOVERNANCE AND INTERNATIONAL BUSINESS REGULATIONS

At a time when U.S. executives are being investigated and, in some cases criminally charged, the rest of the world is very different. Regulations and enforcement efforts in many Asian, European, and Latin American countries are, by comparison, very weak. For example, the Japan's Securities and Exchange Surveillance Commission operates with about 10 percent of the employees at the SEC in the United States. In Taiwan, the Securities and Futures Commission lacks the power to conduct its own investigations. Italy recently decriminalized false accounting and made it a misdemeanor. A German executive recently compared his country's regulatory climate to the "Wild West" as he criticized toothless regulators. Such investigative and enforcement lapses could undermine growth and confidence in world markets.

by a foreign firm intended to affect the exports of a U.S. business may be sanctioned as well. (See the box above.)

The following case represents the most recent judicial examination of extraterritoriality in a case involving the U.S. prosecution of a foreign corporation for price-fixing that took place entirely in Japan.

UNITED STATES V. NIPPON PAPER INDUSTRIES CO., LTD.

109 F. 3D 1 (1ST CIR. 1997)

A federal grand jury handed down an indictment naming as a defendant Nippon Paper Industries Co., Ltd. (NPI), a Japanese manufacturer of facsimile paper. The indictment alleged that NPI and certain unnamed co-conspirators held a number of meetings in Japan which culminated in an agreement to fix the price of thermal fax paper throughout North America. NPI and other manufacturers who were privy to the scheme purportedly accomplished their objective by selling the paper in Japan to unaffiliated trading houses on condition that the latter charge specified (inflated) prices for the paper when they resold it in North America. The trading houses then shipped and sold the paper to their subsidiaries in the United States who in turn sold it to American consumers at swollen prices. The indictment further related that NPI sold thermal fax paper worth approximately $6,100,000 for eventual import into the United States; and that in order to ensure the success of the venture, NPI monitored the paper trail and confirmed that the prices charged to end users were those that it had arranged. These activities, the indictment claims, had a substantial adverse effect on commerce in the United States and unreasonably restrained trade in violation of Section One of the Sherman Act.

NPI moved to dismiss, claiming that if the conduct attributed to NPI occurred at all, it took place entirely in Japan, and, thus, the indictment failed to limit an offense under Section One of the Sherman Act. The government opposed this initiative on two grounds. First, it claimed that the law deserved a less grudging reading and that, properly read, Section One of the Sherman Act applied criminally to wholly foreign conduct as long as that conduct produced substantial and intended effects within the United States. Second, it claimed that the indictment, too, deserved a less grudging reading and that, properly read, the bill alleged a vertical conspiracy in restraint of trade that involved overt acts by certain co-conspirators within the United States. Accepting a restrictive reading of both the statute and the indictment, the district court dismissed the case.

[CONTINUED]

POPOFSKY, J.: This case raises an important, hitherto unanswered question. In it, the United States attempts to convict a foreign corporation under the Sherman Act, a federal antitrust statute, alleging that price-fixing activities which took place entirely in Japan are prosecutable because they were intended to have, and did in fact have, substantial effects in this country. The district court, declaring that a criminal antitrust prosecution could not be based on wholly extraterritorial conduct, dismissed the indictment.

Our law has long presumed that legislation of Congress, unless a contrary intent appears, is meant to apply only within the territorial jurisdiction of the United States. In this context, the Supreme Court has charged inquiring courts with determining whether Congress has clearly expressed an affirmative desire to apply particular laws to conduct that occurs beyond the borders of the United States. . . .

The case law now conclusively establishes that civil antitrust actions predicated on wholly foreign conduct which has an intended and substantial effect in the United States come within Section One's jurisdictional reach. Were this a civil case, our journey would be complete. But here the United States essays a criminal prosecution for solely extraterritorial conduct rather than a civil action. This is largely uncharted terrain; we are aware of no authority directly on point, and the parties have cited none.

Be that as it may, one [point] sticks out like a sore thumb: in both criminal and civil cases, the claim that Section One applies extraterritorially is based on the same language in the same section of the same statute: "Every contract, combination in the form of trust or otherwise, or conspiracy, in restraint of trade or commerce among the several states, or with foreign nations, is declared to be illegal." Words may sometimes be chameleons, possessing different shades of meaning in different contexts, but common sense suggests that courts should interpret the same language in the same section of the same statute uniformly, regardless of whether the impetus for interpretation is criminal or civil. . . .

NPI makes much of the fact that this appears to be the first criminal case in which the United States endeavors to extend Section One to wholly foreign conduct. We are not impressed. There is a first time for everything, and the absence of earlier criminal actions is probably more a demonstration of the increasingly global nature of our economy than proof that Section One cannot cover wholly foreign conduct in the criminal milieu.

There is simply no comparable tradition or rationale for drawing a criminal/civil distinction with regard to extraterritoriality, and neither NPI nor [the Japanese Government] have alluded to any case which does so. NPI and the district court both sing the praises of the Restatement (Third) of Foreign Relations Law (1987), claiming that it supports a distinction between civil and criminal cases on the issue of extraterritoriality. The passage to which they pin their hopes states:

> In the case of regulatory statutes that may give rise to both civil and criminal liability, such as the United States antitrust and securities laws, the presence of substantial foreign elements will ordinarily weigh against application of criminal law. In such cases, legislative intent to subject conduct outside the state's territory to its criminal law should be found only on the basis of express statement or clear implication.

We believe that this statement merely reaffirms the classic presumption against extraterritoriality—no more, no less.

The next arrow which NPI yanks from its quiver is the rule of lenity. The rule itself is venerable; it provides that, in the course of interpreting statutes in criminal cases, a reviewing court should resolve ambiguities affecting a statute's scope in the defendant's favor. Put bluntly, the rule of lenity cannot be used to create ambiguity when the meaning of a law, even if not readily apparent, is, upon inquiry, reasonably clear.

. . . The conduct with which NPI is charged is illegal under both Japanese and American laws, thereby alleviating any founded concern about NPI being whipsawed between separate sovereigns. . . . We live in an age of international commerce, where decisions reached in one corner of the world can reverberate around the globe in less time than it takes to tell the tale. Thus, a ruling in NPI's favor would create perverse incentives for those who would use nefarious means to influence markets in the United States, rewarding them for erecting as many territorial firewalls as possible between cause and effect.

The combined force of these commitments requires that we accept the government's cardinal argument, reverse the order of the district court, reinstate the indictment, and remand for further proceedings. **Reversed and remanded.**

CASE QUESTIONS

1. Why did NPI and the Japanese Government claim that a U.S. criminal case could not be initiated under these facts?

2. What reasons did the Court of Appeals offer for permitting prosecution here even though the criminal conduct occurred outside the United States?

3. Given this action by the United States, what additional risks are now posed to U.S. businesses and their employees when engaged in foreign trade?

---

concept SUMMARY   *Risks Involved in International Trade*

1. Expropriation and nationalization are risks involved in international business.

2. Expert controls seek to balance national security interests against global trade.

3. The Foreign Corrupt Practices Act seeks to stop the bribery of foreign government officials.

4. The extraterritorial application of U.S. antitrust laws has generated considerable international controversy.

RESOLVING INTERNATIONAL DISPUTES

12. SUING FOREIGN GOVERNMENTS IN THE UNITED STATES

The doctrine of **sovereign immunity** provides that a foreign sovereign is immune from suit in the United States. Under the doctrine of sovereign immunity, the foreign sovereign claims to be immune from suit entirely based on its status as a state.

Until approximately 1952, this notion was absolute. From 1952 until 1976, U.S. courts adhered to a *restrictive theory* under which immunity existed with regard to sovereign or public acts but not with regard to private or commercial acts. In 1976, Congress enacted the **Foreign Sovereign Immunities Act (FSIA),** which codifies this restrictive theory and rejects immunity for *commercial acts* carried on in the United States or having direct effects in this country. (See box, below.)

SOVEREIGN IMMUNITY AND INTERNET DOMAIN NAMES

In the case of *Virtual Countries, Inc. v. Republic of South Africa,* 300 F.2d 230 (2d Cir. 2002), the appellate court protected South Africa from a lawsuit filed over the ownership of an Internet domain name on the basis of the doctrine of sovereign immunity. Virtual Countries, Inc., owned the Internet name "southafrica.com" and sought to protect its usage by the Republic of South Africa which contended that sovereign countries have the right to use their own domain names. The court dismissed Virtual Countries' lawsuit by finding that South Africa had sovereign immunity under the Foreign Sovereign Immunities Act (FSIA).

The Supreme Court has held that the doctrine should not be extended to foreign governments acting in a commercial capacity and "should not be extended to include the repudiation of a purely commercial obligation owed by a foreign sovereign or by one of its commercial instrumentalities." This interpretation recognizes that governments also may act in a private or commercial capacity and, when doing so, will be subjected to the same rules of law as are applicable to private individuals. Of course, a nationalization of assets probably will be considered an act in the "public interest" and immune from suit under the FSIA. The limitations of the FSIA is demonstrated in the following case.

DOLE FOOD COMPANY V. DEAD SEA BROMINE CO. AND BROMINE COMPOUNDS, LTD.

123 S. CT. 1655 (2003)

The plaintiffs, a group of farm workers from Latin America, filed a state-court action against Dole Food Company and others alleging injury from chemical exposure. The Dole Company sued Dead Sea Bromine Co. and Bromine Compounds, Ltd. (collectively, the Dead Sea Companies) claiming that Dead Sea Companies would be liable if Dole lost the case. The Dole Company removed the action to federal court, arguing that the federal common law of foreign relations provided federal-question jurisdiction. Dead Sea Companies claimed they could not be sued because they were acting as an instrumentality of Israel.

KENNEDY, J.: Foreign states may invoke certain rights and immunities in litigation under the *Foreign Sovereign Immunities Act.* Some of the Act's provisions also may be invoked by a corporate entity that is an "instrumentality" of a foreign state as defined by the Act. The corporate entities in this action claim instrumentality status to invoke the Act's provisions allowing removal of state-court actions to federal court. As the action comes to us, it presents two questions. The first is whether a corporate subsidiary can claim instrumentality status where the foreign state does not own a majority of its shares but does own a majority of the shares of a corporate parent one or more tiers above the subsidiary. The second question is whether a corporation's instrumentality status is defined as of the time an alleged tort or other actionable wrong occurred or, on the other hand, at the time suit is filed.

The FSIA defines "foreign state" to include an "agency or instrumentality of a foreign state."

The lower court resolved the question of the FSIA's applicability by holding that a subsidiary of an instrumentality is not itself entitled to instrumentality status. Its holding was correct.

The State of Israel did not have direct ownership of shares in either of the Dead Sea Companies at any time pertinent to this suit. Rather, these companies were, at various times, separated from the State of Israel by one or more intermediate corporate tiers. For example, Israel wholly owned a company called Israeli Chemicals, Ltd.; which owned a majority of shares in another company called Dead Sea Works, Ltd.; which owned a majority of shares in Dead Sea Bromine Co., Ltd.; which owned a majority of shares in Bromine Compounds, Ltd.

The Dead Sea Companies, as indirect subsidiaries of the State of Israel, were not instrumentalities of Israel under the FSIA at any time. Those companies cannot come within the statutory language which grants status as an instrumentality of a foreign state to an entity a majority of whose shares or other ownership interest is owned by a foreign state or political subdivision thereof. We hold that only direct ownership of a majority of shares by the foreign state satisfies the statutory requirement.

A basic tenet of American corporate law is that the corporation and its shareholders are distinct entities. A corporate parent which owns the shares of a subsidiary

[CONTINUED]

does not, for that reason alone, own or have legal title to the assets of the subsidiary; and, it follows with even greater force, the parent does not own or have legal title to the subsidiaries of the subsidiary.

Applying these principles, it follows that Israel did not own a majority of shares in the Dead Sea Companies. The State of Israel owned a majority of shares, at various times, in companies one or more corporate tiers above the Dead Sea Companies, but at no time did Israel own a majority of shares in the Dead Sea Companies. Those companies were subsidiaries of other corporations.

Where Congress intends to refer to ownership in other than the formal sense, it knows how to do so. The absence of this language instructs us that Congress did not intend to disregard structural ownership rules.

The reason for the official immunities in those cases does not apply here. The immunities for government officers prevent the threat of suit from "crippling the proper and effective administration of public affairs."

Foreign sovereign immunity, by contrast, is not meant to avoid chilling foreign states or their instrumentalities in the conduct of their business but to give foreign states and their instrumentalities some protection from the inconvenience of suit as a gesture of comity between the United States and other sovereigns.

Any relationship recognized under the FSIA between the Dead Sea Companies and Israel had been severed before suit was commenced. As a result, the Dead Sea Companies would not be entitled to instrumentality status even if their theory that instrumentality status could be conferred on a subsidiary were accepted.

For these reasons, we hold first that a foreign state must itself own a majority of the shares of a corporation if the corporation is to be deemed an instrumentality of the state under the provisions of the FSIA; and we hold second that instrumentality status is determined at the time of the filing of the complaint.

It is so ordered.

CASE QUESTIONS

1. When may a corporate entity invoke the FSIA as a defense in court?

2. What is the policy rationale for exempting governments from the threat of lawsuits?

3. Why did the court rule against the Dead Sea Companies?

13. SUING FOREIGN FIRMS IN THE UNITED STATES

As foreign products and technology are imported into the United States, disputes may arise over either the terms of contract or the performance of the goods. In order to sue a foreign firm in the United States, the Supreme Court recently has held that the plaintiff must establish "minimum contacts" between the foreign defendant and the forum court. The plaintiff must demonstrate that exercise of personal jurisdiction over the defendant "does not offend traditional notions of fair play and substantial justice."

Once the plaintiff decides to sue in the United States, he or she also must comply with the terms of the Hague Service Convention when serving the foreign defendant notice of the lawsuit. The Hague Service Convention is a treaty that was formulated "to provide a simpler way to serve process abroad, to assure that defendants sued in foreign jurisdictions would receive actual and timely notice of suit, and to facilitate proof of service abroad." Many countries, including the United States, have approved the convention. The primary requirement of the agreement is to require each nation to establish a central authority to process requests for service of documents from other countries. After the central authority receives the request in proper form, it must serve the documents by a method prescribed by the internal law of the receiving state or by a method designated by the requester and compatible with the law.

In the case that follows, the court considers a lawsuit against a foreign firm over whether U.S. employment laws can be imposed on its domestic employees.

MORELLI V. CEDEL

141 F. 3D 39 (2D CIR. 1998)

CUDAHY, J.: This appeal requires us to decide whether the domestic employees of certain foreign corporations are protected under the Age Discrimination and Employment Act of 1967 (the ADEA), and, if so, whether a foreign corporation's foreign employees are counted for the purpose of determining whether the corporation has enough employees to be subject to the ADEA. We answer both questions in the affirmative.

After the defendant fired the plaintiff, the plaintiff sued the defendant. The plaintiff's amended complaint asserted that the defendant violated the ADEA, the Employment Retirement Security Act (ERISA), and New York State's Human Rights Law. The district court dismissed the complaint on the grounds that the defendant was not subject to the ADEA.

As alleged in the complaint, the facts relevant to this appeal are as follows. The plaintiff, Ida Morelli, was born on April 11, 1939. The defendant is a Luxembourg bank. On or about June 29, 1984, the defendant hired the plaintiff to work in its New York office. On or about February 26, 1993, the plaintiff became an assistant to Dennis Sabourin, a manager in the defendant's New York office. Mr. Sabourin summoned the then 54-year-old plaintiff to his office on January 18, 1994, handed her a separation agreement, and insisted that she sign it.

Under the terms of the separation agreement, the plaintiff would resign, effective April 30, 1994. She would continue to receive her salary and benefits until the effective date of her resignation, but she would be relieved of her duties as an employee, effective immediately. Both the defendant and the employee would renounce all claims arising out of "their past working relationship." Mr. Sabourin told the plaintiff that she would receive the three months' severance pay, medical coverage for three months, and her pension only

on the condition that she sign the agreement on the spot. The plaintiff had never seen the separation agreement before and had no warning that she was going to be asked to resign. But in the face of Mr. Sabourin's ultimatum, she did sign the agreement immediately and returned it to him. The defendant, however, never provided her with a pension distribution.

The ADEA was enacted to prevent arbitrary discrimination by employers on the basis of age. In order to determine whether the defendant is subject to the ADEA, we must first determine whether the ADEA generally protects the employees of a branch of a foreign employer located in the United States.

[T]he ADEA provides that the prohibitions of [the ADEA] shall not apply where the employer is a foreign person not controlled by an American employer. At a minimum, this provision means that the ADEA does not apply to the foreign operations of foreign employers—unless there is an American employer behind the scenes. An absolutely literal reading of [the statute] might suggest that the ADEA also does not apply to the domestic operations of foreign employers. But the plain language is not necessarily decisive if it is inconsistent with Congress' clearly expressed legislative purpose. Congress' purpose was not to exempt the domestic workplaces of foreign employers from the ADEA's prohibition of age discrimination. . . .

We have previously concluded that even when a foreign employer operating in the United States can invoke a Friendship, Commerce and Navigation treaty to justify employing its own nationals, this does not give the employer license to violate American laws prohibiting discrimination in employment. Although the Supreme Court vacated our judgment in that case on the grounds that the defendant could

[CONTINUED]

not invoke the treaty, the Court observed that "the highest level of protection afforded by commercial treaties" to foreign corporations operating in the United States is generally no more than "equal treatment with domestic corporations." Here equal treatment would require that antidiscrimination rules apply to foreign enterprises' U.S. branches, since defending personnel decisions is a fact of business life in contemporary America and is a burden that the domestic competitors of foreign enterprise have been required to shoulder. Also, U.S. subsidiaries of foreign corporations are generally subject to U.S. antidiscrimination laws, and, absent treaty protection—not an issue in this case—a U.S. branch of a foreign corporation is not entitled to an immunity not enjoyed by such subsidiaries.

Cedel will still not be subject to the ADEA by virtue of its U.S. operations unless Cedel is an "employer" under the ADEA. A business must have at least twenty "employees" to be an "employer." Cedel maintains that, in the case of foreign employers, only domestic employees should be counted. The district court agreed, and, since Cedel had fewer than 20 employees in its U.S. branch, the court granted Cedel's motion to dismiss for lack of subject matter jurisdiction without considering the number of Cedel's overseas employees.

The district court reasoned that the overseas employees of foreign employers should not be counted because they are not protected by the ADEA. But there is no requirement that an employee be protected by the ADEA to be counted; an enumeration, for the purpose of ADEA coverage of an employer, includes employees under age 40, who are also unprotected. The nose count of employees relates to the scale of the employer rather than to the extent of protection.

Cedel contends that because it has fewer than 20 employees in the United States, it is the equivalent of a small U.S. employer. This is implausible with respect to compliance and litigation costs; their impact on Cedel is better gauged by its worldwide employment. Cedel would not appear to be any more a boutique operation in the United States than would a business with ten employees each in offices in, say, Alaska and Florida, which would be subject to the ADEA. Further, a U.S. corporation with many foreign employees but fewer than 20 domestic ones would certainly be subject to the ADEA.

Accordingly, in determining whether Cedel satisfies the ADEA's 20-employee threshold, employees cannot be ignored merely because they work overseas. We therefore vacate the judgment on the plaintiff's ADEA count.

So ordered.

CASE QUESTIONS

1. What is the purpose behind the ADEA?
2. How did the court find that the ADEA covered a U.S. branch of a foreign employer?
3. Why did the court count foreign employees of the firm in determining whether the employer was subject to the ADEA?

14. INTERNATIONAL ARBITRATION

International businesses now are focusing on the need for new methods of resolving international commercial disputes and, as a result, are frequently resorting to the use of arbitration. The advantages of arbitration in domestic transactions, previously discussed in Chapter 5, are more pronounced in international transactions where differences in languages and legal systems make litigation costs still more costly.

The United Nations Convention on the Recognition and Enforcement of Foreign Arbitral Awards of 1958 (New York Convention), which has been adopted in more than 50 countries, encourages the use of arbitration in commercial agreements made by companies in the signatory countries. Under the New York Convention it is easier to compel arbitration, where previously agreed upon by the parties, and to enforce the arbitrator's award once a decision has been reached.

Once the parties to an international transaction have agreed to arbitrate disputes between them, the U.S. courts are reluctant to disturb that agreement. In the case of *Mitsubishi Motors v. Soler Chrysler-Plymouth* (473 U.S. 614 [1985]) the Supreme Court upheld an international agreement even where it required the parties to arbitrate all disputes, including federal antitrust claims. The Court decided that the international character of the undertaking required enforcement of the arbitration clause even as to the antitrust claims normally heard in a U.S. court.

The advantages of arbitrating international disputes are many. The arbitration process likely will be more streamlined and easier for the parties to understand than litigating the dispute in a foreign court. Moreover, the parties can avoid the unwanted publicity that often results in open court proceedings. Finally, the parties can agree, before the dispute even arises, on a neutral and objective third party to act as the arbitrator. Several organizations, such as the International Chamber of Commerce in Paris and the Court of International Arbitration in London, provide arbitration services for international disputes.

KEY TERMS

Bill of lading   549
Convention on the International Sale of
    Goods (CISG)   546
European Union (EU)   547
Export controls   554
Expropriation   553
Foreign Corrupt Practices Act (FCPA)
    557
Foreign Sovereign Immunities Act
    (FSIA)   561
Foreign subsidiary   552
Franchise   552
General Agreement on Tariffs and
    Trade (GATT)   545

International Court of Justice (ICJ)
    543
Irrevocable letter of credit   549
Joint venture   552
License   552
Nationalization   553
North American Free Trade Agreement
    (NAFTA)   548
Private international law   542
Public international law   542
Sovereign immunity   561
United Nations   544
World Trade Organization (WTO)
    545

REVIEW QUESTIONS AND PROBLEMS

International Law and Organizations

1. *Sources of International Law*
    (a)   What are the essential differences between the International Court of Justice and the U.S. Supreme Court?
    (b)   How does the ICJ determine international law?

2. *International Organizations and Agreements Affecting Trade*
    (a)   What are the three major principles of the World Trade Organization?
    (b)   Has adherence to those principles improved international trade?

3. *The European Union*
    (a)   Describe the organization of the European Union.
    (b)   How is it similar to the structure of the government of the United States?

4. *The North American Free Trade Agreement*

What are some of the key benefits that NAFTA has produced for member countries?

Methods of Transacting International Business

5. *Foreign Sales*

BMW, a German buyer, opens an irrevocable letter of credit in favor of Goodyear, an American seller, for the purchase of tires on BMW automobiles. BMW confirms the letter of credit with Goodyear's bank in New York, Bankers Trust. How will the seller obtain payment?

6. *Licenses or Franchises*

    (a)   How should a licensor protect its investment in a foreign country?

    (b)   Is licensing a less risky approach for the seller than direct foreign investment?

7. *Direct Foreign Investment*

What are the advantages and disadvantages of a joint venture with a foreign firm?

Risks Involved in International Trade

8. *Expropriation and Nationalization*

Explain the "modern traditional theory" of compensation related to the taking of private property by a foreign government.

9. *Export Controls*

    (a)   Why is the future of export controls in doubt?

    (b)   What are some of the dangers associated with having an inadequate export control regime as nations combat terrorism?

10. *Pressures for Bribes*

XYZ Company, a U.S. firm, is seeking to obtain business in Indonesia. XYZ learns that one of its major competitors, a German firm, is offering a key Indonesian governmental official a trip around the world for choosing their firm in the transaction. Can XYZ report this bribe to the Department of Justice and have the German firm prosecuted under the Foreign Corrupt Practices Act?

11. *Conflicts with U.S. Antitrust Laws*

What are some of the practical and political dangers associated with the United States attempting to apply its laws to business activity in foreign nations?

Resolving International Disputes

12. *Suing Foreign Governments in the United States*

Belgium arrests an American citizen, while he is visiting Brussels, on suspicion that he is an international drug smuggler. After a thorough investigation, Belgium realizes that it has arrested the wrong person. Can the American citizen successfully sue Belgium in the United States for false arrest?

13. *Suing Foreign Firms in the United States*

What is the primary requirement of the Hague Service Convention and how does it help a plaintiff when filing a lawsuit?

14. *International Arbitration*

Why are arbitration clauses in international agreements favored by the courts and likely to be enforced when conflicts arise between the contracting parties?

TERMINOLOGY REVIEW

For each term in the left-hand column, match the most appropriate description in the right-hand column.

1. International Court of Justice
2. World Trade Organization
3. CISG
4. Letter of credit
5. License
6. Expropriation
7. Export Controls
8. FCPA
9. Sovereign immunity
10. Arbitration agreements

a. Seizure of foreign-owned private property by a government
b. The traditional place for ascertaining what is public international law
c. Ensures payment and delivery of goods in international transactions
d. The umbrella organization for regulating international trade
e. Governmental restrictions placed on the sale of products and technology abroad
f. Typical method for controlling the transfer of information regarding a product or service
g. Document followed by many nations that outlines standard international contract rules for the sale of goods
h. An increasingly common method of resolving international disputes
i. Law designed to stop bribery of foreign officials by U.S. firms
j. Provides immunity for foreign governments from lawsuits in the United States

BUSINESS DISCUSSION

Now that relations with Vietnam have been normalized, you have been sent overseas by your employer, Global Communications, to obtain a contract with its government to upgrade the communication network between the capital and several outlying villages. After arriving in Vietnam, you are approached by a member of the Parliament, who offers to serve as a consultant and use her influence to help you land the desired contract with the Vietnamese government. She demands a nonrefundable retainer of $100,000 and an additional commission of $1 million should your firm succeed in obtaining the contract. Because this contract is worth nearly $100 million and could result in a hefty profit for your firm, you are considering her offer very seriously. You really need an "inside" link to the government, and she seems to be your best bet.

> Do you call your home office to ask for advice?
>
> Do you agree to her terms and avoid the risk that the boss may say no?
>
> If the boss says to pay the money, should you do it?
>
> What legal problems, if any, are presented by the payment?

appendix

THE CONSTITUTION OF THE UNITED STATES OF AMERICA

We, the People of the United States, in Order to form a more perfect Union, establish Justice, insure domestic Tranquility, provide for the common defense, promote the general Welfare, and secure the Blessings of Liberty to ourselves and our Posterity, do ordain and establish this Constitution for the United States of America.

ARTICLE I

Section 1.　All legislative Powers herein granted shall be vested in a Congress of the United States, which shall consist of a Senate and House of Representatives.

Section 2.　The House of Representatives shall be composed of Members chosen every second Year by the People of the several States, and the Electors in each State shall have the Qualifications requisite for Electors of the most numerous Branch of the State Legislature.

No Person shall be a Representative who shall not have attained the Age of twenty five Years, and been seven Years a Citizen of the United States, and who shall not, when elected, be an Inhabitant of that State in which he shall be chosen.

Representatives and direct Taxes shall be apportioned among the several States which may be included within this Union, according to their respective Numbers, which shall be determined by adding the whole Number of free Persons, including those bound to Service for a Term of Years, and excluding Indians not taxed, three-fifths of all other Persons. The actual Enumeration shall be made within three Years after the first Meeting of the Congress of the United States, and within every subsequent Term of ten Years, in such Manner as they shall by Law direct. The Number of Representatives shall not exceed one for every thirty Thousand, but each State shall have at Least one Representative; and until such enumeration shall be made, the State of New Hampshire shall be entitled to chuse three, Massachusetts eight, Rhode Island and Providence Plantations one, Connecticut five, New-York six, New Jersey four, Pennsylvania eight, Delaware one, Maryland six, Virginia ten, North Carolina five, South Carolina five, and Georgia three.

When vacancies happen in the Representation from any State, the Executive Authority thereof shall issue Writs of Election to fill such Vacancies.

The House of Representatives shall chuse their Speaker and other Officers; and shall have the sole Power of Impeachment.

Section 3.　The Senate of the United States shall be composed of two Senators from each State, chosen by the Legislature thereof, for six Years; and each Senator shall have one Vote.

Immediately after they shall be assembled in Consequence of the Election, they shall be divided as equally as may be into three Classes. The Seats of the Senators of the first Class shall be vacated at the Expiration of the second Year, of the second Class at the Expiration of the fourth Year, and of the third Class at the Expiration of the sixth Year, so that one third may be chosen every second Year; and if Vacancies happen by Resignation, or otherwise, during the Recess of the Legislature of any State, the Executive thereof may make temporary Appointments until the next Meeting of the Legislature, which shall then fill such Vacancies.

No Person shall be a Senator who shall not have attained to the Age of thirty Years, and been nine Years a Citizen of the United States, and who shall not, when elected, be an Inhabitant of that State for which he shall be chosen.

The Vice President of the United States shall be President of the Senate, but shall have no Vote, unless they be equally divided.

The Senate shall chuse their other Officers, and also a President pro tempore, in the Absence of the Vice President, or when he shall exercise the Office of the President of the United States.

The Senate shall have the sole Power to try all Impeachments. When sitting for that Purpose, they shall be on Oath or Affirmation. When the President of the United States is tried, the Chief Justice shall preside: and no Person shall be convicted without the Concurrence of two-thirds of the Members present.

Judgment in Cases of Impeachment shall not extend further than to removal from Office, and disqualification to hold and enjoy any Office of honor, Trust or Profit under the United States: but the Party convicted shall nevertheless be liable and subject to Indictment, Trial, Judgment and Punishment, according to Law.

Section 4.   The Times, Places and Manner of holding Elections for Senators and Representatives, shall be prescribed in each State by the Legislature thereof: but the Congress may at any time by Law make or alter such Regulations, except as to the Places of chusing Senators.

The Congress shall assemble at least once in every Year, and such Meeting shall be on the first Monday in December, unless they shall by Law appoint a different Day.

Section 5.   Each House shall be the Judge of the Elections, Returns and Qualifications of its own Members, and a Majority of each shall constitute a Quorum to do Business; but a smaller Number may adjourn from day to day, and may be authorized to compel the Attendance of absent Members, in such Manner, and under such Penalties as each House may provide.

Each House may determine the Rules of its Proceedings, punish its Members for disorderly Behaviour, and, with the concurrence of two thirds, expel a Member.

Each House shall keep a Journal of its Proceedings, and from time to time publish the same, excepting such Parts as may in their Judgment require Secrecy; and the Yeas and Nays of the Members of either House on any question shall, at the Desire of one-fifth of those Present, be entered on the Journal.

Neither House, during the Session of Congress, shall, without the Consent of the other, adjourn for more than three days, nor to any other Place than that in which the two Houses shall be sitting.

Section 6.   The Senators and Representatives shall receive a Compensation for their Services, to be ascertained by Law, and paid out of the Treasury of the

United States. They shall in all Cases, except Treason, Felony and Breach of the Peace, be privileged from Arrest during their Attendance at the Session of their respective Houses, and in going to and returning from the same; and for any Speech or Debate in either House, they shall not be questioned in any other Place.

No Senator or Representative shall, during the Time for which he was elected, be appointed to any civil Office under the Authority of the United States, which shall have been created, or the Emoluments whereof shall have been encreased during such time; and no Person holding any Office under the United States, shall be a Member of either House during his Continuance in Office.

Section 7.   All Bills for raising Revenue shall originate in the House of Representatives; but the Senate may propose or concur with Amendments as on other Bills.

Every Bill which shall have passed the House of Representatives and the Senate, shall, before it become a Law, be presented to the President of the United States; If he approve, he shall sign it, but if not he shall return it, with his Objections to that house in which it shall have originated, who shall enter the Objections at large on their Journal, and proceed to reconsider it. If after such Reconsideration two thirds of that House shall agree to pass the Bill, it shall be sent, together with the Objections, to the other House, by which it shall likewise be reconsidered, and if approved by two thirds of that House, it shall become a Law. But in all such Cases the Votes of both Houses shall be determined by Yeas and Nays, and the Names of the Persons voting for and against the Bill shall be entered on the Journal of each House respectively. If any Bill shall not be returned by the President within ten Days (Sundays excepted) after it shall have been presented to him, the Same shall be a Law, in like Manner as if he had signed it, unless the Congress by their Adjournment prevent its Return, in which Case it shall not be a Law.

Every Order, Resolution, or Vote to which the Concurrence of the Senate and House of Representatives may be necessary (except on a question of Adjournment) shall be presented to the President of the United States; and before the Same shall take Effect, shall be approved by him, or being disapproved by him, shall be repassed by two thirds of the Senate and House of Representatives, according to the Rules and Limitations prescribed in the Case of a Bill.

Section 8.   The Congress shall have the Power to lay and collect Taxes, Duties, Imposts and Excises, to pay the Debts and provide for the common Defence and general Welfare of the United States; but all Duties, Imposts and Excises shall be uniform throughout the United States;

To borrow Money on the credit of the United States;

To regulate Commerce with foreign Nations, and among the several States, and with the Indian Tribes;

To establish an uniform Rule of Naturalization, and uniform Laws on the subject of Bankruptcies throughout the United States;

To coin Money, regulate the Value thereof, and of foreign Coin, and fix the Standard of Weights and Measures;

To provide for the Punishment of counterfeiting the Securities and current Coin of the United States;

To establish Post Offices and post Roads;

To promote the Progress of Science and useful Arts, by securing for limited Times to Authors and Inventors the exclusive Right to their respective Writings and Discoveries;

To constitute Tribunals inferior to the supreme Court;

To define and punish Piracies and Felonies committed on the high Seas, and Offenses against the Law of Nations;

To declare War, grant Letters of Marque and Reprisal, and make rules concerning Captures on Land and Water;

To raise and support Armies, but no Appropriation of Money to that use shall be for a longer Term than two Years;

To provide and maintain a Navy;

To make Rules for the Government and Regulation of the land and naval Forces;

To provide for calling forth the Militia to execute the Laws of the Union, suppress Insurrections and repel Invasions;

To provide for organizing, arming and disciplining, the Militia, and for governing such Part of them as may be employed in the Service of the United States, reserving to the States respectively, the Appointment of the Officers, and the Authority of training the Militia according to the discipline prescribed by Congress;

To exercise exclusive Legislation in all Cases whatsoever, over such District (not exceeding ten Miles square) as may, by Cession of particular States, and the acceptance of Congress, become the Seat of the Government of the United States, and to exercise like Authority over all Places purchased by the Consent of the Legislature of the State in which the Same shall be, for the Erection of Forts, Magazines, Arsenals, dock-Yards, and other needful buildings;—And

To make all Laws which shall be necessary and proper for carrying into Execution the foregoing Powers, and all other Powers vested by the Constitution in the Government of the United States, or in any Department or Officer thereof.

Section 9.   The Migration or Importation of such Persons as any of the States now existing shall think proper to admit, shall not be prohibited by the Congress prior to the Year one thousand eight hundred and eight, but a Tax or Duty may be imposed on such Importation, not exceeding ten dollars for each Person.

The Privilege of the Writ of Habeas Corpus shall not be suspended, unless when in Cases of Rebellion or Invasion the public Safety may require it.

No Bill of Attainder or ex post facto Law shall be passed.

No Capitation, or other direct, Tax shall be laid, unless in Proportion to the Census or Enumeration herein before directed to be taken.

No Tax or Duty shall be laid on Articles exported from any State.

No Preference shall be given by any Regulation of Commerce or Revenue to the Ports of one State over those of another: nor shall Vessels bound to, or from, one State, be obliged to enter, clear, or pay Duties in another.

No Money shall be drawn from the Treasury, but in Consequence of Appropriations made by Law; and a regular Statement and Account of the Receipts and Expenditures of all public Money shall be published from time to time.

No Title of Nobility shall be granted by the United States: And no Person holding any Office or Profit or Trust under them, shall, without the Consent of the Congress, accept of any present, Emolument, Office, or Title, of any kind whatever, from any King, Prince, or foreign State.

Section 10. No State shall enter into any Treaty, Alliance, or Confederation; grant Letters of Marque and Reprisal; coin Money; emit Bills of Credit; make any Thing but gold and silver Coin a Tender in Payment of Debts; pass any Bill of Attainder, ex post facto Law, or Law impairing the Obligation of Contracts, or grant any Title of Nobility.

No State shall, without the Consent of the Congress, lay any Imposts or Duties on Imports or Exports, except what may be absolutely necessary for executing its inspection Laws: and the net Produce of all Duties and Imposts, laid by any State on Imports or Exports, shall be for the Use of the Treasury of the United States; and all such Laws shall be subject to the Revision and Control of the Congress.

No State shall, without the Consent of Congress, lay any Duty of Tonnage, keep Troops, or Ships of War in time of Peace, enter into any Agreement or Compact with another State, or with a foreign Power, or engage in War, unless actually invaded, or in such imminent Danger as will not admit of delay.

ARTICLE II

Section 1. The executive Power shall be vested in a President of the United States of America. He shall hold Office during the Term of four Years, and, together with the Vice President, chosen for the same Term, be elected as follows:

Each State shall appoint, in such Manner as the Legislature thereof may direct, a Number of Electors, equal to the whole Number of Senators and Representatives to which the State may be entitled in the Congress: but no Senator or Representative, or Person holding an Office or Trust or Profit under the United States, shall be appointed an Elector.

The Electors shall meet in their respective States, and vote by Ballot for two Persons, of whom one at least shall not be an Inhabitant of the same State with Themselves. And they shall make a List of all the Persons voted for, and of the Number of Votes for each; which List they shall sign and certify, and transmit sealed to the Seat of the Government of the United States, directed to the President of the Senate. The President of the Senate shall, in the Presence of the Senate and House of Representatives, open all the Certificates, and the Votes shall then be counted. The Person having the greatest Number of Votes shall be the President, if such Number be a Majority of the whole Number of Electors appointed; and if there be more than one who have such Majority, and have an equal Number of Votes, then the House of Representatives shall immediately chuse by Ballot one of them for President; and if no Person have a Majority, then from the five highest on the List the said House shall in like Manner chuse the President. But in chusing the President, the Votes shall be taken by States, the Representation from each State having one Vote; a quorum for this Purpose shall consist of a Member or Members from two thirds of the States, and a Majority of all the States shall be necessary to a Choice. In every Case, after the Choice of the President, the Person having the greatest Number of Votes of the Electors shall be the Vice President. But if there should remain two or more who have equal Votes, the Senate shall chuse from them by Ballot the Vice President.

The Congress may determine the Time of chusing the Electors, and the Day on which they shall give their Votes; which Day shall be the same throughout the United States.

No Person except a natural born Citizen, or a Citizen of the United States, at the time of the Adoption of this Constitution, shall be eligible to the Office of President; neither shall any Person be eligible to that Office who shall not have attained to the Age of thirty five Years, and been fourteen Years a Resident within the United States.

In Case of the Removal of the President from Office, or of his Death, Resignation, or Inability to discharge the Powers and Duties of the said Office, the Same shall devolve on the Vice President, and the Congress may by Law provide for the Case of Removal, Death, Resignation, or Inability, both of the President and Vice President, declaring what Officer shall then act as President, and such Officer shall act accordingly, until the Disability be removed, or a President shall be elected.

The President shall, at stated Times, receive for his Services, a Compensation, which shall neither be increased nor diminished during the Period for which he shall have been elected, and he shall not receive within that Period any other Emolument from the United States, or any of them.

Before he enter on the Execution of his Office, he shall take the following Oath or Affirmation:—"I do solemnly swear (or affirm) that I will faithfully execute the Office of President of the United States, and will to the best of my Ability, preserve, protect and defend the Constitution of the United States."

Section 2.   The President shall be Commander in Chief of the Army and Navy of the United States, and of the Militia of the several States, when called into the actual Service of the United States; he may require the Opinion, in writing, of the principal Officer in each of the executive Departments, upon any Subject relating to the Duties of their respective Offices, and he shall have Power to grant Reprieves and Pardons for Offenses against the United States, except in Cases of Impeachment.

He shall have Power, by and with the Advice and Consent of the Senate, to make Treaties, providing two thirds of the Senators present concur; and he shall nominate, and by and with the advice and consent of the Senate, shall appoint Ambassadors, other public Ministers and Consuls, Judges of the supreme Court, and all other Officers of the United States, whose Appointments are not herein otherwise provided for, and which shall be established by Law: but the Congress may by Law vest the Appointment of such inferior Officers, as they think proper, in the President alone, in the Courts of Law, or in the Heads of Departments.

The President shall have the Power to fill up all Vacancies that may happen during the Recess of the Senate, by granting Commissions which shall expire at the End of their next Session.

Section 3.   He shall from time to time give to the Congress Information of the State of the Union, and recommend to their Consideration such Measures as he shall judge necessary and expedient; he may, on extraordinary Occasions, convene both Houses, or either of them, and in Case of Disagreement between them, with Respect to the Time of Adjournment, he may adjourn them to such Time as he shall think proper; he shall receive Ambassadors and other public Ministers; he shall take Care that the Laws be faithfully executed, and shall Commission all the Officers of the United States.

Section 4.   The President, Vice President, and all civil Officers of the United States, shall be removed from Office on Impeachment for, and Conviction of, Treason, Bribery, or other high Crimes and Misdemeanors.

ARTICLE III

Section 1.   The judicial Power of the United States, shall be vested in one supreme Court, and in such inferior Courts as the Congress may from time to time ordain and establish. The Judges, both of the supreme and inferior Courts, shall hold their Offices during good Behaviour, and shall, at stated Times, receive for their Services, a Compensation, which shall not be diminished during their Continuance in Office.

Section 2.   The judicial Power shall extend to all Cases, in Law and Equity, arising under this Constitution, the Laws of the United States, and Treaties made, or which shall be made, under their Authority;—to all Cases affecting Ambassadors, other public Ministers and Consuls;—to all Cases of admiralty and maritime Jurisdiction;—to Controversies to which the United States shall be a Party;—to Controversies between two or more States;—between a State and Citizens of another State;—between Citizens of different States;—between Citizens of the same State claiming Lands under Grants of different States, and between a State, or the Citizens thereof, and foreign States, Citizens or Subjects.

In all Cases affecting Ambassadors, other public Ministers and Consuls, and those in which a State shall be Party, the supreme Court shall have original Jurisdiction. In all the other Cases before mentioned, the supreme Court shall have appellate Jurisdiction, both as to Law and Fact, with such Exceptions, and under such Regulations as the Congress shall make.

The Trial of all Crimes, except in Cases of Impeachment, shall be by Jury; and such Trial shall be held in the State where the said Crimes shall have been committed; but when not committed within any State, the Trial shall be at such Place or Places as the Congress may by Law have directed.

Section 3.   Treason against the United States, shall consist only in levying War against them, or in adhering to their Enemies, giving them Aid and Comfort. No Person shall be convicted of Treason unless on the Testimony of two Witnesses to the same overt Act, or on Confession in open Court.

The Congress shall have Power to declare the Punishment of Treason, but no Attainder of Treason shall work Corruption of Blood, or Forfeiture except during the Life of the Person attainted.

ARTICLE IV

Section 1.   Full Faith and Credit shall be given in each State to the public Acts, Records, and judicial Proceedings of every other State. And the Congress may by general Laws prescribe the Manner in which such Acts, Records and Proceedings shall be proved, and the Effect thereof.

Section 2.   The Citizens of each State shall be entitled to all Privileges and Immunities of Citizens in the several states.

A person charged in any State with Treason, Felony, or other Crime, who shall flee Justice, and be found in another State, shall on Demand of the executive Authority of the State from which he fled, be delivered up, to be removed to the state having Jurisdiction of the Crime.

No Person held to Service or Labour in one State, under the Laws thereof, escaping into another, shall, in Consequence of any Law or Regulation therein, be discharged from such Service or Labour, but shall be delivered up on Claim of the Party to whom such Service or Labour may be due.

Section 3.   New States may be admitted by the Congress into this Union; but no new State shall be formed or erected within the Jurisdiction of any other State, nor any State be formed by the Junction of two or more States, or Parts of States, without the Consent of the Legislatures of the States concerned, as well as of the Congress.

The Congress shall have Power to dispose of and make all needful Rules and Regulations respecting the Territory or other Property belonging to the United States; and nothing in this Constitution shall be so construed as to Prejudice any Claims of the United States, or of any particular State.

Section 4.   The United States shall guarantee to every State in this Union a Republican form of Government, and shall protect each of them against Invasion; and on Application of the Legislature, or of the Executive (when the Legislature cannot be convened) against domestic Violence.

ARTICLE V

The Congress, whenever two thirds of both Houses shall deem it necessary, shall propose Amendments to this Constitution, or, on the Application of the Legislatures of two thirds of the several States, shall call a Convention for proposing Amendments, which, in either Case, shall be valid to all Intents and Purposes, as Part of this Constitution, when ratified by the Legislatures of three fourths of the several States, or by Conventions in three fourths thereof, as the one or the other Mode of Ratification may be proposed by the Congress; Provided that no Amendment which may be made prior to the Year One thousand eight hundred and eight shall in any Manner affect the first and fourth Clauses in the Ninth Section of the first Article; and that no State, without its Consent, shall be deprived of its equal Suffrage in the Senate.

ARTICLE VI

All Debts contracted and Engagements entered into, before the Adoption of this Constitution, shall be as valid against the United States under this Constitution, as under the Confederation.

This Constitution, and the Laws of the United States which shall be made in Pursuance thereof; and all Treaties made, or which shall be made, under the Authority of the United States, shall be the supreme Law of the Land; and the Judges in every State shall be bound thereby, any Thing in the Constitution or Laws of any State to the Contrary notwithstanding.

The Senators and Representatives before mentioned, and the Members of the several State Legislatures, and all executive and judicial Officers, both of the United States and of the several States, shall be bound by Oath or Affirmation, to support this Constitution; but no religious Test shall ever be required as a Qualification to any Office or public Trust under the United States.

ARTICLE VII

The Ratification of the Conventions of nine States, shall be sufficient for the Establishment of this Constitution between the States so ratifying the Same.

AMENDMENT I [1791]

Congress shall make no law respecting an establishment of religion, or prohibiting the free exercise thereof; or abridging the freedom of speech, or of the press; or the right of the people peaceably to assemble, and to petition the Government for a redress of grievances.

AMENDMENT II [1791]

A well regulated Militia, being necessary to the security for a free State, the right of the people to keep and bear Arms, shall not be infringed.

AMENDMENT III [1791]

No Soldier shall, in time of peace be quartered in any house, without the consent of the Owner, nor in time of war, but in a manner to be prescribed by law.

AMENDMENT IV [1791]

The right of the people to be secure in their persons, houses, papers, and effects, against unreasonable searches and seizures, shall not be violated, and no Warrants shall issue, but upon probable cause, supported by Oath or affirmation, and particularly describing the place to be searched, and the persons or things to be seized.

AMENDMENT V [1791]

No person shall be held to answer for a capital, or otherwise infamous crime, unless on a presentment or indictment of a Grand Jury, except in cases arising in the land or naval forces, or in the Militia, when in actual service in time of War or public danger; nor shall any person be subject for the same offense to be twice put in jeopardy of life or limb; nor shall be compelled in any criminal case to be a witness against himself, nor be deprived of life, liberty, or property, without due process of law; nor shall private property be taken for public use without just compensation.

AMENDMENT VI [1791]

In all criminal prosecutions, the accused shall enjoy the right to a speedy and public trial, by an impartial jury of the State and district wherein the crime shall have been committed, which district shall have been previously ascertained by law, and to be informed of the nature and cause of the accusation; to be confronted with the Witnesses against him; to have compulsory process for obtaining witnesses in his favor, and to have the Assistance of counsel for his defense.

AMENDMENT VII [1791]

In suits at common law, where the value in controversy shall exceed twenty dollars, the right of trial by jury shall be preserved, and no fact tried by a jury, shall be otherwise re-examined in any Court of the United States, than according to the rules of the common law.

AMENDMENT VIII [1791]

Excessive bail shall not be required, nor excessive fines imposed, nor cruel and unusual punishments inflicted.

AMENDMENT IX [1791]

The enumeration in the Constitution, of certain rights, shall not be construed to deny or disparage others retained by the people.

AMENDMENT X [1791]

The powers not delegated to the United States by the Constitution, nor prohibited by it to the States, are reserved to the States respectively, or to the people.

AMENDMENT XI [1798]

The Judicial power of the United States shall not be construed to extend to any suit in law or equity, commenced or prosecuted against one of the United States by Citizens of another State, or by Citizens or Subjects of any Foreign State.

AMENDMENT XII [1804]

The Electors shall meet in their respective states and vote by ballot for President and Vice-President, one of whom, at least, shall not be an inhabitant of the same state with themselves; they shall name in their ballots the person voted for as President, and in distinct ballots the person voted for as Vice-President, and they shall make distinct lists of all persons voted for as President, and of all persons voted for as Vice-President, and of the number of votes for each, which lists they shall sign and certify, and transmit sealed to the seat of the government of the United States, directed to the President of the Senate;—The President of the Senate shall, in the presence of the Senate and House of Representatives, open all the certificates and the votes shall then be counted;—The person having the greatest number of votes for President, shall be the President, if such number be a majority of the whole number of Electors appointed; and if no person have such majority, then from the persons having the highest numbers not exceeding three on the list of those voted for as President, the House of Representatives shall choose immediately, by ballot, the President. But in choosing the President, the votes shall be taken by states, the representation from each state having one vote; a quorum for this purpose shall consist of a member or members from two-thirds of the states, and a majority of all the states shall be necessary to a choice. And if the House of Representatives shall not choose a President whenever the right of choice shall devolve upon them, before the fourth day of March next following, then the Vice-President shall act as President. The person having the greatest number of votes as Vice-President, shall be the Vice-President, if such number be a majority of the whole number of electors appointed, and if no person have a majority, then from the two highest numbers on the list, the Senate shall choose the Vice-President; a quorum for the purpose shall consist of two-thirds of the whole number of Senators, and a majority of the whole number shall be necessary to a choice. But no person constitutionally ineligible to the office of President shall be eligible to that of the Vice-President of the United States.

AMENDMENT XIII [1865]

Section 1.   Neither slavery nor involuntary servitude, except as a punishment for crime whereof the party shall have been duly convicted, shall exist within the United States, or any place subject to their jurisdiction.

Section 2.   Congress shall have power to enforce this article by appropriate legislation.

AMENDMENT XIV [1868]

Section 1.   All persons born or naturalized in the United States, and subject to the jurisdiction thereof, are citizens of the United States and of the State wherein they reside. No State shall make or enforce any law which shall abridge the privileges or immunities of citizens of the United States; nor shall any State deprive any person of life, liberty, or property, without due process of law; nor deny to any person within its jurisdiction the equal protection of the laws.

Section 2.   Representatives shall be appointed among the several States according to their respective numbers, counting the whole number of persons in each State, excluding Indians not taxed. But when the right to vote at any election for the choice of electors for President and Vice President of the United States, Representatives in Congress, the executive and judicial officers of a State, or the members of the Legislature thereof, is denied to any of the male inhabitants of such State, being twenty-one years of age, and citizens of the United States, or in any way abridged, except for participation in rebellion, or other crime, the basis of representation therein shall be reduced in the proportion which the number of such male citizens shall bear to the whole number of male citizens twenty-one years of age in such State.

Section 3.   No person shall be a Senator or Representative in Congress, or elector of President and Vice President, or hold any office, civil or military, under the United States, or under any State, who, having previously taken an oath, as a member of Congress, or as an officer of the United States, or as a member of any State legislature, or as an executive or judicial officer of any State, to support the Constitution of the United States, shall have engaged in insurrection or rebellion against the same, or given aid or comfort to the enemies thereof. But Congress may by a vote of two-thirds of each House, remove such disability.

Section 4.   The validity of the public debt of the United States, authorized by law, including debts incurred for payment of pensions and bounties for services in suppressing insurrection or rebellion, shall not be questioned. But neither the United States nor any State shall assume or pay any debt or obligation incurred in aid of insurrection or rebellion against the United States, or any claim for the loss or emancipation of any slave; but all such debts, obligations and claims shall be held illegal and void.

Section 5.   The Congress shall have the power to enforce, by appropriate legislation, the provisions of this article.

AMENDMENT XV [1870]

Section 1.   The right of citizens of the United States to vote shall not be denied or abridged by the United States or by any State on account of race, color, or previous condition of servitude.

Section 2.   The Congress shall have power to enforce this article by appropriate legislation.

AMENDMENT XVI [1913]

The Congress shall have power to lay and collect taxes on incomes, from whatever sources derived, without apportionment among the several States, and without regard to any census or enumeration.

AMENDMENT XVII [1913]

The Senate of the United States shall be composed of two Senators from each State, elected by the people thereof, for six years; and each Senator shall have one vote. The electors in each State shall have the qualifications requisite for electors of the most numerous branch of the State legislatures.

When vacancies happen in the representation of any State in the Senate, the executive authority of such State shall issue writs of election to fill such vacancies: *Provided,* That the legislature of any State may empower the executive thereof to make temporary appointments until the people fill the vacancies by election as the legislature may direct.

This amendment shall not be so construed as to affect the election or term of any Senator chosen before it becomes valid as part of the Constitution.

AMENDMENT XVIII [1919]

Section 1. After one year from the ratification of this article the manufacture, sale, or transportation of intoxicating liquors within, the importation thereof into, or the exportation thereof from the United States and all territory subject to the jurisdiction thereof for beverage purposes is hereby prohibited.

Section 2. The Congress and the several States shall have concurrent power to enforce this article by appropriate legislation.

Section 3. This article shall be inoperative unless it shall have been ratified as an amendment to the Constitution by the legislatures of the several States, as provided in the Constitution, within seven years from the date of the submission hereof to the States by the Congress.

AMENDMENT XIX [1920]

The right of citizens of the United States to vote shall not be denied or abridged by the United States or by any State on account of sex.

Congress shall have power to enforce this article by appropriate legislation.

AMENDMENT XX [1933]

Section 1. The terms of the President and the Vice President shall end at noon on the 20th day of January, and the terms of Senators and Representatives at noon on the 3d day of January, of the years in which such terms would have ended if this article had not been ratified; and the terms of their successors shall then begin.

Section 2. The Congress shall assemble at least once in every year, and such meeting shall begin at noon on the 3d day of January, unless they shall by law appoint a different day.

Section 3. If, at the time fixed for the beginning of the term of the President, the President elect shall have died, the Vice President elect shall become President. If a President shall not have been chosen before the time fixed for the beginning of his term, or if the President elect shall have failed to qualify, then the Vice President elect shall act as President until a President shall have qualified; and the Congress may by law provide for the case wherein neither a President elect nor a Vice President shall have qualified, declaring who shall then act as President, or the manner in which one who is to act shall be selected, and such person shall act accordingly until a President or Vice President shall have qualified.

Section 4.   The Congress may by law provide for the case of the death of any of the persons from whom the House of Representatives may choose a President whenever the right of choice shall have devolved upon them, and for the case of the death of any of the persons from whom the Senate may choose a Vice President whenever the right of choice shall have devolved upon them.

Section 5.   Sections 1 and 2 shall take effect on the 15th day of October following the ratification of this article.

Section 6.   This article shall be inoperative unless it shall have been ratified as an amendment to the Constitution by the legislatures of three-fourths of the several States within seven years from the date of its submission.

AMENDMENT XXI [1933]

Section 1.   The eighteenth article of amendment to the Constitution of the United States is hereby repealed.

Section 2.   The transportation or importation into any State, Territory, or possession of the United States for delivery or use therein of intoxicating liquors, in violation of the laws thereof, is hereby prohibited.

Section 3.   This article shall be inoperative unless it shall have been ratified as an amendment to the Constitution by conventions in the several States, as provided in the Constitution, within seven years from the date of the submission hereof to the States by the Congress.

AMENDMENT XXII [1951]

Section 1.   No person shall be elected to the office of the President more than twice, and no person who has held the office of President, or acted as President, for more than two years of a term to which some other person was elected President shall be elected to the office of President more than once. But this Article shall not apply to any person holding the office of President when this Article was proposed by the Congress, and shall not prevent any person who may be holding the office of President, or acting as President, during the term within which this Article becomes operative from holding the office of President or acting as President during the remainder of such term.

Section 2.   This article shall be inoperative unless it shall have been ratified as an amendment to the Constitution by the legislatures of three-fourths of the several States within seven years from the date of its submission to the States by the Congress.

AMENDMENT XXIII [1961]

Section 1.   The District constituting the seat of Government of the United States shall appoint in such manner as the Congress may direct:

A number of electors of President and Vice President equal to the whole number of Senators and Representatives in Congress to which the District would be entitled if it were a State, but in no event more than the least populous State; they shall be in addition to those appointed by the States, but they shall be considered, for the purposes of the election of President and Vice President, to be electors appointed by a State; and they shall meet in the District and perform such duties as provided by the twelfth article of amendment.

Section 2.   The Congress shall have power to enforce this article by appropriate legislation.

AMENDMENT XXIV [1964]

Section 1.   The right of citizens of the United States to vote in any primary or other election for President or Vice President, for electors for President or Vice President, or for Senator or Representative in Congress, shall not be denied or abridged by the United States or any State by reason of failure to pay poll tax or any other tax.

Section 2.   The Congress shall have power to enforce this article by appropriate legislation.

AMENDMENT XXV [1967]

Section 1.   In case of the removal of the President from office or of his death or resignation, the Vice President shall become President.

Section 2.   Whenever there is a vacancy in the office of the Vice President, the President shall nominate a Vice President who shall take the office upon confirmation by a majority vote of both Houses of Congress.

Section 3.   Whenever the President transmits to the President pro tempore of the Senate and the Speaker of the House of Representatives his written declaration that he is unable to discharge the powers and duties of his office, and until he transmits to them a written declaration to the contrary, such powers and duties shall be discharged by the Vice President as Acting President.

Section 4.   Whenever the Vice President and a majority of either the principal officers of the executive departments or of such other body as Congress may by law provide, transmit to the President pro tempore of the Senate and the Speaker of the House of Representatives their written declaration that the President is unable to discharge the powers and duties of his office, the Vice President shall immediately assume the powers and duties of the office as Acting President.

Thereafter, when the President transmits to the President pro tempore of the Senate and the Speaker of the House of Representatives his written declaration that no inability exists, he shall resume the powers and duties of his office unless the Vice President and a majority of either the principal officers of the executive departments or of such other body as Congress may by law provide, transmit within four days to the President pro tempore of the Senate and the Speaker of the House of Representatives their written declaration that the President is unable to discharge the powers and duties of his office. Thereupon Congress shall decide the issue, assembling within forty-eight hours for that purpose if not in session. If the Congress, within twenty-one days after receipt of the latter written declaration, or, if Congress is not in session, within twenty-one days after Congress is required to assemble, determines by two-thirds vote of both houses that the President is unable to discharge the powers and duties of his office, the Vice President shall continue to discharge the same as Acting President; otherwise, the President shall resume the powers and duties of his office.

AMENDMENT XXVI [1971]

Section 1.   The right of citizens of the United States, who are eighteen years of age or older, to vote shall not be denied or abridged by the United States or any State on account of age.

Section 2.   The Congress shall have power to enforce this article by appropriate legislation.

AMENDMENT XXVII [1992]

No law, varying the compensation for the services of the Senators and Representatives shall take effect, until an election of Representatives shall have intervened.

glossary

Abatement   Decrease, reduction, or diminution.

Acceptance   The contractual communication of agreeing to another's offer. The acceptance of an offer creates a *contract*.

Accession   Property acquired by adding something to an owned object.

Accessory   A term used at the state level that is similar to "aiding and abetting." Accessory to a crime generally is either before the criminal act or after it.

Accord and satisfaction   Payment of money, or other thing of value, usually less than the amount demanded, in exchange for cancellation of a debt that is uncertain in amount.

Actual authority   The authority a principal expressly or implicitly gives to an agent in an agency relationship. This authority may be written, spoken, or derived from the circumstances of the relationship.

Ad infinitum   Without limit; endlessly.

Adjudication   The judicial determination of a legal proceeding.

Adjustment   Under the Bankruptcy Act the procedure followed when a debtor's debts are partly reduced and partly rearranged for repayment.

Administrative agency   An organization, usually a part of the executive branch of government, that is created to serve a specific purpose as authorized by the legislative branch. An agency's function usually is characterized as quasi-legislative or quasi-judicial.

Administrative law   The branch of public law dealing with the operation of the various agency boards and commissions of government.

Administrative law judge   The individual employed by an administrative agency who is in charge of hearing the initial presentations in a quasi-judicial case.

ADRs   An abbreviation for alternative dispute resolution systems that may be used in lieu of litigation.

Ad substantiation **program**   A program of the Federal Trade Commission under which the FTC demands that an advertiser substantiate any claims made in advertising. Even if the claims are not provably untrue, they are considered deceptive if they cannot be substantiated.

Ad valorem   According to value.

Adverse possession   Property ownership acquired through open, notorious, actual, exclusive, continuous, and wrongful possession of land for a statutorily prescribed period of time.

Advisory opinion   A formal opinion by a judge, court, regulatory agency, or law officer upon a question of law.

Affidavit   A sworn written statement made before an officer authorized by law to administer oaths.

Affirmative action   Positive steps taken in order to alleviate conditions resulting from past discrimination or from violations of a law.

Affirmative action program   A program designed to promote actively the position of minority workers with regard to hiring and advancement.

Affirmative defenses   Defenses that must be raised and proved by the defendant.

A fortiori   Even more clearly; said of a conclusion that follows with even greater logical necessity from another that is already included in the argument.

Agent   The person who on behalf of a principal deals with a third party.

Aiding and abetting   A criminal action that arises from association with and from assistance rendered to a person guilty of another criminal act.

Alter-ego theory   One method used by courts to pierce the corporate veil when a shareholder fails to treat the corporate organization as a separate legal entity.

Amicus curiae   A friend of the court who participates in litigation though not a party to the lawsuit.

Annual percentage rate   A rate of interest that commercial lenders charge persons who borrow money. This rate is calculated in a standardized fashion required by the Truth-in-Lending Act.

Annuity   A contract by which the insured pays a lump sum to the insurer and later receives fixed annual payments.

Answer   The responsive pleading filed by a defendant.

Apparent authority   The authority that a third party in an agency relationship perceives to exist between the principal and the agent. In fact, no actual authority does exist. Sometimes also called *ostensible authority.*

Appeal   The right of the litigation parties to have the legal decisions of the trial judge reviewed by an appellate court.

Appellant   The party seeking review of a lower court decision.

Appellate court   A court that decides whether a trial judge has made a mistake of law.

Appellee   The party responding to an appeal; the winner in the trial court.

Apportionment   The concept used by states to divide a company's taxable income so that no one state burdens a company with an unfair tax bill.

Arbitration   Submission of a dispute to an extrajudicial authority for decision.

Arbitrator   The individual or panel members authorized by disputing parties to resolve a dispute through the arbitration process.

Arguendo   For the sake of argument.

Articles of incorporation   The legal document that forms the application for a state charter of incorporation.

Articles of organization   The document used to create a limited liability company. Its purpose corresponds to the purpose of the articles of partnership and the articles of incorporation.

Articles of partnership   Another name for a formally drafted partnership agreement.

Artisan's lien   The lien that arises in favor of one who has expended labor upon, or added value to, another person's personal property. The lien allows the person to possess the property as security until reimbursed for the value of labor or materials. If the person is not reimbursed, the property may be sold to satisfy the claim.

Assault   The intentional creation of immediate apprehension of injury or lack of physical safety.

Assignee   One who receives a transfer of contractual rights from an assignor.

Assignment   A transfer of contractual rights.

Assignor   One who sells or transfers contractual rights to an assignee.

Assumed-name statute   A state law that requires partners to make a public filing of their identities if their partnership operates under a name that does not reveal the partners' identities.

Assumption of risk   Negligence doctrine that bars the recovery of damages by an injured party on the ground that such a party acted with actual or constructive knowledge of the hazard causing the injury.

Attachment   The term *attachment* has three meanings. First, attachment is a method of acquiring in rem jurisdiction of a nonresident defendant who is not subject to the service of process to commence a lawsuit. By "attaching" property of the nonresident defendant, the court acquires jurisdiction over the defendant to the extent of the value of the property attached. Second, attachment is a procedure used to collect a judgment. A plaintiff may have the property of a defendant seized, pending the outcome of a lawsuit, if the plaintiff has reason to fear that the defendant will dispose of the property before the court renders its decision. Third, attachment is the event that creates an enforceable security interest under the Uniform Commercial Code (UCC). In order that a security interest attach, there must be a signed, written security agreement, or possession of the collateral by the secured party; the secured party must give value to the debtor; and the debtor must maintain rights in the collateral.

Award   The decision announced by an arbitrator.

Bait-and-switch promotion   An illegal promotional practice in which a seller attracts consumer interest by promoting one product, the "bait," then once interest has been attracted switches it to a second, higher-priced product by making the "bait" unavailable or unattractive.

Balance of trade   The difference between the amount of exports and imports of goods by a nation. A favorable balance would indicate more exports than imports. The United States has run an unfavorable balance of trade for several years.

Bank Merger Acts   Federal laws passed in 1960 and 1966 that require approval of the appropriate administrative agency prior to the merger of banks.

Bankruptcy crime   An action involving the falsification of documents filed in a bankruptcy case.

Bargained for   A term used in conjunction with the requirement of contractual consideration to represent the exchange of benefits and burdens between the contracting parties.

Battery   The cause of action for physical contact that is not consented to and is offensive.

Beneficiary   A person entitled to the possession, use, income, or enjoyment of an interest or right to which legal title is held by another; a person to whom an insurance policy is payable.

Best evidence rule   A principle requiring that the original of a document be submitted to the court as proof of the document's contents.

Beyond a reasonable doubt   The burden of proof required in a criminal case. The prosecution in a criminal case has the burden of proving the defendant is guilty, and the jury must have no reasonable doubt about the defendant's guilt. See also *Burden of proof.*

Bilateral contract An agreement that contains mutual promises, with each party being both a promisor and a promisee.

Bill of lading A document issued by a carrier indicating that goods to be shipped have been received by the carrier.

Bill of particulars In legal practice, a written statement furnished by one party to a lawsuit to another, describing in detail the elements upon which the claim of the first party is based.

Battery An intentional, unpermitted, offensive contact or touching.

Biodegradable Capable of being decomposed by organic action.

Blue sky laws Securities law enacted by States.

Bona fide In good faith; innocently; without fraud or deceit.

Bona fide occupational qualification (BFOQ) A qualification that permits discriminatory practices in employment if a person's religion, sex, or national origin is reasonably related to the normal operation of a particular business.

Breach of contract A party's failure to perform some contracted-for or agreed-upon act, or failure to comply with a duty imposed by law.

Brief A written document produced by a party for a reviewing court that contains the facts, propositions of law, and argument of a party. It is in this document that the party argues the desired application of the law and any contentions as to the rulings of the lower court.

Bubble concept A procedure by which the Environmental Protection Agency (EPA) allows a business to treat its entire plant complex as though encased in a bubble. The business suggests its own methods of cleanup, provided the total pollution does not exceed certain limits.

Bulk transfer A transfer made outside the ordinary course of the transferor's business involving a major part of the business's inventory. Bulk transfers are subject to Article 6 of the Uniform Commercial Code (UCC).

Burden of proof The term *burden of proof* has two meanings. It may describe the party at a trial with the burden of coming forward with evidence to establish a fact. The term also describes the party with the burden of persuasion. This party must convince the judge or jury of the disputed facts in issue or else lose that issue. There are various degrees of proof. See also *Beyond a reasonable doubt, Preponderance of evidence,* and *Clear and convincing proof.*

Burglary Theft by breaking and entering.

Business judgment rule A legal principle used by the courts to uphold the decisions of corporate directors and officers who have exercised good faith and due care in their business practices.

Business necessity defense An affirmative defense under Title VII of the Civil Rights Act. It is raised to disparate impact claims and asserts that a facially neutral but discriminatory policy is job related.

Buy and sell agreement A contract, usually among partners, but perhaps among shareholders, wherein one party agrees to buy the ownership interest held by another party or the first party agrees to sell such an interest to the other party. These contractual provisions help provide for a transition of owners without harming the business of the organization.

Capacity Mental ability to make a rational decision that includes the ability to perceive and appreciate all relevant facts. A required element of a contract.

Case law   The legal principles that are developed by appellate judges through their written opinions. See *Common law.*

Categorical imperative   A concept by the philosopher Kant that a person should never act in a certain way unless he or she is willing to have everyone else act in the same way.

Caucus   The name used for a private meeting between a mediator and one of the parties involved in a mediation.

Cause in fact   The actual cause of an event; the instrument that is the responsible force for the occurrence of a certain event. A required element of a tort.

Cause of action   This phrase has several meanings, but it is commonly used to describe the existence of facts giving rise to a judicially enforceable claim.

Caveat emptor   Let the buyer beware; rule imposing on a purchaser the duty to inform him- or herself as to defects in the property being sold.

Caveat venditor   Let the seller beware; it is the seller's duty to do what the ordinary person would do in a similar situation.

Cease and desist order   The sanction that may be issued by an administrative agency to prevent a party from violating the law.

Celler-Kefauver Amendment   Passed in 1950 to amend the Clayton Act by broadening the scope of Section 7 on mergers and acquisitions.

Certification mark   A mark used by someone other than its owner to certify the quality, point of origin, or other characteristic of goods or services. The Good Housekeeping "Seal of Approval" is an example.

Certiorari   A Latin word that means "to be informed of." This is the name of a writ that a higher court grants permitting the review of a lower court's ruling.

Changing conditions defense   A defense to a price discrimination (Section 2 of the Clayton Act) case wherein the defendant seeks to justify charging different customers different prices due to a change in the conditions of the product or marketplace.

Charter   The legal document issued by a state when creating a new corporation.

Circuit court   This term frequently is used to describe two distinct courts. First, the appellate courts in the federal court system often are called circuit courts of appeals. Second, the trial courts of general subject matter jurisdiction in some state court systems also are referred to as circuit courts.

Citation   The reference identifying how to find a case.

Civil law   The area of law governing the rights and duties between private parties as compared with the criminal law. This term also describes the system of codifying law in many countries as compared with the judicial orientation of the common law system.

Civil rights   The area of law designed to protect an individual's right to freedom from discrimination. In employment, this area of law prohibits unequal treatment based on race, color, national origin, religion, and sex.

Class-action suit   A method of litigation that allows one or more plaintiffs to file a lawsuit on behalf of a much larger group of persons, all of whom have a common interest in the claims being litigated.

Clayton Act   Legislation passed in 1914 that exempts labor unions from the Sherman Act. This law expanded the national antitrust policy to cover price discrimination, exclusive dealings, tying contracts, mergers, and interlocking directors.

Clean-hands doctrine   An equitable principle that requires a party seeking an equitable remedy to be free from wrongdoing.

Clear and convincing proof   A burden of proof that requires the party with the burden to establish clearly the existence of the alleged facts. This burden requires more proof than merely having a preponderance of evidence on one's side.

Closed shop   A contractual agreement between an employer and a union that all applicants for a job with the employer will have to join the union. This type of agreement was outlawed by the Taft-Hartley Act.

Closely held   An organization that is owned by only a few people.

Code   A compilation of legislation enacted by a federal, state, or local government.

Colgate doctrine   The legal principle that allows a form of vertical price fixing in that manufacturers may maintain the resale price of their products by announcing their pricing policy and refusing to deal with customers who fail to comply with the policy.

Collective bargaining   The process used by an employer and a union representing employees to discuss and resolve differences so that the parties can agree to a binding contract.

Collective mark   A mark representing membership in a certain organization or association. The "union label" is an example.

Commerce clause   A provision in Article I, Section 8, of the U.S. Constitution that grants the federal government the power to regulate business transactions.

Commercial impracticability   A Uniform Commercial Code (UCC) defense to contractual nonperformance based on happenings that greatly increase the difficulty of performance and that violate the parties' reasonable commercial expectations.

Commercial speech   Speech that has a business-oriented purpose. This speech is protected under the First Amendment, but this protection is not as great as that afforded to noncommercial speech.

Common law   That body of law deriving from judicial decisions as opposed to legislatively enacted statutes and administrative regulations.

Comparable worth   Jobs that, although different, produce substantially equal value for the employer.

Comparative negligence   A doctrine that compares the plaintiff's contributory fault with the defendant's fault and allows the jury to reduce the plaintiff's verdict by the percentage of the plaintiff's fault.

Comparative responsibility   A doctrine that compares the plaintiff's contributory fault with the defendant's fault and allows the jury to reduce the plaintiff's verdict by the percentage of the plaintiff's fault. Also called *comparative negligence*.

Compensatory damages   Usually awarded in breach-of-contract cases to pay for a party's losses that are a direct and foreseeable result of the other party's breach. The award of these damages is designed to place the nonbreaching party in the same position as if the contract had been performed.

Complaint   In legal practice, the first written statement of the plaintiff's contentions, which initiates the lawsuit.

Complete performance   Degree of performance recognizing that each contracting party has performed every duty required by the contract.

Compulsory bargaining issue   Mandatory bargaining issue regarding wages, hours, or other terms or conditions of employment. Refusal to engage in good-faith bargaining with regard to these issues is an unfair labor practice.

Concealment   An intentional misrepresentation of a material fact occurring through the silence of a party.

Concerted activities   Those activities involving an agreement, contract, or conspiracy to restrain trade that may be illegal under the Sherman Antitrust Act.

Concurrent conditions   Mutual conditions under which each party's contractual performance is triggered by the other party's tendering (offering) performance.

Condition precedent   An event in the law of contracts that must occur before a duty of immediate performance of the promise arises. Contracts often provide that one party must perform before there is a right to performance by the other party. For example, completion of a job is often a condition precedent to payment for that job. One contracting party's failure to perform a condition precedent permits the other party to refuse to perform, cancel the contract, and sue for damages.

Condition subsequent   A fact that will extinguish a duty to make compensation for breach of contract after the breach has occurred.

Conduct   Under the Uniform Commercial Code (UCC) the conduct of contracting parties (i.e., their actions) is important in determining the meaning of a sales contract.

Confiscation   The seizure of property without adequate compensation.

Conflict of law   Rules of law the courts use to determine that substantive law applies when there is an inconsistency between laws of different states or countries.

Confusion   Property ownership that arises when identical masses of objects, such as grain, are mixed together.

Conglomerate merger   The merger resulting when merging companies have neither the relationship of competitors nor that of supplier and customer.

Consent order   Any court or regulatory order to which the opposing party agrees; a contract of the parties entered upon the record with the approval and sanction of a court.

Consequential damages   The amount of money awarded in a breach-of-contract case to the non-breaching party to pay for the special damages that exceed the normal compensatory damages. Lost opportunities may create consequential damages if the breaching party was aware of the special nature of the contract.

Consequentialism   An ethical system that concerns itself with the moral consequences of actions. Also called *teleology.*

Consideration   An essential element in the creation of a contract obligation that creates a detriment to the promisee or a benefit to the promisor.

Consolidation   The process by which two or more corporations are joined to create a new corporation.

Conspiracy   A combination or agreement between two or more persons for the commission of a criminal act.

Constitutional law   The legal issues that arise from interpreting the U.S. Constitution or a state constitution.

Constructive discharge   The event of an employee resigning because the employer has made working conditions too uncomfortable for continued employment.

Consumer   An individual who buys goods and services for personal use rather than for business use.

Consumer investigative report   A report on a consumer's character, general reputation, mode of living, etc., obtained by personal interviews in the community where the consumer works or lives.

Contempt of court   An order by a judge to punish wrongdoing with respect to the court's authority.

Contingency fee   An arrangement whereby an attorney is compensated for services in a lawsuit according to an agreed percentage of the amount of money recovered.

Contract   A legally enforceable promise.

Contract clause   The constitutional provision that prohibits states from enacting laws that interfere with existing contracts. The Supreme Court has refused to interpret this clause in an absolute manner.

Contract law   The law of legally enforceable promises.

Contribution   The right of one who has discharged a common liability to recover from another also liable the proportionate share of the common liability.

Contributory negligence   A failure to use reasonable care by the plaintiff in a negligence suit.

Controlling person   The person who has the control of, or is controlled by, the issuer of securities in securities laws.

Convention on the International Sale of Goods (CISG)   A treaty adopted by most major trading countries that outlines standard commercial rules for international contracts involving the sale of goods.

Conversion   An unlawful exercise of dominion and control over another's property that substantially interferes with property rights.

Cooling-off period   A time provided by the Taft-Hartley Act during which labor and management must suspend the work stoppage (strike or lockout) and continue their working relationship while negotiating a resolution of the dispute. This period is for 80 days.

Copyright   A statutorily created property in creative expression that protects authors.

Corporate governance   The regulation of business organizations, specifically including regulation of the legal relationship of directors, managers, and owners.

Corporation   An artificial, but legal, person created by state law. As a business organization, the corporation's separation of owners and managers gives it a high level of flexibility.

Corrective advertising   A Federal Trade Commission (FTC) remedy that requires companies that have advertised deceptively to run ads that admit the prior errors and correct the erroneous information.

Cost justification defense   A defense to a price discrimination (Section 2 of the Clayton Act) case wherein the defendant seeks to justify charging different customers different prices due to that defendant's costs varying because of the differing quantities purchased by the customers.

Counterclaim   Any claim filed by the defendant in a lawsuit against the plaintiff in the same suit.

Counterdefendant   The party involved in litigation against whom a counterclaim is filed. This party is the original plaintiff.

Counteroffer   An offer made in response to another's offer. Usually made in place of an acceptance. A counteroffer usually terminates an offer.

Counterplaintiff   The party involved in litigation who files a counterclaim. This party is the original defendant who is making a claim against the original plaintiff.

Course of dealing   The way parties to a contract have done business in the past. Important in helping to determine the meaning of a contract for the sale of goods.

Covenant   An agreement or promise in writing by which a party pledges that something has been done or is being done. The term is often used in connection with real estate to describe the promises of the grantor of the property.

Covenant not to compete   An agreement in which one party agrees not to compete directly with the business of the other party; may be limited by geography or length of time.

Criminal law   That area of law dealing with wrongs against the state as representative of the community at large, to be distinguished from civil law, which hears cases of wrongs against persons.

Cross-examination   The process of questioning a witness by the lawyer who did not call the witness to testify on behalf of that lawyer's client.

Cruel and unusual punishment   Protection against such punishment is provided by the Eighth Amendment of the U.S. Constitution. To be cruel and unusual, the punishment must be disproportionately harsh when compared to the offense committed.

Damages   Monetary compensation recoverable in a court of law.

D.B.A.   Doing business as.

Decree   The decision of a court of equity.

Deed   A document representing the title or ownership of land.

Defamation   The publication of anything injurious to the good name or reputation of another.

Default   The failure of a defendant to answer a plaintiff's complaint within the time period allowed by the court. Upon the defendant's default, a judgment is entered in the plaintiff's favor.

Defect   Something that makes a product not reasonably safe for a use that can be reasonably anticipated.

Defendant   The party involved in a lawsuit that is sued; the party required to respond to the plaintiff's complaint.

Defined benefit plan   A money-purchase plan that guarantees a certain retirement income based on the employee's service and salary under the Employee Retirement Income Security Act. The benefits are fixed, and the contributions vary.

Defined contribution plan   A money-purchase plan that allows employers to budget pension costs in advance under the Employee Retirement Income Security Act. The contribution is fixed, and the benefits vary.

Delivery   The physical transfer of something. In sale-of-goods transactions, delivery is the transfer of goods from the seller to the buyer.

Demurrer   A formal statement by the defendant that the facts alleged by the plaintiff are insufficient to support a claim for legal relief in common law pleading.

De novo **judicial review** A proceeding wherein the judge or hearing officer hears the case as if it had not been heard before.

Deontology An ethical system that affirms an absolute morality. Also called *formalism.*

Deposited acceptance rule The contractual doctrine that a binding acceptance of an offer occurs when a mailed acceptance is irrevocably placed with the postal service.

Deposition A discovery process outside the court's supervision that involves the sworn questioning of a potential witness. This oral questioning is reduced to a written form so that a record is established.

Derivative action A lawsuit filed by a shareholder of a corporation on behalf of the corporation. This action is filed to protect the corporation from the mismanagement of its officers and directors.

Derivative suit A lawsuit filed by one or more shareholders of a corporation against that organization's management. This suit is brought to benefit the corporation directly and its shareholders indirectly.

Design defect A defect arising when a product does not meet society's expectation for a safely designed product.

Dicta Statements made in a judicial opinion that are not essential to the decision of the case.

Directed verdict A motion for a directed verdict requests that the judge direct the jury to bring in a particular verdict if reasonable minds could not differ on the correct outcome of the lawsuit. In deciding the motion, the judge will view in the light most favorable to the nonmoving party, and if different inferences may be drawn by reasonable people, then the court cannot direct a verdict. In essence, a directed verdict removes the jury's discretion.

Direct examination The process of questioning a witness conducted by the lawyer who called the witness to testify on behalf of that lawyer's client.

Directors Those individuals who are elected by the shareholders to decide the goals and objectives for the corporate organization.

Disability Any physical or mental impairment that substantially limits a major life activity.

Disaffirm To void. Used to describe a minor's power to get out of a contract because of age.

Discharge In bankruptcy the forgiving of an honest debtor's debts. In contract law an act that forgives further performance of a contractual obligation.

Discovery Procedures by which one party to a lawsuit may obtain information relevant to the case from the other party or from third persons.

Discretionary function exception An exception to the waiver of the doctrine of sovereign immunity. Officials of administrative agencies are exempt from personal liability if their performance or lack thereof is based on a discretionary function.

Discrimination in effect The discriminatory result of policies that appear to be neutral.

Disparate impact A term of employment litigation that refers to the disproportionate impact of a policy neutral on its face on some protected class (e.g., race or sex).

Disparate treatment   A term of employment litigation that refers to the illegal discriminatory treatment of an individual in some protected class (e.g., race or sex).

Dissolution   The cancellation of an agreement, thereby rescinding its binding force. A partnership is dissolved anytime there is a change in partners. A corporation's dissolution occurs when that business entity ceases to exist.

Diversity of citizenship   The plaintiffs filing a lawsuit must be from states different from those of the defendants. This requirement, along with over $50,000 at stake, is one method a federal district court gains jurisdiction over the subject matter of a lawsuit.

Divestiture   The antitrust remedy that forces a company to get rid of assets acquired through illegal mergers or monopolistic practices.

Docket   A book containing a brief summary of all acts done in court in the conduct of each case.

Doctrine of abstention   A principle used by federal courts to refuse to hear a case. When used by the federal courts, the lawsuit involved is sent to the state court system.

Domestic corporation   A business organization created by the issuance of a state charter that operates in the state that issued the charter.

Domicile   That place that a person intends as his or her fixed and permanent legal residence; place of permanent abode, as contrasted with a residence, which may be temporary; a person can have a number of residences but only one domicile; the state of incorporation of a corporation.

Dominant commerce clause concept   The impact of the commerce clause as a means of limiting state and local governments' powers to regulate business activities.

Donee beneficiary   A noncontracting third party who receives as a gift the benefits of a contract made between two other parties. This third party is empowered to enforce the contract to ensure the receipt of the contract's benefits.

Double jeopardy   A constitutional doctrine that prohibits an individual from being prosecuted twice by the same governing body based on the same factual situation.

Double tax   A disadvantage of a corporate form of organization in that the corporation must pay a tax on the money earned and the shareholder pays a second tax on the dividends distributed.

Dram shop acts   Statutes adopted in many states that impose strict liability upon tavern owners for injuries to third parties caused by their intoxicated patrons.

Due diligence defense   A defense that experts may assert in a 1933 Securities Act case involving the failure to register securities or the failure to provide accurate documents. The expert utilizing this defense attempts to prove his or her reasonable investigation into all available information.

Due process   Fundamental fairness. As applied to judicial proceedings, adequate notice of a hearing and an opportunity to appear and defend in an orderly tribunal.

Due process clause   A provision found in the Fifth and Fourteenth Amendments of the U.S. Constitution. This clause assures all citizens of fundamental fairness in their relationship with the government.

Dumping   The practice of selling foreign goods in one country at less than the comparable price in the country where the goods originated.

Duress   Action by a person that compels another to do what he or she would not otherwise do. It is a recognized defense to any act that must be voluntary in order to create liability in the actor.

Duty   A legal obligation imposed by the law.

Duty of performance   In contract law the legal obligation of a party to a contract.

Duty of reasonable care   The legal duty owed under negligence doctrine.

Easement   The right of one other than the owner of land to some use of that land.

Economic boycott   Used in three basic forms (primary, secondary, and tertiary), a practice aimed at cutting off trade opportunities for enemy countries.

Eighty-day cooling-off period   A provision in the Taft-Hartley Act that allows the president to require that laborers continue working and that the laborers' representatives and management continue bargaining for at least 80 days during which it is intended that federal mediation will resolve the dispute. This provision can be utilized by the president only when there is a determination that the work stoppage is adversely affecting the national health and safety.

Ejusdem generis   Of the same kind or class; a doctrine of legislative interpretation.

Embezzlement   The fraudulent appropriation by one person, acting in a fiduciary capacity, of the money or property of another.

Eminent domain   The government's constitutional power to take private property for public use upon the payment of just compensation.

Emissions reduction banking   The policy stating that businesses that lower pollution beyond the requirements of the law may use the additional reductions in the future.

Employment at will   A hiring for an indefinite period of time.

En banc   Proceedings by or before the court as a whole rather than any single judge.

Endangerment of workers   A criminal act that involves placing employees at risk with respect to their health and safety in the work environment.

Enforceable contract   A contract that can be enforced in court.

Enjoin   To require performance of or abstention from some act through issuance of an injunction.

Environmental impact statement   A filing of documents required by the National Environmental Policy Act that forces governmental agencies to consider the environmental consequences of their actions.

Equal protection clause   A provision in the Fourteenth Amendment of the U.S. Constitution that requires all citizens to be treated in a similar manner by the government unless there is a sufficient justification for the unequal treatment.

Escrow   A deed, bond, or deposit that one party delivers for safekeeping by a second party who is obligated to deliver it to a third party upon the fulfillment of some condition.

Establishment clause   A provision in the First Amendment of the U.S. Constitution that prohibits the federal government from establishing any government-supported religion or church.

Estate   The bundle of rights and powers of real property ownership.

Estoppel   The legal principle that one may not assert facts inconsistent with one's own prior actions.

Ethics   A systematic statement of right and wrong together with a philosophical system that both justifies and necessitates rules of conduct.

European Union (EU)   Created by the Treaty of Rome, an organization that seeks to facilitate the free movement of goods, services, labor, professions, transportation, and capital among European countries.

Exclusive dealing   A buyer agrees to purchase a certain product exclusively from the seller or the seller agrees to sell all of his or her production to the buyer.

Exclusive remedy rule   The rule that limits an injured employee's claim against the employer to worker's compensation.

Exculpatory clause   A provision in a contract whereby one of the parties attempts to relieve itself of liability for breach of a legal duty.

Exculpatory contract   A contract that excuses one from accepting responsibility or blame. For example, a contract that excuses one from having to accept liability for one's negligence or another's injury or loss.

Executed contract   A contract that is fully accomplished or performed, leaving nothing unfulfilled.

Execution   To carry out some action to completion. With respect to enforcing a court's judgment, an execution involves the seizure of the debtor's property, a sale of the property, and the payment of proceeds to the creditor.

Executory contract   An agreement that is not completed. Until the performance required in a contract is completed, it is executory.

Exemplary damages   Punitive damages. Monetary compensation in excess of direct losses suffered by the plaintiff that may be awarded in intentional tort cases where the defendant's conduct deserves punishment.

Exhaustion of remedies   A concept used in administrative law that requires any party to an administrative proceeding to give the administrative agency every opportunity to resolve the dispute before appealing to the court system.

Experience rating system   A system of sliding taxation under which employers are charged less unemployment compensation tax as they lay off fewer workers due to economic conditions.

Export controls   Action taken on a national and multilateral basis to prevent the exportation of controlled goods and technology to certain destinations.

Express authority   Actual authority that arises from specific statements made by the principal to the agent.

Express conditions   Conditions that are explicitly set out in a contract.

Express contract   A contract in which parties show their agreement in words.

Express warranty   Any statement of fact or promise about the performance of a product made by a seller.

Expropriation   A foreign government's seizure of privately owned property.

Extortionate picketing   Picketing by employees in an attempt to force an employer to pay money to union officials or other individuals when these payments provide personal benefit to the officials or individuals instead of benefiting the union membership generally.

Extradition   The process that one state uses to have another state transfer to the jurisdiction of the first state a person accused of criminal activities.

Failing-company doctrine   A merger between a failing company and a competitor may be allowed, although such a merger would be illegal if both companies were viable competitors.

Fair use   A statutorily permitted use of another's copyright for criticism, comment, news reporting, teaching, scholarship, or research.

False advertising   Untrue and fraudulent statements and representations made by way of advertising a product or a service.

False imprisonment   The tort of an intentional, unjustified confinement of a nonconsenting person who knows of the confinement.

Family resemblance test   A legal principle used to determine whether or not promissory notes or other similar investment opportunities are securities.

Featherbedding   A term used in the labor laws to describe workers who are paid although they do not perform any work. Under the Taft-Hartley Act, featherbedding is an unfair labor practice by unions.

Federal Employer's Liability Act   The federal act covering transportation workers that establishes an employer's liability to employees for negligence.

Federalism   A term used to describe the vertical aspect of the separation of powers. The coexistence of a federal government and the various state governments, with each having responsibilities and authorities that are distinct but overlap, is called federalism.

Federal question   Litigation involving the application or interpretation of the federal Constitution, federal statutes, federal treaties, or federal administrative agencies. The federal court system has subject matter jurisdiction over these issues.

Federal Rules of Civil Procedure   A law passed by Congress that provides the procedural steps to be followed by the federal courts when handling civil litigation.

Federal Trade Commission Act   Passed in 1914, this legislation created the Federal Trade Commission (FTC) and authorized it to protect society against unfair methods of competition. The law was amended in 1938 (by the Wheeler-Lea amendment) to provide the FTC with authority to regulate unfair or deceptive trade practices.

Fee schedule   A plan, usually adopted by an association, that establishes minimum or maximum charges for a service or product.

Fee simple   The maximum bundle of rights, or estate, permitted by law.

Fellow-servant doctrine   The doctrine that precludes an injured employee from recovering damages from his employer when the injury resulted from the negligent act of another employee.

Felony   A criminal offense of a serious nature, generally punishable by death or imprisonment in a penitentiary; to be distinguished from a misdemeanor.

Fiduciary   One having a duty to act for another's benefit in the highest good faith.

Finance charge   Any charge for an extension of credit, which specifically includes interest, service charges, and other charges.

Financing statement   An established form that a secured party files with a public officer, such as a state official or local court clerk, to perfect a security interest under the Uniform Commercial Code (UCC). It is a simple form that contains basic information such as a description of the collateral, names, and addresses. It is designed to give notice that the debtor and the secured party have entered into a security agreement.

Firm offer   An offer in signed writing by a merchant to buy or sell goods; it gives assurances that the offer will be held open for acceptance under the Uniform Commercial Code (UCC).

Fixture   Personal property that has become real property, generally through physical attachment (annexation).

Foreclosure   If a mortgagor fails to perform his or her obligations as agreed, the mortgagee may declare the whole debt due and payable, and she or he may foreclose on the mortgaged property to pay the debt secured by the mortgage. The usual method of foreclosure authorizes the sale of the mortgaged property at a public auction. The proceeds of the sale are applied to the debt.

Foreign corporation   A business organization, created by the issuance of a state charter, that operates in states other than the one issuing the charter.

Foreign Corrupt Practices Act   A U.S. law that seeks to ban the payment of bribes to foreign officials in order to obtain business.

Foreign Sovereign Immunities Act   A federal law passed in 1976 that codifies the restrictive theory of *sovereign immunity* and rejects immunity for commercial acts carried on in the United States or having direct effects in this country.

Foreign subsidiary   A practice common in a multinational corporation that conducts part of its business operations in a foreign country.

Formalism   An ethical system that affirms an absolute morality. Also called *deontology*.

Forum non conveniens   The doctrine under which a court may dismiss a lawsuit in which it appears that for the convenience of the parties and in the interest of justice the action should have been brought in another court.

Franchise   A marketing technique whereby one party (the franchisor) grants a second party (the franchisee) the right to manufacture, distribute, or sell a product using the name or trademark of the franchisor.

Fraud   A false representation of fact made with the intent to deceive another that is justifiably relied upon to the injury of that person.

Free exercise clause   A provision in the First Amendment of the U.S. Constitution that allows all citizens the freedom to follow or believe any religious teaching.

Frolic and detour   The activity of an agent or an employee who has departed from the scope of the agency and is not, therefore, a representative of his or her employer.

Full faith and credit clause   A provision in the U.S. Constitution that requires a state to recognize the laws and judicial decisions of all other states.

Full-line forcing   An arrangement in which a manufacturer refuses to supply any portion of the product line unless the retailer agrees to accept the entire line.

Functional discount   A reduction in price as the result of the buyer performing some service that usually is provided by the seller.

Garnishment   A legal proceeding whereby a creditor may collect directly from a third party who is obligated to the debtor.

General Agreement on Tariffs and Trade (GATT)   An international treaty that requires member countries to abide by the principles of open and free trade.

General counsel   An individual who is responsible for coordinating all law-related issues, such as the quasi-judicial hearings in administrative agencies. This term is also used to describe the principal lawyer of a company.

General partner   The owner of a limited partnership that enjoys the control of the partnership's operation. This type of partner is personally liable for the debts of the limited partnership.

General partnership   A business organization wherein all owners (partners) share profits and losses and all are jointly and severally liable for the organization's debts.

Generic   To lose distinctiveness in reference to the source of goods and thus to lose trademark protection.

Geographic extension merger   A combining of companies involved with the same product or service that do not compete in the same geographical regions or markets.

Geographic market   The relevant section of the country affected by a merger.

Going bare   A professional practicing (in her or his field of expertise) without liability insurance.

Good, the   In philosophy the moral goals and objectives that people choose to pursue.

Good faith   Honesty in dealing; innocence; without fraud or deceit.

Good-faith meeting of competition   A bona fide business practice that is a defense to a charge of violation of the Robinson-Patman Act. The Robinson-Patman Act is an amendment to the Clayton Act, which outlaws price discrimination that might substantially lessen competition or tends to create a monopoly. This exception allows a seller in good faith to meet the equally low price, service, or facility of a competitor. The good-faith exception cannot be established if the purpose of the price discrimination has been to eliminate competition.

Goods   Tangible (touchable), movable personal property.

Greenmail   Forcing a corporation to buy back some of its own stock at an inflated price to avoid a takeover.

Guardian   One charged with the duty of care and maintenance of another person such as a minor or incompetent under the law.

Guardian *ad litem*   A guardian appointed to prosecute or defend a lawsuit on behalf of an incompetent or a minor.

Guidelines   A result of an administrative agency's quasi-legislative function that assists parties being regulated to understand the agency's functions and intentions. Guidelines do not have the force of the law, but they can be helpful in anticipating the application of an agency's regulations.

Habeas corpus   The name of a writ that orders one holding custody of another to produce that individual before the court for the purpose of determining whether such custody is proper.

Hearsay evidence   Evidence of statements made or actions performed out of court that is offered to prove the truth thereof.

Hearsay rule   The exclusion, with certain exceptions, of hearsay evidence because of the lack of opportunity to cross-examine the original source of the evidence.

Holder in due course   One who has acquired possession of a negotiable instrument through proper negotiation for value, in good faith, and without notice of any defenses to it. Such a holder is not subject to personal defenses that would otherwise defeat the obligation embodied in the instrument.

Horizontal merger   Merger of corporations that were competitors prior to the merger.

Horizontal price fixing   A per se illegal agreement among competitors as to the price all of them will charge for their similar products.

Horizontal territorial agreement   An arrangement between competitors with respect to geographical areas in which each will conduct its business to the exclusion of the others. This type of agreement is illegal per se under the Sherman Act.

Hostile working environment   Under Title VII an environment where coworkers make offensive sexual comments or propositions, engage in suggestive touching, show nude pictures, or draw sexual graffiti.

Hot-cargo contract   An agreement whereby an employer agrees to refrain from handling, using, selling, transporting, or otherwise dealing in the products of another employer or to cease doing business with any other person.

Illegal search and seizure   The area covered by the Fourth Amendment that protects individuals and organizations from unreasonable intrusion without a court-issued warrant.

Immunity   Status of exemption from lawsuits or other legal obligations.

Implied authority   Actual authority that is incidental to express authority.

Implied conditions   Conditions to a contract that are implied by law rather than by contractual agreement.

Implied contract   A legally enforceable agreement inferred from the circumstances and conduct of the parties. Also called an *implied-in-fact contract.*

Implied-in-fact contract   A legally enforceable agreement inferred from the circumstances and conduct of the parties.

Implied-in-law contract   A quasi-contract.

Implied warranty   A warranty implied by law rather than by express agreement of the parties to a contract.

Implied warranty of fitness for a particular purpose   An implied Uniform Commercial Code (UCC) warranty that arises when a buyer specifies a purpose for a product, then relies on the seller's skill and judgment to select the product.

Implied warranty of habitability   A warranty implied by law in a number of states that guarantees the quality of new home construction.

Implied warranty of merchantability   A warranty (implied) that the goods are reasonably fit for general purpose for which they are sold.

Impossibility of performance   A defense to contractual nonperformance based on special circumstances that render the performance illegal, physically impossible, or so difficult as to violate every reasonable expectation the parties have regarding performance.

Incidental beneficiary   A person who may incidentally benefit from the creation of a contract. Such a person cannot enforce any right to incidental benefit.

Incorporators   Those individuals who are responsible for bringing a corporation into being.

Indefiniteness   When the terms of an agreement are not sufficiently specific, the agreement does not rise to the level of a contract because of the doctrine of indefiniteness.

Indictment   A document issued by a grand jury formally charging a person with a felony.

Individual retirement account   A retirement account for persons who can make either tax deductible contributions, which are taxed on withdrawal, or contributions that are taxed, which produce tax-free withdrawals. This latter type of account is known as a Roth IRA.

Industry guide   An issue of the Federal Trade Commission (FTC) defining the agency's view of the legality of an industry's trade practice.

Infliction of mental distress   An intentional tort of the emotions that causes both mental distress and physical symptoms as a result of the defendant's outrageous behavior.

Infringement   The tort establishing violation of intellectual property rights.

Injunction   A court order directing a party to do or to refrain from doing some act.

Injurious falsehood   A statement of untruth that causes injury or damage to the party against whom it is made.

In pari materia   Concerning the same subject matter. A rule of statutory construction that two such statutes will be construed together.

In personam   The jurisdiction of a court to affect the rights and duties of a specific individual.

In rem   The jurisdiction of a court to affect property rights with respect to a specific thing.

Insider   A person who owns 10 percent or more of a company or who is a director or officer of the company; a term used in securities law. This term is also used to describe a person possessing nonpublic information.

Intangible property   Something that represents value but has no physical attributes, such as a copyright, patent, or franchise right.

Intellectual property   A type of property in information and its application or expression. Patents and copyrights are examples.

Intent   A legal doctrine indicating that parties meant to do what they did.

Intentional interference with contractual relations   The tort of causing another to break a contract.

Intentional tort   Noncontractual legal wrong caused by one who desires to cause the wrong or where the wrong is substantially likely to occur from the behavior.

Intent to defraud   Applies to an individual who knowingly and willfully makes a misrepresentation of a material fact that is relied on and thereby causes injury or harm.

Interference with contractual relations   A business tort in which persons are induced to breach binding agreements.

International Court of Justice   The judicial branch of the United Nations, which sits at The Hague in the Netherlands and consists of 15 judges representing the world's major legal systems.

Interpleader   A legal procedure by which one holding a single fund subject to conflicting claims of two or more persons may require the conflicting claimants to come into court and litigate the matter between themselves.

Interrogatory   A written question propounded by one party to a lawsuit to another; a type of discovery procedure.

Inter se   Between themselves.

Intestate   A person who dies without a will.

Invasion of privacy   A tort based on misappropriation of name or likeness, intrusion upon physical solitude, or public disclosure of objectionable, private information.

Involuntary petition   The document filed by a creditor to initiate bankruptcy proceedings against a debtor.

Irrevocable letter of credit   Reduces the risk to parties in cases where business is extended across national borders between strangers by providing guarantees of payment and delivery of goods.

Issuer   The term in securities law for an individual or business organization offering a security for sale to the public.

Jointly and severally liable   The legal principle that makes two or more people, usually partners, liable for an entire debt as individuals or in any proportional combination.

Joint tenancy   A property ownership that is undivided (common) and equal between two or more owners. Permits survivorship.

Joint venture   Two or more persons or business organizations agreeing to do business for a specific and limited purpose.

Judgment   Official adjudication of a court of law.

Judgment notwithstanding the verdict   The decision of a court that sets aside the verdict of a jury and reaches the opposite result.

Judgment on the pleadings   A principle of litigation, in the form of a motion, whereby one party tests the validity of the allegations contained in the complaint and answer. Upon this motion a judge might determine that the pleadings contain no issues of fact or law and thus grant a judgment prior to a trial.

Judicial activism   An activist judge tends to abide by the following judicial philosophies: (1) The political process cannot adequately handle society's difficult issues; (2) the courts can correct society's ills through the decision-making process; (3) following precedent is not crucial; and (4) "judge-made law" is often necessary to carry out the legislative intent of the law. See also *Judicial restraint.*

Judicial restraint   A judge who abides by the judicial restraint philosophy (1) believes that the political process, and not the courts, should correct society's ills; (2) decides an issue on a narrow basis, if possible; (3) follows precedent whenever possible; and (4) does not engage in "judge-made law" but interprets the letter of the law. See also *Judicial activism.*

Judicial review   The power of courts to declare laws enacted by legislative bodies and actions by the executive branch to be unconstitutional.

Jurisdiction   The power and authority of a court or other governmental agency to adjudicate controversies and otherwise deal with matters brought before it.

Jurisdictional strike   A stoppage of work that arises from a dispute between two or more unions as to what work should be assigned to the employees belonging to the disputing unions. This work stoppage is an unfair labor practice. This dispute between the unions should be resolved by the NLRB.

Jurisprudence   The science of the law; the practical science of giving a wise interpretation of the law.

Jury instruction   A statement made by the judge to the jury informing them of the law applicable to the case the jury is bound to accept and apply.

Knowingly   Intentionally.

Laches   Defense to an equitable action based on the plaintiff's unreasonable delay in bringing the action.

Landrum-Griffin Act   The federal law passed in 1959 that provides union members with a "Bill of Rights" and requires union officers to file reports with the Department of Labor. This law, which is known as the Labor-Management Reporting and Disclosure Act, also added unfair labor practices by unions.

Lanham Act   A federal law regulating unfair methods of competition regarding trademarks.

Larceny   The unlawful taking of personal property with the intent to deprive the right owner of this property.

Law of agency   That body of law concerning one's dealing with another on behalf of a principal.

Leading question   A question that indicates the appropriate answer because of the way or manner in which it is asked. Typically, such questions are allowed during the cross-examination of a witness but not during the direct examination.

Leashold estate   The property granted to tenants (lessees) by a landlord (lessor).

Legacy   A gift of money under a will. It is a type of bequest, which is a gift of personal property. The word *devise* is used in connection with real property distributed by will.

Legal capacity   The ability of a business organization to sue and be sued in its own name rather than having to sue or be sued in the name of its owners.

Legal clinic   A term referring to a law firm that specializes in low-cost, generally routine legal procedures.

Legislation   Laws passed by an elected body such as Congress, a state legislation, or local council/commission. Those laws enacted at the federal and state levels are called statutes. At the local level, such laws are often referred to as ordinances.

Legislative history   A technique used by courts in interpreting statutes. Courts often examine the record of the legislators' debate in an attempt to determine what was intended by the legislation.

Letter of credit   A document commonly used in international transactions to ensure payment and delivery of goods.

Libel   A defamatory written statement communicated to a third party.

License   A common method of controlling product or technology transfers across national borders.

Lien   A claim to an interest in property in satisfaction of a debt or claim.

Life estate   A property that grants land ownership for the lifetime of a specified person.

Limited liability   This term is used to describe the exposure of business owners to pay the debts of their businesses when such exposure does not exceed the owner's investment in the business.

Limited liability company (LLC)   A type of business organization that has characteristics of both a partnership and a corporation. The owners of an LLC are called members, and their personal liability is limited to their capital contributions. The LLC, as an organization, is not a taxable entity.

Limited liability partnership   A hybrid business partnership.

Limited partners   Those owners of a limited partnership who forgo control of the organization's operation in return for their liability being limited to the amount of their investment.

Limited partnership   A partnership in which one or more individuals are general partners and one or more individuals are limited partners. The limited partners contribute assets to the partnership without taking part in the conduct of the business. Such individuals are liable for the debts of the partnership only to the extent of their contributions.

Limited personal liability   See *Limited liability.*

Liquidated damages clause   A contractual provision that specifies a predetermined amount of damages or a formula for such a determination to be utilized if a breach of contract occurs.

Liquidation   The process of winding up the affairs of a business for the purpose of paying debts and disposing of assets. May be voluntary or under court order.

Litigation   The process of utilizing the court system to resolve a legal dispute.

Long-arm statute   A state statute that gives extraterritorial effect to process (summons) in specified cases. It allows state courts to obtain jurisdiction in civil actions over defendants who are beyond the border of the state provided the defendants have minimum contact with the state sufficient to satisfy due process.

Mailbox rule   The rule that an acceptance is effective once it is sent. See *Deposited acceptance rule.*

Mail fraud   The use of the United States Postal Service or any interstate carrier to conduct fraudulent activities with the intent to deprive an owner of property.

Malfeasance   Doing of some wrongful act.

Malice   The state of mind that accompanies the intentional doing of a wrongful act without justification or excuse.

Malicious prosecution   An action for recovery of damages that have resulted to person, property, or reputation from previous unsuccessful civil or criminal proceedings that were prosecuted without probable cause and with malice.

Mandamus   A court order directing the holder of an office to perform his or her legal duty.

Mandatory arbitration   A form of resolving a dispute, as an alternative to litigation, that is required by a statute.

Manifest system   A documentary system required by the Resource Conservation and Recovery Act. Used in the disposal of toxic chemicals.

Market extension merger   An acquisition in which the acquiring company increases its market through product extension or geographical extension.

Master   The term used in an agency relationship to describe the principal (employer) of a servant (employee) who is involved in a tort.

Material breach   A level of performance below what is reasonably acceptable. A substantial failure, without excuse, to perform a promise that constitutes the whole or part of a contract. A party who has materially breached cannot sue the other party for performance and is liable for damages.

Mayhem   Unlawfully depriving a human being of a member of his or her body.

Mechanic's lien   A lien on real estate that is created by statute to assist suppliers and laborers in collecting their accounts and wages. Its purpose is to subject the owner's land to a lien for material and labor expended in the construction of buildings and other improvements.

Med-Arb   An abbreviation for an alternative dispute resolution system that involves parties going through mediation and agreeing to resolve as many issues as possible. These parties agree that any matters not resolved in the mediation process will then be arbitrated.

Mediation   An alternative to litigation whereby a third party attempts to assist the disputing parties in reaching a settlement. The third-party mediator lacks authority to impose on the parties a binding solution to the dispute.

Mediator   An individual who assists disputing parties in their efforts to resolve their differences. Mediators must rely on their persuasive abilities since they have no authority to settle the dispute.

Members   The individuals or business entities that belong to a limited liability company.

Merchant   A person who deals in goods of the kind or otherwise by his or her occupation presents himself or herself as having knowledge or skill peculiar to the practice or goods involved.

Merger   The extinguishment of a corporate entity by the transfer of its assets and liabilities to another corporation that continues in existence.

Minimum rationality   A legal test used by courts to test the validity of governmental action, such as legislation, under the equal protection clause of the U.S. Constitution. To satisfy this test, the government needs to demonstrate that there is a good reason for the government's action.

Minimum wage   Minimum hourly wages, established by Congress under the Fair Labor Standards Act, to maintain the health, efficiency, and general well-being of workers.

Ministerial duty   An example of a definite duty regarding that nothing be left to discretion or judgment.

Minitrial   An alternative dispute resolution system that involves lawyers presenting both sides of a business dispute to the executives of the organizations involved.

Mirror image rule   The common law rule that the terms of an acceptance offer must mirror exactly the terms of the offer. Any variation of terms would make the attempted acceptance a counteroffer.

Misappropriation theory   The legal doctrine supported by the Securities and Exchange Commission (SEC) and the courts that any person who shares nonpublic information with another party or who trades on the information violates the securities laws if that information was intended to be kept confidential.

Misdemeanor   A criminal offense of less serious nature than a felony, generally punishable by fine or jail sentence other than in a penitentiary.

Misfeasance   A misdeed or trespass.

Misrepresentation   An untrue manifestation of fact by word or conduct; it may be unintentional.

Mitigate   To lessen the consequences of. Usually used to refer to the contractual duty to lessen damages following breach of contract.

Mock trial   An alternative dispute resolution system that involves lawyers presenting their clients' cases to a group of citizens who render their opinion about the relative merits of the parties' positions.

Monopoly   Exclusive control of a market by a business entity.

Morality   The values of right and wrong.

Mortgage   A transfer of an interest in property for the purpose of creating a security for a debt.

Motion   The process by which the parties make written or oral requests that the judge issue an order or ruling.

Mutual assent   A contractual doctrine requiring that the minds of the contracting parties must meet before there exists a binding contract.

Mutual mistake   A situation in which parties to a contract reach a bargain on the basis of an incorrect assumption common to both parties.

Nationalization   A claim made by a foreign government that it owns expropriated property.

National Labor Relations Board (NLRB)   The federal administrative agency created in 1935 to conduct certification/decertification elections of unions and to conduct quasi-judicial hearings arising from the labor-management relationship.

Necessaries of life   Food, clothing, shelter, medical care, and, in some states, education. A minor is legally responsible to pay a reasonable value for purchased necessaries of life.

Negligence   A person's failure to exercise reasonable care that foreseeably causes another injury.

Negotiable instrument or document   A special type of written promise to pay money (instrument) or deliver goods (document). Personal defenses do not apply against the holder in due course of a negotiable instrument or document.

Negotiated settlement   A voluntary but binding agreement that settles a legal dispute, such as one involving a contractual breach or a tort lawsuit.

Nexus   A logical connection.

NLRB   National Labor Relations Board

Noerr-Pennington doctrine   This doctrine exempts from the antitrust laws concerted efforts to lobby government officials regardless of the anticompetitive purposes. It is based on the First Amendment freedom of speech.

No-fault laws   Laws barring tort actions by injured persons against third-party tortfeasors and requiring such persons to obtain recovery from their own insurers.

Nolo contendere   A plea entered by the defendant in a criminal case that neither admits nor denies the crime allegedly committed but, if accepted by the court, permits the judge to treat the defendant as guilty.

Nontrading partnership   A business organization made up of two or more partners engaged in buying and selling goods.

Norris-LaGuardia Act   The federal legislation adopted in 1932 that attempted to increase union membership by prohibiting the use of injunctions issued by federal courts against certain union activities and by outlawing yellow-dog contracts.

North American Free Trade Agreement (NAFTA) An agreement reached in 1993 among the United States, Mexico, and Canada to increase economic growth through mutual trade.

Noscitur a sociis The principle that the scope of general words is defined by specific accompanying words; a doctrine of legislative interpretation.

Notary public A public officer authorized to administer oaths and certify certain documents.

Notice Communication sufficient to charge a reasonable person with knowledge of some fact.

Novation The substitution of a new contract in place of an old one.

Nuisance A physical condition constituting an unreasonable and substantial interference with the rights of individuals or the public at large.

Obligee One who is entitled to receive a payment or performance under a contract.

Obligor One who is obligated to pay or perform under a contract.

Obstruction of justice A criminal act involving the interference of the administration of the laws during the investigations and conduct of trials.

Offer A contractual communication that contains a specific promise and a specific demand. The offer initiates the process of making a contract.

Officers Those individuals appointed by directors of a corporation to conduct the daily operations of the corporate organization.

Oligopoly Control of the supply and price of a commodity or service in a given market by a small number of companies or suppliers.

Opinion The decision of a judge, usually issued in a written form.

Option A contractual arrangement under which one party has for a specified time the right to buy certain property from or sell certain property to the other party. It is essentially a contract to not revoke an offer.

Oral argument Attorneys appear in person before the appellate court to explain orally to the court their position in the case and answer the court's questions about the case.

Ordinance The legislative enactment of a city, county, or other municipal corporation.

Organizers The parties responsible for bringing a limited liability company into existence. These parties correspond to the functions of incorporators with respect to corporations.

Overbreadth doctrine A principle used by courts to invalidate legislation that is broader in scope than is necessary to regulate an activity. This doctrine may be utilized to protect constitutional rights, such as freedom of speech, against a wide sweep of some governmental action.

Overt act An essential element of a crime. Without this action by a party, the intent to engage in criminal activity is not wrongful.

Ownership The property right that makes something legally exclusive to its owner.

Paper fortress A term referring to the documentation an employer should keep about an employee's performance.

Parker v. Brown doctrine   The name given to the state action exemption to the Sherman Act. See also *State action exemption.*

Parol evidence   Legal proof based on oral statements; with regard to a document, any evidence extrinsic to the document itself.

Parol evidence rule   Parol evidence is extrinsic evidence. In contracts, the parol evidence rule excludes the introduction of evidence of prior written or oral agreements that may vary, contradict, alter, or supplement the present written agreement. There are several exceptions to this rule. For example, when the parties to an agreement do not intend for that agreement to be final and complete, then parol evidence is admissible.

Partnership   A business organization involving two or more persons agreeing to conduct a commercial venture while sharing its profits and losses.

Part performance   The contractual doctrine that says when a buyer of land has made valuable improvements in it or has paid part or all of the purchase price, the statute of frauds does not apply to prevent an oral land sales contract from being enforceable.

Patent   A statutorily created property in inventions.

Per capita   By or for each individual.

Per curiam   By the court; said of an opinion expressing the view of the court as a whole as opposed to an opinion authored by any single member of the court.

Peremptory challenge   The power granted each party to reject a limited number of potential jurors during voir dire examination. No reason for the rejection need be given.

Perfection   The status ascribed to security interests after certain events have occurred or certain prescribed steps have been taken, e.g., the filing of a financing statement.

Perjury   The giving of false testimony under oath.

Per se   In itself.

Per se illegality   Under the Sherman Act, agreements and practices are illegal only if they are unreasonable. The practices that are conclusively presumed to be unreasonable are per se illegal. If an activity is per se illegal, only proof of the activity is required, and it is not necessary to prove an anticompetitive effect. For example, price fixing is per se illegal. See also *Rule of reason.*

Personal jurisdiction   The power of a court over the parties involved in the litigation process.

Personal property   All property that does not involve land and interests in land.

Petitioner   The party filing either a case in equity or a petition for a writ of *certiorari* before a supreme court.

Petit jury   The fact-finding body during a trial. Also called a trial or traverse jury.

Petty offenses   Criminal acts that are viewed as minor and thus are typically punished by a fine only.

Piercing the corporate veil   The legal doctrine used by courts to disregard the existence of a corporation thereby holding the shareholders personally liable for the organization's debts.

Plaintiff   The person who initiates a lawsuit.

Plan termination insurance   The insurance required by federal law on regulated pension plans. It protects against plan termination that leaves pension benefits underfunded.

Pleadings   The process by which the parties to a lawsuit present formal written statements of their contentions to create the issues of the lawsuit.

Plenary   Entire; complete in all respects.

Point source   Any source of air pollution that must be licensed under the Clean Air Act.

Police power   The authority a state or local government has to protect the public's health, safety, morals, and general welfare.

Possession   Dominion and control over property; the holding or detention of property in one's own power or command.

Precedent   A prior judicial decision relied upon as an example of a rule of law.

Predatory conduct   An anticompetitive action that is intended to drive competitors out of business. A common example occurs when a business lowers its prices in the hope of gaining such a large market share that it can then raise prices without the fear of competition.

Predatory pricing   A policy of lowering the price charged to customers for the purpose of driving competitors out of business. Typically, this policy involves prices that are below the seller's costs of the products sold with resulting losses to the seller.

Preemption   A condition when a federal statute or administrative rule governs an issue to the extent that a state or local government is prohibited from regulating that area of law.

Preemptive right   A corporation's shareholder's right to maintain the same percentage ownership of the organization whenever newly authorized stock is sold.

Preferred stock   A type of stock issued by a corporation that entitles the owner to receive a dividend before owners of common stock.

Prejudicial error   An error in judicial proceedings that may have affected the result in the case.

Preponderance of evidence   In the judgment of the jurors, evidence that has greater weight and overcomes the opposing evidence and presumptions.

Presumption of innocence   The basis of requiring the government to prove a criminal defendant's guilt beyond a reasonable doubt.

Prevention of significant deterioration   A rule implemented under the Clean Air Act that prohibits the degradation of air quality in regions where air quality is better than required by primary air quality standards.

Price discrimination   A seller charging different purchasers different prices for the same goods at the same time.

Price fixing   An agreement or combination by which the conspirators set the market price, whether high or low, of a product or service whether being sold or purchased.

Prima facie   On the face of it; thus, presumed to be true unless proved otherwise.

Primary air quality standards   The standards necessary to protect human health. Secondary air quality standards are stricter standards necessary to protect various environmental amenities.

Primary jurisdiction   A doctrine used by reviewing courts to determine whether a case is properly before the courts or whether it should be heard by an administrative agency first since such an agency might have expertise superior to the courts'.

Principal   The person who gives an agent authority.

Prior consideration   Service or gift from the past that presently induces one to make a promise. Prior consideration does not enable that promise to bind one. It is not legal consideration.

Prior restraint   A principle applicable under the freedom of press and speech clauses of the First Amendment of the U.S. Constitution. The courts have announced decisions that encourage governments to allow the publication or expression of thoughts rather than to restrain such thoughts in advance of their publication or expression.

Private international law   A body of rules that utilizes treaties, agreements, and individual laws of nations to resolve international business disputes between private firms.

Private law   A classification of legal subject matters that deals most directly with relationships between legal entities. The law of contracts and the law of property are two examples of this classification.

Private nuisance   An unreasonable use of one's land so as to cause substantial interference with the enjoyment or use of another's land.

Privilege   A special advantage accorded by law to some individual or group; an exemption from a duty or obligation generally imposed by law.

Privileged communication   A rule of evidence that protects conversations that society deems to be confidential. For example, a witness cannot be required to disclose communications between an attorney and a client.

Privileges and immunities clause   A provision found in Article IV and the Fourteenth Amendment of the U.S. Constitution that prevents a state government from discriminating in favor of its citizens and against citizens from another state. This clause, while not interpreted to be absolute, has emphasized national rather than state citizenship.

Privity   Interest derived from successive relationship with another party; a contractual connection.

Probable cause   The reasonable basis on which law enforcement officials convince a judge that criminal activity has occurred. This is the basis that must be satisfied before a judge will issue a criminal search warrant.

Procedural due process   The process or procedure ensuring fundamental fairness that all citizens are entitled to under the U.S. Constitution.

Procedural law   The body of rules governing the manner in which legal claims are enforced.

Product extension merger   A merger that extends the products of the acquiring company into a similar or related product but one that is not directly in competition with existing products.

Production defect   A defect arising when a product does not meet its manufacturer's own standards.

Product liability   The liability that sellers have for the goods they sell.

Promissory estoppel   Court enforcement of an otherwise unbinding promise if injustice can be avoided only by enforcement of the promise. A substitute for consideration.

Property   A bundle of private, exclusive rights in people to acquire, possess, use, and transfer scarce resources.

Proportionality review   The process that appellate courts use to determine the appropriateness of a criminal sentence.

Prospectus   The legal document required by the 1933 Securities Act to be made available to potential purchasers of securities.

Pro tanto   So far as it goes.

Protestant ethic   A set of beliefs urging that human desire and indulgence be bent to God's will through hard work, self-denial, and rational planning.

Proximate causation   The doctrine that limits an actor's liability to consequences that could reasonably be foreseen to have resulted from the act.

Proxy   The legal document whereby a shareholder appoints an agent to vote the stock at a corporation's shareholders' meeting.

Public international law   A body of rules that examines relationships among nations and seeks to bind them to common principles in the international community.

Public law   A classification of legal subject matters that regulates the relationship of individuals and organizations to society.

Publicly held   A business organization that has hundreds, if not thousands, of owners who can exchange their ownership interests on public exchanges.

Public nuisance   An owner's use of land that causes damage or inconvenience to the general public.

Public policy   Accepted standards of behavior. For instance, a contract is illegal if it violates public policy.

Punitive damages   Monetary damages in excess of a compensatory award, usually granted only in intentional tort cases where defendant's conduct involved some element deserving punishment. Also called *exemplary damages.*

Purchase-money security interest   A security interest given to the party that loans the debtor the money that enables the debtor to buy the collateral.

Qualified disabled   A disabled person who can perform the duties of a job.

Qualified pension plan   A private retirement plan that gains favorable income tax treatment from the Internal Revenue Service (IRS). A qualified pension plan allows for the deduction of contributions made to fund the plan. Also, earnings from fund investments are not taxable, and employees defer personal income tax liability until payments are received after retirement. To qualify, the plan must cover a high percentage of workers (usually 70 percent) or cover classifications of employees that do not discriminate in favor of management or shareholders.

Quantity discount   The practice of giving a lower per unit price to businesses that buy a product in volume than to their competitors that do not.

Quasi-contract   A quasi-contract, often referred to as an implied-in-law contract, is not a true contract. It is a legal fiction that the courts use to prevent unjust enrichment and wrongdoing. Courts permit the person who conferred a benefit to recover the reasonable value of that benefit. Nonetheless, the elements of a true contract are not present.

Quasi-judicial   Administrative actions involving factual determinations and the discretionary application of rules and regulations.

Quasi-legislative   This term describes the rule-making functions of administrative agencies.

Quasi-strict scrutiny   A legal test used by courts to test the validity of governmental action, such as legislation, under the equal protection clause of the U.S. Constitution. To satisfy this test, the government needs to demonstrate that the purpose of the action is substantially related to an important governmental objective.

Quick-look analysis   A process of review used by courts in antitrust cases to determine the legality of an anticompetitive act. This analysis is something greater than the per se determination of illegality and less than the full consideration of the rule of reason analysis.

Quid pro quo   The exchange of one thing of value for another.

Quitclaim deed   The transfer by deed of all the grantor's rights, title, and interest in property.

Quo warranto   An action brought about by the government to test the validity of some franchise, such as the privilege of doing business as a corporation.

Racketeering   A crime under RICO involving a pattern of actions that are indictable under state or federal laws.

Railway Labor Act   The federal law passed in 1926 to encourage collective bargaining in the railroad industry. The law also created the National Mediation Board.

Ratio decidendi   Logical basis of judicial decision.

Real property   Property in land and interests in land.

Reasonable accommodation   The actions that an employer must take under Title VII of the Civil Rights Act and under the Americans with Disabilities Act to adapt employment conditions to an employee's religious belief or disability.

Reciprocal dealing   A contract in which two parties agree to mutual actions so that each party can act as both a buyer and a seller. The agreement violates the Clayton Act if it results in a substantial lessening of competition.

Redlining   An act or refusal to act that results in a discriminatory practice. For example, refusing to make loans in low-income areas can discriminate against minorities in granting credit.

Reformation   A contractual remedy exercised by a court to correct a mistake of drafting or some other nonessential mistake. After reformation the parties remain bound to the contract.

Registration statement   The legal document required to be filed with the Securities and Exchange Commission (SEC) prior to securities being offered for sale to the public.

Reimbursement   Restoration; to pay back or repay that expended; the act of making one whole.

Rejection   The refusal of an offer. A rejection terminates an offer.

Release   The relinquishment of a right or claim against another party.

Remand The return of a case by an appellate court for further action by the lower court.

Remedial statute Legislation designed to provide a benefit or relief to a victim of a violation of law.

Remedy The action or procedure that is followed in order to enforce a right or to obtain damages for injury to a right; the means by which a right is enforced or the violation of a right is prevented, redressed, or compensated.

Reorganization The legal process of forming a new corporation after bankruptcy or foreclosure.

Replevin An action for the recovery of goods wrongfully taken or kept.

Representational standing The requirements that must be satisfied for an organization to have the right to file a lawsuit on behalf of its members.

Request for an admission A method of discovery used to narrow the issues to be litigated by having a party request that the other party admit the facts are not in dispute.

Request for production of documents A method of discovery whereby one party asks the other to provide documents for the requesting party's review.

Requirements contract A contract under which the buyer agrees to buy a certain item only from the seller.

Res A thing, object, or status.

Resale price maintenance Manufacturer control of a brand- or trade-name product's minimum resale price.

Rescind To cancel or annul a contract and return the parties to their original positions.

Rescission A contractual remedy that cancels the agreement and returns the consideration exchanged to each party.

Res ipsa loquitur The thing speaks for itself. A rule of evidence whereby negligence of the alleged wrongdoer may be inferred from the mere fact that the injury occurred.

Res judicata The doctrine that deems a former adjudication conclusive and prevents a retrial of matters decided in the earlier lawsuit.

Respondeat superior The doctrine imposing liability on one for torts committed by another person who is in his or her employ and subject to his or her control.

Respondent The party answering a petition in equity or petition for a writ of *certiorari*.

Restitution A contractual remedy involving one party returning to another the value previously received.

Restraint of trade Monopolies, combinations, and contracts that impede free competition.

Restrictive covenants Private agreements that restrict land use.

Retaliatory trade practices Actions by aggrieved nations responding to tariffs and other unfair trade restrictions imposed by foreign governments.

Reverse Overturn or vacate the judgment of a court.

Reverse discrimination The advancement and recruitment of minority workers ahead of similarly qualified nonminority workers.

Revocation   The contractual communication of withdrawing an offer.

RICO   The Racketeer Influenced and Corrupt Organizations Act.

Right of redemption   The right to buy back. A debtor may buy back or redeem his or her mortgaged property when he or she pays the debt.

Right-to-work law   A state statute that outlaws a union-shop contract—one by which an employer agrees to require membership in the union sometime after an employee has been hired as a condition of continued employment.

Robbery   Illegally taking something by force.

Robinson-Patman Act   The amendment to Section 2 of the Clayton Act covering price discrimination. As originally adopted, the Robinson-Patman Act outlawed price discrimination in interstate commerce that might substantially lessen competition or tends to create a monopoly.

Rule of law   The general and equal application of laws, even to lawmakers.

Rule of reason   Under the Sherman Act, contracts or conspiracies are illegal only if they constitute an unreasonable restraint of trade or attempt to monopolize. An activity is unreasonable if it adversely affects competition. An act is reasonable if it promotes competition. The rule of reason requires that an anticompetitive effect be shown. See also *Per se illegality.*

Rules of evidence   The laws governing the admission of evidence, such as testimony and documents, during the trial of a case.

Sale of business doctrine   The legal principle in securities law that might be used to remove the sale of corporate stock from the securities laws' protection if the purchaser of such stock is to operate the business instead of relying on others to do so.

Sanctions   Penalties imposed for violation of a law.

Sarbanes-Oxley Act of 2002   The law enacted to correct inadequacies in the law that existed and allowed numerous examples of corporate fraud. In essence, through increased criminal sanctions and specific requirements, this law attempts to make corporate CEOs more responsible.

Scienter   With knowledge; particularly, guilty knowledge.

Scoping   A regulatory step required of a federal agency by the Council on Environmental Quality. Before preparing an environmental impact statement, an agency must designate which environmental issues of a proposed action are most significant.

S corporation   A business organization that is formed as a corporation but, by a shareholders' election, is treated as a partnership for taxation purposes.

Search warrant   A court order required by the Fourth Amendment of the U.S. Constitution to be obtained from governmental officials prior to private property being searched or seized.

Secondary air quality standards   Clean Air Act standards designed to protect environmental quality other than human health.

Secondary boycott   Conspiracy or combination to cause the customers or suppliers of an employer to cease doing business with that employer.

Section 402A   That section of the Second Restatement of Torts that imposes strict liability on product sellers who sell a product in a "defective condition unreasonably dangerous to the user or consumer or his property."

Section 1981   That provision of the Civil Rights Act of 1866 that forbids racial discrimination in the making of contracts.

Secured transactions   Any credit transaction creating a security interest; an interest in personal property that secures the payment of an obligation.

Securities Act of 1933   The federal law that regulates (through disclosure requirements) the initial sale of securities to the public.

Securities and Exchange Commission (SEC)   The federal administrative agency that regulates the securities industry.

Securities Exchange Act of 1934   The federal law that regulates sales (other than the initial sale) of securities. This law governs the resale of securities whether by individuals or through brokers and exchanges.

Security   Under the securities law, an investment in which the investor does not participate in management.

Seller   In commercial law, a person who sells or contracts to sell goods.

Seniority system   A plan giving priority to employees based on the length of time an employee has worked for an employer. An employer may apply different standards pursuant to a good-faith seniority system if the differences are not the result of an intention to discriminate.

Sentencing guidelines   Adopted by the U.S. Sentencing Commission as a means of standardizing the sentences given to similar criminals committing similar crimes.

Separation of powers   The doctrine that holds that the legislative, executive, and judicial branches of government function independently of one another and that each branch serves as a check on the others.

Servant   The person hired to act on behalf of a principal in an agency relationship.

Service mark   Any mark, word, picture, or design that attaches to a service and indicates its source.

Set-off   A counterclaim by a defendant against a plaintiff that grows from an independent cause of action and diminishes the plaintiff's potential recovery.

Sexual harassment   Under Title VII, for an employer or workplace supervisor to promise benefits or threaten loss if an employee does not give sexual favors.

Shareholders   The owners of corporations. Typically these owners vote on major decisions impacting their corporations, most commonly the election of a board of directors.

Shark repellent   Corporate action to make a threatened acquisition unattractive to the acquiring company.

Shelf registration   The process in securities law under Securities and Exchange Commission (SEC) Rule 415 that allows an issuer to satisfy the registration statement requirements, thereby allowing the issuer immediately to offer securities for sale.

Sherman Act   An 1890 congressional enactment designed to regulate anticompetitive behavior in interstate commerce.

Short-swing profits   The proceeds gained by an insider buying and selling, or vice versa, securities within a six-month time period. Such profits are considered to be illegal.

Simplified employee pension A type of pension permitted by the Revenue Act of 1978. Under this pension type, employers contribute up to a specified amount to employee individual retirement accounts.

Slander An oral defamatory statement communicated to a third person.

Small-claims court A court of limited jurisdiction, usually able to adjudicate claims up to a certain amount, such as $3,000, depending on the state.

Social contract theory A theory by John Rawls that proposes a way for constructing a just society.

Sole proprietorship The simplest form of business organization, created and controlled by one owner.

Sovereign immunity A doctrine of state and international law that permits a foreign government to claim immunity from suit in the courts of other nations.

Specific performance Equitable remedy that requires defendants in certain circumstances to do what they have contracted to do.

Standing The doctrine that requires the plaintiff in a lawsuit to have a sufficient legal interest in the subject matter of the case.

Standing to sue The requirement that a plaintiff must satisfy by demonstrating a personal interest in the outcome of litigation or an administrative hearing.

Stare decisis The doctrine that traditionally indicates that a court should follow prior decisions in all cases based on substantially similar facts.

State action exemption The Sherman Act exemption of the sovereign action of a state that replaces competition with regulation if the state actively supervises the anticompetitive conduct.

State-of-the-art defense A defense that the defendant's product or practice was compatible with the current state of technology available at the time of the event in question.

States' relations article Article IV of the U.S. Constitution. Among its purposes, this article prevents a state from favoring its citizens over the citizens of another state, thereby making the United States one nation as opposed to 50 subgroups.

Status quo The conditions or state of affairs at a given time.

Statute A legislative enactment.

Statute of frauds Legislation that states that certain contracts will not be enforced unless there is a signed writing evidencing the agreement.

Statute of limitations A statute that sets a date after which a lawsuit may not be brought. The statute begins running after the happening of a certain event, such as the occurrence of an injury or the breach of a contract.

Statute of repose A statute that applies to product liability cases. It prohibits initiation of litigation involving products more than a certain number of years (e.g., 25) following their manufacture.

Statutory construction The rules courts use in interpreting the meaning of legislation.

Strict liability The doctrine under which a party may be required to respond in tort damages without regard to such party's use of due care.

Strict products liability The cause of action under which commercial sellers of defective products are held liable without negligence.

Strict scrutiny   A legal test used by courts to test the validity of governmental action, such as legislation, under the equal protection clause of the U.S. Constitution. To satisfy this test, the government needs to demonstrate that there is a compelling state interest justifying the government's action.

Structured settlement   A periodic payment of damages, usually taking the form of a guaranteed annuity.

Subject matter jurisdiction   The authority of a court to hear cases involving specific issues of law.

Submission   The act or process of referring an issue to arbitration.

Subpoena   A court order directing a witness to appear or to produce documents in his or her possession.

Substantial performance   Degree of performance recognizing that a contracting party has honestly attempted to perform but has fallen short. One who has substantially performed is entitled to the price promised by the other less that party's damages.

Substantive due process   The use of the due process provision of the U.S. Constitution to make certain that the application of a law does not unfairly deprive persons of property rights.

Substantive law   A body of rules defining the nature and extent of legal rights.

Summary judgment   A judicial determination that no genuine factual dispute exists and that one party to the lawsuit is entitled to judgment as a matter of law.

Summons   An official notice to a person that a lawsuit has been commenced against him or her and that he or she must appear in court to answer the charges.

Superfund   The Comprehensive Environmental Response, Compensation, and Liability Act of 1980.

Supremacy clause   Article VI of the U.S. Constitution, which states that the Constitution, laws, and treaties of the United States shall be the "supreme law of the land" and shall take precedence over conflicting state laws.

Supreme Court   The highest appellate court.

Surety   One who incurs a liability for the benefit of another. One who undertakes to pay money in the event that his or her principal is unable to pay.

Symbolic speech   Non-verbal expression.

Taft-Hartley Act   The federal law enacted in 1947 to increase the bargaining power of management by creating unfair labor practices by unions, by outlawing the closed shop, by creating an 80-day cooling-off period, by permitting states to adopt right-to-work laws, and by creating the Federal Mediation and Conciliation Service.

Tangible property   Physical property.

Teleology   An ethical system that concerns itself with the moral consequences of actions. Also called *consequentialism.*

Tenancy in common   A property ownership that is undivided (common) but not necessarily equal between two or more owners.

Tender offer   An invited public offer by a company or organization to buy shares from existing shareholders of another public corporation under specified terms.

Testator   One who has made a will.

Third party   One who enters into a relationship with a principal by way of interacting with the principal's agent.

Third-party beneficiaries Persons who are recognized as having enforceable rights created for them by a contract to which they are not parties and for which they have given no consideration.

Third-party defendant A party who is not a party (plaintiff or defendant) to the original litigation. Typically, a defendant might file a claim against a third party stating that if the defendant is liable to the plaintiff, then this third party will be liable to the defendant.

Tippee A person who learns of nonpublic information about a security from an insider.

Title A synonym for ownership. Sometimes represented as a document.

Tort A civil wrong other than a breach of contract.

Trade disparagement The publication of untrue statements that disparage the plaintiff's ownership of property or its quality.

Trademark A statutorily created property in a mark, word, picture, or design that attaches to goods and indicates their source.

Trademark dilution Using someone's trademark in such a way so as to reduce the value of the trademark's significance, reputation, and goodwill even if the public is not confused by the use.

Trade practice regulation A term generally referring to laws that regulate competitive practices.

Trade secret Any formula, pattern, machine, or process of manufacturing used in one's business that may give the user an opportunity to obtain an advantage over its competitors. Trade secrets are legally protectable.

Trade usage Refers to the particular use of a word in business that may differ from its common use.

Trading partnership A business organization made up of two or more partners engaged in providing services.

Treason Breach of allegiance to one's government, specifically by levying war against such government or by giving aid and comfort to the enemy.

Treaty of Rome A historic agreement reached by six European countries in 1957 to achieve economic unity in the European Community. The latter is now known as the European Union, and its membership has grown to 15 nations.

Treble damages See *Triple damages.*

Trespass An act done in an unlawful manner so as to cause injury to another; an unauthorized entry upon another's land.

Trial court The level of any court system that initially resolves the dispute of litigants. Frequently, but not always, a jury serves as a fact-finding body while the judge issues rulings on the applicable law.

Triple damages (or treble damages) An award of damages allowable under some statutes equal to three times the amount found by the jury to be a single recovery.

Trust A fiduciary relationship whereby one party (trustee) holds legal title for the benefit of another (beneficiary).

Trustee One who holds legal title to property for the benefit of another.

Truth in lending A federal law that requires the disclosure of total finance charges and the annual percentage rate for credit in order that borrowers may be able to shop for credit.

Tying contract   A contract that ties the sale of one piece of property (real or personal) to the sale or lease of another item of property.

Ultra vires   Beyond the scope of corporate powers granted in the charter.

Unconscionable   In the law of contracts, provisions that are oppressive, overreaching, or shocking to the conscience.

Underwriter   The party that, in securities law, guarantees the issuer that the securities offered for sale will be sold.

Undue burden   Under the Civil Rights Act of 1964 and the Americans with Disabilities Act an employer need not take action that is excessively costly or creates excessive inefficiency in order to accommodate an employee's religious beliefs or disability. This is the concept of undue burden.

Undue influence   Influence of another destroying the requisite free will of a testator or donor, which creates a ground for nullifying a will or invalidating a gift. A contract will not be binding if one party unduly influences the other since the parties have not dealt on equal terms.

Unenforceable contract   A contract that cannot be enforced in court.

Unfair competition   A group of statutory torts that include misappropriation of trademarks, patent violations, and copyright breaches. One aspect of the Federal Trade Commission's authority. Section 5 of the FTC Act makes unfair methods of competition illegal.

Unfair labor practices   Activities by management or labor unions that have been declared to be inappropriate by the Wagner Act and Taft-Hartley Act, respectively.

Uniform Commercial Code (UCC)   The most successful attempt to have states adopt a uniform law. This code's purpose is to simplify, clarify, and modernize the laws governing commercial transactions.

Unilateral contract   A contract in which the promisor does not receive a promise as consideration; an agreement whereby one makes a promise to do, or refrain from doing, something in return for a performance, not a promise.

Unilateral mistake   Arises when only one of the parties to a contract is wrong about a material fact. It is not usually a basis for rescinding a contract.

Union shop   This term applies, in labor law, to an agreement by management and labor that all employees of a business will be or become union members. Union shops are not allowed in states with right-to-work laws.

Unreasonable search and seizure   A violation of the Fourth Amendment of the U.S. Constitution that occurs when a valid search warrant is not obtained or when the scope of a valid warrant is exceeded.

Usury   A loan of money at interest above the legal rate.

Utilitarianism   A form of consequentialist ethics.

Valid contract   A contract that contains all of the proper elements of a contract.

Venue   The geographical area over which a court presides. Venue designates the court in which the case should be tried. Change of venue means moving to another court.

Verdict   Findings of fact by the jury.

Vertical merger   A merger of corporations where one corporation is the supplier of the other.

Vertical price fixing   An agreement between a seller and a buyer (for example, between a manufacturer and a retailer) to fix the resale price at which the buyer will sell goods.

Vertical territorial agreement   Arrangement between a supplier and its customers with respect to the geographical area in which each customer will be allowed to sell that supplier's products. This type of agreement is analyzed under the rule of reason to determine whether it violates the Sherman Act. Limitations on intrabrand competition may be permitted if there is a corresponding increase in interbrand competition.

Vested rights   Rights that have become so fixed that they are not subject to being taken away without the consent of the owner.

Voidable contract   Capable of being declared a nullity, though otherwise valid.

Void contract   A contract that is empty, having no legal force; ineffectual, unenforceable.

Voir dire   The preliminary examination of prospective jurors for the purpose of ascertaining bias or interest in the lawsuit.

Voluntary arbitration   A method of resolving a dispute, as an alternative to litigation, that the parties agree to utilize. This agreement may be made before or after a dispute arises.

Voluntary bargaining issue   Either party may refuse to bargain in good faith regarding matters other than wages, hours, and other terms and conditions of employment. This refusal does not constitute an unfair labor practice. An issue over which parties may bargain if they choose to do so.

Voluntary petition   The document filed by a debtor to initiate bankruptcy proceedings.

Wagner Act   The federal law passed in 1935 that recognizes employees' rights to organize. This law also created the National Labor Relations Board and defined unfair labor practices by management. It is formally known as the National Labor Relations Act.

Waiver   An express or implied relinquishment of a right.

Warrant   A judicial authorization for the performance of some act.

Warranty of authority   An agent's implied guarantee that he or she has the authority to enter into a contract. The agent is liable for breaching the warranty if he or she lacks proper authority.

Warranty of merchantability   A promise implied in a sale of goods by merchants that the goods are reasonably fit for the general purpose for which they are sold.

Wheeler-Lea amendment   Legislation passed in 1938 that expanded the Federal Trade Commission's authority to protect society against unfair or deceptive practices.

White-collar crime   Violations of the law by business organizations or by individuals in a business-related capacity.

White knight   A slang term that describes the inducement of a voluntary acquisition when an involuntary acquisition is threatened. The voluntary acquisition group is a white knight since it saves the corporation from an unfriendly takeover.

Willful and wanton negligence   Extremely unreasonable behavior that causes injury.

Willfully   With intent to defraud or deceive.

Wire fraud   The use of radio, television, telephone, Internet, or other wired forms of communication to conduct fraudulent activities with the intent to deprive an owner of property.

Workers' compensation   A plan for the compensation for occupational diseases, accidental injuries, and deaths of employees that arise out of employment. Compensation includes medical expenses and burial costs and lost earnings based on the size of the family and the wage rate of the employee.

Work rules   A company's regulations governing the workplace, the application of which often becomes an issue in the ability of employees to organize for their mutual benefit and protection.

World Trade Organization (WTO)   Mechanism for enforcing the General Agreement on Tariffs and Trade that allows GATT member countries to bring complaints and seek redress.

Wright-Line doctrine   Establishes procedures for determining the burden of proof in cases involving mixed motivation for discharge.

Writ of certiorari   A discretionary proceeding by which an appellate court may review the ruling of an inferior tribunal.

Writ of habeas corpus   A court order to one holding custody of another to produce that individual before the court for the purpose of determining whether such custody is proper.

Yellow-dog contract   An agreement in which a worker agrees not to join a union and that discharge will result from a breach of the contract.

Zoning ordinance   Laws that limit land use based usually on residential, commercial, or industrial designations.

PHOTO *credits*

A complete set of individual photos of current members of the United States Supreme Court was provided by Jerry Goldman, Director of the OYEZ project at Northwestern University.

index